CEQA Deskbook

Ronald E. Bass

Albert I. Herson

Kenneth M. Bogdan

Solano Press Books
Point Arena, Californ·

CEQA Deskbook
1999 [Second] Edition
Includes 2001 Supplement

Third printing
April 2002

Solano Press Books
Post Office Box 773
Point Arena, California 95468
telephone (800) 931-9373
facsimile (707) 884-4109

email spbooks@solano.com
internet www.solano.com

Cover design by Christy Anderson, Jones &
  Stokes Associates, Inc. and Solano Press Books
Book design by Solano Press Books
Index by Paul Kish, Rohnert Park, California
Printed by Centaur Print Partners, Provo, Utah

ISBN 0-923956-58-1

IMPORTANT NOTICE

Before you rely on the information in this
book, please be sure you have the latest
edition and are aware that some changes
in statutes, guidelines, or case law may
have gone into effect since the date of
publication. The book, moreover, provides
general information about the law. Readers
should consult their own attorneys before
relying on the representations found herein.

The authors wish to dedicate this book to Robert Jones (1917-1994) who was instrumental in the early development of the California Environmental Quality Act. In 1970 he served as the lead consultant to the State Assembly Select Committee on Environmental Quality. The committee's report, known as the Environmental Bill of Rights, contained the recommendation to enact CEQA. A year later the Legislature followed Bob's advice, and California became the first state to have an environmental impact assessment law. His leadership in guiding CEQA through the Legislature and his subsequent founding of one of the state's first environmental consulting firms were truly pioneering efforts in the field of environmental management in California.

Preface

The California Environmental Quality Act is California's most important environmental law. It requires state, local, and other agencies subject to the jurisdiction of California to evaluate the environmental implications of their actions. Furthermore, it aims to prevent environmental effects of the agency actions by requiring agencies to avoid or reduce, when feasible, the significant environmental impacts of their decisions.

CEQA establishes a series of action-forcing procedures to ensure that agencies accomplish the purposes of the law. In addition, under the direction of CEQA, the California Resources Agency has adopted regulations, known as the State CEQA Guidelines, which provide detailed procedures that agencies must follow to implement the law. The key to compliance with CEQA is understanding the procedural steps and key decision points involved in the environmental review process established by the statute (Public Resources Code 21000 et seq.), the Guidelines (14 Cal. Code Reg. 15000 et seq.), local CEQA procedures, if applicable, and relevant court decisions.

In its almost three decades of existence, CEQA has been praised by some as giving members of the public the power to challenge or stop environmentally damaging projects, and vilified by others as a major impediment to California's economic progress and development. In the 1990s, however, many agency representatives, academics, interest groups, and environmental practitioners recognized that CEQA has become inextricably woven into the fabric of California governance, decisionmaking, and politics. This recognition by these groups coalesced in a series of initiatives to streamline CEQA, fix practical problems, and make CEQA more effective in achieving its objectives. These initiatives were reflected in comprehensive revisions to the CEQA Guidelines in 1998.

The authors of this deskbook have devoted their careers to implementing CEQA with excellence. They participated in many of the CEQA improvement efforts of the 1990s, and deeply believe that they owe an obligation to everyone that CEQA touches to clearly explain CEQA's legal requirements, identify opportunities for improvement in both CEQA law and CEQA practice, and take action on those opportunities for improvement.

CEQA Deskbook: A Step-by-Step Guide on How to Comply with the California Environmental Quality Act presents the user with a handy, illustrated approach to CEQA. This 1999 edition contains new and improved materials designed to help public agency staff, consultants, attorneys, developers, and interested citizens understand the environmental review process, and identifies, in a simplified fashion, most of the key steps, requirements, and decision points necessary to comply with the law. This edition reflects the most recent changes to CEQA, including all legislative and regulatory changes adopted through 1998 and effective in 1999. Additionally, it includes the author's practical advice to help CEQA practitioners through the process of environmental review. This completely new book is intended to supersede and replace both the *Successful CEQA Compliance: A Step-by-Step Approach* and the 1996 *CEQA Deskbook* published by Solano Press.

With this book users will be better able to:

- Learn when a Negative Declaration is appropriate or whether an Environmental Impact Report must be prepared
- Prepare a legally defensible Negative Declaration, Mitigated Negative Declaration, or EIR
- Prepare a Master EIR or program EIR and know when and how it can be applied to specific projects
- Write adequate, feasible, and effective mitigation measures
- Effectively review and evaluate an EIR
- Prepare joint CEQA/NEPA documents
- Understand the environmental review process and determine the roles and requirements of state and local agencies

The book is intended to be used as a general guide to implementing the provisions of CEQA; therefore, for more detailed interpretations, users should consult the CEQA statute, the State CEQA Guidelines, and relevant case law.

The legal citations in the book are not exhaustive but, rather, whenever possible, refer to the CEQA Guidelines alone. The handbook selectively cites CEQA (Pub. Res. Code Secs. 21000–21178.1), other statutes, case law, and other references only when the Guidelines do not provide sufficient authority for a particular legal requirement. For detailed legal citations, users should refer to the additional CEQA publications listed in the suggested reading section after the appendices.

In 1993, the California Association of Environmental Professionals recognized *Successful CEQA Compliance: A Step-by-Step Approach* with an Award of Excellence in the category of "Outstanding Public Involvement and Education Programs."

Acknowledgments

The authors wish to thank the following staff members at Jones & Stokes Associates for their assistance in producing this book: Christy Anderson and Tim Messick, graphic artists, Pat Anderson, production assistance, and Vicki Axiaq, technical editor. In addition, the authors wish to thank the staff at Jones & Stokes, including Terry Rivasplata, former chief of the State Clearinghouse of the Governor's Office of Planning and Research, for their helpful comments in revising the *CEQA Deskbook.*

Special thanks also belong to the many environmental professionals who have attended CEQA workshops and shared with the authors their ideas for improving the book.

About the Authors

Ronald E. Bass is a principal with Jones & Stokes Associates, Inc., a leading West Coast consulting firm providing services in environmental planning and natural resource management. He was formerly Director of the State Clearinghouse in the Governor's Office of Planning and Research, where he was responsible for the administration of CEQA, Mr. Bass received a J.D. from the Washington College of Law at American University and an M.A. in Environmental Planning from California State University, Sacramento. Mr. Bass is a past President of the Association of Environmental Professionals and the California Chapter American Planning Association (CCAPA). As a result of his extensive environmental work teaching classes and seminars and writing publications on CEQA and the National Environmental Policy Act, Mr. Bass was recognized in 1993 by the CCAPA with a distinguished leadership award. In 1998–1999. Mr. Bass taught environmental law in Slovenia as a Fulbright Scholar.

Albert I. Herson, President of Jones & Stokes Associates, Inc., frequently assists private and public clients on how to comply with CEQA, NEPA, and other environmental laws. He has served on the State Bar Environmental Law Section's Executive Committee and CEQA Review Committee and regularly teaches workshops on environmental compliance. He is a past President of CCAPA, which gave him the distinguished leadership award for a professional planner in 1996. Mr. Herson received a J.D. from the University of the Pacific McGeorge School of Law and an M.A. in Urban Planning from the University of California, Los Angeles.

Mr. Bass and Mr. Herson are co-authors of *Mastering NEPA: A Step-by-Step Approach,* published by Solano Press Books, as well as contributing authors of *California Environmental Law and Land Use Practice,* published by Matthew-Bender and Company, Inc. They also serve on the editorial board of Matthew-Bender's *California Environmental Law Reporter.*

Kenneth M. Bogdan, Environmental Counsel for Jones & Stokes Associates, Inc., specializes in analyzing issues for private and public projects regarding compliance with environmental laws and regulations, including CEQA, NEPA, wetlands regulation, and the state and federal Endangered Species Acts. He has extensive experience analyzing land use and regulatory issues associated with all types of projects, including water resources, and construction of bridges, pipelines, large-scale development, and other large facilities. Mr. Bogdan received a J.D. from the University of California, Davis, School of Law, and a B.S. in Environmental Management from Rutgers University, Cook College, New Brunswick, New Jersey. He speaks regularly on environmental law topics, has authored several articles on environmental regulations and is coauthor, with Mr. Herson, of *Wetlands Regulation: A Complete Guide to Federal and California Programs,* published by Solano Press Books.

Chapters at a Glance

Contents

Contents

Contents

Contents

Contents

Chapter 8

Is CEQA Effective?

Short Articles

Figures

Contents

Chapter 1

Background and Implementation of CEQA

Overview

Objectives

The California Environmental Quality Act is regarded as the foundation of environmental law and policy in California. Unlike other single-topic environmental laws, CEQA encourages the protection of all aspects of the environment by requiring state and local agencies to prepare multidisciplinary environmental impact analyses and to make decisions based on those studies' findings regarding the environmental effects of the proposed action. Since its enactment, CEQA has been praised, criticized, amended often, and subject to considerable litigation. In spite of this, it has maintained its position as the backbone of California's environmental legislation. The full text of CEQA is found in Appendix 1.

Through its comprehensive policies and rigorous procedural requirements, CEQA has made an indelible mark on both government and private decision making in California. CEQA's main objectives are to disclose to decision makers and the public the significant environmental effects of proposed activities and to require agencies to avoid or reduce the environmental effects by implementing feasible alternatives or mitigation measures (consistent with constitutional requirements). Other objectives of CEQA focus on public disclosure regarding the reasons for agency approval of projects with significant environmental effects, interagency coordination in the review of projects, and enhancement of public participation in the planning process. Pub. Res. Code secs. 21000–21004; California State CEQA Guidelines, California Administrative Code (Guidelines), secs. 15002, 15086, 15087. *See* Appendix 2 for the full text of the Guidelines.

Application to Government Activities in California

CEQA applies to all discretionary activities proposed to be carried out or approved by California public agencies, including state, regional, county,

---

Objectives of CEQA

- To disclose to decision makers and the public the significant environmental effects of proposed activities

- To identify ways to avoid or reduce environmental damage

- To prevent environmental damage by requiring implementation of feasible alternatives or mitigation measures

- To disclose to the public reasons for agency approval of projects with significant environmental effects

- To foster interagency coordination in the review of projects

- To enhance public participation in the planning process

CEQA = California Environmental Quality Act

In enacting the California Environmental Quality Act, the Legislature sought to protect California's renowned aesthetic, natural, and scenic qualities.

and local agencies, unless an exemption applies. CEQA applies to private activities that require discretionary governmental approvals. Pub. Res. Code secs. 21001.1, 21002, 21080; Guidelines sec. 15002(c).

Policies Encouraging Protection of the Environment

CEQA sets forth a series of sweeping policy statements encouraging environmental protection. Pub. Res. Code secs. 21000–21004; Guidelines secs. 15002, 15003. These policy statements in CEQA provide that:

- Maintenance of a quality environment is of statewide concern
- There is a need to maintain ecological systems and the general welfare of the people
- Government agencies should identify critical thresholds for health and safety and prevent conditions from reaching those thresholds
- Every citizen has the responsibility to preserve and enhance the environment
- Public and private interests must make systematic and concerted efforts to enhance environmental quality and control pollution
- Government agencies must give major consideration to preventing environmental damage
- All actions necessary to protect, rehabilitate, and enhance the environmental quality of the state should be taken
- All actions necessary to provide the people with clean air and water and the enjoyment of aesthetic, natural, scenic, and historic qualities should be taken
- The elimination of fish and wildlife species should be prevented by ensuring that their populations do not drop below self-perpetuating levels

Broad, environmentally oriented policies have led the courts to interpret CEQA "so as to afford the fullest protection of the environment within the reasonable scope of the statutory language."

These broad, environmentally oriented policies have led the courts to interpret CEQA "so as to afford the fullest protection of the environment within the reasonable scope of the statutory language." *Friends of Mammoth v. Board of Supervisors* (1972) 8 Cal. 3d 247.

Policies Encouraging Efficient and Streamlined Implementation

In addition to encouraging the protection of the environment, CEQA also encourages agencies to implement CEQA in an efficient and streamlined manner through policies that require them to:

- Integrate CEQA with other planning and environmental laws to encourage concurrent review and processing
- Organize and write environmental documents to make them useful to decision makers and the public
- Omit unnecessary project descriptions and emphasize feasible alternatives and mitigation measures
- Incorporate information from environmental impact reports (EIRs) into a database that can be used to reduce delays and duplication in preparing subsequent documents

EIR = Environmental impact report

- Carry out CEQA efficiently and expeditiously to conserve financial, governmental, physical, and social resources so that those resources may be applied toward mitigation of environmental impacts
- Make decisions with environmental consequences in mind
- Consider the whole of an action, not simply its constituent parts, when determining whether it will have a significant environmental effect
- Prepare sufficient but not necessarily technically perfect informational documents that are complete and contain a good-faith effort at full disclosure
- Make decisions that are informed and balanced and not use CEQA as an instrument for the oppression and delay of social, economic, or recreational development or advancement

Pub. Res. Code sec. 21003; Guidelines secs. 15003, 15006.

Procedural and Substantive Requirements

CEQA requires all California public agencies to comply with both procedural and substantive requirements. Pub. Res. Code sec. 21080; Guidelines sec. 15002. Failure to follow either set of requirements may be considered a violation of CEQA and an agency's decision may be set aside by a court. Pub. Res. Code secs. 21005, 21168, 21168.5.

Failure to follow both procedural and substantive requirements may be considered a violation of CEQA and an agency's decision may be set aside by a court.

CEQA Objectives	CEQA Procedural Requirements to Meet Objectives
Disclose environmental impacts	• Initial studies • Negative declarations • Environmental impact reports
Identify and prevent environmental damage	• Mitigation measures • Alternatives • Mitigation monitoring
Disclose agency decision making	• Findings • Statements of overriding consideration
Enhance public participation	• Scoping • Public notice requirement • Response to comments • Legal enforcement procedures • Citizen access to the courts
Foster intergovernmental coordination	• Early consultation • Scoping meetings • Notices of preparation • State Clearinghouse review

**Figure 1-1
CEQA Objectives
and Procedures**

Procedural Requirements. CEQA sets forth a series of detailed procedural requirements to ensure that each of the law's objectives are accomplished. The fundamental premise on which CEQA is based is that environmental protection can be achieved through compliance with rigorous, action-forcing procedures. Figure 1-1 outlines some of the procedural requirements designed to accomplish each objective. These procedural requirements are

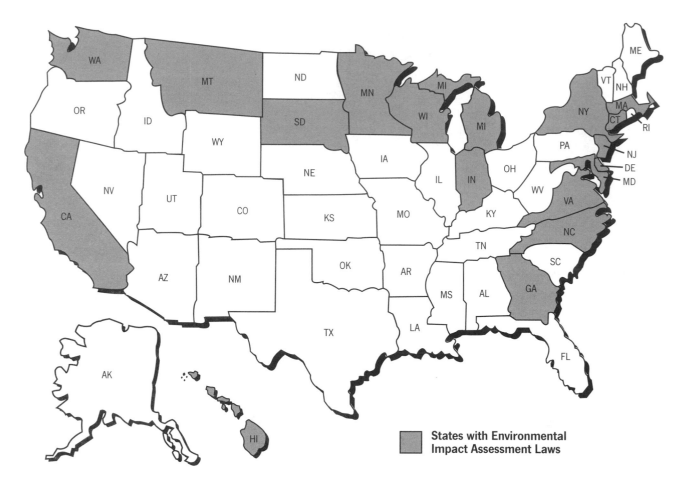

States with Environmental
Impact Assessment Laws

Figure 1-2
States with Environmental
Impact Assessment Laws

linked with specific timing requirements that must be met in order for an agency to have complied with CEQA. Detailed procedural requirements are discussed throughout this book.

Substantive Requirements. CEQA also contains substantive provisions requiring agencies to address environmental impacts disclosed in an EIR. Therefore, to comply with CEQA, it is not enough for agencies to prepare a report that meets the procedural requirements. Rather, the agencies must actually avoid or minimize environmental damage when feasible. Pub. Res. Code sec. 21002; Guidelines secs. 15002, 15021. When avoiding or minimizing environmental damage is not feasible, CEQA requires agencies to prepare a written statement of overriding considerations when they decide to approve a project that will cause one or more significant effects on the environment. Pub. Res. Code sec. 21002; Guidelines sec. 15021(a).

Authorities Granted to Public Agencies

No New Powers. Although it requires agencies to mitigate or avoid significant impacts when feasible, CEQA does not grant an agency new, independent powers to impose or carry out mitigation measures. Rather, an agency must rely on its existing discretionary powers to mitigate or avoid significant environmental effects. However, all empowering statutes available to an agency can be used, in conjunction with CEQA, to effect environmental mitigation (e.g., using an agency's power of condemnation in order to effectuate mitigation measures associated with the agency's proposed project). Pub. Res. Code sec. 21004; Guidelines sec. 15040.

Authorities Granted. CEQA grants public agencies five basic types of authority to enable them to carry out the objectives of the law. CEQA authorizes all public agencies to comment on other agencies' environmental documents. Pub. Res. Code sec. 21104; Guidelines sec. 15044. CEQA authorizes Lead Agencies to require feasible changes in a project to substantially lessen or avoid significant effects, when feasible, or disapprove a project to avoid significant effects. Pub. Res. Code sec. 21002.1; Guidelines secs. 15041(a), 15042. CEQA authorizes Lead Agencies, public agencies that have principal responsibility for carrying out or approving a project and for implementing CEQA, to approve a project with significant effects if there is no feasible way to lessen or avoid the significant effects and the project's benefits outweigh these effects. Pub. Res. Code sec. 21002.1; Guidelines sec. 15043. CEQA allows Lead Agencies to impose fees on project applicants for CEQA implementation, including preparing environmental documents and for procedures necessary to comply with CEQA for an applicant's project. Litigation expenses are not, however recoverable under this authorization to charge fees. Pub. Res. Code sec. 21089; Guidelines sec. 15045(a).

Responsible Agencies, public agencies other than the Lead Agency that have responsibility for carrying out or approving a project and for complying with CEQA, have a more limited authority to require changes in the project to lessen or avoid, or refuse to approve the project to avoid, only the effects of that part of the project that they will be called on to carry out or approve. Pub. Res. Code secs. 21104(c), 21153(c); Guidelines secs. 15041(b), 15042. Agencies participating in the CEQA process other than the Lead Agency— including Responsible Agencies, Trustee Agencies (state agencies having jurisdiction by law over natural resources affected by a project that are held in trust for the people of the State of California), and other commenting agencies—are not authorized under CEQA to impose fees for CEQA implementation (*see* Payment of Environmental Review Fees to California Department of Fish and Game, page 51). However, these agencies may charge permit application and review fees pursuant to their own enabling authorities.

> **CEQA Authorizes Agencies to:**
> - Require changes in a project to lessen or avoid significant effects, when feasible. Guidelines sec. 15041(a).
> - Disapprove a project to avoid significant effects. Guidelines sec. 15042.
> - Approve a project with significant effects if there is no feasible way to lessen or avoid the significant effects and the project's benefits outweigh these effects. Guidelines sec. 15043.
> - Impose fees on project applicants for CEQA implementation. Guidelines sec. 15045(a).

Legislative and Judicial History

Enactment and Early Enforcement

Enacted in 1970, CEQA was modeled after the National Environmental Policy Act (NEPA) [42 U.S.C. 4321–4327]. California was the first of 15 states to enact an environmental impact assessment law modeled after NEPA. *See* Figure 1-2. NEPA and CEQA require agencies to prepare environmental impact assessments of proposed projects with significant environmental effects and to circulate these documents to other agencies and the public for comment before making decisions. However, NEPA's requirements are more procedural than substantive; unlike CEQA, NEPA does not contain an explicit directive requiring federal agencies to avoid or mitigate impacts disclosed in an

NEPA = National Environmental Policy Act

NEPA and CEQA require agencies to prepare environmental impact assessments of proposed projects with significant environmental effects and to circulate these documents to other agencies and the public for comment before making decisions.

environmental impact statement (EIS) (which is equivalent to an EIR) regardless of feasibility. *See* chapter 6 for a detailed comparison of CEQA and NEPA.

CEQA was drafted in response to a report by a joint legislative committee on environmental quality. It originated with a report, issued by the California Assembly Select Committee on Environmental Quality in 1970, entitled *The Environmental Bill of Rights.* This report called for adoption of an environmental quality act modeled after NEPA, which had been enacted by Congress in 1969. The Environmental Bill of Rights included a proposal to make CEQA a constitutional amendment, but the Legislature instead chose to enact CEQA as a statute. Following the recommendation of the Assembly Select Committee on Environmental Quality, the full Legislature enacted CEQA, and it was signed by Governor Reagan later in 1970.

Subsequent Amendments

Since its enactment, CEQA has been amended almost every year. Most of the amendments have been minor; however, fundamental changes have been made every few years. For example, in 1972 CEQA was amended to codify the key holding of *Friends of Mammoth v. Board of Supervisors of Mono County* (1972) 8 Cal. 3d 247, 104 Cal. Rptr. 76 (that CEQA applies not only to public projects but also to private activities requiring discretionary governmental approval; *see* page 7). Other important amendments, generally intended to streamline CEQA, were enacted in 1976, 1978, 1984, and 1989.

The CEQA Revision Acts of 1993, the latest major legislative amendments enacted, resulted in numerous technical revisions intended to streamline the CEQA process. These revisions included such measures as requiring an update of the Guidelines every two years, expediting the Responsible Agency permit process, streamlining the process of granting CEQA compliance for environmentally mandated projects, limiting judicial remedies, and new procedures for preparing master and focused EIRs. Since 1993, the Legislature has adopted only relatively minor revisions to CEQA.

The Politics of CEQA Compliance

Discretion and Risk. CEQA is a flexible law that gives broad discretionary powers to agencies responsible for its implementation. With this discretion comes considerable responsibility, risk, and challenges from conflicting interests. Throughout the environmental review process, public agencies must make a series of important decisions, any one of which may be challenged by project opponents. Lead Agencies must continually balance the time, effort, and expense of full compliance against the risks of losing tax revenue-generating projects or facing litigation. To a great extent, the success of CEQA depends on the way in which agencies manage this risk.

In practice, the agency required to comply with CEQA is often subject to political and economic influences, exerted by project proponents, to shorten the process by either allowing the project to proceed under an

Lead Agencies often balance the time, effort, and expense of full compliance against the risks of losing tax revenue-generating projects or facing litigation.

exemption when a Negative Declaration (*see* chapter 2) may be more appropriate, or preparing a Negative Declaration when an EIR (*see* chapter 3) may be more appropriate. When deciding which type of document to prepare, the agency should be mindful of the legal and political risks inherent in taking shortcuts. Generally, the risk of being challenged in court (and potentially losing the challenge) increases as less time and effort is devoted to preparing the CEQA document and the record on which the agency has based its decision (Figure 1-3).

Variations in CEQA Compliance among Projects and Agencies. An additional challenge for public agencies is that the degree of public scrutiny of their actions or community concern regarding a type of project or sensitive resource is generally a factor in determining the level of CEQA compliance. Consequently, the standard for determining adequate compliance often differs from project to project and from community to community. For example, a project that requires an EIR in one community may require only a Negative Declaration in another because of differing environmental thresholds generated by the level of public scrutiny or community concerns. Recent changes to the Guidelines have attempted to reduce the discretion and variability between some agencies when determining impact significance. Guidelines secs. 15064, 15064.7, Appendix G.

One way to think of these levels of CEQA compliance is: "bare legal minimum," "good practice," and "overkill." Examples of these levels can vary between different California jurisdictions, and within the same jurisdiction depending on the Lead Agency's desire to ward off legal challenges.

CEQA as a Bridge between Science and Politics. In addition to being highly discretionary and subject to local variations, CEQA compliance is also a challenge because of

Friends of Mammoth v. Board of Supervisors: Court Establishes That CEQA Applies to Government Approval of Private Projects

CEQA was not taken seriously by many public agencies during the first year following its enactment, and the law was not originally applied to private development projects requiring government permits. Early EIRs looked more like the Negative Declarations prepared by today's standards.

This approach changed with the California Supreme Court's decision in *Friends of Mammoth v. Board of Supervisors* (1972) 8 Cal. 3d 247, which specifically addressed whether CEQA applied to government approval of private projects. In this case, Mono County, assuming that its action was not subject to the newly enacted law, approved a conditional use permit for a complex of 184 condominium units, a restaurant, and specialty shops without any environmental study. An unincorporated association sought a writ of mandate to set aside the county's approval, pending compliance with CEQA.

Although the Superior Court held for the county, the State Supreme Court reversed the lower court's decision, holding that the county's grant of a conditional use permit was a "project" as defined under CEQA. The court stated that the State Legislature enacted CEQA to require an agency, in its regulatory capacity, to analyze the significant environmental effects of its actions, including privately-initiated projects for which government approvals are needed; therefore, the term "project" includes not only agency actions that directly involve physical impacts on the environment, but also activities such as approving permits, which have indirect environmental effects. In addition to holding that CEQA applied to issuance of permits for private projects, the court announced that all aspects of CEQA should be interpreted expansively "so as to afford the fullest protection of the environment within the reasonable scope of the statutory language." In 1972, the Legislature amended the law to indicate that CEQA clearly applied to government approval of private projects as well as to direct government activities.

The California Supreme Court's decision in *Friends of Mammoth* established the courts as the ultimate enforcers of CEQA and provided a clear message that agency noncompliance would not be tolerated. However, it should be noted that, in 1993, the State Legislature specifically amended CEQA to limit a court's review of agency actions in compliance with CEQA so that courts will not "interpret [CEQA or the Guidelines] in a manner which imposes procedural or substantive requirements beyond those explicitly stated in [CEQA and the Guidelines]." Pub. Res. Code sec. 21083.1.

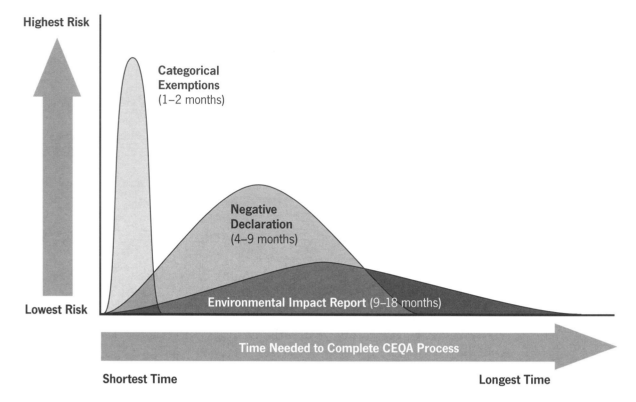

Highest Risk

Categorical
Exemptions
(1–2 months)

Negative
Declaration
(4–9 months)

Lowest Risk

Environmental Impact Report (9–18 months)

Time Needed to Complete CEQA Process

Shortest Time

Longest Time

**Figure 1-3
Risk versus Approximate
Time in CEQA Compliance**

OPR = Governor's Office
of Planning and Research

the interdisciplinary nature of many environmental impacts. As described in chapter 2, CEQA requires an agency to review the effects of its actions on numerous environmental resources, including air, water, fish, and wildlife. Proper implementation requires delicate coordination between a variety of professional disciplines. The goal of CEQA's interdisciplinary focus is to ensure that government agencies consider a broad range of environmental factors and that trade-offs between various resources are publicly considered.

Prior to the passage of CEQA, government decision making was often two-dimensional, focusing only on economic and technical factors. Environmental issues rarely entered into the political debate. Generally, the negative aspects of a project, often environmental in nature, were not even presented to the public.

By requiring multi-disciplinary scientific inquiry, CEQA has clearly filled a void. The EIR, in particular, has proved to be a valuable tool for bridging the gap between science and politics, fostering informed public debate over a broad range of environmental impacts.

Administration and Oversight

In General

Two state agencies, the Governor's Office of Planning and Research (OPR) and the Resources Agency, are responsible for CEQA administration and oversight. Their responsibilities center on administering some of CEQA's procedural requirements and issuing the Guidelines. The Guidelines (Figure 1-4) are the official administrative interpretation of CEQA for agency implementation. For a complete copy of the Guidelines, *see* Appendix 2.

OPR Responsibilities

OPR is responsible for the following CEQA-related activities:

NOP = Notice of Preparation
SCH = State Clearinghouse

- Reviewing and recommending changes to the Guidelines
- Recommending categorical exemptions
- Assisting in identifying Responsible Agencies
- Ensuring that Responsible Agencies respond to Notices of Preparation (NOPs)
- Operating the State Clearinghouse (SCH)
- Resolving Lead Agency disputes
- Posting notices of completion and determination
- Publishing the SCH newsletter
- Collecting California Department of Fish and Game review fees
- Providing education and training on CEQA
- Maintaining a database to assist agencies in CEQA implementation

Pub Res. Code secs. 21080.4, 21083; Guidelines sec. 15023.

Resources Agency Responsibilities

The Resources Agency is responsible for the following CEQA-related activities:

- Formal rule making and adoption of the Guidelines, including determination of classes of projects that will not have a significant effect on the environment and therefore be given a categorical exemption
- Certifying state agency regulatory programs
- Maintenance of Internet information about CEQA

Pub. Res. Code sec. 21083(c); Guidelines sec. 15024.

CEQA Guidelines. The State CEQA Guidelines, adopted by the Resources Agency, are the primary rules and source of interpretation of CEQA. Pub. Res. Code sec. 21083. The process for adoption of the Guidelines typically starts with recommendations from OPR or through a request from a public agency. The Resources Agency certifies and adopts the Guidelines after proposing a draft that goes through public notice and comment. After adoption but prior to the Guidelines becoming effective, the California Office of Administrative Law reviews the adopted Guidelines to ensure compliance with state requirements for promulgating regulations. Compliance with amendments to the Guidelines does not become mandatory until the 120th day after the amendments have become "effective," although a public agency may choose to implement the amendment beginning on the Guideline amendment's effective date. Guidelines sec. 15007.

Although the Guidelines are adopted with public notice and comment, in the same manner as other state regulations, there is an ongoing legal question as to whether the Guidelines are regulatory mandates or merely aids to interpretation of CEQA. Courts, however, generally defer to the Guidelines. The choice of the term "Guidelines," however, has led some courts to question the Guidelines' legal authority. The Guidelines themselves state that they contain "mandatory, advisory, [and] permissive" directives. Guidelines sec. 15005.

Figure 1-4. CEQA Guidelines Contents

Article 1	General Provisions
Article 2	General Responsibilities
Article 3	Authorities Granted to Public Agencies by CEQA
Article 4	Lead Agency
Article 5	Preliminary Review of Project and Conduct of Initial Study
Article 6	Negative Declaration Process
Article 7	EIR Process
Article 8	Time Limits
Article 9	Contents of EIR
Article 10	Considerations in Preparing EIRs
Article 11	Types of EIRs
Article 12	Special Situations
Article 13	Review and Evaluations of EIRs and Negative Declarations
Article 14	Projects Also Subject to NEPA
Article 15	Litigation
Article 16	EIR Monitor
Article 17	Exemptions for Certified State Regulatory Programs
Article 18	Statutory Exemptions
Article 19	Categorical Exemptions
Article 20	Definitions
	Appendices

Revision and Update of CEQA Guidelines. Despite the requirement to periodically review and recommend changes to the Guidelines [Pub. Res. Code sec. 21087; Guidelines sec. 15007], the Guidelines were not comprehensively amended between 1984 and 1992. In 1992, the Resources Agency revised the Guidelines to reflect some of the legislative changes that had occurred through 1991. This, however, was not a comprehensive revision. In 1994, an important but relatively limited set of amendments to the Guidelines was adopted.

Not happy with the pace of Guideline amendments, in 1995 the Legislature amended CEQA to require OPR to review and recommend changes to the Guidelines every two years. In the same legislation, the Resources Agency was required to adopt amendments every two years. Pub. Res. Code sec. 21087. This requirement is intended to ensure that the Guidelines remain up to date and reflect recent legislation, new judicial interpretations, and current CEQA practice. Pub. Res. Code sec. 21087. OPR and the Resources Agency were specifically directed to adopt new Guidelines by March 1995 to reflect 1993 and 1994 CEQA amendments.

In response to these legislative mandates, the Resources Agency has recently adopted two sets of Guideline amendments, one in May 1997 and another in October 1998. The purpose of the May 1997 Guidelines amendments was to bring the Guidelines up-to-date with regard to legislation adopted during the past several years. The October 1998 amendments, however, were more comprehensive, reflecting not only recent legislation, but also relevant court decisions and changes in agency practice. The complete text of the CEQA Guidelines, including the most recent amendments, can be found in Appendix 2 or is available on-line at: http://ceres.ca.gov/ceqa. An unofficial copy of the entire California Code of Regulations is available on the Internet, through the State Office of Administrative Law, at http://ccr.oal.ca.gov/ccrmain.htm.

Although the Guidelines are now relatively up-to-date, practitioners are always advised to review the latest judicial opinions for the most recent interpretations of CEQA. CEQA cases are also reported on the CERES website.

Other Responsibilities of OPR

Beginning in March 1994, OPR has been required to implement a public assistance and information program to help agencies implement CEQA. As part of this program, OPR commenced a CEQA technical advice series to explain complex issues that frequently arise in CEQA practice. To date, it has issued the following very useful advice memoranda (*see* Appendices 4 through 11):

- *Tracking Mitigation Measures under AB 3180* (March 1996)
- *Focusing on Master EIRs* (November 1997)
- *CEQA and Archaeological Resources* (April 1994)
- *CEQA and Historical Resources* (May 1996)
- *Mitigated Negative Declarations* (December 1997)
- *CEQA, NEPA, and Base Closure: Recipes for Streamlining Environmental Review* (March 1996)

- *Thresholds of Significance: Criteria for Defining Environmental Significance* (September 1994)
- *Circulation and Notice Under the California Environmental Quality Act* (January 1998)

Additionally, OPR is required to maintain an information database to help agencies prepare environmental documents. Pub. Res. Code sec. 21159.9. A listing of recent environmental documents submitted to the State Clearinghouse is available through the CERES website (discussed below).

State Clearinghouse

In 1973, the SCH was established within OPR as the single point of contact in state government to receive and distribute environmental documents prepared pursuant to NEPA and to coordinate the environmental review process under CEQA when state agencies are involved. The categories of documents required to be sent to the SCH are described in chapter 3. The SCH does not actually review CEQA documents, but instead circulates them for review to those state agencies likely to be interested in the projects and receives and transmits comments from those state agencies to the agencies responsible for preparing the CEQA documents.

The SCH maintains a computerized database of all environmental documents it receives for state review. Although the SCH does not receive all EIRs, its database is the only source of information regarding the number of EIRs prepared in California.

California Resources Agency–California Environmental Resource Evaluation System

CERES is an information system developed by the State of California to facilitate access to a variety of electronic data describing California's environment. The goal of CERES is to improve environmental analysis and planning by integrating natural and cultural resource information from multiple contributors and by making it available and useful to a wide variety of users.

Within CERES, the user will find the Land Use Planning Information Network (LUPIN) which contains considerable data sources on land use planning in California. LUPIN contains the text of CEQA, the regulations, including proposed amendments, and a growing collection of on-line environmental documents. CERES and LUPIN may be found on-line at: http://ceres.ca.gov. Information available on-line includes, but is not limited to:

CERES = California Environmental Resource Evaluation System

LUPIN = Land Use Planning Information Network

- The CEQA Statute
- The CEQA Guidelines, including proposed amendments
- Recent CEQA court decisions
- OPR technical advice series
- Database of CEQA documents submitted to the state for review
- Directory of CEQA judges
- Other information related to CEQA

As a component of CERES, California recently developed an interactive CEQA process flow chart, an innovative legal research tool to help CEQA practitioners. Using the interactive version of the familiar CEQA flow chart, a person may select any aspect of the environmental review process and the following information will immediately appear:

- A narrative summary of that component of the process
- The relevant Public Resources Code sections
- The CEQA Guideline references related to that topic
- A list of the most significant cases dealing with that topic

The flow chart helps bring the details of CEQA's legal framework to anyone who uses it. Additionally, it helps bridge the gap between the visually oriented world of planners and the written world of attorneys.

CEQA Implementation by Public Agencies

CEQA applies to all California government agencies at all levels, including local agencies, regional agencies, and state agencies, boards, commissions, and special districts.

CEQA applies to all California government agencies at all levels, including local agencies, regional agencies, and state agencies, boards, commissions, and special districts. Pub. Res. Code secs. 21000, 21001; Guidelines secs. 15002, 15368, 15379, 15383. However, proposals for legislation; continuing administrative or maintenance activities, personnel-related actions, certain emergency actions, general policy and procedure-making; submittal of proposal to vote; creation of general government funding mechanisms; and political activity of the government that does not result in physical changes in the environment are not subject to CEQA's environmental review. Guidelines sec. 15378.

Agency Requirement to Adopt CEQA Procedures

Each state and local agency must adopt CEQA implementation procedures that are consistent with CEQA and the Guidelines. A public agency's implementing procedures should contain the provisions for:

- Identifying activities that are exempt from CEQA
- Conducting initial studies
- Preparing Negative Declarations
- Consulting with other agencies
- Ensuring adequate opportunities for public review and comment
- Evaluating and responding to comments
- Assigning responsibility for determining the adequacy of environmental documents
- Reviewing and considering environmental documents by decision makers
- Filing environmental documents
- Submitting comments to other agencies
- Assigning CEQA functions to agency staff
- Providing time periods for performing CEQA functions

Pub. Res. Code sec. 21082; Guidelines sec. 15022.

A public agency may adopt the Guidelines by reference, but the agency's procedures must still include specific provisions to tailor the general provisions to its specific operations. Guidelines sec. 15022.

In practice, most state and local agency CEQA procedures have not been updated and tend to mainly incorporate the Guidelines by reference. However, agencies should consider updating their CEQA procedures to maximize CEQA's usefulness within their jurisdiction.

Because public participation is an essential part of the CEQA process, each public agency should include provisions in its CEQA procedures to encourage both formal and informal public involvement. Such procedures should be designed to receive and evaluate public comments on environmental issues related to agency activities. *See* chapter 4. Additionally, an agency's CEQA procedures should include, whenever possible, making environmental information available in electronic format on the Internet, on a website maintained or utilized by the public agency. Guidelines sec. 15201.

Because public participation is an essential part of the CEQA process, each public agency should include provisions in its CEQA procedures to encourage both formal and informal public involvement.

Key Participants in the CEQA Process

For any given project, many agencies and groups may be involved in the CEQA process. *See* Figure 1-5. The potential roles of the various agencies involved in CEQA are described below. Agencies serve in different roles for different projects.

Lead Agency. A Lead Agency is the California government agency that has the principal responsibility for carrying out or approving a project and therefore the principal responsibility for preparing CEQA documents. A Lead Agency is responsible for deciding whether a negative declaration or an

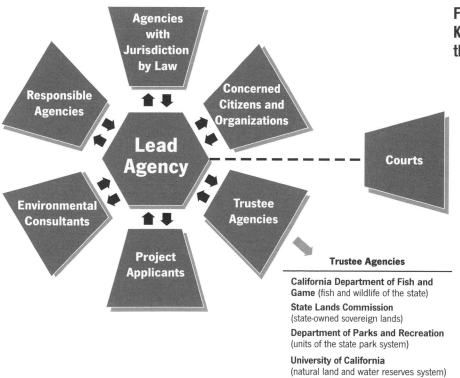

**Figure 1-5
Key Participants in
the CEQA Process**

Trustee Agencies

California Department of Fish and Game (fish and wildlife of the state)

State Lands Commission (state-owned sovereign lands)

Department of Parks and Recreation (units of the state park system)

University of California (natural land and water reserves system)

A Responsible Agency must actively participate in the Lead Agency's CEQA process, review the Lead Agency's CEQA document, and use that document when making a decision on the project.

EIR will be required and for determining the scope and content of that document. Additionally, the Lead Agency is responsible for the preparation and adequacy of the document. Pub. Res. Code sec. 21067; Guidelines secs. 15367, 15050. *See* chapter 2. A Lead Agency has a duty to produce a comprehensive environmental document that can be used by a Responsible Agency (*see* page 15) in making decisions. As stated above, a Lead Agency is required to make changes in a project to lessen or avoid significant effects, when feasible, or to disapprove a project to avoid significant effects unless the project's benefits outweigh these effects.

For public projects subject to CEQA, a public agency is the Lead Agency for its own projects, even if the project will be located within the jurisdiction of another agency. For private projects requiring government approval, an agency with general governmental powers (e.g., city or county) prevails as the Lead Agency over an agency with a single or limited purpose; for rezoning, the city doing the rezoning will be the Lead Agency. When criteria are equal, the agency that acts first becomes the Lead Agency. However, agencies may designate a Lead Agency by mutual agreement. Guidelines sec. 15051.

Lead Agency disputes may be submitted to OPR for resolution. Pub. Res. Code sec. 21165; Guidelines secs. 15023, 15053. OPR issued Lead Agency dispute regulations setting forth procedures agencies must follow to formally resolve disputes. *See* Cal. Code Regs. secs. 16012 et seq. and OPR's Regulations for Designation of Lead Agency, Appendix 3.

Although OPR has informally mediated numerous Lead Agency disputes, there have been only three occasions since 1995 where the OPR director has had to formally designate a Lead Agency.

Responsible Agency. A Responsible Agency is an agency other than the Lead Agency that has a legal responsibility for also carrying out or approving a project. A Responsible Agency must actively participate in the Lead Agency's CEQA process, review the Lead Agency's CEQA document, and use that document when making a decision on the project. Pub. Res. Code sec. 21069; Guidelines secs. 15096, 15381. A Responsible Agency is required to rely on the Lead Agency's environmental document in acting on whatever aspect of the project requires its approval but must prepare and issue its own findings regarding the project. Guidelines sec. 15096. A Responsible Agency generally must consider the Lead Agency's CEQA document legally adequate, subject to narrow exceptions. Pub. Res. Code sec. 21167.3; Guidelines secs. 15052, 15096. *See* chapter 4. In certain cases, a Responsible Agency may take over a Lead Agency's role. Guidelines sec. 15052.

Trustee Agencies. Trustee Agencies have jurisdiction over certain resources held in trust for the people of California but do not have a legal authority over approving or carrying out the project. Guidelines sec. 15386. Only four agencies are designated by the Guidelines as Trustee Agencies, the California Department of Fish and Game, with regard to fish and wildlife of the state, native plants designated as rare or endangered, game refuges, and ecological reserves; the State Lands Commission, with regard to state-owned "sovereign" lands, such as the beds of navigable waters and state school lands; the California Department of Parks and Recreation, with regard to units of the state park system; and the University of California, with regard to sites within the Natural Land and Water Reserves System. Guidelines sec. 15386. Although other agencies have jurisdiction by law over certain resources (*see below*), they are not considered to hold these resources "in trust" for the people of California. Trustee Agencies are generally required to be notified of CEQA documents relevant to their jurisdiction, whether or not these agencies have actual permitting authority or approval power over aspects of the underlying project. Guidelines sec. 15086.

The Department of Fish and Game is a trustee agency for the state's wildlife.

Agencies with Jurisdiction by Law. In addition to contacting all Responsible and Trustee Agencies, the Lead Agency, when preparing an EIR, must consult with and seek comments from every public agency that has jurisdiction by law with respect to the project; each city or county that borders on a city or county within which the project is located; and state, federal, and local agencies that exercise authority over resources that may be affected by the project. Pub. Res. Code secs. 21104, 21153; Guidelines sec. 15086.

Public Participation

Importance of Public Involvement

Public involvement is an essential feature of CEQA. Guidelines sec. 15201. The environmental review process introduced by CEQA has greatly expanded the opportunities for interested citizens to participate in project planning and government decision making. The EIR has become a well-established tool by which the public can gain access to information and influence the outcome of a broad variety of projects. In fact, the California Supreme Court has stated that members of the public hold a "privileged position" in the CEQA process. *Concerned Citizens of Costa Mesa v. 32nd District Agricultural Association* (1986) 42 Cal. 3d 929.

Public involvement is an essential feature of CEQA. In fact, the California Supreme Court has stated that members of the public hold a "privileged position" in the process.

The environmental review process established by CEQA provides ample opportunities for the public to participate through scoping [Guidelines sec. 15083], public notice and public review of CEQA documents [Guidelines secs. 15072, 15087], and public hearings, and by requiring agencies to respond to public comments in Final EIRs [Guidelines sec. 15088].

Also, the public plays a major role in the judicial enforcement of CEQA. The vigilance of private citizens has been instrumental in ensuring that agencies comply with the law. Without the active involvement of citizen "watchdogs," many instances of noncompliance would have gone unchallenged. Many Californians have come to expect full compliance with CEQA and are ready and willing to challenge agencies that do not take CEQA seriously.

Lead Agency Responsibilities

The success of CEQA as an environmental disclosure and problem-solving law is based on open decision making. Therefore, state and local agencies must make diligent efforts to involve the public in implementing CEQA throughout the environmental review process. Each public agency must include provisions in its CEQA procedures for wide public involvement, both formal and informal, to encourage the public to react to environmental issues related to the agency's proposed projects. Guidelines sec. 15201. The objectives of public review of agency proposals include sharing expertise, disclosing agency analysis, checking for accuracy, detecting omissions, discovering public concerns, and soliciting counter proposals. Guidelines sec. 15200.

Effective Public Participation in the CEQA Process

CEQA provides ample opportunities for members of the public to participate in the environmental review process. Citizens should learn the organizational structure, the decision-making lines of authority, and the administrative appeal process for the agencies of concern and identify the key individuals who may be responsible for CEQA implementation within the agency. It is important for citizens to write to those individuals and request to be put on the list of persons to be notified of CEQA actions. Joining forces with established associations, environmental groups, and other organizations will assist citizens to address similar environmental issues and pool financial resources. It is helpful for concerned citizens to regularly monitor local newspapers for any formal announcements of or articles about agency activities in your community. When concerned about a particular agency action, citizens should submit comments at every possible opportunity afforded by the agency and make sure that the comments are substantive, well written or presented, and supported by the weight of evidence. Citizens must be willing to meet with agency staff to discuss views about the proposed actions. If all other efforts to influence agency decision making are unsuccessful, a person or organization may challenge the agency's decision through litigation.

A vigilant, informed, and well-prepared citizenry is the key to the enforcement of CEQA and better environmental decision making by state and local officials.

Timing of CEQA Implementation

When to Comply with CEQA

CEQA documents should be prepared during the agency planning process and must be completed and certified before project "approval," which is the decision committing an agency to a definite course of action on the project. Guidelines sec. 15352(a). CEQA documents should be prepared early enough in the planning process to enable environmental factors to influence project design, but late enough so that useful information is available for environmental assessment. Guidelines sec. 15004(b). *See* chapter 2 for discussion of the particular timing requirements for Lead and Responsible Agencies under CEQA and the Permit Streamlining Act.

With public projects, the project sponsors must incorporate environmental considerations into project conceptualization, design, and planning.

The objectives of public review of agency proposals include sharing expertise, disclosing agency analysis, checking for accuracy, detecting omissions, discovering public concerns, and soliciting counter proposals.

CEQA documents should be prepared early enough in the planning process to enable environmental factors to influence project design, but late enough so that useful information is available for environmental assessment.

With private projects, the Lead Agency must encourage the project proponent to incorporate environmental considerations in their project conceptualization, design, and planning at the earliest feasible time. In either case, public agencies must not undertake any action concerning a proposed project which would have a significant adverse effect or limit the choice of alternatives or mitigation measures before completion of CEQA compliance.

Additionally, an agency may not formally make a decision to proceed with the use of a site until after CEQA compliance. However, an agency may designate a preferred site for CEQA review and may enter into a land acquisition agreement, so long as the agreement is conditioned on any future use of the site being subject to CEQA compliance.

Further, an agency may not commit or solicit funding for a project or otherwise take any action which gives impetus to a planned-for foreseeable project in a manner that forecloses alternatives or mitigation measures that would ordinarily be part of CEQA compliance. Guidelines sec. 15004.

An agency may not commit or solicit funding for a project or otherwise take any action which gives impetus to a planned-for foreseeable project in a manner that forecloses alternatives or mitigation measures that would ordinarily be part of CEQA compliance.

Integration with Existing Planning Procedures

The environmental review process established by CEQA is not an independent process; it must be integrated into project planning and decision making. To the maximum extent feasible, these procedures should run concurrently, not consecutively. Guidelines sec. 15004(c). *See* Figure 1-6. As described in detail in chapter 4, CEQA should be coordinated with the project planning process, when CEQA requirements are directly linked to the phases of the agency's planning process.

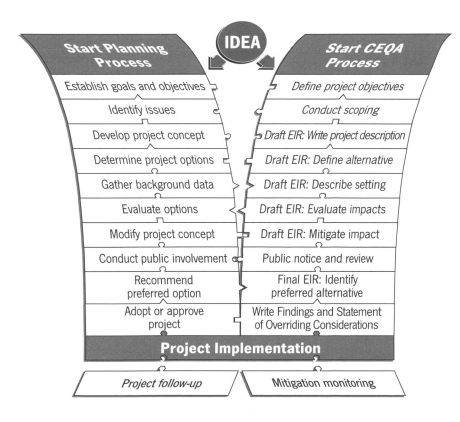

**Figure 1-6
Integrating CEQA
with Planning**

Integration with Related Environmental Review Requirements

To the fullest extent possible, the Lead Agency should integrate CEQA with other state and federal environmental review and consultation requirements. Guidelines sec. 15124. CEQA document preparers need to proactively determine all applicable environmental review requirements applicable to a proposed project and develop a comprehensive environmental review strategy. *See* chapter 6 for discussion of coordinating CEQA, NEPA, and various environmental review requirements.

Chapter 2

Preliminary Review, Exemptions, and Negative Declarations

Phases in the Environmental Review Process

Generally, the implementation of CEQA entails three separate phases:

- The first phase consists of preliminary review of a project to determine whether it is subject to CEQA.
- The second phase involves preparation of an Initial Study to determine whether the project may have a significant environmental effect.
- The third phase is preparation of an EIR if the project may have a significant environmental effect or of a Negative Declaration or Mitigated Negative Declaration if no significant effects will occur.

Guidelines sec. 15002(k)

Figure 2-1 presents an overview of the three phases of CEQA, incorporating the steps of CEQA's environmental review requirements. Figure 2-2 presents the questions raised during the three phases of CEQA and the resulting documents that are prepared depending on the answers to the questions.

> **Phases in the Environmental Review Process under CEQA**
>
> - Preliminary review of an agency action to determine whether the action is subject to CEQA or the underlying project is exempt from CEQA
> - Preparation of an Initial Study to determine whether the project may have a significant environmental effect
> - Preparation of an EIR if the project may have a significant environmental effect or of a Negative Declaration or Mitigated Negative Declaration if no significant effects will occur

Phase One: Preliminary Review

Determining Whether an Action Is a "Project" as Defined by CEQA

Review for Application of CEQA. During the preliminary review phase of CEQA, the Lead Agency must determine whether CEQA applies to the activity being evaluated. The agency must conduct a preliminary screening to determine whether the activity is a "project," or whether it is exempt. A government activity is only subject to CEQA if it involves the exercise of an agency's discretionary powers, has the potential to result in a direct or reasonably foreseeable indirect physical change in the environment, and falls within the definition of a "project" as defined by the Guidelines. Guidelines sec. 15060. All of these concepts are discussed further below.

A government activity is only subject to CEQA if it involves the exercise of an agency's discretionary powers, has the potential to result in a direct or reasonably foreseeable indirect physical change in the environment, and falls within the definition of a project as defined by the Guidelines.

Figure 2-1. Three Phases of the CEQA Process

Phase 1	**Preliminary Review**

- ◆ Pre-application consultation
- ◆ Application submitted to Lead Agency
- ○ Application determined to be complete
  (30 days from submittal; start of EIR/Negative Declaration time limits)
- ◆ Determination that project is subject to CEQA
- ◆ Review for exemptions

Phase 2	**Initial Study**

- ◆ Checklist completed
- ◆ Consultation with responsible and trustee agencies
- ○ Decision to prepare EIR or Negative Declaration
  (30 days from acceptance of complete application)

Phase 3

Environmental Impact Report	*or*	**Negative Declaration**

Environmental Impact Report

- ◆ Notice of Preparation sent to responsible and trustee agencies
- ○ Responses to Notice of Preparation sent to Lead Agency (30 days from acceptance)
- ○ Contract for EIR preparation executed (45 days from decision to prepare EIR)
- ◆ Preliminary Draft EIR prepared
- ◆ Independent review by Lead Agency
- ◆ Draft EIR completed and submitted for review
- ◆ Notice of completion filed
- ◆ Public notice and review of Draft EIR
- ○ Public hearing on Draft EIR (optional) (30–45 days)
- ◆ Written comments received
- ◆ Responses to comments prepared
- ○ Responses sent to commenting agencies (10 days before decision)
- ○ Final EIR certified by Lead Agency (1 year from acceptance)
- ○ Lead Agency makes decision on project (6 months from final EIR certification)
- ◆ Findings written and adopted
- ◆ Mitigation reporting and monitoring program adopted
- ○ Notice of Determination filed (5 days from approval)
- ○ Notice of Determination posted (24 hours from filing)
- ○ Responsible agency makes decision on project (180 days from Lead Agency decision)

Negative Declaration

- ○ Contract for Negative Declaration preparation executed (45 days from decision to prepare Negative Declaration)
- ◆ Mitigation measures identified and agreed to by project proponent
- ◆ Draft Negative Declaration prepared
- ○ Public notice and review (20–30 days)
- ◆ Responses to Negative Declaration received
- ◆ Comments considered
- ○ Negative Declaration completed (180 days from acceptance)
- ◆ Commenting agencies notified of date of hearing on project
- ◆ Negative Declaration adopted
- ○ Mitigation reporting and monitoring program adopted
- ○ Lead Agency makes determination on project (2 months from Negative Declaration adoption)
- ○ Notice of Determination filed (5 days from project approval)
- ○ Notice of Determination posted (24 hours from filing)
- ○ Responsible agency makes decision on project (180 days from Lead Agency decision)

Legend

- ◆ CEQA process actions
- ○ CEQA process actions with time constraints

CEQA Process Complete

Definition of a Project. CEQA applies only to discretionary government activities that are defined as "projects." A project is defined as the whole of an action which has the potential for resulting in either a direct physical change in the environment or a reasonably foreseeable indirect physical change in the environment. Guidelines sec. 15378(a); Pub. Res. Code sec. 21065.

A "project" under CEQA is considered to be an activity directly undertaken by a public agency, an activity that is supported, in whole or in part, through public agency contracts, grants, subsidies, loans, or other assistance from a public agency, or an activity involving the public agency issuance of a lease, permit, license, certificate, or other entitlement for use by a public agency. As used in CEQA, the term "project" is very broad. In considering whether an activity is a "project" an agency must look at all of the parts, components, and phases of the activity.

Project Segmenting Not Permitted. An agency is generally not permitted to "segment" or "piecemeal" a project into small parts if the effect is to avoid full disclosure of environmental impacts. This rule arises from the definition of "project" under CEQA which includes the phrase "whole of the action." This phrase has been interpreted by the California Supreme Court to mean that it is generally inappropriate to chop a project into small segments to avoid preparing an EIR. *See Bozung v. Local Agency Formation Commission* (1975) 13 Cal. 3d 263. Therefore, an agency may not treat each separate permit or approval as a separate project for purposes of

> ### Definition of a Project
>
> - An activity directly undertaken by a public agency, including:
>   - Public works construction activities
>   - Clearing or grading of land
>   - Improvements to existing public structures
>   - Enactment and amendment of zoning ordinances
>   - Adoption and amendment of local general plans
> - An activity that is supported, in whole or in part, through public agency contracts, grants, subsidies, loans, or other assistance from a public agency
> - An activity involving the public agency issuance of a lease, permit, license, certificate, or other entitlement for use by a public agency

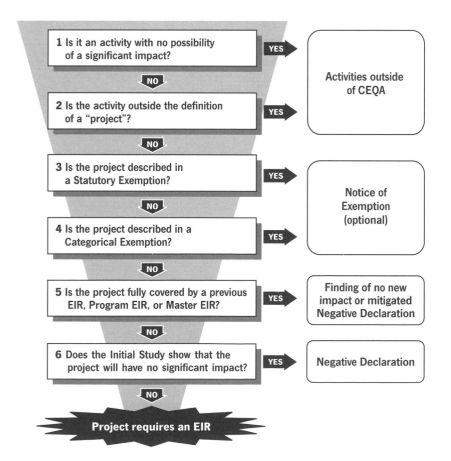

Figure 2-2
Screening Projects for CEQA Applicability

evaluating environmental impacts. *See* chapter 4 for more detail on requirements of the project description in an EIR.

"Project" refers to the underlying activity being approved by an agency, not just the government permits necessary to develop such an undertaking. Guidelines sec. 15378(c). Therefore, an agency may not treat each separate permit or approval as a separate project for purposes of evaluating environmental impacts.

The rule against segmenting does not, however, mean that every activity related to a proposed project must be included in a single CEQA document. Rather, the California Supreme Court held that related actions only had to be included in a CEQA document when they were reasonably foreseeable, but not when they were remote and speculative. *See Laurel Heights Improvement Association v. Regents of the University of California* (1988) 47 Cal. 3d 376. In *Laurel Heights,* the court also noted the decision whether related actions must be evaluated in a single CEQA document was to be determined by the facts and circumstances of each case.

A variety of other exceptions to the "segmenting" rule have also been recognized. Figure 2-3 summarizes the current state of the law regarding when related activities must be considered in a single environmental document and when they may be segmented into separate environmental documents or deferred to future documents. In the table "Action A" refers to the proposed project under current evaluation, and "Action B" refers to the related activity in question (often a future activity). Many of the concepts in the table are discussed in greater detail throughout this book.

Nonprojects. Some government activities are not subject to CEQA because they do not fall within the meaning of the term "project" as defined by the law. Although they are listed separately in CEQA, for practical purposes "nonprojects" are treated the same as statutory exemptions. Guidelines sec. 15378. CEQA does not consider the following actions to be within the definition of a "project":

- Proposals for legislation to be enacted by the State Legislature
- Certain continuing administrative or maintenance activities
- Submissions of proposals to a statewide or local vote, except for CEQA projects requiring later voter ratification
- School closing and student transfer when the only physical changes involved are categorically exempt
- A city council action placing a voter initiative on the ballot
- Creation of government funding mechanisms or other government fiscal activities that do not involve any commitment to any specific project that may result in physical environmental impacts
- Organizational or administrative activities of governments that are political or that are not physical changes in the environment

Exemptions from CEQA

Review for Exemptions. Once a Lead Agency has determined that an activity is a "project" subject to CEQA, it must then determine whether an exemption applies. Exemptions fall into four categories: "statutory exemptions,"

Figure 2-3. Evaluation of Related Activities in a CEQA Document

When must related activities be evaluated in the same CEQA document?	When may related activities be deferred to a future CEQA document? *
When "Action B" is a reasonably foreseeable consequence of "Action A" *Bozung v. Local Agency Formation Commission* (1975) 13 Cal. 3d 263 (successive government approvals for the same underlying project must be considered together); *Laurel Heights Improvement Association v. Regents of the University of California* (1988) 47 Cal.3d 376 (future phases of a single building must be evaluated in the EIR on the first phase because they are foreseeable) **When "Action B" is a future expansion of "Action A" and will be significant because it will likely change the scope, nature, and impacts of "Action A"** *Laurel Heights Improvement Association v. Regents of the University of California* (1988) 47 Cal.3d 376 (future phases of a single building must be evaluated in the EIR on the first phase because they will contribute to the project's impacts) **When "Action A" cannot proceed without essential public services that would be provided by "Action B"** *Santiago County Water District v. County of Orange* (1981) 118 Cal. App. 3d 818 (EIR on a mining project must include impacts of water delivery system to serve the project); *San Joaquin Raptor/Wildlife Rescue Center v. County of Stanislaus* (1995) 27 Cal. App. 4th 713 (EIR on a housing project must include impacts of additional sewer capacity to serve the project) **When "Action A" and "Action B" are integral parts of the same project** *No Oil, Inc. v. City of Los Angeles* (1987) 196 Cal. App. 3d 223 (Pipelines to deliver oil must be evaluated in an EIR for an oil drilling project)	**When "Action A" is being evaluated at a time when meaningful information about "Action B" is not capable of being obtained (e.g., is "remote and speculative")** *No Oil, Inc. v. City of Los Angeles* (1987) 196 Cal. App. 3d 223 (information about pipeline locations was not yet available and did not have to be evaluated in an EIR on an oil drilling project) **When information about "Action B" is not necessary to make an intelligent decision whether to proceed with "Action A"** *No Oil, Inc. v. City of Los Angeles* (1987) 196 Cal. App. 3d 223 (detailed information about pipelines to deliver oil was not necessary for a decision to be made whether to approve an oil drilling project) **When "Action A" is being evaluated in a first-tier EIR and "Action B" will be evaluated in a second-tier EIR.** *Rio Vista Farm Bureau Center v. County of Solano* (1992) 5 Cal. App. 4th 351 (program EIR on hazardous waste management plan need not evaluate project-specific impacts of activities that will be subject to future, second-tier EIRs) **When "Action A" merely establishes criteria for "Action B" but does not commit to its implementation** *Rio Vista Farm Bureau Center v. County of Solano* (1992) 5 Cal. App. 4th 351 (EIR on hazardous waste management plan need not evaluate future facilities that might be developed under the plan) **When "Action B" is independent of, and not a contemplated future part of, "Action A"** *Christward Ministry v. County of San Diego* (1993) 13 Cal. App. 4th 31 (EIR for a proposed landfill expansion need not evaluate impacts of other solid waste projects in the county) **When "Action A" is part of a large highway project with logical termination points and independent utility and does not foreclose consideration of alternatives** *Del Mar Terrace Conservancy, Inc. v. City Council of the City of San Diego* (1992) 10 Cal. App 4th. 712 (EIR on 1.8 mile highway project was appropriate because it had independent use for local and state service even if no other phases were constructed)

* When a Lead Agency elects to exclude or limit the evaluation of related activities, it should include the following in the CEQA document:

    1) A description of the potential future activities and how they relate to the proposed project

    2) A brief explanation of the types of impacts that those related actions might produce

    3) A discussion of why it is not necessary or possible to evaluate the related actions at the current time

    4) An explanation of when, and in what type of CEQA document, the related actions will be evaluated (e.g., second-tier EIR)

"categorical exemptions," "general rule" exemptions where it can be seen with certainty that there is no possibility that the activity may have a significant effect on the environment, and "disapproved project" exemptions. Guidelines sec. 15061(b). There is also a partial exemption for "certified regulatory programs." Guidelines secs. 15250–15253.

Statutory Exemptions. Because CEQA is a legislative in origin, the State Legislature has the authority to exempt activities from its jurisdiction. A project that falls within a statutory exemption is not subject to CEQA even if it has the potential to significantly affect the environment. The Legislature has established a variety of statutory exemptions from CEQA. *See* Figure 2-4. A project that is statutorily exempt is entitled to a blanket exemption from all of CEQA's procedures and policies as delineated by the statutory language. Although there are dozens of statutory exemptions from CEQA, most are very specific to certain types of projects. However, there are several categories that are of general application and more commonly used. Some of the more commonly used statutory exemptions are discussed below.

"Ministerial" describes a decision applying fixed, objective standards with little or no judgment required as to the wisdom or manner of carrying out the project.

Ministerial Projects. The exemption from CEQA review for ministerial projects is the most widely used statutory exemption. "Ministerial" describes a decision applying fixed, objective standards with little or no judgment required as to the wisdom or manner of carrying out the project. Pub. Res. Code sec. 21080(b)(1); Guidelines secs. 15268, 15369.

A "discretionary project," on the other hand, requires the exercise of judgment or deliberation when a project decision is made. Guidelines sec. 15357. If a project contains both ministerial and discretionary elements, it is not exempt. Guidelines sec. 15268(d). Examples of ministerial projects include final subdivision map approvals and most building permits. A building permit is considered ministerial if the ordinance requiring the permit limits the public official to determining whether the zoning allows the structure to be built in the requested location, the structure will meet the requirements of the Uniform Building Code, and the applicant has paid the required fee.

Building, grading, and demolition permits, although often ministerial, are considered discretionary if the particular permit ordinance allows the exercise of at least some discretion that can be used to reduce environmental impacts. Generally, courts have interpreted the scope of the ministerial project exemption narrowly, and it should therefore be applied with caution.

Emergency repairs for public service facilities may be statutorily exempt from CEQA.

Emergency Projects. Most emergency projects are exempt from CEQA review. Pub. Res. Code secs. 21080(b)(2), (3), (4); Guidelines sec. 15269. A situation is considered an "emergency" if it is a sudden, unexpected occurrence involving a clear and imminent danger that demands immediate action to prevent or mitigate loss of or damage to life, health, property, or essential public services. Emergencies include such occurrences as fires, floods, earthquakes, or other soil or geologic movements, as well as riots, accidents, or sabotage. Pub. Res. Code sec. 21060.3; Guidelines sec. 15359.

The following types of emergency actions are covered by this exemption:

- Projects to maintain, repair, restore, demolish, or replace property or facilities damaged or destroyed as a result of a disaster in a disaster stricken area in which a state of emergency has been proclaimed by the Governor. This includes projects that would adversely affect historical resources when that resource represents an imminent threat to bodily harm or damage to adjacent properties.

- Emergency repairs to publicly or privately owned service facilities necessary to maintain service essential to the public health, safety, or welfare.

- Specific actions necessary to prevent or mitigate an emergency, but not including long-term projects undertaken to fix short-term problems.

- Projects carried out or approved by a public agency to maintain, repair, or restore an existing highway damaged by a natural disaster, excluding official state scenic highways and excluding projects to expand or widen highways initiated within one year of the occurrence of damage.

- Certain seismic work on highways and bridges.

Pub. Res. Code secs. 21080(b)(2), (3), (4); Guidelines sec. 15269.

Rejected or Disapproved Projects. Rejected or disapproved projects are exempt from CEQA review when the public agency determines that the application for project approval will not be approved. Public agencies are allowed an initial screening of projects on their merits, allowing quick disapproval of a project prior to initiation of the CEQA process when the agency can determine at that point that the project cannot be approved. This exemption does not relieve an applicant from paying the costs associated with preparing an environmental document for a project prior to the agency's disapproval but after normal evaluation and processing. Pub. Res. Code sec. 21080(b)(5); Guidelines sec. 15270.

Rejected or disapproved projects are exempt from CEQA review when the public agency determines that the application for project approval will not be approved.

Setting of Certain Rates, Tolls, Fares, or Charges. The setting, modification, structuring, or restructuring of certain rates, tolls, fares, or charges other than rate increases to fund system expansions are exempt from CEQA review. These fees must be for the purpose of meeting operating expenses, including employee wage rates and fringe benefits; purchasing or leasing supplies, equipment, or materials; meeting financial reserve needs and requirements; or obtaining funds for capital projects necessary for maintenance of services within an existing service area or as authorized by city charter. Rate increases to fund capital projects for the expansion of a system are subject to CEQA. Pub. Res. Code sec. 21080(b)(8); Guidelines sec. 15273.

The setting, modification, structuring, or restructuring of certain rates, tolls, fares, or charges other than rate increases to fund system expansions are exempt from CEQA review.

Feasibility or Planning Studies for Possible Future Actions. Also exempt from CEQA review are feasibility or planning studies carried out by a public agency when the agency has not approved, adopted, or funded any particular action. This provision does not apply to adoption of any plan that would have a legally binding effect on later activities (e.g., a city or county general plan). Pub. Res. Code secs. 21102, 21150.

Categorical Exemptions. CEQA directs the Resources Agency to designate classes of projects that should be exempt from CEQA review. Pub.

Figure 2-4. Statutory Exemptions

The Legislature has enacted a variety of statutory exemptions from CEQA. This table summarizes the exemptions and provides citations to the appropriate code sections. Please refer to the statutory provision for the complete statutory language. The table does not include certain project-specific exemptions for certain facilities already approved or constructed.

Type of Action	Exempt Activities	Statutory Provision
Agency Actions	• Ministerial projects (e.g., issuance of building permits or business licenses)	Pub. Res. Code 21080(b)(1)
	• Projects that a public agency rejects or disapproves	Pub. Res. Code 21080(b)(5)
	• Local actions implementing a state rule or regulation pursuant to a state-certified regulatory program, except certain site-specific activities	Pub. Res. Code 21080(b)(15)
	• Feasibility or planning studies for possible future actions that the agency has not approved, adopted, or funded	Pub. Res. Code 21102, 21150
Emergency Actions	• Emergency repairs to public service facilities necessary to maintain service	Pub. Res. Code 21080(b)(2)
	• Projects to maintain, repair, restore, demolish, or replace property or facilities damaged or destroyed in an area proclaimed as an emergency by the Governor	Pub. Res. Code 21080(b)(3)
	• Actions necessary to prevent or mitigate an emergency (not including long-term projects with low probability of short-term occurrence)	Pub. Res. Code 21080(b)(4)
	• Projects to maintain, repair, or restore an existing highway	Pub. Res. Code 21080.33
Energy Projects	• Actions relating to thermal power plants	Pub. Res. Code 21080(b)(6)
	• Local ordinances regarding solar shade control requirements	Pub. Res. Code 25985
Transportation-Related Projects	• Actions to establish, modify, or restructure rates, tolls, fares, or other charges for certain designated public purposes	Pub. Res. Code 21080(b)(8)
	• Projects instituting or increasing passenger or commuter service on existing rail or highway rights-of-way	Pub. Res. Code 21080(b)(10)
	• Projects instituting or increasing passenger or commuter service on existing high-occupancy vehicle lanes	Pub. Res. Code 21080(b)(11)
	• Mass transit extensions of less than 4 miles for the transfer of passengers	Pub. Res. Code 21080(b)(12)
	• Regional or state transportation improvement programs	Pub. Res. Code 21080(b)(13)
	• Congestion Management Program by a county agency	Pub. Res. Code 21080(b)(13)
	• Railroad grade separation projects	Pub. Res. Code 21080.12
	• Restriping of streets or highways to reduce traffic congestion	Pub. Res. Code 21080.19
	• Transportation rights-of-way in designated transportation corridors for which an EIR was certified	Pub. Res. Code 33911
Categorically Exempt Projects	• All classes of projects designated pursuant to Pub. Res. Code 21084 (i.e., categorical exemptions)	Pub. Res. Code 21080(b)(9)
Out-of-State/ NEPA Projects	• Projects or portions of projects located in another state that will be subject to NEPA or state environmental review consistent with NEPA	Pub. Res. Code 21080(b)(14)
Housing-Related Projects	• Housing or neighborhood commercial facilities in urbanized areas that are consistent with a comprehensive regulatory document and meet certain criteria	Pub. Res. Code 21080.7
	• Conversion of existing rental mobile home parks to condominium ownership	Pub. Res. Code 21080.8
	• Adoption of ordinances related to certain senior citizen units or second units	Pub. Res. Code 21080.17
	• Approval of day-care homes providing family daycare for up to 12 children	Health and Safety Code 1597.46
	• Actions related to the construction, conversion, or use of low-income agricultural employee housing	Pub. Res. Code 21801.01

(continued next page)

Type of Action	Exempt Activities	Statutory Provision
Housing-Related Projects (continued)	• Actions related to the construction, conversion, or use of lower-income housing projects of 100 units or less in urban areas	Pub. Res. Code 21080.14
	• Regional housing needs determinations made by the Department of Housing and Community Development, a council of governments, or a city or county	Govt. Code 65584
Local Coastal Programs	• Activities and approvals by local governments or state colleges and universities related to local coastal programs	Pub. Res. Code 21080.9
School Projects	• Closing of any K–12 public school or the transfer of students from such a school, if the associated physical changes are categorically exempt	Pub. Res. Code 21080.18
Timberland Preserve Projects	• Local adoption of timberland preserve zones	Govt. Code 51119
Water-Related Projects	• Temporary water transfers of up to 1 year in duration	Water Code 1729
	• Repiping, redesign, or use of reclaimed water for certain irrigation, cooling, or air conditioning purposes	Water Code 13552.4(c)(1), 13552.8(c)(1)
	• Minor alterations to utilities to comply with public water system fluoridation requirements	Pub. Res. Code 21080.26
	• Preparation and adoption of Urban Water Management Plans	Water Code 10652
Waste Disposal Projects	• Non-disposal facilities of local solid waste management plans	Pub. Res. Code 41375
	• Certain pipelines for the transport of certain hazardous or volatile wastes	Pub. Res. Code 21080.23
	• Cooperative agreements for the development of solid waste management facilities on Indian lands	Pub. Res. Code 44203(g)
Specific Agency Actions	• General plan time extensions granted by the Office of Planning and Research	Pub. Res. Code 21080.10a
	• General plan actions required to comply with a court order	Govt. Code 65759
	• Funding of low- or moderate-income housing projects by the California Department of Housing and Community Development or Housing Finance Agency	Pub. Res. Code 21080.10(b)
	• Settlements of title and boundary problems and related exchanges and leases by the State Lands Commission	Pub. Res. Code 21080.11
	• Adoption of waste discharge requirements under the federal Clean Water Act, except for certain new sources, by the State Water Resources Control Board and Regional Water Quality Control Boards	Water Code 13372, 13389
	• Issuance of bonds by the California Pollution Control Financing Authority	Health and Safety Code 44561
	• Local general plan amendments required by the Delta Protection Commission	Pub. Res. Code 21080.22
	• Issuance, modification, or renewal of "Title V" permits under the Clean Air Act that do not involve physical or operational changes by an Air Quality Management District	Pub. Res. Code 21080.24 Pub. Res. Code 21080.24
	• Issuance of permits relating to automotive painting by an Air Quality Management District	Chapter 1131 Statutes of 1993, Section 1
	• Bidding, hosting, or staging of and funding and carrying out of the Olympic Games	Pub. Res. Code 21080(b)(7)
	• Notification of discovery of Native American burial sites	Pub. Res. Code 5097.98(c)
	• Specified prison facilities	Pub. Res. Code 21080.01, 21080.03, 21080.07
	• Purchase of rail right-of-way for the San Francisco Peninsula commute service	Pub. Res. Code 21080.05
	• Project funding by the Rural Economic Development Infrastructure Panel	Pub. Res. Code 21080.08
	• Installation of new or repair or removal of an existing pipeline under 1 mile	Pub. Res. Code 21080.21
	• Actions by the Industrial Development Authority	Govt. Code 91543

Res. Code secs. 21080(b)(9), 21084. A categorical exemption is an exemption from CEQA for a class of projects that the Secretary for Resources determines generally will not have a significant effect on the environment, unless an exception to the categorical exemption exists (*see* page 30). The Resources Agency has established 32 classes of categorical exemptions. *See* Figure 2-5. Guidelines secs. 15301–15332. Each public agency must establish its own list of specific activities falling within each class. Guidelines sec. 15300.

As with statutory exemptions, some categorical exemptions are more commonly used than others. The following are generalized summaries of the conditions of some of the more frequently used categorical exemptions. Agencies interested in relying on a particular exemption must refer to the Guidelines to make sure the proposed activity falls within the exemption.

Class 1: Existing Facilities. This categorical exemption applies to the operation, repair, maintenance, permitting, leasing, licensing, or minor alteration of existing public or private structures, facilities, mechanical equipment, or topographical features involving negligible or no expansion of use beyond that existing at the time of the Lead Agency's determination. The exemption includes interior or exterior alterations. Guidelines sec. 15301.

Class 2: Replacement or Reconstruction. This categorical exemption applies to the replacement or reconstruction of existing structures and facilities where the new structure will be located on the same site as the original one and will have substantially the same purpose and capacity as the original. The exemption includes replacement or reconstruction of existing schools or hospitals for earthquake retrofit. Guidelines sec. 15302.

Class 3: New Construction or Conversion of Small Facilities. This categorical exemption applies to the construction and location of limited numbers of new small facilities or structures; the installation of small new equipment and facilities in small structures; and the conversion of existing small structures from one use to another when only minor modifications are made to the exterior of the structure. The exemption includes a list of structures with maximum allowable sizes. For example, it applies to the construction of three or fewer single-family homes in urbanized areas. Guidelines sec. 15303.

Class 4: Minor Alterations to Land. This categorical exemption applies to minor public or private alterations in the condition of land, water, or vegetation that do not involve removal of healthy, mature, scenic trees except for forestry and agricultural purposes. The exemption includes grading on land with a slope of less than ten percent or new gardening or landscaping. Guidelines sec. 15304.

Class 5: Minor Alterations in Land Use Limitations. This categorical exemption applies to minor alterations in land use limitations in areas with an average slope of less than twenty percent when they do not result in any changes in land use or density. The exemption includes lot line adjustments and variances that do not create new parcels. Guidelines sec. 15305.

Class 6: Information Collection. This categorical exemption applies to basic data collection, research, experimental management, and resource evaluation activities that do not result in a serious or major disturbance to an

Figure 2-5. Categorical Exemptions

The Secretary for Resources has adopted a variety of categorical exemptions from CEQA. This table summarizes the exemptions (referred to as "classes") and provides citations to the appropriate Guidelines sections. Many of the categories include special limitations and examples of exempt projects. Please refer to the Guidelines section for complete Guidelines language. Also, unlike statutory exemptions, categorical exemptions are subject to certain exceptions found in Guidelines Section 15300.2.

Class	Exempt Activity	Guidelines Section
Class 1	Operation, repair, maintenance, or minor alteration of existing structures or facilities not expanding existing uses	15301
Class 2	Replacement or reconstruction of existing structures or facilities on the same site having substantially the same purpose and capacity	15302
Class 3	New construction of limited small new facilities; installation of small, new equipment and facilities in small structures; and conversion of the use of small existing structures (e.g., construction of three or fewer single-family homes in urban areas)	15303
Class 4	Minor alterations in the condition of the land, such as grading, gardening, and landscaping, that do not affect sensitive resources	15304
Class 5	Minor alterations to land use limitations, such as lot line adjustments, variances, and encroachment permits on land with a slope of less than 20%, that do not result in changes in land use or density	15305
Class 6	Basic data collection, research, experimental management, and resource evaluation activities that do not result in major disturbances to an environmental resource	15306
Class 7	Certain actions by regulatory agencies to maintain, restore, or enhance natural resources, other than construction activities, where the regulatory process includes procedures to protect the environment	15307
Class 8	Certain actions by regulatory agencies to maintain, restore, or enhance the environment, other than construction activities, where the regulatory process includes procedures to protect the environment	15308
Class 9	Inspections to check for the performance of an operation, or for quality, health, or safety of a project	15309
Class 10	Certain Department of Veterans Affairs loans and mortgages for purchases of certain existing structures	15310
Class 11	Construction or placement of minor structures accessory to existing facilities (e.g., signs, small parking lots, portable structures)	15311
Class 12	Sales of surplus government property, except in environmentally sensitive areas	15312
Class 13	Acquisition of land for fish and wildlife habitat conservation purposes	15313
Class 14	Minor additions to existing schools that do not increase capacity by more than 25%	15314
Class 15	Subdivision of certain properties in urban areas into four or fewer parcels	15315
Class 16	Certain acquisitions or sales of land in natural condition or containing cultural resource sites to establish a park	15316
Class 17	Establishment of agricultural preserves, making and renewal of Williamson Act contracts, and acceptance of open space property	15317
Class 18	Designation of wilderness areas under the California Wilderness System	15318
Class 19	Annexations of certain areas containing existing structures and certain small parcels	15319
Class 20	Local government reorganizations requiring no changes in the areas where previous powers were exercised, such as the establishment of subsidiary districts, consolidations, and mergers	15320
Class 21	Actions by regulatory agencies to enforce a lease, permit license, or other entitlement; actions by law enforcement officials	15321
Class 22	Actions related to educational or training programs involving no exterior physical changes	15322
Class 23	Normal operations of existing facilities for public gatherings for which the facilities were designed	15323
Class 24	Actions taken by regulatory agencies related to wages, hours, and working conditions	15324
Class 25	Transfers of interest in land to preserve open space	15325
Class 26	Actions needed to implement a housing assistance plan by acquiring an interest in housing units	15326
Class 27	Leasing of new or unoccupied private facilities in a building exempt from CEQA	15327
Class 28	Installations of certain hydroelectric facilities of less than 5 megawatts capacity at existing facilities	15328
Class 29	Installation of certain cogeneration equipment of less than 50 megawatts capacity at existing facilities	15329
Class 30	Minor actions to prevent, minimize, stabilize, mitigate, or eliminate the release or threat of release of hazardous waste or substances	15330
Class 31	Historical resource restoration or rehabilitation consistent with Secretary of Interior guidelines	15331
Class 32	Certain in-fill development projects in urban areas	15332

environmental resource. These activities may involve information gathering only or be part of a study that leads to an action not yet approved, adopted, or funded by the public agency. Guidelines sec. 15306.

Classes 7 and 8: Actions by Regulatory Agencies for Protection of Natural Resources or the Environment. These two closely related categories consist of actions taken by regulatory agencies, as authorized by state law or local ordinance, to ensure the maintenance, restoration, or enhancement of natural resources or the environment when regulatory processes involve procedures for environmental protection. This exemption does not apply to any construction activities or relaxation of standards allowing environmental degradation. Guidelines secs. 15307, 15308.

Class 9: Inspections. This categorical exemption applies to activities limited entirely to inspections to check for performance of an operation or for the quality, health, or safety of a project, including related activities such as inspection for possible mislabeling, misrepresentation, or adulteration of products. Guidelines sec. 15309.

Exceptions to Categorical Exemptions. Categorical exemptions represent activities that generally do not result in significant environmental impacts. However, unlike statutory exemptions, these exemptions are not absolute. There are six exceptions to categorical exemptions. Pub. Res. Code secs. 21084(b), (c), (e); Guidelines sec. 15300.2. A person challenging the use of a categorical exemption must produce substantial evidence that the project has the potential for significant environmental impacts and that, therefore, an exception applies. The Lead Agency is not required by CEQA to write findings to explain why the exceptions to the exemption do not apply. It is recommended, however, that the Lead Agency prepare enough information within the administrative record to support the use of a categorical exemption.

A categorical exemption does not apply if unusual circumstances create a reasonable possibility that the activity may have a significant environmental impact or if cumulative impacts would be significant. A categorical exemption does not apply if the project occurs in certain specified sensitive environments, affects scenic resources within official state scenic highways, or is located on listed hazardous waste sites maintained by the California Environmental Protection Agency. Also, a categorical exemption does not apply if the project causes substantial adverse changes in the significance of a historical resource.

Notice of Exemption. A public agency has the option to file a Notice of Exemption when it decides that a project is either statutorily or categorically exempt from CEQA and approves or determines to carry out the project. If a Notice of Exemption is filed at all, it should include a brief description of the project, a finding that the project is exempt, citations to the applicable exemption in the law or State Guidelines, and a brief statement of reasons supporting the finding of exemption [Guidelines sec. 15062], and is filed after approval of the project. Appendix E of the CEQA Guidelines (*see* Appendix 2 of this book) is a recommended Notice of Exemption form.

A Categorical Exemption Does Not Apply If:

- A reasonable possibility exists that the activity may have a significant environmental impact because of unusual circumstances
- Project cumulative impacts would be considerable and therefore significant
- A project within certain categories of exemption occurs in certain specified sensitive environments
- A project affects scenic resources within official state scenic highways
- A project is located on a toxic site listed by the California Environmental Protection Agency
- A project causes substantial adverse changes in significant historic resources

---

Notice of Exemption

- A brief description of the project
- A finding that the project is exempt
- Citations to the applicable exemption in the law or State Guidelines
- A brief statement of reasons supporting the finding of exemption

---

In practice, agencies are strongly advised to file a Notice of Exemption with the county clerk or OPR, depending on the public agency filing notice. Notices of Exemption must be posted and made available for public inspection on a weekly basis. In addition to posting Notices of Exemption in the customary manner, agencies are encouraged to make postings of the notices available in electronic format on the Internet.

If the Notice of Exemption is filed and posted, a 35-day statute of limitations will commence from the date of project approval; if the notice is not filed, a 180-day statute of limitations will apply. Guidelines sec. 15062(d). *See* the discussion of CEQA litigation in chapter 7. Thus, lead agencies are encouraged to file Notices of Exemption to limit their exposure to legal challenge.

Partial Exemptions for Certified Regulatory Programs

Certification. The Secretary of Resources has certified certain state regulatory programs, exempting them from CEQA's requirements to prepare EIRs and Negative Declarations. Pub. Res. Code sec. 21080.5; Guidelines secs. 15250–15253. A certified program, however, remains subject to other provisions of CEQA, such as the requirement to avoid significant adverse effects on the environment where feasible. To qualify for this partial exemption, which is based on the theory that one of the agency's purposes is to protect the environment, the program requires preparation of a "substitute document" that must include several specific environmental protection requirements. Guidelines sec. 15252. The state-certified regulatory programs are as follows:

- Regulation of timber harvesting operations by the California Department of Forestry and Fire Protection and the State Board of Forestry
- The regulatory program of the Fish and Game Commission
- The regulatory program of the California Air Resources Board involving protection and enhancement of ambient air quality
- The regulatory program of the State Board of Forestry under the Forest Practices Act
- California Coastal Commission preparation, approval, and certification of local coastal programs
- The water quality control and Section 208 planning programs of the State Water Resources Control Board and the Regional Water Quality Control Board
- The permit and planning programs of the San Francisco Bay Conservation and Development Commission
- The pesticide regulatory program administered by the Department of Pesticide Regulation of the California Environmental Protection Agency and the county agricultural commissioners
- California Department of Water Resources regulation of water resources management projects
- The power plant site certification program of the Energy Resources Conservation and Development Commission

A categorical exemption does not apply if an activity may have a significant impact because of unusual circumstances (such as an endangered species habitat).

PSA = Permit Streamlining Act

- The regulatory program of the State Water Resources Control Board to establish instream beneficial use protection programs
- The planning program of the Sacramento–San Joaquin Delta Protection Commission
- Portions of the regulatory program of the South Coast Air Quality Management District

Guidelines sec. 15251.

The California Supreme Court has held that the California Fish and Game Commission's regulatory program under the California Endangered Species Act falls within the Commission's previously approved certified program for hunting and fishing regulation. *Mountain Lion Foundation v. Fish and Game Commission* (1997) 16 Cal. 4th 105.

Duties of Agencies with Certified Programs. Agencies responsible for implementing a certified program must continue to comply with CEQA's goals and policies, provide public review of the substitute document, respond to comments, and adopt CEQA findings. Also, an agency must consider the cumulative effects of its actions. In the "substitute document," however, the agency must evaluate impacts and identify alternatives and mitigation measures. The substitute document must include a description of the project activity, along with either alternatives to the activity and mitigation measures to avoid or reduce the significant environmental effects or a statement, and supporting checklist or other documentation, that there would be no significant environmental effects and therefore no alternatives or mitigation measures proposed. Guidelines sec. 15252. Responsible Agencies are required to use these substitute documents for CEQA compliance if certain conditions are met. Guidelines sec. 15253. *See* Figure 2-6.

Review of Entitlement Applications under the Permit Streamlining Act

Purpose of the Permit Streamlining Act. During the preliminary review phase of CEQA for project proposals from non-public entities, the Lead Agency must determine whether the project being evaluated is subject to the Permit Streamlining Act (PSA). The PSA is a related law that requires government agencies complying with CEQA for certain types of private development projects to process those projects within state-mandated time limits (*see* Figure 2-7). It was enacted to ensure that government agencies process certain private development projects expeditiously. The PSA applies only to "development projects," as defined by the act, and not to legislative actions, such as rezoning or general plan amendments. Waiver of the PSA requirements is not permitted. Gov. Code secs. 65920–65960.

Preapplication Consultation. A Lead Agency must, upon request by a project applicant, provide for consultation concerning CEQA compliance prior to the filing of a permit application. The purpose of this preapplication consultation is for the Lead Agency to discuss with the applicant the scope and content of the CEQA requirements for the project. The objective of a preapplication meeting is to identify as many issues as possible early in the permit process to encourage efficient and expeditious CEQA compliance. Among the topics that should be discussed at the preapplication meeting are:

- The range of actions the project would include
- The potential alternatives to be evaluated in the environmental document
- The likely significant environmental impacts of the project
- Mitigation measures for any significant impacts

Pub. Res. Code sec. 21080.1(b); Guidelines sec. 15060.5.

Review for Completeness of Application. The Lead Agency or Responsible Agency, during "preliminary review," is allowed 30 days to review a permit application for completeness. The PSA does not apply to legislative acts (e.g., general plan amendments) or to adjudicative actions requiring legislative changes (e.g., zoning changes).

The application will be deemed complete if the agency does not make a determination as to whether an application is complete within 30 days of receipt. Gov. Code sec. 65943(a); Guidelines sec. 15101. If the application is returned as incomplete, the applicant may complete and resubmit the application, and the agency again has 30 days to determine the completeness of the resubmitted application. Gov. Code sec. 64943(b); Guidelines sec. 15060.

Each agency must publish and make available to the project applicant the information required for submitting entitlement applications. An agency may require enough information to determine whether an EIR must be prepared, but may not require the informational equivalent of an EIR as a condition of accepting an application as complete. Gov. Code sec. 65941. The purpose of this prohibition is to encourage simultaneous CEQA and permit processing. However, accepting an application as complete does not limit the authority of the Lead Agency to require the applicant to submit additional information needed for environmental evaluation of the project. Requiring such additional information after the application is complete does not change the status of the application. Guidelines sec. 15060.

> **Preapplication Consultation**
>
> A potential project applicant may request a meeting with the Lead Agency to consider:
> - Range of actions
> - Potential alternatives
> - Mitigation measures
> - Potential significant effects on the environment
>
> **The Lead Agency may involve:**
> - Responsible agencies
> - Trustee agencies
> - Other interested agencies

Environmental Document Time Limits	• 30 days from application's acceptance as complete: Lead Agency must decide to prepare Negative Declaration or EIR • 45 days from decision to prepare Negative Declaration or EIR: Lead Agency must execute consultant contract • 180 days from application's acceptance as complete: Lead Agency must complete Negative Declaration • 1 year from application's acceptance as complete: Lead Agency must certify EIR
Lead Agency Project Approval Time Limits	• 2 months from exemption decision or adoption of Negative Declaration • 6 months from date of EIR certification
Responsible Agency Project Approval Time Limits	• 180 days after responsible agency accepts application as complete or after Lead Agency action, whichever is later

**Figure 2-7
Permit Streamlining Act
Time Limits**

The Lead Agency must decide whether to prepare an EIR or a Negative Declaration within 30 days, complete a Negative Declaration within 180 days, and complete an EIR within one year. An applicant's unreasonable delay in providing information will, however, suspend these time limits.

PSA and CEQA Time Limits Initiated by Completion of the Application. CEQA, in coordination with the PSA, contains strict time limits that a Lead Agency must follow. Once an application is deemed complete, a Lead Agency must determine if the activity is subject to CEQA before conducting an Initial Study (*see* page 35). Guidelines sec. 15060. The Lead Agency must decide whether to prepare an EIR or a Negative Declaration within 30 days, complete a Negative Declaration within 180 days, and complete an EIR within one year. Guidelines secs. 15102, 15107, 15108. An applicant's unreasonable delay in providing information will, however, suspend these time limits. Guidelines sec. 15109. *See* Figure 2-7.

Project Approval by the Lead Agency. The PSA requires the Lead Agency to approve or disapprove the project within 60 days from the date of adoption of a Negative Declaration or the determination that a project is exempt. For projects involving an EIR, the Lead Agency must approve or disapprove the project within 180 days from the date of certification of the EIR. Gov. Code sec. 65950. If a combined EIR and environmental impact statement is prepared in compliance with CEQA and NEPA, the Lead Agency must approve or disapprove the project within 90 days after the document was completed and adopted. Gov. Code sec. 65951.

An agency may not, however, disapprove an application for a development project merely for the purpose of satisfying the time limits in the PSA. Rather, any disapproval of an application must specify the reasons for disapproval, other than failure to meet the specified time limits. Gov. Code sec. 65959.

Project Approval by the Responsible Agency. A Responsible Agency, at the request of a project applicant, must begin processing a permit application for a development project prior to final Lead Agency action on the project, to the extent that needed information is available. Gov. Code sec. 65941(c).

A Responsible Agency must act within 180 days either of accepting the application as complete or of the Lead Agency's action, whichever is later. Gov. Code sec. 65952.

Execution of Consultant Contracts. If an EIR or Negative Declaration is to be prepared by a private consultant under contract with the Lead Agency, the contract must be executed within 45 days from the Lead Agency's determination that either a Negative Declaration or an EIR is required. The Lead Agency may take longer to execute the contract if compelling circumstances exist and the project applicant consents. This requirement, however, may result in practical timing difficulties, especially if consultant contracts must be placed on an agenda and formally approved by Lead Agency decision-making bodies. Pub. Res. Code secs. 21100.2(a), 21151.5(b).

The Permit Streamlining Act allows for a one-time, limited extension for most of the time limits with mutual consent of the project applicant and Lead Agency.

Extensions. The PSA allows for a one-time, limited extension for most of the time limits with mutual consent of the project applicant and Lead Agency. The PSA specifically disallows any other extensions or waivers of the time limits. Gov. Code sec. 65957.

Enforcement. The project may be "deemed approved" if an agency fails to act within the time limits for project approval, provided public notice requirements have been met. Gov. Code sec. 65956(b). However, it should be noted that the PSA is a confusing law subject to conflicting judicial interpretations. For projects subject to the law, public agencies must carefully document the dates on which permit applications are submitted and determined to be complete. Although in practice few projects are "deemed approved" by a lapsed time limit, decision-making agencies should avoid such inadvertent lapses because the courts have occasionally deemed projects approved under such circumstances and allowed project implementation without CEQA review and requirement of appropriate mitigation.

Because the Permit Streamlining Act is a confusing law subject to conflicting judicial interpretations, public agencies must carefully document the dates on which permit applications are submitted and determined to be complete and must carefully adhere to the prescribed time limits.

Phase Two: Preparation of an Initial Study to Determine Whether to Prepare a Negative Declaration or an EIR

Legislatively Mandated EIRs

Although the decision whether or not to prepare an EIR is generally discretionary with the Lead Agency, the State Legislature has decided that certain types of project approvals should always require EIRs; therefore, no Initial Study is required and the Lead Agency must go forward with preparation of an EIR. The following projects always require an EIR:

- Construction of new facilities involving the burning of municipal wastes, hazardous wastes, or refuse-derived fuel, including tires. Pub. Res. Code sec. 21151.1(a).
- Expansion of an existing facility that burns hazardous waste increasing capacity by more than ten percent. Pub. Res. Code sec. 21151.1(a).
- Issuance of a hazardous waste facilities permit to a land disposal facility or large treatment facility. Pub. Res. Code sec. 21151.1(a).
- Location of a campus or development of a long-range development plan for all public community colleges, the California State University, and the University of California. Pub. Res. Code sec. 21080.09(b).
- Open pit mining operations subject to the Surface Mining and Reclamation Act (Pub. Res. Code sec. 2710 et seq.) that utilize a cyanide heap-leaching process for producing gold or other precious metals.

Guidelines sec. 15081.5.

Requirement to Prepare an Initial Study

Once it determines that an activity is subject to CEQA and no statutory or categorical exemptions apply, a Lead Agency generally prepares an Initial Study. The Lead Agency, however, may determine at the outset that the proposed activity does have the potential to significantly affect the environment and preparation of an EIR will be required and bypass preparation of the Initial Study. Guidelines sec. 15063. Because an Initial Study serves to focus the EIR on only the potentially significant effects, it is recommended that the Lead Agency prepare an Initial Study even if it has already concluded that an EIR is required.

Because an Initial Study serves to focus the EIR on only the potentially significant effects, the Lead Agency should prepare an Initial Study even if it has already concluded that an EIR is required.

Purposes of an Initial Study

An Initial Study is a preliminary analysis prepared by a Lead Agency, in consultation with other relevant agencies, to determine whether an EIR or a Negative Declaration is needed. If the Initial Study concludes that the project, without mitigation, may have a significant effect on the environment, an EIR should be prepared; otherwise, the Lead Agency may prepare a Negative Declaration or Mitigated Negative Declaration. Guidelines sec. 15063.

If an EIR is to be prepared, the Initial Study is used to focus the EIR on the potential significant effects and allows the Lead Agency to avoid unnecessary analysis on those effects that are not potentially significant. If a Negative Declaration is to be prepared, the Initial Study is used to support the finding that a project will not have a significant unmitigated environmental impact. Guidelines sec. 15063(c). The Initial Study can be used to assist a Lead Agency in avoiding preparation of an unnecessary EIR when, prior to public review of the Negative Declaration, appropriate measures can be incorporated into the project description to mitigate the potential significant impacts identified and, therefore, allow for preparation of a Mitigated Negative Declaration.

If, after preparing and issuing the Initial Study for public review, the Lead Agency determines that there is substantial evidence that any aspect of the project, either individually or cumulatively, may cause a significant effect on the environment, regardless of whether the overall effect of the project is adverse or beneficial, it must either prepare an EIR, use a previously prepared EIR that adequately analyzes the project at hand, or use one of CEQA's allowable tiering methods to determine which of the project's effects have already been adequately examined in an earlier EIR or Negative Declaration. Guidelines sec. 15063(b)(1).

If the Lead Agency determines that there is no substantial evidence that the project may cause a significant effect on the environment, it must prepare a Negative Declaration. Guidelines sec. 15063(b)(2).

Contents of Initial Study

CEQA requires Initial Studies to include a description of the project, environmental setting, potential environmental impacts, and mitigation measures for any significant effects. In describing the project, the Initial Study must look at all phases including project planning, implementation, and operation. The Initial Study must also address consistency of the proposed project with plans and policies. Names of preparers of the Initial Study are also required for inclusion in the Initial Study. Guidelines sec. 15063(d).

When describing potential environmental effects in an Initial Study, the Lead Agency may use a checklist, matrix, or other form so long as the entries are briefly explained to indicate that evidence exists to support the entries. The brief explanation may be provided through either a narrative or a reference to another information source such as attached maps, photographs, or earlier EIRs or Negative Declarations. A reference to another document should include, where appropriate, a citation to the page or pages where the information is found. Guidelines sec. 15063(d)(3).

In preparing an Initial Study, the Lead Agency may rely upon expert opinion supported by facts, technical studies, or other substantial evidence to document its conclusions. However, an Initial Study is neither intended nor required to include the level of detail that is typically found in an EIR. Guidelines sec. 15063(a)(3). However, many provisions of the CEQA

Guidelines dealing with EIR preparation may be helpful in preparing an Initial Study. Additionally, in preparing an Initial Study, the Lead Agency may use an Environmental Assessment prepared by a federal agency pursuant to NEPA, if one has been prepared. Guidelines sec. 15063(a)(2).

In preparing an Initial Study, the Lead Agency may use an Environmental Assessment prepared by a federal agency pursuant to NEPA, if one has been prepared.

Format of Initial Study

The Initial Study may use a checklist format but must explain the factual data or evidence used to reach conclusions regarding impact significance. An Initial Study without appropriate explanations is sometimes referred to as a "naked checklist" and should be avoided. The Lead Agency must undertake a reasonable investigation of potential impacts when it prepares an Initial Study. Thus, fact-based explanations must be used to support the checklist.

Some public agencies rely on Initial Studies composed of checklists similar to the model checklist found in Appendix G of the Guidelines. In the 1998 amendments to the CEQA Guidelines, the model Initial Study checklist was changed. The checklist now contains a more organized, comprehensive listing of potential environmental impacts, many tied to other environmental laws and regulations, and including those from the old Appendix G ("Effects that may be deemed significant"). Although the items presented in the checklist are not treated as presumptions of significance, a Lead Agency may use them when determining whether the proposed project effects are significant. Even with the revised more comprehensive checklist, a Lead Agency may want to develop its own, comprehensive checklist adding issues that are unique to its jurisdiction.

The model checklist includes four possible levels of environmental effects: "potentially significant impact," "less than significant with mitigation incorporation," "less than significant impact," and "no impact." These possible checklist responses correspond directly to the legal standards for preparing EIRs, Negative Declarations, and Mitigated Negative Declarations. Guidelines sec. 15063(f) and Appendix G of the Guidelines.

Conclusions of an Initial Study

When Must an EIR Be Prepared? As stated above, CEQA requires preparation of an EIR for certain projects. Guidelines sec. 15981.5. An EIR must be prepared when the Lead Agency determines that it can be fairly argued, based on substantial evidence, in light of the whole record, that a project may have a significant effect on the environment. Pub. Res. Code secs. 21080(d), 21082.2(d). If such substantial evidence of significant impacts is presented, the Lead Agency must prepare an EIR, even though it may be presented with other substantial evidence that the project would not have significant impacts. Guidelines sec. 15064. Sometimes known as the "fair argument" standard, this standard for preparation of an EIR may turn on expert, factual, or other substantial evidence where, if there is conflicting evidence on the record (e.g., if two experts disagree) regarding the potential for significant effect, the Lead Agency is still required to prepare an EIR.

The "fair argument" standard creates a very low threshold for EIR preparation and may turn on expert, factual, or other substantial evidence where, if there is conflicting evidence on the record regarding the potential for significant effect, the Lead Agency is still required to prepare an EIR.

Definition of Substantial Evidence. The term "substantial evidence" includes facts, fact-related reasonable assumptions, and expert opinion. According to

Substantial evidence for an initial study means enough relevant information and reasonable inferences from that information to make a fair argument and consists of:

- Facts
- Reasonable assumptions predicated on facts
- Expert opinion supported by facts

Substantial evidence does not include:

- Argument
- Speculation
- Unsubstantiated opinion or narrative
- Evidence that is clearly erroneous or inaccurate
- Evidence of social or economic impacts that do not contribute to or are not caused by physical impacts on the environment

Making the Threshold Decision: Are Effects Potentially Significant?

Factors to consider which must be based on substantial evidence in the record:

- Direct effects
- Reasonably foreseeable indirect effects
- Expert disagreement
- "Considerable" contribution to cumulative effects
- Special thresholds for historical and archaeological resources

Factors not relevant:

- Speculative indirect physical changes to the environment
- Public controversy
- Economic and social effects
- Existing plan build-out

CEQA, substantial evidence does not include arguments, speculation, unsubstantiated opinion or narrative, clearly inaccurate or erroneous evidence, or socioeconomic impacts not related to the physical environment. Pub. Res. Code secs. 21080(e), 21082.2(c); Guidelines sec. 15384.

When May a Negative Declaration Be Prepared? A Negative Declaration may only be prepared when no substantial evidence exists, in light of the whole record, that the project may have a significant environmental effect. Pub. Res. Code sec. 21080(c); Guidelines sec. 15070. In practice, this rule establishes a very low threshold for preparing an EIR. Thus, if there is any substantial evidence of a potentially significant effect (and the requirements of a Mitigated Negative Declaration cannot be met), a Lead Agency may not prepare a Negative Declaration.

When May a Mitigated Negative Declaration Be Prepared? A Mitigated Negative Declaration may be prepared if the Initial Study identifies a potentially significant effect for which the project's proponent, before public release of a proposed Negative Declaration, has made or agrees to make project revisions that clearly mitigate the effects. Additionally, a Mitigated Negative Declaration may not be used if any substantial evidence indicates that the revised project with mitigation may still have a significant environmental effect. Pub. Res. Code sec. 21064.5; Guidelines sec. 15070. For such a Mitigated Negative Declaration, specific mitigation measures must be developed and agreed to before project approval. *See Sundstrom,* page 39. Although no format is specified in CEQA, the project proponent's agreement regarding mitigation commitments may take the form of a letter or revised project application. For additional information about Mitigated Negative Declarations, *see* "Mitigated Negative Declarations," a CEQA advice memorandum published by OPR (December 1997) (Appendix 8).

Determining Whether Effects Are Potentially Significant

Determining whether a project may have a significant effect on the environment calls for careful judgment on the part of the Lead Agency. To the extent feasible, the decision should be based on scientific and factual data. An ironclad definition of "significant effect" is not possible because the significance of an activity may vary with the setting. For example, an activity that may not be significant in an urban area may be significant in a rural one. Guidelines sec. 15064(b). The Guidelines' recommended tools for determining the potential for significant environmental effects include the model Initial Study checklist [Appendix G of the Guidelines], CEQA's mandatory findings of significance [Guidelines sec. 15065], consultation with other agencies, and particular agency thresholds of significance.

A significant effect on the environment is generally defined as a substantial or potentially substantial adverse change in the physical environment. Guidelines sec. 15358. "Environment" as used in this definition means the physical conditions that exist within the area affected by a proposed project, including, but not limited to, land, air, water, minerals, flora, fauna, ambient noise, and objects of historical or aesthetic significance. The "environment" includes both natural and man-made conditions. "The area that will be affected" means the area in which significant effects would occur either directly or indirectly as a result of the project. Guidelines sec. 15360.

CEQA's Mandatory Findings of Significance

CEQA sets forth certain mandatory findings of significance. Pub. Res. Code sec. 21083; Guidelines sec. 15065. According to CEQA, a project would have a significant effect on the environment if the project would substantially degrade environmental quality or reduce fish or wildlife habitat; cause a fish or wildlife habitat to drop below self-sustaining levels; threaten to eliminate a plant or animal community; reduce the numbers or range of a rare, threatened, or endangered species; eliminate important examples of the major periods of California history or prehistory; or achieve short-term goals to the disadvantage of long-term goals. If the project's possible environmental effects are individually limited but cumulatively considerable, when viewed in connection with past, current, and reasonably anticipated future projects, the project would be deemed to have a significant effect. Also, if the project would have environmental effects that will directly or indirectly cause substantial adverse effects on human beings, the project would be deemed to have a significant effect. Guidelines sec. 15065. In addition, the Guidelines specify that a project with an effect that may cause a substantial adverse change in the significance of an historical resource will have a significant effect on the environment. Guidelines sec. 15064.5.

A potential impact will be considered significant if a Lead Agency determines that any of the mandatory findings of significance apply

Sundstrom v. County of Mendocino: Court Establishes Rules for Initial Studies and Negative Declarations

In *Sundstrom v. County of Mendocino* (1988) 202 Cal. App. 3d 296, court interpretation of Negative Declarations came to a head. An individual citizen challenged the Mendocino County Board of Supervisors' decision to approve construction of a sewage treatment plant to serve an existing development consisting of a small motel, restaurant, and filling station, to which a larger motel, a restaurant, and apartments would be added.

The county had prepared an Initial Study supporting a Negative Declaration for the proposed project. The Initial Study/Negative Declaration conditioned certain mitigation measures to be developed and implemented at a later date. One of the reasons the Initial Study/ Negative Declaration concluded there would be no potential for significant effects was because it required the applicant to prepare a future hydrologic study to evaluate the project's potential environmental effects on soil stability, erosion, sediment transport, and flooding of downslope properties. This future study was required to recommend appropriate mitigation measures for the significant impacts reported.

The Court of Appeal held that the Initial Study/Negative Declaration violated CEQA. The court stated that, before approving the project, the county must first resolve the uncertainties regarding the project's potential significant environmental effects. The court concluded that the success of the mitigation determined by a later study was uncertain; therefore, the county could not have reasonably concluded that the project would not have the potential to have significant environmental effects. Also, the court found that the county's deferral of the analysis of significant effects to a study the applicant was preparing in the future was an inappropriate delegation of its CEQA duties. Although the county had included a permit condition requiring subsequent county approval of a sludge disposal plan, the court found it inadequate because there was evidence that an environmentally sound disposal plan might not be achievable. The court also noted that both the county public works department and the Coastal Commission had recommended project denial until the potential problems could be solved.

The court held that the Initial Study/Negative Declaration was ultimately invalid because of a lack of substantial evidence supporting the county's finding of no potential for significant impact. The court stated that the county had "evaded its responsibility to engage in comprehensive environmental review." This fact pattern and associated court ruling have been used as a reference guide for assessing the adequacy of mitigation included in Initial Study/Negative Declarations. An Initial Study/Negative Declaration that relies on a future study to determine if there are potentially significant effects is considered a failure to comply with CEQA.

and thereby require preparation of an EIR. However, these mandatory findings of significance are somewhat open to Lead Agency interpretation as to when a project meets the trigger for significance (e.g., when a project feature would reduce the range of an endangered species). Another issue rests with whether the mandatory findings of significance should be applied before or after project mitigation. For example, in order to obtain an incidental take permit under section 2081 of the California Endangered Species Act, the Department of Fish and Game (DFG) must ensure that the impacts of the taking are "fully mitigated." Fish and Game Code sec. 2081. If a project has incorporated the DFG required mitigation, yet the mandatory findings of significance were applied before project mitigation was factored in the analysis (and assuming there were no other potential significant environmental effects), an EIR would be required even though DFG made a separate finding when issuing the 2081 permit that the impact was fully mitigated.

Consultation with Other Agencies

In determining whether to prepare an EIR, a Lead Agency must formally consult with responsible and trustee agencies. Additionally, a Lead Agency is authorized to consult informally with these agencies as well as any other agency with jurisdiction over resources affected by the proposed project. Pub. Res. Code sec. 21080.3. The purpose of interagency consultation is to ensure that all affected agencies have a voice in the threshold decision.

If an agency with jurisdiction over an affected environmental resource recommends that an EIR be prepared and presents substantial evidence to support that recommendation, the Lead Agency should either prepare an EIR or develop mitigation measures that satisfy the requirements of the other agency for inclusion in a Mitigated Negative Declaration.

Thresholds of Significance

Each public agency is encouraged to develop and publish thresholds of significance to aid that agency in determining the significance of environmental effects. A threshold of significance is an identifiable quantitative, qualitative, or performance level of a particular environmental effect. Noncompliance with this performance level would normally be determined to be significant by the agency and compliance would normally be determined to be considered less than significant. Guidelines sec. 15064.7.

Thresholds of significance to be adopted for general use must be developed though a public review process with advance public notice. If thresholds are formally adopted, they must be adopted by ordinance, resolution, rule, or regulation. Thresholds must be supported by substantial evidence. Guidelines sec. 15064.7.

OPR's CEQA Technical Advice Series report, *Thresholds of Significance: Criteria for Defining Environmental Significance* (September 1994), contains guidance for agencies interested in setting thresholds and information about the advantages of doing so. It also contains examples of thresholds adopted by various public agencies. This technical advice memorandum is reproduced in Appendix 10. *See also* chapter 4 for discussion of thresholds of significance.

Mandatory Findings of Significance

A project will have a significant effect if it will:

- Substantially degrade environmental quality
- Substantially reduce fish or wildlife habitat
- Cause a fish or wildlife habitat to drop below self-sustaining levels
- Threaten to eliminate a plant or animal community
- Reduce the numbers or range of a rare, threatened, or endangered species
- Eliminate important examples of the major periods of California history or prehistory
- Achieve short-term goals to the disadvantage of long-term goals
- Have possible environmental effects that are individually limited but cumulatively considerable when viewed in connection with past, current, and reasonably anticipated future projects
- Have environmental effects that will directly or indirectly cause substantial adverse effects on human beings

---

Tools for Determining Whether Environmental Effects Are Significant

- Model Initial Study Checklist (Appendix G of the Guidelines)
- CEQA's mandatory findings of significance
- Agency adopted regulatory standards
- Consultation with other agencies
- Agency thresholds of significance

Relationship to Adopted Regulatory Standards

Except as otherwise provided in the mandatory Findings of Significance, a change in the environment is not a significant effect if it complies with a standard that meets all of the following criteria:

- The standard contains a quantitative, qualitative, or performance requirement found in a statute, ordinance, resolution, rule, regulation, order, or other standard of general application
- The standard was adopted for the purpose of environmental protection
- The standard was adopted by a public agency though a public review process to implement, interpret, or make specific the law enforced or administered by that agency
- The standard governs the same environmental effect which the change in the environment is impacting
- The standard applies within the jurisdiction where the project is located

A project will normally have a significant environmental effect if it substantially interferes with the movement of resident or migrating wildlife.

A Lead Agency's own thresholds of significance are included within this definition if they meet the above criteria.

If there is a conflict between standards, the Lead Agency must select the appropriate standard on the basis of substantial evidence in light of the whole record. If the Lead Agency determines on the basis of substantial evidence in the record that a standard is inappropriate to determine the significance of an effect for a particular project, it must determine the significance of the effect based on other criteria in the Guidelines. Guidelines sec. 15064(h).

CEQA practitioners should apply the 1998 Guidelines amendments on the use of "standards" with caution because the change to section 15064 was very controversial and thus litigation prone. If a standard is used to render an impact less than significant, care should be taken that all the elements of the definition of a standard described above are met. Conversely, if a Lead Agency chooses to use a significance threshold stricter than an arguably relevant standard, the Lead Agency should document the reasons for choosing the stricter threshold in the Initial Study.

Direct and Indirect Effects. In evaluating the significance of an impact, the Lead Agency must consider both the direct and indirect impacts of the project. Guidelines sec. 15064(c). A more detailed discussion of direct and indirect impacts can be found in chapter 5.

Socioeconomic Effects. An economic or social change alone is not considered a significant environmental effect, but an economic or social change causally related to a physical change may be considered when the significance of the physical change is determined. Guidelines secs. 15064(f), 15382.

Cumulative Effects. In assessing whether a cumulative effect requires an EIR, the Lead Agency must consider whether the cumulative impact is significant and whether the project's contribution to the cumulative problem is "cumulatively considerable." An EIR must be prepared if the cumulative impact is significant and the project's incremental effect, though individually limited, is cumulatively considerable. "Cumulatively considerable" means that the incremental effects of an individual project are considerable when viewed in connection with the effects of past, current, and probable future projects.

"Cumulatively considerable" means that the incremental effects of an individual project are considerable when viewed in connection with the effects of past, current, and probable future projects.

Figure 2-8. Environmental Effects That May Be Considered Significant

This table lists effects that may be considered significant under CEQA. See the model Initial Study Checklist, Appendix G of the CEQA Guidelines, for a complete listing.

Resource Category	Type of Activity A project may be considered to have a significant environmental effect if it will:
Aesthetics	• Adversely affect a scenic vista • Damage scenic resources • Degrade existing visual character • Create a new source of light or glare
Agricultural Resources	• Convert Prime Farmland, Unique Farmland, or Farmland of Statewide Importance • Conflict with existing zoning for agricultural use or Williamson Act contracts • Cause other impacts on or conversions of Farmland
Air Quality	• Conflict with or obstruct implementation of air quality plan • Violate air quality standards • Contribute a cumulatively considerable net increase of a criteria pollutant in a non-attainment area • Expose sensitive receptors to substantial pollutant concentrations • Create objectionable odors affecting a substantial number of people
Biological Resources	• Adversely affect endangered, threatened, or rare species • Adversely affect habitat of such species • Adversely affect wetlands under jurisdiction of Section 404 of the Clean Water Act • Interfere with movement of native resident or migratory species • Conflict with policies or ordinances protecting biological resources • Conflict with an adopted Habitat Conservation Plan or other type of approved biological habitat management plan
Cultural Resources	• Adversely affect the significance of a historical resource (defined by Guidelines sec. 15064.5) • Adversely affect the significance of an archaeological resource (defined by Guidelines sec. 15064.5) • Destroy a unique paleontological resource or geologic feature • Disturb any human remains
Geology and Soils	• Expose people or structures to risk of loss, injury, or death from (1) earthquake, (2) strong seismic groundshaking, (3) seismic-related ground failure, including liquefaction, or (4) landslides • Result in substantial soil erosion or loss of topsoil • Be located on unstable soil • Be located on expansive soil • Have soils incapable of supporting proposed septic system use
Hazards and Hazardous Materials	• Create a public hazard through transport, use, or disposal of hazardous materials • Create a public hazard through upset or accident involving release of hazardous materials • Emit hazardous emissions or involve handling hazardous materials within one-quarter mile of an existing or proposed school • Be located on a site that is listed as hazardous by CAL-EPA • Result in safety hazards near a public or public-use airport or private airstrip • Impair implementation of an adopted emergency response or evacuation plan • Expose people or structures to risk of loss, injury, or death involving wildland fires
Hydrology and Water Quality *(continued next page)*	• Violate water quality standards or waste discharge requirements • Substantially deplete groundwater supplies or interfere with groundwater recharge • Substantially alter existing drainage patterns, resulting in substantial increase in erosion or surface runoff and causing flooding • Create or contribute to runoff that exceeds drainage system capacity • Otherwise substantially degrade water quality • Place housing within a 100-year flood hazard area • Impede or redirect flood flows within a 100-year flood hazard area • Expose people or structures to significant risk of loss, injury, or death from flooding • Contribute to inundation by seiche, tsunami, or mudflow

Resource Category	Type of Activity A project may be considered to have a significant environmental effect if it will:
Land Use Planning	• Physically divide an established community • Conflict with land use plans, policies, or regulations • Conflict with Habitat Conservation Plans or other type of approved biological habitat management plan
Mineral Resources	• Result in loss of a known valuable mineral resource • Result in the loss of availability of a locally important mineral resource identified in an approved land use plan
Noise	• Expose persons to noise levels exceeding established standards • Expose persons to excessive groundborne vibration • Substantially increase ambient noise (temporary, periodic, or permanent) • Expose people to excessive noise near a public-use airport or private airstrip
Population and Housing	• Induce substantial population growth • Displace a substantial number of existing housing units or people, necessitating construction of replacement housing
Public Services	• Result in substantial adverse physical effects from construction of new or altered governmental facilities needed to maintain acceptable service ratios, response times, or other performance objectives for (1) fire protection, (2) police protection, (3) schools, (4) parks, or (5) other public services
Recreation	• Increase the use of existing neighborhood and regional parks, resulting in physical deterioration • Result in substantial adverse physical effects from construction of new or altered recreational facilities
Transportation and Traffic	• Substantially increase traffic relative to existing load and capacity • Exceed an established level-of-service standard • Result in a change in air traffic patterns • Substantially increase hazards due to design or incompatible uses • Result in inadequate emergency access • Result in inadequate parking capacity • Conflict with adopted alternative transportation policies, plans, or programs
Utilities and Service Systems	• Fail to comply with wastewater treatment requirements of Regional Water Quality Control Board • Require or result in the construction of new or expanded water or wastewater treatment facilities • Require or result in the construction of new or expanded stormwater drainage facilities • Exceed existing water supplies • Exceed existing wastewater capacity • Exceed existing landfill capacity • Conflict with federal, state, and local statutes and regulations related to solid waste

Guidelines secs. 15064(i)(1), 15130; *San Joaquin Raptor/Wildlife Rescue Center v. County of Stanislaus* (1996) 42 Cal. App. 4th 608.

A Lead Agency may determine in an Initial Study that a project's contribution to a significant cumulative impact will be rendered less than cumulatively considerable and thus is not potentially significant. When a project might contribute to a significant cumulative impact, but is rendered less than cumulatively considerable through mitigation, the Initial Study must briefly indicate and explain how the contribution has been mitigated. Guidelines sec. 15064(i)(2).

A Lead Agency may determine that a project's contribution to a cumulative impact is not "cumulatively considerable" if the project will comply with the requirements in a previously approved plan or mitigation program that provides specific requirements that will avoid or substantially lessen the cumulative problem within the geographic area in which the project is located. Such plans or programs must be specified in law or adopted by the public agency with jurisdiction over the affected resources through a public review process. Examples of this concept include project-specific compliance with mitigation measures in a water quality control plan, air quality plan, or integrated waste management plan. Guidelines sec. 15064(i)(3).

A Lead Agency may determine that the incremental impacts of a project are not "cumulatively considerable" when they are so small that they make a *de minimus* contribution to a significant cumulative impact caused by other projects that would exist in the absence of the project. Such *de minimus* incremental impacts, by themselves, do not trigger the obligation to prepare an EIR. A *de minimus* contribution means that the environmental conditions would essentially be the same whether or not the project is implemented. Guidelines sec. 15064(i)(4).

In view of this provision, agencies should consider establishing quantitative *de minimus* thresholds, under which a project's incremental contribution to cumulative impacts would not be "cumulatively considerable." For example, if a project's incremental contribution to cumulatively significant environmental impacts only represents 1/1000th of the problem, an agency might not consider the contribution to be "considerable." By establishing such a *de minimus* threshold, a Lead Agency would be able to avoid having to prepare an EIR for every project within an area that already has an unavoidable cumulative environmental problem. The mere existence of significant cumulative impacts caused by other projects alone does not constitute substantial evidence that the proposed project's incremental effects are cumulatively considerable. Guidelines sec. 15064(i)(5).

Public Opinion and Controversy. A Lead Agency must consider public opinion when determining whether an impact is beneficial or adverse. Pub. Res. Code secs. 21080(c)(2), 21082.2(b); Guidelines sec. 15064(c). However, the existence of public controversy alone does not result in an EIR being required if no substantial evidence in light of the whole record shows that a project may have a significant environmental effect. In marginal cases in which it is unclear whether substantial evidence of a potential significant effect exists, the presence of public controversy may indicate that an EIR is necessary if the controversy is related to the project's environmental effects. Guidelines sec. 15064(h).

Expert Disagreement. As discussed above regarding the "fair argument standard" for determining whether to prepare an EIR, if experts disagree about the significance of an effect and their opinions are based on substantial evidence, then the effect must be considered significant. Guidelines sec. 15064(h).

Baseline for Comparison for Land Use Planning Changes. A Lead Agency assessing whether an EIR is required for a general plan amendment, rezoning, or other land use change must compare the newly authorized uses with existing environmental conditions rather than with those environmental conditions anticipated if development goes on as authorized under existing land use designations. Also, mere conformity of a project with a general plan does not independently justify a finding of no significant effect. A more detailed discussion of setting the baseline or "environmental setting" for significance determinations can be found in chapter 5.

Historical and Archaeological Resources. CEQA provides special rules for determining whether historical and archaeological resources are potentially significant. As stated above, the Guidelines specify that a substantial adverse change in the significance of an historical resource is a significant effect requiring preparation of an EIR. The demolition, destruction, relocation, or alteration of an historical resource would be considered a substantial adverse change and therefore, a significant effect. Guidelines sec. 15064.5. These rules are described in greater detail in chapter 5 under the Contents of an EIR.

CEQA has special detailed procedures for determining the significance of impacts to archaeological and historic resources.

Phase Three: Preparation of Negative Declarations, Including Mitigated Negative Declarations

Unless otherwise noted, all discussions regarding Negative Declarations in the following section also apply to Mitigated Negative Declarations; *see also* OPR's CEQA advice memoranda, "Mitigated Negative Declarations" (Appendix 8). Chapters 3, 4, and 5 include discussion of the third phase of CEQA as it pertains to preparation of an EIR if the project may have a significant environmental effect.

During the preparation of the Initial Study, the Lead Agency must make a determination whether it can be fairly argued based on substantial evidence in light of the whole record that a project may have a significant effect on the environment. If the Lead Agency concludes that there is no substantial evidence that a project may cause a significant effect, a Negative Declaration should be prepared. Guidelines sec. 15063.

Contents of a Negative Declaration

A Negative Declaration is a written statement, briefly explaining why a proposed project will not have a significant environmental effect. It must include a brief description of the project and location, identification of the project proponent, and a proposed finding of no significant effect. The Negative Declaration is also required to include a copy of the Initial Study justifying the finding. For Mitigated Negative Declarations, the Negative Declaration must describe the mitigation measures included in the project description to avoid potentially significant effects. Guidelines sec. 15371; Pub. Res. Code sec. 21092.6(a).

Although the requirements for preparing a Negative Declaration are quite limited, in practice, a Lead Agency may want to incorporate many of the rules governing the preparation and content of EIRs. For example, while a Negative Declaration need not evaluate alternatives, in many cases alternatives are included to support the administrative record. Therefore, persons preparing Negative Declarations should familiarize themselves with the required procedural requirements (*see* chapter 4) and contents of EIRs (*see* chapter 5) and include relevant information in a Negative Declaration when necessary to improve the planning and decision-making process.

> **Required Contents of a Negative Declaration**
>
> - Project description
> - Project location
> - Identification of project proponent
> - Proposed finding of no significant effect
> - Attached copy of the Initial Study justifying the finding
> - For Mitigated Negative Declarations, mitigation measures included in the project description to avoid significant effects

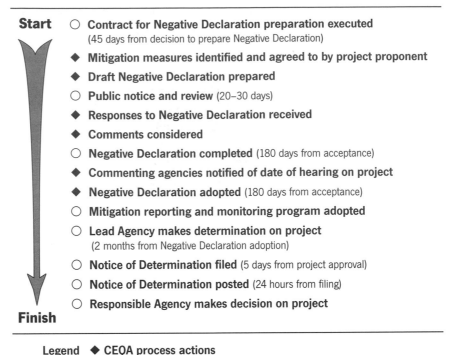

Figure 2-9
Negative Declaration Process

Start ○ **Contract for Negative Declaration preparation executed**
(45 days from decision to prepare Negative Declaration)

◆ **Mitigation measures identified and agreed to by project proponent**

◆ **Draft Negative Declaration prepared**

○ **Public notice and review** (20–30 days)

◆ **Responses to Negative Declaration received**

◆ **Comments considered**

○ **Negative Declaration completed** (180 days from acceptance)

◆ **Commenting agencies notified of date of hearing on project**

◆ **Negative Declaration adopted** (180 days from acceptance)

○ **Mitigation reporting and monitoring program adopted**

○ **Lead Agency makes determination on project**
(2 months from Negative Declaration adoption)

○ **Notice of Determination filed** (5 days from project approval)

○ **Notice of Determination posted** (24 hours from filing)

○ **Responsible Agency makes decision on project**

Finish

Legend ◆ CEQA process actions
○ CEQA process actions with time constraint

Preparation and Review of a Negative Declaration

The preparation and review of a Negative Declaration (including the Initial Study) involves a process similar to, but more abbreviated than, the EIR process. *See* Figure 2-9. If a Negative Declaration for non-public projects is to be prepared under contract, the contract must be executed within 45 days from the Lead Agency's determination that a Negative Declaration is required. The Lead Agency may take longer to execute the contract if compelling circumstances exist and the project applicant consents. The Negative Declaration for non-public projects must be completed and approved within 180 days from determination that the application was complete. Pub. Res. Code sec. 21151.5(c); Guidelines sec. 15107.

The Negative Declaration for non-public projects must be completed and approved within 180 days from determination that the application was complete.

Mitigated Negative Declaration

As authorized by the Guidelines, Mitigated Negative Declarations have been used by numerous agencies for many years. However, it was not until the Legislature approved the 1993 CEQA amendments that specific legislation authorized the use of Mitigated Negative Declarations.

In practice, the Mitigated Negative Declaration is more of a process than a document. After preparing an Initial Study and identifying a project's potentially significant environmental impacts, a Lead Agency may avoid preparing an EIR if it develops mitigation measures to clearly avoid or mitigate significant impacts and those measures are agreed to by the project proponent prior to public review of the proposed Mitigated Negative Declaration and Initial Study. This relatively straightforward concept sometimes leads to extended negotiations between the Lead Agency, the project proponent, other concerned agencies, and even concerned individuals or organizations. Such negotiations are often informal and, with the concurrence of a project applicant, may prolong the formal Negative Declaration review process for months. However, the goals of CEQA are often better achieved through such negotiations, making the extra time worthwhile.

The flexibility permitted by the Mitigated Negative Declaration has been praised by its supporters and criticized by its detractors. People favoring its use cite as the main advantage the guarantee of mitigation. Unlike the use of an EIR, which allows unavoidable significant impacts to ultimately be overridden by decision makers, the use of a Mitigated Negative Declaration is only permissible if all potentially significant impacts are definitely mitigated. Therefore, many people feel that the Mitigated Negative Declaration is a far more effective tool than an EIR to ensure environmental protection.

Although it is now officially authorized in CEQA, critics of the Mitigated Negative Declaration cite three main problems. First is the sometimes "behind-the-scenes" negotiation process that leads to development of a mitigation agreement. Although the agreed-to mitigation is ultimately subjected to public review, some people feel that meaningful participation by the public is eliminated when an EIR is not prepared. A second criticism is that alternatives need not be evaluated in a Mitigated Negative Declaration. Critics therefore feel that agencies sometimes jump directly to mitigating a project's impacts rather than considering how to avoid those impacts by adopting alternatives to the project. Finally, some people feel that the Mitigated Negative Declaration relegates the full EIR process to little more than a threat for a project applicant not agreeing to mitigation measures, a use which was clearly not intended by the Legislature when it enacted CEQA. Despite the pros and cons, the unique procedures permitted by the Mitigated Negative Declaration have become a commonly used method of CEQA compliance.

Unlike the use of an EIR, which allows unavoidable significant impacts to ultimately be overridden by decision makers, the use of a Mitigated Negative Declaration is only permissible if all potentially significant impacts are definitely mitigated.

Public Review

The notice of intent to adopt a Negative Declaration or Mitigated Negative Declaration must specify the review period, identify any public meetings or hearings on the project, briefly describe the project, and state where the proposed Negative Declaration and all reference documents are available for review. Pub. Res. Code sec. 21092(b)(1). A copy of the notice of intent and the proposed Negative Declaration must be mailed to responsible and trustee agencies and agencies with jurisdiction by law and to all parties previously requesting notice. Guidelines secs. 15073, 15072. The notice of intent must be posted in the county clerk's office for 20 days. Pub. Res. Code sec. 21092.3. The clerk must post the notice within 24 hours of receipt. Pub. Res. Code sec. 21092.3. In addition, where a state agency is a responsible agency or a trustee agency's involvement is required, or where the project is of statewide, regional, or areawide importance, the proposed Negative Declaration is required to be sent to the State Clearinghouse.

The minimum public review period for a proposed Negative Declaration or Mitigated Negative Declaration is 20 days. When the document is sent to the State Clearinghouse for review, the public review period must be 30 days unless a shorter period (not less than 20 days) is approved by the SCH

Required Contents of a Notice of Intent to Adopt a Negative Declaration or Mitigated Negative Declaration

- Brief description of project and location
- Starting and ending dates for public review
- Date, time, and place of any scheduled public meetings or hearings
- Address where copies of the Negative Declaration or Mitigated Negative Declaration are available for review
- Whether any listed toxic sites are present
- Other information required by statute or regulation for a particular type of project

(*see* chapter 4 for discussion of where SCH distribution procedures apply). Pub. Res. Code sec. 21091(b). For a Mitigated Negative Declaration, project modifications must be identified before circulation of the proposed Negative Declaration. Pub. Res. Code sec. 21064.5; Guidelines sec. 15070(b)(1).

Recirculation of a Negative Declaration

If a Negative Declaration must be substantially revised after public review and before adoption, the Lead Agency is required to recirculate the proposed Negative Declaration for an additional public review period. A Negative Declaration is considered to be "substantially revised" if:

- A new, avoidable significant effect is identified and mitigation measures or project revisions must be added to reduce the effect to a less than significant level or
- The Lead Agency determines that the proposed mitigation measures or project revisions will not reduce potential significant effects and new measures or revisions must be required

Recirculation is not required under the following circumstances:

- Mitigation measures are replaced with equal or more effective measures (*see* page 49)
- New project revisions are added in response to comments on the project's effects identified in the proposed Negative Declaration which are not new avoidable significant effects
- Measures or conditions of project approval are added after circulation of the proposed Negative Declaration which are not required by CEQA, which do not create new significant environmental effects, and are not necessary to mitigate an avoidable significant effect
- New information is added to the Negative Declaration which merely clarifies, amplifies, or makes insignificant modifications to the Negative Declaration

Guidelines secs. 15073.5(a), (b), (c).

Switching from a Negative Declaration to an EIR

If during the Negative Declaration process there is substantial evidence that the project may have a significant effect on the environment which cannot be mitigated or avoided, the Lead Agency must prepare a draft EIR and certify a Final EIR prior to project approval.

If during the Negative Declaration process there is substantial evidence, in light of the whole record, that the project, as revised, may have a significant effect on the environment which cannot be mitigated or avoided, the Lead Agency must prepare a draft EIR and certify a Final EIR prior to project approval. When it circulates the EIR for consultation and public review, the Lead Agency must advise reviewers in writing that a proposed Negative Declaration had previously been circulated for the project. Guidelines sec. 15073.5(d).

Consideration of Comments on the Proposed Negative Declaration and Consideration of Adoption of the Negative Declaration

The Lead Agency must consider the Negative Declaration, together with any comments received, before approving the project. Pub. Res. Code sec. 21091(f); Guidelines sec. 15074. The Lead Agency has no affirmative duty to prepare formal responses to comments on the proposed Negative Declaration but should have adequate information on the record explaining why the comment does not affect the conclusion that there are no potential significant environmental effects. The Lead Agency is required, however, to notify in writing any commenting agencies of the date of the public hearing on the project for which a Negative Declaration is prepared. Pub. Res. Code sec. 21092.5(b); Guidelines sec. 15073.

Substitution of Mitigation Measures

Before approving the project for which a Mitigated Negative Declaration was prepared, the Lead Agency is permitted to substitute equivalent mitigation measures without having to recirculate the Mitigated Negative Declaration. The Lead Agency, however, must hold a hearing on the matter and find that the new mitigation measures are at least as effective as the original ones in mitigating significant environmental impacts and do not themselves cause any potentially significant effects. A Lead Agency may also use this process, and avoid new environmental review, if a court or administrative body sets aside a condition of project approval. Pub. Res. Code secs. 21080(f), (g); Guidelines sec. 15074.1.

The ability to substitute one mitigation measure for another provides agencies with considerable flexibility in the project approval process. However, this provision is also subject to potential abuse if an agency substitutes weaker measures that have not been reviewed by the public. Therefore, to ensure that substitution of mitigation is legally adequate and justified, the Lead Agency must not only hold the required hearing but also carefully explain, on the record, why the original mitigation measure is not feasible and why the newly proposed mitigation is "equivalent." This explanation must be supported by substantial evidence.

Mitigation Monitoring

When approving a Mitigated Negative Declaration, the Lead Agency must also adopt a monitoring or reporting program for those mitigation measures included in the Mitigated Negative Declaration or made a condition of project approval to mitigate or avoid significant environmental effects. Pub. Res. Code sec. 21081.6; Guidelines sec. 15074(d). *See* chapter 5 for a full discussion of mitigation monitoring and reporting.

Notice of Determination

A Notice of Determination (NOD) for approval of a project based on a Negative Declaration or Mitigated Negative Declaration must be filed with OPR (for state Lead Agencies or where state Responsible Agencies are involved) and the county clerk (for local Lead Agencies) within five working days after approval of a project for which a Negative Declaration has been prepared. The Department of Fish and Game filing fee (*see* page 51) must accompany the NOD. The Notice of Determination must be posted by the county clerk within 24 hours of receipt. Pub. Res. Code sec. 21092.3; Guidelines sec. 15075. The Notice of Determination for a Negative Declaration must identify and describe the project, indicate the date of project approval, and state

---

Substitution of Mitigation Measures in a Mitigated Negative Declaration

A Lead Agency may substitute one mitigation measure for another if:

- The new measure is equivalent or more effective
- Agency considers the matter at a public meeting
- Agency adopts a written finding that:
  - New measure is equivalent or more effective
  - New measure will not cause a significant effect

NOD = Notice of Determination

Required Contents of an NOD on a Project for Which a Negative Declaration or Mitigated Negative Declaration Has Been Approved

- Project name
- Project description
- Project location
- Date of project approval
- Determination that the project will not have any significant effects on the environment
- Statement that a Negative Declaration or Mitigated Negative Declaration has been prepared
- Address where the document may be reviewed

that the project will have no significant environmental effect and that a Negative Declaration has been prepared. In addition to the customary noticing and posting requirements, agencies are encouraged to make copies of all Notices of Determination available in electronic format on the Internet. Guidelines sec. 15075(f).

Subsequent Negative Declarations

Generally, only one Negative Declaration is adopted for a project. Once a project has been approved, the Lead Agency's role in it is completed unless further discretionary approval on that project is required. Information appearing after an approval usually does not require reopening that approval. However, if the Lead Agency does have to exercise further discretionary approvals and if new information arises, then further environmental review may be necessary.

An agency must prepare a subsequent Negative Declaration or Mitigated Negative Declaration for a project if it determines, on the basis of substantial evidence in light of the whole record, that one or more of the following has occurred (and there is no substantial evidence in light of the whole record that the project may have a significant effect on the environment):

- Substantial changes are proposed for the project that will require major revision of a previous Negative Declaration due to the involvement of new, significant environmental effects or a substantial increase in the severity of previously identified effects.
- Substantial changes occur with respect to the circumstances under which the project is undertaken, requiring major revision to a previous Negative Declaration due to the involvement of new significant environmental effects or a substantial increase in the severity of previously identified ones.
- New information of substantial importance that was not known or could not have been known without the exercise of reasonable diligence at the time the previous Negative Declaration was adopted shows any of the following:
  - The project will have one or more significant effects not discussed in the previous Negative Declaration.
  - Significant effects previously examined will be substantially more severe than shown in the previous Negative Declaration.
  - Mitigation measures or alternatives previously found not to be feasible would in fact be feasible and would substantially reduce one or more significant effects of the project, but the project proponents decline to adopt them.
  - Mitigation measure or alternatives that are considerably different from those analyzed in the previous document would substantially reduce one or more significant effects, but the project proponents decline to adopt them.

Guidelines sec. 15162(a).

If the project was approved prior to the occurrence of conditions that trigger preparation of a subsequent Negative Declaration, the subsequent document must be prepared by the public agency that grants the next discretionary approval for the project. Guidelines sec. 16162(c). If no further

A Subsequent Negative Declaration Is Required When:

- Substantial changes are proposed for the project that will involve new, significant environmental effects or substantially increase the severity of previously identified effects
- Substantial changes occur with respect to the circumstances under which the project is undertaken that involve new significant environmental effects or substantially increase the severity of previously identified ones
- New information of substantial importance shows:
  - The project will have one or more significant effects not discussed in the previous Negative Declaration
  - Significant effects previously examined will be substantially more severe than shown in the previous Negative Declaration
  - Mitigation measures or alternatives previously found not to be feasible would in fact be feasible and would substantially reduce one or more significant effects of the project, but the project proponents decline to adopt them
  - Mitigation measure or alternatives that are considerably different from those analyzed in the previous document would substantially reduce one or more significant effects, but the project proponents decline to adopt them
- There is no substantial evidence in light of the whole record that a project, or a project with mitigation agreed to by the project proponent, may have a significant effect on the environment

discretionary authorities are necessary for the project to move forward, no supplemental document is required.

A subsequent Negative Declaration is subject to the same notice and public review requirements as the original document and must state whether the previous document is available for review. Guidelines sec. 15162(d).

Addendum to a Negative Declaration

An agency may prepare an addendum to an adopted Negative Declaration if only minor technical changes or additions are necessary or if none of the conditions triggering a subsequent Negative Declaration are present. An addendum need not be circulated for public review but can be included in or attached to the adopted Negative Declaration. The decision-making body shall consider the addendum with the adopted Negative Declaration before making a decision on the project. A brief explanation supported by substantial evidence justifying the decision not to prepare a subsequent Negative Declaration or EIR should be included in the addendum or elsewhere in the record. Guidelines sec. 15164.

Judicial Review of Negative Declarations

An EIR, rather than a Negative Declaration, must be prepared if it can be "fairly argued on the basis of substantial evidence in light of the whole record" that the project may have a

Payment of Environmental Review Fees to California Department of Fish and Game

The California Fish and Game Code was amended in the late 1980s to require payment of environmental review fees to the California Department of Fish and Game for all Negative Declarations and EIRs prepared pursuant to CEQA. The requirement was that, at the time the Notice of Determination is filed, the Lead Agency or the private applicant pay a fee of $1,250 for Negative Declarations and $850 for EIRs to the county clerk (or to the Governor's Office of Planning and Research in the case of a state Lead Agency) The fee was then transmitted to DFG to fund its environmental review staff. A project approval was not considered final until the fee was paid. California Fish and Game Code sec. 711.4.

Payment of this fee was not contingent on the amount of DFG review time, if any, or on the underlying project's potential environmental effects on fish and wildlife resources. The fee for Negative Declaration "review" was higher than the fee for "review" of an EIR because DFG stated that it spent more time reviewing a Negative Declaration and negotiating with the Lead Agency.

From the outset, the requirement for these review fees was controversial. Private applicants disliked the requirement because of the added costs to prepare a Negative Declaration or EIR and being required to pay a "tax" without a definable relationship to actual DFG review. Public agencies other than DFG disliked the requirement because of their added administrative burden to collect and distribute the fees and because many other agencies' review time was not covered by similar fees.

In June 1995, the Sacramento Superior Court held that the DFG environmental review fees were unconstitutional. In response, DFG agreed to refund the fees to the challengers and stop collecting any future review fees. DFG also agreed to submit to the Legislature a proposal to unconditionally repeal the particular California Fish and Game Code section requiring the review fees. In response to the court holding, DFG directed that any parties seeking refunds of previously paid fees may submit requests to the State Board of Control. It should be noted that some counties collect an administrative fee of $25 associated with collection of the DFG review fee. Reimbursement of this fee was not addressed in the DFG settlement.

The DFG environmental review fee issue is still not resolved, however. The California Association of Professional Scientists, representing DFG staff, succeeded in a suit challenging DFG's agreement to stop collection of the review fees. The court agreed that DFG had no legal authority to refuse to enforce the California Fish and Game Code without appropriate statutory authority. However, the court acknowledged that, absent a Court of Appeals ruling or action by the Legislature, DFG cannot stop complying with a statute. Although DFG began again collecting environmental review fees, the monies are being retained in a trust account because the state expects an appellate court or legislation to require refunding the fees.

"Substantial evidence" for an impact significance determination means enough relevant information and reasonable inferences from that information to make a fair argument to support a conclusion, even though other conclusions might also be reached.

significant environmental effect, even though the agency has other substantial evidence that the project will not have a significant effect. Pub. Res. Code secs. 21080(d), 21082.2(d); Guidelines sec. 15064(g)(1). "Substantial evidence" means enough relevant information and reasonable inferences from that information to make a fair argument to support a conclusion, even though other conclusions might also be reached. Pub. Res. Code secs. 21080(e), 21082.2(c); Guidelines sec. 15384(a).

Thus, in reviewing an agency decision to rely on a Negative Declaration, the court will review the entire record to determine whether any substantial evidence was presented to the Lead Agency that a significant impact could occur. Substantial evidence must include facts, fact-based reasonable assumptions, and expert opinion. It does not include speculation or clearly inaccurate evidence. Pub. Res. Code secs. 21080(e), 21082.2(e).

Chapter 3

Types of Environmental
Impact Reports

Definition and Purpose of an EIR

The preparation of an EIR is part of the third phase of CEQA's environmental review process. After the public agency decides that an activity is a project, is not exempt from CEQA, and potentially causes significant effects on the environment that could not be addressed by a Mitigated Negative Declaration, an EIR must be prepared. Pub. Res. Code secs. 21080(d), 21082.2(d); Guidelines sec. 15064. An EIR is a detailed informational document prepared by a Lead Agency that analyzes a project's potential significant effects and identifies mitigation measures and reasonable alternatives to avoid the significant effects. Guidelines secs. 15121(a), 15362. The primary purposes of an EIR are to inform decision makers and the public about a project's significant environmental effects and ways to reduce them, to demonstrate to the public that the environment is being protected, and to ensure political accountability by disclosing to citizens the environmental values held by their elected and appointed officials. Guidelines secs. 15003, 15121(a). CEQA does not require technical perfection in an EIR, but rather adequacy, completeness, and a good faith effort at full disclosure. Guidelines sec. 15003(i).

> **Purposes of an EIR**
>
> - Inform decision makers and the public about a project's significant environmental effects and ways to reduce them
> - Demonstrate to the public that the environment is being protected
> - Ensure political accountability by disclosing to citizens the environmental values held by their elected and appointed officials

Matching the EIR to the Decision-Making Process

A Lead Agency should select the appropriate type of EIR based on the particular decision-making process and project. Although CEQA requirements for EIR procedure and content are generally applicable to all types of EIRs, certain types of EIRs may assist the Lead and Responsible Agencies in streamlining and focusing the environmental review of the proposed action. Figure 3-1 lists various project types that may require an EIR and the correlated type of EIR that may be prepared to most appropriately review the potential effects of the proposed project. Appendix J of the CEQA Guidelines compares and contrasts the different types of EIRs.

Figure 3-1
Types of EIRs

Activity	Type of EIR
Specific Project	• Project EIR • Joint EIR/EIS (federal agency involvement) • Focused EIR (when based on Master EIR) • Staged EIR
Plan or Study	• Program EIR • Master EIR • General Plan EIR
EIR Already Certified	• Supplemental EIR • Subsequent EIR • Addendum to EIR

Tiering

Tiering refers to the preparation of environmental documents using a multi-level approach where the first-tier includes analysis of general matters contained in a broader EIR (e.g., analyzing the impacts of an entire plan, program, or policy) and subsequent tiers include analysis of narrower projects with later EIRs and Negative Declarations (incorporating by reference the general discussions from the broader EIR and focusing only on the impacts of individual projects that implement the plan, program, or policy). Guidelines sec. 15152. *See* Figure 3-2.

First-tier documents are usually Program EIRs, Master EIRs, General Plan EIRs, Staged EIRs, Redevelopment Plan EIRs, or similar EIRs that evaluate the broad-scale impacts of an entire plan, program, or policy. Second-tier documents are typically Project EIRs, Focused EIRs, or Mitigated Negative Declarations that evaluate the impacts of a single activity undertaken to implement the plan, program, or policy.

Tiering is a method to streamline EIR preparation by allowing a Lead Agency to focus on the issues that are ripe for decision and exclude from consideration issues already decided or not yet ready for decision.

Tiering is a method to streamline EIR preparation by allowing a Lead Agency to focus on the issues that are ripe for decision and exclude from consideration issues already decided or not yet ready for decision. Guidelines secs. 15152; 15385.

Agencies are encouraged to tier the environmental analyses whenever possible when they prepare CEQA analyses for separate but related projects including general plans, zoning changes, and developments projects. This approach can eliminate repetitive discussions of the same issues and focus the later EIR or negative declaration on the actual issues ripe for decision at each level of environmental review. Tiering is appropriate when the sequence of analysis is from an EIR prepared for a general plan, policy, or program to an EIR or negative declaration for another plan, policy, or program of lesser scope, or to a site-specific EIR or negative declaration. Tiering does not excuse the Lead Agency from adequately analyzing reasonable foreseeable significant environmental effects of the project and does not justify deferring such analysis to a later tier EIR or negative declaration. However, the level of detail contained in a first-tier EIR need not be greater than that of the program, plan, policy, or ordinance being analyzed. Guidelines sec. 15152(b).

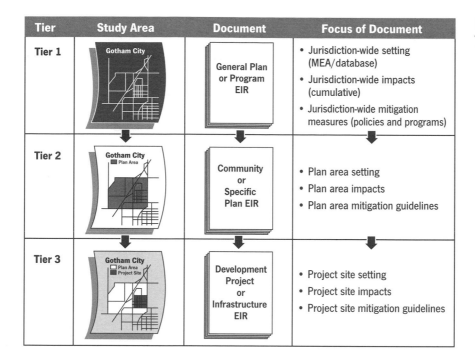

Figure 3-2
Tiering under CEQA

Where a Lead Agency is using the tiering process in connection with an EIR for a large-scale planning approval, such as a general plan or component thereof (e.g., an area plan or community plan), the development of detailed, site-specific information may not be feasible but can be deferred, in many instances, until such time as the Lead Agency prepares a future environmental document in connection with a project of a more limited geographical scale, as long as deferral does not prevent adequate identification of significant effects of the planning approval at hand. Guidelines sec. 15152(c).

Additionally, a first-tier EIR may contain generalized mitigation criteria and policy-level alternatives. The subsequent tiered CEQA documents contain the focused analysis for site-specific mitigation requirements and a specific set of alternatives. For example, tiered CEQA documents for development projects that are consistent with a general plan or community plan may be limited to those site-specific issues or worsened significant effects not disclosed in the first-tier EIR. Pub. Res. Code sec. 21083.3.

Where an EIR has been prepared and certified for a program, plan, policy, or ordinance consistent with CEQA's tiering requirements, any Lead Agency for a later project pursuant to or consistent with the program, plan, policy, or ordinance should limit the EIR or negative declaration on the later project to effects which were not examined as significant effects on the environment in the prior EIR or are susceptible to substantial reduction or avoidance by the choice of specific revisions in the project, by the imposition of conditions, or other means. Tiering under this section shall be limited to situations where the project is consistent with the general plan and zoning of the city or county in which the project is located, except that a project requiring a rezone to achieve or maintain conformity with a general plan may be subject to tiering. Guidelines secs. 15152(d), (e).

Tiered CEQA documents for development projects that are consistent with a general plan or community plan may be limited to site-specific issues or worsened significant effects not disclosed in the first-tier EIR.

When using a tiered analysis, a Lead Agency should prepare an Initial Study to decide whether and to what extent the first-tier document is still adequate. A later EIR shall be required when the initial study or other analysis finds that the later project may cause significant effects on the environment that were not adequately addressed in the prior EIR. Otherwise, a negative declaration shall be required.

Cumulative effects have been a difficult issue to address for later-tiered CEQA documents. CEQA clarifies that where a Lead Agency determines that a cumulative effect has been adequately addressed in the prior EIR, that effect is not treated as significant for purposes of the later EIR or negative declaration, and need not be discussed in detail. When assessing whether there is a new significant cumulative effect, the Lead Agency shall consider whether the incremental effects of the project would be considerable when viewed in the context of past, present, and probable future projects. At this point, the question is not whether there is a significant cumulative impact, but whether the effects of the project are cumulatively considerable. Guidelines secs. 15064(i), 15152(f).

For purposes of tiering, significant environmental effects have been "adequately addressed" in the first-tier document if the Lead Agency determines that the significant environmental effects:

- Have been mitigated or avoided as a result of the prior EIR and findings adopted in connection with that prior EIR;
- Have been examined at a sufficient level of detail in the prior EIR to enable those effects to be mitigated or avoided by site-specific revisions, the imposition of conditions, or by other means in connection with the approval of the later project; or
- Cannot be mitigated to avoid or substantially lessen the significant impacts despite the project proponent's willingness to accept all feasible mitigation measures, and the only purpose of including analysis of such effects in another EIR would be to put the agency in a position to adopt a statement of overriding considerations with respect to the effects.

When a Lead Agency decides to prepare a second-tier CEQA document, the document must include a statement that it is a "tiered" EIR or Negative Declaration, make reference to the first-tier CEQA document, and indicate where the first-tier document is available for review. Guidelines sec. 15152.

Tiering can be used in a variety of situations under CEQA. These options and the projects to which they apply are summarized in Figure 3-3.

Appendix J of the CEQA Guidelines further explains the concept of tiering with examples of tiered situations.

Specific Types of EIRs

Project EIR

The most common type of EIR, the "Project EIR" analyzes the impacts of an individual activity or specific project. The Project EIR, like all EIRs, must include the contents required by CEQA and the Guidelines and must examine

---

Various Types of EIRs That May Be Used in a Tiering Situation

- General Plan EIR
- Staged EIR
- Program EIR
- Master EIR
- Multiple-family residential development/residential and commercial or retail mixed-use development
- Redevelopment project
- Housing/neighborhood commercial facilities in an urbanized area
- Projects consistent with community plan, general plan, or zoning

Figure 3-3. Types of EIRs or Other Documents for Which Tiering May Be Appropriate

EIR Type (Authority)	Applicable Programs or Projects
Program EIR (14 CCR 15168)	Programs composed of a series of actions that are: • related geographically • logical parts in a chain of contemplated actions • connected as part of a continuing program • carried out under same authorizing statute or regulatory authority and have similar environmental impacts that can be mitigated in similar ways
Master EIR (Pub. Res. Code sec. 21156–21158.5)	Programs for approval of: • general plan (including individual elements and amendments) • specific plan • project consisting of smaller, phased projects • regulation to be implemented by subsequent projects • project pursuant to or furthering a redevelopment plan • state highway or transit project subject to multiple reviews or approvals • Department of Fish and Game hunting and fishing regulations
Staged EIR (14 CCR 15167)	Programs or projects that are larger in nature and will: • involve many years of planning • require numerous discretionary approvals from several government agencies, some of which would be required before detailed project plans would be formulated • require several approvals, one of which is scheduled to occur more than 2 years before construction will begin

Community Plan EIR/ Zoning Ordinance EIR	• A project with proposed land uses that are consistent with zoning/community plan designations that were evaluated in a previous community plan EIR (Pub. Res. Code sec. 21083.3)
	• A multifamily residential development of not more than 100 units or residential and commercial or retail mixed-use development of not more than 100,000 square feet that is consistent with a community plan or zoning ordinance for which an EIR was prepared within the preceding 5 years if the project site:
	  – is surrounded by immediately contiguous urban development
	  – was previously developed with urban uses
	  – is within 0.5 mile of an existing rail transit station (Pub. Res. Code sec. 21158.5)

General Plan/Specific Plan/ Coastal Program EIR	• A housing or neighborhood commercial facilities development project in an urbanized setting that is consistent with a specific plan or coastal program adopted within the preceding 5 years (Pub. Res. Code sec. 21080.7)
	• A residential development project consistent with a specific plan for which an EIR was certified after January 1, 1980 (Govt. Code sec. 65457)
	• A multifamily residential development of not more than 100 units or residential and commercial or retail mixed-use development of not more than 100,000 square feet that is consistent with a community plan or zoning ordinance for which an EIR was prepared within the preceding 5 years if the project site:
	  – is surrounded by immediately contiguous urban development
	  – was previously developed with urban uses
	  – is within 0.5 mile of an existing rail transit station (Pub. Res. Code sec. 21158.5)

Redevelopment Plan EIR	• A project that is consistent with a redevelopment plan (Pub. Res. Code sec. 21090)
Environmentally Mandated Projects	• A project undertaken to comply with a performance standard or treatment requirement of the Air Resources Board or an air quality management or control district, the State Water Resources Control Board, a regional water quality control board, the Department of Toxic Substances Control, or the Integrated Waste Management Board (Pub. Res. Code sec. 21159.2)
Installation of Pollution Control Equipment	• Installation of pollution control equipment required by a rule or regulation of the Air Resources Board or an air quality management or control district, the State Water Resources Control Board, a regional water quality control board, the Department of Toxic Substances Control, or the Integrated Waste Management Board (Pub. Res. Code sec. 21159.1)
Environmental Analysis of Rivers and Wetlands	• Adoption of rules and regulations by the Air Resources Board, Department of Toxic Substances Control, Integrated Waste Management Board, State Water Resources Control Board or Regional Water Quality Control Boards, and Air Pollution Control Districts

all phases of the project, including planning, construction, operation, and reasonably foreseeable future phases. Guidelines sec. 15161.

Program EIR

When Applicable. The Program EIR, a type of first-tier document (*see* Tiering, page 54), is prepared for an agency program or series of actions that can be characterized as one large project. Typically, such a project involves actions that are closely related either geographically or temporally. Program EIRs are also prepared for agency plans, policies, or regulatory programs. Program EIRs generally analyze broad environmental effects of the program with the acknowledgment that site-specific environmental review may be required for particular aspects of portions of the program when those aspects are proposed for implementation. Guidelines sec. 15168.

A state or local agency should prepare a Program EIR, rather than a Project EIR, when the agency proposes a program or series of related actions that are linked geographically, are logical parts of a chain of contemplated events, rules, regulations, or plans that govern the conduct of a continuing program, or are individual activities carried out under the same authorizing statutory or regulatory authority and having generally similar environmental effects that can be mitigated in similar ways. Guidelines sec. 15168(a).

Environmental Review of Subsequent Activities. Once a Program EIR has been prepared, subsequent activities within the program must be evaluated to determine whether an additional CEQA document needs to be prepared. However, the Lead Agency may not need to prepare a new CEQA document. When the subsequent activities involve site-specific operations, the Lead Agency should use a written checklist to document its determination that the environmental effects of the operation were covered in the Program EIR. If the Program EIR addresses the program's effects as specifically and comprehensively as possible, many subsequent activities could be found to be within the Program EIR scope and additional environmental documents would not be required. Guidelines sec. 15168(c).

If a subsequent activity would have effects that are not within the scope of the Program EIR, the Lead Agency must prepare a new Initial Study leading to either a Negative Declaration, Mitigated Negative Declaration, or an EIR. In this case, the Program EIR still serves a valuable purpose as the first-tier environmental analysis. The Program EIR can be incorporated by reference into the subsequently prepared document to address program wide issues such as cumulative impacts and policy alternatives, allowing the subsequent environmental document to focus on new or site-specific impacts. Guidelines secs. 15168(d), 15152. Chapter 4 includes a more detailed discussion of cumulative impact analysis.

When a Program EIR is relied on during implementation of subsequent activities, the Lead Agency must incorporate feasible mitigation measures and alternatives developed in the Program EIR into the subsequent activities. Guidelines sec. 15168(c)(3). If a public notice is required for the subsequent activities, the Lead Agency must state in that notice that the proposed activity is within the scope of the Program EIR. Guidelines sec. 15168(e).

Types of Actions That May Require a Program EIR

- Activities that are linked geographically
- Activities that are logical parts of a chain of contemplated events
- Rules, regulations, or plans that govern the conduct of a continuing program
- Individual activities carried out under the same authorizing statutory or regulatory authority and having generally similar environmental effects that can be mitigated in similar ways

When a Program EIR is relied on during implementation of subsequent activities, the Lead Agency must incorporate feasible mitigation measures and alternatives developed in the Program EIR into the subsequent activities.

Advantages of Program EIRs. The Guidelines encourage the use of Program EIRs, citing five advantages:

- Provision for a more exhaustive consideration of impacts and alternatives than would be practical in an individual EIR
- Focus on cumulative impacts that might be slighted in a case-by-case analysis
- Avoidance of continual reconsideration of recurring policy issues
- Consideration of broad policy alternatives and programmatic mitigation measures at an early stage when the agency has greater flexibility to deal with them
- Reduction of paperwork by encouraging the reuse of data (through tiering)

Guidelines sec. 15168(b).

Practical Implications of Program EIRs. Although the legally required contents of a Program EIR are the same as those of a Project EIR, in practice there are considerable differences in level of detail. Because of the general nature of the programs being evaluated, Program EIRs are typically more conceptual and abstract. Courts have indicated that a Program EIR may contain a more general discussion of impacts, alternatives, and mitigation measures.

In developing a Program EIR, the Lead Agency should try to anticipate likely future scenarios that could ultimately develop under the program. Uncertainty over future scenarios often leads agencies to prepare Program EIRs as alternative-based documents, evaluating more than one possible set of future outcomes in equal levels of detail. In a Program EIR, once a reasonable range of assumptions about the future is developed, the agency will generally evaluate the impacts using quantitative and qualitative methods similar to those used for project-specific EIRs.

Lack of adequate funding is sometimes a deterrent to the use of Program EIRs for public projects, because CEQA does not provide a system for recouping the cost from future projects that develop under the program. Nevertheless, some agencies have developed innovative funding systems relying on CEQA's general authority to impose fees for implementation.

Lack of adequate funding is sometimes a deterrent to the use of Program EIRs for public projects, because CEQA does not provide a system for recouping the cost from future projects that develop under the program.

Despite these shortcomings, the Program EIR, used by a variety of agencies, is considered a useful tool for evaluating community-wide and regional impacts and for saving agencies time and money as they comply with CEQA on subsequent projects.

General Plan and Other Plan-Level EIR

Scope and Content. A General Plan EIR is one prepared for a city or county general plan, and usually meets the requirements for either a Program EIR or a Master EIR. The plan itself may serve as the EIR if all required topics in CEQA are covered and identified. Guidelines sec. 15166. Preparation of the EIR parallels the development of the general plan; evaluation of the effects of land uses on the environment should dictate where land uses are located. Although in some cases combining the two documents may not be practical, preparing a General Plan EIR allows an economizing of time and money and results in a more comprehensive document. For further information and advice about preparing General Plan EIRs, *see* the *General Plan Guidelines* issued by OPR.

The environmental review process for a General Plan EIR should be initiated at the outset of general plan preparation. The local agency would prepare a General Plan EIR on the proposed general plan overall land use designations. When combined with an EIR, the general plan must address all the points required for an EIR by CEQA and the Guidelines and must contain a special section or cover sheet identifying where the general plan document addresses each of the points required in an EIR. The development and evaluation of alternatives for the general plan can be the basis for the alternatives analysis of the General Plan EIR. Special studies prepared for the general plan may provide useful information for the analysis of the environmental effects in the General Plan EIR (e.g., a study developed to analyze traffic of various land use intensities can be used to evaluate traffic impacts).

All CEQA reviews on subsequent actions as authorized by the general plan should be based on the General Plan EIR using CEQA's tiering provision. A well-prepared General Plan EIR covering a broad geographic area can increase the possibility that Negative Declarations can be issued at a later time for specific project proposals within the planning area.

Projects Consistent with General Plan, Community Plan, or Zoning. A project that is consistent with the development density established by existing general plan, community plan, or zoning policies for which an EIR was certified shall not require additional environmental review, except where there are project-specific significant impacts which are peculiar to the project or the site. When relying on this form of tiering, the Lead Agency shall limit its examination of environmental effects to those that the agency determines in an Initial Study or other analysis to be impacts peculiar to the project or project site that were not evaluated in the first-tier EIR. It must also determine if there are any potentially significant off-site impacts or cumulative impacts that were not discussed in the prior EIR. Further, it must determine if any impacts identified in the prior EIR are more severe than previously determined, due to substantial new information.

An effect of a project on the environment shall not be considered "peculiar to the project or the parcel" for the purposes of this tiering provision, if uniformly applied development policies or standards have been previously adopted by the city or county with a finding that the development policies or standards will substantially mitigate that environmental effect when applied to future projects, unless substantial new information shows that the policies or standards will not substantially mitigate the environmental effect. The finding shall be based on substantial evidence which need not include an EIR. Such development policies or standards need not apply throughout the entire city or county, but can apply only within the zoning district in which the project is located, or within the area subject to the community plan on which the Lead Agency is relying. Moreover, such policies or standards need not be part of the general plan or any community plan, but can be found within another pertinent planning document such as a zoning ordinance. Where a city or county, in previously adopting

A project consistent with the development density established by existing general plan, community plan, or zoning policies for which an EIR was certified shall not require additional review, except where project-specific significant impacts are peculiar to the project or the site.

uniformly applied development policies or standards for imposition on future projects, failed to make a finding as to whether such policies or standards would substantially mitigate the effects of future projects, the decision-making body of the city or county, prior to approving such a future project pursuant to this section, may hold a public hearing for the purpose of considering whether, as applied to the project, such standards or policies would substantially mitigate the effects of the project. Such a public hearing need only be held if the city or county decides to apply the standards or policies as permitted in this section. Guidelines sec. 15183.

Redevelopment Projects. All public and private activities or undertakings pursuant to or in furtherance of a redevelopment plan are considered a single project, and are deemed approved at the time of adoption of the redevelopment plan by the legislative body. Therefore, once an EIR is prepared for a redevelopment plan, no EIR need be prepared for activities undertaken under the plan, unless the rules governing Subsequent or Supplemental EIRs trigger the need for further CEQA compliance. Pub. Res. Code sec. 21090; Guidelines sec. 15180.

Once an EIR is prepared for a redevelopment plan, no EIR need be prepared for activities undertaken under the plan, unless the rules governing Subsequent or Supplemental EIRs trigger the need for further CEQA compliance.

Housing and Neighborhood Commercial Facilities in Urban Areas. An agency may approve the construction of housing or neighborhood commercial facilities in urbanized areas using an EIR or Negative Declaration previously prepared for a comprehensive regulatory document with no new CEQA compliance. The agency approving the facilities must find that the comprehensive regulatory document was adopted in the last five years pursuant to Article 8 of Chapter 3 of Title 7 of the Government Code or adopted, in the coastal zone, pursuant to a local coastal program certified pursuant to the California Coastal Act. In either case, the plan or program must have been subject to an EIR that is of sufficient detail to address the significant effects of the facilities and the measures to mitigate or avoid those effects. The agency is required to prepare CEQA findings for the approval of the facilities pursuant to the prior EIR and file a Notice of Decision on the proposed action, pursuant to the requirements of CEQA. Pub. Res. Code sec. 21080.7.

Military Base Reuse Projects. An EIR for a military base reuse project is subject to special rules and procedures. Among these procedures are the authority to use the federal EIS as the EIR, the establishment of a specific baseline for impact analysis, and the requirement to conduct a special public hearing on the project. Pub. Res. Code secs. 21083.8, 21083.81. The OPR has prepared a CEQA Technical Advice Series report entitled *CEQA, NEPA, and Base Closure: Recipes for Streamlining Environmental Review* (March 1996), which provides specific guidance on the preparation of environmental documents for base closure and reuse projects. The full report is found in Appendix 9.

An EIR for a military base reuse project is subject to special rules and procedures, including: the authority to use the federal EIS as the EIR; the establishment of a specific baseline for impact analysis; and the requirement to conduct a special public hearing on the project.

Staged EIR

A "Staged EIR," similar to a Program EIR, may be prepared for large-scale, capital-intensive projects that are planned and developed over a long period of time, or similar actions. The first stage of a Staged EIR must include a general discussion of the entire project, including cumulative impacts; however, unlike a Program EIR, the first stage EIR contemplates that there will be future environmental documentation, including project EIRs, prepared. The second-stage EIR supplements the first, focusing on more detailed impact analysis related to second-stage approval. Guidelines sec. 15167.

Master EIR

In General. Master EIRs are a relatively new type of first-tier document that are similar to Program EIRs, Staged EIRs, and other tiered environmental reviews. According to CEQA, Master EIRs may be prepared for general plans (including elements and amendments), specific plans, projects consisting of smaller individual projects to be implemented in phases, regulations to be implemented by subsequent projects, state highway or transit projects subject to multiple reviews or approvals, regional transportation plans, congestion management plans, California Department of Fish and Game regulations for hunting and fishing, and federal military base reuse plans. Pub. Res. Code secs. 21157(a), (c).

OPR's CEQA Technical Advice Series report, *Focusing on Master EIRs: Examining AB 1888 of 1993* (November 1997), contains guidance for agencies interested in preparing Master EIRs. This technical advice memorandum is found in Appendix 5.

Background. The Legislature intended in its 1993 amendments to CEQA to include the provision for Master EIRs to streamline the CEQA process by allowing that a Master EIR evaluate cumulative, growth-inducing, and irreversible significant environmental effects of subsequent projects to the greatest extent feasible. The Legislature further intended that environmental review of subsequent projects be substantially reduced to the extent that the Master EIR reviews project impacts and sets forth mitigation measures. Pub. Res. Code secs. 21156–21159.

Specific Requirements. A Master EIR must describe and present sufficient information about anticipated subsequent projects within its scope. Information required about subsequent projects includes size, location, intensity, and scheduling. The Master EIR must also preliminarily describe potential impacts of anticipated subsequent projects for which insufficient information is available to support a full impact assessment. A Lead Agency may develop a fee program to pay for a Master EIR. Pub. Res. Code secs. 21157(a), (c). *See* Figure 3-4.

Limited Environmental Review for Subsequent Projects. The Lead Agency and Responsible Agencies identified in the Master EIR may use the Master EIR to limit review of subsequent projects. There are several alternative ways that a Lead Agency may limit the scope of a subsequent document. Whenever it is evaluating a subsequent project, the first step is for the Lead Agency to prepare an Initial Study to determine whether the subsequent project and its alternatives, impacts, and mitigation measures were already addressed in the Master EIR. *See* Figure 3-5.

If the Lead Agency determines that the subsequent project is "within the scope" of the Master EIR and therefore will have no additional significant

Master EIRs May Be Prepared for:

- General plans (including elements and amendments)
- Specific plans
- Projects consisting of smaller individual projects to be implemented in phases
- Regulations to be implemented by subsequent projects
- Projects pursuant to or furthering a redevelopment plan
- State highway or transit projects subject to multiple reviews or approvals
- Regional transportation plans
- Congestion management plans
- Federal military base reuse plans
- California Department of Fish and Game for hunting and fishing regulations

environmental effect, and that no new mitigation measures or alternatives may be required, it may prepare a written finding to that effect without preparing a new environmental document or findings. The Lead Agency must provide public notice of its intent to approve or carry out the project and incorporate all feasible applicable mitigation measures or alternatives. Guidelines sec. 15177. *See* Figure 3-5.

Projects "Identified in" the Master EIR. If the subsequent project is not within the scope of the Master EIR, but has been "identified in" the Master EIR and the Lead Agency cannot make the above findings, it may prepare either a Mitigated Negative Declaration or a Focused EIR for the subsequent project. Guidelines sec. 15178.

Small Residential and Mixed Use Project Not Identified in the Master EIR. Even if the subsequent project was not identified in the Master EIR, it may nevertheless be the subject of a Focused EIR if it is a multiple-family residential projects of 100 units or less or residential and commercial or retail mixed use projects of not more than 100,000 square feet and meets certain specific criteria. Guidelines sec. 15179.5.

Restrictions on Use and Practical Implications of Master EIRs. The Master EIR cannot be used to limit subsequent project reviews if it was certified more than five years before the application for a subsequent project was filed. The five-year limitation does not apply if the Lead Agency finds that no substantial changes or no new information related to the Master EIR exist, or if it certifies a subsequent or supplemental EIR that makes appropriate modifications to the Master EIR. Guidelines sec. 15179. *See* Figure 3-5.

A Master EIR is not allowed to be used to streamline approvals of subsequent projects if it did not describe the project and if that project may affect the adequacy of the environmental review in the Master EIR for any subsequent project. Pub. Res. Code sec. 21157.7.

If a subsequently approved project that is not within the scope of the Master EIR makes substantial changes or provides new, relevant information to the Master EIR, the Lead Agency for the Master EIR must take one of three steps:

- Prepare a subsequent or supplemental Master EIR to include additional subsequent projects

- Prepare a Mitigated Negative Declaration for a subsequent project within the scope of the Master EIR

- Prepare a focused EIR for all subsequent projects within the scope of the Master EIR

The Master EIR (and Focused EIR) (*see below*) provisions added to CEQA establish for the first time a detailed statutory process for tiering CEQA documents. Agencies using the new processes will have greater certainty about their ability to withstand legal challenges to tiered documents.

The provisions for Master EIRs (and Focused EIRs), however, do have several shortcomings. The new procedures for use of the Master EIR for subsequent project review are detailed and highly complex, and the Master EIR may be difficult to use for this purpose more than five years after preparation.

**Figure 3-4
Master EIR Contents**

- Anticipated future projects
  - Type
  - Location
  - Intensity
  - Scheduling of capital improvements
  - Location of alternative sites
- Preliminary evaluation of anticipated future project-specific impacts and mitigation measures
- Cumulative impacts
- Growth-inducing impacts
- Significant irreversible environmental changes

Limited Environmental Review Process for Projects within the Scope of a Master EIR

No new EIR or findings are required if the Lead Agency:

- Incorporates in the project all feasible mitigation measures or alternatives as set forth in the Master EIR
- Prepares initial study that concludes:
  - The proposed project was described in Master EIR
  - No additional significant impacts would result
- Prepares findings that:
  - Project is within scope of Master EIR
  - No additional significant impacts would result
  - No new additional mitigation or alternatives would be required
- Prepares public notice pursuant to Guidelines section 15075

Figure 3-5
Relationship between
Master EIR and
Subsequent Documents

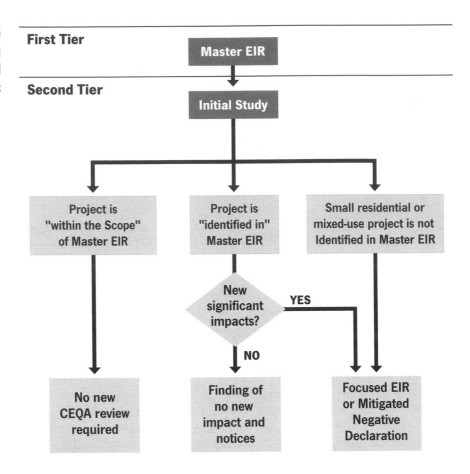

A tiered EIR or Program EIR may more simply achieve many of the stream-lining benefits of a Master EIR.

Also, a subsequent project can be found to be within the scope of a Master EIR through an Initial Study and administrative finding, without a new Negative Declaration being circulated for public and agency review. However, CEQA does not specify the procedures and standards of review for judicial challenges to such an administrative finding.

Focused EIR

In General. A Focused EIR, also provided for by the legislation creating Master EIRs, is an EIR for a subsequent project identified in a Master EIR. It may be used only if the Lead Agency finds that the Master EIR analyses of cumulative, growth-inducing, and irreversible significant environmental effects are adequate for the subsequent project. Pub. Res. Code sec. 21158(a). *See* Figure 3-5. Focused EIRs may be prepared for future projects that were identified in the Master EIR, small multifamily and mixed-use projects not identified in a Master EIR (subject to certain conditions), and installation of pollution control equipment required by specific agency regulation (subject to certain conditions).

The Focused EIR must analyze additional project-specific significant environmental effects not addressed in the Master EIR and any new mitigation measures or alternatives not included in the Master EIR. It must also

---

Focused EIRs May Be Prepared for:

- Future projects that were identified in the Master EIR
- Small multifamily and mixed-use projects not identified in a Master EIR
- Installation of pollution control equipment required by specific agency regulation

examine significant effects discussed in the Master EIR for which substantial new information exists showing that those effects may be more significant than described in the Master EIR. The Focused EIR must also examine those mitigation measures found to be infeasible in the Master EIR for which substantial new information exists that shows those measures may now be feasible. Guidelines secs. 15178, 15179.5. *See* Figure 3-6.

Focused EIRs for Small Multifamily and Mixed-Use Projects (not analyzed in Master EIR). A Focused EIR may be prepared for a multifamily residential project not exceeding 100 units or a mixed-use residential project not exceeding 100,000 square feet, even though the project was not identified in a Master EIR, if the following conditions are met:

- The project is consistent with a general plan, specific plan, or zoning ordinance for which an EIR was prepared within five years of the focused EIR's certification

- The project does not require preparation of a subsequent or supplemental EIR

- The parcel is bordered by urban development, was previously developed by urban uses, or is within one-half mile of a rail transit station

A Focused EIR for these projects should be limited to analyzing site-specific significant effects and significant effects that substantial new information shows will be more significant than described in the Master EIR. Guidelines sec. 15178.

Focused EIRs for Installation of Pollution Control Equipment. If certain conditions are met, a Focused EIR may be prepared for a project consisting solely of the installation of pollution control equipment required by a regulation of the Air Resources Board, local air pollution control districts, the State Water Resources Control Board, the Regional Water Quality Control Boards, the Department of Toxic Substances Control, and the Integrated Waste Management Board. The agency must have certified an EIR on the regulation or reviewed it pursuant to a certified regulatory program within five years of certification of the Focused EIR. The scope of the Focused EIR must be limited to project-specific, potentially significant effects not discussed in the prior environmental analysis and to alternative means of compliance with the regulation. Pub. Res. Code sec. 21159.1; Guidelines sec. 15188. These provisions overlap considerably with those for preparation of EIRs for environmentally mandated projects. Pub. Res. Code secs. 21159–21159.4; Guidelines sec. 15187.

Use of Certified EIRs for Subsequent Development

A Lead Agency may reuse an EIR, previously prepared and certified for one project, for a later project if an Initial Study shows that the previous EIR adequately describes the later project's setting, impacts, alternatives, and mitigation measures. Prior to the reuse of a previous EIR, the Lead Agency must: (1) provide public notice that the previous EIR will be used as a Draft EIR; (2) respond to public comments received in response to the notice; and (3) complete the remaining steps in the CEQA process. Guidelines sec. 15153.

> **Figure 3-6. Focused EIR Contents Must...**
>
> - Focus on project-specific impacts and mitigation measures
>
> - Evaluate any new significant effects not in Master EIR
>
> - Include no new evaluation of:
>   – Cumulative impacts
>   – Growth-inducing impacts
>   – Significant irreversible environmental changes

A Focused EIR may be prepared for a subsequent project identified in a Master EIR.

When reusing an EIR, it is inappropriate for a Lead Agency to use a Negative Declaration procedure. However, a Negative Declaration may refer to an EIR prepared for an earlier project as evidence that the later project will not have a significant environmental effect.

Master Environmental Assessment

MEA = Master Environmental Assessment

The Master Environmental Assessment (MEA) is not the same thing as a Master EIR, but rather an inventory of resources within a jurisdiction. Guidelines sec. 15169. It is recommended as a tool to identify environmental characteristics and constraints of an area during the first phase of comprehensive planning. Preparation of an MEA does not replace the need to prepare an EIR; however, an MEA may be incorporated by reference into an EIR for addressing the environmental characteristics of the proposed project site. In practice, MEAs are rarely prepared as stand-alone documents. Rather, the "environmental setting" section of a Program EIR or a Master EIR is sometimes referred to as a MEA.

Environmental Impact Report / Environmental Impact Statement

An environmental impact statement is the NEPA equivalent of an EIR.

An environmental impact statement is the NEPA equivalent of an EIR. An EIR/EIS is a document prepared jointly by a Lead Agency subject to CEQA and a federal Lead Agency to satisfy the requirements of both CEQA and NEPA. Guidelines sec. 15170. *See* chapter 6 for a complete discussion of EIR/EISs and other joint CEQA/NEPA documents.

Substitute Document for Certified Regulatory Programs

As described in chapter 2, an agency's actions when involving the implementation of certain state regulatory programs (certified by the Secretary of Resources) are exempt from the CEQA requirement to prepare an EIR. For an action to qualify for this partial exemption, the regulatory program requires preparation of a "substitute document" that must include several specific environmental protection requirements. The substitute document prepared for the agency action within the certified regulatory program must comply with CEQA requirements for preparation of an EIR, including the requirement to avoid significant adverse effects on the environment where feasible. *See* Partial Exemptions for Certified Regulatory Programs, page 31.

Environmental Analysis for Adoption of New Regulations for Environmentally Mandated Projects

CEQA provides special rules for environmental analyses of regulations adopted by the Air Resources Board, local air pollution control districts, the State Water Resources Control Board, the Regional Water Quality Control Boards, the Department of Toxic Substances Control, and the Integrated Waste Management Board. These agencies, when adopting a regulation, must conduct an environmental review of reasonably foreseeable methods of compliance (e.g., installation of pollution control equipment). The regulatory review must include reasonably foreseeable impacts of methods of compliance, mitigation measures, and alternative means of compliance. This requirement will be satisfied by an EIR prepared when a regulation is adopted. Pub. Res. Code sec. 21159; Guidelines sec. 15187.

If a subsequent project consists solely of compliance with a performance standard or treatment requirement imposed by the above-listed regulatory agencies, the Lead Agency must use the previously prepared regulatory review to the greatest extent feasible. Any EIR required for the compliance project must be limited in scope to project-specific issues not discussed in sufficient detail in the regulation's environmental review, mitigation measures for significant environmental effects only, and alternative means for compliance with the regulation. Pub. Res. Code secs. 21159.2, 21159.3. These procedures overlap considerably with those for preparation of Focused EIRs for installation of pollution control equipment.

An EIR required for a compliance project must be limited in scope to project-specific issues not discussed in sufficient detail in the regulation's environmental review, mitigation measures for significant environmental effects only, and alternative means for compliance with the regulation.

Subsequent EIR, Supplemental EIR, and Addendum

Subsequent EIRs, Supplemental EIRs, and Addenda to an EIR are required when there is a change in the conditions analyzed in an EIR, after the EIR has been certified but before all Lead or Responsible Agency discretionary authorities have been granted for the project. These documents are discussed in chapter 4 under Subsequent EIR, Supplemental EIR, and Addendum to an EIR.

Chapter 4

Preparation and Review of an EIR and Agency Decision Making

EIR Preparation Process

After the Lead Agency decides, either through preparation of an Initial Study or at the outset of project planning, that there is substantial evidence in light of the whole record that the proposed project may have a significant effect on the environment, an EIR shall be prepared. EIR preparation is a multiple-step process designed to provide opportunities to integrate environmental factors into project planning and decision making. Guidelines sec. 15080. *See* Figure 4-1. The primary steps for the Lead Agency in the EIR process include: determination of scope, content, and focus of EIR; issuance of a Draft EIR/analysis of significant environmental impacts; circulation of the Draft EIR for agency and public comment; issuance of a Final EIR/response to substantive issues raised during comments; adoption of findings regarding significant impacts and appropriate mitigation; and adoption of Statement of Overriding Considerations for significant and unavoidable impacts.

These steps and all other steps in the EIR process are discussed in this chapter and in chapter 5.

Time of Preparation of the EIR

The incorporation of environmental factors into all levels of government planning and project implementation is one of the fundamental objectives of CEQA. To accomplish this goal, EIR preparation should begin as early as possible in the planning process to allow environmental considerations to influence project design, but late enough to provide meaningful information for environmental assessment. Guidelines sec. 15004(b). *See* Timing of CEQA Implementation, page 17. Too often, the design of projects is finalized before beginning the CEQA process. This often leads to costly design changes and a project proponent's resistance to analyzing alternatives and including mitigation measures.

> **Lead Agency Requirements for EIR Preparation**
>
> - Determination of scope, content, and focus
> - Issuance of a Draft EIR/analysis of significant environmental impacts
> - Circulation of the Draft EIR for agency and public comment
> - Issuance of a Final EIR/response to substantive issues raised during comments
> - Adoption of findings regarding significant impacts and appropriate mitigation
> - Adoption of Statement of Overriding Considerations for significant and unavoidable impacts
> - Adoption of a mitigation monitoring or reporting program

Figure 4-1
EIR Process

Start

◆ Notice of Preparation sent to Responsible and Trustee Agencies
○ Responses to Notice of Preparation sent to Lead Agency
   (30 days from acceptance)
○ Contract for EIR preparation executed
   (45 days from decision to prepare EIR)
◆ Preliminary Draft EIR prepared
◆ Independent review by Lead Agency
◆ Draft EIR completed and submitted for review
◆ Notice of completion filed
◆ Public notice and review of Draft EIR (30–45 days)
○ Public hearing on Draft EIR (optional)
◆ Written comments received
◆ Responses to comments prepared
○ Responses sent to commenting agencies (10 days before decision)
○ Final EIR certified by Lead Agency (1 year from acceptance)
○ Lead Agency makes decision on project
   (6 months from final EIR certification)
◆ Findings written and adopted
◆ Mitigation reporting and monitoring program adopted
○ Notice of Determination filed (5 days from approval)
○ Notice of Determination posted (24 hours from filing)

Finish ○ Responsible Agency makes decision on project
   (180 days from Lead Agency decision)

Legend
◆ CEQA process actions
○ CEQA process actions with time constraints

For private development projects, EIR preparation and the project decision are to be completed within one year from the time an application is accepted as complete by the Lead Agency. *See* Figure 2-7.

Determining the Scope, Focus, and Content of the EIR

Purpose of Scoping

As a result of scoping, the Lead Agency may limit EIR discussion of nonsignificant environmental effects to a brief explanation of why those effects are not considered potentially significant.

The process of determining the scope, focus, and content of an EIR is known as "scoping." Scoping helps to identify the range of actions, alternatives, environmental effects, methods of assessment, and mitigation measures to be analyzed in depth, and eliminates from detailed study those issues that are not important to the decision at hand. Scoping is also an effective way to bring together and resolve the concerns of interested federal, state, and local agencies; the proponent of the action; and other interested persons, including opponents of the project. Guidelines sec. 15083. As a result of scoping, including preparation of an Initial Study, the Lead Agency may limit EIR discussion of nonsignificant environmental effects to a brief explanation of why those effects are not considered potentially significant. Pub. Res. Code sec. 21002.1; Guidelines sec. 15143.

Tools used to determine the scope of an EIR include the Initial Study, early public and inter-agency consultation, the NOP, and scoping meetings with agencies and the public. Of these tools, only the NOP is mandatory under CEQA for preparation of an EIR.

Early Public and Agency Consultation

The Lead Agency may, either prior to or during preparation of an EIR, want to consult with any person, organization, or government agency it believes will be concerned with the environmental effects of the project. Guidelines sec. 15083. Many Lead Agencies have found that early consultation solves potential problems that would arise in more serious forms later in the review process.

Notice of Preparation

Immediately after deciding that an EIR is required, the Lead Agency must send an NOP soliciting participation in determining the scope of the EIR to Responsible and Trustee Agencies and involved federal agencies; to the State Clearinghouse, if a state agency is a Responsible Agency for the proposed action or if a Trustee Agency is involved; and to parties previously requesting notice in writing. Guidelines sec. 15082(a). Although not required, the Lead Agency should consider sending the NOP to all parties that may be interested in the project, including neighboring landowners. Pub. Res. Code sec. 21092.2; Guidelines sec. 15082. CEQA requires an NOP (of sufficient detail to allow for a "meaningful response"), including a brief description of the proposed project and project location; probable environmental effects of the project; date, time, and place of the public hearing (if the Lead Agency decides to hold one); address where documents or files relating to the proposed project are available for review and where written comments on the scope of the EIR may be sent; and the deadline for submitting comments. Guidelines sec. 15082.

A sample NOP form can be found in Appendix I of the Guidelines (Appendix 2 of this book). The NOP must be posted in the county clerk's office for 30 days. Pub. Res. Code sec. 21092.3. The county clerk must post the notice within 24 hours of receipt. Pub. Res. Code sec. 21092.3.

Responses to a Notice of Preparation. Responses to the NOP regarding the scope of the EIR by each Responsible Agency must be submitted to the Lead Agency within 30 days of issuance of the NOP. The response shall provide specific detail about the scope and content of the environmental information related to the Responsible Agency's jurisdiction to be included in the EIR. If no response is issued within 30 days (and there is no well-justified request for additional time), the Lead Agency may presume the Responsible Agency has no comment. The Lead Agency must include in the EIR any information requested in response to the NOP. Guidelines sec. 15082.

Scoping Meetings

Formal scoping meetings are not required by CEQA when a Lead Agency has decided to prepare an EIR. At the Lead Agency's discretion, however, scoping meetings with Responsible and Trustee Agencies, and other interested agencies or the public, may be a useful opportunity for obtaining information about the scope and content of an EIR.

> **Required Contents of a Notice of Preparation**
>
> - Brief description of the proposed project
> - Description of the proposed project's location
> - Date, time, and place of the public hearing (if the Lead Agency decides to hold one)
> - Address where documents or files relating to the proposed project are available for review
> - Address where written comments on the scope of the EIR may be sent
> - Deadline for submitting comments

Early public and agency consultation will assist the Lead Agency in developing the appropriate scope and methodology for surveying for special status species to be included in setting the environmental baseline.

Scope of State-Mandated Local Projects

An EIR prepared for a local project mandated by state agency order must be limited to factors and alternatives consistent with the order. Guidelines sec. 15184.

If a local agency undertakes a project to implement a rule or regulation imposed by a certified state regulatory program listed in the Guidelines section 15251, the project is exempt from CEQA with regard to the significant effects analyzed in the document prepared by the state agency as a substitute for an EIR. The local agency shall comply with CEQA with regard to site-specific effects of the project that were not analyzed by the certified state agency as a significant effect on the environment. The local agency is not required to reexamine the general environmental effects of the state rule or regulation. *See also* Partial Exemptions for Certified Regulatory Programs, page 31, and Substitute Document for Certified Regulatory Programs, page 66.

Preparation of a Draft EIR

Although the Lead Agency is required to allow for 30 days from issuance of the NOP to accept comments regarding the scope of the EIR, the Lead Agency may start collecting the preliminary information and preparing the impact analysis for the EIR directly after deciding to prepare an EIR. The Lead Agency cannot circulate a Draft EIR for public review before the time period for responses to the NOP has expired. Guidelines sec. 15082(a)(4).

Contents of a Draft EIR

See chapter 5 for more detail on the contents of an EIR. The scoping process assists the Lead Agency in determining the basic substantive content of the EIR. Through scoping, the Lead Agency should have identified the range of actions, alternatives, environmental effects, and mitigation measures to be analyzed in depth. The EIR's discussion of nonsignificant environmental effects may be limited to a brief explanation of why those effects are not considered potentially significant. Pub. Res. Code sec. 21002.1; Guidelines sec. 15143. CEQA and the Guidelines contain general content requirements for a Draft EIR as follows:

- Table of contents or index
- Summary of discussion contained in the Draft EIR
- Project description
- Environmental setting
- Significant environmental effects of the project (including direct, indirect, short-term, long-term, cumulative, and unavoidable impacts)
- Areas of known controversy
- Alternatives to the proposed project, including the No-Project Alternative, and identification of the environmentally superior alternative
- Mitigation measures for the significant environmental effects
- Growth-inducing impacts
- Significant irreversible changes due to the proposed project (required only for EIRs on plans, policies, ordinances, local agency formation commission actions, and EIR/EISs)

Required Contents of a Draft EIR

- Table of contents or index
- Summary of discussion contained in the Draft EIR
- Project description
- Environmental setting
- Presentation of the significant environmental effects of the project (including direct, indirect, short-term, long-term, cumulative, and unavoidable impacts)
- Areas of known controversy
- Alternatives to the proposed project, including the No-Project Alternative, and identification of the environmentally superior alternative
- Mitigation measures for the significant environmental effects
- Growth-inducing impacts
- Expected significant irreversible changes due to the proposed project (required only for EIRs on plans, policies, ordinances, LAFCO actions, and EIR/EISs)

Who May Prepare a Draft EIR

While the Lead Agency is ultimately responsible for the adequacy of the Draft (and Final) EIR under CEQA, including the scope, content, and impact conclusions of the Draft EIR, a Draft (and Final) EIR may be prepared by Lead Agency staff, another public or private entity, project applicant or project applicant's consultant, or a combination of these parties. Additionally, the Lead Agency may rely on another Lead Agency's EIR and use the previously prepared EIR as its own. Guidelines sec. 15084(d).

The preparation of an environmental impact report is a difficult and challenging task that is sometimes beyond the expertise or time constraints of an agency's own staff. Consequently, many Lead Agencies rely on private consultants to prepare EIRs.

When the Lead Agency is considering a private applicant's proposal, there is a wide variety of preferences for approaches to the preparation of an EIR. Even when they use consultants, most Lead Agencies maintain a firm control on the scope, content, and adequacy of the EIR. These agencies typically send requests for proposals to private consultants and directly retain the consultants under a two-party contract. In these situations, the private applicants are given only minimal, if any, involvement in the process, even though they typically pay the cost of EIR preparation under a separate fee arrangement with the Lead Agency. Guidelines sec. 15045.

Other Lead Agencies utilize a three-party contract under which the agency, consultant, and applicant all participate in EIR preparation. In these situations, applicants are often given a limited degree of review of the EIR while it is being prepared. Still other agencies allow project applicants to have the primary role in consultant selection and contracting. Because of the appearance of inappropriateness for an applicant-funded consultant to prepare an EIR, every Lead Agency should review its consultant selection procedures and its standard consultant contract to ensure that they support the concept that the Lead Agency should control all aspects of the CEQA process. Any agency that gives too much control to project applicants may jeopardize its ability to defend an EIR if one is ever challenged by an applicant. However, as discussed below, the Lead Agency must subject the Draft EIR to its own review and analysis. Guidelines sec. 15084(e).

Lead Agency Responsibilities. CEQA requires that, no matter who prepares the initial version of an EIR, the EIR must be subject to the Lead Agency's own review and analysis and reflect the Lead Agency's independent judgment with regard to the scope, content, and adequacy. The Lead Agency is responsible for the objectivity of the Draft EIR. When a Draft EIR is prepared by another party, such as the applicant or a consultant, the Lead Agency should review preliminary or administrative drafts of the EIR to enable the Lead Agency to exercise its independent judgment concerning the EIR's scope, content, and general CEQA adequacy. At the time of certifying the EIR (*see below*), the Lead Agency must specifically make a written finding that the EIR does in fact reflect the Lead Agency's independent judgment. Pub. Res. Code sec. 21082.1(c); Guidelines sec. 15084(e).

> ### A Draft EIR May Be Prepared by...
>
> - Lead Agency staff
> - Another public or private entity
> - Project applicant or project applicant's consultant
> - Third-party contractor involving the Lead Agency, project applicant, and consultant

No matter who prepares the initial version of an EIR, the EIR must be subject to the Lead Agency's own review and analysis and reflect the Lead Agency's independent judgment with regard to the scope, content, and adequacy.

Time Limits for Consultant Contracting. If a Draft EIR is to be prepared under contract with a consultant, the contract must be executed within 45 days of the decision of the Lead Agency to prepare the Draft EIR. Pub. Res. Code sec. 21151.5(c). To assist in meeting this time constraint, some Lead Agencies maintain a list of qualified consultants from which to choose for preparing the EIR; other Lead Agencies enter into "indefinite quantities" contracts with consultants for on-call service to prepare EIRs as applications are submitted.

Public Notice and Review of a Draft EIR

Once a Draft EIR is prepared, the Lead Agency must issue notices of availability and completion (*see below*) and distribute the document for review and comment and consultation with other agencies. The Lead Agency must ensure that the public has been adequately notified of the availability of the Draft EIR. *See* OPR's CEQA Technical Advice Series report, "Circulation and Notice under CEQA," found in Appendix 11.

Consultation with Other Agencies Concerning a Draft EIR

A Lead Agency must consult with and request comments on a Draft EIR from the following agencies:

- Responsible Agencies
- Trustee Agencies
- Any other state, local, or federal agencies that have jurisdiction by law with respect to the project
- Any city or county which borders on the city or county within which the project is located
- For a project of statewide, regional, or areawide significance, the transportation planning agency and other agencies that have major transportation facilities within their jurisdiction
- For development projects meeting the requirements of Guidelines section 15083.5, water agencies affected by the project
- For a state Lead Agency when the EIR is prepared for a highway or freeway project, the State Air Resources Board
- For a subdivision project located within one mile of the State Water Project, the California Department of Water Resources

In addition to these required consultations, a Lead Agency may consult with any person or agency who is interested in or has expertise with regard to the project. Guidelines sec. 15086.

Public Notice of Draft EIR Availability

In General. As discussed in chapter 1, public involvement is one of the fundamental objectives of CEQA. Thus, adequate notification to the public of the availability of a Draft EIR is important to achieving this objective. CEQA requires state and local agencies to make diligent efforts to involve the public throughout the environmental review process. Each Lead Agency must include provisions in its CEQA procedures for wide public involvement, both formal and informal, to encourage the public to react to environmental issues

---

Contents of a Public Notice of Draft EIR

- Brief description of the proposed project and location
- Dates of review period
- List of anticipated significant environmental effects
- Location for public review of documents
- Presence of any hazardous waste sites

A Notice of Draft EIR Availability Must Contain...

- Project description
- Project location
- Identification of significant environmental impacts
- Specification of the review period
- Identification of the public hearing date, time, and place (if applicable)
- Address where the Draft EIR is available for review
- Identification of the location of documents referenced in the Draft EIR
- Statement of whether the project site is a listed toxic site

related to the agency's proposed projects. In addition to the notice requirements discussed below, an agency should whenever possible, making environmental information available in electronic format on the Internet, on a website maintained or utilized by the public agency. Guidelines sec. 15201.

Notice of Availability. The notice that the Draft EIR is available for review must contain a description of the project and location; identification of significant environmental impacts; specification of the review period; identification of the public hearing date, time, and place (if applicable); address where the Draft EIR and documents referenced in the Draft EIR are available for review; and a statement of whether the project site is a listed toxic site. Pub. Res. Code secs. 21092(b), 21092.6; Guidelines secs. 15087, 15105.

Methods of Notice of Availability. CEQA requires that the public notice announcing that the Draft EIR is available for review be issued to the county clerk, all Responsible and Trustee Agencies (*see below*), and any person or organization requesting, or who previously requested, a copy. The public notice must either be published in a newspaper of general circulation, posted on and off the project site, or directly mailed to owners and occupants of contiguous property. If the Lead Agency uses a newspaper notice, and if more than one area will be affected, the notice must be published in the newspaper of largest circulation from among the newspapers of general circulation in the affected areas. Pub. Res. Code secs. 21092(b), 21092.3; Guidelines secs. 15087(a).

The notice must be posted in the county clerk's office for 30 days. The clerk must post the notice within 24 hours of receiving it. Pub. Res. Code sec. 21092.3.

Notice to Public Agencies. CEQA requires that the Lead Agency must consult with, and request comments on the Draft EIR from, all Responsible and Trustee Agencies, agencies with jurisdiction by law, and representatives from cities and counties adjacent to the project site. Pub. Res. Code secs. 21104, 21153; Guidelines sec. 15086. Typically, notice for these agencies involves transmittal of the Draft EIR with a specific request for comments.

Notice of Completion

At the same time the Lead Agency provides public notice of the availability of a Draft EIR, the Lead Agency must file a Notice of Completion with the State Clearinghouse. The notice must include a brief project description and information on the project location, the address where the Draft EIR is available, and the public review period. Guidelines sec. 15085. Where the EIR will be reviewed through the state review process handled by the SCH (*see below*), the cover form required by the SCH will serve as the Notice of Completion. The Notice of Completion may be filed as a printed hard copy or electronically by way of a diskette or e-mail. Guidelines sec. 15085.

State Review Process Administered by the State Clearinghouse

The SCH was established to coordinate the systematic review of environmental documents by state agencies. The SCH must be used to distribute

---

Objectives of Public Review of Agency Proposals

- Sharing expertise
- Disclosing agency analysis
- Checking for accuracy
- Detecting omissions
- Discovering public concerns
- Soliciting counterproposal

Public Notice of a Draft EIR Must Be Sent to...

- County clerk
- All Responsible and Trustee Agencies
- Any person or organization requesting, or who previously requested, a copy

---

Public Notice of a Draft EIR Must Be Issued in at Least Any One of the Following...

- Publication in a newspaper of general circulation
- Posting on and off the project site
- Direct mailing to owners and occupants of contiguous property

---

A Lead Agency Assures Public Participation by Providing for...

- Issuance of the Notice of Preparation
- Scoping meetings
- Public notice and public review of the Draft EIR
- Public hearings on the Draft EIR
- Response to public comments in the Final EIR
- Public hearing on the project decision

Draft EIRs (and Negative Declarations) whenever the project meets any of the criteria shown in the box. Guidelines secs. 15205, 15206.

The Lead Agency is required to identify to the SCH those state agencies that are likely to be interested in the project. The Lead Agency must send at least ten copies of the Draft EIR to the SCH. The SCH transmits the Draft EIR to those agencies identified for review and receives comments on the Draft EIR from reviewing agencies for transmittal to the Lead Agency. In addition to submitting printed copies of environmental documents to the State Clearinghouse, the Lead Agency must include a copy of the document in electronic format, on a diskette or by E-mail, if available. Guidelines sec. 15205. *See* Figure 4-2.

Public Comments

As stated in chapter 1, public participation is an essential part of CEQA. Guidelines sec. 15201. Although a member of the public is free to comment on any aspect of a proposed project, when reviewing Draft EIRs, people should focus on the sufficiency of the document regarding the identification of environmental impacts and methods to avoid or mitigate those impacts. Guidelines sec. 15204. The Lead Agency is required, when responding to comments on the Draft EIR, to respond to the significant environmental issues raised. Guidelines sec. 15088.

Persons who submit comments or otherwise participate in the public review process provided by CEQA are afforded protection from legal retaliation by project proponents who may disagree with their comments. Such lawsuits, known as "strategic lawsuits against public participation" (SLAPP) have been frowned on by the courts in California and the legislature has enacted an anti-SLAPP law to deter this type of offensive litigation. *Dixon v. Superior Court* (1994) 30 Cal. App. 4th 733; Code Civ. Proc. sec. 425.16.

Agency Comments

A public agency, however, is limited to submitting comments on only those aspects of a project which are within its area of expertise or which are required to be carried out or approved by the agency. Agency comments must be supported by substantial evidence. Guidelines secs. 15204(f), 15209.

If, in commenting on a Draft EIR, a Responsible or Trustee Agency identifies any significant environmental effects, it should submit mitigation measures to address those effects and must notify the Lead Agency of detailed performance objectives for mitigating those impacts or refer the Lead Agency to readily available guidelines or reference documents

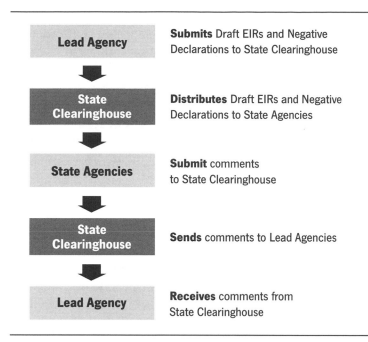

Lead Agency	**Submits** Draft EIRs and Negative Declarations to State Clearinghouse
↓	
State Clearinghouse	**Distributes** Draft EIRs and Negative Declarations to State Agencies
↓	
State Agencies	**Submit** comments to State Clearinghouse
↓	
State Clearinghouse	**Sends** comments to Lead Agencies
↓	
Lead Agency	**Receives** comments from State Clearinghouse

Agencies frequently involved in reviewing CEQA documents:

- Air Resources Board
- Bay Conservation and Development Commission
- California Coastal Commission
- California Environmental Protection Agency
- Department of Conservation
- Department of Fish and Game
- Department of Forestry and Fire Protection
- Department of Parks and Recreation
- Department of Transportation
- Department of Water Resources
- Integrated Waste Management Board
- State Lands Commission
- Water Resources Control Board

concerning mitigation measures. If the Responsible or Trustee Agency is not aware of any appropriate mitigation measures, it must state that to the Lead Agency. Guidelines secs. 15204(f), 15086.

**Figure 4-2
State Clearinghouse
Operation**

How to Comment Effectively

To effectively participate in the CEQA review process, members of the public as well as interested organizations and agencies must be diligent and focused in their comments. In reviewing EIRs, people should address the sufficiency of the document in identifying and analyzing possible significant environmental impacts and how they may be avoided or mitigated. Comments are most helpful when they disclose additional possible impacts, alternatives, or mitigation measures. Commenters should explain the basis for their comments and should support them by substantial evidence such as data, references, expert opinion, or other facts. At the same time, commenters should be aware that the adequacy of an EIR is determined in terms of what is reasonable. CEQA does not, however, require a Lead Agency to conduct every test or perform all research, study, and experimentation recommended or demanded by commenters. Guidelines secs. 15151, 15204.

The State Clearinghouse coordinates systematic review of environmental documents by state agencies.

All commenters should include with their comments the name of a contact person who would be available for later consultation if necessary. Guidelines sec. 15204(d).

Exhausting Administrative Remedies. Under the legal doctrine known as "exhaustion of administrative remedies," a court generally will not allow a person or organization to bring a legal challenge to an agency's decision unless that person or organization has participated during the agency's administrative review process. Pub. Res. Code. sec. 21177. To most effectively participate in the environmental review process, as well as to

Shorter review periods are not available for projects of statewide, regional, or area-wide significance.

preserve the right to later bring a legal action regarding particular CEQA issues, a person should take advantage of every opportunity afforded by CEQA, the Guidelines, and the Lead Agency's own procedures to make his or her views known.

Additionally, exhaustion of administrative remedies requires that a person preparing written or oral comments on an environmental document must allege specific violations of CEQA procedures or findings. Mere objections to the project, as opposed to the procedures, are not sufficient to alert an agency to an objection based on CEQA. For more information on legal remedies, *see* chapter 7, CEQA Litigation.

Failure to Comment or Late Comment

When a person or organization who has been consulted with regard to a Draft EIR (or Negative Declaration) fails to comment within the time limits provided by the Lead Agency, the Lead Agency may assume that the person or agency has no comment. Although a Lead Agency need not respond to late comments, it may choose to do so. Guidelines sec. 15207.

An individual or organization serious about being involved in the environmental review process should never submit a late comment. However, should this occur, the Lead Agency must handle the late comments carefully. While the Guidelines and judicial precedent indicate that a Lead Agency need not respond to a late comment, the agency should exercise discretion, because all comments, including late ones, become part of the project's administrative record. Therefore, a Lead Agency should attempt to respond to the comment and include it in the final environmental document. If the final document has already been prepared, the Lead Agency should include the late comment in its staff report with at least a minimal response.

Review Periods

In General. The minimum public review period for a Draft EIR is 30 days and the maximum is generally 60 days. When a Draft EIR is sent to the SCH for review, the public review period must be 45 days unless a shorter period (of not less than 30 days) is approved by the SCH. When the SCH review period is longer than the public review period established by the Lead Agency, the Lead Agency must adhere to the review period approved by the SCH. Pub. Res. Code secs. 21091, 15087, 15105. Any agency or member of the public may request an extension of the Draft EIR comment period. Although the Lead Agency is not required to extend the comment period beyond that required by CEQA, in practice the Lead Agency will extend the comment period if a reasonable request is made.

Requests for Shortened Review. OPR establishes criteria for granting shortened review periods for Draft EIRs (and Negative Declarations) requiring SCH review. Requests must be made by the Lead Agency's decision-making body or its designee. Shorter review periods are not available for projects of statewide, regional, or areawide significance. Approval of shortened review periods must be shown in the notice that the Draft EIR (or Negative Declaration) is available for review. Pub. Res. Code sec. 21091; Guidelines sec. 15105; Guidelines Appendix K.

Public Hearings

CEQA does not require a public hearing on Draft EIRs [Guidelines sec. 15087(I)], although in practice most agencies conduct such hearings. This type of "hearing" is typically held for the Lead Agency to receive comments on the Draft EIR and is not a formal evidentiary hearing. Participants have no right to cross-examine the preparers of the Draft EIR, and the Lead Agency is not required to respond to questions or comments raised at the hearing. If the Lead Agency conducts a hearing on the merits of the project during the Draft EIR phase of CEQA compliance, the agency should include Draft EIR review as part of that larger hearing. To the extent that an agency maintains or utilizes an Internet website, notice of all public hearings should be made available in electronic format on that site. Guidelines sec. 15202.

Participants have no right to cross-examine the preparers of a Draft EIR, and the Lead Agency is not required to respond to questions or comments raised at the hearing.

Preparation of a Final EIR

Final EIR Process

The Lead Agency must prepare a Final EIR responding to all environmental comments received on the Draft EIR and certify the Final EIR before approving the project. The responses to comments on a Draft EIR must include good faith, well-reasoned responses to all comments received on the Draft EIR. Guidelines secs. 15088, 15132.

In responding to comments, CEQA does not require a Lead Agency to conduct every test or perform all research, study, or experimentation recommended or demanded by commenters. Rather, a Lead Agency need only respond to significant environmental issues and does not need to provide all information requested by reviewers, as long as a good faith effort at full disclosure is made in the EIR. Guidelines secs. 15088, 15204.

A Lead Agency need only respond to relevant environmental issues and does not need to provide information requested by reviewers outside the scope of the CEQA analysis, as long as a good faith effort at full disclosure is made in the EIR.

For example, if the Lead Agency has studied the traffic impacts of a project using a particular computer model with a particular set of assumptions, it need not reevaluate those impacts using another computer model, just because a commenter makes that suggestion. However, in this situation, the Lead Agency should explain the reason why it used the particular approach and why that approach constituted a good-faith effort at full disclosure.

The Final EIR must include a list of persons, agencies, and organizations commenting on the Draft EIR; copies of comments received during public review of the Draft EIR; and the Lead Agency's response to those comments. The responses may take the form of a revision to the Draft EIR or may be a separate action in the Final EIR. Guidelines sec. 15132.

The Lead Agency must also provide a copy of its responses to any public agency that submitted comments at least ten days prior to certifying the Final EIR. Pub. Res. Code sec. 21092.5(a). In practice, before project approval, most agencies provide at least a short public review period. Guidelines sec. 15089(b). *See* chapter 5 for further discussion of the contents of a Final EIR.

The Lead Agency must provide a copy of its responses to any public agency that submitted comments at least ten days prior to certifying the Final EIR.

If a significant revision is limited to a few chapters or portions of an EIR, the Lead Agency need only recirculate the chapters or portions that have been modified.

Recirculation of a Draft EIR

When Recirculation Is Required. "If "significant new information" is added to the EIR after the close of the public comment period on the Draft EIR but before certification of the Final EIR, the Lead Agency must provide a second public review period and recirculate the Draft EIR for comments. The standards for determining when to recirculate a Draft EIR are similar to, but slightly broader than, those for preparing a Subsequent or Supplemental EIR. *See* Subsequent EIR and Supplemental EIR, page 87. Under the Guidelines, recirculation is required when new significant information identifies:

- Significant new environmental impact resulting from the project or from a new mitigation measure proposed to be implemented

- Substantial increase in the severity of an environmental impact unless mitigation measures are adopted that reduce the impact to a level of insignificance

- Feasible project alternative or mitigation measure, considerably different from others previously analyzed, that clearly would lessen the environmental impacts of the project but that the project's proponents decline to adopt

- The Draft EIR was so fundamentally and basically inadequate and conclusory in nature that meaningful public review and comment were precluded.

Guidelines sec. 15088.5(a).

Recirculation of a Draft EIR is not required where the new information merely clarifies, amplifies, or makes minor modifications to an adequate EIR. Guidelines sec. 15088.5(b).

The decision not to recirculate an EIR must be supported by substantial evidence in the administrative record. Guidelines sec. 15088.5(e). Given the rules on recirculation of an EIR, if a Lead Agency decides not to recirculate a Draft EIR after receiving public comments, it should clearly explain in the Final EIR that recirculation of the draft was not necessary. This explanation should indicate that all the comments received merely clarified, amplified, or made insignificant modifications to the Draft EIR.

Recirculation of an EIR is subject to the same public notice and consultation requirements that applied to the original Draft EIR. Guidelines sec. 15088.5(d). If the "significant" revision is limited to a few chapters or portions of the EIR, however, the Lead Agency need only recirculate the chapters or portions that have been modified. Guidelines sec. 15088.5(c).

What to Include in a Recirculated EIR

Recirculating an EIR can result in a Lead Agency receiving more than one set of comments from reviewers. To avoid confusion of which comments are subject to formal response, the CEQA Guidelines provide two approaches a Lead Agency can follow to handle the recirculation.

- **EIR is substantially revised.** When the EIR is substantially revised and the entire document is recirculated, the Lead Agency may require that reviewers submit new comments and need not respond to those comments received during the earlier circulation period. In this situation, the Lead Agency must advise reviewers, either in the text of the revised EIR, or by an attachment, that new comments must be submitted.

Additionally, the Lead Agency must directly notify every entity that commented on the prior Draft EIR specifying that new comments must be submitted.

After recirculation, the Lead Agency need only respond to those comments submitted in response to the recirculated, revised EIR. Although the original comments are part of the administrative record, the Lead Agency need not respond to them in the Final EIR. Guidelines sec. 15088.5(f)(1).

- **EIR is partially revised.** When the EIR is only partially revised the Lead Agency may recirculate only the revised chapters or portions. In that situation, the Lead Agency may request that reviewers limit their comments to the revised chapters or portions. The request to limit the scope of comments must be included either within the text of the revised EIR or in an attachment to it.

  In responding to comments on a partial recirculation, the Lead Agency must respond to both sets of comments on the unrevised portion of the EIR, but may limit its responses to the second set of comments on the revised portions. Guidelines sec. 15085.5(f)(2).

When recirculating a revised EIR, in whole or in part, the Lead Agency must include, in the revision or as an attachment, a summary of the revisions made to the previously circulated EIR. Guidelines sec. 15088.5(g).

When recirculating a revised EIR, in whole or in part, the Lead Agency must include, in the revision or as an attachment, a summary of the revisions made to the previously circulated EIR.

Consideration and Certification of a Final EIR

Consideration

A decision-making body is required to read and consider the information in an EIR before making a decision. The Lead Agency's administrative record on the proposed project must show that the Lead Agency reviewed and considered the Final EIR before acting on a project. Guidelines sec. 15090.

Certification

Before approving the project, the Lead Agency must certify that the Final EIR was prepared in compliance with CEQA and was presented to the Lead Agency's decision-making body, which reviewed and considered the Final EIR before approving the project. Guidelines sec. 15090. In addition, the Lead Agency must certify that the EIR reflects the independent judgment of the Lead Agency. Pub. Res. Code sec. 21082.1(c)(3). Responsible Agencies are not required under CEQA to make any additional certifications regarding the preparation or adequacy of the Final EIR. However, *see* Responsible Agency Consideration, page 86. Guidelines sec. 15096.

Certification may be conducted by the decision-making body of the Lead Agency or may be delegated to an advisory body (e.g., a planning commission) or to staff (e.g., a planning director). However, in the case of a

---

Final EIR Certification Requirements

Before approving a project, a Lead Agency must certify that:

- The Final EIR has been completed in compliance with CEQA
- The Final EIR was reviewed and considered by the decision-making body
- The Final EIR represents the Lead Agency's independent judgment and analysis
- If certification is by a nonelected body, an appeal to the elected body must be allowed

Lead Agency with an elected decision-making body, when a Final EIR is certified by a nonelected decision-making body, certification must be appealable to the agency's elected decision-making body. Pub. Res. Code sec. 21151(c); Guidelines sec. 15090(b).

Prior to certifying a Final EIR for a project involving the purchase of a school site or the construction of a new elementary or secondary school by a school district, the Lead Agency must determine whether the site is currently or formerly a hazardous waste or solid waste disposal site and whether the wastes have been removed.

Prior to certifying the Final EIR for any project involving the purchase of a school site or the construction of a new elementary or secondary school by a school district, the Lead Agency must make the determination of whether the site is currently or formerly a hazardous waste disposal site or solid waste disposal site and, if so, whether the wastes have been removed. Pub. Res. Code sec. 21151.8(a); Guidelines sec. 15186. In the case of a large project without an identified source of water, the Lead Agency must determine, at the time it makes a decision on the proposed project, whether the projected water supplies presented in the EIR will be sufficient to satisfy the demands of the proposed project. *See* Impacts on Public Water Systems, page 105.

Taking Action on Projects for Which an EIR Was Prepared

Lead and Responsible Agency Authority

In General. CEQA gives Lead and Responsible Agencies broad range of authority to deal with a project after the Lead Agency certifies an EIR. In reaction to the EIR, a Lead or Responsible Agency may disapprove a project because the project may cause significant environmental effects or the agency may require changes in a project to reduce or avoid a significant environmental effect. The Lead or Responsible Agency may approve a project despite its significant environmental effects, if the proper findings and statement of overriding considerations are adopted (*see* Findings, page 83, and Statement of Overriding Considerations, page 84); however, an agency need not select the most environmentally superior alternative. *Laurel Hills Homeowners Association v. City Council* (1978) 83 Cal. App. 3d 515; Guidelines secs. 15042, 15043.

In Response to an EIR, a Lead Agency May...

- Disapprove a project because it has significant environmental effects
- Require changes in a project to reduce or avoid a significant environmental effect
- Approve a project despite its significant environmental effects, if the proper findings and statement of overriding considerations are adopted; an agency need not select the most environmentally superior alternative

---

Limitations on Authority. An agency does not have unlimited authority to impose mitigation measures or alternatives discussed in an EIR that would reduce the environmental effects of the proposed project to a less than significant level. Rather, a public agency is subject to both general and specific limitations on its authority. In mitigating or avoiding a project's significant environmental effects, an agency may exercise only those express or implied powers provided by law, aside from those provided by CEQA. Where another law grants an agency discretionary powers, CEQA authorizes its use. Guidelines sec. 15040.

The U.S. Constitution limits an agency's authority to impose conditions to those situations where there is a clear nexus between the impact and the mitigation measure.

In addition, the U.S. Constitution limits an agency's authority to impose conditions to those situations where there is a clear "nexus" between the impact and the mitigation measure; otherwise, the exercise of government authority may be considered a "taking" of private property without just compensation. *Nollan v. California Coastal Commission* (1988) 107 S.Ct. 3141. Thus, the mitigation proposed for a project must relate directly to the impacts caused. In addition to the required "nexus," the U.S. Supreme court held, in *Dolan v. City of Tigard* [(1994) 512 U.S. 854], that there must be "rough proportionality" between the environmental problems caused by a development project and the mitigation measure imposed on the project applicant. While the court held that there was no precise mathematical formula for determining "rough proportionality," some form of individualized determination is required. Guidelines secs. 15041, 15126.4(a)(4).

One method for a Lead Agency to determine the appropriateness of certain mitigation measures, to justify that there is a clear "nexus" or connection between the impact and the mitigation measure, would be to calculate an applicant's pro rata share of a problem and impose no more than a pro rata share of the solution on the applicant by way of mitigation. Thus, for example, if an applicant's project is contributing ten percent of the traffic on a roadway, then the applicant may be required to pay for only ten percent of the mitigation. The EIR (or Negative Declaration) should be used to document such a determination of "rough proportionality." For a detailed discussion of limitations on agency authority to impose mitigation, *see Public Needs and Private Dollars* by Abbott, Moe, and Hanson, Solano Press Books, 1993).

CEQA sets forth certain specific limits on the authority of an agency to mitigate impacts to archaeological and historic resources, schools, housing, and public water systems. *See* chapter 5 for further information regarding the limitations of Lead Agencies on requiring mitigation.

Findings

In General. To support its decision on the project for which an EIR was prepared, a Lead and Responsible Agency must prepare written findings of fact for each significant environmental impact identified in the EIR. Guidelines secs. 15091, 15096(h). A statement of overriding considerations (*see below*) does not substitute for the requirement to prepare findings. Guidelines sec. 15091(f). Findings are one of the least understood aspects of CEQA implementation. Simply stated, a finding is a written statement made by the decision-making body of the Lead and Responsible Agency than explains how it dealt with each significant impact and alternative in the EIR. Each finding must contain an ultimate conclusion regarding each significant impact, substantial evidence supporting the conclusion, and an explanation of how the substantial evidence supports the conclusion. Guidelines sec. 15091.

Specifically, the agencies must make findings for each significant impact that the project has been changed (including adoption of mitigation measures) to avoid or substantially reduce the magnitude of the impact. The agency must ensure that adopted mitigation measures are fully enforceable through permit conditions, agreements, or other measures. If the Lead or Responsible Agency cannot make these findings, it must make the finding either that changes to the project are within another agency's jurisdiction, and such changes have been or should be adopted, or specific economic, social, legal, technical, or other considerations, such as employment opportunities for highly trained workers, make the mitigation measure or alternative infeasible. Guidelines sec. 15091.

> **For Each Significant Impact, an Agency Must Make One of the Following Findings...**
>
> - Changes in the project have been made (including adoption of mitigation measures) to avoid or substantially reduce the magnitude of the impact. (The agency must ensure that adopted mitigation measures are fully enforceable through permit conditions, agreements, or other measures.)
> - Changes to the project are within another agency's jurisdiction and have been or should be adopted
> - Specific economic, social, legal, technical, or other considerations make mitigation measures or alternatives infeasible.

The findings must be based on substantial evidence in the administrative record and must include an explanation that bridges the gap between evidence in the record and the conclusions required by CEQA. Guidelines sec. 15091(b). *See* Figure 4-3. Responsible Agencies, in granting subsequent approvals for projects studied in an EIR, cannot rely on the Lead Agency's findings, but must make their own findings. Guidelines sec. 15096(h).

Timing. Findings are made at the time a project is approved. In practice, however, tentative findings, often written by agency legal or planning staff (although the agency's decision-making body cannot delegate the issuance of findings), are presented to the decision-making body with the project staff report and recommendation. They are then rewritten and adopted to conform to the final decision shortly after the decision-making body approves the project. The findings become part of the project's administrative record and are available to the public, but they do not have to be circulated for public review.

Drafting Findings. In drafting findings, agency decision makers and their staff should remember that one of the stated objectives of CEQA is public accountability. Therefore, the findings should be presented in a clear, well organized manner that enables the reader to understand how the agency addressed every significant impact and alternative. *See* sidebar for examples of findings.

Infeasibility of Mitigation Measures or Alternatives. If it finds a mitigation measure or an alternative to be infeasible, the Lead or Responsible Agency must explain the specific reasons for rejecting the identified mitigation measure or alternative. Guidelines sec. 15091(a)(3). A mitigation measure or alternative is considered feasible if it is capable of being accomplished in a successful manner within a reasonable period of time, taking into account economic, environmental, legal, social, and technological factors, as well as considerations for employment of highly trained workers. Pub. Res. Code sec. 21081(c). When economics is used as a factor to support a finding of infeasibility, the agency must support the finding with specific data showing that the additional cost or lost profits are great enough to make it impractical to proceed with the project. The mere fact that an alternative may be more expensive does not necessarily make it infeasible.

Mitigation Reporting or Monitoring

When it makes findings on significant effects identified in an EIR (or adopts a Negative Declaration containing mitigation measures) an agency must also adopt a program for reporting

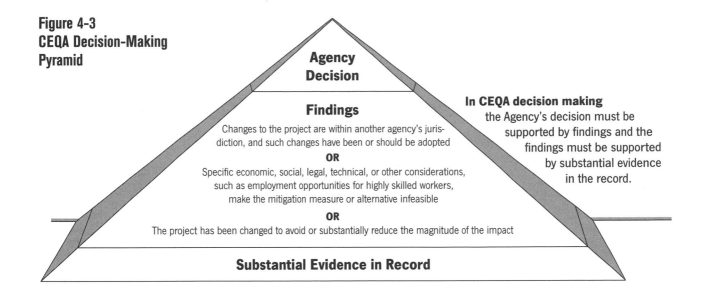

**Figure 4-3
CEQA Decision-Making
Pyramid**

Agency
Decision

Findings

Changes to the project are within another agency's jurisdiction, and such changes have been or should be adopted

OR

Specific economic, social, legal, technical, or other considerations,
such as employment opportunities for highly skilled workers,
make the mitigation measure or alternative infeasible

OR

The project has been changed to avoid or substantially reduce the magnitude of the impact

Substantial Evidence in Record

In CEQA decision making
the Agency's decision must be
supported by findings and the
findings must be supported
by substantial evidence
in the record.

or monitoring mitigation measures that were adopted or made conditions of project approval. Pub. Res. Code sec. 21081.6(a); Guidelines secs. 15091(d), 15097. The reporting or monitoring program must ensure compliance with mitigation measures during project implementation. *See* chapter 5 for more details on mitigation monitoring and reporting.

Statement of Overriding Considerations

In General. After considering the Final EIR in conjunction with making findings, the Lead Agency must not approve the project if the project will have a significant effect on the environment after imposition of feasible mitigation or alternatives, unless the Lead and Responsible Agencies find that the benefits of a proposed project outweigh the unavoidable adverse environmental effects. Guidelines secs. 15092, 15096(h). However, when approving a project with unavoidable significant environmental effects, the Lead and Responsible Agency are required by CEQA to prepare a Statement of Overriding Considerations. The Statement of Overriding Considerations is a written statement explaining why the agency is willing to accept each significant effect [Pub. Res. Code sec. 21081; Guidelines sec. 15093]; in this way, CEQA requires the decision maker to balance the benefits of a proposed project against unavoidable environmental risks in determining whether to approve the project. *See* Figure 4-4. The statement setting forth the specific overriding social, economic, legal, technical, or other benefi-cial project aspects supporting the agency's decision must be based on substantial evidence in the Final EIR or elsewhere in the record. A State-ment of Overriding Considerations must be included in the record of proj-ect approval and must be mentioned in the Notice of Determination (*see* discussion below). Guidelines sec. 15093(c).

Drafting Statements of Overriding Considerations. Typically, the Statement of Overriding Considerations begins with a summary of the unavoidable impacts and then lists specific social, economic, or other factors that justify approving the project despite these impacts. As with findings, a Statement of Overriding

---

Example of a Statement of Overriding Considerations

"The City Council hereby finds that, for the reasons set forth below, the economic, social, and other considerations of the project outweigh the unavoid-able traffic and air quality im-pacts identified in the findings. First, the need for housing, as identified in the housing ele-ment of the general plan, is of paramount importance to the city. Second, the commercial aspects of the project will en-able the city to achieve its plans for revitalization of the cen-tral business district. Third, the commercial base of the project will enhance the tax base, cre-ate more jobs, and provide di-verse shopping opportunities for residents of the city. The data to support these overriding factors are found in the "Popu-lation, Employment, and Hous-ing" section of the EIR and in the demographic data submit-ted by the project applicant."

A Lead Agency may use a Statement of Overriding Considerations to find that a project's socioeconomic benefits justify its unavoidable adverse environmental effects.

Considerations should clearly enable the reader to understand the rationale for the agency's decision and must be supported by substantial evidence. *See* sidebar for an example of a Statement of Overriding Consideration.

Notice of Determination

In General. A Lead Agency must file a Notice of Determination after deciding to approve a project for which an EIR is prepared. No Notice of Determination is required if the agency decides to disapprove the project. The Notice of Determination must include the project name, description, and location and date of project approval. The Notice of Determination also must summarize the project's significant impacts and state whether mitigation measures were adopted as conditions of approval, findings were prepared, and Statement of Overriding Considerations were adopted. The notice must state that the Final EIR is available for public review and disclose the location where the Final EIR and record of project approval is available for review. Guidelines sec. 15094.

Filing and Posting. Within five days of project approval, if the Lead Agency is a local agency, the Notice of Determination must be filed with the county clerk (or several county clerks if the project is located in more than one county) and, if state discretionary approval is also involved, with OPR. The county clerk must post the notice within 24 hours of receipt. Pub. Res. Code secs. 21092.3, 21152(a)(c); Guidelines sec. 15094. If the Lead Agency is a state agency, the Notice of Determination must be filed with OPR. The notice must be posted for 30 days and retained in the agency files for nine months. Guidelines sec. 15094. The Notice must also be sent to anyone previously requesting notice. Pub. Res. Code sec. 21092.2.

A Department of Fish and Game review fee of $850 must generally be paid at the time the Notice of Determination is filed. *See* page 51.

Statute of Limitations. Posting the Notice of Determination starts a 30-day statute of limitations period for parties wanting to challenge the Lead Agency's decision under CEQA. Pub. Res. Code sec. 21167(c); Guidelines sec. 15094(f). If more than one notice is filed for the same project, the 30-day period begins on the day the last notice is posted.

Lead Agency Disposition of a Final EIR

After project approval, the Lead Agency must: (1) file the Final EIR with the planning agency of any city or county where significant effects may occur; (2) include the Final EIR in any regular project report used for project review or budgeting; (3) retain the Final EIR as a public record for a reasonable time; and (4) require the project applicant to provide copies of the Final EIR to Responsible Agencies. Guidelines sec. 15095. Pub. Res. Code sec. 21105.

Responsible Agency Consideration

Each Responsible Agency must use the Final EIR, prepared by the Lead Agency, to reach a project decision, make its own CEQA findings, and, if

---

Contents of a Notice of Determination

- Project name
- Project description
- Project location
- Date of project approval
- Statement that the EIR was prepared and certified
- Summary of project's significant effects
- Whether mitigation measures were made conditions of project approval
- Whether findings were made and a Statement of Overriding Considerations adopted
- Address where Final EIR may be reviewed

Notice of Determination Filing and Posting Time Periods

- Lead Agency files with county clerk or OPR within five days
- County clerk posts notice within 24 hours
- Notice kept posted for 30 days
- Notice retained for nine months

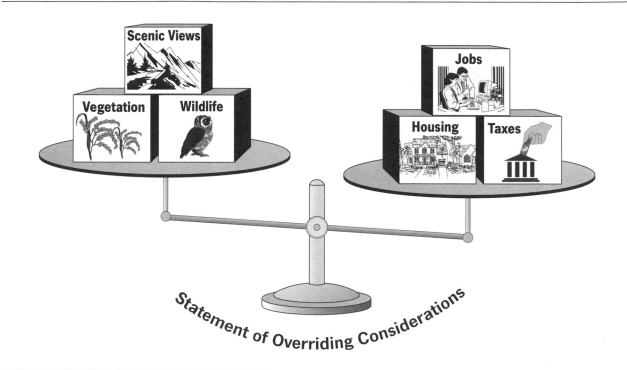

Statement of Overriding Considerations

necessary, adopt a Statement of Overriding Considerations. If a Responsible Agency believes that an EIR is not adequate for its own use, it may: (1) file a CEQA court challenge against the Lead Agency as long as the 30-day statute of limitations period has not elapsed; (2) be deemed to have waived objections to the Final EIR, and proceed to use the adequacy of the Final EIR in project decision making; (3) prepare a Subsequent EIR, if required (*see below*); or (4) assume the Lead Agency role and prepare its own EIR if the previous Lead Agency failed to prepare any CEQA document or failed to consult with the Responsible Agency. Guidelines sec. 15096.

Figure 4-4
Balancing Environmental Damage against Social, Economic, and Other Factors

CEQA Compliance after an EIR Is Prepared

Subsequent EIR and Supplemental EIR

In General. Only one EIR is typically prepared for a project. However, an agency must prepare a Subsequent or Supplemental EIR for a project if the agency has continuing discretionary authority over the project [Guidelines sec. 15162(c)] and if it determines, on the basis of substantial evidence in light of the whole record, that substantial changes proposed in the project will require major revisions to the previous EIR because of the involvement of new significant environmental effects or a substantial increase in the severity of previously identified effects; substantial changes occur with respect to the circumstances under which the project is undertaken that will require major revision of a previous EIR because of the involvement of new significant environmental effects or a substantial increase in the severity of previously identified effects; or new information of substantial importance that was not known or could not have been known without the exercise of reasonable diligence at the time the previous EIR was certified shows any of the following:

- The project will have one or more significant effects not discussed in the previous EIR.
- Significant effects previously examined will be substantially more severe than shown in the previous EIR.
- Mitigation measures or alternatives previously found not to be feasible would, in fact, be feasible and would substantially reduce one or more significant effects of the project, but the project proponents decline to adopt them.
- Mitigation measures or alternatives that are considerably different from those analyzed in the previous document would substantially reduce one or more significant effects, but the project proponents decline to adopt them.

Guidelines sec. 15162(a).

A Subsequent or Supplemental EIR is subject to the same notice and public review requirements as the original EIR and is required to state whether the previous document is available for review. Guidelines sec. 15162(d). An Initial Study should be used to determine whether the changes or new information lead to significant environmental effects. If the conditions described above has not occurred, the agency must either prepare a subsequent Negative Declaration or Addendum to the EIR. Guidelines sec. 15162(b).

If the project was approved before the occurrence of the conditions that trigger a Subsequent or Supplemental EIR, then the subsequent document must be prepared by the public agency that grants the next discretionary approval for the project. Guidelines sec. 15162(c).

Differences between Subsequent EIR and Supplemental EIR. A Subsequent EIR is prepared if the previous EIR requires major revisions, whereas a Supplemental EIR may be prepared if the revisions are not considered major. Both must be recirculated for public review, following the requirements of the original EIR. Guidelines secs. 15162, 15163(c). *See* Figure 4-5.

Standard of Judicial Review. In reviewing an agency's refusal to prepare a Subsequent or Supplemental EIR, the courts do not use the low threshold standard used for determining whether an EIR should initially have been prepared (the "fair argument" test), but instead employ a more deferential, traditional "substantial evidence," standard. If an agency makes substantial changes to a project and fails to prepare a Subsequent or Supplemental EIR, the 180-day statute of limitations period starts when a project opponent knew, or reasonably should have known, of the changes.

Addendum to an EIR

An agency must prepare an Addendum to the previously certified EIR if the Lead or Responsible Agency's role in the project is not complete and some changes or additions are necessary to the project but none of the conditions triggering a Subsequent EIR, Negative Declaration, or Supplemental EIR have occurred. Guidelines sec. 15164(a). An addendum should be prepared if only minor technical changes or additions are necessary. Guidelines sec. 15164(b). *See* Figure 4-5. An addendum need not be circulated for public review but can be included in or attached to the Final EIR. Guidelines sec. 15164(c). The decision-making body is required to consider the addendum with the Final EIR before making a decision on the project. Guidelines sec. 15164(d). A brief explanation of the decision not to prepare a subsequent EIR should be included in the addendum, in the findings, or elsewhere in the record. The explanation must be supported by substantial evidence in the administrative record. Guidelines sec. 15164(e).

Environmental issues not anticipated in the CEQA analysis with regard to new development may require supplemental CEQA documentation in certain instances.

Document	Requirement
Subsequent EIR	Should be prepared for important project revisions resulting in significant impacts
Supplemental EIR	Should be prepared for minor project additions or changes resulting in significant impacts
Addendum to an EIR	Should be prepared for minor technical project changes with no significant impacts

* The agency must retain some discretionary authority over the project.

**Figure 4-5
Differences in Documentation
Requirements for a Project
after an EIR Has Been Certified***

Chapter 5

Contents of an EIR

Overall Requirements for a Draft EIR

As discussed in chapter 3, an EIR is a detailed informational document prepared by a Lead Agency that analyzes a project's potential significant effects and identifies mitigation measures and reasonable alternatives to avoid those significant effects. Guidelines secs. 15121(a), 15362. This chapter discusses the substantive requirements of a Draft EIR, focusing on the project description, environmental setting, environmental impacts, alternatives, mitigation measures, and monitoring. CEQA requires that a Draft EIR include a table of contents or index, a summary (including areas of known controversy), a description of the project, environmental setting, significant environmental impacts, alternatives, and mitigation measures. Draft EIRs for certain projects must also present the significant irreversible changes (for EIRs on plans, policies, ordinances, LAFCO actions, and joint NEPA documents) associated with the project, organizations and persons consulted, and list of preparers of the Draft EIR. *See* Figure 5-1.

General Rules

Format and Scope of a Draft EIR

CEQA requires that each Lead Agency develop a standard format for EIR preparation, whenever feasible. Pub. Res. Code sec. 21100(a). Regardless of the format used by an agency, every EIR must include all the required contents set forth in CEQA and the Guidelines. Pub. Res. Code sec. 21100; Guidelines secs. 15084(a), 15120, 15160. An EIR should be organized to best fit the decision-making process for which it is prepared.

Style and Page Limits

An EIR must be written in plain language that is understandable by decision makers and the public. An EIR should be no longer than 150 pages for a

---

**Figure 5-1
Required Contents of an EIR**

- Table of contents or index
- Summary
- Project description
- Environmental setting
- Significant environmental impacts
  - Direct
  - Indirect
  - Short-term
  - Long-term
  - Cumulative
  - Unavoidable
- Areas of known controversy
- Alternatives
  - No Project alternative
  - Environmentally superior alternative
- Mitigation measures
- Growth-inducing impacts
- Significant irreversible changes (required only in EIRs on plans, policies, ordinances, LAFCO actions, and joint NEPA documents)

normal project and no longer than 300 pages for an unusually complex project. Guidelines secs. 15140, 15141.

Emphasis

An EIR should focus on a project's significant environmental effects with discussions proportional to their severity and probability.

An EIR should focus on the project's significant environmental effects. Discussions should be proportional to the severity and probability of these effects. EIRs should be analytic rather than encyclopedic. Guidelines secs. 15006(o), 15143. The Lead Agency may limit discussion of other (nonsignificant) effects to a brief explanation of why those effects are not potentially significant. Pub. Res. Code sec. 21002.1. In practice, however, Lead Agencies typically include presentation of complete analysis even if the EIR determines the effects of the action to be less than significant. As discussed in chapter 7, the fear of litigation often causes Lead Agencies to prepare EIRs that go beyond the minimum legal requirement for analysis of environmental effects.

Forecasting and Speculation

If an agency finds, after thorough investigation, that an impact is too speculative to evaluate, it should note this conclusion and proceed. CEQA does not require a worst-case analysis.

An agency must use its best efforts to predict impacts but is not required to predict the unforeseeable. If it finds, after thorough investigation, that an impact is too speculative to evaluate, an agency should note this conclusion and proceed. Guidelines secs. 15144, 15145. CEQA does not require, in these instances, a "worst-case" analysis.

Level of Specificity

The specificity required in an EIR should correspond to the specificity of the underlying activity being evaluated. For example, an EIR prepared for a development project should be more specific than one prepared for a zoning ordinance or general plan. Guidelines sec. 15146. For a discussion of various types of EIRs, *see* Specific Types of EIRs, page 56.

Citations, Consultations, and List of Preparers

An EIR must cite all documents used in its preparation, and the Lead Agency must make them available for public review.

An EIR must cite all documents used in its preparation. Guidelines sec. 15148. The Lead Agency is required to make all documents cited in the EIR available for public review. Pub. Res. Code sec. 21092(b). The EIR must identify all federal, state, or local agencies; other organizations; and private individuals consulted in preparation of the document. The EIR is required to identify the persons, firm, or agency that actually prepared it, by contract or other authorization. Guidelines sec. 15129.

Incorporation by Reference

An EIR may incorporate portions or all of any publicly available document, including EIRs prepared for other projects. The incorporated document must be summarized or described briefly, its relationship to the EIR must be summarized, and the EIR must state where the document will be made available for public inspection. Guidelines sec. 15150. When a Lead Agency relies on tiering, the information from the first-tier EIR is generally incorporated by reference in the subsequent tier documents. Guidelines sec. 15152.

Restrictions on Disclosure of Certain Information

Although an EIR is a disclosure document, there may be some information that is subject to disclosure restrictions. Guidelines sec. 15120(d). Specifically, an EIR (or any other document prepared under CEQA) must not include any:

- "Trade secrets" (as defined by Govt. Code sec. 6254.7)
- Information about the specific location of archaeological sites or sacred lands
- Any other information that is not subject to public disclosure under the California Public Records Act

Govt. Code sec. 6254.

Table of Contents or Index

The EIR is required to contain at least a table of contents or an index to assist readers in finding particular resource analyses and issues. Guidelines sec. 15122.

Summary

The EIR's summary should be clear, concise, and normally no longer than 15 pages. It must identify each significant effect; proposed mitigation measures; areas of known controversy, including issues raised by agencies and the public; and unresolved issues. Guidelines sec. 15123. For practical purposes, the summary should be written and formatted in a manner that will facilitate preparation of CEQA findings on significant impacts. *See* chapter 4. The summary should specifically identify which impacts are significant, what specific mitigation measures have been recommended to reduce each significant impact, and whether each significant impact will be reduced to a less-than-significant level following mitigation. A matrix format is often useful.

Project Description

In General

The Guidelines require that the EIR's project description include a discussion of the project objectives. The project description must include a discussion of project location, including presentation of a local and regional map and identification of site boundaries. When discussing project characteristics, the project description should include project concept, proposed buildings and facilities, construction activities, build-out assumptions, conceptual drawings, supporting public services, and reasonably foreseeable future phases. The project description must also include a list of the required approvals for the project, including agencies using the EIR and required permits and the related environmental review and consultation requirements. Guidelines sec. 15124.

The project description is not required to supply extensive detail beyond that needed for evaluation and review of the environmental impacts. Guidelines sec. 15124(b). Writing the project description is often considered one of the most challenging aspects of EIR preparation because

---

The Draft EIR Project Description Should Include...

- Project objectives
- Project location
  - Local map
  - Regional map
  - Identification of site boundaries
- Project characteristics
  - Project concept
  - Proposed buildings
  - Construction activities
  - Build-out assumptions
  - Conceptual drawings
  - Supporting public services
- Reasonably foreseeable future phases
- Required approvals
  - Agencies using the EIR
  - Required permits

The summary should identify significant impacts, mitigation measures recommended to reduce each impact, and whether each impact will be reduced to a less-than-significant level following mitigation.

The description should include project concept, proposed buildings and facilities, construction activities, build-out assumptions, conceptual drawings, supporting public services, and reasonably foreseeable future phases.

The EIR's project description should include a presentation depicting exactly where the project will be sited in comparison to natural conditions.

The description of project characteristics should discuss all actions necessary to achieve the project objectives, including the proposal for secondary support facilities.

An agency may not segment a larger project into pieces, thereby avoiding an analysis of the cumulative impacts of the larger project.

Cal–EPA = California Environmental
Protection Agency

Lead Agencies often begin the EIR process before having complete knowledge about a project and its characteristics. However, an accurate, complete, and final project description is essential to preparing an adequate EIR. To avoid problems, the Lead Agency should write a detailed project description as early as possible (preferably before it distributes the Notice of Preparation), to enable technical environmental analysts and reviewing agencies to fully understand the project being evaluated or reviewed.

Statement of Objectives

The Guidelines require that the project description contain a clearly written statement of objectives, including the underlying purpose of the project. Guidelines sec. 15124(b). The statement of objectives is important in helping the Lead Agency develop a reasonable range of alternatives to evaluate in the EIR and will aid the decision makers in preparing findings and a statement of overriding considerations, if necessary. *See* chapter 4.

Project Location

The project description should include a discussion of the precise location and boundaries of the proposed project. This information should be presented on a detailed local map, preferably topographic. The location of the project site should also be presented on a regional map. Guidelines sec. 15124(a).

Project Characteristics

The project description should include a narrative explaining the project concept, and, if relevant, proposed buildings and facilities, and construction activities, build-out activities and assumptions, diagrams and conceptual drawings, and proposed supporting public services. Guidelines sec. 15124(c). The description of characteristics should discuss all actions necessary to achieve the project objectives, including the proposal for secondary support facilities.

Scope of Project

When an individual project is part of a larger project, the EIR project description and impact analysis must address the larger project. An agency may not segment a larger project into pieces (i.e., "piecemeal" a project), thereby avoiding an analysis of the cumulative impacts of the larger project. Guidelines sec. 15165.

An EIR must describe and analyze "reasonably foreseeable future phases" of a project, except certain highway projects, if the larger project is a reasonably foreseeable consequence of the initial project and the future project will be significant because it will likely change the scope or nature of the initial project or its environmental effects. *See* Project Segmenting, page 21. The rule against project segmenting applies even if the Lead Agency has not yet formally approved the larger future project and it is impossible to predict precisely the future project's environmental effects, as long as these effects can be discussed generally. *Laurel Heights Improvement Association v. Regents of University of California* (1988) 47 Cal. 3d 376. However, this rule does not apply to tiered EIRs. For more information on project segmenting and tiering, *see* chapter 3.

Approvals Required

The project description must describe how the Lead and Responsible Agencies intend to use the EIR, and must include a list of the agencies that expect to use the EIR in their decision making and a list of the approvals for which the EIR will be used. It must also include a list of the related environmental review and consultation requirements required by federal, state, or local laws, regulations, or policies. To the fullest extent possible, these Lead Agency should integrate CEQA review with these requirements. Guidelines sec. 15124(d). *See* chapter 6 for a discussion of the integration of CEQA with other requirements.

The State Permit Handbook, published by the Office of Permit Assistance in the Trade and Commerce Agency, and consultation with SCH are useful guides to help the Lead Agency identify the state agencies that would be involved in a project.

Environmental Setting

The EIR is required to include a description of the physical environmental conditions in the vicinity of the project from both a local and regional perspective, as it exists at the time the NOP is published or, if no NOP is published, at the time the environmental analysis is commenced. The environmental setting will normally constitute the baseline physical conditions by which a Lead Agency determines whether an impact is significant. The description should be no longer than is necessary to support an analysis of the significant environmental effects of the proposed project and its alternatives. Guidelines sec. 15125. If applicable, the EIR must include a statement indicating that the project is located on a toxic site listed by the California Environmental Protection Agency (Cal–EPA). Pub. Res. Code sec. 21092.6(a).

By implication, the Guidelines allow the Lead Agency to use a different baseline than that described above in "non-normal" circumstances. The Lead Agency should, however, explain its rationale for choosing a different baseline. For example, a baseline defined by past conditions might be appropriate where a project site has been illegally modified prior to the start of environmental review. A baseline defined by anticipated future conditions might be appropriate if future infrastructure components are reasonably certain to exist by the time the proposed project would be operational.

Knowledge of the regional setting is critical to the assessment of environmental impacts. Special emphasis should be placed on resources that are rare or unique to that region. The EIR must demonstrate that the project's significant effects were adequately investigated and discussed and must permit the significant effects to be considered in the full environmental context. Guidelines sec. 15125(c).

The EIR must identify the policy and planning context in which the project is proposed. Specifically, it must discuss any

Laurel Heights Improvement Association v. Regents of the University of California: Court Rules on When EIR Should Include Foreseeable Future Actions

In *Laurel Heights Improvement Association v. Regents of the University of California* (1988) 47 Cal. 3d 376, the California Supreme Court aided CEQA practitioners in determining the scope of an EIR through its ruling on the adequacy of the University of California's EIR prepared for the expansion of the School of Pharmacy's biomedical research operations and the creation of a new research facility in a residential and commercial area of San Francisco. A citizens association brought suit to set aside the Regents of the University of California's decision to certify the EIR for the research facility.

The University prepared an EIR for the initial research operations, occurring in 100,000 square feet of a 354,000-square-foot building. Although there was potential that the University would expand into the remainder of the building in the next five years, the University's EIR did not consider the expansion because no formal proposal had been approved.

The State Supreme Court held the EIR inadequate for not including the assessment of the full use of the research facility. The court rejected the argument that an EIR need not analyze future actions that were not yet formally approved. The court stated that there was evidence in the record that indicated the University's ultimate plans to expand into the entire research facility. Because the expansion was reasonably foreseeable, and was likely to change the scope of the proposed project's environmental effects, the EIR should have disclosed the environmental effects that were likely to result from this expansion.

inconsistencies between the proposed project and any applicable general plans and regional plans. When a proposed project is compared with an adopted plan, the analysis must examine existing physical conditions at the time the Notice of Preparation is published or, if no NOP is published, at the time the environmental analysis is commenced, as well as future potential conditions discussed in the plan. Guidelines sec. 15125(e). When preparing an EIR for a plan for the reuse of a military base, special rules applies with regard to the baseline. *See* Guidelines section 15229.

The EIR should include only enough setting information necessary to provide a meaningful context for the discussions of environmental impacts, alternatives, and mitigation measures.

In practice, one of the most common criticisms of the CEQA process is the inclusion of voluminous and unnecessary background data in the section of an EIR dealing with the environmental setting. However, the Guidelines state that the EIR should include only enough setting information necessary to provide a meaningful context for the discussions of environmental impacts, alternatives, and mitigation measures. Guidelines sec. 15125. Highly detailed and technical background reports should be summarized in the setting and included, in full, in technical appendices. To ensure a proper balance between setting and impact evaluation, some EIR preparers recommend writing the impact section first and then writing the setting section to match the evaluation of impacts.

The rules and practices described for defining the environmental setting should be applied to the preparation of Initial Studies and Negative Declarations, as well as EIRs.

Environmental Impacts

General

An EIR must identify and focus on the significant environmental effects of all phases of the proposed project, including planning, acquisition, development, and operation of the proposed project. Guidelines sec. 15126. In assessing the impacts of a proposed project, the Lead Agency should limit its examination to changes in the existing physical conditions in the affected area as they exist at the time the NOP is published. Guidelines sec. 15126.2.

Direct and indirect impacts must be clearly identified and described, giving due attention to both the short-term and long-term effects. The discussion should include, but not be limited to, relevant specifics of the area, the resources involved, physical alterations to ecological systems, changes induced in population distribution and concentration, the human use of the land, health and safety problems caused by physical changes, and aspects of the resource base such as water, historic resources, scenic quality, and public services.

An EIR must analyze any significant environmental effects the project might cause by bringing development and people into the area affected.

An EIR must also analyze any significant environmental effects the project might cause by bringing development and people into the area affected. Guidelines sec. 15126.2(a). For example, an EIR on a subdivision astride an active earthquake fault should identify as a significant effect the seismic hazard to future occupants of the subdivision. The subdivision would have the effect of attracting people to the location and exposing them to the hazards found there. Guidelines sec. 15126.2(a).

The specific issues evaluated in an EIR will vary from project to project depending upon the location and the nature of the project. An EIR should include a discussion of any environmental impacts that are determined to be "significant" or "potentially significant" on the Initial Study checklist found in Appendix G, or similar checklist developed by the Lead Agency.

Significance Determination

In general, the EIR should define the threshold of significance and explain the criteria used to judge whether an impact is above or below that threshold. Guidelines sec. 15064(f). *See* Figure 5-2. As stated in chapter 2, determining whether a project may have a significant effect on the environment should be based on scientific and factual data; however, an ironclad definition of "significant effect" is not possible because the significance of an activity may vary with the setting. Guidelines sec. 15064(b).

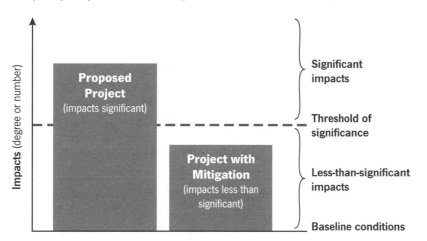

**Figure 5-2
Determining the
Significance of Impacts**

Determining Thresholds of Significance. The tools used to make significance determinations for an EIR are the same as those available to the Lead Agency during preparation of an Initial Study to determine whether there is a possibility of a significant effect on the environment. These tools include CEQA's Mandatory Findings of Significance, Appendix G of the Guidelines (the model Initial Study checklist), Agency Regulatory Standards, consultation with other agencies, and the Lead Agency's specific thresholds of significance. *See* Determining Whether Effects Are Potentially Significant, page 38, and Appendix 10, OPR's CEQA Technical Advice Series report *Thresholds of Significance: Criteria for Defining Environmental Significance.*

Lead Agencies should use the relationship of the environmental effect of the proposed project to an established regulatory or legislative standard to presume the significance of the environmental effect. However, this may not be appropriate if there is a conflict between standards or substantial evidence in the record indicates that the standard is inappropriate. Guidelines sec. 15064(h).

Disagreement among Experts. Disagreement among experts concerning the significance of a proposed project's environmental effect does not require the Lead Agency to follow the evidence concluding an impact is significant. In contrast to the "fair argument" test used when a Lead Agency is deciding whether to prepare an EIR or Negative Declaration, when

Disagreement among experts concerning the significance of a proposed project's environmental effect does not necessarily require the Lead Agency to follow the evidence concluding an impact is significant in an EIR.

experts disagree on impact significance in an EIR, the Lead Agency need only summarize the main points of disagreement and explain its choice of expert opinions. Guidelines secs. 15064(f)(7), 15151.

Presentation of Impact Significance. In describing the significance of impacts, the Lead Agency should identify whether the impacts are less than significant (where the environmental effect of the proposed project does not reach the threshold of significance); avoidable (where the environmental effect of the proposed project reaches the threshold of significance but feasible mitigation measures are available to reduce the impact to a less-than-significant level); unavoidable (where the environmental effect of the proposed project reaches the threshold of significance but no feasible mitigation is available to reduce the impact to a less-than-significant level); or beneficial (where the environmental effect of the proposed project will improve the environment regardless of the threshold of significance). Guidelines secs. 15126, 15126.2.

When unavoidable impacts would result from the project, the EIR should explain their implications and the reasons why the project is being proposed notwithstanding these impacts. Guidelines sec. 15126.2(b).

In preparing the impact analysis, the Lead Agency should avoid using unclear terminology that may confuse the reader. Using modifiers such as "somewhat," "potentially," "very," "major," "minor," or "partially" for impacts does not provide sufficient information as to whether the Lead Agency determines the impact to be significant.

Types of Impacts

Direct impacts, also referred to as primary effects, are those caused by the project and that occur at the same time and place.

Direct Impacts. Direct impacts, also referred to as primary effects, are those caused by the project and that occur at the same time and place. Guidelines sec. 15358. An example of direct effects is the construction of a sewage treatment plant and possible odors from operation of the plant. Guidelines sec. 15064(d)(1).

Indirect impacts, also referred to as secondary effects, are those caused by a project that may occur either later in time or at some distance from the project site but that are still reasonably foreseeable.

Indirect Impacts. Indirect impacts, also referred to as secondary effects, are those caused by a project that may occur either later in time or at some distance from the project site but that are still reasonably foreseeable. Guidelines sec. 15358. An example of indirect effects is the effects of population growth facilitated by the increase in sewage treatment capacity. Guidelines sec. 15064(d)(2). An indirect physical change is to be considered only if that change is a reasonably foreseeable impact that may be caused by the project. Guidelines sec. 15064(d)(3).

Short- and Long-Term Impacts. Short-term impacts are those of a limited duration, such as the impacts that would occur during the construction of a project. Long-term impacts are those of greater duration, including those that would endure for the life of a project and beyond. The Guidelines do not provide a specific definition or dividing duration between short and long term for these types of impacts. Whether they are characterized as short- or long-term impacts, these impacts should be analyzed in the EIR.

Irreversible Environmental Changes. An EIR must identify any significant irreversible environmental changes which would be caused by the proposed project. Irreversible environmental changes may include current or future commitments to using non-renewable resources, secondary, or growth-inducing impacts that commit future generations to similar uses. Also irreversible change can result from accidents associated with the project. Irretrievable commitments of resources should be evaluated to assure that such current consumption is justified. CEQA Guidelines sec. 15126.2(c).

Growth-Inducing Impacts. The EIR must discuss how the proposed project if implemented could induce growth. Growth inducement is sometimes characterized as a secondary or indirect project impact. A project may be growth-inducing if it directly or indirectly fosters economic or population growth or the construction of additional housing, removes obstacles to population growth or taxes community service facilities to the extent that the construction of new facilities would be necessary, or encourages or facilitates other activities that cause significant environmental effects. Guidelines sec. 15126.2(d).

A Lead Agency must evaluate the growth-inducing impacts of water supply projects.

A project EIR need not evaluate general growth within a community if that growth is not caused, in part, by the project being evaluated.

In practice, the evaluation of growth-inducing impacts is often treated in a far too cursory manner. Although the Guidelines do not specify any particular level of analysis, to ensure adequate treatment of such impacts, a Lead Agency should consider the following approach:

- Estimate amount, location, and time frame of growth to occur as a result of the project
- Apply impact assessment methodology (either quantitatively or qualitatively)
- Determine significance of secondary impacts from growth
- Determine mitigation measures to reduce significant impacts to a less-than-significant level

The best time to evaluate growth-inducing impacts is in a first-tier EIR, such as a Program EIR or Master EIR prepared for plans, programs, policies, or ordinances. If the impacts of future growth are adequately evaluated in a first-tier document, then second-tier or Focused EIRs on specific projects may be able to incorporate the prior discussions by reference, thereby avoiding repetitive analysis.

Some agencies avoid use of the term "growth inducing" because it has a negative connotation, substituting instead the phrase "growth accommodating." Although the impacts of induced growth clearly must be discussed in an EIR, the Guidelines also indicate that growth should not be assumed to be either beneficial or detrimental. Guidelines sec. 15126.2(d). Agencies should therefore spend less time worrying about the terminology and devote greater effort to ensuring that the impacts of induced growth are properly evaluated.

Cumulative Impacts

Cumulative impacts refer to two or more individual impacts that, when considered together, are considerable or that compound or increase other environmental impacts. The cumulative impact of several projects is the change in the environment that results from the incremental impact of the project when added to other, closely related past, present, or reasonably

> **Growth-Inducing Project Directly or Indirectly...**
>
> - Fosters economic or population growth or additional housing
> - Removes obstacles to growth
> - Taxes community services or facilities to such an extent that new services or facilities would be necessary
> - Encourages or facilitates other activities that cause significant environmental effects

Cumulative impacts are two or more individual impacts that, when considered together, are considerable or that compound or increase other environmental impacts.

The best time to evaluate cumulative impacts is in a first-tier EIR, such as a Program EIR or Master EIR prepared for plans, programs, policies, or ordinances.

foreseeable, probable future projects. Cumulative impacts can result from individually minor but collectively significant projects taking place over a period of time. Guidelines sec. 15355.

An EIR must discuss the cumulative impacts of a project when the project's incremental effect is cumulatively considerable. *See also* the discussion in chapter 2. When a Lead Agency is examining a project with an incremental effect that is not "cumulatively considerable," a Lead Agency need not consider that effect significant, but must briefly describe its basis for concluding that the incremental effect is not cumulatively considerable. Guidelines secs. 15064(i), 15130(a).

An EIR need not discuss cumulative impacts which do not result in part from the project evaluated in the EIR. An EIR may determine that a project's contribution of a significant cumulative impact will be mitigated to a less-than-significant level and thus is not significant. A project's contribution is less than cumulatively considerable and therefore less than significant if the project is required to implement or fund its fair share of mitigation measures designed to alleviate the cumulative impact. Guidelines secs. 15130(a)(1), (2), (3).

An EIR may determine that a project's contribution to a significant cumulative impact is *de minimis* and thus not significant. A *de minimis* contribution means that the environmental conditions would essentially be the same whether or not the proposed project is implemented. Guideline sec. 15130(a)(4).

In contrast to the Initial Study stage of CEQA, at the EIR stage a Lead Agency must prepare a more detailed evaluation of cumulative impacts. The EIR must contain a reasonable analysis of the significant cumulative impacts of a project. The EIR's cumulative impact analysis must identify related projects through a "list" or "projection" approach, summarize effects of the related projects, and reasonably analyze the cumulative impacts of the proposed project and recommend mitigation measures for the significant cumulative impacts. Guidelines sec. 15130(b).

The discussion of cumulative impacts must reflect their severity and likelihood of occurring, but the discussion need not be as detailed as the discussion of a project's direct effects. The discussion should focus on the cumulative impact to which the identified other projects contribute rather than the attributes of the other projects which do not contribute to the cumulative impact. For example if another project contributes only to the cumulative water supply problem, its impacts on air quality need not be discussed. Guidelines secs. 15064(i), 15130(b).

As discussed in chapter 2, in determining the significance of a cumulative impact, the Lead Agency's analysis should focus on whether the project's incremental contribution to cumulative impacts is considerable. As with growth-inducing impacts, the best time to evaluate cumulative impacts is in a first-tier EIR, such as a Program EIR or Master EIR prepared for plans, programs, policies, or ordinances; however, using the list or projection approach in an EIR may be appropriate if no first-tier analysis was performed, or the analysis does not include the proposed project within its assessment of projected cumulative impacts.

List Approach. Under the list approach, the Lead Agency must identify all past, present, and probable future projects that could contribute to a significant cumulative environmental impact. If necessary, these projects must include those that may be outside the Lead Agency's control. Guidelines 15130(b).

When EIR preparers utilize the list approach, factors to consider in determining whether to include a related project should include the nature of each environmental resource being examined, the location of the project, and its type. Location may be important, for example, when water supply impacts are at issue since projects outside the watershed would probably not contribute to a cumulative effect. Type may be important, for example, when the impact is specialized, such a particular air pollutant or mode of traffic. Guidelines sec. 15130(b). When utilizing the list approach, the Lead Agency should define the geographic scope of the area affected by the cumulative effect and provide a reasonable explanation for the geographic limitation used. *See* Figure 5-3.

"Probable future projects" may be limited to those projects requiring agency approval for an application which has been received at the time the NOP is released, unless a project has been abandoned by the applicant. " Probable future projects" also include public projects for which money has been budgeted or included in an adopted capital improvement program, general plan, regional transportation plan, or other similar plan. They also include projects from a summary of projects in a general plan or similar plan and those projects anticipated as later phases of a previously approved project.

In practice, when EIR preparers rely on the list approach to evaluate cumulative impacts, several practical issues are frequently encountered in developing adequate lists. First, EIR preparers should be aware that project lists may differ from subject to subject (e.g., water-type projects for effects related to fish and may differ from traffic-type projects for effects related to traffic, air, and noise). Second, EIR preparers must recognize that related-project lists are constantly changing. Although this may lead to frustration, minor changes in a list will not cause an EIR to be inadequate if the Lead Agency can demonstrate that a good-faith effort was made to address

---

"Probable Future Projects" Include:

- Private projects requiring agency approval for an application which has been received at the time the NOP is released, unless a project has been abandoned by the applicant.
- Public projects for which money has been budgeted or included in an adopted capital improvement program, general plan, regional transportation plan, or other similar plan.
- Projects included in a summary of projects in a general plan or similar plan
- Projects anticipated as later phases of a previously approved project.

List past, present, and "reasonably foreseeable" future projects producing related impacts, including those outside the control of the Lead Agency

Factors to consider

- **Location of other projects**
- **Jurisdiction of other projects**
- **Types of other projects**
- **Size of other projects**

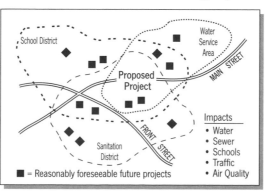

**Figure 5-3
Cumulative Impacts:
List Approach**

cumulative impacts. To enhance the adequacy of the EIR, an agency should clearly explain how it is evaluating the cumulative impacts of each subject and how it developed its related-project list.

Projection Approach. In lieu of using the list approach, a Lead Agency may base the cumulative impact analysis on a summary of projections contained in an adopted general plan or related planning document, or in a prior environmental document which has been adopted or certified. Pub. Res. Code sec. 21100(d). In using this approach, the Lead Agency must be certain that the adopted plan actually described or evaluated regional or areawide conditions contributing to the cumulative impact. Guidelines sec. 15130(b)(1).

Evaluation of the Cumulative Effects–General Rules. Regardless of whether the Lead Agency uses the list approach or the projection approach, certain general rules apply to the evaluation of cumulative impacts. The analysis must include a summary of the expected environmental effects to be produced by those projects with specific reference to additional information stating where that information is available. Additionally, the cumulative impact assessment must include a reasonable analysis of the relevant projects and must examine reasonable, feasible options for mitigating or avoiding the project's contribution to the cumulative impacts. With some projects, the only feasible mitigation for cumulative impacts may involve the adoption of ordinances or regulations rather than the imposition of conditions on a project-by-project basis. Guidelines secs. 15130(b)(2), (3)(c).

Previously approved land use documents such as general plans, specific plans, and local coastal plans may be used in cumulative impact analysis. A pertinent discussion of cumulative impacts contained in one or more previously certified EIRs may be incorporated by reference pursuant to the provisions for "tiering," Master EIRs, and program EIRs. No further cumulative impacts analysis is required when a project is consistent with a general, specific, master, or comparable programmatic plan where the Lead Agency determines that the regional or areawide cumulative impacts of the project have already been adequately addressed in a certified EIR for that plan. Guidelines sec. 15130(d).

Further, if a cumulative impact was adequately addressed in a prior EIR for a community plan, zoning action, or general plan, and the project is consistent with that plan or action, then an EIR for such a project should not further analyze that cumulative impact. Guidelines sec. 15130(e).

Economic and Social Effects

Effects analyzed under CEQA must be related to a physical change in the environment. Guidelines sec. 15358(b). Economic and social effects are not considered environmental effects under CEQA. These effects need to be considered in EIRs only if they would lead to an environmental effect. For example, an EIR is not required to analyze the economic effect on small businesses of construction of a large shopping mall; however, the Lead Agency should analyze the environmental effect of the change in traffic patterns that would result from the closing of the small businesses and opening of the shopping mall. The evaluation of economic or social effects is generally treated as optional; agencies may, but are not required to, evaluate

If a cumulative impact was adequately addressed in a prior EIR for a community plan, zoning action, or general plan, and the project is consistent with that plan or action, then the project's EIR should not further analyze that cumulative impact.

them and sometimes do include an analysis of economic or social effects of the proposed project. Guidelines sec. 15131.

Impact Assessment Methodology

Lead Agencies are free to develop or utilize any methodology regarding assessment of the environmental effects of a proposed project. In general, neither CEQA nor the Guidelines contain any specific requirement for how or at what level of detail impacts must be evaluated. However, CEQA provides some guidance on the analysis of impacts on agricultural land, archaeological and historic resources, and public water systems, and projects within airport planning areas and school-related facilities.

Neither CEQA nor the CEQA Guidelines contain any specific requirement for how or at what level of detail impacts must be evaluated.

Impacts on Agricultural Land

CEQA includes a finding stating that the conversion of agricultural lands to nonagricultural uses threatens the long-term health of the state's agricultural industry and that CEQA should play an important role in the preservation of agricultural land. Therefore, CEQA encourages agencies to make wise and efficient land use decisions by adopting and using the Land Evaluation and Site Assessment (LESA) criteria developed by the U.S. Natural Resources Conservation Service (formerly called the Soil Conservation Service) to implement the federal Farmland Protection Policy Act. Chapter 812, Statutes of 1993.

LESA = Land Evaluation and Site Assessment

To assist Lead Agencies in accomplishing this objective, the California Department of Conservation is required to develop a state model LESA system. Pub. Res. Code sec. 21095(b). The state LESA system is intended to be modified by Lead Agencies and adopted as a decision-making methodology for assessing the potential environmental impact of state and local projects on agricultural land. Pub. Res. Code sec. 21061.2. The Department of Conservation developed the model system in 1997. However, Lead Agencies which lack the time or resources to modify the state model for their own use may want to use the federal LESA system, which is routinely used under NEPA, to evaluate the effects of projects on agricultural resources.

The LESA system requires agencies to systematically quantify and evaluate the effect of their activities on farmland. In addition to the traditional emphasis on soil classification, the LESA procedures require that agencies assign a numeric rating to a variety of other factors affecting the viability of agricultural operations that are threatened by non-agricultural land uses.

Historical Resources

In determining if there is a significant impact to an historic resources, there is a two-part test: (1) Is the resource "historically significant" and (2) would the project cause a "substantial adverse change" in the significance of the resource. The term "historic resource" is given a broad definition with three categories of significance. Guidelines sec. 15064.5(a).

If the resource is considered "historically significant" and the project would cause a "substantial adverse change" in the significance of the resource, the Lead Agency must conclude that the impact is significant.

California Register of Historical Resources. An historic resource is deemed to be significant if it is a resource listed in, or determined to be eligible for listing in, the California Register of Historical Resources. An historic resource is eligible if it:

Definition of Significant "Historic Resources"

- Resources on or eligible for the California Register of Historical Resources
- Resources on or eligible for the National Register of Historic Places
- Resources locally designated as historically significant
- Resources the Lead Agency finds to be historically significant based on substantial evidence

- Is associated with events that have made a significant contribution to the broad patterns of California's history and cultural heritage
- Is associated with the lives of persons important in our past
- Embodies the distinctive characteristics of a type, period, region, or method of construction, or represents the work of an important creative individual, or possesses high artistic value
- Has yielded, or may be likely to yield, information about prehistory or history

Historic resources that are on or eligible for inclusion in the National Register of Historic Places fall within this definition.

Locally Designated Historic Resources. Historic resources included in a local register of historical resources or identified as significant in an historical resource survey meeting certain requirements shall be presumed to be historically or culturally significant. Public agencies must treat such resources as significant unless the preponderance of the evidence demonstrates that they are not historically or culturally significant.

Other Historically Significant Resources. Any object, building, structure, site, area, place, record, or manuscript which a Lead Agency determines to be historically significant in the architectural, engineering, scientific, economic, agricultural, educational, social, political, military, or cultural annals of California may be considered to be an historic resource, provided the Lead Agency's determination is supported by substantial evidence in light of the whole record.

Substantial Adverse Changes to Historic Resources. A project with an effect that may cause a "substantial adverse change" in the significance of an historical resource is a project that may have a significant effect on the environment. "Substantial adverse change" means physical demolition, destruction, relocation, or alteration in the resource, such that the resource is "materially impaired." The significance of an historical resource is considered to be materially impaired when a project demolishes or materially alters the physical characteristics that justify the determination of its significance. Guidelines sec. 15064.5(b).

"Substantial adverse change" means physical demolition, destruction, relocation, or alteration in the resource, such that the resource is "materially impaired."

When a project will affect state-owned historical resources, any state Lead Agency must consult with the State Historic Preservation Office (SHPO). Consultation should be coordinated in a timely manner with the preparation of the environmental document. Although not required, local Lead Agencies are also advised to consult with the SHPO. Guidelines sec. 15064.5(b)(5).

SHPO = State Historic Preservation Office

Archaeological Resources

When a project will have an impact on an archaeological site, a Lead Agency must first determine whether the site falls within the definition of an historical resource as described above. If the archaeological site meets the definition of an historical resource, then it shall be treated like any other historical resource.

If an archaeological site does not fall within the definition of an historical resource, but does meet the definition of a "unique archaeological resource" [Pub. Res. Code 21083.2], then the site must be treated in accordance with the special provisions for such resources, including the time and cost limitations for implementing mitigation. An archaeological resource will be "unique" if it:

- Is associated with an event or person of recognized significance in California or American history or recognized scientific importance in prehistory
- Can provide information that is of demonstrable public interest and is useful in addressing scientifically consequential and reasonable research questions
- Has a special or particular quality such as oldest, best example, largest, or last surviving example of its kind
- Is at least 100 years old and possesses substantial stratigraphic integrity
- Involves important research questions that historical research has shown can be answered only with archaeological methods

Pub. Res. Code sec. 21083.2.

In practice, most archaeological resources that meet the definition of a "unique" will also meet the definition of an "historical resource."

If an archaeological site is neither a "unique archaeological resource" nor an "historical resource," any effect to it shall not be considered significant. The environmental document must include an explanation supporting such conclusion and no further consideration is necessary. Guidelines sec. 15064.5(c).

Native American Human Remains. When an environmental document identifies the existence of, or the probable likelihood of, Native American human remains within a project, the Led Agency shall work with the most likely descendant as designated by the Native American Heritage Commission and special rules apply. Guidelines sec. 15064.5(d).

Accidental Discovery of Resources. As a part of its CEQA procedures, a Lead Agency should make provisions for historical or archaeological resources that are accidentally discovered during construction. Special rules apply in those situations. Guidelines sec. 15064.5(e).

As a part of its CEQA procedures, a Lead Agency should make provisions for historical or archaeological resources that are accidentally discovered during construction.

In preparing an EIR, any information about the specific location of archaeological sites and sacred lands need not be included. Guidelines sec. 15120(d).

Impacts on Public Water Systems

Special requirements apply for evaluating the impacts of certain large projects on public water systems. Pub. Res. Code sec. 21151.9; Water Code Part 2.10, Division 6, Section 10910; Guidelines sec. 15083.5. In practice, many Lead Agencies fail to comply with these requirements, foregoing an opportunity to improve land use and water supply assessments.

Whenever a Lead Agency prepares an NOP of an EIR for certain projects, it must identify the public water system that will serve the project and must request that the water agency assess whether the projected water demand associated with the project is covered by the water agency's master water management plan. The projects subject to this provision are residential projects of more than 500 dwelling units; shopping centers and businesses that would employ more than 1,000 people or have more than 500,000 square feet of floor space; commercial office buildings where more than 1,000 persons would be employed or that would have more than 250,000 square feet of floor space; hotels or motels with more than 500 rooms; industrial, manufacturing, processing plant, or industrial park projects that would employ more than 1,000 persons, occupy more than 40 acres, or have more than 650,000 square feet of floor space; and mixed-use projects that would demand an amount of water equal to or greater than the amount required by a housing project of 500 dwelling units.

A public water system that is notified by a Lead Agency must prepare an assessment indicating whether its total projected water supplies will meet the projected water demand of the proposed project, in addition to the other planned future uses of water. The governing body of the public water system must approve the assessment, at one of its official meetings, no later than 30 days after the date on which the request for the assessment was received. If the public water system fails to submit the assessment to the Lead Agency in a timely manner, the Lead Agency may assume that the water system has no information to submit.

If, as a result of the assessment, the public water system concludes that its supplies are insufficient, it must submit to the Lead Agency its plans for additional water supplies, including the following:

- Estimated total costs, and methods of financing the costs, associated with acquiring the additional water supplies
- A list of all federal, state, and local permits, approvals, or other entitlements necessary to acquire or develop the additional water supplies
- Estimated time frames for acquiring the additional water supplies.

The Lead Agency must include the water assessment in the EIR, but the length of such discussion may not exceed ten pages unless the Lead Agency determines that additional information is necessary. Also, at the time it makes a decision on the project, the Lead Agency must determine whether the projected water supplies will be sufficient to satisfy the demands of the proposed project, in addition to existing and planned future uses. If the Lead Agency determines that water supplies will not be sufficient, it must include that determination in its findings.

Projects within Airport Comprehensive Land Use Plan Areas

In preparing EIRs on projects within the purview of an airport comprehensive land use plan or within two nautical miles of a public use airport, the Lead Agency must evaluate the impacts on safety and noise.

In preparing EIRs on projects within the purview of an airport comprehensive land use plan or within two nautical miles of a public or public use airport, the Lead Agency must evaluate the impacts on safety and noise by using the handbook prepared by the California Department of Transportation, Division of Aeronautics. Pub. Res. Code sec. 21096; Guidelines sec. 15154.

Projects Involving Schools

Special requirements apply to certain school projects and projects near schools to ensure that potential health impacts resulting from exposure to hazardous materials, wastes, and substances will be carefully examined and disclosed in an EIR (or in a Negative Declaration). Guidelines sec. 15186. Specifically, for any project located within one-quarter mile of a school which is expected to involve the construction or alteration of a facility which might reasonably be anticipated to emit hazardous material above certain limits, the Lead Agency must consult with the affected school district during preparation of the document and notify the district within 30 days prior to certification.

When a project involves purchase of a school site or construction of a secondary or elementary school, the EIR must disclose:

- Any sites of current or former hazardous waste disposal and their status
- Records of any hazardous substance releases
- Any buried or above ground pipelines which carry hazardous substances.

Additionally, the Lead Agency must consult with and notify the appropriate air pollution control district or air quality management agency.

In preparing findings for the project, the school board must find that no hazardous facilities were present or, if such facilities exist, that

- No health risks from the facilities will endanger the public health of persons attending or working at the school, and
- Corrective action will mitigate all hazardous air emissions before the school is occupied.

These provisions of the CEQA Guidelines involving school facilities are very specific and include various cross references to the California Health and Safety Code. Guidelines sec. 15186.

The provisions of the CEQA Guidelines involving school facilities are very specific and include various cross references to the California Health and Safety Code.

Significant Irreversible Changes

Uses of nonrenewable resources during the initial and continued phases of the project may be irreversible since a large commitment of such resources makes removal or nonuse thereafter unlikely. Therefore, for EIRs on plans, policies, ordinances, LAFCO actions, and joint NEPA documents, the EIR must analyze and justify the extent to which the proposed project will commit nonrenewable resources to uses that future generations will probably be unable to reverse (e.g., construction of access to previously inaccessible areas or use of nonrenewable fuel resources for construction). The focus should be on both primary and, particularly, secondary impacts that generally commit future generations to similar uses and also on the irreversible damage that could result from environmental accidents associated with the project. Pub. Res. Code sec. 21100(a); Guidelines secs. 15126(c), 15126.2(c), 15127.

Alternatives

In General

A Draft EIR must describe a reasonable range of feasible alternatives to the project or project location that could feasibly attain most of the basic project objectives and would avoid or substantially lessen any of the significant environmental impacts of the proposed project. Additionally, the No-Project Alternative (*see below*) must also be analyzed in a Draft EIR. The EIR

Determining the Feasibility of Alternatives

General feasibility factors

- Economic
- Legal
- Social
- Technical
- Environmental

must evaluate the comparative merits of the alternatives. Guidelines secs. 15126(d), 15126.6(a).

There is no ironclad rule governing the nature or scope of the alternatives to be discussed other than the rule of reason. The discussion of alternatives must focus on those alternatives that are capable of avoiding or substantially lessening the significant environmental effects of the proposed project, even if the alternative could impede to some degree the attainment of all the project objectives or would be more costly. Guidelines sec. 15126.6(b). The EIR must identify the environmentally superior alternative other than the No-Project Alternative and explain why alternatives other than the proposed project were rejected. Guidelines sec. 15126.6(c).

The treatment of alternatives in an EIR should be based on the following methodology (*see* Figure 5-4):

- Describe the project objectives
- Assess the proposed project's significant environmental effects
- Develop screening criteria for feasibility of alternatives
- Select a reasonable range of alternatives that:
  - Meet some or all of the project objectives
  - May be located on alternative sites
  - Substantially avoid or lessen the proposed project's significant environmental effects
  - Are feasible based on specific economic, social, legal, or technical considerations
- Explain why other alternatives have been rejected from evaluation
- Provide meaningful evaluation and analysis of environmental effects of the reasonable range of alternatives and the No-Project Alternative in comparison with environmental effects of the proposed project
- Identify the environmentally superior alternative

**Figure 5-4
Alternatives
Screening Process**

Develop project objectives

Determine significant impacts to be avoided

Develop broad list of potential alternatives

Develop screening criteria for feasibility

Screen alternatives down to "reasonable range"

If alternative is infeasible: **Explain** why

If alternative is potentially feasible: **Conduct** detailed evaluation

Evaluation and Comparison of Alternatives

The EIR must include sufficient information about each alternative to allow meaningful evaluation, analysis, and comparison with the proposed project. A matrix displaying the major characteristics and impacts of each alternative may be used to summarize the comparison. When possible, the comparison should rely on quantitative factors. Generalized qualitative factors (e.g., "Alternative A is better than Alternative B") may not be adequate. However, the discussion of environmental effects of alternatives may be in less detail than the discussion of the impacts of the project as proposed. Guidelines sec. 15126.6(d).

No-Project Alternative

The EIR must always evaluate and analyze the impacts of the no-project alternative. The purpose of evaluating the no-project alternative is to allow decision makers to compare the impacts of approving the project with the impacts of not approving the project. However the no-project alternative is not the baseline for determining whether the proposed project's impacts are significant unless it is identical to the existing environmental setting analysis that establishes the baseline. Guidelines secs. 15125, 15126.6(e).

The no-project analysis must discuss the existing conditions at the time the Notice of Preparation is published as well as what would be reasonably expected to occur in the foreseeable future if the project were not approved, based on current plans and consistent with available infrastructure and community services. If the environmentally superior alternative is the no-project alternative, then the EIR must also identify another environmentally superior alternative. Guidelines sec. 15126.6(e).

The no-project analysis must discuss the existing conditions at the time the NOP is published as well as what would be reasonably expected to occur in the foreseeable future if the project were not approved.

The discussion of the no-project alternative will usually proceed along one of two lines. When the project is the revision of an existing land use or regulatory plan, policy, or ongoing operation, the no-project alternative will be the continuation of the plan, policy, or operation into the future (not the plan at full buildout). If, on the other hand, the project is an individual development project on identifiable location, the no-project alternative should compare the environmental effects of the property remaining in its exiting state. If, however, other future uses of the land are predictable, such uses should also be discussed as possible no-project conditions and the project should be compared to them. Guidelines sec. 15126.6(e)(3).

Selection of Range of Alternatives

Rule of Reason. The range of alternatives required in an EIR is governed by a "rule of reason" that requires an EIR to set forth only those alternatives necessary to permit a reasoned choice. An EIR need not consider every conceivable alternative to a project.

An EIR need not consider every conceivable alternative to a project.

Rather, the alternatives must be limited to ones that meet the project objectives, are ostensibly feasible, and would avoid or substantially lessen at least one of the significant environmental effects of the project. Of those alternatives, the EIR need only examine in detail the ones that the Lead Agency determines could feasibly attain most of the basic objectives of the project. The range of reasonable alternatives must be selected and discussed in a manner to foster meaningful public participation and informed decision making. Guidelines sec. 15126.6(f).

Alternatives should be developed that would avoid or substantially lessen significant environmental effects of the project.

The EIR must briefly describe the rationale for selection and rejection of alternatives and the information the Lead Agency relied on in making the selection. It should also identify any alternatives that were considered by the Lead Agency but were rejected as infeasible during the scoping process and briefly explain the reasons for their exclusion. Additional information explaining the choice of alternatives may be included in the administrative record. Alternatives may be eliminated from detailed consideration in the EIR if they fail to meet most of the basic project objectives, are infeasible, or do not avoid any significant environmental effects. Guidelines sec. 15126.6(c). *See* Figure 5-5.

Figure 5-5
Developing a Reasonable
Range of Alternatives

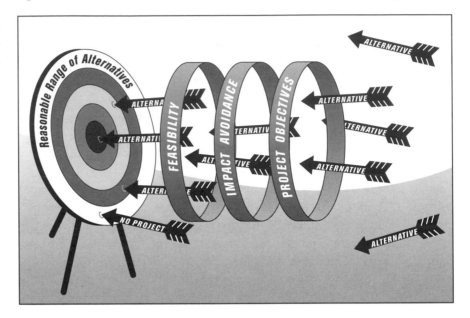

Importance of a Clear Statement of Project Objectives. In developing a range of alternatives, a Lead Agency should focus on those alternatives that meet most or all of the project objectives. Guidelines sec. 15126.6(a). Clearly written project objectives will help in the development of a reasonable range of alternatives. The statement of objectives should include the underlying purpose of the project. Guidelines sec. 15124(b).

Although CEQA does not define the term "objective," a dictionary definition distinguishes between an "action" ("the project") and the goal of the action ("the objective"). If the term "objective" is viewed in this manner, even a private project (e.g., a "housing development") can be described as having a public objective (e.g., providing housing for the community). A Lead Agency may narrow the range of alternatives to be evaluated by defining a relatively narrow objective. For example, an EIR for a bay-oriented aquarium need not evaluate alternatives that do not include siting the project near the bay, which was one of the stated objectives of the project. Although the Lead Agency should not describe the objective so narrowly as to preclude any alternatives, one court has found an EIR that contained only one alternative (other than the No-Project Alternative) to be adequate because of the very explicit and narrow project objective. *Marin Municipal Water District v. K.G. Land Corporation* (1991) 235 Cal. App. 3d 1652. On the other hand, if the project has multiple objectives, every alternative need not satisfy every objective. It is sufficient if each alternative meets most of the project's objectives. *City of Carmel-by-the Sea v. United States Department of Transportation* (9th Cir. 1997) 123 Fed. 3d 1142.

If a project has multiple objectives, every alternative need not satisfy every objective. It is sufficient if each alternative meets most of the project's objectives.

Feasibility. No single factor establishes a fixed limit on the scope of reasonable alternatives. In determining whether alternatives are feasible, Lead

Agencies are guided by the general definition of feasibility found in CEQA: "capable of being accomplished in a successful manner within a reasonable period of time, taking into account economic, environmental, legal, social, and technological factors." Guidelines sec. 15364. In addition, the Lead Agency should consider site suitability, economic viability, availability of infrastructure, general plan consistency, other regulatory limitations, jurisdictional boundaries, and proponent's control over alternative sites in determining the range of alternatives to be evaluated in an EIR. Guidelines sec. 15126.6(f).

Lead Agencies should be guided by CEQA's general definition of feasibility: "capable of being accomplished in a successful manner within a reasonable period of time, taking into account economic, environmental, legal, social, and technological factors."

Alternative Locations. Alternative locations need not be evaluated in every case. The key question is determining whether to evaluate alternative locations is whether any of the significant environmental effects of the project would be avoided or substantially lessened by putting the project in another location. Only locations that would avoid or substantially lessen any significant effects need be evaluated in the EIR. If the Lead Agency determines that no feasible alternative locations exist, it must disclose the reasons for this conclusion in the EIR. When alternative locations are evaluated in an EIR, to the extent possible, they should rely on previous documents (e.g. plan, policy, or program level EIRs) that have already analyzed a range of reasonable alternative locations. Guidelines sec. 15126.6(f).

If the Lead Agency determines that no feasible alternative locations exist, it must disclose the reasons for this conclusion in the EIR.

Relationship to Comprehensive Planning. Alternative locations for projects are best evaluated in Program or Master EIRs prepared for plans, programs, or policies. A project-level EIR should not ordinarily be an occasion for the reconsideration or overhaul of fundamental land use policy. However, the fact that an alternative site may require a legislative change (e.g., general plan amendment or rezoning) does not necessarily exclude it from consideration in an EIR.

Adopted regional and local plans may be relied on when the feasibility of alternative sites is being determined and may result in those sites being eliminated from detailed discussion in an EIR. At the same time, if they have been identified in adopted plans, feasible alternative sites may be included in an EIR. Additionally, the inconsistency of an alternative site with an adopted plan may be a factor in its being determined to be infeasible. Guidelines sec. 15126.6(f)(2).

Rationale for Rejecting Alternatives. The Lead Agency may, as part of the scoping process, make an initial determination as to which alternatives are feasible and merit in-depth consideration and which do not. Although an EIR should generally set forth the alternatives that the Lead Agency considered and rejected as infeasible during the scoping process, and the reasons for their rejection, such explanations may be found elsewhere in the administrative record. Thus, the entire administrative record, and not merely the EIR, may be studied to assess the degree of discussion any particular alternative deserves, based on its feasibility and the stage in the decision-making process at which it is brought to the attention of the Lead Agency. Alternatives that are brought to the Lead Agency's attention after the public review period must also be considered, but the Lead Agency may address these alternatives by means of administrative findings, rather than in a supplemental EIR. *Citizens of Goleta Valley v. Board of Supervisors* (1990) 52 Cal. App. 3d 553.

Alternatives that are brought to the Lead Agency's attention after the public review period must be considered, but the Lead Agency may address these alternatives by means of administrative findings, rather than in a supplemental EIR.

Alternatives that are remote or speculative, or the effects of which cannot be reasonably predicted, need not be considered. However, alternatives may not be rejected merely because they are beyond an agency's authority, would require new implementing legislation, or would be too costly. Guidelines sec. 15126(f)(2).

An EIR should analyze alternatives even if mitigation measures can reduce the impacts of the proposed project to less-than-significant levels. If it concludes that no feasible alternatives exist, an EIR must present the reasons why alternatives were rejected in sufficient detail to enable meaningful public review. The Lead Agency's responsibility to provide an adequate analysis of alternatives does not depend on project opponents first showing that feasible alternatives exist.

Mitigation Measures

In General

> **For Each Significant Impact, the Lead Agency Must...**
>
> - Discuss whether the measure avoids or substantially reduces the significant environmental effect
> - Distinguish measures proposed by project proponents
> - Identify responsibility of implementation for each measure
> - Discuss the basis for selecting a particular measure (when several measures are available)
> - Discuss significant impacts associated with implementation of each mitigation measure
> - Consider special limits for archaeological resources, school facilities, housing units, and public water systems

In general, CEQA requires that, for each significant impact identified in the EIR, the EIR must discuss feasible measures to avoid or substantially reduce the project's significant environmental effect. Guidelines 15126.4(a).

In practice, the EIR preparer should include all measures that it considers to be ostensibly feasible, even though the ultimate determination of feasibility is not made until the decision makers prepare Findings later in the project approval process. A measure brought to the attention of the Lead Agency staff should not be left out of the EIR unless it is infeasible on its face. *Los Angeles Unified School District v. City of Los Angeles* (1997) 58 Cal. App. 4th 1019.

The EIR must distinguish between the measures which are proposed by the project proponents to be included in the project from other measures proposed by the Lead, Responsible, or Trustee Agency which are not included but could reasonably be expected to reduce the adverse impacts if required as conditions of approving the project. Where several measures are available to mitigate an impact, each should be discussed and the basis for selecting a particular measure should be identified. Guidelines sec. 15126.4(a).

The Guidelines provide for five categories of mitigation—measures that avoid, minimize, rectify, reduce or eliminate, or compensate for the significant environmental effect of the proposed project. Guidelines sec. 15370. *See* Figure 5-6.

Drafting Adequate Mitigation Measures

To be considered adequate, mitigation measures should be specific, feasible actions that will actually improve adverse environmental conditions.

Adequacy and Feasibility. To be considered adequate, mitigation measures should be specific, feasible actions that will actually improve adverse environmental conditions. Mitigation measures should be measurable to allow monitoring of their implementation. Mitigation measures consisting only of further studies, or consultation with regulatory agencies that are not tied to a specific action plan, may not be adequate and should therefore be avoided. *See* Figure 5-7. *Sundstrom v. County of Mendocino* (1998) 202 Cal. App. 3d 296; *see* discussion of the details of this case on page 39. It may be appropriate, however, for a Lead Agency to list alternative mitigation

Figure 5-6
Types of Mitigation

Mitigation Action	Explanation
Avoid	Avoid the impact altogether by not taking certain actions or parts of actions
Minimize	Minimize impacts by limiting the degree or magnitude of the action and its implementation
Rectify	Rectify the impact by repairing, rehabilitating, or restoring the affected environment
Reduce or Eliminate	Reduce or eliminate the impact over time by preservation and maintenance during the life of the action
Compensate	Compensate for the impact by replacing or providing substitute resources or environments

Figure 5-6
Types of Mitigation

measures in an EIR if the agency commits to mitigating the impacts and the measures are tied to measurable performance standards.

While a Lead Agency should attempt to apply mitigation consistently, CEQA does not mandate that the same mitigation measures be applied to similar projects. For example, historically applied ratios (e.g., 3:1 wetland replacement) may not be applicable to future projects with different circumstances.

When drafting mitigation measures, agencies should include only those that are feasible. A mitigation measure is considered feasible if it is capable of being accomplished in a successful manner within a reasonable period of time, taking into consideration economic, environmental, legal, social, and technological factors. Guidelines sec. 15364. However, the final determination of the feasibility of a mitigation measure is made by the decision makers when they prepare findings. *See* Findings, page 83.

Effective Mitigation Measures. In practice, drafting a good mitigation measure involves clearly explaining its objectives—specifically how it will be implemented, who is responsible for its implementation, where it will occur, and when it will occur. *See* Figure 5-8. In drafting or reviewing mitigation measures, a Lead Agency may use the five factors in Figure 5-6 as a test of a

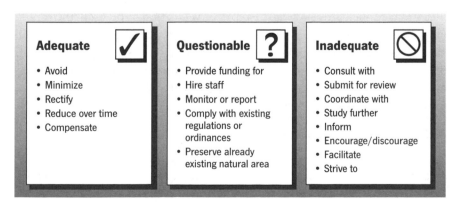

Figure 5-7
Adequacy of
Mitigation Measures

Figure 5-8
Five Questions for Effective
Mitigation Measures

Question	Requirement
WHY	State the objective of the mitigation measure and why it is recommended
WHAT	Explain the specifics of the mitigation measure and how it will be designated and implemented Identify measurable performance standards by which the success of the mitigation can be determined Provide for contingent mitigation if monitoring reveals that the success standards are not satisfied
WHO	Identify the agency, organization, or individual responsible for implementing the measure
WHERE	Identify the specific location of the mitigation measure
WHEN	Develop a schedule for implementation

SEIR = Supplemental EIR

measure's adequacy. If they are not specific, mitigation measures are less likely to be implemented, effective, and capable of being monitored.

Analysis of Impacts of Mitigation

The EIR must include discussion of the environmental effects of implementation of the mitigation measures, in addition to those caused by the proposed project. The discussion of a mitigation measure's significant effects may be less detailed than those of the proposed project. Guidelines sec. 15126.4(a).

Mitigation May Not Be Deferred

Formulation of mitigation measures should not be deferred until some future time. However, measures may specify performance standards which would mitigate the significant effect of the project and which may be accomplished in more than one specified way. For example, if a mitigation measure for wildlife habitat loss is to create replacement habitat, the detailed design of the new habitat may be deferred to the future so long as the EIR includes performance standards such as the types of vegetation to be used, the timing of implementation, and contingency plans if the replanting is not successful. Additionally, if the activity being evaluated in the EIR is a plan or program, the mitigation measures will typically consist of policy statements included in the program that will serve to guide project-specific mitigation in the future. Guidelines sec. 15126.4(a).

Authority to Mitigate Impacts

Subject to the limitations discussed below, CEQA gives a public agency the authority to require feasible changes in any or all activities involved in a project to substantially lessen or avoid significant effects on the environment.

Deferred mitigation measures in an EIR prepared for the Sacramento Convention Center expansion were upheld in a controversial judicial decision (Sacramento Old City Association v. City Council (1991) 229 Cal.App.3d 1011).

Guidelines sec. 15041. An agency does not, however, have unlimited authority to impose mitigation measures. *See* Limitations on Authority, page 82.

CEQA's Limitations. CEQA contains both general and specific limitations on an agency's authority to mitigate impacts. As discussed in chapter 4, in mitigating a project's significant environmental effects, an agency may exercise only those express or implied powers provided by law, aside from those provided by CEQA. Where another law grants an agency discretionary powers, CEQA authorizes its use. Guidelines sec. 15040. However, if under other law, an agency lacks the legal authority to impose those mitigation measures for a significant environmental impact, CEQA does not provide that authority.

If the Lead Agency determines that a mitigation measure cannot be legally imposed, the measure need not be proposed or analyzed. Instead, the EIR may simply reference that fact and briefly explain the reasons underlying the Lead Agency's determination. Guidelines sec. 15126.4(a).

Constitutional Limitations. In addition, the U.S. Constitution limits an agency's authority to impose conditions to those situations where there is a clear "nexus" between the impact and the mitigation measure; otherwise, the agency may be accused of "taking" private property without "just compensation." *Nollan v. California Coastal Commission* (1988) 107 S.Ct. 3141. Thus, the mitigation proposed for a project must relate directly to the impacts caused. There must be "rough proportionality" between the environmental problems caused by a development project and the mitigation measure imposed on the project applicant. *Dolan v. City of Tigard* (1994) 512 U.S. 374; CEQA Guidelines secs. 15041, 15126.4.

Historical Resources

A Lead Agency must identify any potentially feasible measures to mitigate significant adverse changes in the significance of an historical resource. Any adopted mitigation measures must be made fully enforceable through permits, conditions, agreements, or other measures. Guideline secs. 15064.5(b)(3–5).

Mitigation measures that do not truly reduce or avoid the impact to the significant historical resources are inadequate under CEQA. For example, measures such as placing historical markers on a

Citizens of Goleta Valley v. Board of Supervisors (1990) 52 Cal. App. 3d 553: Court Rules on Offsite Alternatives to Be Analyzed in an EIR

The California Supreme Court clarified the circumstances under which public agencies may evaluate alternative sites in EIRs. This case involved a decade-long struggle of the Hyatt Corporation's attempt to develop a coastal resort hotel in Goleta, a community in Santa Barbara County. After the Court of Appeal held that the EIR prepared for the coastal resort hotel was deficient in that it failed to examine any alternative sites for the proposed project (*see Citizens of Goleta Valley v. Board of Supervisors [Goleta I]* (1988) 197 Cal. App. 3d 1167), Santa Barbara County prepared a Supplemental EIR (SEIR) analyzing the potential for developing alternative sites. This SEIR analyzed a single alternative site rather than a range of sites. Although the appellate court again declared the EIR inadequate in that it did not evaluate a reasonable range of alternatives and did not explain why other ostensibly feasible alternatives were eliminated from consideration (*see Citizens of Goleta Valley v. Board of Supervisors [Goleta II]* (1989) 214 Cal. App. 3d 264), the California Supreme Court reversed, holding that the SEIR was legally sufficient and that substantial evidence supported the County's decision approving the project.

The County's Draft SEIR contained a brief discussion of an alternative site on the Santa Barbara coast the County believed could feasibly accommodate a resort hotel of the scale proposed for the project. In comments on the Draft SEIR, the County was requested to include more detail about this alternative site and to discuss any other feasible alternative sites (including other coastal and specific inland sites). The Final SEIR included an expanded discussion of the alternate coastal site but rejected it because of anticipated environmental impacts and the fact that the site was not zoned for this use and was not available to the project proponents. The Final SEIR justified not analyzing other coastal sites by referencing a staff report separately prepared that concluded no other sites along the coast could accommodate a resort hotel. The Final SEIR justified not analyzing inland sites because coastal access was an essential aspect of the proposed project objectives. During the hearings on the Final SEIR, the County was requested to analyze seven additional alternative sites; although the County did not revise the Final SEIR, in its findings on the project, the County specifically addressed the feasibility of and rejected the seven additional alternatives.

In upholding the SEIR, the high court stated that the range of alternatives, governed by the "rule of reason," should offer "substantial environmental advantages over the proposed project" and are "feasibly accomplished in a successful manner considering economic, environmental, social, and technical factors." The Court emphasized that there is no "categorical legal imperative" as to the scope of alternatives and that each case "must be evaluated on its facts" to determine whether the purposes of CEQA have been achieved. The Court stated that generally the EIR should set forth the reasons for rejecting certain alternatives as infeasible but added that such reasons may be found elsewhere in the administrative record. For specific alternative sites brought to the Lead Agency's attention after the public review process, the Lead Agency must consider them but may address them "by means of administrative findings, rather than by commissioning a Supplemental EIR."

The Court stated also that an EIR was "not ordinarily an occasion for the reconsideration or overhaul of fundamental land use policy;" however, the Court recognized that although an alternative may require a legislative change (e.g., general plan amendment or zoning change), that should not preclude it from consideration in an EIR. The Court held that adopted regional and local plans may be relied on by a Lead Agency in determining the infeasibility of alternative sites. The Court identified certain circumstances under which the inclusion of alternative sites would be appropriate, including the project being a public project (because of the power of eminent domain); the project proponent owning or controlling, having the ability to purchase or lease, or having access to feasible alternative sites; or two or more developers seeking approval for the same type of development at different locations. The Court also noted that the existence of alternative sites outside the Lead Agency's jurisdiction does not necessarily preclude them from consideration in an EIR.

site, writing a report, or consulting with an historic society do not adequately mitigate for the demolition of an historical building. Guidelines sec. 15126.4(b)(2).

Generally, a project that seeks to improve an historical resource in accordance with either of the following publications will be considered as mitigated to a level of less-than-significant:

- Secretary of Interior's *Standards for the Treatment of Historic Properties with Guidelines for Preserving, Rehabilitating, Restoring, and Reconstructing Historic Buildings*
- Secretary of Interior's *Standards for Rehabilitation and Guidelines for Rehabilitating Historic Buildings*

Guidelines sec. 15064.5(b)(3)

Archaeological Resources

Public agencies should, whenever possible, seek to avoid damaging effects to any archaeological resources. Preservation in place to maintain the relationship between the artifacts and the archaeological context is the preferred manner of mitigating impacts to archaeological sites. Preservation may be accomplished by:

- Planning construction to avoid archaeological sites;
- Incorporating sites within parks, greenspace, or other open space;
- Covering the sites with a layer of chemically stable soil;
- Deeding the site into a permanent conservation easement.

When in-place mitigation is not feasible, data recovery through excavation may be necessary. A data recovery plan, which makes provisions for adequately recovering the scientifically consequential information about the site, shall be prepared and adopted prior to any excavation being undertaken. Such studies must be deposited with the California Historical Resources Regional Information Center. Special rules apply to any archaeological sites known to contain human remains. Health and Safety Code sec. 7050.5; Guidelines sec. 15126.4(b).

Data recovery shall not be required if the Lead Agency determines that testing or studies already completed have adequately recovered the necessary data, provided that the data have already been documented in another EIR and are available for review at the California Historical Resource Regional Information Center. Guidelines sec. 15126.4(b).

CEQA expressly limits a public agency's ability to mitigate the impacts on unique archaeological resources by imposing cost limitations on the amount of mitigation that can be required of project applicants. These complex limitations are discussed in CEQA itself and, in practice, are rarely used. Pub. Res. Code sec. 21082.2.

School Impacts

State law prohibits a local agency from either denying approval of a land use project because of inadequate school facilities or imposing school impact mitigation measures other than designated fees. For residential developments, mitigation for schools, imposed as fees, is limited to $1.93 per square foot of assessable space; for commercial or industrial developments, mitigation is limited to $0.31 per square foot of chargeable covered and enclosed space. Govt. Code sec. 65995. These amounts are adjusted for inflation every two years beginning in the year 2000. The Leroy F. Greene School Facilities Act of 1998 (SB 50) and bond procedures under Proposition 1A of 1998 regulate school facilities financing and mitigation of land use approvals by setting fee caps, removing application denial authority, and setting the CEQA standard for full and complete school facilities mitigation.

Reductions in Housing Density

In accordance with state laws, requiring a reduction in the density of a housing development project as a condition of approval is only permissible if the project would have a specific adverse impact on health or safety that cannot be mitigated except by lowering of the density. Govt. Code sec. 65589.5.

Trip Reduction Programs

Employee or shopping center trip reduction programs cannot be required as mitigation for transportation or air quality impacts. Health and Safety Code secs. 40929(a), 40717.6.

Mitigation Reporting or Monitoring

In General

As discussed in chapter 4, when it makes findings on significant effects identified in an EIR (or when adopting a Negative Declaration containing mitigation measures), an agency must also adopt a program for reporting or monitoring mitigation measures that were adopted or made conditions of project approval. Pub. Res. Code sec. 21081.6(a); Guidelines secs. 15091(d), 15097. However, many Lead Agencies choose to include draft mitigation monitoring programs in the Draft EIR to obtain public comment. The monitoring program is implemented to ensure that the mitigation measures and project revisions identified in the EIR (or Negative Declaration) are implemented. Therefore, the monitoring program must include all changes in the proposed project either adopted by the project proponent or

---

League for Protection of Oakland's Architectural and Historical Resources v. City of Oakland: Court Requires EIR for Demolition of Historic Building and Declares Mitigation Measures Inadequate

In a decision with potentially far reaching implications for practice of historical resource protection, under CEQA, the court of appeals held that demolition of an identified historic structure was, in and of itself, a significant environmental impact. The court also held that some of the most common methods of mitigating impacts to historic buildings were not adequate under CEQA.

League for Protection of Oakland's Architectural and Historical Resources v. City of Oakland [(1997) 52 Cal. App. 4th 60] involved the proposed demolition of the old Montgomery Ward's building in one of Oakland's warehouse districts. The City of Oakland had identified the building as an historic structure in its General Plan, although it was not listed either on the national or state listings of historic buildings. A developer proposed to demolish the building to construct a new one. In response to this proposal, the city prepared a Mitigated Negative Declaration. The proposed mitigation for the loss of the building consisted of the following measures, which until this decision, were commonly used throughout California:

- Prepare an historic resource documentation report to provide historic material for the city's archives
- Conduct a historic building survey to further document the historic structure

- Design the replacement building to reflect the historic elements of the old building
- Display a plaque or marker commemorating the building; and
- Consult with a qualified archaeologist to monitor excavation for discovery of any possible cultural elements

The court first found that the historic building was a "significant" historical resource even though it was on neither the state nor federal listing of historic structures. On the question of whether a historic resource is "significant" the court established three possible criteria:

Mandatory significance—an historical resource must be considered significant if it is on or eligible for listing on the National Register of Historic Places or the California Register of Historic Resources.

Presumptive Significance—an historical resource is presumed to be significant if it is listed on a local register of historical resources unless the preponderance of the evidence demonstrates otherwise.

Discretionary Significance—An historical resource may still be considered significant even it is not on a federal, state, or local list if substantial evidence demonstrates it's significance.

Having found that the Montgomery Wards building was significant, the court also held that the proposed package of mitigation measures was not adequate under CEQA. The court concluded that, even taken together, this package of mitigation measures would not reduce the effects of the building's demolition to a less than significant level.

In view of this decision, agencies should re-evaluate their standards for preparing EIRs when historical resources would be effected as well as their practices on historical resource mitigation.

made conditions of approval by the Lead or Responsible Agency that would mitigate or avoid each significant environmental effect identified in the EIR. Guidelines sec. 15097. CEQA authorizes the Lead Agency to levy fees to pay for the monitoring program. *See* Figure 5-9 and OPR's CEQA Technical Advice Series report, *Tracking Mitigation Measures under AB 3180* (March 1996), Appendix 4.

The reporting or monitoring program must ensure compliance with mitigation measures during project implementation. In addition to ensuring implementation of mitigation measures, monitoring serves to ensure implementation of mitigation measures during project implementation, provide feedback to agency staff and decision makers about the effectiveness of their actions and learning opportunities for improving mitigation measures on future projects, and identify the need for enforcement action before irreversible environmental damage occurs.

A public agency may delegate reporting or monitoring responsibilities to another public agency or to a private entity which accepts the delegation. However, until the mitigation measures have been completed, the Lead Agency remains responsible for ensuring that the implementation of the measures occurs in accordance with the program. Guidelines sec. 15097(a).

Where the project consists of the adoption of a general plan, specific plan, or other plan-level document, the monitoring plan shall apply to any policies in the plan that are designed to mitigate environmental effects. The monitoring plan may consist of policies included in such plan-level documents. Guidelines sec. 15097(b).

Differences between Monitoring and Reporting

A public agency may choose whether its program will monitor mitigation, report on mitigation, or both. However, there is often no clear distinction between reporting and monitoring and the program best suited to ensuring compliance in any given project will usually involve elements of both. Guidelines sec. 15097(c).

Reporting. Reporting generally consists of a written compliance review that is presented to the decision-making body or authorized staff person. A report may be required at various stages of a project. Reporting is suited to projects which have readily measurable or quantitative mitigation measures or which already involve regular review under some other law or ordinance. For example a report may be required upon final occupancy for a project whose mitigation measures were confirmed by a building inspection. Guidelines sec. 15097(c)(1).

Monitoring. Monitoring is generally an ongoing process of project oversight and is suited to projects with complex mitigation which exceed the expertise of the local agency's expertise, expected to be implemented over a period of time, or require

Figure 5-9
**Mitigation Monitoring and
Reporting Requirements**

Trigger	• Agency adopts a Mitigated Negative Declaration
	• Agency makes finding after adopting an EIR
CEQA Requirement	• Agency must adopt a "reporting or monitoring" program for changes in the project adopted or made as conditions of approval to mitigate or avoid significant effects
Provisions for Mitigation Measures	• Mitigation measures must be made express conditions of project approval
	• Agencies with jurisdiction by law over natural resources must provide the Lead Agency with performance standards for mitigation measures
	• Agencies with jurisdiction by law over natural resources may be required to prepare monitoring programs if their recommended mitigation measures are adopted by the Lead Agency
	• Responsible agencies and agencies with jurisdiction over natural resources must identify mitigation performance objectives
Payment for Monitoring Program	• CEQA authorizes levy fees to pay for monitoring program

careful implementation to assure compliance. Wetland restoration or archaeological recovery activities are examples of such mitigation measures. Guidelines sec. 15097(c)(2).

Coordination between Lead and Responsible Agencies

Generally, Lead and Responsible Agencies will adopt separate and different monitoring and reporting programs for the same project. This often occurs because the agencies have adopted and are responsible for different mitigation measures, have made their decision on the project at different times or have their own expertise. Although Lead and Responsible Agencies have the discretion to choose their own approach to monitoring and reporting, they should coordinate their mitigation monitoring programs where possible. Guidelines sec. 15097(d).

Role of Responsible Agencies and Agencies with Jurisdiction over Natural Resources

Before the close of the public review period for the Draft EIR (or Mitigated Negative Declaration), a Responsible Agency, or agencies with jurisdiction by law over natural resources, must provide the Lead Agency with detailed performance standards for mitigation measures subject to their jurisdiction. Any mitigation measures submitted to the Lead Agency must be limited to those that mitigate impacts subject to that agency's jurisdiction. Pub. Res. Code sec. 21080.6(c). That agency may be required to prepare a monitoring program for the recommended mitigation measures that are adopted by the Lead Agency. Guidelines sec. 15097(f).

Mitigation monitoring requirements were added to CEQA in 1989.

Public Policy Objectives Served by Monitoring

• To ensure implementation of mitigation measures during project implementation

• To provide feedback to agency staff and decision makers about the effectiveness of their actions

• To provide learning opportunities for improving mitigation measures on future projects

• To identify the need for enforcement action before irreversible environmental damage occurs

When a project is of statewide, regional, or areawide importance, any transportation information generated by a required monitoring program must be submitted to the transportation planning agency in the region where the project is located.

When a project is of statewide, regional, or areawide importance, any transportation information generated by a required monitoring or reporting program must be submitted to the transportation planning agency in the region where the project is located. Each transportation planning agency shall adopt guidelines for the submittal of such information. Guidelines sec. 15097(g).

Enforcement of Mitigation Measures

CEQA does not give an agency the authority to remedy violations of mitigation requirements. Most public agencies, however, have considerable authority under other state laws or local ordinances to ensure compliance. These other legal enforcement procedures may be used to remedy violations of mitigation requirements discovered by monitoring. Such enforcement provisions may include "stop work" orders, denial of building occupancy permits, revocation of project approval, misdemeanor criminal sanctions, performance bonds, and recording with county recorder.

Procedures to Ensure Mitigation Requirement Compliance

- "Stop work" orders
- Denial of building occupancy permits
- Revocation of project approval
- Misdemeanor criminal sanctions
- Performance bonds
- Recording with county recorder

Effectiveness of Mitigation Monitoring: An Independent Study

An independent Bay Area study found that most public planners and policy makers believe that implementation of CEQA's mitigation monitoring requirements has been slow and generally ineffective, stemming primarily from the vagueness of the monitoring legislation. The survey, which resulted in responses from 68 public agencies in a 17-county area, found that formal programs for mitigation monitoring remain the exception to the rule. Additionally, the study found that the intensity of monitoring is generally inconsistent from agency to agency and project to project. The study is the first comprehensive study of mitigation monitoring and provides useful insights into how agencies and the Legislature may improve monitoring in the future. *See* "Mitigation Monitoring Programs," by Dominic Roques, in The Environmental Monitor, The Association of Environmental Professionals, Fall 1993.

Mitigation Monitoring Programs: Practical Experience

Monitoring the Success of Mitigation. Monitoring the success of a mitigation measure, although not required by CEQA unless success monitoring is already included in a mitigation measure, may be included in mitigation monitoring program. Descriptions of monitoring approaches should be, but are not required to be, included in the EIR to ensure that mitigation measures are capable of being monitored, to take advantage of the technical expertise of the EIR preparer, and to allow for public review.

Incorporation into a Draft EIR. Although the project-specific monitoring program is not required to be included in the EIR or Negative Declaration, in practice, many agencies are incorporating monitoring into their documents so that members of the public, Responsible Agencies, and others can review them before they are adopted. Including the monitoring program in the environmental documents is also recommended to ensure that mitigation measures will be specific enough to be monitored effectively (i.e., drafting the mitigation measure with monitoring in mind may ensure that the measure is written in a way to provide for effective monitoring).

Phased Monitoring Programs. Generally, agencies are implementing the mitigation monitoring requirement in two phases. First, many agencies are voluntarily adopting jurisdiction-wide, comprehensive monitoring programs in which the basic framework for monitoring is established for all projects. Second, agencies are developing detailed, project-specific monitoring plans as individual projects are approved.

At its discretion, an agency may adopt standardized policies and requirements to guide individually adopted monitoring or reporting programs. Such a jurisdiction-wide program may include, but is not limited to:

- The relative responsibilities of various departments within the agency

- The role, if any, of project proponents
- Agency guidelines for preparing monitoring or reporting programs
- General standards for determining project compliance with the mitigation measures
- Enforcement procedures for noncompliance, including provisions for administrative appeals
- Processes for informing staff and decision makers of the relative success of mitigation measures and using those results to improve future mitigation measures

Guidelines section 15097(e).

In practice, the components of a project-specific monitoring program typically include the following:

- Description of specific performance standards
- Master mitigation checklist
- Identification of project-specific monitoring activities:
  - Assignment of responsibilities
  - Development of schedule
- Specific reporting requirements
  - Field visit verification reports

Applicant Compliance Reports

Future of Mitigation Monitoring. Although it was an important first step in solving the monitoring loophole (*see* sidebar), enactment of the monitoring law is not a cure-all for all problems arising under CEQA's requirement to mitigate or avoid all significant effects of the proposed project where feasible. In addition to being overly general and providing agencies with few specific details on what a monitoring program should entail, the law requires agencies to monitor only the implementation of mitigation measures; the success of those measures is only an optional component. Guidelines sec. 15097(e)(6). For example, if a mitigation measure recommends that trees be replanted, the agency's responsibility is only to monitor the planting and not to determine whether the trees survive. For the law truly to meet the objective of successful mitigation, agencies should write much more specific mitigation measures that include measurable performance standards by which success can be determined.

Contents of a Final EIR

After the public review period, the Lead Agency must prepare a Final EIR. Guidelines secs. 15089, 15132. The Final EIR is required to include the Draft EIR, or a revision of the Draft EIR, copies or a summary of comments and recommendations received during public review of the Draft EIR, a list of persons and entities commenting on the Draft EIR, Lead Agency responses to the comments received on the Draft EIR, and any other information added by the Lead Agency.

The responses to comments in the Final EIR must demonstrate good faith and a well-reasoned analysis, and may not be conclusory. Pub. Res.

Code sec. 21091(d); Guidelines sec. 15088(b). When responding to comments, the Lead Agency need only respond to significant environmental issues and does not need to provide all information requested by reviewers. Guidelines sec. 15204(a). To respond to the comments, the Lead Agency may revise portions of or the entire Draft EIR, add new material to the Draft EIR, or both. These changes may be a separate section of the Final EIR. Guidelines sec. 15088(c). However, changes to the Draft EIR considered to be "significant new information" or substantial changes may require the Lead Agency to recirculate the EIR. *See* Preparation of a Final EIR, page 79.

Judicial Standards for EIR Adequacy

If no action or proceeding alleging that the Lead Agency violated CEQA requirements is brought forth before the expiration of the statute of limitations, the CEQA document shall be conclusively presumed to comply with CEQA. Pub. Res. Code sec. 21167.2.

Judicial review of the content of EIRs typically incorporates the "rule of reason" standard to assess whether the Lead Agency has complied with the requirements of CEQA. The courts do not hold an agency to a standard of absolute perfection, but rather require only that an EIR show that an agency has made an objective, good-faith attempt at full disclosure. Guidelines sec. 15151. In reviewing an EIR for adequacy, courts will make sure that all required contents are included. Courts will assess whether the Lead Agency applied an objective, good-faith effort toward full disclosure. Disagreement among experts regarding conclusions in the EIR is acceptable, and perfection is not required. Also, exhaustive treatment of issues is not required in an EIR. Minor technical defects identified in an EIR are not necessarily fatal. Guidelines sec. 15151.

The scope of judicial review does not extend to the correctness of an EIR's conclusions, but only to the EIR's sufficiency as an informative document for decision makers and the public. Guidelines sec. 15003(i). *See* chapter 7 for more information regarding CEQA litigation.

Chapter 6

Projects Subject to CEQA and NEPA

Background and Implementation of NEPA

The National Environmental Policy Act was signed into law on January 1, 1970 in response to an overwhelming national sentiment that federal agencies should take a lead in providing greater protection for the environment. NEPA established an environmental review process that is separate from but similar to that under CEQA. However, NEPA applies only to federal agencies. For further information on NEPA, *see Mastering NEPA: A Step-by-Step Approach,* published by Solano Press Books. Additional NEPA references are listed in Suggested Reading, page 407.

Under NEPA, all federal agencies are authorized and directed, to the fullest extent possible, to carry out their regulations, policies, and programs in accordance with NEPA's policies of environmental protection. 42 U.S.C. 4332; 40 C.F.R. 1500.2. To ensure the policies are achieved, NEPA requires that every federal agency prepare an EIS for proposed legislation or other major federal actions significantly affecting the quality of the human environment. 42 U.S.C. 4332; 40 C.F.R. 1501.

NEPA requires that every federal agency prepare an EIS for proposed legislation or other major federal actions significantly affecting the quality of the human environment.

As presented in NEPA and the Council on Environmental Quality's (Council's) NEPA Regulations [40 C.F.R. secs. 1500 et seq.], the overall environmental review process under NEPA, parallel to CEQA (*see* Figure 6-1), involves three key phases:

- Review of a project for categorical exclusions or other exemptions

- Preparation on an Environmental Assessment to determine whether there is a possibility of significant environmental effects

- Preparation of an EIS or Finding of No Significant Impact (FONSI)

FONSI = Finding of No Significant Impact

The similarities and differences between NEPA and CEQA are discussed on page 127 under the heading "Similarities and Differences between CEQA and NEPA."

Figure 6-1
CEQA and NEPA:
Parallel Processes

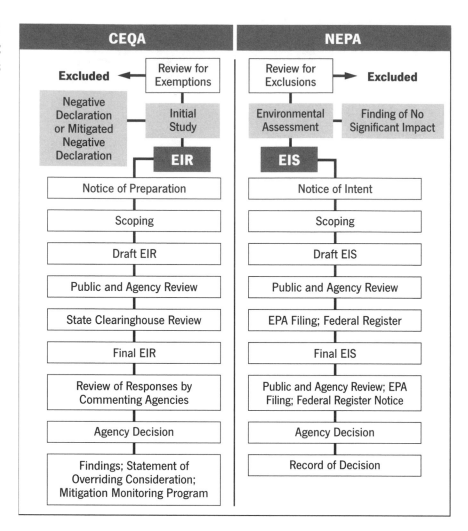

NEPA-Related Information on the Internet

Two sites of particular interest are described below.

Council on Environmental Quality–NEPANET

The Council on Environmental Quality is responsible for adopting NEPA regulations and providing advice and assistance to federal agencies on NEPA compliance.

The Council on Environmental Quality, within the Executive Office of the President, is responsible for the implementation of NEPA, including adopting NEPA regulations and providing advice and assistance to federal agencies on NEPA compliance. The Council's home page includes "NEPANET," a database of NEPA-related resources on the law, regulations, publications issued by the Council, and links to other federal agency data sources. Users may reach NEPANET at: http:ceq.eh.doe.gov/nepa/nepanet/html.

U.S. Environmental Protection Agency– Office of Federal Activities

OFA = Office of Federal Activities

The Environmental Protection Agency's Office of Federal Activities (OFA) is responsible for review and comment on all Environmental Impact Statements. OFA's home page provides a broad variety of NEPA-related information, including a complete listing of EISs submitted to EPA for review and EPA's comments on those documents. Users may reach the OFA home page at: http:/es.inel.gov/oeca/ofa/index/html.

OFA's home page includes a complete listing of EISs submitted to EPA for review and EPA's comments on those documents.

CEQA Projects Subject to NEPA

The CEQA Guidelines contain a separate section for projects that are also subject to NEPA. A project that is subject to CEQA will also be subject to NEPA when it is jointly carried out by a federal agency; requires a federal discretionary permit, entitlement, authorization, or federal funding; or occurs on federal land.

Joint Environmental Reviews

When a project is subject to both CEQA and NEPA, state and local agencies are encouraged to cooperate with federal agencies, to the fullest extent possible, through such measures as joint planning, research, hearings, and preparation of environmental documents. Guidelines sec. 15226.

If a Lead Agency finds that an EIS or FONSI for a project would not be prepared by the federal agency by the time the Lead Agency would need to consider an EIR or Negative Declaration, the Lead Agency should try to prepare a combined EIR–EIS or Negative Declaration–FONSI. To avoid the need for the federal agency to prepare a separate document for the same project, the Lead Agency must involve the federal agency in the preparation of the joint document. This involvement is necessary because federal law generally prohibits a federal agency from using an EIR prepared by a state agency unless the federal agency was involved in the preparation of the document.

A Project Is Subject to NEPA If It:

- Is jointly carried out by a federal agency
- Requires a federal permit, entitlement, or authorization
- Requires federal funding
- Will occur on federal land

Federal law generally prohibits a federal agency from using an EIR prepared by a state agency unless the federal agency was involved in the preparation of the document.

Use of NEPA Documents to Satisfy CEQA

In General. State and local agencies are encouraged to use NEPA documents to replace CEQA documents if the NEPA process is proceeding faster than the CEQA process and the NEPA document complies with CEQA. Guidelines sec. 15221. The state or local agency may use the NEPA document without recirculation if the NEPA document is circulated as broadly as required by CEQA, and if the agency gives notice that it intends to use the NEPA document. Guidelines sec. 15225.

Special Rules for Military Bases. For approvals related to a local military base reuse plan (prepared as a general plan or amendment, specific plan, redevelopment plan, or other plan), the Lead Agency is authorized to use the EIS on the military base closure as the basis for preparing an EIR under CEQA. Pub. Res. Code sec. 21083.81; Guidelines sec. 15229. *See* OPR's CEQA Technical Advice Series report, *CEQA, NEPA, and Base Closure: Recipes for Streamlining Environmental Review* (March 1996), Appendix 9.

If an EIS has been prepared and filed pursuant to NEPA on the closure and reuse of a military base and the Lead Agency decides that the EIS does not fully meet the requirements of CEQA or has not been circulated for public review as state and local law require, the Lead Agency responsible for

For approvals related to a local military base reuse plan, the Lead Agency is authorized to use the EIS on the military base closure as the basis for preparing an EIR under CEQA.

Closure of military bases such as Hamilton Army Airfield has heightened the need to integrate NEPA and CEQA compliance.

The Lead Agency must state the specific economic or social reasons that support selection of the baseline physical conditions.

preparation of an EIR for a reuse plan for the same base should prepare and circulate a NOP. The notice must include a description of the reuse plan, a copy of the EIS, an address to which to send comments, and the deadline for submitting comments. The notice must state that the Lead Agency intends to utilize the EIS as a Draft EIR and requests comments on whether the EIS provides adequate information to serve as a Draft EIR and what specific additional information, if any, is necessary. Upon the close of the comment period, the Lead Agency may proceed with preparation and circulation for comment of the Draft EIR for the reuse plan. To the greatest extent feasible, the Lead Agency must avoid duplication and utilize the EIS or information in the EIS as all or part of the Draft EIR. Guidelines sec. 15225(b).

The EIR for a plan for reuse of a military base should base its significance determination on the physical conditions that were present at the time the federal decision for the closure or realignment of the base or reservation became final. Impacts that do not exceed the baseline physical conditions shall not be considered significant. The Lead Agency must consult with Responsible and Trustee Agencies prior to the public hearing as to the application of their regulatory authority and permitting standards to the proposed baseline physical conditions, the proposed reuse plan, and specific, planned future nonmilitary land uses of the base or reservation. These agencies have 30 days, prior to the public hearing, to review the proposed baseline physical conditions and the proposed reuse plan and to submit comments to the Lead Agency.

The Lead Agency must hold a public hearing to discuss the federal EIS prepared for, or being prepared for, the closure or realignment of the military base or reservation. Before the close of the hearing, the Lead Agency must specify the baseline physical conditions that it intends to adopt for the reuse plan EIR and specify particular physical conditions, if any, that it will examine in greater detail than were examined in the EIS. In addition, the Lead Agency must state specifically how it intends to integrate its discussion of the baseline physical conditions in the EIR with the reuse planning process, taking into account the adopted environmental standards of the community, including but not limited to, the adopted general plan, specific plan, or redevelopment plan, and including other applicable provisions of adopted congestion management plans, habitat conservation plans, air quality management plans, integrated waste management plans, and county hazardous waste management plans. The Lead Agency must also state the specific economic or social reasons, including but not limited to, new job creation, opportunities for employment of skilled workers, availability of low- and moderate-income housing, and economic continuity that support selection of the baseline physical conditions.

An EIR prepared for military base reuse should identify any adopted baseline physical conditions in the environmental setting section. The No-Project Alternative analyzed in the EIR must discuss the conditions on the base as they exist at the time of preparation, as well as what could be reasonably expected to occur in the foreseeable future if the reuse plan were not approved, based on current plans and consistent with available infrastructure and services.

Joint Environmental Documents

State and local agencies are encouraged to prepare a joint EIR/EIS or Negative Declaration/FONSI (the NEPA equivalent to a Negative Declaration). Guidelines sec. 15222. The two laws establish essentially similar processes. *See* Figure 6-1. The Lead Agency is required to approve the project for which a joint EIR/EIS was prepared within 90 days after the joint document was completed and adopted. Govt. Code sec. 65951.

In practice, there are several recommendations that may facilitate state and local agency interaction with federal Lead Agencies when preparing joint CEQA/NEPA documents. First, a written memorandum of understanding (MOU) between the two Lead Agencies should spell out the roles and responsibilities of each agency, expected schedule, other expectations regarding the preparation of the environmental document (including assumptions regarding impact analysis), and dispute resolution procedures. Second, because NEPA and CEQA are somewhat different with regard to procedural and content requirements (*see* Figure 6-2), the agencies should agree at the outset to apply whichever requirements are more stringent. Third, the scope and content of the EIR/EIS, and the respective responsibilities for reviewing interim drafts, should be clearly spelled out.

MOU = Memorandum of Understanding

Using CEQA Documents to Satisfy NEPA

There is no express provision in NEPA or the Council's NEPA Regulations that authorizes a federal agency to use a CEQA document to comply with NEPA. A narrow exception exists allowing a federal agency only to use an EIR to satisfy NEPA if a state agency with statewide jurisdiction prepares the EIR for a federal grant project and the federal agency actively participates in the environmental review process. 40 C.F.R. 1506.2. This provision would typically apply only to Caltrans in the federal-aid highway program.

In practice federal agencies typically utilize CEQA documents as important background information to prepare NEPA documents. To ensure that the procedural requirements of NEPA are met, the federal agency, in using a CEQA document for NEPA compliance, should make sure the record shows that there was independent review of the CEQA document and that the federal agency is preparing its own NEPA document based on the CEQA document (and not that the NEPA document is replaced by the CEQA document).

No express provision in NEPA or the Council on Environmental Quality's NEPA Regulations authorizes a federal agency to use a CEQA document to comply with NEPA.

Similarities and Differences between CEQA and NEPA

In general, CEQA and NEPA contain many similar terms and concepts (*see* Figure 6-3); yet, despite their similarities, they also have several important differences. *See* Figure 6-2. Both laws require the preparation of a detailed environmental study to evaluate the environmental effects of proposed governmental activities. Both laws establish multi-step procedures for evaluating projects and preparing environmental impact documents. Generally, the differences between CEQA and NEPA may be classified into categories of terminology, procedures, environmental document content, and substantive mandates to protect the environment.

Both laws require the preparation of a detailed environmental study to evaluate the environmental effects of proposed governmental activities.

Difference	Subject Area	CEQA	NEPA
Substantive Differences	Agency Decision on Project	Agencies must mitigate project impacts when feasible	Agencies need not mitigate project impacts, even if feasible, unless required by agency regulations
Procedural Differences	Public Notice and Review	Public Notice required for Negative Declarations	Public Notice not always required for FONSIs
		Public Notice required for Draft EIRs	Notice in Federal Register required for Draft EIS
		Public Notice and review not required for Final EIRs but Commenting Agencies must receive responses prior to the Final EIR	Notice in Federal Register and 30-day review required for Final EIS
	Time Limits	Non-agency projects subject to the Permit Streamlining Act	No time limits for preparation of environmental documents
	Agency Decision to Prepare EIR or EIS	Agencies must prepare if "fair argument" can be made that project may have significant impact	Agencies must prepare only if there is substantial evidence that project may have significant impact
	Statutes of Limitation	CEQA provides short statute of limitation for legal challenges	NEPA contains no specific statute of limitation
Document Content Differences	Decision Document	"Findings" must explain whether each impact has been mitigated and if each has not, why	"Record of Decision" need only explain why the decision was made
	Alternatives Analysis	EIR must compare alternatives, but may evaluate them in less detail than the proposed project	EIS must treat alternatives in relatively similar level of detail

**Figure 6-2
Major Differences
between CEQA and NEPA**

The term and concept of "Lead Agency" are the same under NEPA and CEQA.

Terminology

Proposal for Action. NEPA defines a federal undertaking as a "proposal" for "action" [42 U.S.C. sec. 4332(2)(C)], whereas CEQA uses the term "project" [Pub. Res. Code sec. 21080]. As with CEQA's definition of "project," an "action" under NEPA includes policies, rules, regulations, plans, programs, and specific projects, including private undertakings requiring federal agency permits or regulatory decisions. 40 C.F.R. sec. 1508.18; Guidelines sec. 15378. Continuing or ongoing activities of federal agencies may also be considered actions under NEPA. A proposal for action exists at the stage of planning when a federal agency has a goal and is actively preparing to make a decision furthering that goal. 40 C.F.R. sec. 1508.23.

Lead Agency. The term and concept of "Lead Agency" are the same under NEPA and CEQA. The NEPA regulations define that term to mean the agency having primary responsibility for preparing an EIS. 40 C.F.R. sec. 1508.16. The Guidelines define "Lead Agency" as the agency carrying out the project or having the greatest responsibility for supervising or approving a project.

Figure 6-3
Similarities in Terminology between CEQA and NEPA

CEQA Term	Correlated NEPA Term
Lead Agency	Lead Agency
Responsible Agency	Cooperating Agency
Categorical Exemption	Categorical Exclusion
Initial Study	Environmental Assessment
Negative Declaration	Finding of No Significant Impact
Environmental Impact Report	Environmental Impact Statement
Notice of Preparation	Notice of Intent
Findings	Record of Decision

Guidelines sec. 15051. Although the Guidelines contain a more elaborate definition of "Lead Agency," the concept is essentially the same.

Both NEPA and CEQA provide similar procedures and criteria for resolving Lead Agency disputes. Lead Agency disputes are submitted to the Council under NEPA and to OPR under CEQA. 40 C.F.R. sec. 1501.5(e); Guidelines secs. 16000–16041.

Cooperating Agency. Under NEPA, agencies other than the Lead Agency that are involved in EIS preparation are referred to as "Cooperating Agencies." The concept of a Cooperating Agency under NEPA is broader than that of a "Responsible Agency" under CEQA. A NEPA Cooperating Agency is any federal agency other than the Lead Agency with jurisdiction over the project by law, or with special expertise regarding the impacts of the action. 40 C.F.R. sec. 1508.5. Under CEQA, Responsible Agencies are only those state or local agencies that issue permits or provide funding for the project. Guidelines sec. 15381. Under NEPA, a Cooperating Agency is expected to participate in the preparation of the EIS when requested to do so by a Lead Agency, whereas under CEQA, a Responsible Agency generally serves in a more passive commenting role. 40 C.F.R. sec. 1501.6; Guidelines sec. 15096.

Under NEPA a Cooperating Agency is any federal agency other than the Lead Agency with jurisdiction over the project by law, or with special expertise regarding the impacts of the action.

Categorical Exclusion. A "categorical exclusion" is NEPA's equivalent to a categorical exemption under CEQA. Guidelines sec. 15354. Each federal agency, in its NEPA-implementing regulations, has identified certain types of proposed federal actions that it has determined would not have a significant effect on the environment. These actions are categorically excluded from the requirement to prepare further NEPA environmental documentation. A categorical exclusion will not apply if any "extraordinary circumstances" (as opposed to CEQA's "exceptions" designated by the federal agency) exist. 40 C.F.R. sec. 1508.4.

A categorical exclusion is NEPA's equivalent to a categorical exemption under CEQA.

Practitioners should be aware that the range of federal actions that have been categorically excluded is very broad. Unlike the Guidelines, which list 32 standard categories of exemptions to which all state and local agencies must adhere [Guidelines secs. 15300–15332], each federal agency has identified its own list of categorical exclusions that differ substantially from agency to agency. Thus, a careful reading of a particular agency's NEPA regulations is necessary to determine which proposed actions are categorically excluded.

An Environmental Assessment is the NEPA analog to CEQA's Initial Study.

Environmental Assessment. An "Environmental Assessment" is the NEPA analog to an Initial Study under CEQA. Guidelines sec. 15063. After determining that a proposed action is not categorically excluded, a federal agency generally prepares an Environmental Assessment. Like a CEQA Initial Study, an Environmental Assessment has several purposes. It helps the federal agency determine whether an EIS is required by briefly evaluating whether a proposed action may have significant environmental effects. If an agency decides that an EIS is not required, the Environmental Assessment provides the documentation to support a FONSI (discussed below). When an agency decides an EIS must be prepared, the Environmental Assessment helps determine the scope and content of the EIS. An Environmental Assessment is a formally recognized part of the NEPA process and should be distinguished from informal studies that are often referred to as environmental assessments. 40 C.F.R. secs. 1501.4(b), 1508.9.

The required contents of an Environmental Assessment are similar to those of an Initial Study. One difference, however, is that an Environmental Assessment must discuss alternatives to a proposed action, whereas an Initial Study is not required to discuss alternatives. *See below* for differences in legal standards for determining whether to prepare an EIS as opposed to an EIR. 40 C.F.R. sec. 1508.9(b); Guidelines sec. 15063(d).

A FONSI is NEPA's equivalent to CEQA's Negative Declaration. Like a Negative Declaration, which must be supported by an Initial Study, a FONSI must be supported by an Environmental Assessment.

Finding of No Significant Impact. A FONSI is NEPA's equivalent to CEQA's Negative Declaration. Guidelines secs. 15070–15075. A FONSI is a public document that briefly describes why an action that is otherwise not excluded from NEPA will not have any significant environmental effect and why the action will not require an EIS. A federal agency preparing an Environmental Assessment must prepare a FONSI if it decides not to prepare an EIS. 40 C.F.R. secs. 1501.4(e), 1508.13. Like a Negative Declaration, which must be supported by an Initial Study [Guidelines sec. 15071(d)], a FONSI must be supported by an Environmental Assessment. 40 C.F.R. sec. 1508.13.

A federal agency may prepare a "mitigated FONSI" when an Environmental Assessment indicates that environmental effects of a proposed action are potentially significant but that, with mitigation, they may be reduced or avoided. Unlike CEQA's Mitigated Negative Declaration, however, a mitigated FONSI has no official status or recognition in the Council's NEPA Regulations, and, until recently, the Council has discouraged their preparation. In practice, federal agencies go through the process of a mitigated FONSI, calling the final document a FONSI (that includes mitigation commitments).

Both an EIR and an EIS are disclosure documents designed to ensure that environmental factors are taken into consideration in government decision making.

Environmental Impact Statement. An EIS prepared under NEPA is essentially the same as an EIR prepared under CEQA. Both are disclosure documents designed to ensure that the environmental factors are taken into consideration in government decision making. Like CEQA, NEPA requires a federal Lead Agency to prepare an EIS in draft and final stages. 40 C.F.R. secs. 1502.9, 1508.11; Guidelines secs. 15084–15089. For a discussion of the differences in content between an EIS and EIR, *see* Environmental Document Content, page 134.

Notice of Intent. A Notice of Intent serves the same functional purpose as an NOP under CEQA [Guidelines sec. 15082]; the Notice of Intent is the first formal step in EIS preparation. As soon as practical after its decision to prepare an EIS but before the scoping process begins, a federal Lead Agency must publish a Notice of Intent in the Federal Register. A Notice of Intent must briefly describe the proposed federal action and alternatives, the agency's scoping process and the opportunity to participate in scoping meetings, and the name and address of persons to contact within the Lead Agency regarding the EIS. 40 C.F.R. secs. 1501.7, 1508.22.

Record of Decision. A Record of Decision is analogous to the findings and Statements of Overriding Considerations under CEQA. Guidelines secs. 15091, 15093. The Record of Decision is a written record explaining why the federal agency has taken a particular course of action. It must include:

Analogous to CEQA's findings and Statement of Overriding Considerations, NEPA's Record of Decision is a written record explaining why a federal agency has taken a particular course of action.

- A statement explaining the decision
- An explanation of other alternatives that were considered and rejected
- A description of social, economic, and environmental factors considered by the agency in making its decision
- A summary of any mitigation measures that were adopted and an explanation for any that were not adopted
- A monitoring and enforcement program for any adopted mitigation measures

40 C.F.R. sec. 1505.2

Unlike findings under CEQA, NEPA does not require that a Record of Decision expressly find each unadopted mitigation measure to be infeasible. *See* Guidelines sec. 15091(a)(3).

Procedures

Role of Agency NEPA Regulations. In California, CEQA and the Guidelines set forth universal requirements to which all state and local agencies must adhere. Although each state and local agency is required to adopt its own CEQA procedures that are consistent with the Guidelines [sec. 15022], in practice, most of these procedures vary little from agency to agency.

Under NEPA, the Council has adopted regulations that, like CEQA, require federal agencies to adopt their own regulations tailored to their unique situations. 40 C.F.R. sec. 1507.3(a). However, unlike CEQA, the Council's regulations are very general and the NEPA regulations of each federal agency often contain significant differences in practice and interpretation from agency to agency. Thus, practitioners must become familiar not only with the Council's NEPA Regulations, but also with those NEPA regulations adopted by any particular agency with which they deal. Some of the more common federal agency NEPA regulations that may be encountered by California practitioners are those of the U.S. Army Corps of Engineers [33 C.F.R. secs. 230.1–230.26]; U.S. Department of Agriculture [7 C.F.R. secs. 1(b)(1)–(b)(4)]; U.S. Environmental Protection Agency [40 C.F.R. secs. 6.100–6.1007]; and the Federal Highway Administration [23 C.F.R. secs. 771.101–771.137]. *See* Coordinated Environmental Review Requirements, page 139.

Unlike CEQA, the NEPA regulations of each federal agency often contain significant differences in practice and interpretation from agency to agency.

Additionally, some federal agencies have prepared detailed procedural manuals or handbooks for NEPA compliance.

Public Review of FONSIs. CEQA requires all state and local agencies to adhere to the same public notice and review requirements for Negative Declarations; the content of such notices and time periods for review (minimum 20 days) are standardized. Pub. Res. Code sec. 21091(b). Although the NEPA Regulations require federal agencies to provide notice of the availability of FONSIs, practice concerning public review of FONSIs differs substantially from agency to agency; there are no standard requirements for the content of public notices, and only certain actions require a minimum 30-day public review. Specifically, NEPA requires a FONSI to be made available for a 30-day period if the proposal is unusual or precedent setting, or is similar to one normally requiring an EIS. Additionally, the Council advises agencies to make a FONSI available for 30 days in borderline situations in which there is a reasonable argument that an EIS should have been prepared, if the proposal is controversial, or if the proposal is located in a floodplain or wetland. In practice, however, most federal agencies provide a public review period for most FONSIs. *See* Council on Environmental Quality, "Memorandum: Forty Most Asked Questions Concerning CEQ's NEPA Regulations," 46 Fed. Reg. 18026 [March 23, 1981].

Under NEPA, there are no standard requirements for the content of public notices, and only certain actions require a minimum 30-day public review.

CEQ = Council on Environmental Quality

Scoping. Although scoping is used under both NEPA and CEQA to determine the focus and content of an EIS or EIR, it is a more formalized process under NEPA. NEPA requires a formal scoping process for each EIS. 40 C.F.R. secs. 1501.7(a), (b). Additionally, the Council has issued formal guidance to assist federal agencies in the scoping process. Council on Environmental Quality, "Memorandum: Scoping Guidance" (April 30, 1981). Under CEQA, scoping is a permissive process that differs considerably from agency to agency.

Public Notice and Review Requirements for an EIS. After preparing a Draft EIS, a federal Lead Agency must request comments from other federal agencies, project applicants, Native American tribes, state and local agencies, and the general public. 40 C.F.R. sec. 1503.1(a). As with FONSIs, the specific requirements for giving public notice of the availability of Draft EISs differ considerably from agency to agency; each federal agency's regulations must be consulted to determine the specifics. However, a requirement that federal agencies send their EISs for filing and review to EPA does exist. 42 U.S.C. sec. 7609. In addition to conducting reviews of EISs, EPA files a notice of the availability of the EIS in the Federal Register. 40 C.F.R. sec. 1506.10(a).

A federal agency preparing an EIS in California must also send the draft document to OPR for state agency review.

The requirement for a federal Lead Agency to obtain the comments of other federal agencies is similar to that under CEQA. A federal agency preparing an EIS in California must also send the draft document to OPR for state agency review. OPR serves as the state's single point of contact for review of NEPA documents under Presidential Executive Order 12372 (July 14, 1982) and the Guidelines [sec. 15205(b)(4)].

EPA Review of Draft EISs. EPA's Office of Federal Activities [40 C.F.R. sec. 1.37(a)] reviews and rates all EISs for adequacy and to determine whether the proposed action is environmentally damaging.

Under CEQA, OPR distributes EIRs to other agencies for review, but there is no formal system for OPR review and rating of EIRs. Because of inadequate staffing during the past decade, there has been little active review of Draft EIRs by OPR.

Notice Requirements for a Final EIS. CEQA does not require public notice and review of a Final EIR, although some agencies provide such notice. The only provision for review of a Final EIR is the new law that requires a Lead Agency to send other agencies any responses to their comments prior to certifying an EIR. Pub. Res. Code sec. 21092.5. Under NEPA, however, a Final EIS must be given similar public review, typically for 30 days, and notice as the Draft EIS, including filing with EPA and notification in the Federal Register. 40 C.F.R. secs. 1502.19, 1506.10(a).

Time Limits. For environmental documents prepared on "development projects," CEQA and the Permit Streamlining Act [Govt. Code secs. 65920–65963.1] impose mandatory time limits for completing EIRs or Negative Declarations and approving projects. Govt. Code sec. 65950; Guidelines secs. 15107, 15108. NEPA contains no such universal standardized time limits.

CEQA and the Permit Streamlining Act impose mandatory time limits for completing EIRs or Negative Declarations and approving projects. NEPA contains no such universal standardized time limits.

Although the NEPA Regulations contain minimum review periods for the Federal Register notice of draft EISs (45 days) and final EISs (30 days), they do not require completion of the entire EIS preparation process within specified periods. 40 C.F.R. sec. 1506.10. There is a provision allowing time limits to be established for preparing an EIS [40 C.F.R. sec. 1501.8]; however, in practice, few time limits are established.

Statutes of Limitation. CEQA imposes very short limitation periods for initiating litigation challenging agency action: 30 days if a Notice of Determination is filed, 180 days if no Notice of Determination is filed, and 35 days if a Notice of Exemption is filed. Pub. Res. Code sec. 21167. NEPA, on the other hand, has no statute of limitations. Actions challenging federal agencies under NEPA are subject only to the common law equitable defense of "laches" under which excessive delays in filing may result in dismissal at the discretion of the court. Because of the uncertainty of the laches defense, federal agencies appear to be subject to longer periods of potential legal vulnerability under NEPA than state or local agencies under CEQA.

Actions challenging federal agencies under NEPA are subject only to the common law equitable defense of "laches" under which excessive delays in filing may result in dismissal at the discretion of the court.

Legal Standard for Determining Whether to Prepare an EIS. Under CEQA, a Lead Agency must prepare an EIR if it is presented with a fair argument, based on substantial evidence, that a project may have a significant effect on the environment. Guidelines sec. 15064(g). A significant effect on the environment is defined as a "substantial or potentially substantial adverse change in any of the physical conditions in the area affected by the project." Guidelines sec. 15382.

Under NEPA, a federal agency must prepare an EIS for any "proposals for legislation and other major federal actions significantly affecting the quality of the human environment." 42 U.S.C. sec. 4332(2)(C). "Significantly" is defined with regard to the context and the intensity of the impact. 40 C.F.R. sec. 1508.27.

Although the relevant CEQA and NEPA definitions are similar, the courts have applied very different standards of review to agency determinations of significance. Under CEQA, the "fair argument" standard of review has been interpreted by the California courts as a very low threshold for EIR preparation; by this standard, virtually any credible information showing potentially significant impacts can support a fair argument that significant impacts may occur.

Under NEPA, however, the federal courts generally rely on an "arbitrary and capricious" standard when reviewing agency decisions not to prepare an EIS. This standard is far more deferential to agency decisions. Thus, challenging a federal agency's decision that impacts are not significant is considerably more difficult as long as the agency has not acted arbitrarily.

These different legal standards are part of the reason that more EIRs are prepared by state and local agencies in California each year than the total number of EISs prepared by federal agencies nationwide. The difference in the legal standard is also part of the reason a project may have an EIR prepared for CEQA compliance and a FONSI for NEPA compliance.

Environmental Document Content

In general, an EIS prepared under NEPA differs very little from an EIR prepared under CEQA. Both documents must include a description of the proposed activity, the environmental setting, an analysis of significant environmental impacts (direct, indirect, and cumulative), and a discussion of mitigation measures to reduce or avoid those impacts. 40 C.F.R. secs. 1502.11–1502.25; Guidelines secs. 15120–15132. "Mitigation" is defined exactly the same under NEPA and CEQA. 40 C.F.R. sec. 1508.20; Guidelines sec. 15370.

The technical impact analysis of topical issues (e.g., biology and air quality) generally does not differ between NEPA and CEQA because neither the law nor its implementing regulations prescribe any particular type or level of analysis. Rather, the practices of each federal agency and the facts and circumstances of each proposed action determine the scope and content of the documents.

There are, however, several key differences in document content between the two laws.

Analysis of Alternatives. The most important difference in document content between an EIS and an EIR is the treatment of alternatives. Although both NEPA and CEQA require that the documents evaluate a "reasonable range" of alternatives, NEPA requires that an EIS rigorously evaluate and compare all reasonable alternatives to provide a clear basis for choice of options. Although no particular level of treatment is required, the degree of analysis devoted to each alternative must be substantially similar to that devoted to the proposed action. 40 C.F.R. sec. 1502.14. This standard differs from CEQA, which does not require substantially equal treatment of alternatives. Under CEQA, the comparative merits of the alternatives must be evaluated; however, such evaluation may be considerably less detailed than the evaluation of the proposed project. Guidelines sec. 15126.6(d).

Incomplete or Unavailable Information. A second difference between an EIS and an EIR is the treatment given to incomplete or unavailable information. Before 1986, the NEPA Regulations required federal agencies confronted with incomplete or unavailable information to conduct a "worst-case analysis." In 1986, the Council revoked the worst-case analysis requirement because it often resulted in expensive and unreasonable technical studies and analyses. Under the new regulations, when information is incomplete or unavailable, it must be obtained if the costs are not exorbitant. If the costs are exorbitant, the agency must state that the information is incomplete or unavailable, state the relevance of the information to evaluating reasonably foreseeable impacts, summarize the credible scientific evidence that exists about the topic, and evaluate the impacts based on scientifically accepted methods. 40 C.F.R. sec. 1502.22.

Socioeconomic impacts associated with development are treated somewhat differently between CEQA and NEPA.

Despite the repeal of the worst-case analysis requirement, NEPA's requirement for evaluating unknown or speculative impacts is still greater than CEQA's. Under CEQA, drafting an EIR generally involves some degree of forecasting. Although forecasting the unforeseeable is not possible, an agency must use its best efforts to discover and disclose all it reasonably can about an issue. Guidelines sec. 15144. However, if after thorough investigation, a Lead Agency finds that a particular impact is too speculative for evaluation, the agency should note its conclusion and terminate discussion of the impact. Guidelines sec. 15145. In practice, this standard enables a state or local agency to cut off discussion of speculative impacts more easily than a federal agency can under NEPA.

Socioeconomic Impacts. NEPA and CEQA differ somewhat with regard to the requirement to evaluate social and economic impacts. Under NEPA, the definition of "human environment" states that economic or social effects are not intended, by themselves, to require preparation of an EIS. However, when an EIS is prepared, the economic and social effects must be discussed if they are interrelated to the natural or physical environmental effects. 40 C.F.R. sec. 1508.14. The definition of the term "effects" also includes economic and social factors. 40 C.F.R. sec. 1508.8.

Under CEQA, economic and social changes resulting from a project are not treated as significant effects on the environment. Guidelines sec. 15064(f). Effects analyzed in an EIR must be related to a physical change in the environment. Guidelines sec. 15358(b). However, economic or social changes may be used to determine that a physical change is significant. Additionally, if a physical change in the environment will result in economic and social changes, which in turn have secondary physical effects, those effects may be evaluated in an EIR. Guidelines sec. 15064(f).

NEPA's requirement to consider socioeconomic impacts is slightly broader than CEQA's; in practice federal agencies generally include more economic and social information in EISs than state or local agencies include in EIRs.

Integration of NEPA with Other Federal Environmental Laws. One of the most complex aspects of EIS preparation is the requirement that federal agencies integrate NEPA with other federal environmental review and consultation requirements. Generally, proposed federal actions that trigger review under NEPA also require compliance with a variety of other federal environmental laws. Each federal agency has an obligation to identify and list in the EIS

One of the most complex aspects of EIS preparation is the requirement that federal agencies integrate NEPA with other federal environmental review and consultation requirements.

Requirement	Scoping Process	Draft Document	Final Document	Decision Making
NEPA	Notice of Intent	Draft EIS	Final EIS	Lead Agency decision and Record of Decision
CEQA	Notice of Preparation	Draft EIR	Final EIR	Lead Agency decision and Notice of Decision
Endangered Species Act, section 7	Request species list	Biological Assessment	Biological Opinion	
Clean Water Act, section 404 (Individual Permit)	Define objectives; screen alternatives; submit permit application	Draft sec. 404(b)(1) analysis	Final sec. 404(b)(1) analysis	Corps of Engineers issues sec. 404 permit (after sec. 401 certification or waiver)
National Historic Preservation Act, section 106	Identify and evaluate historic and archaeological properties	Draft effects assessment	Memorandum of Agreement	
Clean Air Act Conformity (non-transportation project)	Determine whether the conformity requirement applies	Preliminary analysis (comparison to de minimus levels)	Detailed modeling analysis if necessary	Federal agency issues conformity determination
Public involvement	Scoping meetings	Public comment; Public hearing	Public comment	Public hearing

**Figure 6-4
Approach to Integrating
Environmental Review
Requirements**

—

NEPA review should be integrated with Clean Water Act Section 404 compliance for projects requiring wetlands fill.

all other federal environmental requirements that may be applicable to the proposed action. Additionally, NEPA requires that, to the fullest extent possible, agencies integrate the NEPA process with the review processes established by these other laws. 40 C.F.R. sec. 1502.25(a).

Each proposed federal action will trigger a different set of related environmental requirements, depending on the type of activity being proposed and its location (*see* Figures 6-4 and 6-5). For example, the replacement of a historic bridge across a navigable river could trigger the need for U.S. Army Corps of Engineers permits under Section 404 of the Clean Water Act [33 U.S.C. sec. 1344], consultation with the U.S. Fish and Wildlife Service under Section 7 of the federal Endangered Species Act [16 U.S.C. sec. 1536], and review of historic resources under Section 106 of the National Historic Preservation Act [16 U.S.C. sec. 470(f)]. Under this example, the review, consultation, evaluation, and documentation requirements of these other laws should be completed during EIS preparation, and the results should be incorporated into the EIS. Such integration of environmental review requirements is designed to avoid duplication and delay.

CEQA requires that the EIR's project description contain a list of related environmental reviews and consultations required by federal, state, or local laws, regulations, or policies. To the fullest extent possible, the Lead Agency must integrate CEQA review with these related environmental review and consultation requirements. Guidelines sec. 15124(d). Although similar integration of state and local environmental review is encouraged and often occurs under CEQA, CEQA's integration mandate is much weaker than NEPA's and is generally easier to handle because fewer agencies are involved. When a joint EIS/EIR is prepared, the complexities of integration are compounded.

Coordinated Environmental Review Requirements

A goal of "one project, one document" should be adopted to minimize the need for costly duplicative environmental reviews by many agencies. Key federal agency environmental review requirements that often are relevant include the following:

- U.S. Fish and Wildlife Service: Section 7 consultation or Section 10 Incidental Take Permit and Habitat Conservation Plan pursuant to the federal Endangered Species Act. 16 U.S.C. 1536.
- U.S. Army Corps of Engineers: Section 404 permit including section 404(b)(1) alternatives analysis, for discharges of dredged or fill material into wetlands and waters of the United States pursuant to the federal Clean Water Act. 33 U.S.C. 1344.
- Advisory Council on Historic Preservation and State Historic Preservation Office: Section 106 consultation pursuant to the National Historic Preservation Act. 16 U.S.C. 470.
- U.S. Environmental Protection Agency and State Air Quality Management Districts: conformity analysis pursuant to the federal Clean Air Act. 42 U.S.C. 7401.

Figure 6-4 presents an approach to integrating CEQA and NEPA with the key federal agency environmental review requirements and public involvement. Figure 6-5 presents a comprehensive overview of the federal and state environmental compliance requirements for CEQA/NEPA projects. *See also The California Permit Handbook,* Governor's Office of Planning and Research, 1994.

Substantive Mandates to Protect the Environment

Although NEPA and CEQA contain similar requirements to evaluate impacts and identify mitigation measures, CEQA's statutory mandate to protect the environment is much stronger. Neither law requires that the environment be protected in all cases, but CEQA expressly requires state and local agencies to avoid or mitigate significant environmental impacts whenever feasible. Guidelines secs. 15021, 15091. NEPA, on the other hand, is essentially procedural. It does not require federal agencies preparing an EIS to avoid or mitigate impacts even if mitigation is feasible. *Robertson v. Methow Valley Citizens Council* (1989) 490 U.S. 332. Although a record of decision must generally explain the federal agency's reason for taking a proposed action, it does not require that each rejected mitigation measure be found infeasible. 40 C.F.R. sec. 1505.2.

In practice, NEPA has, however, become more mitigation driven over time. This is because the use of FONSIs, supported by project mitigation is much more the preference for federal agencies' NEPA compliance than EISs. In addition, many federal agencies have, in their own NEPA regulations, added provisions that do require impacts to be mitigated for certain types of projects.

NEPA is essentially procedural, and does not require federal agencies preparing an EIS to avoid or mitigate impacts even if mitigation is feasible.

Figure 6-5. Environmental Review Requirements That May Require Integration

Regulated Activity and Resource	Implementing Agency	Regulatory Authority
Activities affecting species listed as "endangered" and "threatened"	U.S. Fish and Wildlife Service National Marine Fisheries Service	Sections 7 and 10, Endangered Species Act (16 USC 1536, 1538, 1539)
	California Department of Fish and Game	California Endangered Species Act (Fish and Game Code sec. 2081)
Activities affecting general fish and wildlife concerns	U.S. Fish and Wildlife Service National Marine Fisheries Service California Department of Fish and Game	Fish and Wildlife Coordination Act (16 USC 661–666)
Discharge of dredged or fill material into "waters of the United States" (including wetlands) or construction in "navigable waters" or activities within a floodplain	U.S. Army Corps of Engineers	Section 404, Clean Water Act (33 USC 1344) Section 10, Rivers and Harbors Act of 1899 (33 USC 403)
	Federal Lead Agency	Executive Order 11990, Protection of Wetlands Executive Order 11988, Floodplain Management
	California Department of Fish and Game	Streambed Alteration Agreement (Calif. Fish and Game Code secs. 1600–1608)
Activities affecting clean air standards	California Air Quality Management Districts	Section 176, Clean Air Act (42 USC 7506)
Activities affecting cultural resources	Federal Lead Agency (The Advisory Council on Historic Preservation/State Historic Preservation Officer have oversight responsibilities relative to implementation of the National Historic Preservation Act)	National Historic Preservation Act (16 USC 470) American Indian Religious Freedom Act (42 USC 1996) Native American Graves Protection and Repatriation Act (25 USC 3001) Antiquities Act (16 USC 431) Archaeological Resources Protection Act (16 USC 470)
	State Lead Agency	State laws governing treatment of Native American remains: • Calif. Pub. Res. Code secs. 5097.94, 5097.98, 5097.99 • Calif. Health and Safety Code sec. 7050.5
Transportation or other activities affecting recreation areas and parks and historic sites	U.S. Federal Highway Administration	Sec. 4(f), Department of Transportation Act of 1966 (49 USC 303)
Activities affecting agricultural land	Natural Resources Conservation Service	Farmland Protection Policy Act (7 USC 4201) Food Security Act (16 USC 3811)
	California Department of Conservation	California Land Conservation Act of 1965 (Williamson Act) (Govt. Code sec. 51200)
Activities involving hazardous materials or hazardous waste	U.S. Environmental Protection Agency	Comprehensive Environmental Response, Compensation and Liability Act (43 USC 9601) Superfund Amendments and Reauthorization Act (42 USC 9601) Resource Conservation Recovery Act (42 USC 692) Toxic Substances Control Act (15 USC 2601)
(continued next page)	California Environmental Protection Agency	Hazardous Waste Control Law (Calif. Health and Safety Code sec. 25100 et seq.)

Regulated Activity and Resource	Implementing Agency	Regulatory Authority
Activities within the coastal zone	National Oceanic and Atmospheric Administration	Coastal Zone Management Act (16 USC 1451)
	California Coastal Commission	California Coastal Act (Pub. Res. Code sec. 30000 et seq.)
	Local Coastal Commissions	Local Coastal Programs
Activities affecting wild and scenic rivers	U.S. Forest Service U.S. Bureau of Land Management U.S. Fish and Wildlife Service National Park Service	National Wild and Scenic Rivers Act (16 USC 1271)
	California Resources Agency	California Wild and Scenic Rivers Act (Pub. Res. Code sec. 5093.50 et seq.)
Activities affecting minority and low-income populations	Federal Lead Agency	Executive Order 12898, Federal Actions to Address Environmental Justice in Minority Populations and Low-Income Populations
Activities involving water quality	California State Water Resources Control Board/Regional Water Quality Control Boards	Section 401, Clean Water Act (33 USC 1341) Section 402, Clean Water Act (33 USC 1342) Porter-Cologne Water Quality Control Act (Division 7, California Water Code)
Activities affecting water rights	California State Water Resources Control Board	State Water Rights Law (Calif. Water Code sec. 1000 et seq.)
Activities affecting submerged lands and tidelands	California State Lands Commission	California Pub. Res. Code sec. 60001 et seq.
Activities involving dams or reservoirs	California Department of Water Resources, Division of Safety of Dams	California Water Code sec. 6000 et seq.
Activities affecting designated wilderness areas	U.S. Bureau of Land Management	Federal Land Policy and Management Act of 1976 (43 USC 1701)
	U.S. Bureau of Land Management U.S. Forest Service National Park Service	Wilderness Act of 1964 (16 USC 1131)
	California Resources Agency	California Wilderness Act (Pub. Res. Code sec. 5093.30 et seq.)
Mining operations	CEQA Lead Agency	Surface Mining and Reclamation Act of 1975 (Calif. Pub. Res. Code sec. 2710)
	U.S. Bureau of Land Management	General Mining Law of 1872 (30 USC 22) Surface Mining Control and Reclamation Act of 1977 (30 USC 1201)
Activities involving timber harvests on private land	California Department of Forestry and Fire Protection	Z-Berg-Nejedly Forest Practice Act (Calif. Pub. Res. Code sec. 4511 et seq.)
Activities affecting federal forests	U.S. Bureau of Land Management	Federal Land Policy and Management Act of 1976 (43 USC 1701)
	U.S. Forest Service	National Forest Management Act of 1976 (16 USC 1600) Multiple-Use and Sustained-Yield Act of 1960 (16 USC 528) Organic Administration Act of 1897 (16 USC 473)
Management of grazing land	U.S. Bureau of Land Management U.S. Forest Service	Taylor Grazing Act of 1934 (43 USC 315)

Chapter 7

CEQA Litigation

The Role of Litigation

Legal Enforcement

CEQA is generally enforced through litigation brought by private citizens, organizations, and public agencies. Neither OPR nor the California Resources Agency has authority to enforce the requirements of CEQA. For a complete discussion of CEQA and CEQA case law and litigation issues, *see Guide to the California Environmental Quality Act* by Remy, Thomas, Moose, and Manley, published by Solano Press Books.

The courts have played a major role in extending CEQA's applicability and effect and, in general, have interpreted CEQA's statutory provisions liberally. Of particular importance in CEQA's judicial development is the California Supreme Court's statement in *Friends of Mammoth v. Board of Supervisors* that CEQA "is to be interpreted to afford the fullest possible protection to the environment within the reasonable scope of the statutory language." Since the *Friends of Mammoth* case, few CEQA cases have reached the California Supreme Court, but the court has consistently used those opportunities to strengthen the law. Overall, the Supreme Court's interpretation of legislative intent has strongly influenced lower court decisions throughout CEQA's history.

Since the Friends of Mammoth *case, few CEQA cases have reached the California Supreme Court, but the court has consistently used those opportunities to strengthen the law.*

The tendency of the courts to construe CEQA liberally led the Legislature to amend the law in 1993 to provide some limits on court interpretations. The Legislature declared its intent that courts, consistent with generally accepted rules of statutory interpretation, shall not interpret either CEQA or the Guidelines in a manner that imposes procedural or substantive requirements beyond those explicitly stated in CEQA or the Guidelines. Pub. Res. Code sec. 21083.1. Recently, the courts have looked critically at persons or organizations using litigation to advance economic interests.

In 1993, the Legislature declared its intent that courts shall not interpret either CEQA or the Guidelines in a manner that imposes procedural or substantive requirements beyond those explicitly stated in CEQA or the Guidelines.

Effect of Potential for Litigation on CEQA Compliance

ABAG = Association of Bay Area Governments

As stated in chapter 1, Lead Agencies are mindful of the legal and political risks inherent in taking shortcuts when deciding whether to comply with CEQA and which document to prepare to comply with CEQA. Generally, the risk of being threatened to be challenged in court (and potentially losing the challenge) increases as less time is devoted to preparing the CEQA document (*see* Figure 1-3). Although litigation has been a major factor in CEQA "enforcement," a study by the Association of Bay Area Governments (ABAG) indicated that fewer than one percent of project applications subject to CEQA are ever the object of actual litigation. That same study, based on a survey of local planning directors, indicated that the outcome of most CEQA judicial decisions favored the public agency. *See* chapter 8.

Typical Issues and Trends in Litigation

Definition of a Project and Exemptions. The judicial history of CEQA is marked by more than 300 appellate decisions with several noticeable trends. First, beginning with *Friends of Mammoth,* the numerous court decisions have dealt with the applicability of CEQA to various types of activities and have rejected many would-be exemptions.

Failure to Prepare an EIR. A second category of activities, giving rise to considerable litigation, has been use of the "fair argument" standard to reject many Negative Declarations. While the Legislature intended the EIR to become the predominant method for CEQA compliance, in practice the Negative Declaration has become the most frequently prepared form of documentation. In response to the expansive role of Negative Declarations, the courts have taken a hard look at their use and have created a relatively low threshold for mandating the preparation of an EIR. The judicial message has been clear: an agency choosing not to prepare an EIR does so at its own risk, unless the Negative Declaration is clearly justified and documented.

The judicial message has been clear: an agency choosing not to prepare an EIR does so at its own risk, unless the Negative Declaration is clearly justified and documented.

Adequacy of an EIR. A third line of cases has established the parameters of an adequate EIR. In evaluating EIR adequacy, the courts have established a "rule of reason" that is now embodied in the Guidelines. Guidelines sec. 15151. As a result of this standard, challenges to the adequacy of EIRs are difficult to win and have, therefore, become less frequent; however, three notable exceptions have occurred in challenges to inadequate project descriptions, alternatives analysis, and cumulative impacts analysis. Current litigation on the adequacy of EIRs typically focuses on these three areas.

Current litigation on the adequacy of EIRs typically focuses on challenges to inadequate project descriptions, alternatives analysis, and cumulative impacts analysis.

As discussed in chapter 5, the courts do not hold an agency to a standard of absolute perfection, but rather require only that an EIR show that an agency has made an objective, good-faith attempt at full disclosure. Guidelines secs. 15003(i), 15151. Courts generally look to see that all required contents are included and accept that experts may disagree and do not hold the Lead Agency to the same fair argument standard in making impact significance determinations. Courts do not require that the EIR have an exhaustive treatment of the environmental issues. In addition, courts will not hold an EIR as inadequate for minor technical defects. The scope of judicial review does not extend to the correctness of an EIR's conclusions, but only to the EIR's sufficiency as an informative document for decision makers and the public.

Procedural Requirements. The fourth trend in judicial interpretation has been an emphasis on strict procedural compliance. Many times, appellate courts have reversed agency decisions based on procedural violations, declaring them to be prejudicial abuses of discretion. The cases on inadequate findings are but one example.

Overview of the CEQA Litigation Process

The following sections summarize the legal procedures under CEQA and are merely intended to provide a general framework for the nonlawyers involved in CEQA litigation. Attorneys involved in litigation should refer to one of the more detailed references listed in Suggested Reading, page 407.

Statute of Limitations

When deciding whether to pursue litigation through CEQA, parties must be mindful of CEQA's statutes of limitation. CEQA has several unusually short statutes of limitation. The statutes of limitation cut off the right of another party from filing a court action challenging approval of the project after the specified time period has expired. Parties wishing to challenge agency approval of a project under CEQA must seek court review within:

- 35 days after an agency has filed and posted a Notice of Exemption
- 30 days after an agency has filed and posted a Notice of Determination (for either a Negative Declaration or EIR)
- 180 days after an agency decides to carry out or approve a project, or 180 days from commencement of a project for projects without formal decision (when no Notice of Exemption or Notice of Determination has been filed)

Guidelines sec. 15112(c).

If an agency substantially changes a project after completing an EIR without preparing a Subsequent or Supplemental EIR, the 180-day limitation period begins when a petitioner knows or should have known of the project changes.

Procedural Pretrial Requirements

In General

CEQA contains the following special pretrial procedural requirements that must be strictly adhered to in order to pursue a lawsuit under CEQA:

- Petition for writ of mandate
- Notice to the Lead Agency of commencement of action
- Petition for writ of mandate filed with the court
- Notice to the agency to prepare the administrative record
- Service to the defendant agency
- Service of pleadings to the State Attorney General
- Motion requesting a hearing (within 90 days of filing a petition)
- Briefing schedule established by the court (within 30 days of motion requesting hearing)

CEQA's Statutes of Limitations

- 35 days after an agency has filed and posted a Notice of Exemption
- 30 days after an agency has filed and posted a Notice of Determination (for either a Negative Declaration or EIR)
- 180 days after an agency decides to carry out or approve a project, or 180 days from commencement of a project for projects without formal decision (when no Notice of Exemption or Notice of Determination has been filed)

Special Considerations

Petition for a Writ of Mandate. A party seeking to challenge an action under CEQA must file a petition for a writ of mandate. The petition for a writ of mandate is a request that the court issue an order requiring the Lead Agency to do something to remedy the perceived infraction, typically to correct the CEQA violation.

Notice of a Lawsuit. A petitioner must serve the public agency with notice of the commencement of a CEQA lawsuit no later than ten days after filing the CEQA lawsuit and must file proof of service of such notice with the initial pleading. Pub. Res. Code sec. 21167.5. A petitioner must furnish copies of the pleadings to the State Attorney General. Pub. Res. Code sec. 21167.7.

Request for Administrative Record. Also within ten days after filing a CEQA action, the petitioner must request that the agency being challenged prepare a record of administrative proceedings related to the action. Pub. Res. Code sec. 21167.6. The public agency must prepare and certify the administrative record within 60 days. Pub. Res. Code sec. 21167.6(b). If the public agency fails to prepare and certify the record within the prescribed time limit, the petitioner may move for sanctions, and the court may, upon that motion, grant appropriate sanctions. Pub. Res. Code sec. 21167.6(d).

For purposes of judicial review in CEQA litigation, the public agency is required to include in the administrative record the project application and all supplementary materials, all staff reports regarding the proposed project, project public hearing records, all public notices, written comments received regarding the project, proposed decisions and findings on the project, and any other documents relating to the agency decision on the project Pub. Res. Code sec. 21167.6.

Pretrial Settlement. CEQA provides detailed procedures for pretrial settlement, including the requirement of pretrial settlement conferences. As a part of these procedures, a party must file a notice with the court no later than 20 days after filing a petition or complaint setting forth the time and place at which all the parties shall meet to attempt to settle the litigation. The meeting must be scheduled within 45 days of the date of the service of petition or complaint. Pub. Res. Code sec. 21167.8.

Optional Mediation Procedures. Optional mediation procedures are provided to resolve land use disputes, including CEQA challenges. Govt. Code sec. 66030. The optional mediation procedures provide for an alternative to CEQA litigation. The mediation procedures allow a superior court judge to invite litigants to CEQA suits. Within five days of the deadlines for filing a response to a lawsuit, the superior court judge can ask the litigants to select a mutually acceptable mediator. In selecting a mediator, the parties may want to ask the Council of Governments or the State Office of Permit Assistance to provide a mediator. Alternatively, the parties may select a mediator of their own choosing. If the parties do not select a mediator within 30 days, the lawsuit will proceed. However, the parties can still use a mediator at any other time.

If the parties do enter into mediation, the time limits that usually apply to lawsuits will be suspended while the mediation continues. The

---

Materials Included in the Administrative Record

- Project application and all supplementary materials
- All staff reports regarding the proposed project
- Project public hearing records
- All public notices
- Written comments received regarding the project
- Proposed decisions and findings on the project
- All other documents relating to the agency decision on the project

---

Under optional mediation, within five days of the deadlines for filing a response to a lawsuit, the superior court judge can ask the litigants to select a mutually acceptable mediator. If the parties do not select a mediator within 30 days, the lawsuit will proceed.

procedures exempt the mediation from requirements of the state's open meeting laws. However, public agencies implementing a mediated settlement must still comply with current law. Ninety days after mediation starts, the case is reactivated unless the mediation was successful or unless the parties agree to another 90 days of mediation.

If mediation does not resolve the issues, the judge can set up a settlement conference. If the case still moves ahead, the settlement judge cannot hear the suit, except in counties with only one superior court judge. Unless all parties agree, the procedures prohibit a mediator from filing court declarations or findings, except for a statement of agreement or nonagreement. At the end of the mediation, the mediator must submit a report to the Office of Permit Assistance describing the mediation.

The CEQA process should disclose to the public both the environmental impacts and the benefits of a project. CEQA documents analyzing projects with public benefits, such as recreation, may be less likely to be challenged in court if the public is aware of the proposed project's benefits.

By January 1, 2001, the Office of Permit Assistance must report to the Legislature on the implementation of the mediation program. Unless extended by the Legislature on that date, the law expires.

Request for a Hearing. The petitioner must file a motion requesting a hearing within 90 days of filing the petition. Guidelines sec. 15232. Upon the filing of a request for hearing, the court is required to establish a briefing schedule and hearing date. The briefing must be completed within 90 days of filing of the request and the hearing must be within 30 days thereafter. Pub. Res. Code sec. 21167.4. Failure to meet either of these schedules can result in dismissal of the case. The requirement for petitioners to request a hearing within 90 days of filing a petition may be relaxed when a case is transferred to a different judicial forum. Additionally, the petitioner must serve notice of the request for a hearing on all parties to the litigation within 14 day of filing the request. Pub. Res. Code sec. 21167.4(b).

Calendar Preference. Both trial and appellate courts are required to give CEQA actions calendar preference over other civil actions. Pub. Res. Code sec. 21167.1. Additionally, to expedite the litigation process the courts must regulate the briefing schedule so that, to the extent feasible, a hearing on appeal commences within one year of the date the appeal is filed. Pub. Res. Code sec. 21167.1(a). To further ensure that actions or proceedings challenging CEQA compliance are heard and determined quickly in the lower courts, the superior courts in all counties with a population of more than 200,000 must designate one or more judges to develop expertise in CEQA and related land use and environmental laws so that those judges will be available to hear, and quickly resolve, CEQA actions. Pub. Res. Code sec. 21167.1(b).

Both trial and appellate courts are required to give CEQA actions calendar preference over other civil actions. To expedite the process the courts must regulate the briefing schedule so that, to the extent feasible, a hearing on appeal commences within one year of the date the appeal is filed.

Typical Defenses

Procedural Defenses

The procedural defenses commonly asserted during CEQA litigation include statute of limitations (*see* page 143), standing, and exhaustion of administrative remedies.

Standing. CEQA does not have strict standing rules. Parties may sue under CEQA if they are property owners, taxpayers, or voters within the area affected by the project. The party must show a clear, present, and beneficial

---

Typical Procedural Defenses

- Statute of limitations
- Standing
- Exhaustion of administrative remedies

right to performance of the duty that the agency allegedly failed to perform. Code Civ. Proc. sec. 1086. Because courts, in practice, usually apply liberal standards for standing in CEQA cases, standing has not been a problem for would-be CEQA litigants.

Exhaustion of Administrative Remedies. A CEQA lawsuit may not be filed unless the alleged CEQA violations were raised orally or in writing during the public comment period or before the close of the public hearing and the issuing of the Notice of Determination, as long as an agency properly provided an opportunity for the public to comment. Pub. Res. Code sec. 21177. Courts disagree on the specificity with which objections must be stated during the administrative proceedings. Objections need not be raised before a lower administrative agency (e.g., a planning commission), provided they are raised before the decision-making body (e.g., a board of supervisors). If a party submits comments after the public review period provided by CEQA, but before the project decision is made, the exhaustion doctrine will, nevertheless be satisfied *Galante Vineyards v. Monterey Peninsula Water District* (1997) 60 Cal. App. 4th 1109.

The primary purpose of this doctrine is to ensure that public agencies are given the opportunity to receive and respond to particular environmental or procedural issues prior to litigation. To ensure that the agency has been given the opportunity to respond to objections, the specific issues pertaining to the litigation must have been raised during the administrative process; however, the issues do not have to be personally raised by the petitioner, as long as someone else presented the objections to the agency. Pub. Res. Code sec. 21177(a). The petitioner must have objected to the agency's approval of the project sometime during the administrative process, during the public comment period, or before the close of the public hearing and the issuing of the Notice of Determination. Pub. Res. Code sec. 21177(b).

Substantive Defenses

As stated above, agencies are not held to a standard of perfection; therefore, the agency's substantive defense focuses on whether the agency has made an objective, good-faith attempt at full disclosure. Guidelines secs. 15003(i), 15151. The agency's defense should include the fact that all required procedures have been followed and contents of the CEQA document are adequate. Challengers to the agency action based on an EIR will generally not be successful if the challenge centers around the fact that experts disagree in regard to significance determinations or the adequacy of mitigation. However, as noted below, the standard is different when the agency decision based on a Negative Declaration is challenged.

Judicial Standards of Review

In General

Review is by "administrative mandamus" if the challenged agency decision is based on an evidentiary hearing; otherwise, review is by traditional "mandamus." Pub. Res. Code secs. 21168, 21168.5. Under either proceeding,

A CEQA lawsuit may not be filed unless the alleged violations were raised orally or in writing during the public comment period or before the close of the public hearing and the issuing of the Notice of Determination.

The agency's substantive defense focuses on whether the agency has made an objective, good-faith attempt at full disclosure.

a court may overturn an agency decision only if the agency did not proceed as required by law or if the decision was not supported by substantial evidence. *Western States Petroleum Association v. The Superior Court of Los Angeles County* (1995) 9 Cal. 4th 559. In either case, the court generally may not receive evidence outside the administrative record.

Reviewing courts generally defer to the agencies' substantive judgments while requiring strict compliance with the procedural aspects of CEQA. Courts cannot overturn agencies' discretionary decisions and substitute their own opinions as to what constitutes appropriate public policy. In this regard, the courts cannot pass judgment on the correctness of the EIR's environmental conclusions, but only upon its sufficiency as an informative document.

Courts cannot overturn an agency's discretionary decisions and substitute their own opinions as to what constitutes appropriate public policy.

Special Standard of Review

A special standard favorable to the petitioner, the "fair argument" standard, is used when a court reviews an agency decision to prepare a Negative Declaration. *See* Conclusions of an Initial Study, page 37. When reviewing the contents of an EIR for adequacy, the courts employ the "rule of reason" standard of review. The scope of judicial review does not extend to the correctness of an EIR's conclusions, but only to the EIR's sufficiency as an informative document for decision makers and the public.

Remedies

Remedies in General

The court reviewing the CEQA challenge is required to address each of the alleged grounds for noncompliance. Pub. Res. Code sec. 21005. A court finding a CEQA violation may void the agency action, suspend all agency and relevant project actions that could have environmental impacts until CEQA compliance is achieved, or order the agency to comply with CEQA.

The court must issue a peremptory writ of mandate specifying what actions are needed to comply with CEQA. A court may limit the writ of mandate to include only those specific project activities that are out of compliance with CEQA if it determines that the project is severable, that severance would not prejudice CEQA compliance, and that the remainder of the project is in compliance. Pub. Res. Code sec. 21168.9(a)(1). The trial court must retain continuing jurisdiction over the agency's proceedings until determining that the agency has complied with CEQA. Pub. Res. Code sec. 21168.9. Monetary damages for CEQA violations are not available.

> **Court-Ordered Remedies for CEQA Violations**
>
> - Void the agency action
> - Suspend all agency and relevant project actions that could have environmental impacts until CEQA compliance is achieved
> - Order the agency to comply with CEQA

Injunctions

In deciding whether to grant an injunction, the court will consider whether an injunction is necessary to further CEQA's primary purpose of protecting the environment and whether the injunction would unduly prejudice the agency or the public. A court may only enjoin project implementation upon finding that a specific activity will prejudice the consideration or implementation of a particular mitigation measure or alternative. Pub. Res. Code sec. 21168.9(a)(2).

A court may only enjoin project implementation upon finding that a specific activity will prejudice the consideration or implementation of a particular mitigation measure or alternative.

A court has discretion to issue an injunction stopping project construction if it finds a CEQA violation.

Other CEQA Litigation Issues

Effect of Ongoing Litigation on Responsible Agencies

If a CEQA lawsuit has been filed and an injunction has been granted against the Lead Agency, a decision by a Responsible Agency will be conditional; however, the agency is required to act on the project within mandated time limits. If an interim injunction has not been granted, the Responsible Agency must assume Lead Agency CEQA compliance and act on the project within mandated time limits. Guidelines sec. 15233.

Appeals

CEQA contains specific provisions to expedite the judicial appeals process. Pub. Res. Code secs. 21167.6, 21168.3.

Attorneys' Fees

Awards of attorneys' fees may be authorized by the court in CEQA cases if the action resulted in enforcement of an important public right affecting the public interest, significant benefit would be conferred on the public or a large class, and necessity and financial burden of private enforcement of CEQA make the award appropriate. Code Civ. Proc. sec. 1021.5.

Courts tend to be sympathetic to requests for attorneys' fees by successful CEQA plaintiffs. However, it is up to the discretion of the court to grant the fees.

Summary of California Supreme Court Decisions

Early California Supreme Court decisions generally supported the challengers to state and local agencies in most cases. The court consistently held that public agencies should interpret CEQA "so as to afford the fullest protection of the environment within the reasonable scope of the statutory language." *Friends of Mammoth v. Board of Supervisors* (1972) 8 Cal. 3d 247, 104 Cal. Rptr. 76. The court's early pro-CEQA attitude has been an important factor in ensuring proper implementation of CEQA by public agencies throughout California.

Since the early 1990s, the Supreme Court has demonstrated a tendency to side with agencies and has taken a less expansive view of CEQA. Additionally, a 1993 CEQA amendment specifically instructed the courts not to add requirements beyond CEQA and the Guidelines. Pub. Res. Code sec. 21083. The following summaries present some of the California Supreme Court's key CEQA decisions. For a complete treatment of published CEQA court decisions, please *see Guide to the California Environmental Quality Act* by Remy, Thomas, Moose, and Manley, Solano Press Books.

Friends of Mammoth v. Board of Supervisors of Mono County (1972) 8 Cal. 3d 247, 104 Cal. Rptr. 76

The Mono County Board of Supervisors violated CEQA by not complying with the law prior to approving a conditional use permit for a private development project. The court determined that the Legislature intended CEQA to apply not only to public agency actions that directly affect the physical environment, but also to permit approvals of private actions that indirectly affect the environment.

No Oil, Inc. v. City of Los Angeles
(1975) 13 Cal. 3d 68, 118 Cal. Rptr. 34

The City of Los Angeles violated CEQA by not preparing an EIR before enacting an ordinance allowing oil drilling within the city limits. The court held that an EIR is required if substantial evidence is produced that could support a fair argument that the project may have a significant effect on the environment. The court cautioned Lead Agencies that to be significant a potential impact need not be momentous or of a permanent or long enduring nature, but can range from not trivial, to appreciable, to important as well as momentous.

Bozung v. Local Agency Formation Commission
(1975) 13 Cal. 3d 263, 118 Cal. Rptr. 249

The Ventura County LAFCO violated CEQA by not preparing an EIR on an annexation of a property to a city. The Court held than annexation was the first step in the project approval process, and, because the property was clearly destined to be developed, its environmental impacts could be evaluated.

Wildlife Alive v. Chickering
(1976) 18 Cal. 3d 190, 132 Cal. Rptr. 377

The California Fish and Game Commission violated the law when it did not comply with CEQA prior to its decision to authorize the hunting of black bear. The court held that the commission's decision was neither statutorily nor constitutionally exempt from CEQA and that the authorization of bear hunting could have a significant effect on the environment.

Fullerton Joint Union High School District v. State
Board of Education (1982) 32 Cal. 3d 779, 187 Cal. Rptr. 398

The State Board of Education violated CEQA when it made a decision to place an initiative on the ballot that would create a new school district out of an existing district. The court held that the voters were entitled to the benefit of environmental analysis prior to voting on such an initiative.

Concerned Citizens of Costa Mesa, Inc. v. 32nd District
Agricultural Association (1986) 42 Cal. 3d 929, 231 Cal. Rptr. 748

The court allowed a citizens' association to maintain a CEQA challenge against an agency's failure to prepare a Supplemental EIR, even though the lawsuit was filed after the normal 180-day statute of limitations period (from the date of the agency decision) had expired. The court held that the statute of limitations period begins only after the plaintiff knew or should have known of a change in the project.

Laurel Heights Improvement Association v. Regents of the
University of California (1988) 47 Cal. 3d 376, 253 Cal. Rptr. 426

The EIR of the Regents of the University of California on the decision to occupy an existing building to be used for biomedical research was inadequate. The court held that the Regents' EIR should have analyzed reasonably

---

California Supreme Court CEQA Decisions

- Friends of Mammoth v. Board of Supervisors of Mono County (1972)
- No Oil, Inc. v. City of Los Angeles (1975)
- Bozung v. Local Agency Formation Commission (1975)
- Wildlife Alive v. Chickering (1976)
- Fullerton Joint Union High School District v. State Board of Education (1982)
- Concerned Citizens of Costa Mesa, Inc. v. 32nd District Agricultural Association (1986)
- Laurel Heights Improvement Association v. Regents of the University of California (1988)
- Napa Valley Wine Train, Inc. v. Public Utilities Commission (1990)
- Citizens of Goleta Valley et al. v. Board of Supervisors (1990)
- Laurel Heights Improvement Association of San Francisco v. Regents of the University of California (1993)
- Western States Petroleum Association v. The Superior Court of Los Angeles County (1995)
- Mountain Lion Foundation v. Fish and Game Commission (1997)

The Napa Valley Wine Train project was statutorily exempt from CEQA.

foreseeable (although tentative) future phases of the project, as well as alternative sites.

Napa Valley Wine Train, Inc. v. Public Utilities Commission (1990) 50 Cal. 3d 370, 267 Cal. Rptr. 569

The Public Utilities Commission should have exempted the proposed Wine Train from complying with CEQA because the project qualified for an exemption for mass transit projects that initiate or increase passenger or commuter services on rail or highway rights-of-way already in use. The proposed route for the Wine Train was already in use because the rail line, although used only sporadically, had not been formally abandoned.

Citizens of Goleta Valley et al. v. Board of Supervisors (1990) 52 Cal. 3d 553, 276 Cal. Rptr. 410

Santa Barbara County properly excluded alternative sites for a coastal resort hotel from consideration in an EIR because the sites were not within the applicant's control, could require a local coastal plan/general plan amendment, and were outside the Lead Agency's permitting jurisdiction.

Laurel Heights Improvement Association of San Francisco v. Regents of the University of California (1993) 6 Cal. 4th 1112

Recirculation of a Draft EIR for public comment is required where significant new information is added to the EIR after the close of the public comment period but before certification. The new information is significant when it results in a new or more severe impact, or consists of a new mitigation measure or alternative that could reduce the significance of an impact. Information that merely clarifies or amplifies the Draft EIR is not significant.

Western States Petroleum Association v. The Superior Court of Los Angeles County (1995) 9 Cal. 4th 559

In a challenge to the adoption of California Air Resources Board air quality regulations, the court held that in a traditional mandamus proceeding under CEQA, the parties are severely limited as to submission of extra-record evidence.

Mountain Lion Foundation v. Fish and Game Commission (1997) 16 Cal. 4th 105

The California Fish and Game Commission violated CEQA when it failed to prepare an environmental document consistent with its certified regulatory program for hunting and fishing prior to its decision to delist the Mojave ground squirrel as a threatened species under the California Endangered Species Act. The California Supreme Court held that the delisting decision was subject to neither an implied exemption nor a categorical exemption. The court held that the Commission's decisions under the Endangered Species Act fall within its hunting and fishing certified regulatory program. The court found that in this case, however, the Commission failed to comply with its own regulatory program.

Chapter 8

Is CEQA Effective?

Have CEQA's Objectives Been Achieved?

During the past twenty-five years, CEQA has become a legal and regulatory institution in California. State and local officials have become accustomed to relying on environmental impact documents in making their decisions. Citizens are also used to relying on information provided in EIRs and Negative Declarations to alert them to pending decisions and to provide opportunities to effectively participate in the agency project-approval process. Yet, despite these benefits, CEQA remains a highly controversial statute because it is often used by project opponents to delay or stop projects.

During the past twenty-five years, CEQA has become a legal and regulatory institution in California. Yet, despite all the benefits, CEQA remains highly controversial because it is often used by project opponents to delay or stop projects.

While agency officials, developers, attorneys, and environmentalists have all pondered CEQA's effectiveness at various times over the past twenty-five years, there is no simple answer to the question of whether CEQA's objectives have been achieved. One reason for the difficulty in answering the question is that, as indicated in chapter 1, CEQA has six stated objectives that are not exactly consistent:

- To disclose to decision makers and the public the significant environmental effects of government decisions before they are made
- To identify ways to avoid or reduce environmental damage
- To prevent environmental damage by requiring implementation of feasible alternatives or mitigation measures
- To disclose to the public the reasons why agencies sometime approve projects despite their environmental damage
- To foster interagency coordination in the review of projects
- To enhance public participation in the planning process

Additionally, because CEQA applies to all types of state and local agencies and to most of the projects that they approve or carry out, any serious evaluation of its effectiveness will vary depending upon which objective is being evaluated, the type of agency involved, and the nature of the project being studied.

CEQA was found by one study to be somewhat successful in achieving the objective of informing the public about environmental impacts.

The ABAG study was one of the first in the state to provide current data on how many environmental studies are typically conducted under CEQA in each jurisdiction.

While almost everyone involved in the CEQA process has strong opinions about the advantages and disadvantages of the law, to date relatively few independent studies have been conducted that evaluate CEQA's effectiveness. Several studies of CEQA were conducted in the 1970s and 1980s. While researchers of CEQA's implementation may find these older studies interesting, the results are somewhat dated. However, between 1990 and 1995, a series of new studies were conducted that shed considerable light about current CEQA practice as well as local government attitudes about CEQA's effectiveness.

Association of Bay Area Governments CEQA Study (1991)

In 1991, the Association of Bay Area Governments conducted a comprehensive study of CEQA implementation by local governments in the San Francisco Bay Area. ABAG surveyed all city and county planning directors and city and county attorneys in the San Francisco Bay Area and approximately 275 private CEQA consultants.

The study was one of the first in the state to provide current data on how many environmental studies are typically conducted under CEQA in each jurisdiction. Bay Area planning directors reported receiving an average of 65 project applications that were subject to CEQA each year. Of the 65 applications, respondents report an average of four EIRs were prepared. The remaining projects were processed either as Negative Declarations or were determined to be exempt from CEQA.

With regard to meeting CEQA's objectives, the survey found that most local governments felt that they were fairly well achieved. Respondents ranked the achievement of CEQA's objectives on a scale of 1 to 3 (1 = very well, 2 = fairly well, 3 = poorly):

Objective	Relative Achievement
Informing decision makers and the public about environmental impacts	1.5
Identifying ways to avoid or reduce environmental damage	1.8
Preventing avoidable environmental damage	2.0
Disclosing the reasons for agency decisions	2.2

Despite these favorable responses with regard to CEQA's overall objectives, respondents identified six issue areas where considerable uncertainty clouded CEQA's implementation:

- Alternatives analysis
- Cumulative impact requirements
- Recirculation requirements when new information is added to a document
- The lack of "thresholds" of significance
- The definition of "substantial evidence"
- Mitigation monitoring requirements

The survey also revealed that the greatest dissatisfaction with CEQA was the poor relationship between the environmental review and the ultimate project decision.

One of the most interesting aspects of the study was the data relating to CEQA litigation. Although some critics complain that litigation drives the CEQA process, the survey disclosed that the actual numbers of CEQA lawsuits is quite small. According to the city attorneys and county counsels responding, fewer than one percent of project applications were the object of litigation. Further, it showed that of those that were subject to litigation, a majority (76 percent) were decided in favor of the public agency being challenged. Thus, the survey reflects a relatively low level of CEQA litigation activity and demonstrates that CEQA challenges are generally not successful. Nevertheless, over half of the respondents believed that legal defensibility, rather than improved information disclosure, drives the preparation of most EIRs. ABAG concluded that, while the actual level of litigation is relatively low, the perceived threat of litigation is very influential in determining the type of environmental document prepared (e.g., EIR versus Negative Declaration versus categorical exemption) and the scope and content of the documents. *See* Association of Bay Area Governments, *CEQA Process and Practices,* Oakland, California, 1991.

California Planning Department Survey (1992)

In the first truly comprehensive, statewide study of CEQA's effectiveness, a researcher from the University of Illinois concluded that most professional planners feel that CEQA has done a fairly good job of accomplishing its stated objectives. Robert Olshansky, formerly of the University of California, Berkeley, surveyed planning departments throughout California to determine attitudes regarding CEQA implementation. To ensure its professional acceptability, the survey was reviewed by representatives of the Governor's Office of Planning and Research, the California Chapter of the American Planning Association, and the California Association of Environmental Professionals. After this independent review, the survey was mailed to all cities and counties in the state. Of the 500 departments that received the questionnaires, 350 or 70.9 percent responded. This rate of return is considered excellent for such a survey.

Like the ABAG effort, this study revealed some interesting statistical data regarding CEQA implementation. For example, it showed that, on average, a city or county prepares only 2.4 environmental impact reports per year (this is less than the average of 4 in the Bay Area). Of greater interest, however, were the attitudinal responses of planning officials regarding the accomplishment of CEQA's objectives. Respondents were asked to rate how successful CEQA has been in accomplishing each of its stated objectives. Respondents ranked the following CEQA functions on a scale of 1 to 8, with 1 being the best score.

The greatest dissatisfaction with CEQA was the poor relationship between the environmental review and the ultimate project decision.

The ABAG study found that, while the actual level of litigation is relatively low, the perceived threat of litigation is very influential in determining the type of environmental document prepared and its scope and contents.

CEQA's Objective	Score	Relative Accomplishment
Ensuring thorough analysis of environmental impacts	2.39	most successful
Causing the adoption of mitigation measures	3.26	
Informing the public about environmental impacts	3.59	
Protecting the environment	3.63	
Coordinating public agency review	4.90	
Facilitating citizen participation	5.04	
Making local officials accountable for their decisions	5.33	least successful

According to local professional planners, CEQA has been more successful in achieving environmental protection than it has been in achieving government procedural reform.

This study confirms that professional planners feel that CEQA has been fairly successful at accomplishing most of its intended objectives. It is notable, however, that according to local planners, CEQA has been more successful in achieving environmental protection than it has in achieving government procedural reform. *See The California Environmental Quality Act: Implications for Local Land Use Planning* by Robert B. Olshansky, Department of Urban and Regional Planning, University of Illinois, Champaign-Urbana, Illinois, 1991.

Bay Area Mitigation Monitoring Study (1993)

The Bay Area Mitigation Monitoring study concluded that CEQA's mitigation monitoring requirements have been generally ineffective in accomplishing its objectives of improving mitigation practices.

In this effort, a private researcher in the San Francisco Bay Area conducted a limited study that focused only on the effectiveness of the mitigation monitoring requirements of CEQA which were added to the law in the late 1980s. That study, which was also based on a survey of local government planning departments in the seventeen-county area of northern California, concluded that CEQA's mitigation monitoring requirements have been generally ineffective in accomplishing its objectives of improving mitigation practices (*see* Effectiveness of Mitigation Monitoring: An Independent Study, page 100). Specifically, the study revealed that formal programs for mitigation monitoring remained the exception rather than the rule and that the extent monitoring varied dramatically from jurisdiction to jurisdiction. *See* "Mitigation Monitoring Programs" by Dominic Roques, *The Environmental Monitor*, published by California Association of Environmental Professionals, Fall 1993.

State Bar CEQA Review Committee (1994–1995)

The State Bar CEQA Review Committee developed a list of fourteen key issues and solicited input from over 2,500 members of the Environmental Law Section, interested agencies, bar associations, and others.

In 1995, the Environmental Law Section of the State Bar of California completed a comprehensive legal evaluation of CEQA. The study was initiated in response to strongly voiced requests of State Bar members and other professionals to conduct a careful legal review of CEQA. To accomplish this, the Executive Committee of the Environmental Law Section appointed a select CEQA Review Committee consisting of attorneys who represent a diverse group of clients affected by CEQA including government agencies, citizens' groups, developers, and industry interests. The committee developed a list of fourteen key issues and solicited input from over 2,500 members of the Environmental Law Section, interested agencies, bar associations, and others about these issues.

In arriving at its recommendations, the committee reached consensus that the overall intent and underlying policies of CEQA were fundamentally sound, but that various areas needed improvement. Under each of these issue areas, the committee conducted a detailed analysis of the statutory provisions, the CEQA Guidelines, and relevant case law. Additionally, for each problem, detailed recommendations for improving CEQA were presented. The following are the problem areas that are addressed in the report.

- Timing of environmental review—particularly the lack of clear rules for deferring analysis to future stages of decision making
- Tiering—the lack of clear rules when to use it and how it works
- Thresholds of significance—the lack of standards for making significance determinations
- Mitigation measures—the need for clarification regarding specificity, enforceability, feasibility, effectiveness, and monitoring
- Alternatives—the lack of clear rules regarding the selection of a reasonable range of alternatives
- Cumulative impacts—particularly the problems that occur when a project contributes a small increment to an already existing significant environmental problem
- Public review and participation—specifically relating to translation of EIRs into other languages, the submittal of late comments, and the lack of required public hearings
- Model guidance and documents—the lack of regular, informal guidance from the Resources Agency
- Statewide indexing of EIRs—the need for the Resources Agency to create an EIR data bank from documents filed with the State Clearinghouse so that such data may be accessed by future EIR preparers
- Compliance with other applicable environmental laws—the fact that CEQA is poorly integrated with other environmental laws and regulations
- Certified regulatory programs—the need for greater clarity with regard to these programs
- Findings and integration of environmental review into agency decisions—the lack of clarity over how these procedures should work in practice
- Revisiting CEQA documents—the need to revise or clarify the test for when a previously circulated CEQA document must be revised and recirculated
- CEQA litigation—the study identified several different problems with CEQA litigation

After evaluating each of these issue areas in detail, the Environmental Law Section's report provides an affirmative answer to the two more fundamental questions established by the committee at the outset: (1) Given CEQA's policy objectives, the CEQA process can be restructured to improve environmental decisions and to provide greater certainty to all parties regarding the adequacy of CEQA compliance; (2) Given CEQA's general procedural framework, the CEQA process can be made more cost-effective and less time-consuming. Environmental Law Section, State Bar of California *The California*

The Environmental Law Section's report found that, given CEQA's general procedural framework, the process can be made more cost-effective and less time-consuming.

Environmental Policy Act: Assessment and Recommendations, Final Report, Sacramento, California, 1995.

California Policy Seminar CEQA Study (1995)

Research in the California Policy Seminar CEQA Study was based on detailed evaluation of local CEQA practices in fourteen selected communities throughout California, chosen to represent the fullest possible range of local governments.

The most recent effort to determine CEQA's effectiveness was undertaken in 1995 by the California Policy Seminar, a joint program of the University of California and state government, which completed a comprehensive survey of CEQA practice at the local government level. This study was directed by Professor John Landis of U.C. Berkeley, and was essentially a continuation of the work done by Olshansky in 1991. The research was based on detailed evaluation of local CEQA practices in fourteen selected communities throughout California. The communities were chosen to represent the fullest possible range of local governments.

For each of the selected communities, the research team first determined the total level of CEQA reviews, the number of EIRs and Negative Declarations, and the frequency of CEQA litigation. Against this background, the researchers then compared and contrasted local practices with regard to all aspects of the environmental review process. The study not only includes empirical data about the environmental review process in each community, but also the opinions of various local officials and others about the effectiveness of CEQA as well as case studies of specific projects. The study also compares practices in California to those in other states with laws similar to CEQA.

While the study concluded that most local government planners generally feel that CEQA's general objectives have been achieved, it identified eight specific problems areas with the law's implementation:

- State and regional agencies do not play a predictable role in local CEQA reviews
- Within local agencies, environmental review is often uncertain and inconsistent
- CEQA review cannot effectively mitigate cumulative impacts
- Alternatives analysis is generally inadequate and inconsistent
- CEQA lacks incentives for timely dispute resolution
- The State Clearinghouse does not provide a meaningful role in CEQA
- There are too few incentives and too little funding for advance planning
- There is a lack of consistent data with which to conduct environmental review

For each of the identified problem areas, the study recommended proposed solutions and concluded with an interesting evaluation of the common myths about CEQA and recommendations for change.

For each of these identified problem areas, the study recommended proposed solutions.

The study concluded with an interesting evaluation of the common "myths" about CEQA and recommendations for change.

Myth 1. CEQA applies to a much broader range of projects than similar laws in other states. The study revealed that CEQA did apply to more types of projects than the similar laws in the other sixteen states with environmental impact assessment requirements, but that the complexity or extent of environmental review was relatively similar from state to state.

Myth 2. CEQA encourages the unnecessary writing of EIRs, often for projects that should not require them. The study revealed quite the contrary. The vast majority of initial studies result in Negative Declarations, not EIRs. Nearly a quarter of the communities responding reported that they did not initiate a single EIR in 1990. Another 22 percent reported preparing only one EIR that year. On average, agencies prepared twenty Negative Declarations for every EIR.

Myth 3. EIRs are unnecessarily costly and time-consuming and add little substantive information to the decision-making process. The study revealed that while there are occasional EIR "horror stories," the average cost of an EIR in 1990 was only $38,124. Further, most EIRs are completed in less than one year and many in less than six months. These numbers support the conclusion that a typical EIR is neither excessively costly nor time-consuming. With regard to usefulness, while no quantitative data exists on this issue, nearly 90 percent of the planning directors responding believed CEQA to have been successful in providing a thorough analysis of environmental impacts.

The study found that most EIRs are completed in less than one year and many in less than six months. The numbers support the conclusion that a typical EIR is neither excessively costly nor time-consuming.

Myth 4. CEQA reviews are usually associated with litigation. The study results were consistent with the findings in the ABAG research that litigation is relatively rare under CEQA. Most communities reported no CEQA litigation in the years between 1986 and 1990. The average number of lawsuits was one for every 354 initial studies and one for every 18 draft EIRs respectively.

Myth 5. The costs and uncertainties associated with CEQA discourage businesses from relocating or expanding in California. The study provided insufficient evidence to support this assertion. The only evidence the researchers found was anecdotal information from several other studies of the effects of government regulation on California's businesses. While CEQA may contribute to what some perceive as "overregulation," the study concluded that it is difficult to hold CEQA solely responsible for delays and difficulties in project reviews.

CEQA can be most effective where mitigation can be incorporated into the project design.

Myth 6. CEQA review is poorly integrated with other forms of federal, state, regional, and local planning and environmental regulations. Case studies provided ample evidence of the truth of this assertion. The study revealed problems with integrating CEQA with other local planning activities. It also demonstrated problems integrating local CEQA activities with state and regional environmental regulations.

Myth 7. While valuable in theory, in practice, the evaluation of alternatives, cumulative impacts, and growth-inducing impacts are usually incomplete, poorly done, and confusing. As with Myth 6, the study provided strong support for this assertion. With regard to alternatives, the study revealed that time and budget constraints cause most agencies to evaluate alternatives on only a cursory basis. With regard to cumulative and growth-inducing impacts, it revealed that there is often a lack of data and a deficiency in analytical models with which to evaluate the impacts. Further, most respondents felt that, even with a thorough analysis, there is little that agencies can do to mitigate these problems. *See* "Fixing CEQA: Options and Opportunities for Reforming the California Environmental Quality Act," California Policy Seminar, University of California, Berkeley, 1995.

CEQA: Making It Work Better (1997) by the Legislative Analyst's Office

This study, conducted by the Legislative Analyst's Office, was prepared in response to concerns expressed by California's business community that CEQA has had a detrimental effect on economic development in the state. In particular, the business community was concerned about the complexity and unpredictability of the CEQA process, the costs of compliance, and the ease of making legal challenges that impede development.

The study concluded that some of these problems exist but that their extent is unclear. Additionally, it found that little information exists about the cost-effectiveness of public agency mitigation measures. Furthermore, the study found that CEQA has become a substitute for general, long-term planning in some jurisdictions even though it is not well suited to do the job.

The study responds to some of the concerns about CEQA with a series of recommendations that fall into three broad categories:

- Measures to make the process more efficient, thereby making it less costly and time consuming for project developers and public agencies
- Measures to make mitigation of environmental impacts more cost effective
- Measures to improve the resolution of CEQA disputes

According to the study, these recommendations, if adopted, would in large measure address the concerns identified by the business community and would make CEQA work better at achieving its goals.

Conclusion

Taken together, these five most recent studies reveal considerable common ground about the CEQA's effectiveness. Most observers agree that CEQA is an important part of California's scheme for protecting the environment that is anchored by a strong legal foundation and based on sound public policy. There is also considerable agreement that CEQA is misunderstood by many of its critics and poorly implemented by some agencies. There is clearly a wide gulf between the myths surrounding CEQA and the reality of how it is carried out. For example, the studies concluded that agencies are not burdened by excessive numbers of EIRs. Nor are projects typically held up by CEQA-related litigation.

On the other hand, there is considerable agreement that many aspects of CEQA practice are cumbersome and should be streamlined. The studies have also revealed that, while reforms are needed, neither the State Legislature nor the two oversight agencies (OPR and the Resources Agency) have been successful in achieving reform. Some observers have noted that there is a need for greater legislative and regulatory oversight and, in particular, a need for further guidance about how to implement the law successfully.

Hopefully, these research efforts will lead the Legislature, the Resources Agency, and OPR to continue the quest to streamline CEQA without removing the effective CEQA provisions. And, those involved in the CEQA process can, even in the absence of legislative or regulatory changes, play an important role in implementing CEQA successfully.

Appendix 1

California Environmental Quality Act Statutes

Public Resources Code, Division 13, Sections 21000–21177

Source

CEQA: California Environmental Quality Act Statutes (1998). These sections of the Public Resources Code were reprinted with the cooperation and permission of the California Resources Agency (December 1998)

The statutory language in this appendix is current as of February 1, 1999. Readers are advised to use the most current version of these statutory sections. In the past, a current unofficial version of these sections has been available on the Internet at **http://ceres.ca.gov/ceqa**. An unofficial version of the California Codes, including the Public Resources Code, has been available at **http://www.leginfo.ca.gov/calaw.html**.

Solano Press Books has made every effort to see that no changes have been made to the contents of this state document as a result of reformatting and reprinting. Any omissions or changes to the contrary are entirely the responsibility of Solano Press Books and not the State of California.

CEQA Statutes
Table of Contents

Revised December 1998

California Environmental Quality Statutes

Public Resources Code, Division 13, §§ 21000–21177

Chapter 1. Policy
Sections 21000 to 21006

21000   Legislative Intent–Policies

The Legislature finds and declares as follows:

(a) The maintenance of a quality environment for the people of this state now and in the future is a matter of statewide concern.

(b) It is necessary to provide a high-quality environment that at all times is healthful and pleasing to the senses and intellect of man.

(c) There is a need to understand the relationship between the maintenance of high-quality ecological systems and the general welfare of the people of the state, including their enjoyment of the natural resources of the state.

(d) The capacity of the environment is limited, and it is the intent of the Legislature that the government of the state take immediate steps to identify any critical thresholds for the health and safety of the people of the state and take all coordinated actions necessary to prevent such thresholds being reached.

(e) Every citizen has a responsibility to contribute to the preservation and enhancement of the environment.

(f) The interrelationship of policies and practices in the management of natural resources and waste disposal requires systematic and concerted efforts by public and private interests to enhance environmental quality and to control environmental pollution.

(g) It is the intent of the Legislature that all agencies of the state government which regulate activities of private individuals, corporations, and public agencies which are found to affect the quality of the environment, shall regulate such activities so that major consideration is given to preventing environmental damage, while providing a decent home and satisfying living environment for every Californian.

(Amended: Chapter 947, Statutes of 1979)

21001   Additional Policies

The Legislature further finds and declares that it is the policy of the state to:

(a) Develop and maintain a high-quality environment now and in the future, and take all action necessary to protect, rehabilitate, and enhance the environmental quality of the state.

(b) Take all action necessary to provide the people of this state with clean air and water, enjoyment of aesthetic, natural, scenic, and historic environmental qualities, and freedom from excessive noise.

(c) Prevent the elimination of fish or wildlife species due to man's activities, ensure that fish and wildlife populations do not drop below self-perpetuating levels, and preserve for future generations representations of all plant and animal communities and examples of the major periods of California history.

(d) Ensure that the long-term protection of the environment, consistent with the provision of a decent home and suitable living environment for every Californian, shall be the guiding criterion in public decisions.

(e) Create and maintain conditions under which man and nature can exist in productive harmony to fulfill the social and economic requirements of present and future generations.

(f) Require governmental agencies at all levels to develop standards and procedures necessary to protect environmental quality.

(g) Require governmental agencies at all levels to consider qualitative factors as well as economic and technical factors and long-term benefits and costs, in addition to short-term benefits and costs and to consider alternatives to proposed actions affecting the environment.

(Amended: Chapter 947, Statutes of 1979)

21001.1   Review of Public Agency Projects

The Legislature further finds and declares that it is the policy of the state that projects to be carried out by public agencies be subject to the same level of review and consideration under this division as that of private projects required to be approved by public agencies.

(Added: Chapter 1514, Statutes of 1984)

21002   Approval of Project

The Legislature finds and declares that it is the policy of the state that public agencies should not approve projects as proposed if there are feasible alternatives or feasible mitigation measures available which would substantially lessen the significant environmental effects of such projects, and that the procedures required by this division are intended to assist public agencies in systematically identifying both the significant effects of proposed projects and the feasible alternatives or feasible mitigation measures which will avoid or substantially lessen such significant effects. The Legislature further finds and declares that in the event specific economic, social, or other conditions make infeasible such project alternatives or such mitigation measures, individual projects may be approved in spite of one or more significant effects thereof.

(Amended: Chapter 676, Statutes of 1980)

21002.1 Use of Environmental Impact Reports

In order to achieve the objectives set forth in Section 21002, the Legislature hereby finds and declares that the following policy shall apply to the use of environmental impact reports prepared pursuant to this division:

(a) The purpose of an environmental impact report is to identify the significant effects on the environment of a project, to identify alternatives to the project, and to indicate the manner in which those significant effects can be mitigated or avoided.

(b) Each public agency shall mitigate or avoid the significant effects on the environment of projects that it carries out or approves whenever it is feasible to do so.

(c) If economic, social, or other conditions make it infeasible to mitigate one or more significant effects on the environment of a project, the project may nonetheless be carried out or approved at the discretion of a public agency if the project is otherwise permissible under applicable laws and regulations.

(d) In applying the policies of subdivisions (b) and (c) to individual projects, the responsibility of the lead agency shall differ from that of a responsible agency. The lead agency shall be responsible for considering the effects, both individual and collective, of all activities involved in a project. A responsible agency shall be responsible for considering only the effects of those activities involved in a project which it is required by law to carry out or approve. This subdivision applies only to decisions by a public agency to carry out or approve a project and does not otherwise affect the scope of the comments that the public agency may wish to make pursuant to Section 21104 or 21153.

(e) To provide more meaningful public disclosure, reduce the time and cost required to prepare an environmental impact report, and focus on potentially significant effects on the environment of a proposed project, lead agencies shall, in accordance with Section 21100, focus the discussion in the environmental impact report on those potential effects on the environment of a proposed project which the lead agency

has determined are or may be significant. Lead agencies may limit discussion on other effects to a brief explanation as to why those effects are not potentially significant.

(Amended: Chapter 1230, Statutes of 1994)

21003 Additional Policies

The Legislature further finds and declares that it is the policy of the state that:

(a) Local agencies integrate the requirements of this division with planning and environmental review procedures otherwise required by law or by local practice so that all those procedures, to the maximum feasible extent, run concurrently, rather than consecutively.

(b) Documents prepared pursuant to this division be organized and written in a manner that will be meaningful and useful to decisionmakers and to the public.

(c) Environmental impact reports omit unnecessary descriptions of projects and emphasize feasible mitigation measures and feasible alternatives to projects.

(d) Information developed in individual environmental impact reports be incorporated into a data base which can be used to reduce delay and duplication in preparation of subsequent environmental impact reports.

(e) Information developed in environmental impact reports and negative declarations be incorporated into a data base which may be used to make subsequent or supplemental environmental determinations.

(f) All persons and public agencies involved in the environmental review process be responsible for carrying out the process in the most efficient, expeditious manner in order to conserve the available financial, governmental, physical, and social resources with the objective that those resources may be better applied toward the mitigation of actual significant effects on the environment.

(Amended: Chapter 1130, Statutes of 1993)

21003.1 Further Findings by the Legislature

The Legislature further finds and declares it is the policy of the state that:

(a) Comments from the public and public agencies on the environmental effects of a project shall be made to lead agencies as soon as possible in the review of environmental documents, including, but not limited to, draft environmental impact reports and negative declarations, in order to allow the lead agencies to identify, at the earliest

possible time in the environmental review process, potential significant effects of a project, alternatives, and mitigation measures which would substantially reduce the effects.

(b) Information relevant to the significant effects of a project, alternatives, and mitigation measures which substantially reduce the effects shall be made available as soon as possible by lead agencies, other public agencies, and interested persons and organizations.

(c) Nothing in subdivisions (a) or (b) reduces or otherwise limits public review or comment periods currently prescribed either by statute or in guidelines prepared and adopted pursuant to Section 21083 for environmental documents, including, but not limited to, draft environmental impact reports and negative declarations.

(Added: Chapter 85, Statutes of 1985)

21004 Declaration of Legislative Intent

In mitigating or avoiding a significant effect of a project on the environment, a public agency may exercise only those express or implied powers provided by law other than this division. However, a public agency may use discretionary powers provided by such other law for the purpose of mitigating or avoiding a significant effect on the environment subject to the express or implied constraints or limitations that may be provided by law.

(Added: Chapter 1438, Statutes 1982)

Uncodified declaration of legislative intent

The Legislature finds and declares as follows:

(a) The enactment of Section 21004 of the Public Resources Code by this act is intended to clarify the scope and meaning of various provisions of Division 13 (commencing with Section 21000) of the Public Resources Code.

Such clarification is necessary because of contentions that the provisions of Division 13 (commencing with Section 21000) of the Public Resources Code, by themselves, confer on public agencies independent authority to levy fees, impose exactions, and take other actions in order to comply with the general requirement of that division that significant effects on the environment be mitigated or avoided whenever it is feasible to do so.

The provisions of Division 13 (commencing with Section 21000) of the Public Resources Code confer no such independent authority. Rather, the provisions of that division are intended to be used in conjunction with discretionary powers granted to a public agency by other law in order to achieve the objective of mitigating or avoiding significant effects on the environment when it is feasible to do so. Compliance with the requirements of that division identifies the manner in which significant effects of a project can be mitigated or avoided, and imposes an additional requirement that these mitigating or avoiding actions be taken whenever it is feasible to do so. In order to fulfill that latter requirement, a public agency is required to select from the various powers which have been conferred upon it by other law, those which it determines may be appropriately and legally exercised to avoid or mitigate the significant effects of the project as required by that division.

Thus, for example, if the California Constitution, a charter, a statute, or some other law generally confers upon a public agency the authority to levy a fee or to impose another type of exaction for public welfare purposes, that public agency may, to the extent expressly or impliedly permitted by such other law, choose to impose that fee or exaction for the purpose of mitigating or avoiding a significant effect on the environment which has been identified pursuant to Division 13 (commencing with Section 21000) of the Public Resources Code. Or, if a public agency is generally authorized to exercise the power of condemnation, it may, to the extent expressly or impliedly permitted by such other law, choose to do so in order to mitigate or avoid a significant effect on the environment which has been identified pursuant to that division.

The provisions of Section 21004 of the Public Resources Code do not modify the holdings expressed in *Golden Gate Bridge etc. Dist. v. Muzzi*, (1978) 83 Cal. App. 3d 707; and *San Diego Trust & Savings Bank v. Friends of Gill*, (1981) 121 Cal. App. 3d 203.

(b) There is currently in litigation the question of whether or not Division 13 (commencing with Section 21000) of the Public Resources Code, prior to its amendment by this act, does, or does not, confer on public agencies an authorization to impose fees and other exactions, which is wholly separate and independent from any authorization conferred on such agencies by other law. The Legislature, therefore, declares that, by adding Section 21004 to Division 13 (commencing with Section 21000) of the Public Resources Code, it makes no statement, either directly or by indirection, as to whether that division, prior to its amendment by this act, did or did not confer on public agencies independent authority to impose fees or other exactions.

(Added: Chapter 1438, Statutes of 1982)

21005   Information Disclosure Provisions

(a) The Legislature finds and declares that it is the policy of the state that noncompliance with the information disclosure provisions of this division which precludes relevant information from being presented to the public agency, or noncompliance with substantive requirements of this division, may constitute a prejudicial abuse of discretion within the meaning of Sections 21168 and 21168.5, regardless of whether a different outcome would have resulted if the public agency had complied with those provisions.

(b) It is the intent of the Legislature that, in undertaking judicial review pursuant to Sections 21168 and 21168.5, courts shall continue to follow the established principle that there is no presumption that error is prejudicial.

(c) It is further the intent of the Legislature that any court, which finds, or, in the process of reviewing a previous court finding, finds, that a public agency has taken an action without compliance with this division, shall specifically address each of the alleged grounds for noncompliance.

(Amended: Chapter 1230, Statutes of 1994)

21006   Legislative Intent

The Legislature finds and declares that this division is an integral part of any public agency's decisionmaking process, including, but not limited to, the issuance of permits, licenses, certificates, or other entitlements required for activities undertaken pursuant to federal statutes containing specific waivers of sovereign immunity.

(Added: Chapter 272, Statutes of 1998)

Chapter 2. Short Title
Section 21050

21050   Citation

This division shall be known and may be cited as the California Environmental Quality Act.

(Amended: Chapter 1312, Statutes of 1976)

Chapter 2.5. Definitions
Sections 21060 to 21069

21060   Application of Definitions

Unless the context otherwise requires, the definitions in this chapter govern the construction of this division.

21060.1   Agricultural Land

(a) "Agricultural land" means prime farmland, farmland of statewide importance, or unique farmland, as defined by the United States Department of Agriculture land inventory and monitoring criteria, as modified for California.

(b) In those areas of the state where lands have not been surveyed for the classifications specified in subdivision (a), "agricultural land" means land that meets the requirements of "prime agricultural land" as defined in paragraph (1), (2), (3), or (4) of subdivision (c) of Section 51201 of the Government Code.

(Added: Chapter 812, Statutes of 1993)

21060.3   Emergency

"Emergency" means a sudden, unexpected occurrence, involving a clear and imminent danger, demanding immediate action to prevent or mitigate loss of, or damage to, life, health, property, or essential public services. "Emergency" includes such occurrences as fire, flood, earthquake, or other soil or geologic movements, as well as such occurrences as riot, accident, or sabotage.

(Added: Chapter 1312, Statutes of 1976)

21060.5   Environment

"Environment" means the physical conditions which exist within the area which will be affected by a proposed project, including land, air, water, minerals, flora, fauna, noise, objects of historic or aesthetic significance.

(Added: Chapter 1154, Statutes of 1972)

21061   Environmental Impact Report

"Environmental impact report" means a detailed statement setting forth the matters specified in Sections 21100 and 21100.1; provided that information or data which is relevant to such a statement and is a matter of public record or is generally available to the public need not be repeated in its entirety in such statement, but may be specifically cited as the source for conclusions stated therein; and provided further that such information or data shall be briefly described, that its relationship to the environmental impact report shall be indicated, and that the source thereof shall be reasonably available for inspection at a public place or public building. An environmental impact report also includes any comments which are obtained pursuant to Section 21104 or 21153, or which are required to be obtained pursuant to this division.

An environmental impact report is an informational document which, when its preparation is required by this division, shall be considered by every public agency prior to its approval or disapproval of a project. The purpose of an environmental impact report is to provide public agencies and the public in general with detailed information about the effect which a proposed project is likely to have on the environment; to list ways in which the significant effects of such a project might be minimized; and to indicate alternatives to such a project.

In order to facilitate the use of environmental impact reports, public agencies shall require that such reports contain an index or table of contents and a summary. Failure to include such index, table of contents, or summary shall not constitute a cause of action pursuant to Section 21167.

(Amended: Chapter 1312, Statutes of 1976)

21061.1   Feasible

"Feasible" means capable of being accomplished in a successful manner within a reasonable period of time, taking into account economic, environmental, social, and technological factors.

(Added: Chapter 1312, Statutes of 1976)

21061.2   Land Evaluation and Site Assessment

"Land evaluation and site assessment" means a decisionmaking methodology for assessing the potential environmental impact of state and local projects on agricultural land.

(Added: Chapter 812, Statutes of 1993)

21062   Local Agency

"Local agency" means any public agency other than a state agency, board, or commission. For purposes of this division, a redevelopment agency and a local agency formation commission are local agencies, and neither is a state agency, board, or commission.

(Amended: Chapter 222, Statutes of 1975)

21063   Public Agency

"Public agency" includes any state agency, board, or commission, any county, city and county, city, regional agency, public district, redevelopment agency, or other political subdivision.

(Added: Chapter 1154, Statutes of 1972)

21064   Negative Declaration

"Negative declaration" means a written statement briefly describing the reasons that a proposed project will not have a significant effect on the environment and does not require the preparation of an environmental impact report.

(Added: Chapter 1312, Statutes of 1976)

21064.5   Mitigated Negative Declaration

"Mitigated negative declaration" means a negative declaration prepared for a project when the initial study has identified potentially significant effects on the environment, but (1) revisions in the project plans or proposals made by, or agreed to by, the applicant before the proposed negative declaration and initial study are released for public review would avoid the effects or mitigate the effects to a point where clearly no significant effect on the environment would occur, and (2) there is no substantial evidence in light of the whole record before the public agency that the project, as revised, may have a significant effect on the environment.

(Added: Chapter 1130, Statutes of 1993; Amended: Chapter 1230, Statutes of 1994)

21065   Project

"Project" means an activity which may cause either a direct physical change in the environment, or a reasonably foreseeable indirect physical change in the environment, and which is any of the following:

(a) An activity directly undertaken by any public agency.

(b) An activity undertaken by a person which is supported, in whole or in part, through contracts, grants, subsidies, loans, or other forms of assistance from one or more public agencies.

(c) An activity that involves the issuance to a person of a lease, permit, license, certificate, or other entitlement for use by one or more public agencies.

(Amended: Chapter 1230, Statutes of 1994)

21065.5   Geothermal Exploratory Project

"Geothermal exploratory project" means a project as defined in Section 21065 composed of not more than six wells and associated drilling and testing equipment, whose chief and original purpose is to evaluate the presence and characteristics of geothermal resources prior to commencement of a geothermal field development project as defined in Section 65928.5 of the Government Code. Wells included within a geothermal exploratory project must be located at least one-half mile from geothermal development wells which are capable of producing geothermal resources in commercial quantities.

(Added: Chapter 1271, Statutes of 1978)

21066   Person

"Person" includes any person, firm, association, organization, partnership, business, trust, corporation, limited liability company, company, district, county, city and county, city, town, the state, and any of the agencies and political subdivisions of * * * those entities, and, to the extent permitted by federal law, the United States, or any of its agencies or political subdivisions.

(Amended: Chapter 272, Statutes of 1998)

21067   Lead Agency

"Lead Agency" means the public agency which has the principal responsibility for carrying out or approving a project which may have a significant effect upon the environment.

21068   Significant Effect on the Environment

"Significant effect on the environment" means a substantial, or potentially substantial, adverse change in the environment.

(Added: Chapter 1312, Statutes of 1976)

21068.5   Tiering or Tier

"Tiering" or "tier" means the coverage of general matters and environmental effects in an environmental impact report prepared for a policy, plan, program or ordinance followed by narrower or site-specific environmental impact reports which incorporate by reference the discussion in any prior environmental impact report and which concentrate on the environmental effects which (a) are capable of being mitigated, or (b) were not analyzed as significant effects on the environment in the prior environmental impact report.

(Added: Chapter 967, Statutes of 1983)

21069   Responsible Agency

"Responsible Agency" means a public agency, other than the lead agency, which has responsibility for carrying out or approving a project.

(Added: Chapter 1312, Statutes of 1976)

Chapter 2.6. General
Sections 21080 to 21096

21080   **Application to Discretionary Projects; Olympic Games; Rates–Tolls– Fares; Proposition 13 Adjustments; Categorical Exemptions; Rail Service; Commuter Service; Mass Transit Service; Regional Transportation Programs; Out- of-State Projects; Local Agency Implementation of State Regulation Pursuant to Certified Regulatory Program; Negative Declarations**

(a) Except as otherwise provided in this division, this division shall apply to discretionary projects proposed to be carried out or approved by public agencies, including, but not limited to, the enactment and amendment of zoning ordinances, the issuance of zoning variances, the issuance of conditional use permits, and the approval of tentative subdivision maps unless the project is exempt from this division.

(b) This division does not apply to any of the following activities:

(1) Ministerial projects proposed to be carried out or approved by public agencies.

(2) Emergency repairs to public service facilities necessary to maintain service.

(3) Projects undertaken, carried out, or approved by a public agency to maintain, repair, restore, demolish, or replace property or facilities damaged or destroyed as a result of a disaster in a disaster-stricken area in which a state of emergency has been proclaimed by the Governor pursuant to Chapter 7 (commencing with Section 8550) of Division 1 of Title 2 of the Government Code.

(4) Specific actions necessary to prevent or mitigate an emergency.

(5) Projects which a public agency rejects or disapproves.

(6) Actions undertaken by a public agency relating to any thermal powerplant site or facility, including the expenditure, obligation, or encumbrance of funds by a public agency for planning, engineering, or design purposes, or for the conditional sale or purchase of equipment, fuel, water (except groundwater), steam, or power for a thermal powerplant, if the powerplant site and related facility will be the subject of an environmental impact report, negative declaration, or other document, prepared pursuant to a regulatory program certified pursuant to Section 21080.5, which will be prepared by the State Energy Resources Conservation and Development Commission, by the Public Utilities Commission, or by the city or county in which the powerplant and related facility would be located if the environmental impact report, negative declaration, or document includes the environmental impact, if any, of the action described in this paragraph.

(7) Activities or approvals necessary to the bidding for, hosting or staging of, and funding or carrying out of, an Olympic games under the authority of the International Olympic Committee, except for the construction of facilities necessary for the Olympic games.

(8) The establishment, modification, structuring, restructuring, or approval of rates, tolls, fares, or other charges by public agencies which the public agency finds are for the purpose of (A) meeting operating expenses, including employee wage rates and fringe benefits, (B) purchasing or leasing supplies, equipment, or materials, (C) meeting financial reserve needs and requirements, (D) obtaining funds for capital projects necessary to maintain service within existing service areas, or (E) obtaining funds necessary to maintain those intracity transfers as are authorized by city charter. The public agency shall incorporate written findings in the record of any proceeding in which an exemption under this paragraph is claimed setting forth with specificity the basis for the claim of exemption.

(9) All classes of projects designated pursuant to Section 21084.

(10) A project for the institution or increase of passenger or commuter services on rail or highway rights-of-way already in use, including modernization of existing stations and parking facilities.

(11) A project for the institution or increase of passenger or commuter service on high-occupancy vehicle lanes already in use, including the modernization of existing stations and parking facilities.

(12) Facility extensions not to exceed four miles in length which are required for the transfer of passengers from or to exclusive public mass transit guideway or busway public transit services.

(13) A project for the development of a regional transportation improvement program, the state transportation improvement program, or a congestion management program prepared pursuant to Section 65089 of the Government Code.

(14) Any project or portion thereof located in another state which will be subject to environmental impact review pursuant to the National Environmental Policy Act of 1969 (42 U.S.C. Sec. 4321 et seq.) or similar state laws of that state. Any emissions or discharges that would have a significant effect on the environment in this state are subject to this division.

(15) Projects undertaken by a local agency to implement a rule or regulation imposed by a state agency, board, or commission under a certified regulatory program pursuant to Section 21080.5. Any site-specific effect of the project which was not analyzed as a significant effect on the environment in the plan or other written documentation required by Section 21080.5 is subject to this division.

(c) If a lead agency determines that a proposed project, not otherwise exempt from this division, would not have a significant effect on the environment, the lead agency shall adopt a negative declaration to that effect. The negative declaration shall be prepared for the proposed project in either of the following circumstances:

(1) There is no substantial evidence, in light of the whole record before the lead agency, that the project may have a significant effect on the environment.

(2) An initial study identifies potentially significant effects on the environment, but (A) revisions in the project plans or proposals made by, or agreed to by, the applicant before the proposed negative declaration and initial study are released for public review would avoid the effects or mitigate the effects to a point where clearly no significant effect on the environment would occur, and (B) there is no substantial evidence, in light of the whole record before the lead agency, that the project, as revised, may have a significant effect on the environment.

(d) If there is substantial evidence, in light of the whole record before the lead agency, that the project may have a significant effect on the environment, an environmental impact report shall be prepared.

(e) (1) For the purposes of this section and this division, substantial evidence includes fact, a reasonable assumption predicated upon fact, or expert opinion supported by fact.

*** (2) Substantial evidence is not argument, speculation, unsubstantiated opinion or narrative, evidence that is clearly inaccurate or erroneous, or evidence of social or economic impacts that do not contribute to, or are not caused by, physical impacts on the environment* * *.

(f) As a result of the public review process for a mitigated negative declaration, including administrative decisions and public hearings, the lead agency may conclude that certain mitigation measures identified pursuant to paragraph (2) of subdivision (c) are infeasible or otherwise undesirable. In those circumstances, the lead agency, prior to approving the project, may delete those mitigation measures and substitute for them other mitigation measures that the lead agency finds, after holding a public hearing on the matter, are equivalent or more effective in mitigating significant effects on the environment to a less than significant level and that do not cause any potentially significant effect on the environment. If those new mitigation measures are made conditions of project approval or are otherwise are made part of the project approval, the deletion of the former measures and the substitution of the new mitigation measures shall not constitute an action or circumstance requiring recirculation of the mitigated negative declaration.

(g) Nothing in this section shall preclude a project applicant or any other person from challenging, in an administrative or judicial proceeding, the legality of a condition of project approval imposed by the lead agency. If, however, any condition of project approval set aside by either an administrative body or court was necessary to avoid or lessen the likelihood of the occurrence of a significant effect on the environment, the lead agency's approval of the negative declaration and project shall be invalid and a new environmental review process shall be conducted before the project can be reapproved, unless the lead agency

substitutes a new condition that the lead agency finds, after holding a public hearing on the matter, is equivalent to, or more effective in, lessening or avoiding significant effects on the environment and that does not cause any potentially significant effect on the environment.

(Amended: Chapter 547, Statutes of 1996; Chapter 1230, Statutes of 1994; Chapter 1131, Statutes of 1993)

21080.01 California Men's Colony West Facility; Reopening and Operation

This division shall not apply to any activity or approval necessary for the reopening and operation of the California Men's Colony West Facility in San Luis Obispo County.

(Added: Chapter 958, Statutes of 1983)

21080.02 Kings County Prison Facilities

This division shall not apply to any activity or approval necessary for and incidental to planning, design, site, acquisition, construction, operation, or maintenance of the new prison facility at or in the vicinity of Corcoran in Kings County as authorized by the act that enacted this section.

(Added: Chapter 931, Statutes of 1985)

21080.03 Kings and Amador (Ione) Counties Prison Facilities

This division shall not apply to any activity or approval necessary for or incidental to the location, development, construction, operation, or maintenance of the prison in the County of Kings, authorized by Section 9 of Chapter 958 of the Statutes of 1983, as amended, and of the prison in the County of Amador (Ione), authorized by Chapter 957 of the Statutes of 1983, as amended.

(Added: Chapter 931, Statutes of 1985)

21080.04 Rocktram-Krug Passenger Rail Service Project

(a) Notwithstanding paragraph (10) of subdivision (b) of Section 21080, this division applies to a project for the institution of passenger rail service on a line paralleling State Highway 29 and running from Rocktram to Krug in the Napa Valley. With respect to that project, and for the purposes of this division, the Public Utilities Commission is the lead agency.

(b) It is the intent of the Legislature in enacting this section to abrogate the decision of the California Supreme Court "that Section 21080, subdivision (b)

(11), exempts Wine Train's institution of passenger service on the Rocktram-Krug line from the requirements of CEQA" in *Napa Valley Wine Train, Inc. v. Public Utilities Com.*, 50 Cal.3d 370.

(c) Nothing in this section is intended to affect or apply to, or to confer jurisdiction upon the Public Utilities Commission with respect to, any other project involving rail service.

(Amended: Chapter 91, Statutes of 1995)

21080.05 San Francisco Peninsula Commute Service Project

This division does not apply to a project by a public agency to lease or purchase the rail right-of-way used for the San Francisco Peninsula commute service between San Francisco and San Jose, together with all branch and spur lines, including the Dumbarton and Vasona lines.

(Added: Chapter 1283, Statutes of 1989)

21080.07 Riverside and Del Norte Counties Prison Facilities

This division shall not apply to any activity or approval necessary for or incidental to planning, design, site acquisition, construction, operation, or maintenance of the new prison facilities located in any of the following places:

(a) The County of Riverside.

(b) The County of Del Norte.

(Added: Chapter 933, Statutes of 1985)

21080.08 Funding by Rural Economic Development Infrastructure Panel

This division shall not apply to any activity or approval necessary for or incidental to project funding, or the authorization for the expenditure of funds for the project, by the Rural Economic Development Infrastructure Panel pursuant to Article 5 (commencing with Section 15373.6) of Chapter 2.5 of Part 6.7 of Division 3 of Title 2 of the Government Code.

(Added: Chapter 1286, Statutes of 1987)

21080.09 Public Higher Education

(a) For purposes of this section, the following definitions apply:

(1) "Public higher education" has the same meaning as specified in Section 66010 of the Education Code.

(2) "Long range development plan" means a physical development and land use plan to meet the academic and institutional objectives for a particular campus or medical center of public higher education.

(b) The selection of a location for a particular campus and the approval of a long range development plan are subject to this division and require the preparation of an environmental impact report. Environmental effects relating to changes in enrollment levels shall be considered for each campus or medical center of public higher education in the environmental impact report prepared for the long range development plan for the campus or medical center.

(c) The approval of a project on a particular campus or medical center of public higher education is subject to this division and may be addressed, subject to the other provisions of this division, in a tiered environmental analysis based upon a long range development plan environmental impact report.

(d) Compliance with this section satisfies the obligations of public higher education pursuant to this division to consider the environmental impact of academic and enrollment plans as they affect campuses or medical centers, provided that any such plans shall become effective for a campus or medical center only after the environmental effects of those plans have been analyzed as required by this division in a long range development plan environmental impact report or tiered analysis based upon that environmental impact report for that campus or medical center, and addressed as required by this division.

(Added: Chapter 659, Statutes of 1989)

21080.1   Determining Environmental Impact

(a) The lead agency shall be responsible for determining whether an environmental impact report, a negative declaration, or a mitigated negative declaration shall be required for any project which is subject to this division. That determination shall be final and conclusive on all persons, including responsible agencies, unless challenged as provided in Section 21167.

(b) In the case of a project described in subdivision (c) of Section 21065, the lead agency shall, upon the request of a potential applicant, provide for consultation prior to the filing of the application regarding the range of actions, potential alternatives, mitigation measures, and any potential and significant effects on the environment of the project.

(Amended: Chapter 1230, Statutes of 1994; Chapter 1130, Statutes of 1993)

21080.2   30 Days

In the case of a project described in subdivision (c) of Section 21065, the determination required by Section 21080.1 shall be made within 30 days from the date on which an application for a project has been received and accepted as complete by the lead agency. This period may be extended 15 days upon the consent of the lead agency and the project applicant.

(Amended: Chapter 586, Statutes of 1984)

21080.3   Consultation With Other Agencies

(a) Prior to determining whether a negative declaration or environmental impact report is required for a project, the lead agency shall consult with all responsible agencies and with any other public agency which has jurisdiction by law over natural resources affected by the project which are held in trust for the people of the State of California. Prior to that required consultation, the lead agency may informally contact any such agency.

(b) In order to expedite the requirements of subdivision (a), the Office of Planning and Research, upon request of a lead agency, shall assist the lead agency in determining the various responsible agencies for a proposed project. In the case of a project described in subdivision (c) of Section 21065, the request may also be made by the project applicant.

(Amended: Chapter 1130, Statutes of 1993)

21080.4   Notices of Preparation; Scope and Content; OPR Assistance

(a) If a lead agency determines that an environmental impact report is required for a project, the lead agency shall immediately send notice of that determination by certified mail or an equivalent procedure to each responsible agency and to those public agencies having jurisdiction by law over natural resources affected by the project that are held in trust for the people of the State of California. Upon receipt of the notice, each responsible agency and each public agency having jurisdiction by law over natural resources affected by the project that are held in trust for the people of the State of California shall specify to the lead agency the scope and content of the environmental information that is germane to the statutory responsibilities of that responsible agency or public agency in connection with the proposed project and which, pursuant to the requirements of this division, shall

be included in the environmental impact report. The information shall be specified in writing and shall be communicated to the lead agency by certified mail or equivalent procedure not later than 30 days after the date of receipt of the notice of the lead agency's determination. The lead agency shall request similar guidance from appropriate federal agencies.

(b) * * * To expedite the requirements of subdivision (a), the lead agency or any responsible agency or public agency having jurisdiction by law over natural resources affected by the project that are held in trust for the people of the State of California may request one or more meetings between representatives of those agencies for the purpose of assisting the lead agency to determine the scope and content of the environmental information that any of those responsible agencies or public agencies may require. In the case of a project described in subdivision (c) of Section 21065, the request may also be made by the project applicant. The meetings shall be convened by the lead agency as soon as possible, but not later than 30 days * * * after the date that the meeting was requested.

(c) * * * To expedite the requirements of subdivision (a), the Office of Planning and Research, upon request of a lead agency, shall assist the lead agency in determining the various responsible agencies, public agencies having jurisdiction by law over natural resources affected by the project that are held in trust for the people of the State of California, and any federal agencies that have responsibility for carrying out or approving a proposed project. In the case of a project described in subdivision (c) of Section 21065, such a request may also be made by the project applicant.

(d) If a state agency is a responsible agency or a public agency having jurisdiction by law over natural resources affected by the project that are held in trust for the people of the State of California, subject to the requirements of subdivision (a), the Office of Planning and Research shall ensure that the information required by subdivision (a) is transmitted to the lead agency, and that affected agencies are notified regarding meetings to be held upon request pursuant to subdivision (b), within the required time period.

(Amended: Chapter 1201, Statutes of 1992; Amended: Chapter 415, Statutes of 1997)

21080.5 Certified Regulatory Programs

(a) * * * <u>Except as provided in Section 21158.1,</u> when the regulatory program of a state agency * * * requires a plan or other written documentation, containing environmental information and complying with * * * paragraph (3) of subdivision (d), to be submitted in support of any * * * <u>activity</u> listed in subdivision (b), the plan or other written documentation may be submitted in lieu of the environmental impact report required by this division * * * <u>if</u> the Secretary of the Resources Agency has certified the regulatory program pursuant to this section.

(b) This section * * * <u>applies</u> only to regulatory programs or portions thereof which involve either of the following:

(1) The issuance to a person of a lease, permit, license, certificate, or other entitlement for use.

(2) The adoption or approval of standards, rules, regulations, or plans for use in the regulatory program.

(c) A regulatory program certified pursuant to this section is exempt from * * * Chapter 3 (commencing with Section 21100)<u>,</u> and Chapter 4 (commencing with Section 21150)<u>,</u> and Section 21167<u>, except as provided in Article 2 (commencing with Section 21157) of Chapter 4.5</u>.

(d) * * * <u>To</u> qualify for certification pursuant to this section, a regulatory program shall require <u>the</u> utilization of an interdisciplinary approach <u>that</u> will ensure the integrated use of the natural and social sciences in decisionmaking and <u>which</u> shall meet all of the following criteria:

(1) The enabling legislation of the regulatory program * * * <u>does both of the following</u>:

* * * <u>(A)</u> <u>Includes</u> protection of the environment among its principal purposes.

* * * <u>(B)</u> <u>Contains</u> authority for the administering agency to <u>adopt</u> rules and regulations for the protection of the environment, guided by standards set forth in the enabling legislation.

(2) The rules and regulations adopted by the administering agency * * * <u>for the regulatory program do all of the following</u>:

<u>(A)</u> Require that an activity will not be approved or adopted as proposed if there are feasible alternatives or feasible mitigation measures available which would substantially lessen any significant adverse <u>effect</u> which the activity may have on the environment.

<u>(B)</u> Include guidelines for the orderly evaluation of proposed activities and the preparation of the plan or other written documentation in a manner consistent with the environmental protection purposes of the regulatory program.

<u>(C)</u> Require the administering agency to consult with all public agencies which have jurisdiction, by law, with respect to the proposed activity.

<u>(D)</u> Require that final action on the proposed activity include the written responses of the issuing authority to significant environmental points raised during the evaluation process.

<u>(E)</u> Require the filing of a notice of the decision by the administering agency on the proposed activity with the Secretary of the Resources Agency. Those notices shall be available for public inspection, and a list of the notices shall be posted on a weekly basis in the Office of the Resources Agency. Each list shall remain posted for a period of 30 days.

<u>(F)</u> Require notice of the filing of the plan or other written documentation to be made to the public and to any person who requests, in writing, notification. The notification shall be made in a manner that will provide the public or any person requesting notification with sufficient time to review and comment on the filing.

(3) The plan or other written documentation required by the regulatory program * * * <u>does both of the following</u>:

* * * <u>(A)</u> <u>Includes</u> a description of the proposed activity with alternatives to the activity, and mitigation measures to minimize any significant adverse * * * <u>effect on the environment of the activity</u>.

* * * <u>(B)</u> <u>Is</u> available for a reasonable time for review and comment by other public agencies and the general public.

(e) <u>(1)</u> The Secretary of the Resources Agency shall certify a regulatory program which the secretary determines meets all the qualifications for certification set forth in this section, and withdraw certification on determination that the regulatory program has been altered so that it no longer meets those qualifications. Certification and withdrawal of certification shall occur only after compliance with Chapter 3.5 (commencing with Section 11340) of Part 1 of Division 3 of Title 2 of the Government Code.

<u>(2)</u> In determining whether or not a regulatory program meets the qualifications for certification set forth in this section, the inquiry of the <u>secretary</u> * * * shall extend only to the questions of whether the regulatory program meets the generic requirements of subdivision (d). The inquiry shall not extend to individual decisions to be reached under the regulatory program, including the nature of specific alternatives or mitigation measures which might be proposed to lessen any significant adverse * * * <u>effect on the environment</u> of the activity.

* * * <u>(3)</u> <u>If</u> the <u>secretary</u> * * * determines that the regulatory program submitted for certification does not meet the qualifications for certification set forth in this section, the secretary shall adopt findings setting forth the reasons for the determination.

(f) After a regulatory program has been certified pursuant to this section, any proposed change in the program which could affect compliance with the qualifications for certification specified in subdivision (d) may be submitted to the Secretary of the Resources Agency for review and comment. The scope of the secretary's review shall extend only to the question of whether the regulatory program meets the generic requirements of subdivision (d). The review shall not extend to individual decisions to be reached under the regulatory program, including specific alternatives or mitigation measures which might be proposed to lessen any significant adverse * * * <u>effect on the environment</u> of the activity. The secretary shall have 30 days * * * <u>from the date of</u> receipt of the proposed change to notify the state agency * * * whether the proposed change will alter the regulatory program so that it no longer meets the qualification for certification established in this section and will result in a withdrawal of certification as provided in this section.

(g) Any action or proceeding to attack, review, set aside, void, or annul a determination or decision of a state agency * * * approving or adopting a proposed activity under a regulatory program which has been certified pursuant to this section on the basis that the plan or other written documentation prepared pursuant to paragraph (3) of subdivision (d) does not comply with this * * * section shall be commenced <u>not</u> later than 30 days from the date of the filing of notice of the approval or adoption of the activity.

(h) <u>(1)</u> Any action or proceeding to attack, review, set aside, void, or annul a determination of the Secretary of the Resources Agency to certify a regulatory program pursuant to this section on the basis that the regulatory program does not comply with * * * this section shall be commenced within 30 days * * * <u>from the date of certification by the secretary.</u>

<u>(2)</u> In any action brought * * * <u>pursuant to paragraph (1)</u>, the inquiry shall extend only to whether there was a prejudicial abuse of discretion by the secretary * * * . Abuse of discretion is established if the secretary has not proceeded in a manner required by law or if the determination is not supported by substantial evidence.

(i) For purposes of this section, any county agricultural commissioner * * * <u>is</u> a state agency.

(j) For purposes of this section, any air quality management district or air pollution control district * * * <u>is</u> a state agency, except that the approval, if any, by * * * <u>such a district</u> of a nonattainment area plan * * * <u>is</u> subject to this section only if, and to the extent that, the approval adopts or amends rules or regulations.

(Added: Chapter 1284, Statutes of 1987; Amended: Chapter 444, Statutes of 1996)

21080.6

(Added: Chapter 1070, Statutes of 1993; Repealed: January 1, 1997 by its own terms)

21080.7 Housing or Neighborhood Commercial Facilities

(a) No environmental impact report or negative declaration is required for any project involving the construction of housing or neighborhood commercial facilities in an urbanized area if the lead agency does all of the following:

(1) Finds, after giving notice pursuant to subdivision (c) or (d) of Section 21092 and following the procedure prescribed by law or regulation which would be necessary to make a determination pursuant to Section 21080.1, all of the following:

(A) The project is consistent with a comprehensive regulatory document which has been adopted pursuant to Article 8 (commencing with Section 65450) of Chapter 3 of Title 7 of the Government Code or, in the coastal zone, a local coastal program certified pursuant to Article 2 (commencing with Section 30510) of Chapter 6 of Division 20.

(B) For purposes of this section, the plan or program was adopted pursuant to the procedures established by Article 8 (commencing with Section 65450) of Chapter 3 of Title 7 of the Government Code not more than five years prior to the finding made pursuant to this section.

(C) The plan or program has been the subject of an environmental impact report.

(D) The environmental impact report is sufficiently detailed so that the significant effects on the environment of the project and measures necessary to mitigate or avoid those effects can be determined, including any significant physical effects on existing structures and neighborhoods of historical or aesthetic significance that exist in the area covered by the plan or program and measures necessary to mitigate or avoid those effects.

(2) Makes one or more of the findings as required pursuant to Section 21081.

(3) Files a notice of the decision on the proposed activity with the county clerk. Those notices shall be available for public inspection, and a list of the notices shall be posted on a weekly basis in the office of the county clerk. Each list shall remain posted for a period of 30 days.

(b) As used in this section:

(1) "Neighborhood commercial facilities" means those commercial facilities which are an integral part of a project involving the construction of housing and which will serve the residents of the housing.

(2) "Urbanized area" means a central city or cities and surrounding closely settled territory, as defined by the United States Department of Commerce Bureau of the Census in the Federal Register, Volume 39, Number 85, for Wednesday, May 1, 1974, at pages 15202 and 15203, and as periodically updated.

(Amended: Chapter 1130, Statutes of 1993)

21080.8 Mobilehome Park Conversion

This division does not apply to the conversion of an existing rental mobilehome park to a resident initiated subdivision, cooperative, or condominium for mobilehomes if the conversion will not result in an expansion of or change in existing use of the property.

(Added: Chapter 272, Statutes of 1990.)

21080.9 Local Coastal Programs

This division shall not apply to activities and approvals by any local government, as defined in Section 30109, or any state university or college, as defined in Section 30119, as necessary for the preparation and adoption of a local coastal program or long-range land use development plan pursuant to Division 20 (commencing with Section 30000); provided, however, that certification of a local coastal program or long-range land use development plan by the California Coastal Commission pursuant to Chapter 6 (commencing with Section 30500) of Division 20 shall be subject to the requirements of this division. For the purposes of Section 21080.5, a certified local coastal program or long-range land use development plan constitutes a plan for use in the California Coastal Commission's regulatory program.

(Amended: Chapter 961, Statutes of 1979)

21080.10 General Plan Time Extension; Low/Moderate Income Housing

This division shall not apply to any of the following:

(a) An extension of time, granted pursuant to Section 65361 of the Government Code, for the preparation and adoption of one or more elements of a city or county general plan.

(b) Actions taken by the Department of Housing and Community Development or the California Housing Finance Agency to provide financial assistance or insurance for the development and construction of residential housing for persons and families of low or moderate income, as defined in Section 50093 of the Health and Safety Code, if the project which is the subject of the application for financial assistance or insurance will be reviewed pursuant to this division by another public agency.

(c) (1) Any development project which consists of the construction, conversion, or use of residential housing for agricultural employees, as defined in paragraph (2), that is affordable to lower-income households, as defined in Section 50079.5 of the Health and Safety Code, if there is no public financial assistance for the development project and the developer of the development project provides sufficient legal commitments to the appropriate local agency to ensure the continued availability and use of the housing units for lower-income households for a period of at least 15 years, or any development project that consists of the construction, conversion, or use of residential housing for agricultural employees, as defined in paragraph (2), that is affordable to low- and moderate-income households, as defined in paragraph (2) of subdivision (h) of Section 65589.5 of the Government Code, if there is public financial assistance for the development project and the developer of the development project provides sufficient legal commitments to the appropriate local agency to ensure the continued availability and use of the housing units for low- and moderate-income households for a period of at least 15 years, if either type of development project meets all of the following requirements:

(A) (i) If the development project is proposed for an urbanized area, it is located on a project site which is adjacent, on at least two sides, to land that has been developed, and consists of not more than 45 units, or is housing for a total of 45 or fewer agricultural employees if the housing consists of dormitories, barracks, or other group living facilities.

(ii) If the development project is proposed for a nonurbanized area, it is located on a project site zoned for general agricultural use, and consists of not more than 20 units, or is housing for a total of 20 or fewer agricultural workers if the housing consists of dormitories, barracks, or other group living facilities.

(B) The development project is consistent with the jurisdiction's general plan as it existed on the date that the application was deemed complete.

(C) The development project is consistent with the zoning designation, as specified in the zoning ordinance as it existed on the date that the application was deemed complete, unless the zoning is inconsistent with the general plan because the local agency has not rezoned the property to bring it into conformity with the general plan.

(D) The development project is not more than five acres in area, except that a project site located in an area with a population density of at least 1,000 persons per square mile shall not be more than two acres in area.

(E) The development project site can be adequately served by utilities.

(F) The development project site has no value as a wildlife habitat.

(G) The development project site is not included on any list of facilities and sites compiled pursuant to Section 65962.5 of the Government Code.

(H) The development project will not involve the demolition of, or any substantial adverse change, in any structure that is listed, or is determined to be eligible for listing, in the California Register of Historic Resources.

(2) As used in paragraph (1), "residential housing for agricultural employees" means housing accommodations for an agricultural employee, as defined in subdivision (b) of Section 1140.4 of the Labor Code.

(3) As used paragraph (1), "urbanized area" means either of the following:

(A) An area with a population density of at least 1,000 persons per square mile.

(B) An area with a population density of less than 1,000 persons per square mile that is identified as an urban area in a general plan adopted by a local government, and was not designated, on the date that the application was deemed complete, as an area reserved for future urban growth.

(4) This division shall apply to any development project described in this subdivision if a public agency which is carrying out or approving the development project determines that there is a reasonable possibility that the project, if completed, would have a significant effect on the environment due to unusual circumstances, or that the cumulative impact of successive projects of the same type in the same area over time would be significant.

(Amended: Chapter 1058, Statutes of 1994)

21080.11 Title and Boundary Problems

This division shall not apply to settlements of title and boundary problems by the State Lands Commission and to exchanges or leases in connection with those settlements.

(Added: Chapter 1463, Statutes of 1982)

21080.12 Storm Damage Repair

(Added: Chapter 4, Statutes of 1997; repealed January 1, 1999, by its own terms.)

21080.13 Railroad Grade Separation Project

This division shall not apply to any railroad grade separation project which eliminates an existing grade crossing or which reconstructs an existing grade separation.

(Added: Chapter 58, Statutes of 1982)

21080.14 Affordable Housing Projects in Urbanized Areas

(a) Except as provided in subdivision (c), this division does not apply to any development project that consists of the construction, conversion, or use of residential housing consisting of not more than 100 units in an urbanized area that is affordable to lower income households, as defined in Section 50079.5 of the Health and Safety Code, if the developer of the development project provides sufficient legal commitments to the appropriate local agency to ensure the continued availability and use of the housing units for lower income households for a period of at least 15 years, or that is affordable to low- and moderate-income households, as defined in paragraph (2) of subdivision (h) of Section 65589.5 of the Government Code, if the developer of the development project provides sufficient legal commitments to the appropriate local agency to ensure the continued availability and use of the housing units for low- and moderate-income households at monthly housing costs as determined pursuant to paragraph (2) of subdivision (h) of Section 65589.5 of the Government Code, the developer provides sufficient legal commitments to ensure continued availability of units for the lower income households for 30 years as provided in paragraph (3) of subdivision (h) of Section 65589.5 of the Government Code, and the development project meets all of the following requirements:

(1) The development project is consistent with the jurisdiction's general plan or any applicable specific plan or local coastal program as it existed on the date that the application was deemed complete.

(2) The development project is consistent with the zoning designation, as specified in the zoning ordinance as it existed on the date that the application was deemed complete, unless the zoning is inconsistent with the general plan because the local agency has not rezoned the property to bring it into conformity with the general plan.

(3) The project site is an infill site that has been previously developed for urban uses, or the immediately contiguous properties surrounding the project site are, or previously have been, developed for urban uses.

(4) The project site is not more than five acres in area.

(5) The project site can be adequately served by utilities.

(6) The project site has no value as a wildlife habitat.

(7) The project site is not included on any list of facilities and sites compiled pursuant to Section 65962.5 of the Government Code.

(8) The project site is subject to an assessment prepared by a California registered environmental assessor to determine the presence of hazardous contaminants on the site and the potential for exposure of site occupants to significant health hazards from nearby properties and activities. If hazardous contaminants on the site are found, the contaminants shall be removed or any significant effects of those contaminants shall be mitigated to a level of insignificance. If the potential for exposure to significant health hazards from surrounding properties or activities is found to exist, the effects of the potential exposure shall be mitigated to a level of insignificance.

(9) The project will not involve the demolition of, or any substantial adverse change in, any district, landmark, object, building, structure, site, area, or place that is listed, or determined to be eligible for listing, in the California Register of Historical Resources.

(b) As used in subdivision (a), "urbanized area" means an area that has a population density of at least 1,000 persons per square mile.

(c) Notwithstanding subdivision (a), this division does apply to a development project described in subdivision (a) if there is a reasonable possibility that the development project would have a significant effect on the environment or the residents of the development project due to unusual circumstances or due to related or cumulative impacts of reasonably foreseeable projects in the vicinity of the development project.

(Added: Chapter 1230, Statutes of 1994; Amended: Chapter 415, Statutes of 1997)

21080.15

(Repealed: Chapter 912, Statutes of 1983, operative Jan. 1, 1986.)

21080.16

(Repealed: Chapter 912, Statutes of 1983, operative Jan. 1, 1990)

21080.17   Construction of Dwelling Units and Second Units

This division does not apply to the adoption of an ordinance by a city or county to implement the provisions of Section 65852.1 or Section 65852.2 of the Government Code.

(Added: Chapter 1013, Statutes of 1983)

21080.18   Closing of Public School K, 1–12

This division does not apply to the closing of any public school in which kindergarten or any of grades 1 through 12 is maintained or the transfer of students from that public school to another school if the only physical changes involved are categorically exempt under Chapter 3 (commencing with Section 15000) of Division 6 of Title 14 of the California Administrative Code.

(Amended: Chapter 1316, Statutes of 1986)

21080.19   Restriping of Streets or Highways

This division does not apply to a project for restriping of streets or highways to relieve traffic congestion.

(Added: Chapter 750, Statutes of 1984)

21080.21   Right-of-Way

This division does not apply to any project of less than one mile in length within a public street or highway or any other public right-of-way for the installation of a new pipeline or the maintenance, repair, restoration, reconditioning, relocation, replacement, removal, or demolition of an existing pipeline. For purposes of this section, "pipeline" includes subsurface facilities but does not include any surface facility related to the operation of the underground facility.

(Added: Chapter 1650, Statutes of 1984)

21080.22   General Plan Amendments

(a) This division does not apply to activities and approvals by a local government necessary for the preparation of general plan amendments pursuant to Section 29763, except that the approval of general plan amendments by the Delta Protection Commission is subject to the requirements of this division.

(b) For purposes of Section 21080.5, a general plan amendment is a plan required by the regulatory program of the Delta Protection Commission.

(Added: Chapter 898, Statutes of 1992)

21080.23   Existing Hazardous Liquid Pipelines

(a) This division does not apply to any project which consists of the inspection, maintenance, repair, restoration, reconditioning, relocation, replacement, or removal of an existing pipeline, as defined in subdivision (a) of Section 51010.5 of the Government Code, or any valve, flange, meter, or other piece of equipment that is directly attached to the pipeline, if the project meets all of the following conditions:

(1) (A) The project is less than eight miles in length.

(B) Notwithstanding subparagraph (A), actual construction and excavation activities undertaken to achieve the maintenance, repair, restoration, reconditioning, relocation, replacement, or removal of an existing pipeline are not undertaken over a length of more than one-half mile at any one time.

(2) The project consists of a section of pipeline that is not less than eight miles from any section of pipeline that has been subject to an exemption pursuant to this section in the past 12 months.

(3) The project is not solely for the purpose of excavating soil that is contaminated by hazardous materials, and, to the extent not otherwise expressly required by law, the party undertaking the project immediately informs the lead agency of the discovery of contaminated soil.

(4) To the extent not otherwise expressly required by law, the person undertaking the project has, in advance of undertaking the project, prepared a plan that will result in notification of the appropriate agencies so that they may take action, if determined to be necessary, to provide for the emergency evacuation of members of the public who may be located in close proximity to the project.

(5) Project activities are undertaken within an existing right-of-way and the right-of-way is restored to its condition prior to the project.

(6) The project applicant agrees to comply with all conditions otherwise authorized by law, imposed by the city or county planning department as part of any local agency permit process, that are required to mitigate potential impacts of the proposed project, and to otherwise comply with the Keene-Nejedly California Wetlands Preservation Act (Chapter 7 (commencing with Section 5810) of Division 5), the California Endangered Species Act (Chapter 1.5 (commencing with Section 2050) of Division 3 of the Fish and Game Code), and other applicable state laws, and with all applicable federal laws.

(b) If a project meets all of the requirements of subdivision (a), the person undertaking the project shall do all of the following:

(1) Notify, in writing, any affected public agency, including, but not limited to, any public agency having permit, land use, environmental, public health protection, or emergency response authority of the exemption of the project from this division by subdivision (a).

(2) Provide notice to the public in the affected area in a manner consistent with paragraph (3) of subdivision (b) of Section 21092.

(3) In the case of private rights-of-way over private property, receive from the underlying property owner permission for access to the property.

(4) Comply with all conditions otherwise authorized by law, imposed by

the city or county planning department as part of any local agency permit process, that are required to mitigate potential impacts of the proposed project, and otherwise comply with the Keene-Nejedly California Wetlands Preservation Act (Chapter 7 (commencing with Section 5810) of Division 5), the California Endangered Species Act (Chapter 1.5 (commencing with Section 2050) of Division 3 of the Fish and Game Code), and other applicable state laws, and with all applicable federal laws.

(c) Prior to January 1, 1999, this section shall not apply to ARCO Pipeline Company's crude oil pipelines designated as Crude Oil Line 1, from Tejon Station south to its terminus, and Crude Oil Line 90.

(d) This section does not apply to either of the following:

(1) A project in which the diameter of the pipeline is increased.

(2) A project undertaken within the boundaries of an oil refinery.

(Added: Chapter 765, Statutes of 1996)

21080.24 Air Quality Permits

This division does not apply to the issuance, modification, amendment, or renewal of any permit by an air pollution control district or air quality management district pursuant to Title V, as defined in Section 39053.3 of the Health and Safety Code, or pursuant to a district Title V program established under Sections 42301.10, 42301.11, and 42301.12 of the Health and Safety Code, unless the issuance, modification, amendment, or renewal authorizes a physical or operational change to a source or facility.

(b) Nothing in this section is intended to result in the application of this division to any physical or operational change which, prior to January 1, 1995, was not subject to this division.

(Added: Chapter 418, Statutes of 1994)

21080.26 Water Fluoridation

This division does not apply to minor alterations to utilities made for the purposes of complying with Sections 4026.7 and 4026.8 of the Health and Safety Code or regulations adopted thereunder.

(Added: Chapter 660, Statutes of 1995)

21080.32 Publicly Owned Transit Agencies

(a) This section shall only apply to publicly owned transit agencies, but shall not

apply to any publicly owned transit agency created pursuant to Section 130050.2 of the Public Utilities Code.

(b) Except as provided in subdivision (c), and in accordance with subdivision (d), this division does not apply to actions taken on or after July 1, 1995, by a publicly owned transit agency to implement budget reductions caused by the failure of agency revenues to adequately fund agency programs and facilities.

(c) This section does not apply to any action to reduce or eliminate a transit service, facility, program, or activity that was approved or adopted as a mitigation measure in any environmental document authorized by this division or the National Environmental Policy Act (42 U.S.C. Sec. 4321 et seq.) or to any state or federal requirement that is imposed for the protection of the environment.

(d) (1) This section applies only to actions taken after the publicly owned transit agency has made a finding that there is a fiscal emergency caused by the failure of agency revenues to adequately fund agency programs and facilities, and after the publicly owned transit agency has held a public hearing to consider those actions. A publicly owned transit agency that has held such a hearing shall respond within 30 days at a regular public meeting to suggestions made by the public at the initial public hearing. Those actions shall be limited to projects defined in subdivision (a) or (b) of Section 21065 which initiate or increase fees, rates, or charges charged for any existing public service, program, or activity; or reduce or eliminate the availability of an existing publicly owned transit service, facility, program, or activity.

(2) For purposes of this subdivision, "fiscal emergency," when applied to a publicly owned transit agency, means that the agency is projected to have negative working capital within one year from the date that the agency makes the finding that there is a fiscal emergency pursuant to this section. Working capital shall be determined by adding together all unrestricted cash, unrestricted short-term investments, and unrestricted short-term accounts receivable and then subtracting unrestricted accounts payable. Employee retirement funds, including Internal Revenue Code Section 457 deferred compensation plans and Section 401(k)

plans, health insurance reserves, bond payment reserves, workers' compensation reserves, and insurance reserves, shall not be factored into the formula for working capital.

(Added: Chapter 500, Statutes of 1996)

21080.33 Emergency Repairs

This division does not apply to any emergency project undertaken, carried out, or approved by a public agency to maintain, repair, or restore an existing highway, as defined in Section 360 of the Vehicle Code, except for a highway designated as an official state scenic highway pursuant to Section 262 of the Streets and Highways Code, within the existing right-of-way of the highway, damaged as a result of fire, flood, storm, earthquake, land subsidence, gradual earth movement, or landslide, within one year of the damage. This section does not exempt from this division any project undertaken, carried out, or approved by a public agency to expand or widen a highway damaged by fire, flood, storm, earthquake, land subsidence, gradual earth movement, or landslide.

(Added: Chapter 825, Statutes of 1996)

21081 Findings

Pursuant to the policy stated in Sections 21002 and 21002.1, no public agency shall approve or carry out a project for which an environmental impact report has been certified which identifies one or more significant effects on the environment that would occur if the project is approved or carried out unless both of the following occur:

(a) The public agency makes one or more of the following findings with respect to each significant effect:

(1) Changes or alterations have been required in, or incorporated into, the project which mitigate or avoid the significant effects on the environment.

(2) Those changes or alterations are within the responsibility and jurisdiction of another public agency and have been, or can and should be, adopted by that other agency.

(3) Specific economic, legal, social, technological, or other considerations, including considerations for the provision of employment opportunities for highly trained workers, make infeasible the mitigation measures or alternatives identified in the environmental impact report.

(b) With respect to significant effects which were subject to a finding under

paragraph (3) of subdivision (a), the public agency finds that specific overriding economic, legal, social, technological, or other benefits of the project outweigh the significant effects on the environment.

(Amended: Chapter 1294, Statutes of 1994; Chapter 1131, Statutes of 1993)

21081.5 Basis for Findings

In making the findings required by paragraph (3) of subdivision (a) of Section 21081, the public agency shall base its findings on substantial evidence in the record.

(Amended: Chapter 1294, Statutes of 1994)

21081.6 Reporting or Monitoring

(a) When making the findings required by paragraph (1) of subdivision (a) of Section 21081 or when adopting a mitigated negative declaration pursuant to paragraph (2) of subdivision (c) of Section 21080, the following requirements shall apply:

(1) The public agency shall adopt a reporting or monitoring program for the changes made to the project or conditions of project approval, adopted in order to mitigate or avoid significant effects on the environment. The reporting or monitoring program shall be designed to ensure compliance during project implementation. For those changes which have been required or incorporated into the project at the request of a responsible agency or a public agency having jurisdiction by law over natural resources affected by the project, that agency shall, if so requested by the lead agency or a responsible agency, prepare and submit a proposed reporting or monitoring program.

(2) The lead agency shall specify the location and custodian of the documents or other material which constitute the record of proceedings upon which its decision is based.

(b) A public agency shall provide that measures to mitigate or avoid significant effects on the environment are fully enforceable through permit conditions, agreements, or other measures. Conditions of project approval may be set forth in referenced documents which address required mitigation measures or, in the case of the adoption of a plan, policy, regulation, or other public project, by incorporating the mitigation measures into the plan, policy, regulation, or project design.

(c) Prior to the close of the public review period for a draft environmental impact report or mitigated negative declaration, a responsible agency, or a public agency having jurisdiction over natural resources affected by the project, shall either submit to the lead agency complete and detailed performance objectives for mitigation measures which would address the significant effects on the environment identified by the responsible agency or agency having jurisdiction over natural resources affected by the project, or refer the lead agency to appropriate, readily available guidelines or reference documents. Any mitigation measures submitted to a lead agency by a responsible agency or agency having jurisdiction over natural resources affected by the project shall be limited to measures which mitigate impacts to resources which are subject to the statutory authority of, and definitions applicable to, that agency. Compliance or noncompliance by a responsible agency or agency having jurisdiction over natural resources affected by the project with that requirement shall not limit the authority of the responsible agency or agency having jurisdiction over natural resources affected by the project, or the authority of the lead agency, to approve, condition, or deny projects as provided by this division or any other provision of law.

(Amended: Chapter 1294, Statutes of 1994; Chapter 1230, Statutes of 1994; Chapter 1130, Statutes of 1993; Chapter 1070, Statutes of 1992)

21081.7 Transportation Information

Transportation information resulting from the reporting or monitoring program required to be adopted by a public agency pursuant to Section 21081.6 shall be submitted to the transportation planning agency in the region where the project is located when the project has impacts that are of statewide, regional, or areawide significance according to criteria developed pursuant to Section 21083. The transportation planning agency shall adopt guidelines for the submittal of those reporting or monitoring programs.

(Amended: Chapter 626, Statutes of 1989)

21082 Public Agency Implementation

All public agencies shall adopt by ordinance, resolution, rule or regulation, objectives, criteria, and procedures for the evaluation of projects and the preparation of environmental impact reports and negative declarations pursuant to this division. A school district, or any other district, whose boundaries are coterminous with a city, county, or city and county, may utilize the objectives, criteria, and procedures of the city, county, or city and county, as may be applicable, in which case, the school district or other district need not adopt objectives, criteria, and procedures of its own. The objectives, criteria, and procedures shall be consistent with the provisions of this division and with the guidelines adopted by the Secretary of the Resources Agency pursuant to Section 21083. Such objectives, criteria, and procedures shall be adopted by each public agency no later than 60 days after the Secretary of the Resources Agency has adopted guidelines pursuant to Section 21083.

(Amended: Chapter 1312, Statutes of 1976)

21082.1 Preparation of Environmental Documents

(a) Any draft environmental impact report, environmental impact report, or negative declaration prepared pursuant to the requirements of this division shall be prepared directly by, or under contract to, a public agency.

(b) This section is not intended to prohibit, and shall not be construed as prohibiting, any person from submitting information or other comments to the public agency responsible for preparing an environmental impact report, draft environmental impact report, or negative declaration. The information or other comments may be submitted in any format, shall by considered by the public agency, and may be included, in whole or in part, in any report or declaration.

(c) The lead agency shall do all of the following:

(1) Independently review and analyze any report or declaration required by this division.

(2) Circulate draft documents which reflect its independent judgment.

(3) As part of the adoption of a negative declaration or certification of an environmental impact report, find that the report or declaration reflects the independent judgment of the lead agency.

(Amended: Chapter 905, Statutes of 1991)

21082.2 Significant Effect on the Environment; Determination

(a) The lead agency shall determine whether a project may have a significant effect on the environment based on substantial evidence in light of the whole record.

(b) The existence of public controversy over the environmental effects of a project shall not require preparation of an environmental impact report if there is no substantial evidence in light of the whole record before the lead agency that the project may have a significant effect on the environment.

(c) Argument, speculation, unsubstantiated opinion or narrative, evidence which is clearly inaccurate or erroneous, or evidence of social or economic impacts which do not contribute to, or are not caused by, physical impacts on the environment, is not substantial evidence. Substantial evidence shall include facts, reasonable assumptions predicated upon facts, and expert opinion supported by facts.

(d) If there is substantial evidence, in light of the whole record before the lead agency, that a project may have a significant effect on the environment, an environmental impact report shall be prepared.

(e) Statements in an environmental impact report and comments with respect to an environmental impact report shall not be deemed determinative of whether the project may have a significant effect on the environment.

(Amended: Chapter 1131, Statutes of 1993)

21083 State Guidelines

The Office of Planning and Research shall prepare and develop proposed guidelines for the implementation of this division by public agencies. The guidelines shall include objectives and criteria for the orderly evaluation of projects and the preparation of environmental impact reports and negative declarations in a manner consistent with this division.

The guidelines shall specifically include criteria for public agencies to follow in determining whether or not a proposed project may have a "significant effect on the environment." The criteria shall require a finding that a project may have a "significant effect on the environment" if any of the following conditions exist:

(a) A proposed project has the potential to degrade the quality of the environment, curtail the range of the environment, or to achieve short-term, to the disadvantage of long-term, environmental goals.

(b) The possible effects of a project are individually limited but cumulatively considerable. As used in this subdivision, "cumulatively considerable" means that the incremental effects of an individual project are considerable when viewed in connection with the effects of past projects, the effects of other current projects, and the effects of probable future projects.

(c) The environmental effects of a project will cause substantial adverse effects on human beings, either directly or indirectly.

The guidelines shall also include procedures for determining the lead agency pursuant to Section 21165.

The guidelines shall also include criteria for public agencies to use in determining when a proposed project is of sufficient statewide, regional, or areawide environmental significance that it should be submitted to appropriate state agencies for review and comment prior to completion of an environmental impact report or negative declaration thereon.

The Office of Planning and Research shall develop and prepare the proposed guidelines as soon as possible and shall transmit them immediately to the Secretary of the Resources Agency. The Secretary of the Resources Agency shall certify and adopt the guidelines pursuant to Chapter 3.5 (commencing with Section 11340) of Part 1 of Division 3 of Title 2 of the Government Code, which shall become effective upon the filing thereof. However, the guidelines shall not be adopted without compliance with Sections 11346.4, 11346.5, and 11346.8 of the Government Code.

(Amended: Chapter 714, Statutes of 1981)

21083.1 Legislative Intent; Court Interpretations

It is the intent of the Legislature that courts, consistent with generally accepted rules of statutory interpretation, shall not interpret this division or the state guidelines adopted pursuant to Section 21083 in a manner which imposes procedural or substantive requirements beyond those explicitly stated in this division or in the state guidelines.

(Added: Chapter 1070, Statutes of 1993)

21083.2 Significant Effect on Archaeological Resources

(a) As part of the determination made pursuant to Section 21080.1, the lead agency shall determine whether the project may have a significant effect on archaeological resources. If the lead agency determines that the project may have a significant effect on unique archaeological resources, the environmental impact report shall address the issue of those resources. An environmental impact report, if otherwise necessary, shall not address the issue of nonunique archaeological resources. A negative declaration shall be issued with respect to a project if, but for the issue of nonunique archaeological resources, the negative declaration would be otherwise issued.

(b) If it can be demonstrated that a project will cause damage to a unique archaeological resource, the lead agency may require reasonable efforts to be made to permit any or all of these resources to be preserved in place or left in an undisturbed state. Examples of that treatment, in no order of preference, may include, but are not limited to, any of the following:

(1) Planning construction to avoid archaeological sites.

(2) Deeding archaeological sites into permanent conservation easements.

(3) Capping or covering archaeological sites with a layer of soil before building on the sites.

(4) Planning parks, greenspace, or other open space to incorporate archaeological sites.

(c) To the extent that unique archaeological resources are not preserved in place or not left in an undisturbed state, mitigation measures shall be required as provided in this subdivision. The project applicant shall provide a guarantee to the lead agency to pay one-half the estimated cost of mitigating the significant effects of the project on unique archaeological resources. In determining payment, the lead agency shall give due consideration to the in-kind value of project design or expenditures that are intended to permit any or all archaeological resources or California Native American culturally significant sites to be preserved in place or left in an undisturbed state. When a final decision is made to carry out or approve the project, the lead agency shall, if necessary, reduce the specified mitigation measures to those which can be funded with the money guaranteed by the project applicant plus the money voluntarily guaranteed by any other person or persons for those mitigation purposes. In order to allow time for interested persons to provide the funding guarantee referred to in this subdivision, a final decision to carry out or approve a project shall not occur sooner than 60 days after completion of the recommended special environmental impact report required by this section.

(d) Excavation as mitigation shall be restricted to those parts of the unique archaeological resource that would be damaged or destroyed by the project. Excavation as mitigation shall not be required for a unique archaeological resource if the lead agency determines that testing or studies already completed have adequately recovered the scientifically consequential information from and about the resource, if this determination is documented in the environmental impact report.

(e) In no event shall the amount paid by a project applicant for mitigation measures required pursuant to subdivision (c) exceed the following amounts:

(1) An amount equal to one-half of 1 percent of the projected cost of the project for mitigation measures undertaken within the site boundaries of a commercial or industrial project.

(2) An amount equal to three-fourths of 1 percent of the projected cost of the project for mitigation measures undertaken within the site boundaries of a housing project consisting of a single unit.

(3) If a housing project consists of more than a single unit, an amount equal to three-fourths of 1 percent of the projected cost of the project for mitigation measures undertaken within the site boundaries of the project for the first unit plus the sum of the following:

(A) Two hundred dollars ($200) per unit for any of the next 99 units.

(B) One hundred fifty dollars ($150) per unit for any of the next 400 units.

(C) One hundred dollars ($100) per unit in excess of 500 units.

(f) Unless special or unusual circumstances warrant an exception, the field excavation phase of an approved mitigation plan shall be completed within 90 days after final approval necessary to implement the physical development of the project or, if a phased project, in connection with the phased portion to which the specific mitigation measures are applicable. However, the project applicant may extend that period if he or she so elects. Nothing in this section shall nullify protections for Indian cemeteries under any other provision of law.

(g) As used in this section, "unique archaeological resource" means an archaeological artifact, object, or site about which it can be clearly demonstrated that, without merely adding to the current body of knowledge, there is a high probability that it meets any of the following criteria:

(1) Contains information needed to answer important scientific research questions and that there is a demonstrable public interest in that information.

(2) Has a special and particular quality such as being the oldest of its type or the best available example of its type.

(3) Is directly associated with a scientifically recognized important prehistoric or historic event or person.

(h) As used in this section, "nonunique archaeological resource" means an archaeological artifact, object, or site which does not meet the criteria in subdivision (g). A nonunique archaeological resource need be given no further consideration, other than the simple recording of its existence by the lead agency if it so elects.

(i) As part of the objectives, criteria, and procedures required by Section 21082 or as part of conditions imposed for mitigation, a lead agency may make provisions for archaeological sites accidentally discovered during construction. These provisions may include an immediate evaluation of the find. If the find is determined to be a unique archaeological resource, contingency funding and a time allotment sufficient to allow recovering an archaeological sample or to employ one of the avoidance measures may be required under the provisions set forth in this section. Construction work may continue on other parts of the building site while archaeological mitigation takes place.

(j) This section does not apply to any project described in subdivision (a) or (b) of Section 21065 if the lead agency elects to comply with all other applicable provisions of this division. This section does not apply to any project described in subdivision (c) of Section 21065 if the applicant and the lead agency jointly elect to comply with all other applicable provisions of this division.

(k) Any additional costs to any local agency as a result of complying with this section with respect to a project of other than a public agency shall be borne by the project applicant.

(l) Nothing in this section is intended to affect or modify the requirements of Section 21084 or 21084.1.

(Amended: Chapter 375, Statutes of 1993)

21083.3 Use of a Certified EIR with Residential Development or Community Plan

(a) If a parcel has been zoned to accommodate a particular density of development or has been designated in a community plan to accommodate a particular density of development and an environmental impact report was certified for that zoning or planning action, the application of this division to the approval of any subdivision map or other project that is consistent with the zoning or community plan shall be limited to effects upon the environment which are peculiar to the parcel or to the project and which were not addressed as significant effects in the prior environmental impact report, or which substantial new information shows will be more significant than described in the prior environmental impact report.

(b) If a development project is consistent with the general plan of a local agency and an environmental impact report was certified with respect to that general plan, the application of this division to the approval of that development project shall be limited to effects upon the environment which are peculiar to the parcel or to the project and which were not addressed as significant effects in the prior environmental impact report, or which substantial new information shows will be more significant than described in the prior environmental impact report.

(c) Nothing in this section affects any requirement to analyze potentially significant offsite impacts and cumulative impacts of the project not discussed in the prior environmental impact report with respect to the general plan. However, all public agencies with authority to mitigate the significant effects shall undertake or require the undertaking of any feasible mitigation measures specified in the prior environmental impact report relevant to a significant effect which the project will have on the environment or, if not, then the provisions of this section shall have no application to that effect. The lead agency shall make a finding, at a public hearing, as to whether those mitigation measures will be undertaken.

(d) An effect of a project upon the environment shall not be considered peculiar to the parcel or to the project, for purposes of this section, if uniformly applied development policies or standards have been previously adopted by the city or county, with a finding based upon substantial evidence, which need not include an environmental impact report, that the development policies or standards will substantially mitigate that environmental effect when applied to future projects, unless substantial new information shows that the policies or standards will not substantially mitigate the environmental effect.

(e) Where a community plan is the basis for application of this section, any rezoning action consistent with the community plan shall be a project subject to exemption from this division in accordance with this section. As used in this section, "community plan" means a part of the general plan of a city or county which (1) applies to a defined geographic portion of the total area included in the general plan, (2) complies with Article 5 (commencing with Section 65300) of Chapter 3 of Division 1 of Title 7 of the Government Code by including or referencing each of the mandatory elements specified in Section 65302 of the Government Code, and (3) contains specific development policies adopted for the area included in the community plan and identifies measures to implement those policies, so that the policies which will apply to each parcel can be determined.

(f) No person shall have standing to bring an action or proceeding to attack, review, set aside, void, or annul a finding of a public agency made at a public hearing pursuant to subdivision (a) with respect to the conformity of the project to the mitigation measures identified in the prior environmental impact report for the zoning or planning action, unless he or she has participated in that public hearing. However, this subdivision shall not be applicable if the local agency failed to give public notice of the hearing as required by law. For purposes of this subdivision, a person has participated in the public hearing if he or she has either submitted oral or written testimony regarding the proposed determination, finding, or decision prior to close of the hearing.

(g) Any community plan adopted prior to January 1, 1982, which does not comply with the definitional criteria specified in subdivision (e) may be amended to comply with that criteria, in which case the plan shall be deemed a "community plan" within the meaning of subdivision (e) if (1) an environmental impact report was certified for adoption of the plan, and (2) at the time of the conforming amendment, the environmental impact report has not been held inadequate by a court of this state and is not the subject of pending litigation challenging its adequacy.

(Amended: Chapter 1102, Statutes of 1992)

21083.5 Relationship to NEPA; Tahoe Regional Planning Agency

(a) The guidelines prepared and adopted pursuant to Section 21083 shall provide that, when an environmental impact statement has been, or will be, prepared for the same project pursuant to the requirements of the National Environmental Policy Act of 1969 (42 U.S.C. Sec. 4321 et seq.) and implementing regulations, or an environmental impact report has been, or will be, prepared for the same project pursuant to the requirements of the Tahoe Regional Planning Compact (Section 66801 of the Government Code) and implementing regulations, all or any part of that statement or report may be submitted in lieu of all or any part of an environmental impact report required by this division, if that statement or report, or the part which is used, complies with the requirements of this division and the guidelines adopted pursuant thereto.

(b) Notwithstanding subdivision (a), compliance with this division may be achieved for the adoption in a city or county general plan, without any additions or change, of all or any part of the regional plan prepared pursuant to the Tahoe Regional Planning Compact and implementing regulations by reviewing environmental documents prepared by the Tahoe Regional Planning Agency addressing the plan, providing an analysis pursuant to this division of any significant effect on the environment not addressed in the environmental documents, and proceeding in accordance with Section 21081. This subdivision does not exempt a city or county from complying with the public review and notice requirements of this division.

(Amended: Chapter 493, Statutes of 1988)

21083.6 Project Requiring EIR and EIS

In the event that a project requires both an environmental impact report prepared pursuant to the requirements of this division and an environmental impact statement prepared pursuant to the requirements of the National Environmental Policy Act of 1969, an applicant may request and the lead agency may waive the time limits established pursuant to Section 21100.2 or 21151.5 if it finds that additional time is required to prepare a combined environmental impact report-environmental impact statement and that the time required to prepare such a combined document would be shorter than that required to prepare each document separately.

(Added: Chapter 1200, Statutes of 1977)

21083.7   Use of EIS

In the event that a project requires both an environmental impact report prepared pursuant to the requirements of this division and an environmental impact statement prepared pursuant to the requirements of the National Environmental Policy Act of 1969, the lead agency shall, whenever possible, use the environmental impact statement as such environmental impact report as provided in Section 21083.5. In order to implement the provisions of this section, each lead agency to which this section is applicable shall consult, as soon as possible, with the agency required to prepare such environmental impact statement.

(Added: Chapter 1200, Statutes of 1977)

21083.8   Closure and Reuse of Military Base

(a) For the purposed of this section, the following terms have the following meaning:

(1) "Reuse plan" means an initial plan for the reuse of a military base adopted by a local government or a redevelopment agency in the form of a general plan, general plan amendment, specific plan, redevelopment plan, or other planning document.

(2) "Military base" or "base" means any military base or reservation either closed or realigned by, or scheduled for closure or realignment by, the federal government.

(b) If an environmental impact statement on the closure and reuse of a military base has been prepared and filed pursuant to the National Environmental Policy Act of 1969 (42 U.S.C. Sec. 4321 et seq.), the lead agency that is responsible for the preparation of an environmental impact report for a reuse plan for the same base may proceed in the following manner:

(1) A notice of preparation of an environmental impact report on a reuse plan shall be prepared pursuant to either Section 21080.4 or 21080.6 and shall include a description of the reuse plan and a copy of the environmental impact statement. The notice shall indicate that the lead

agency intends to utilize the environmental impact statement as a draft environmental impact report and requests comments on whether, and to what extent, the environmental impact statement provides adequate information to serve as a draft environmental impact report, and what specific additional information, if any, is necessary to comply with this division. The notice shall also indicate the address to which written comments may be sent and the deadline for submitting comments.

(2) Upon the close of the comment period on the notice of preparation, the lead agency may proceed with preparation of the environmental impact report on the reuse plan. The lead agency shall, to the greatest extent feasible, avoid duplication and utilize information in the environmental impact statement consistent with this division. The draft environmental impact report shall consist of all or part of the environmental impact statement and any additional information that is necessary to prepare a draft environmental impact report in compliance with this division.

(3) In all other respects, the environmental impact report for the reuse plan shall be completed in compliance with this division.

(c) This section shall remain in effect only until January 1, 2001, and as of that date is repealed, unless a later enacted statute, which is enacted before January 1, 2001, deletes or extends that date.

(Amended: Chapter 861, Statutes of 1995)

21083.8.1   Baseline Provisions

(a) (1) For purposes of this section, "reuse plan" for a military base or reservation has the same meaning as the term as defined in paragraph (1) of subdivision (a) of Section 21083.8, except that the reuse plan shall also consist of a statement of development policies, include a diagram or diagrams illustrating its provisions, and make the designation required in paragraph (2) of this section.

(2) The reuse plan shall designate the proposed general distribution and general location of development intensity for housing, business, industry, open space, recreation, natural resources, public buildings and grounds, roads and other transportation facilities, infrastructure, and

other categories of public and private uses of land.

(b) (1) When preparing and certifying an environmental impact report for a reuse plan, including when utilizing an environmental impact statement pursuant to Section 21083.5, in addition to the procedure authorized pursuant to subdivision (b) of Section 21083.8, the determination of whether the reuse plan may have a significant effect on the environment may be made in the context of the physical conditions which were present at the time that the federal decision became final for the closure or realignment of the base or reservation. The no project alternative analyzed in the environmental impact report shall discuss the existing conditions on the base, as they exist at the time that the environmental impact report is prepared, as well as what could be reasonably expected to occur in the foreseeable future if the reuse plan were not approved, based on current plans and consistent with available infrastructure and services.

(2) For purposes of this division, all public and private activities taken pursuant to, or in furtherance of, a reuse plan shall be deemed to be a single project. However, further environmental review of any such public or private activity shall be conducted if any of the events specified in Section 21166 have occurred.

(c) Prior to preparing an environmental impact report for which a lead agency chooses to utilize the provisions of this section, the lead agency shall do all of the following:

(A) Hold a public hearing at which is discussed the federal environmental impact statement prepared for, or in the process of being prepared for, the closure of the military base or reservation. The discussion shall include the significant effects on the environment examined in the environmental impact statement, potential methods of mitigating those effects, including feasible alternatives, and the mitigative effects of federal, state, and local laws applicable to future nonmilitary activities. Prior to the close of the hearing, the lead agency may specify the baseline conditions for the reuse plan environmental impact report prepared, or in the process of being prepared, for the closure of the base or reservation. The lead agency may specify particular physical conditions which it will examine in greater detail than were examined in the environmental impact statement. Notice of the hearing shall be given as provided in Section 21092. The hearing may be continued from time to time.

(B) Identify pertinent responsible agencies and trustee agencies and consult with those agencies prior to the public hearing as to the application of their regulatory policies and permitting standards to the proposed baseline for environmental analysis, as well as to the reuse plan and planned future nonmilitary land uses of the base or reservation. The affected agencies shall have not less than 30 days prior to the public hearing to review the proposed reuse plan and to submit their comments to the lead agency.

(C) At the close of the hearing, the lead agency shall state in writing how the lead agency intends to integrate the baseline for analysis with the reuse planning and environmental review process, taking into account the adopted environmental standards of the community, including, but not limited to, the applicable general plan, specific plan, and redevelopment plan, and including other applicable provisions of adopted congestion management plans, habitat conservation or natural communities conservation plans, integrated waste management plans, and county hazardous waste management plans.

(D) At the close of the hearing, the lead agency shall state, in writing, the specific economic or social reasons, including, but not limited to, new job creation, opportunities for employment of skilled workers, availability of low and moderate income housing, and economic continuity, which support the selection of the baseline.

(d) (1) Nothing in this section shall in any way limit the scope of a review or determination of significance of the presence of hazardous or toxic wastes, substances, or materials including, but not limited to, contaminated soils and groundwater, nor shall the regulation of hazardous or toxic wastes, substances, or materials be constrained by prior levels of activity that existed at the time that the federal agency decision to close

the military base or reservation became final.

(2) This section does not apply to any project undertaken pursuant to Chapter 6.5 (commencing with Section 25100) of, or Chapter 6.8 (commencing with Section 25300) of, Division 20 of the Health and Safety Code, or pursuant to the Porter-Cologne Water Quality Control Act (Division 7 (commencing with Section 13000) of the Water Code).

(3) This section may apply to any reuse plan environmental impact report for which a notice of preparation pursuant to subdivision (a) of Section 21092 is issued within one year from the date that the federal record of decision was rendered for the military base or reservation closure or realignment and reuse, or prior to January 1, 1997, whichever is later, if the environmental impact report is completed and certified within five years from the date that the federal record of decision was rendered.

(e) All subsequent development at the military base or reservation shall be subject to all applicable federal, state, or local laws, including, but not limited to, those relating to air quality, water quality, traffic, threatened and endangered species, noise, and hazardous or toxic wastes, substances, or materials.

(Added: Chapter 861, Statutes of 1995)

21083.9   EIR–Transportation Facilities

Notwithstanding Section 21080.4, 21104, or 21153, a lead agency shall call at least one scoping meeting for a proposed project which may affect highways or other facilities under the jurisdiction of the Department of Transportation if the meeting is requested by the department. The lead agency shall call the scoping meeting as soon as possible, but not later than 30 days after receiving the request from the Department of Transportation.

(Added: Chapter 532, Statutes of 1988)

21084   Categorical Exemptions; Projects Damaging Scenic Resources

(a) The guidelines prepared and adopted pursuant to Section 21083 shall include a list of classes of projects which have been determined not to have a significant effect on the environment and which shall be exempt from this division. In adopting the guidelines, the Secretary of the Resources Agency shall make a finding that the listed classes of

projects referred to in this section do not have a significant effect on the environment.

(b) No project which may result in damage to scenic resources, including, but not limited to, trees, historic buildings, rock outcroppings, or similar resources, within a highway designated as an official state scenic highway, pursuant to Article 2.5 (commencing with Section 260) of Chapter 2 of Division 1 of the Streets and Highways Code, shall be exempted from this division pursuant to subdivision (a). This subdivision does not apply to improvements as mitigation for a project for which a negative declaration has been approved or an environmental impact report has been certified.

(c) No project located on a site which is included on any list compiled pursuant to Section 65962.5 of the Government Code shall be exempted from this division pursuant to subdivision (a).

(d) The changes made to this section by Chapter 1212 of the Statutes of 1991 apply only to projects for which applications have not been deemed complete on or before January 1, 1992, pursuant to Section 65943 of the Government Code.

(e) No project that may cause a substantial adverse change in the significance of an historical resource, as specified in Section 21084.1, shall be exempted from this division pursuant to subdivision (a).

(Amended: Chapter 1075, Statutes of 1992)

21084.1   Effects on Historical Resources

A project that may cause a substantial adverse change in the significance of an historical resource is a project that may have a significant effect on the environment. For purposes of this section, an historical resource is a resource listed in, or determined to be eligible for listing in, the California Register of Historical Resources. Historical resources included in a local register of historical resources, as defined in subdivision (k) of Section 5020.1, or deemed significant pursuant to criteria set forth in subdivision (g) of Section 5024.1, are presumed to be historically or culturally significant for purposes of this section, unless the preponderance of the evidence demonstrates that the resource is not historically or culturally significant. The fact that a resource is not listed in, or determined to be eligible for listing in, the California Register of Historical Resources, not included in a local register of historical resources, or not deemed significant pursuant to criteria set forth in subdivision (g) of Section 5024.1 shall not preclude a lead agency from determining whether the resource may be an historical resource for purposes of this section.

(Added: Chapter 1075, Statutes of 1992)

21084.2 Steam Sterilization

The Office of Planning and Research shall, at the next revision of the California Environmental Quality Act Guidelines (Chapter 3 (commencing with Section 15000) of Division 6 of Title 14 of the California Code of Regulations) which takes place after January 1, 1996, pursuant to Section 21087, recommend changes to those guidelines that would determine if Sections 15301, 15302, and 15304 of Title 14 of the California Code of Regulations apply to the treatment of medical waste by steam sterilization. If the office determines that those provisions of the guidelines apply, consistent with existing law, to that treatment, the office shall recommend clarifying revisions to the guidelines to expressly state that the treatment is subject to a categorical exemption under those provisions of the guidelines. If the office determines that those provisions of the guidelines do not categorically exempt that treatment, and if such an exemption is consistent with existing law, the office shall recommend a categorical exemption for the treatment in its recommended revision of the guidelines.

(Added: Chapter 877, Statutes of 1995)

21085 Projects Including Housing Development

With respect to a project which includes housing development, a public agency shall not, pursuant to this division, reduce the proposed number of housing units as a mitigation measure or project alternative for a particular significant effect on the environment if it determines that there is another feasible specific mitigation measure or project alternative that would provide a comparable level of mitigation. This section shall not affect any other requirement regarding the residential density of that project.

(Added: Chapter 1375, Statutes of 1982)

21085.5

(Repealed: Chapter 697, Statutes of 1979)

21085.6

(Repealed: Chapter 697, Statutes of 1979)

21086 Addition or Deletion of Exempt Categories

A public agency may, at any time, request the addition or deletion of a class of projects, to the list designated pursuant to Section 21084. Such a request shall be made in writing to the Office of Planning and Research and shall include information supporting the public agency's position that such class of projects does, or does not, have a significant effect on the environment.

The Office of Planning and Research shall review each such request and, as soon as possible, shall submit its recommendation to the Secretary of the Resources Agency. Following the receipt of such recommendation, the Secretary of the Resources Agency may add or delete the class of projects to the list of classes of projects designated pursuant to Section 21084 which are exempt from the requirements of this division.

The addition or deletion of a class of projects, as provided in this section, to the list specified in Section 21084 shall constitute an amendment to the guidelines adopted pursuant to Section 21083 and shall be adopted in the manner prescribed in Sections 21083, 21084, and 21087.

21087 Review of Guidelines

(a) The Office of Planning and Research shall, at least once every two years, review the guidelines adopted pursuant to Section 21083 and shall recommend proposed changes or amendments to the Secretary of the Resources Agency. The Secretary of the Resources Agency shall certify and adopt guidelines, and any amendments thereto, at least once every two years, pursuant to Chapter 3.5 (commencing with Section 11340) of Part 1 of Division 3 of Title 2 of the Government Code, which shall become effective upon the filing thereof. However, guidelines shall not be adopted or amended without compliance with Sections 11346.4, 11346.5, and 11346.8 of the Government Code.

(b) Within six months of the enactment of AB 314 of the 1993-94 Regular Session of the Legislature, the Office of Planning and Research shall recommend proposed changes and the Secretary of the Resources Agency shall certify and adopt revisions to the guidelines pursuant to Section 21083 to reflect the changes to this division enacted during the 1993-94 Regular Session of the Legislature.

(Amended: Chapter 1294, Statutes of 1994; Chapter 1130, Statutes of 1993)

21087.5

(Repealed: Chapter 1130, Statutes of 1993)

21088 EIR Monitor

The Secretary of the Resources Agency shall provide for the timely distribution to all public agencies of the guidelines and any amendments or changes thereto. In addition, the Secretary of the Resources Agency may provide for publication of a bulletin to provide public notice of the guidelines, or any amendments or changes thereto, and of the completion of environmental impact reports prepared in compliance with this division.

21089 Fees

(a) A lead agency may charge and collect a reasonable fee from any person proposing a project subject to this division in order to recover the estimated costs incurred by the lead agency in preparing a negative declaration or an environmental impact report for the project and for procedures necessary to comply with this division on the project. Litigation expenses, costs, and fees incurred in actions alleging noncompliance with this division under Section 21167 are not recoverable under this section

(b) The Department of Fish and Game may charge and collect filing fees, as provided in Section 711.4 of the Fish and Game Code. Notwithstanding Section 21080.1, a finding required under Section 21081, or any project approved under a certified regulatory program authorized pursuant to Section 21080.5 is not operative, vested, or final until the filing fees required pursuant to Section 711.4 of the Fish and Game Code are paid.

(Amended: Chapter 1201, Statutes of 1992)

21090 Redevelopment Plans

For all purposes of this division, all public and private activities and undertakings pursuant to, or in furtherance of, a redevelopment plan shall be deemed to be a single project. However, further environmental review of any public or private activity or undertaking pursuant to, or in furtherance of, a redevelopment plan shall be conducted if any of the events specified in Section 21166 have occurred.

(Amended: Chapter 1130, Statutes of 1993)

21090.1 Geothermal Exploratory Projects

For all purposes of this division, a geothermal exploratory project shall be deemed to be separate and distinct from any subsequent geothermal field development project as defined in Section 65928.5 of the Government Code.

(Added: Chapter 1271, Statutes of 1978)

21091 Review Periods—DEIR and Negative Declarations

(a) The public review period for a draft environmental impact report shall not be less than 30 days. If the draft environmental impact report is submitted to the State Clearinghouse for review, the review period shall be at least 45 days.

(b) The public review period for a proposed negative declaration shall not be less than 20 days. If the proposed negative declaration is submitted to the State Clearinghouse for review, the review period shall be at least 30 days.

(c) Notwithstanding subdivisions (a) and (b), if a draft environmental impact report or a proposed negative declaration is submitted to the State Clearinghouse for review and the period of review by the State Clearinghouse is longer than the public review period established pursuant to subdivision (a) or (b), whichever is applicable, the public review period shall be at least as long as the period of review by the State Clearinghouse.

(d) (1) The lead agency shall consider any comments it receives on a draft environmental impact report or on a proposed negative declaration, which are received within the public review period.

(2) (A) With respect to the consideration of comments received on a draft environmental impact report, the lead agency shall evaluate any comments on environmental issues that are received from persons who have reviewed the draft and shall prepare a written response pursuant to subparagraph (B). The lead agency may also respond to comments that are received after the close of the public review period.

(B) The written response shall describe the disposition of any significant environmental issue that is raised by commenters. The responses shall be prepared consistent with Section 15088 of Title 14 of the California Code of Regulations, as those regulations existed on June 1, 1993.

(e) (1) Criteria for shorter review periods by the State Clearinghouse for documents which must be submitted to the State Clearinghouse shall be set forth in the written guidelines issued by the Office of Planning and Research and made available to the public.

(2) Those shortened review periods shall not be less than 30 days for a draft environmental impact report and 20 days for a negative declaration.

(3) Any request for a shortened review period shall only be made in writing by the decisionmaking body of the lead agency to the Office of Planning and Research. The decisionmaking body may designate by resolution or ordinance a person authorized to request a shortened review period. Any designated person shall notify the decisionmaking body of this request.

(4) Any request approved by the State Clearinghouse shall be consistent with the criteria set forth in the written guidelines of the Office of Planning and Research.

(5) A shortened review period shall not be approved by the Office of Planning and Research for any proposed project of statewide, regional, or areawide environmental significance as determined pursuant to Section 21083.

(6) Any approval of a shortened review period shall be given prior to, and reflected in, the public notice required pursuant to Section 21092.

(f) Prior to carrying out or approving a project for which a negative declaration has been adopted, the lead agency shall consider the negative declaration together with any comments that were received and considered pursuant to paragraph (1) of subdivision (d).

(Amended: Chapter 1130, Statutes of 1993)

21092 Public Notice

(a) Any lead agency which is preparing an environmental impact report or a negative declaration or making a determination pursuant to Section 21157 shall provide public notice of that fact within a reasonable period of time prior to certification of the environmental impact report or adoption of the negative declaration.

(b) (1) The notice shall specify the period during which comments will be received on the draft environmental impact report or negative declaration, and shall include the date, time, and place of any public meetings or hearings on the proposed project, a brief description of the proposed project and its location, the significant effects on the environment, if any, anticipated as a result of the project, and the address where copies of the draft environmental impact report or negative declaration, and all documents referenced in the draft environmental impact report or negative declaration, are available for review.

(2) This section shall not be construed in any manner which results in the invalidation of an action because of the alleged inadequacy of the notice content, provided that there has been substantial compliance with the notice content requirements of this section.

(3) The notice required by this section shall be given to the last known name and address of all organizations and individuals who have previously requested notice and shall also be given by at least one of the following procedures:

(A) Publication, no fewer times than required by Section 6061 of the Government Code, by the public agency in a newspaper of general circulation in the area affected by the proposed project. If more than one area will be affected, the notice shall be published in the newspaper of largest circulation from among the newspapers of general circulation in those areas.

(B) Posting of notice by the lead agency on- and off-site in the area where the project is to be located.

(C) Direct mailing to the owners and occupants of contiguous property shown on the latest equalized assessment roll.

(c) For any project involving the burning of municipal wastes, hazardous waste, or refuse-derived fuel, including, but not limited to, tires, meeting the qualifications of subdivision (d), notice shall be given to all organizations and individuals who have previously requested notice and shall also be given by at least the procedures specified in subparagraphs (A), (B), and (C) of paragraph (3) of subdivision (b). In addition, notification shall be given by direct mailing to the owners and occupants of property within one-fourth of a mile of any parcel or parcels on which is located a project subject to this subdivision. This subdivision does not apply to any project for which notice has already been provided as of July 14, 1989, in compliance with this section as it existed prior to July 14, 1989.

(d) The notice requirements of subdivision (c) apply to both of the following:

(1) The construction of a new facility.

(2) The expansion of an existing facility which burns hazardous waste which would increase its permitted capacity by more than 10 percent. For purposes of this paragraph, the amount of expansion of an existing facility shall be calculated by comparing the proposed facility capacity with whichever of the following is applicable:

(A) The facility capacity approved in the facility's hazardous waste facilities permit pursuant to Section 25200 of the Health and Safety Code or its grant of interim status pursuant to Section 25200.5 of the Health and Safety Code, or the facility capacity authorized in any state or local agency permit allowing the construction or operation of a facility for the burning of hazardous waste, granted before January 1, 1990.

(B) The facility capacity authorized in the facility's original hazardous waste facilities permit, grant of interim status, or any state or local agency permit allowing the construction or operation of a facility for the burning of hazardous waste, granted on or after January 1, 1990.

(e) The notice requirements specified in subdivision (b) or (c) shall not preclude a public agency from providing additional notice by other means if the agency so desires, or from providing the public notice required by this section at the same time and in the same manner as public notice otherwise required by law for the project.

(Amended: Chapter 1130, Statutes of 1993)

21092.1 Addition—Notice and Consultation

When significant new information is added to an environmental impact report after notice has been given pursuant to Section 21092 and consultation has occurred pursuant to Sections 21104 and 21153, but prior to certification, the public agency shall give notice again pursuant to Section 21092, and consult again pursuant to Sections 21104 and 21153 before certifying the environmental impact report.

(Added: Chapter 1514, Statutes of 1984.)

21092.2 Public Notice Requests

The notices required pursuant to Sections 21080.4, 21092, 21108, and 21152 shall be mailed to any person who has filed a written request for notices with either the clerk of the governing body or, if there is no governing body, the director of the agency. The request may also be filed with any other person designated by the governing body or director to receive these requests. The agency may require requests for notices to be annually renewed. The public agency may charge a fee, except to other public agencies, which is reasonable related to the costs of providing this service. This section shall not be construed in any manner which results in the invalidation of an action because of the failure of a person to receive a requested notice, provided that there has been substantial compliance with the requirements of this section.

(Added: Chapter 907, Statutes of 1989)

21092.3 Posting Requirements

The notices required pursuant to Sections 21080.4 and 21092 for an environmental impact report shall be posted in the office of the county clerk of each county in which the project will be located and shall remain posted for a period of 30 days. The notice required pursuant to Section 21092 for a negative declaration shall be so posted for a period of 20 days, unless otherwise required by law to be posted for 30 days. The county clerk shall post the notices within 24 hours of receipt.

(Amended: Chapter 1130, Statutes of 1993)

21092.4 Consultation—Public Agencies, Transportation Planning Agencies

(a) For a project of statewide, regional, or areawide significance, the lead agency shall consult with transportation planning agencies and public agencies which have transportation facilities within their jurisdictions which could be affected by the project. Consultation shall be conducted in the same manner as for responsible agencies pursuant to this division, and shall be for the purpose of the lead agency obtaining information concerning the project's effect on major local arterials, public transit, freeways, highways, and rail transit service within the jurisdiction of a transportation planning agency or a public agency which is consulted by the lead agency. A transportation planning agency or public agency which provides information to the lead agency shall be notified of, and provided with copies of, environmental documents pertaining to the project.

(b) As used in this section "transportation facilities" includes major local arterials and public transit within five miles of the project site and freeways, highways, and rail transit service within 10 miles of the project site.

(Added: Chapter 626, Statutes 1989)

21092.5 Response to Comments

(a) At least 10 days prior to certifying an environmental impact report, the lead agency shall provide a written proposed response to a public agency on comments made by that agency which conform with the requirements of this division. Proposed responses shall conform with the legal standards established for responses to comments on draft environmental impact reports. Copies of responses or the environmental document in which they are contained, prepared in conformance with other requirements of this division and the guidelines adopted pursuant to Section 21083, may be used to meet the requirements imposed by this section.

(b) The lead agency shall notify any public agency which comments on a negative declaration, of the public hearing or hearings, if any, on the project for which the negative declaration was prepared. If notice to the commenting public agency is provided pursuant to Section 21092, the notice shall satisfy the requirement of this subdivision.

(c) Nothing in this section requires the lead agency to respond to comments not received within the comment periods specified in this division, to reopen comment periods, or to delay acting on a negative declaration or environmental impact report.

(Added: Chapter 905, § 2, Statutes of 1991)

Uncodified language from Statutes of 1991, chapter 905, section 3

The amendments to Section 21082.1 of the Public Resources Code made by this act, and the provisions of Section 21092.5 of the Public Resources Code, apply only to projects for which notice has not been provided pursuant to Section 21092 of the Public Resources Code as of January 1, 1992.

21092.6 Location of Projects on Hazardous Waste Sites List

(a) The lead agency shall consult the lists compiled pursuant to Section 65962.5 of the Government Code to determine whether the project and any alternatives are located on a site which is included on any list. The lead agency shall indicate whether a site is on any list not already identified by the applicant. The lead agency shall specify the list and include the information in the statement required pursuant to subdivision (f) of Section 65962.5 of the Government Code, in the notice required pursuant to Section 21080.4, a negative declaration, and a draft environmental impact report. The requirement in this section to specify any list shall not be construed to limit compliance with this division.

(b) If a project or any alternatives are located on a site which is included on any of the lists compiled pursuant to Section 65962.5 of the Government Code and the lead agency did not accurately specify or did not specify any list pursuant to subdivision (a), the California Environmental Protection Agency shall notify the lead agency specifying any list with the site when it receives notice pursuant to Section 21080.4, a negative declaration, and a draft environmental impact report. The California Environmental Protection Agency shall not be liable for failure to notify the lead agency pursuant to this subdivision.

(c) This section applies only to projects for which applications have not been deemed complete pursuant to Section 65943 of the Government Code on or before January 1, 1992.

(Added: Chapter 1212, Statutes of 1991)

21093 Public Agencies May Tier EIRs

(a) The Legislature finds and declares that tiering of environmental impact reports will promote construction of needed housing and other development projects by (1) streamlining regulatory procedures, (2) avoiding repetitive discussions of the same issues in successive environmental impact reports, and (3) ensuring that environmental impact reports prepared for later projects which are consistent with a previously approved policy, plan, program, or ordinance concentrate upon environmental effects which may be mitigated or avoided in connection with the decision on each later project. The Legislature further finds and declares that tiering is appropriate when it helps a public agency to focus upon the issues ripe for decision at each level of environmental review and in order to exclude duplicative analysis of environmental effects examined in previous environmental impact reports.

(b) To achieve this purpose, environmental impact reports shall be tiered whenever feasible, as determined by the lead agency.

(Amended: Chapter 418, Statutes of 1985)

21094 Later Projects

(a) Where a prior environmental impact report has been prepared and certified for a program, plan, policy, or ordinance, the lead agency for a later project that meets the requirements of this section shall examine significant effects of the later project upon the environment by using a tiered environmental impact report, except that the report on the later project need not examine those effects which the lead agency determines were either (1) mitigated or avoided pursuant to paragraph (1) of subdivision (a) of Section 21081 as a result of the prior environmental impact report, or (2) examined at a sufficient level of detail in the prior environmental impact report to enable those effects to be mitigated or avoided by site specific revisions, the imposition of conditions, or by other means in connection with the approval of the later project.

(b) This sections applies only to a later project which the lead agency determines (1) is consistent with the program, plan, policy, or ordinance for which an environmental impact report has been prepared and certified, (2) is consistent with applicable local land use plans and zoning of the city, county, or city and county in which the later project would be located, and (3) is not subject to Section 21166.

(c) For purposes of compliance with this section, an initial study shall be prepared to assist the lead agency in making the determinations required by this section. The initial study shall analyze whether the later project may cause significant effects on the environment that were not examined in the prior environmental impact report.

(d) All public agencies which propose to carry out or approve the later project may utilize the prior environmental impact report and the environmental impact report on the later project to fulfill the requirements of Section 21081.

(e) When tiering is used pursuant to this section, an environmental impact report prepared for a later project shall refer to the prior environmental impact report and state where a copy of the prior environmental impact report may be examined.

(Amended: Chapter 418, Statutes of 1985)

21095 LESA model; Optional Methodology

(a) The Resources Agency, in consultation with the Office of Planning and Research, shall develop an amendment to Appendix G of the state guidelines, for adoption pursuant to Section 21083, to provide lead agencies an optional methodology to ensure that significant effects on the environment of agricultural land conversions are quantitatively and consistently considered in the environmental review process.

(b) The Department of Conservation, in consultation with the United States Department of Agriculture pursuant to Section 658.6 of Title 7 of the Code of Federal Regulations, and in consultation with the Resources Agency and the Office of Planning and Research, shall develop a state model land evaluation and site assessment system, contingent upon the availability of funding from non-General Fund sources. The department shall seek funding for that purpose from non-General Fund sources, including, but not limited to, the United States Department of Agriculture.

(c) In lieu of developing an amendment to Appendix G of the state guidelines pursuant to subdivision (a), the Resources Agency may adopt the state model land evaluation and site assessment system developed pursuant to subdivision (b) as that amendment to Appendix G.

(Added: Chapter 812, Statutes of 1993)

21096 Airport-Related Safety Hazards and Noise Patterns

(a) If a lead agency prepares an environmental impact report for a project situated within airport comprehensive land use plan boundaries, or, if a comprehensive land use plan has not been adopted, for a project within two nautical miles of a public airport or public use airport, the Airport Land Use Planning Handbook published by the Division of Aeronautics of the Department of Transportation, in compliance with Section 21674.5 of the Public Utilities Code and other documents, shall be utilized as technical resources to assist in the preparation of the environmental impact report as the report relates to airport-related safety hazards and noise problems.

(b) A lead agency shall not adopt a negative declaration for a project described in subdivision (a) unless the lead agency considers whether the project will result in a safety hazard or noise problem for persons using the airport or for persons residing or working in the project area.

(Added: Chapter 438, Statutes of 1994)

Chapter 3. State Agencies, Boards, and Commissions Sections 21100 to 21108

21100 Environmental Impact Reports State Projects; Contents of Environmental Impact Reports

(a) All lead agencies shall prepare, or cause to be prepared by contract, and certify the completion of, an environmental impact report on any project which they propose to carry out or approve that may have a significant effect on the environment. Whenever feasible, a standard format shall be used for environmental impact reports.

(b) The environmental impact report shall include a detailed statement setting forth all of the following:

   (1) All significant effects on the environment of the proposed project.

   (2) In a separate section:

      (A) Any significant effect on the environment that cannot be avoided if the project is implemented.

      (B) Any significant effect on the environment that would be irreversible if the project is implemented.

   (3) Mitigation measures proposed to minimize significant effects on the environment, including, but not limited to, measures to reduce the wasteful, inefficient, and unnecessary consumption of energy.

   (4) Alternatives to the proposed project.

   (5) The growth-inducing impact of the proposed project.

(c) The report shall also contain a statement briefly indicating the reasons for determining that various effects on the environment of a project are not significant and consequently have not been discussed in detail in the environmental impact report.

(d) For purposes of this section, any significant effect on the environment shall be limited to substantial, or potentially substantial, adverse changes in physical conditions which exist within the area as defined in Section 21060.5.

(e) Previously approved land use documents, including, but not limited to, general plans, specific plans, and local coastal plans, may be used in cumulative impact analysis.

(Amended: Chapter 1230, Statutes of 1994; Chapter 1294, Statutes of 1994; Chapter 1130, Statutes of 1993)

21100.1 Information Not Required in Certain Environmental Impact Reports

The information described in subparagraph (B) of paragraph (2) of subdivision (b) of Section 21100 shall be required only in environmental impact reports prepared in connection with the following:

(a) The adoption, amendment, or enactment of a plan, policy, or ordinance of a public agency.

(b) The adoption by a local agency formation commission of a resolution making determinations.

(c) A project which will be subject to the requirements for preparing an environmental impact statement pursuant to the requirements of the National Environmental Policy Act of 1969.

(Amended: Chapter 1230, Statutes of 1994; Chapter 1294, Statutes of 1994)

21100.2 Time Limits

(a)*** (1) For projects described in subdivision (c) of Section 21065, each state agency shall establish, by resolution or order, time limits *** that do not exceed *** the following:

   (A) One year for completing and certifying environmental impact reports ***.

   (B) One hundred eighty days for completing and adopting negative declarations ***.

(2) The time limits specified in paragraph (1) shall apply only to those circumstances in which the state agency is the lead agency for a project. These resolutions or orders may establish different time limits for different types or classes of projects, but all limits shall be measured from the date on which an application requesting approval of the project is received and accepted as complete by the state agency.

(3) No application for a project may be deemed incomplete for lack of a waiver of time periods prescribed in state regulations.

(4) The resolutions or orders required by this section may provide for a reasonable extension of the time period in the event that compelling circumstances justify additional time and the project applicant consents thereto.

(b) If a draft environmental impact report, environmental impact report, or focused environmental impact report *** is prepared under a contract to a state agency, the contract shall be executed within 45 days from the date on which the state agency *** sends a notice of preparation pursuant to Section 21080.4. The state agency may take longer to execute the contract *** if the project applicant and the state agency mutually agree to an extension of the time limit provided by this subdivision.

(Amended: Chapter 808, Statutes of 1996; Chapter 1294, Statutes of 1994)

21100.3

(Repealed: Chapter 39, Statutes of 1987)

21101 Comments on Federal Documents

In regard to any proposed federal project in this state which may have a significant effect on the environment and on which the state officially comments, the state officials responsible for such comments shall include in their report a detailed statement setting forth the matters specified in Section 21100 prior to transmitting the comments of the state to the federal government. No report shall be transmitted to the federal government unless it includes such a detailed statement as to the matters specified in Section 21100.

(Added: Chapter 1433, Statutes of 1970)

21102 Funding Requests

No state agency, board, or commission shall request funds, nor shall any state agency, board, or commission which authorizes expenditures of funds, other than funds appropriated in the Budget Act, authorize funds for expenditure for any project, other than a project involving only feasibility or planning studies for possible future actions which the agency, board, or commission has not approved, adopted or funded, which may have a significant effect on the environment unless such request or authorization is accompanied by an environmental impact report.

Feasibility and planning studies exempted by this section from the preparation of an environmental impact report shall nevertheless include consideration of environmental factors.

(Amended: Chapter 1154, Statutes of 1972)

21104 Consultation with Other Agencies

Prior to completing an environmental impact report, the state lead agency shall consult with, and obtain comments from, each responsible agency, and any public agency which has jurisdiction by law with respect to the project, and any city or county which borders on a city or county within which the project is located unless otherwise designated annually by agreement between the state lead agency and the city or county, and may consult with any person who has special expertise with respect to any environmental impact involved. In the case of a project described in subdivision (c) of Section 21065, the state lead agency shall, upon the request of the applicant, provide for early consultation to identify the range of actions, alternatives, mitigation measures, and significant effects to be analyzed in depth in the environmental impact report. The state lead agency may consult with persons identified by the applicant which the applicant believes will be concerned with the environmental effects of the project and may consult with members of the public who have made a written request to be consulted on the project. A request by the applicant for early consultation shall be made not later than 30 days after the determination required by Section 21080.1 with respect to the project.

(b) The state lead agency shall consult with, and obtain comments from, the State Air Resources Board in preparing an environmental impact report on a highway or freeway project, as to the air pollution impact of the potential vehicular use of the highway or freeway.

(c) A responsible agency or other public agency shall only make substantive comments regarding those activities involved in a project which are within an area of expertise of the agency or which are required to be carried out or approved by the agency. Those comments shall be supported by specific documentation.

(Amended: Chapter 907, Statutes of 1989. Amended: Chapter 732, Statutes of 1990)

21104.2 Effect of Projects on Threatened or Endangered Species

The state lead agency shall consult with, and obtain written findings from, the Department of Fish and Game in preparing an environmental impact report on a project, as to the impact of the project on the continued existence of any endangered species or threatened species pursuant to Article 4 (commencing with Section 2090) of Chapter 1.5 Division 3 of the Fish and Game Code.

(Added: Chapter 1240, Statutes of 1984)

21105 Availability of Environmental Impact Reports

The state lead agency shall include the environmental impact report as a part of the regular project report used in the existing review and budgetary process. It shall be available to the Legislature. It shall also be available for inspection by any member of the general public, who may secure a copy thereof by paying for the actual cost of such a copy. It shall be filed by the state lead agency with the appropriate local planning agency of any city, county, or city and county which will be affected by the project.

(Amended: Chapter 1200, Statutes of 1977)

21106 Funding for Environmental Protection

All state agencies, boards, and commissions shall request in their budgets the funds necessary to protect the environment in relation to problems caused by their activities.

(Added: Chapter 1433, Statutes of 1970)

21107

(Repealed: Chapter 1154, Statutes of 1972)

21108 Notices of Determination; Notices of Exemption; Inspection of Notices

(a) Whenever a state agency, board, or commission approves or determines to carry out a project which is subject to this division, it shall file notice of that approval or that determination with the Office of Planning and Research. The notice shall indicate the determination of the agency, board, or commission whether the project will, or will not, have a significant effect on the environment and shall indicate whether an environmental impact report has been prepared pursuant to this division.

(b) Whenever a state agency, board, or commission determines that a project is not subject to this division pursuant to subdivision (b) of Section 21080 or pursuant to Section 21085 or 21172, and it approves or determines to carry out that project, it, or the person specified in subdivision (b) or (c) of Section 21065, may file notice of the determination with the Office of Planning and Research. Any notice filed pursuant to this subdivision by a person specified in subdivision (b) or (c) of Section 21065 shall have a certificate of determination attached to it issued by the state agency, board, or commission responsible for making the determination that a project is not subject to the provisions of this division pursuant to subdivision

(b) of Section 21080 or pursuant to Section 21085 or 21172. The certificate of determination may be in the form of a certified copy of an existing document or record of the state agency, board, or commission.

(c) All notices filed pursuant to this section shall be available for public inspection, and a list of these notices shall be posted on a weekly basis in the Office of Planning and Research. Each list shall remain posted for a period of 30 days.

(Amended: Chapter 571, Statutes of 1984)

Chapter 4. Local Agencies Sections 21150 to 21155

21150 Environmental Impact Reports for State Funding

State agencies, boards, and commissions, responsible for allocating state or federal funds on a project-by-project basis to local agencies for any project which may have a significant effect on the environment, shall require from the responsible local governmental agency a detailed statement setting forth the matters specified in Section 21100 prior to the allocation of any funds other than funds solely for projects involving only feasibility or planning studies for possible future actions which the agency, board, or commission has not approved, adopted, or funded.

(Amended: Chapter 1154, Statutes of 1972)

21151 Preparing Environmental Impact Reports

(a) All local agencies shall prepare, or cause to be prepared by contract, and certify the completion of, an environmental impact report on any project that they intend to carry out or approve which may have a significant effect on the environment. When a report is required by Section 65402 of the Government Code, the environmental impact report may be submitted as a part of that report.

(b) For purposes of this section, any significant effect on the environment shall be limited to substantial, or potentially substantial, adverse changes in physical conditions which exist within the area as defined in Section 21060.5.

(c) When an environmental impact report is certified by a local agency's decision-making body which is not elected, that certification may be appealed to the agency's elected decisionmaking body, if any.

(Amended: Chapter 1070, Statutes of 1993)

21151.1 Mandatory EIRs; Waste-Burning Projects

(a) Notwithstanding paragraph (6) of subdivision (b) of Section 21080, or Section 21080.5 or 21084, or any other provision of law, except as provided in this section, a lead agency shall prepare or cause to be prepared by contract, and certify the completion of, an environmental impact report or, if appropriate, a modification, addendum, or supplement to an existing environmental impact report, for any project involving any of the following:

(1) (A) The burning of municipal wastes, hazardous waste, or refuse-derived fuel, including, but not limited to, tires, if the project is either of the following:

    (i) The construction of a new facility.

    (ii) The expansion of an existing facility that burns hazardous waste that would increase its permitted capacity by more than 10 percent.

  (B) This paragraph does not apply to any project exclusively burning hazardous waste, for which a final determination under Section 21080.1 has been made prior to July 14, 1989.

(2) The initial issuance of a hazardous waste facilities permit to a land disposal facility, as defined in subdivision (d) of Section 25199.1 of the Health and Safety Code.

(3) The initial issuance of a hazardous waste facilities permit pursuant to Section 25200 of the Health and Safety Code to an offsite large treatment facility, as defined pursuant to subdivision (d) of Section 25205.1 of the Health and Safety Code.

(4) A base reuse plan as defined in Section 21083.8 or 21083.8.1. The Legislature hereby finds that no reimbursement is required pursuant to Section 6 of Article XIII B of the California Constitution for an environmental impact report for a base reuse plan if an environmental impact report is otherwise required for that base reuse plan pursuant to any other provision of this division.

(b) For purposes of clause (ii) of subparagraph (A) of subparagraph (B) of paragraph (1) of subdivision (a), the amount of expansion of an existing facility shall be calculated by comparing the proposed facility capacity with whichever of the following is applicable:

(1) The facility capacity authorized in the facility's hazardous waste facilities permit pursuant to Section 25200 of the Health and Safety Code or its grant of interim status pursuant to Section 25200.5 of the Health and Safety Code, or the facility capacity authorized in any state or local agency permit allowing the construction or operation of a facility for the burning of hazardous waste, granted before January 1, 1990.

(2) The facility capacity authorized in the facility's original hazardous waste facilities permit, grant of interim status, or any state or local agency permit allowing the construction or operation of a facility for the burning of hazardous waste, on or after January 1, 1990.

(c) For purposes of paragraphs (2) and (3) of subdivision (a), the initial issuance of a hazardous waste facilities permit does not include the issuance of a closure or postclosure permit pursuant to Chapter 6.5 (commencing with Section 25100) of Division 20 of the Health and Safety Code.

(d) Paragraph (1) of subdivision (a) does not apply to any project that does any of the following:

(1) Exclusively burns digester gas produced from manure or any other solid or semisolid animal waste.

(2) Exclusively burns methane gas produced from a disposal site, as defined in Section 40122, that is used only for the disposal of solid waste, as defined in Section 40191.

(3) Exclusively burns forest, agricultural, wood, or other biomass wastes.

(4) Exclusively burns hazardous waste in an incineration unit that is transportable and that is either at a site for not longer than three years or is part of a remedial or removal action. For purposes of this paragraph, "transportable" means any equipment that performs a "treatment" as defined in Section 66216 of Title 22 of the California Code of Regulations, and that is transported on a vehicle as defined in Section 66230 of Title 22 of the California Code of Regulations.

(5) Exclusively burns refinery waste in a flare on the site of generation.

(6) Exclusively burns in a flare methane gas produced at a municipal sewage treatment plant.

(7) Exclusively burns hazardous waste, or exclusively burns hazardous waste as a supplemental fuel, as part of a research, development, or demonstration project that, consistent with federal regulations implementing the Resource Conservation and Recovery Act of 1976, as amended (42 U.S.C. Sec. 6901 et seq.), has been determined to be innovative and experimental by the Department of Toxic Substances Control and that is limited in type and quantity of waste to that necessary to determine the efficacy and performance capabilities of the technology or process; provided, however, that any facility that operated as a research, development, or demonstration project and for which an application is thereafter submitted for a hazardous waste facility permit for operation other than as a research, development, or demonstration project shall be considered a new facility for the burning of hazardous waste and shall be subject to subdivision (a) of Section 21151.1.

(8) Exclusively burns soils contaminated only with petroleum fuels or the vapors from these soils.

(9) Exclusively treats less than 3,000 pounds of hazardous waste per day in a thermal processing unit operated in the absence of open flame, and submits a worst-case health risk assessment of the technology to the Department of Toxic Substances Control for review and distribution to the interested public. This assessment shall be prepared in accordance with guidelines set forth in the Air Toxics Assessment Manual of the California Air Pollution Control Officers Association.

(10) Exclusively burns less than 1,200 pounds per day of medical waste, as defined in Section 117690 of the Health and Safety Code, on hospital sites.

(11) Exclusively burns chemicals and fuels as part of firefighter training.

(12) Exclusively conducts open burns of explosives subject to the requirements of the air pollution control district or air quality management district and in compliance with OSHA and Cal-OSHA regulations.

(13) Exclusively conducts onsite burning of less than 3,000 pounds per day of fumes directly from a manufacturing or commercial process.

(14) Exclusively conducts onsite burning of hazardous waste in an industrial

furnace that recovers hydrogen chloride from the flue gas if the hydrogen chloride is subsequently sold, distributed in commerce, or used in a manufacturing process at the site where the hydrogen chloride is recovered, and the burning is in compliance with the requirements of the air pollution control district or air quality management district and the Department of Toxic Substances Control.

(e) Paragraph (1) of subdivision (a) does not apply to any project for which the State Energy Resources Conservation and Development Commission has assumed jurisdiction under Chapter 6 (commencing with Section 25500) of Division 15.

(f) Paragraphs (2) and (3) of subdivision (a) shall not apply if the facility only manages hazardous waste that is identified or listed pursuant to Section 25140 or Section 25141 on or after January 1, 1992, but not before that date, or only conducts activities that are regulated pursuant to Chapter 6.5 (commencing with Section 25100) of Division 20 of the Health and Safety Code on or after January 1, 1992, but not before that date.

(g) This section does not exempt any project from any other requirements of this division.

(h) For purposes of this section, offsite facility means a facility that serves more than one generator of hazardous waste.

(Amended: Chapter 861, Statutes of 1995; Chapter 1104, Statutes of 1994; Chapter 973, Statutes of 1993; Chapter 1343, Statutes of 1992)

21151.2   School Site Proposed Acquisition or Addition; Notice to Planning Commission; Investigation; Report to Governing Board

To promote the safety of pupils and comprehensive community planning the governing board of each school district before acquiring title to property for a new school site or for an addition to a present school site, shall give the planning commission having jurisdiction notice in writing of the proposed acquisition. The planning commission shall investigate the proposed site and within 30 days after receipt of the notice shall submit to the governing board a written report of the investigation and its recommendations concerning acquisition of the site.

The governing board shall not acquire title to the property until the report of the planning commission has been received. If the report does not favor the acquisition of the property for a school site, or for an addition to a present school site, the governing board of the school district shall not acquire title to the property until 30 days after the commission's report is received.

(Added: Chapter 1452, Statutes of 1987)

21151.3

(Repealed: Chapter 1183, Statutes of 1991)

21151.4   Hazardous Air Emissions— School Sites

No environmental impact report or negative declaration shall be approved for any project involving the construction or alteration of a facility within one-fourth of a mile of a school which might reasonably be anticipated to emit hazardous or acutely hazardous air emission, or which would handle acutely hazardous material or a mixture containing acutely hazardous material in a quantity equal to or greater than the quantity specified in subdivision (a) of Section 25536 of the Health and Safety Code, which may pose a health or safety hazard to persons who would attend or would be employed at the school, unless both of the following occur:

(a) The lead agency preparing the environmental impact report or negative declaration has consulted with the school district having jurisdiction regarding the potential impact of the project on the school.

(b) The school district has been given written notification of the project not less than 30 days prior to the proposed approval of the environmental impact report or negative declaration.

(Added: Chapter 1589, Statutes of 1988; amended: Chapter 1183, Statutes of 1991)

21151.5   Time Limits

(a) * * * (1) For projects described in subdivision (c) of Section 21065, each local agency shall establish, by ordinance or resolution, time limits * * * that do not exceed * * * the following:

    (A) One year for completing and certifying environmental impact reports * * *.

    (B) One hundred eighty days for completing and adopting negative declarations * * *.

  (2) The time limits specified in paragraph (1) shall apply only to those circumstances in which the local agency is the lead agency for a project. These ordinances or resolutions

may establish different time limits for different types or classes of projects and different types of environmental impact reports, but all limits shall be measured from the date on which an application requesting approval of the project is received and accepted as complete by the local agency.

  (3) No application for a project may be deemed incomplete for lack of a waiver of time periods prescribed by local ordinance or resolution.

  (4) The ordinances or resolutions required by this section may provide for a reasonable extension of the time period in the event that compelling circumstances justify additional time and the project applicant consents thereto.

(b) If a draft environmental impact report, environmental impact report, or focused environmental impact report * * * is prepared under a contract to a local agency, the contract shall be executed within 45 days from the date on which the local agency * * * sends a notice of preparation pursuant to Section 21080.4. The local agency may take longer to execute the contract * * * if the project applicant and the local agency mutually agree to an extension of the time limit provided by this subdivision.

(Amended: Chapter 1294, Statutes of 1994; Chapter 1130, Statutes of 1993; Chapter 808, Statutes of 1996)

21151.6

(Repealed: Chapter 967, Statutes of 1983)

21151.7   Open-Pit Mining

Notwithstanding any other provision of law, a lead agency shall prepare or cause to be prepared by contract, and certify the completion of, an environmental impact report for any open-pit mining operation which is subject to the permit requirements of the Surface Mining and Reclamation Act of 1975 (Chapter 9 (commencing with Section 2710) of Division 2) and utilizes a cyanide heap-leaching process for the purpose of producing gold or other precious metals.

(Added: Chapter 1097, Statutes of 1990.)

21151.8   School Site Acquisition— Hazardous Waste Disposal

(a) No environmental impact report or negative declaration shall be approved for any project involving the purchase of a schoolsite or the construction of a new elementary or secondary school by a school district unless all of the following occur:

(1) The environmental impact report or negative declaration includes information which is needed to determine if the property proposed to be purchased, or to be constructed upon, is any of the following:

   (A) The site of a current or former hazardous waste disposal site or solid waste disposal site and, if so, whether the wastes have been removed.

   (B) A hazardous substance release site identified by the State Department of Health Services in a current list adopted pursuant to Section 25356 for removal or remedial action pursuant to Chapter 6.8 (commencing with Section 25300) of Division 20 of the Health and Safety Code.

   (C) A site which contains one or more pipelines, situated underground or aboveground, which carries hazardous substances, acutely hazardous materials, or hazardous wastes, unless the pipeline is a natural gas line which is used only to supply natural gas to that school or neighborhood.

(2) The lead agency preparing the environmental impact report or negative declaration has notified in writing and consulted with the administrating agency in which the proposed schoolsite is located, and with any air pollution control district or air quality management district having jurisdiction in the area, to identify facilities within one-fourth of a mile of the proposed schoolsite which might reasonably be anticipated to emit hazardous emissions or handle hazardous or acutely hazardous materials, substances, or waste. The notification by the lead agency shall include a list of the locations for which information is sought.

(3) The governing board of the school district makes one of the following written findings:

   (A) Consultation identified no such facilities specified in paragraph (2).

   (B) The facilities specified in paragraph (2) exist, but one of the following conditions applies:

      (i) The health risks from the facilities do not and will not constitute an actual or potential endangerment of public health to persons who would attend or be employed at the proposed school.

      (ii) Corrective measures required under an existing order by another agency having jurisdiction over the facilities will, before the school is occupied, result in the mitigation of all chronic or accidental hazardous air emissions to levels that do not constitute an actual or potential endangerment of public health to persons who would attend or be employed at the proposed school. If the governing board makes such a finding, it shall also make a subsequent finding, prior to occupancy of the school, that the emissions have been so mitigated.

(4) Each administering agency, air pollution control district, or air quality management district receiving written notification from a lead agency to identify facilities pursuant to paragraph (2) shall provide the requested information and provide a written response to the lead agency within 30 days of receiving the notification. The environmental impact report or negative declaration shall be conclusively presumed to comply with this section as to the area of responsibility of any agency which does not respond within 30 days.

(b) If a lead agency has carried out the consultation required by paragraph (2) of subdivision (a), the environmental impact report or the negative declaration shall be conclusively presumed to comply with this section, notwithstanding any failure of the consultation to identify an existing facility specified in paragraph (2) of subdivision (a).

(c) As used in this section and Section 21151.4, the following definitions shall apply:

(1) "Hazardous substance" means any substance defined in Section 25316 of the Health and Safety Code.

(2) "Acutely hazardous material" means any material defined pursuant to subdivision (a) of Section 25532 of the Health and Safety Code.

(3) "Hazardous waste" means any waste defined in Section 25117 of the Health and Safety Code.

(4) "Hazardous waste disposal site" means any site defined in Section 25114 of the Health and Safety Code.

(5) "Hazardous air emissions" means emissions into the ambient air of air contaminants which have been identified as a toxic air contaminant by the State Air Resources Board or by the air pollution control officer for the jurisdiction in which the project is located. As determined by the air pollution control officer, hazardous air emissions also mean emissions into the ambient air from any substances identified in subdivisions (a) to (f), inclusive, of Section 44321 of the Health and Safety Code.

(6) "Administering agency" means an agency designated pursuant to Section 25502 of the Health and Safety Code.

(7) "Handle" means handle as defined in Article 1 (commencing with Section 25500) of Chapter 6.95 of Division 20 of the Health and Safety Code.

(Amended: Chapter 1183, Statutes of 1991)

21151.9 Water Agency Notification

Whenever a city or county determines that an environmental impact report is required in connection with a project, as defined in Section 10913, and described in Section 10910, of the Water Code, it shall comply with part 2.10 (commencing with Section 10910) of Division 6 of the Water Code.

(Added: Chapter 881, Statutes of 1995)

21152 Notices of Determination; Notices of Exemption; Availability of Notices

(a) Whenever a local agency approves or determines to carry out a project which is subject to this division, it shall file notice of the approval or the determination within five working days after the approval or determination becomes final, with the county clerk of each county in which the project will be located. The notice shall indicate the determination of the local agency whether the project will, or will not, have a significant effect on the environment and shall indicate whether an environmental impact report has been prepared pursuant to this division. The notice shall also include certification that the final environmental impact report, if one was prepared, together with comments and responses, is available to the general public.

(b) Whenever a local agency determines that a project is not subject to this division pursuant to subdivision (b) of Section 21080 or pursuant to Section 21085 or 21172, and it approves or determines to carry out the project, it, or the person specified in subdivision (b) or (c) of Section 21065, may file a notice of the determination with the county clerk of each county in which the project will be located. Any notice filed pursuant to this subdivision by a person specified in subdivision (b) or (c) of Section 21065 shall have a certificate of determination attached to it issued by the local agency responsible for making the determination that the project is not subject to this division pursuant to subdivision (b) of Section 21080 or pursuant to Section 21085 or 21172. The certificate of determination may be in the form of a certified copy of an existing document or record of the local agency.

(c) All notices filed pursuant to this section shall be available for public inspection, and shall be posted within 24 hours of receipt in the office of the county clerk. Each notice shall remain posted for a period of 30 days. Thereafter, the clerk shall return the notice to the local agency with a notation of the period it was posted. The local agency shall retain the notice for not less than nine months.

(Amended: Chapter 1294, Statutes of 1994; Chapter 1130, Statutes of 1993)

21153   Consultation with Other Agencies

(a) Prior to completing an environmental impact report, every local lead agency shall consult with, and obtain comments from, each responsible agency, any public agency that has jurisdiction by law with respect to the project, and any city or county that borders on a city or county within which the project is located unless otherwise designated annually by agreement between the local lead agency and the city or county, and may consult with any person who has special expertise with respect to any environmental impact involved. In the case of a project described in subdivision (c) of Section 21065, the local lead agency shall, upon the request of the project applicant, provide for early consultation to identify the range of actions, alternatives, mitigation measures, and significant effects to be analyzed in depth in the environmental impact report. The local lead agency may consult with persons identified by the project applicant that the applicant believes will be concerned with the environmental effects of the project and may consult with members of the public who have made written request to be consulted on the project. A request by

the project applicant for early consultation shall be made not later than 30 days after the date that the determination required by Section 21080.1 was made with respect to the project. The local lead agency may charge and collect a fee from the project applicant * * * in an amount that does not exceed the actual costs of the consultations.

(b) In the case of a project described in subdivision (a) of Section 21065, the lead agency may provide for early consultation to identify the range of actions, alternatives, mitigation measures, and significant effects to be analyzed in depth in the environmental impact report. At the request of the lead agency, the Office of Planning and Research shall ensure that each responsible agency, and any public agency that has jurisdiction by law with respect to the project, is notified regarding any early consultation.

(c) A responsible agency or other public agency shall only make substantive comments regarding those activities involved in a project that are within an area of expertise of the agency or that are required to be carried out or approved by the agency. Those comments shall be supported by specific documentation.

(Amended: Chapter 907, Statutes of 1989)

21154   State Orders

Whenever any state agency, board, or commission issues an order which requires a local agency to carry out a project which may have a significant effect on the environment, any environmental impact report which the local agency may prepare shall be limited to consideration of those factors and alternatives which will not conflict with such order.

(Added: Chapter 1154, Statutes of 1972)

21155

(Repealed: Chapter 1130, Statutes of 1993)

Chapter 4.5. Streamlined Environmental Review Sections 21156 to 21159.9

Article 1   Findings

21156   Legislative Intent

It is the intent of the Legislature in enacting this chapter that a master environmental impact report shall evaluate the cumulative impacts, growth inducing impacts, and irreversible significant effects on the environment of subsequent projects to the greatest

extent feasible. The Legislature further intends that the environmental review of subsequent projects be substantially reduced to the extent that the project impacts have been reviewed and appropriate mitigation measures are set forth in a certified master environmental impact report.

Article 2   Master Environmental Impact Report

21157   Use; Content; Fee Program

(a) A master environmental impact report may be prepared for any one of the following projects:

(1) A general plan, element, general plan amendment, or specific plan.

(2) A project that consists of smaller individual projects which will be carried out in phases.

(3) A rule or regulation which will be implemented by subsequent projects.

(4) Projects which will be carried out or approved pursuant to a development agreement.

(5) Public or private projects which will be carried out or approved pursuant to, or in furtherance of, a redevelopment plan.

(6) A state highway project or mass transit project which will be subject to multiple stages of review or approval.

(7) A regional transportation plan or congestion management plan

(8) A plan proposed by a local agency for the reuse of a federal military base or reservation that has been closed or that is proposed for closure.

(9) Regulations adopted by the Fish and Game Commission for the regulation of hunting and fishing.

(b) When a lead agency prepares a master environmental impact report, the document shall include all of the following:

(1) A detailed statement as required by Section 21100.

(2) A description of anticipated subsequent projects that would be within the scope of the master environmental impact report, that contains sufficient information with regard to the kind, size, intensity, and location of the subsequent projects, including, but not limited to, all of the following:

(A) The specific type of project anticipated to be undertaken.

(B) The maximum and minimum intensity of any anticipated subsequent project, such as the number of residences in a residential development, and, with regard to a public works facility, its anticipated capacity and service area.

(C) The anticipated location and alternative locations for any development projects.

(D) A capital outlay or capital improvement program, or other scheduling or implementing device that governs the submission and approval of subsequent projects.

(3) A description of potential impacts of anticipated subsequent projects for which there is not sufficient information reasonably available to support a full assessment of potential impacts in the master environmental impact report. This description shall not be construed as a limitation on the impacts which may be considered in a focused environmental impact report.

(c) Lead agencies may develop and implement a fee program in accordance with applicable provisions of law to generate the revenue necessary to prepare a master environmental impact report.

(Amended: Added: Chapter 1130, Statutes of 1993. Amended: Chapter 1229, Statutes of 1994; Chapter 1294, Statutes of 1994; Chapter 444, Statutes of 1996)

21157.1　Review of Subsequent Projects

The preparation and certification of a master environmental impact report, if prepared and certified consistent with this division, may allow for the limited review of subsequent projects that were described in the master environmental impact report as being within the scope of the report, in accordance with the following requirements:

(a) The lead agency for the subsequent project shall be the lead agency or any responsible agency identified in the master environmental impact report.

(b) The lead agency shall prepare an initial study on any proposed subsequent project. This initial study shall analyze whether the subsequent project may cause any significant effect on the environment that was not examined in the master environmental impact report and whether the subsequent project was described in the master environmental impact report as being within the scope of the project.

(c) If the lead agency, based on the initial study, determines that a proposed subsequent project will have no additional significant effect on the environment, as defined in subdivision (d) of Section 21158, that was not identified in the master environmental impact report and that no new or additional mitigation measures or alternatives may be required, the lead agency shall make a written finding based upon the information contained in the initial study that the subsequent project is within the scope of the project covered by the master environmental impact report. No new environmental document nor findings pursuant to Section 21081 shall be required by this division. Prior to approving or carrying out the proposed subsequent project, the lead agency shall provide notice of this fact pursuant to Section 21092 and incorporate all feasible mitigation measures or feasible alternatives set forth in the master environmental impact report which are appropriate to the project. Whenever a lead agency approves or determines to carry out any subsequent project pursuant to this section, it shall file a notice pursuant to Section 21108 or 21152.

(d) Where a lead agency cannot make the findings required in subdivision (c), the lead agency shall prepare, pursuant to Section 21157.7, either a mitigated negative declaration or environmental impact report.

(Added: Chapter 1130, Statutes of 1993. Amended: Chapter 1294, Statutes of 1994)

21157.5　Mitigated Negative Declaration

(a) A proposed mitigated negative declaration shall be prepared for any proposed subsequent project if both of the following occur:

(1) An initial study has identified potentially new or additional significant effects on the environment that were not analyzed in the master environmental impact report.

(2) Feasible mitigation measures or alternatives will be incorporated to revise the proposed subsequent project, before the negative declaration is released for public review, in order to avoid the effects or mitigate the effects to a point where clearly no significant effect on the environment will occur.

(b) If there is substantial evidence in light of the whole record before the lead agency that the proposed subsequent project may have a significant effect on

the environment and a mitigated negative declaration is not prepared, the lead agency shall prepare an environmental impact report or a focused environmental impact report pursuant to Section 21158.

(Added: Chapter 1130, Statutes of 1993)

21157.6　Limit on Use of Master Environmental Impact Report

The master environmental impact report shall not be used for the purposes of this chapter if (1) the certification of the report occurred more than five years prior to the filing of an application for the subsequent project, or (2) if the approval of a project that was not described in the report may affect the adequacy of the environmental review in the report for any subsequent project, unless the lead agency reviews the adequacy of the master environmental impact report and does either of the following:

(a) Finds that no substantial changes have occurred with respect to the circumstances under which the master environmental impact report was certified or that no new information, which was not known and could not have been known at the time that the master environmental impact report was certified as complete, has become available.

(b) Certifies a subsequent or supplemental environmental impact report which has been either incorporated into the previously certified master environmental impact report or references any deletions, additions, or any other modifications to the previously certified master environmental impact report.

(Added: Chapter 1130, Statutes of 1993. Amended: Chapter 1294, Statutes of 1994)

21157.7

(Added: Chapter 1130, Statutes of 1993. Repealed: Chapter 1294, Statutes of 1994)

Article 3　Focused Environmental Impact Report

21158　Purpose and Content

(a) A focused environmental impact report is an environmental impact report on a subsequent project identified in a master environmental impact report. A focused environmental impact report may be utilized only if the lead agency finds that the analysis in the master environmental impact report of cumulative impacts, growth inducing impacts, and irreversible significant effects on the environment is adequate for the subsequent project. The focused environmental impact report shall incorporate, by reference, the master environmental impact report and analyze only the subsequent project's additional significant effects on the environment, as defined in subdivision (d), and any new or additional mitigation measures or alternatives that were not identified and analyzed by the master environmental impact report.

(b) The focused environmental impact report need not examine those effects which the lead agency finds were one of the following:

(1) Mitigated or avoided pursuant to paragraph (1) of subdivision (a) of Section 21081 as a result of mitigation measures identified in the master environmental impact report which will be required as part of the approval of the subsequent project.

(2) Examined at a sufficient level of detail in the master environmental impact report to enable those significant environmental effects to be mitigated or avoided by specific revisions to the project, the imposition of conditions, or by other means in connection with the approval of the subsequent project.

(3) Subject to a finding pursuant to paragraph (2) of subdivision (a) of Section 21081.

(c) A focused environmental impact report on any subsequent project shall analyze any significant effects on the environment where substantial new or additional information shows that the adverse environmental impact may be more significant than was described in the master environmental impact report. The substantial new or additional information may also show that mitigation measures or alternatives identified in the master environmental impact report, which were previously determined to be infeasible, are feasible and will avoid or reduce the significant effects on the environment of the subsequent project to a level of insignificance.

(d) For purposes of this chapter, "additional significant effects on the environment" are those project specific effects on the environment which were not addressed as significant effects on the environment in the master environmental impact report.

(e) Nothing in this chapter is intended to limit or abridge the ability of a lead agency to focus upon the issues that are ripe for decision at each level of environmental review, or to exclude duplicative

analysis of environmental effects examined in previous environmental impact reports pursuant to Section 21093.

(Added: Chapter 1130, Statutes of 1993. Amended: Chapter 1294, Statutes of 1994)

21158.1 Certified Regulatory Programs

When a lead agency is required to prepare an environmental impact report pursuant to subdivision (d) of Section 21157.1 or is authorized to prepare a focused environmental impact report pursuant to Section 21158, the lead agency may not rely on subdivision (a) of Section 21080.5 for that purpose even though the lead agency's regulatory program is otherwise certified in accordance with Section 21080.5.

(Added: Chapter 444, Statutes of 1996)

21158.5 Multi-Family Residential and Mixed-Use Development

(a) Where a project consists of multiple-family residential development of not more than 100 units or a residential and commercial or retail mixed-use development of not more than 100,000 square feet which complies with all of the following, a focused environmental impact report shall be prepared, notwithstanding that the project was not identified in a master environmental impact report:

(1) Is consistent with a general plan, specific plan, community plan, or zoning ordinance for which an environmental impact report was prepared within five years of the certification of the focused environmental impact report.

(2) The lead agency cannot make the finding described in subdivision (c) of Section 21157.1, a negative declaration or mitigated negative declaration cannot be prepared pursuant to Section 21080, 21157.5, or 21158, and Section 21166 does not apply.

(3) Meets one or more of the following conditions:

(A) The parcel on which the project is to be developed is surrounded by immediately contiguous urban development.

(B) The parcel on which the project is to be developed has been previously developed with urban uses.

(C) The parcel on which the project is to be developed is within one-half mile of an existing rail transit station.

(b) A focused environmental impact report prepared pursuant to this section shall

be limited to a discussion of potentially significant effects on the environment specific to the project, or which substantial new information shows will be more significant than described in the prior environmental impact report. No discussion shall be required of alternatives to the project, cumulative impacts of the project, or the growth inducing impacts of the project.

(Added: Chapter 1130, Statutes of 1993)

Article 4 Expedited Environmental Review for Environmentally Mandated Projects

21159 Adoption of a Rule or Regulation

(a) An agency listed in Section 21159.4 shall perform, at the time of the adoption of a rule or regulation requiring the installation of pollution control equipment, or a performance standard or treatment requirement, an environmental analysis of the reasonably foreseeable methods of compliance. In the preparation of this analysis, the agency may utilize numerical ranges or averages where specific data is not available; however, the agency shall not be required to engage in speculation or conjecture. The environmental analysis shall, at minimum, include, all of the following:

(1) An analysis of the reasonably foreseeable environmental impacts of the methods of compliance.

(2) An analysis of reasonably foreseeable feasible mitigation measures.

(3) An analysis of reasonably foreseeable alternative means of compliance with the rule or regulation.

(b) The preparation of an environmental impact report at the time of adopting a rule or regulation pursuant to this division shall be deemed to satisfy the requirements of this section.

(c) The environmental analysis shall take into account a reasonable range of environmental, economic, and technical factors, population and geographic areas, and specific sites.

(d) Nothing in this section shall require the agency to conduct a project level analysis.

(e) For purposes of this article, the term "performance standard" includes process or raw material changes or product reformulation.

(f) Nothing in this section is intended, or may be used, to delay the adoption of any rule or regulation for which an analysis is required to be performed pursuant to this section.

(Added: Chapter 1131, Statutes of 1993)

21159.1   Use of a Focused EIR

(a) A focused environmental impact report may be utilized if a project meets all of the following requirements:

(1) The project consists solely of the installation of pollution control equipment required by a rule or regulation of an agency listed in Section 21159.4 and other components necessary to complete the installation of that equipment.

(2) The agency certified an environmental impact report on the rule or regulation or reviewed it pursuant to a certified regulatory program, and, in either case, the review included an assessment of growth inducing impacts and cumulative impacts of, and alternatives to, the project.

(3) The environmental review required by paragraph (2) was completed within five years of certification of the focused environmental impact report.

(4) An environmental impact report is not required pursuant to Section 21166.

(b) The discussion of significant effects on the environment in the focused environmental impact report shall be limited to project-specific potentially significant effects on the environment of the project which were not discussed in the environmental analysis of the rule or regulation required pursuant to subdivision (a) of Section 21159. No discussion of growth-inducing impacts or cumulative impacts shall be required in the focused environmental impact report, and the discussion of alternatives shall be limited to a discussion of alternative means of compliance, if any, with the rule or regulation.

(Added: Chapter 1130, Statutes of 1993)

21159.2   Later Compliance Projects

(a) If a project consists solely of compliance with a performance standard or treatment requirement imposed by an agency listed in Section 21159.4, the lead agency for the compliance project shall, to the greatest extent feasible, utilize the environmental analysis required pursuant to subdivision (a) of Section 21159 in the preparation of a negative declaration, mitigated negative declaration,

or environmental impact report on the compliance project or in otherwise fulfilling its responsibilities under this division. The use of numerical averages or ranges in an environmental analysis shall not relieve a lead agency of its obligations under this division to identify and evaluate the environmental effects of a compliance project.

(b) If the lead agency determines that an environmental impact report on the compliance project is required, the lead agency shall prepare an environmental impact report which addresses only the project-specific issues related to the compliance project or other issues that were not discussed in sufficient detail in the environmental analysis to enable the lead agency to fulfill its responsibilities under Section 21100 or 21151, as applicable. The mitigation measures imposed by the lead agency for the project shall relate only to the significant effects on the environment to be mitigated. The discussion of alternatives shall be limited to a discussion of alternative means of compliance, if any, with the rule or regulation.

(Added: Chapter 1130, Statutes of 1993)

21159.3   Deadlines for Preparation

In the preparation of any environmental impact report pursuant to Section 21159.1 or 21159.2, the following deadlines shall apply:

(a) A lead agency shall determine whether an environmental impact report should be prepared within 30 days of its determination that the application for the project is complete.

(b) If the environmental impact report will be prepared under contract to the lead agency pursuant to Section 21082.1, the lead agency shall issue a request for proposals for preparation of the environmental impact report as soon as it has enough information to prepare a request for proposals, and in any event, not later than 30 days after the time for response to the notice of preparation has expired. The contract shall be awarded within 30 days of the response date for the request for proposals.

(Added: Chapter 1130, Statutes of 1993)

21159.4   Application of Article

This article shall apply to the following agencies: the State Air Resources Board, any district as defined in Section 39025 of the Health and Safety Code, the State Water Resources Control Board, a California regional water quality control board, the Department

of Toxic Substances Control, and the California Integrated Waste Management Board.

(Added: Chapter 1131, Statutes of 1993)

Article 5   Public Assistance Program

21159.9   Implementation of Program

On or before March 1, 1994, the Office of Planning and Research shall implement, utilizing existing resources, a public assistance and information program, to ensure efficient and effective implementation of this division, to do both of the following:

(a) Establish a public education and training program for planners, developers, and other interested parties to assist them in implementing this division.

(b) Establish a data base to assist in the preparation of environmental documents.

(Added: Chapter 1130, Statutes of 1993)

Chapter 5. Submission of Information Sections 21160 to 21162

21160   Date and Information; Trade Secrets

Whenever any person applies to any public agency for a lease, permit, license, certificate, or other entitlement for use, the public agency may require that person to submit data and information which may be necessary to enable the public agency to determine whether the proposed project may have a significant effect on the environment or to prepare an environmental impact report.

If any or all of the information so submitted is a "trade secret" as defined in Section 6254.7 of the Government Code by those submitting that information, it shall not be included in the impact report or otherwise disclosed by any public agency. This section shall not be construed to prohibit the exchange of properly designated trade secrets between public agencies who have lawful jurisdiction over the preparation of the impact report.

21161   Notices of Completion

Whenever a public agency has completed an environmental impact report, it shall cause a notice of completion of that report to be filed with the Office of Planning and Research. The notice of completion shall briefly identify the project and shall indicate that an environmental impact report has been prepared. Failure to file the notice required by this section shall not affect the validity of a project.

(Amended: Chapter 571, Statutes of 1984)

21162 Notice of Completion

A copy of the notice of completion of an environmental impact report on a project shall be provided, by the State Clearinghouse, to any legislator in whose district the project has an environmental impact, if the legislator request the notice and the State Clearinghouse has received it.

(Added: Chapter 1025, Statutes of 1983)

Chapter 6. Limitations
Sections 21165 to 21178.1

21165 Lead Agency Determination

When a project is to be carried out or approved by two or more public agencies, the determination of whether the project may have a significant effect on the environment shall be made by the lead agency; and such agency shall prepare, or cause to be prepared by contract, the environmental impact report for the project, if such a report is required by this division. In the event that a dispute arises as to which is the lead agency, any public agency, or in the case of a project described in subdivision (c) of Section 21065, the applicant for such project, may submit the question to the Office of Planning and Research, and the Office of Planning and Research shall designate, within 21 days of receiving such request, the lead agency, giving due consideration to the capacity of such agency to adequately fulfill the requirements of this division.

(Amended: Chapter 1200, Statutes of 1977)

21166 Subsequent or Supplemental Environmental Impact Reports

When an environmental impact report has been prepared for a project pursuant to this division, no subsequent or supplemental environmental impact report shall be required by the lead agency or by any responsible agency, unless one or more of the following events occurs:

(a) Substantial changes are proposed in the project which will require major revisions of the environmental impact report.

(b) Substantial changes occur with respect to the circumstances under which the project is being undertaken which will require major revisions in the environmental impact report.

(c) New information, which was not known and could not have been known at the time the environmental impact report was certified as complete, becomes available.

(Amended: Chapter 1200, Statutes of 1977)

21166.1 Effect of Preparation of Impact Report by Lead Agency

The decision of a lead agency to prepare an environmental impact report with respect to environmental impacts within a geographic area or for a group of projects shall not be a basis for determining that an environmental document prepared for an individual project within that area or group is inadequate.

(Added: Chapter 1514, Statutes of 1984)

21167 Statutes of Limitation

Any action or proceeding to attack, review, set aside, void, or annul the following acts or decisions of a public agency on the grounds of noncompliance with this division shall be commenced as follows:

(a) An action or proceeding alleging that a public agency is carrying out or has approved a project which may have a significant effect on the environment without having determined whether the project may have a significant effect on the environment shall be commenced within 180 days from the date of the public agency's decision to carry out or approve the project, or, if a project is undertaken without a formal decision by the public agency, within 180 days from the date of commencement of the project.

(b) Any action or proceeding alleging that a public agency has improperly determined whether a project may have a significant effect on the environment shall be commenced within 30 days from the date of the filing of the notice required by subdivision (a) of Section 21108 or subdivision (a) of Section 21152.

(c) Any action or proceeding alleging that an environmental impact report does not comply with this division shall be commenced within 30 days from the date of the filing of the notice required by subdivision (a) of Section 21108 or subdivision (a) of Section 21152 by the lead agency.

(d) Any action or proceeding alleging that a public agency has improperly determined that a project is not subject to this division pursuant to subdivision (b) of Section 21080 or pursuant to Section 21085 or 21172 shall be commenced within 35 days from the date of the filing by the public agency, or person specified in subdivision (b) or (c) of Section 21065, of the notice authorized by subdivision (b) of Section 21108 or subdivision (b) of Section 21152. If the notice has not been filed, the action or proceeding shall be commenced within 180 days from the date of the public agency's decision to carry out or approve the project, or, if a project is undertaken without a formal decision by the public agency, within 180 days from the date of commencement of the project.

(e) Any action or proceeding alleging that any other act or omission of a public agency does not comply with this division shall be commenced within 30 days from the date of the filing of the notice required by subdivision (a) of Section 21108 or subdivision (a) of Section 21152.

(f) If a person has made a written request to the public agency for a copy of the notice specified in Section 21108 or 21152 prior to the date on which the agency approves or determines to carry out the project, then not later than five days from the date of the agency's action, the public agency shall deposit a written copy of the notice addressed to that person in the United States mail, first-class postage prepaid. The date upon which this notice is mailed shall not affect the time periods specified in subdivisions (b), (c), (d), and (e).

(Amended: Chapter 801, Statutes of 1995; Chapter 1294, Statutes of 1994)

21167.1 Preferential Hearings

(a) In all actions or proceedings brought pursuant to Sections 21167, 21168, and 21168.5, including the hearing of an action or proceeding on appeal from a decision of a lower court, all courts in which the action or proceeding is pending shall give the action or proceeding preference over all other civil actions, in the matter of setting the action or proceeding for hearing or trial, and in hearing or trying the action or proceeding, so that the action or proceeding shall be quickly heard and determined. The court shall regulate the briefing schedule so that, to the extent feasible, the court shall commence hearings on an appeal within one year of the date of the filing of the appeal.

(b) To ensure that actions or proceedings brought pursuant to Sections 21167, 21168, and 21168.5 may be quickly heard and determined in the lower courts, the superior courts in all counties with a population of more than 200,000 shall designate one or more judges to develop expertise in this division and related land use and environmental laws, so that those judges will be available to hear, and quickly resolve, actions or proceedings brought pursuant to Sections 21167, 21168, and 21168.5.

(c) In any action or proceeding filed pursuant to this chapter that is joined with any other cause of action, the court, upon a motion by any party, may grant severance of the actions. In determining whether to grant severance, the court shall consider such as matters judicial economy, administrative economy, and prejudice to any party.

(Amended: Chapter 1294, Statutes of 1994; Chapter 1130, Statutes of 1993)

21167.2   Presumption of Compliance

If no action or proceeding alleging that an environmental impact report does not comply with the provisions of this division is commenced during the period prescribed in subdivision (c) of Section 21167, the environmental impact report shall be conclusively presumed to comply with the provisions of this division for purposes of its use by responsible agencies, unless the provisions of Section 21166 are applicable.

(Added: Chapter 1200, Statutes of 1977)

21167.3   Effect of Litigation

(a) If an action or proceeding alleging that an environmental impact report or a negative declaration does not comply with the provisions of this division is commenced during the period described in subdivision (b) or (c) of Section 21167, and if an injunction or stay is issued prohibiting the project from being carried out or approved pending final determination of the issue of such compliance, responsible agencies shall assume that the environmental impact report or the negative declaration for the project does comply with the provisions of this division and shall issue a conditional approval or disapproval of such project according to the timetable for agency action in Article 5 (commencing with Section 65950) of Chapter 4.5 of Division 1 of Title 7 of the Government Code. A conditional approval shall constitute permission to proceed with a project when and only when such action or proceeding results in a final determination that the environmental impact report or negative declaration does comply with the provisions of this division.

(b) In the event that an action or proceeding is commenced as described in subdivision (a) but no injunction or similar relief is sought and granted, responsible agencies shall assume that the environmental impact report or negative declaration for the project does comply with the provisions of this division and shall approve or disapprove the project according to the timetable for agency action in Article 5 (commencing with

Section 65950) of Chapter 4.5 of Division 1 of Title 7 of the Government Code. Such approval shall constitute permission to proceed with the project at the applicant's risk pending final determination of such action or proceeding.

(Amended: Chapter 131, Statutes of 1980)

21167.4   Request for Hearing

(a) In any action or proceeding alleging noncompliance with this division, the petitioner shall request a hearing within 90 days from the date of filing the petition or shall be subject to dismissal on the court's own motion or on the motion of any party interested in the action or proceeding.

(b) The petitioner shall serve a notice of the request for a hearing on all parties at the time that the petitioner files the request for a hearing.

(c) Upon the filing of a request by the petitioner for a hearing and upon application by any party, the court shall establish a briefing schedule and a hearing date. In the absence of good cause, briefing shall be completed within 90 days from the date that the request for a hearing is filed, and the hearing, to the extent feasible, shall be held within 30 days thereafter. Good cause may include, but shall not be limited to, the conduct of discovery, determination of the completeness of the record of proceedings, the complexity of the issues, and the length of the record of proceedings and the timeliness of its production. The parties may stipulate to a briefing schedule or hearing date that differs from the schedule set forth in this subdivision if the stipulation is approved by the court.

(Amended: Chapter 1294, Statutes of 1994; Chapter 1130, Statutes of 1993)

21167.5   Proof of Service

Proof of prior service by mail upon the public agency carrying out or approving the project of a written notice of the commencement of any action or proceeding described in Section 21167 identifying the project shall be filed concurrently with the initial pleading in such action or proceeding.

(Added: Chapter 1154, Statutes of 1972)

21167.6   Record of Proceedings

Notwithstanding any other provision of law, in all actions or proceedings brought pursuant to Section 21167, except those involving the Public Utilities Commission, all of following shall apply:

(a) At the time that the action or proceeding is filed, the plaintiff or petitioner

shall file a request that the respondent agency prepare the record of proceedings relating to the subject of the action or proceeding. The request, together with the complaint or petition, shall be served upon the public agency not later than 10 business days from the date that the action or proceeding was filed.

(b) (1) The public agency shall prepare and certify the record of proceedings not later than 60 days from the date that the request specified in subdivision (a) was served upon the public agency. Upon certification, the public agency shall lodge a copy of the record of proceedings with the court and shall serve on the parties notice that the record of proceedings has been certified and lodged with the court. The parties shall pay any costs or fees imposed for the preparation of the record of proceedings in conformance with any law or rule of court.

(2) The plaintiff or petitioner may elect to prepare the record of proceedings or the parties may agree to an alternative method of preparation of the record of proceedings, subject to certification of its accuracy by the public agency, within the time limit specified in this subdivision.

(c) The time limit established by subdivision (b) may be extended only upon the stipulation of all parties who have been properly served in the action or proceeding or upon order of the court. Extensions shall be liberally granted by the court when the size of the record of proceedings renders infeasible compliance with that time limit. There is no limit on the number of extensions which may be granted by the court, but no single extension shall exceed 60 days unless the court determines that a longer extension is in the public interest.

(d) If the public agency fails to prepare and certify the record within the time limit established in subdivision (b), or any continuances of that time limit, the plaintiff or petitioner may move for sanctions, and the court may, upon that motion, grant appropriate sanctions.

(e) The record of proceedings shall include, but is not limited to, all of the following items:

(1) All project application materials.

(2) All staff reports and related documents prepared by the respondent public agency with respect to its compliance with the substantive

and procedural requirements of this division and with respect to the action on the project.

(3) All staff reports and related documents prepared by the respondent public agency and written testimony or documents submitted by any person relevant to any findings or statement of overriding considerations adopted by the respondent agency pursuant to this division.

(4) Any transcript or minutes of the proceedings at which the decisionmaking body of the respondent public agency heard testimony on, or considered any environmental document on, the project, and any transcript or minutes of proceedings before any advisory body to the respondent public agency which were presented to the decisionmaking body prior to action on the environmental documents or on the project.

(5) All notices issued by the respondent public agency to comply with this division or with any other law governing the processing and approval of the project.

(6) All written comments received in response to, or in connection with, environmental documents prepared for the project, including responses to the notice of preparation.

(7) All written evidence or correspondence submitted to, or transferred from, the respondent agency with respect to compliance with this division or with respect to the project.

(8) Any proposed decisions or findings submitted to the decisionmaking body of the respondent public agency by its staff, or the project proponent, project opponents, or other persons.

(9) The documentation of the final public agency decision, including the final environmental impact report, mitigated negative declaration, or negative declaration, and all documents, in addition to those referenced in paragraph (3), cited or relied on in the findings or in a statement of overriding considerations adopted pursuant to this division.

(10) Any other written materials relevant to the respondent public agency's compliance with this division or to its decision on the merits of the project, including the initial study, any drafts of any environmental document, or portions thereof, which

have been released for public review, and copies of studies or other documents relied upon in any environmental document prepared for the project and either made available to the public during the public review period or included in the respondent public agency's files on the project, and all internal agency communications, including staff notes and memoranda related to the project or to compliance with this division.

(11) The full written record before any inferior administrative decisionmaking body whose decision was appealed to a superior administrative decisionmaking body prior to the filing of litigation.

(f) In preparing the record of proceedings, the party preparing the record shall strive to do so at reasonable cost in light of the scope of the record.

(g) The clerk of the superior court shall prepare and certify the clerk's transcript on appeal not later than 60 days from the date that the notice designating the papers or records to be included in the clerk's transcript was filed with the superior court, if the party or parties pay any costs or fees for the preparation of the clerk's transcript imposed in conformance with any law or rules of court. Nothing in this subdivision precludes an election to proceed by appendix, as provided in Rule 5.1 of the California Rules of Court.

(h) Extensions of the period for the filing of any brief on appeal may be allowed only by stipulation of the parties or by order of the court for good cause shown. Extensions for the filing of a brief on appeal shall be limited to one 30-day extension for the preparation of an opening brief, and one 30-day extension for the preparation of a responding brief, except that the court may grant a longer extension or additional extensions if it determines that there is a substantial likelihood of settlement that would avoid the necessity of completing the appeal.

(i) At the completion of the filing of briefs on appeal, the appellant shall notify the court of the completion of the filing of briefs, whereupon the clerk of the reviewing court shall set the appeal for hearing on the first available calendar date.

(Amended: Chapter 1294, Statutes of 1994; Chapter 1230, Statutes of 1994; Chapter 1130, Statutes of 1993)

21167.7   Copies of Pleadings

Every person who brings an action pursuant to Section 21167 shall comply with the requirements of Section 389.6 of the Code of Civil Procedure. Every such person shall also furnish pursuant to Section 389.6 of the Code of Civil Procedure a copy of any amended or supplemental pleading filed by such person in such action to the Attorney General. No relief, temporary or permanent, shall be granted until a copy of the pleading has been furnished to the Attorney General in accordance with such requirements.

(Added: Chapter 753, Statutes of 1976)

21167.8   Settlement Meeting; Failure to Participate

(a) Not later than 20 days from the date of service upon a public agency of a petition or complaint brought pursuant to Section 21167, the public agency shall file with the court a notice setting forth the time and place at which all parties shall meet and attempt to settle the litigation. The meeting shall be scheduled and held not later than 45 days from the date of service of the petition or complaint upon the public agency. The notice of the settlement meeting shall be served by mail upon the counsel for each party. If the public agency does not know the identity of counsel for any party, the notice shall be served by mail upon the party for whom counsel is not known.

(b) At the time and place specified in the notice filed with the court, the parties shall meet and confer regarding anticipated issues to be raised in the litigation and shall attempt in good faith to settle the litigation and the dispute which forms the basis of the litigation. The settlement meeting discussions shall be comprehensive in nature and shall focus on the legal issues raised by the parties concerning the project that is the subject of the litigation.

(c) The settlement meeting may be continued from time to time without postponing or otherwise delaying other applicable time limits in the litigation. The settlement meeting is intended to be conducted concurrently with any judicial proceedings.

(d) If the litigation is not settled, the court, in its discretion, may, or at the request of any party, shall, schedule a further settlement conference before a judge of the superior court. If the petition or complaint is later heard on its merits, the judge hearing the matter shall not be the same judge conducting the settlement conference, except in counties that have only one judge of the superior court.

(e) The failure of any party, who was notified pursuant to subdivision (a), to participate in the litigation settlement process, without good cause, may result in an imposition of sanctions by the court.

(f) Not later than 30 days from the date that notice of certification of the record of proceedings was filed and served in accordance with Section 21167.6, the petitioner or plaintiff shall file and serve on all other parties a statement of issues which the petitioner or plaintiff intends to raise in any brief or at any hearing or trial. Not later than 10 days from the date on which the respondent or real party in interest has been served with the statement of issues from the petitioner or plaintiff, each respondent and real party in interest shall file and serve on all other parties a statement of issues which that party intends to raise in any brief or at any hearing or trial.

(Amended: Chapter 801, Statutes of 1995; Chapter 1294, Statutes of 1994; Chapter 1130, Statutes of 1993)

21168   Review of Determination

Any action or proceeding to attack, review, set aside, void or annul a determination, finding, or decision of a public agency, made as a result of a proceeding in which by law a hearing is required to be given, evidence is required to be taken and discretion in the determination of facts is vested in a public agency, on the grounds of noncompliance with the provisions of this division shall be in accordance with the provisions of Section 1094.5 of the Code of Civil Procedure.

In any such action, the court shall not exercise its independent judgment on the evidence but shall only determine whether the act or decision is supported by substantial evidence in the light of the whole record.

(Amended: Chapter 1312, Statutes of 1976)

21168.3

(Repealed: Chapter 1130, Statutes of 1993)

21168.5   Prejudicial Abuse of Discretion Test

In any action or proceeding, other than an action or proceeding under Section 21168, to attack, review, set aside, void or annul a determination, finding, or decision of a public agency on the grounds of noncompliance with this division, the inquiry shall extend only to whether there was a prejudicial abuse of discretion. Abuse of discretion is established if the agency has not proceeded in a manner required by law or if the

determination or decision is not supported by substantial evidence.

(Amended: Chapter 1312, Statutes of 1976)

21168.6   P.U.C. Appeals

In any action or proceeding under Sections 21168 or 21168.5 against the Public Utilities Commission the writ of mandate shall lie only from the Supreme Court to such commission.

(Added: Chapter 1154, Statutes of 1972)

21168.7   Judicial Review

Sections 21168 and 21168.5 are declaratory of existing law with respect to the judicial review of determinations or decisions of public agencies made pursuant to this division.

(Added: Chapter 1154, Statutes of 1972)

21168.9   Public Agency Action Not in Compliance with Article

(a) If a court finds, as a result of a trial, hearing, or remand from an appellate court, that any determination, finding, or decision of a public agency has been made without compliance with this division, the court shall enter an order that includes one or more of the following:

(1) A mandate that the determination, finding, or decision be voided by the public agency, in whole or in part.

(2) If the court finds that a specific project activity or activities will prejudice the consideration or implementation of particular mitigation measures or alternatives to the project, a mandate that the public agency and any real parties in interest suspend any or all specific project activity or activities, pursuant to the determination, finding, or decision, that could result in an adverse change or alteration to the physical environment, until the public agency has taken any actions that may be necessary to bring the determination, finding, or decision into compliance with this division.

(3) A mandate that the public agency take specific action as may be necessary to bring the determination, finding, or decision into compliance with this division.

(b) Any order pursuant to subdivision (a) shall include only those mandates which are necessary to achieve compliance with this division and only those specific project activities in noncompliance with this division. The order shall be made by the issuance of a peremptory writ of mandate specifying what action

by the public agency is necessary to comply with this division. However, the order shall be limited to that portion of a determination, finding, or decision or the specific project activity or activities found to be in noncompliance only if a court finds that (1) the portion or specific project activity or activities are severable, (2) severance will not prejudice complete and full compliance with this division, and (3) the court has not found the remainder of the project to be in noncompliance with this division. The trial court shall retain jurisdiction over the public agency's proceedings by way of a return to the peremptory writ until the court has determined that the public agency has complied with this division.

(c) Nothing in this section authorizes a court to direct any public agency to exercise its discretion in any particular way. Except as expressly provided in this section, nothing in this section is intended to limit the equitable powers of the court.

(Amended: Chapter 1131, Statutes of 1993)

21169   "Grandfather Clause"

Any project defined in subdivision (c) of Section 21065 undertaken, carried out or approved on or before the effective date of this section and the issuance by any public agency of any lease, permit, license, certificate or other entitlement for use executed or issued on or before the effective date of this section notwithstanding a failure to comply with this division, if otherwise legal and valid, is hereby confirmed, validated and declared legally effective. Any project undertaken by a person which was supported in whole or part through contracts with one or more public agencies on or before the effective date of this section, notwithstanding a failure to comply with this division, if otherwise legal and valid, is hereby confirmed, validated and declared legally effective.

(Added: Chapter 1154, Statutes of 1972)

21170   Judicial Proceedings in Progress

(a) Section 21169 shall not operate to confirm, validate or give legal effect to any project the legality of which was being contested in a judicial proceeding in which proceeding the pleadings, prior to the effective date of this section, alleged facts constituting a cause of action for, or raised the issue of, a violation of this division and which was pending and undetermined on the effective date of this section; provided, however, that Section 21169 shall operate to confirm, validate or give legal effect to any project to which this subdivision applies if, prior to the commencement of judicial proceedings and in good faith and in reliance upon the issuance by a public agency of any lease, permit, license, certificate or other entitlement for use, substantial construction has been performed and substantial liabilities for construction and necessary materials have been incurred.

(b) Section 21169 shall not operate to confirm, validate or give legal effect to any project which had been determined in any judicial proceeding, on or before the effective date of this section to be illegal, void or ineffective because of noncompliance with this division.

(Added: Chapter 1154, Statutes of 1972)

21171   Moratorium Provision–
Effective Date

This division, except for Section 21169, shall not apply to the issuance of any lease, permit, license, certificate or other entitlement for use for any project defined in subdivision (c) of Section 21065 or to any project undertaken by a person which is supported in whole or in part through contracts with one or more public agencies until the 121st day after the effective date of this section. This section shall not apply to any project to which Section 21170 is applicable or to any successor project which is the same as, or substantially identical to, such a project.

This section shall not prohibit or prevent a public agency, prior to the 121st day after the effective date of this section, from considering environmental factors in connection with the approval or disapproval of a project and from imposing reasonable fees in connection therewith.

(Added: Chapter 1154, Statutes of 1972)

21172   Emergencies

This division shall not apply to any project undertaken, carried out, or approved by a public agency to maintain, repair, restore, demolish or replace property or facilities damaged or destroyed as a result of a disaster in a disaster stricken area in which a state of emergency has been proclaimed by the Governor pursuant to Chapter 7 (commencing with Section 8550) of Division 1, Title 2 of the Government Code.

21172.5   Existing Procedures

Until the 121st day after the effective date of this section, any objectives, criteria and procedures adopted by public agencies in compliance with this division shall govern the evaluation of projects defined in subdivisions

(a) and (b) of Section 21065 and the preparation of environmental impact reports on such projects when required by this division. Any environmental impact report which has been completed or on which substantial work has been performed on or before the 121st day after the effective date of this section, if otherwise legally sufficient, shall, when completed, be deemed to be in compliance with this division and no further environmental impact report shall be required except as provided in Section 21166.

21173   Severability

If any provision of this division or the application thereof to any person or circumstances is held invalid, such invalidity shall not affect other provisions or applications of this division which can be given effect without the invalid provision or application thereof, and to this end the provisions of this division are severable.

21174   Effect on Other Laws

No provision of this division is a limitation or restriction on the power or authority of any public agency in the enforcement or administration of any provision of law which it is specifically permitted or required to enforce or administer, including, but not limited to, the powers and authority granted to the California Coastal Commission pursuant to Division 20 (commencing with Section 30000). To the extent of any inconsistency or conflict between the provisions of the California Coastal Act of 1976, Division 20 (commencing with Section 30000), and the provisions of this division, the provisions of Division 20 (commencing with Section 30000) shall control.

(Amended: Chapter 285, Statutes of 1991)

21175   LAFCO's Actions

In the event that a local agency formation commission, acting pursuant to the provisions of Chapter 6.6 (commencing with Section 54773) of Part 1 of Division 2 of Title 5 of, or pursuant to Division 1 (commencing with Section 56000) of Title 6 of the Government Code, has approved a project without complying with this division, such approval is hereby confirmed, validated, and declared legally effective notwithstanding the failure to comply with this division; provided that such approval shall have occurred prior to February 7, 1975.

(Added: Chapter 222, Statutes of 1975)

21176   Pending Judicial Proceedings

(a) Section 21175 shall not operate to confirm, validate, or give legal effect to any

project, the legality of which was being contested in a judicial proceeding in which proceeding the pleadings, prior to February 7, 1975, alleged facts constituting a cause of action for, or raised the issue of, a violation of this division, and which was pending and undetermined on February 7, 1975.

(b) Section 21175 shall not operate to confirm, validate, or give legal effect to any project which had been determined in any judicial proceeding, on or before the effective date of this section, to be illegal, void, or ineffective because of noncompliance with this division.

(Added: Chapter 222, Statutes of 1975)

21177   Presentation of Grounds
for Noncompliance

(a) No action or proceeding may be brought pursuant to Section 21167 unless the alleged grounds for noncompliance with this division were presented to the public agency orally or in writing by any person during the public comment period provided by this division or prior to the close of the public hearing on the project before the issuance of the notice of determination.

(b) No person shall maintain an action or proceeding unless that person objected to the approval of the project orally or in writing during the public comment period provided by this division or prior to the close of the public hearing on the project before the issuance of the notice of determination.

(c) This section does not preclude any organization formed after the approval of the project from maintaining an action pursuant to Section 21167 if a member of that organization has complied with subdivision (b).

(d) This section does not apply to the Attorney General.

(e) This section does not apply to any alleged grounds for noncompliance with this division for which there was no public hearing or other opportunity for members of the public to raise those objections orally or in writing prior to the approval of the project, or if the public agency failed to give the notice required by law.

(Amended: Chapter 1131, Statutes of 1993)

21178.1

(Added: Chapter 945, Statutes of 1992; Repealed January 1, 1997 by its own terms.)

Appendix 2

Guidelines for Implementation of the California Environmental Quality Act

California Code of Regulations, Title 14, Division 6,
Chapter 3, Sections 15000–15387 and Appendices A–K

Source

The CEQA Guidelines and Discussions, current as of February 1, 1999, were reprinted with the cooperation and permission of the California Resources Agency. The State CEQA Guidelines are part of the California Code of Regulations, an unofficial copy of which is available on the Internet, through the State Office of Administrative Law, at http://ccr.oal.ca.gov/ccrmain.htm. The Official California Code of Regulations may be ordered from Barclays at (800) 888-3600.

The CEQA Guidelines were substantially amended in 1997 and 1998. The Discussions of the CEQA Guidelines, which are not part of the California Code of Regulations, were revised by OPR staff as of December 1998. While changes to the Guidelines constitute a rulemaking requiring public notice, OPR staff can change the Discussions without such notice. For the most recent version of the Discussions, readers should check the Internet at http://ceres.ca.gov/ceqa.

Solano Press Books has made every effort to see that no changes have been made to the contents of this state document as a result of reformatting and reprinting. Any omissions or changes to the contrary are entirely the responsibility of Solano Press Books and not the State of California.

CEQA Guidelines
Table of Contents

February 16, 1999

Article 1. General
Sections 15000 to 15007

15000 Authority

The regulations contained in this chapter are prescribed by the Secretary for Resources to be followed by all state and local agencies in California in the implementation of the California Environmental Quality Act. These Guidelines have been developed by the Office of Planning and Research for adoption by the Secretary for Resources in accordance with Section 21083. Additional information may be obtained by writing:

Secretary for Resources
1416 Ninth Street, Room 1311
Sacramento, CA 95814

These Guidelines are binding on all public agencies in California.

Note: Authority cited: Sections 21083 and 21087, Public Resources Code. Reference: Sections 21082, 21083 and 21087, Public Resources Code; *City of Santa Ana v. City of Garden Grove*, (1979) 100 Cal.App.3d 521.

Discussion: This section specifies that these regulations are binding on all state and local agencies when implementing CEQA. The section also provides the address where people can write to obtain additional information about the Guidelines.

Section 21082 of CEQA and the court decision cited in the note show that agencies must comply with the Guidelines. The regulations are labeled "Guidelines" because they contain many advisory and permissive interpretations in addition to mandatory requirements. When the Legislature called for the Guidelines to be adopted, it seemed to envision this guidance role in addition to a purely regulatory role.

15001 Short Title

These Guidelines may be cited as the "State CEQA Guidelines." Existing references to the "State EIR Guidelines" shall be construed to be references to the State CEQA Guidelines.

Note: Authority cited: Sections 21083 and 21087, Public Resources Code. Reference: Sections 21083 and 21087, Public Resources Code.

15002 General Concepts

(a) Basic Purposes of CEQA. The basic purposes of CEQA are to:

(1) Inform governmental decisionmakers and the public about the potential, significant environmental effects of proposed activities.

(2) Identify the ways that environmental damage can be avoided or significantly reduced.

(3) Prevent significant, avoidable damage to the environment by requiring changes in projects through the use of alternatives or mitigation measures when the governmental agency finds the changes to be feasible.

(4) Disclose to the public the reasons why a governmental agency approved the project in the manner the agency chose if significant environmental effects are involved.

(b) Governmental Action. CEQA applies to governmental action. This action may involve:

(1) Activities directly undertaken by a governmental agency,

(2) Activities financed in whole or in part by a governmental agency, or

(3) Private activities which require approval from a governmental agency.

(c) Private Action. Private action is not subject to CEQA unless the action involves governmental participation, financing, or approval.

(d) Project. A "project" is an activity subject to CEQA. The term "project" has been interpreted to mean far more than the ordinary dictionary definition of the term. See: Section 15378.

(e) Time for Compliance. A governmental agency is required to comply with CEQA procedures when the agency proposes to carry out or approve the activity. See: Section 15004.

(f) Environmental Impact Reports and Negative Declarations. An environmental impact report (EIR) is the public document used by the governmental agency to analyze the significant environmental effects of a proposed project, to identify alternatives, and to disclose possible ways to reduce or avoid the possible environmental damage.

(1) An EIR is prepared when the public agency finds substantial evidence that the project may have a significant effect on the environment. See: Section 15064(a)(1).

(2) When the agency finds that there is no substantial evidence that a project may have a significant environmental effect, the agency will prepare a "Negative Declaration" instead of an EIR. See: Section 15070.

(g) Significant Effect on the Environment. A significant effect on the environment is defined as a substantial adverse change in the physical conditions which exist in the area affected by the proposed project. See: Section 15382. Further, when an EIR identifies a significant effect, the government agency approving the project must make findings on whether the adverse environmental effects have been substantially reduced or if not, why not. See: Section 15091.

(h) Methods for Protecting the Environment. CEQA requires more than merely preparing environmental documents. The EIR by itself does not control the way in which a project can be built or carried out. Rather, when an EIR shows that a project would cause substantial adverse changes in the environment, the governmental agency must respond to the information by one or more of the following methods:

(1) Changing a proposed project;

(2) Imposing conditions on the approval of the project;

(3) Adopting plans or ordinances to control a broader class of projects to avoid the adverse changes;

(4) Choosing an alternative way of meeting the same need;

(5) Disapproving the project;

(6) Finding that changes in, or alterations, the project are not feasible.

(7) Finding that the unavoidable, significant environmental damage is acceptable as provided in Section 15093.

(i) Discretionary Action. CEQA applies in situations where a governmental agency can use its judgment in deciding whether and how to carry out or approve a project. A project subject to such judgmental controls is called a "discretionary project." See: Section 15357.

(1) Where the law requires a governmental agency to act on a project in a set way without allowing the agency to use its own judgment, the project is called "ministerial," and CEQA does not apply. See: Section 15369.

(2) Whether an agency has discretionary or ministerial controls over a project depends on the authority granted by the law providing the

controls over the activity. Similar projects may be subject to discretionary controls in one city or county and only ministerial controls in another. See: Section 15268.

(j) Public Involvement. Under CEQA, an agency must solicit and respond to comments from the public and from other agencies concerned with the project. (See: Sections 15073, 15086, 15087, and 15088.)

(k) Three Step Process. An agency will normally take up to three separate steps in deciding which document to prepare for a project subject to CEQA.

(1) In the first step the lead agency examines the project to determine whether the project is subject to CEQA at all. If the project is exempt, the process does not need to proceed any farther. The agency may prepare a notice of exemption. See: Sections 15061 and 15062.

(2) If the project is not exempt, the lead agency takes the second step and conducts an initial study (Section 15063) to determine whether the project may have a significant effect on the environment. If the initial study shows that there is no substantial evidence that the project may have a significant effect, the lead agency prepares a negative declaration. See: Sections 15070 et seq.

(3) If the initial study shows that the project may have a significant effect, the lead agency takes the third step and prepares an EIR. See: Sections 15080 et seq.

(l) Certified Equivalent Programs. A number of environmental regulatory programs have been certified by the Secretary of the Resources Agency as involving essentially the same consideration of environmental issues as is provided by use of EIRs and negative declarations. Certified programs are exempt from preparing EIRs and negative declarations but use other documents instead. Certified programs are discussed in Article 17 and are listed in Section 15251.

(m) This section is intended to present the general concepts of CEQA in a simplified and introductory manner. If there are any conflicts between the short statement of a concept in this section and the provisions of other sections of these guidelines, the other sections shall prevail.

Note: Authority cited: Sections 21083 and 21087, Public Resources Code. Reference: Sections 21000–21176, Public Resources

Code; *No Oil, Inc. v. City of Los Angeles*, 13 Cal.3d 68 (1974); *Running Fence Corp. v. Superior Court*, 51 Cal.App.3d 400 (1975).

Discussion: This section is intended to serve as a short introduction to CEQA for people who are unfamiliar with the Act. This section provides a simple outline of the basic concepts, purposes, documents, and processes used in CEQA.

15003   Policies

In addition to the policies declared by the Legislature concerning environmental protection and administration of CEQA in Sections 21000, 21001, 21002, and 21002.1 of the Public Resources Code, the courts of this state have declared the following policies to be implicit in CEQA:

(a) The EIR requirement is the heart of CEQA. (*County of Inyo v. Yorty,* 32 Cal. App.3d 795.)

(b) The EIR serves not only to protect the environment but also to demonstrate to the public that it is being protected. (*County of Inyo v. Yorty*, 32 Cal.App. 3d 795.)

(c) The EIR is to inform other governmental agencies and the public generally of the environmental impact of a proposed project. (*No Oil, Inc. v. City of Los Angeles*, 13 Cal.3d 68.)

(d) The EIR is to demonstrate to an apprehensive citizenry that the agency has, in fact, analyzed and considered the ecological implications of its action. (*People ex rel. Department of Public Works v. Bosio*, 47 Cal.App.3d 495.)

(e) The EIR process will enable the public to determine the environmental and economic values of their elected and appointed officials thus allowing for appropriate action come election day should a majority of the voters disagree. (*People v. County of Kern*, 39 Cal.App.3d 830.)

(f) CEQA was intended to be interpreted in such a manner as to afford the fullest possible protection to the environment within the reasonable scope of the statutory language. (*Friends of Mammoth v. Board of Supervisors*, 8 Cal.3d 247.)

(g) The purpose of CEQA is not to generate paper, but to compel government at all levels to make decisions with environmental consequences in mind. (*Bozung v. LAFCO* (1975) 13 Cal.3d 263)

(h) The lead agency must consider the whole of an action, not simply its constituent parts, when determining whether it will have a significant environmental effect. (*Citizens Assoc. For Sensible

Development of Bishop Area v. County of Inyo (1985) 172 Cal.App.3d 151)

(i) CEQA does not require technical perfection in an EIR, but rather adequacy, completeness, and a good-faith effort at full disclosure. A court does not pass upon the correctness of an EIR's environmental conclusions, but only determines if the EIR is sufficient as an informational document. (*Kings County Farm Bureau v. City of Hanford* (1990) 221 Cal.App.3d 692)

(j) CEQA requires that decisions be informed and balanced. It must not be subverted into an instrument for the oppression and delay of social, economic, or recreational development or advancement. (*Laurel Heights Improvement Assoc. v. Regents of U.C.* (1993) 6 Cal. 4th 1112 and *Citizens of Goleta Valley v. Board of Supervisors* (1990) 52 Cal. 3d 553)

Note: Authority cited: Sections 21083 and 21087, Public Resources Code. Reference: Sections 21000–21176, Public Resources Code.

Discussion: This section highlights court cases that illustrate several essential principles in the application of CEQA. Each of these court opinions has been cited in numerous subsequent holdings. This section cannot reiterate all CEQA principles and should be read in conjunction with the entirety of the statute and Guidelines.

15004   Time of Preparation

(a) Before granting any approval of a project subject to CEQA, every lead agency or responsible agency shall consider a final EIR or negative declaration or another document authorized by these guidelines to be used in the place of an EIR or negative declaration. See the definition of "approval" in Section 15352.

(b) Choosing the precise time for CEQA compliance involves a balancing of competing factors. EIRs and negative declarations should be prepared as early as feasible in the planning process to enable environmental considerations to influence project program and design and yet late enough to provide meaningful information for environmental assessment.

(1) With public projects, at the earliest feasible time, project sponsors shall incorporate environmental considerations into project conceptualization, design, and planning. CEQA compliance should be completed prior to acquisition of a site for a public project.

(2) To implement the above principles, public agencies shall not undertake actions concerning the proposed public project that would have a significant adverse effect or limit the choice of alternatives or mitigation measures, before completion of CEQA compliance. For example, agencies shall not:

   (A) Formally make a decision to proceed with the use of a site for facilities which would require CEQA review, regardless of whether the agency has made any final purchase of the site for these facilities, except that agencies may designate a preferred site for CEQA review and may enter into land acquisition agreements when the agency has conditioned the agency's future use of the site on CEQA compliance.

   (B) Otherwise take any action which gives impetus to a planned or foreseeable project in a manner that forecloses alternatives or mitigation measures that would ordinarily be part of CEQA review of that public project.

(3) With private projects, the Lead Agency shall encourage the project proponent to incorporate environmental considerations into project conceptualization, design, and planning at the earliest feasible time.

(c) The environmental document preparation and review should be coordinated in a timely fashion with the existing planning, review, and project approval processes being used by each public agency. These procedures, to the maximum extent feasible, are to run concurrently, not consecutively. When the lead agency is a state agency, the environmental document shall be included as part of the regular project report if such a report is used in its existing review and budgetary process.

Note: Authority cited: Sections 21083 and 21087, Public Resources Code. Reference: Sections 21003, 21061 and 21105, Public Resources Code; *Friends of Mammoth v. Board of Supervisors*, (1972) 8 Cal.3d 247; *Mount Sutro Defense Committee v. Regents of the University of California*, (1978) 77 Cal.App.3d 20.

Discussion: This section codifies the requirement that EIRs and Negative Declarations be prepared before an agency makes a decision on the project and early enough to help influence the project's plans or design. For

EIRs and Negative Declarations to be effective in serving the purposes of CEQA, the preparation of these documents must be coordinated with the planning, review, and approval processes as described in subsection (c). Early preparation is necessary for the legal validity of the process and for the usefulness of the documents. Early preparation enables agencies to make revisions in projects to reduce or avoid adverse environmental effects before the agency has become so committed to a particular approach that it can make changes only with difficulty.

The 1998 amendment clarifies that public agencies must consider the significant effects of a project before taking actions which may limit their choice of potential project alternatives and mitigation measures. This section also provides examples of how far the agency may proceed in its decision-making prior to initiating the CEQA process.

15005   Terminology

The following words are used to indicate whether a particular subject in the Guidelines is mandatory, advisory, or permissive:

(a) "Must" or "shall" identifies a mandatory element which all public agencies are required to follow.

(b) "Should" identifies guidance provided by the Secretary for Resources based on policy considerations contained in CEQA, in the legislative history of the statute, or in federal court decisions which California courts can be expected to follow. Public agencies are advised to follow this guidance in the absence of compelling, countervailing considerations.

(c) "May" identifies a permissive element which is left fully to the discretion of the public agencies involved.

Note: Authority cited: Sections 21083 and 21087, Public Resources Code. Reference: Sections 21082 and 21083, Public Resources Code.

Discussion: This section explains the terminology used in the Guidelines. The Guidelines contain sections that are clearly mandated, others that are strongly advisory, and still others that are permissive.

The advisory elements are an essential part of the Guidelines. Due to the requirement for state agencies to reimburse local government for any mandates contained in the state regulations, the Guidelines have avoided clear mandates except where they have been required by the CEQA statutes or state court decisions. Nevertheless, as a result of the legislative history of CEQA as interpreted by court decisions such as *Friends of*

Mammoth v. Board of Supervisors, 8 Cal. 3d 247, there are many requirements for the Environmental Impact Statement process under the National Environmental Policy Act that the state courts are likely to apply under CEQA. The use of the term "should" identifies many of these requirements in federal case law which state courts have not yet followed. This language advises individual agencies to follow the provision in the Guidelines unless the agency has a compelling reason to take another approach. This advice helps to implement the preventive law function of the State CEQA Guidelines.

The permissive language serves two functions. First, the language identifies elements made permissive by the statute. Second, the language identifies interpretations where the Guidelines provide that certain activities or short cuts are authorized ways to administer the process. The interpretations are intended to provide certainty, showing administrators that particular approaches are legitimate ways to administer the Act.

15006   Reducing Delay and Paperwork

Public agencies should reduce delay and paperwork by:

(a) Integrating the CEQA process into early planning. (15004(c))

(b) Ensuring the swift and fair resolution of lead agency disputes. (15053)

(c) Identifying projects which fit within categorical exemptions and are therefore exempt from CEQA processing. (15300.4)

(d) Using initial studies to identify significant environmental issues and to narrow the scope of EIRs. (15063)

(e) Using a negative declaration when a project not otherwise exempt will not have a significant effect on the environment. (15070)

(f) Using a previously prepared EIR when it adequately addresses the proposed project. (15153)

(g) Consulting with state and local responsible agencies before and during preparation of an environmental impact report so that the document will meet the needs of all the agencies which will use it. (15083)

(h) Urging applicants, either before or after the filing of an application, to revise projects to eliminate possible significant effects on the environment, thereby enabling the project to qualify for a negative declaration rather than an environmental impact report. (15063(c)(2))

(i) Integrating CEQA requirements with other environmental review and consulting requirements. (Public Resources Code Section 21080.5)

(j) Eliminating duplication with federal procedures by providing for joint preparation of environmental documents with federal agencies and by adopting completed federal NEPA documents. (15227)

(k) Emphasizing consultation before an environmental impact report is prepared, rather than submitting adversary comments on a completed document. (15082(b))

(l) Combining environmental documents with other documents such as general plans. (15166)

(m) Eliminating repetitive discussions of the same issues by using environmental impact reports on programs, policies, or plans and tiering from reports of broad scope to those of narrower scope. (15152)

(n) Reducing the length of environmental impact reports by means such as setting appropriate page limits. (15141)

(o) Preparing analytic rather than encyclopedic environmental impact reports. (15142)

(p) Mentioning only briefly issues other than significant ones in EIRs. (15143)

(q) Writing environmental impact reports in plain language. (15140)

(r) Following a clear format for environmental impact reports. (15120)

(s) Emphasizing the portions of the environmental impact report that are useful to decision-makers and the public and reducing emphasis on background material. (15143)

(t) Using incorporation by reference. (15150)

(u) Making comments on environmental impact reports as specific as possible. (15204)

Note: Authority cited: Sections 21083 and 21087, Public Resources Code. Reference: Sections 21003 and 21083, Public Resources Code.

Discussion: This section encourages agencies to reduce the time and expense previously involved in the administration of CEQA. This section highlights many specific provisions of the Guidelines that are designed to reduce both delay and paperwork. This section is designed to reduce the unnecessary delays and paperwork that have added unjustified costs to the CEQA process. Bringing these provisions together

should help agencies identify and use efficient ways to administer the Act.

15007   Amendments

(a) These Guidelines will be amended from time to time to match new developments relating to CEQA.

(b) Amendments to the Guidelines apply prospectively only. New requirements in amendments will apply to steps in the CEQA process not yet undertaken by the date when agencies must comply with the amendments.

(c) If a document meets the content requirements in effect when the document is set out for public review, the document shall not need to be revised to conform to any new content requirements in guideline amendments taking effect before the document is finally approved.

(d) Public agencies shall comply with new requirements in amendments to the Guidelines beginning with the earlier of the following two dates:

   (1) The effective date of the agency's procedures amended to conform to the new guideline amendments; or

   (2) The 120th day after the effective date of the guideline amendments.

(e) Public agencies may implement any permissive or advisory elements of the guidelines beginning with the effective date of the guideline amendments.

Note: Authority cited: Sections 21083 and 21087, Public Resources Code. Reference: Sections 21082–21087, Public Resources Code; *Stevens v. City of Glendale*, 125 Cal. App.3d 986.

Discussion: Section 15007 is intended to provide a single section that will apply to all past, current, and future amendments. This approach will avoid the need to add a new subsection to the Guidelines to explain the phase-in procedures with every new set of amendments. Subsection (a) recognizes the need to update the Guidelines periodically. Subsection (b) provides the formula for the phase-in of any new requirements.

Section 15007 is intended to provide uniform procedures after the effective date of the new amendments to the Guidelines. If a draft EIR was sent out for public review before the effective date of the amendments and the draft EIR complied with all content requirements at the time, it would not need to be changed even if the contents of a draft EIR were revised in adopted amendments. Any steps taken in processing the draft or final EIR or in making findings

after approving the EIR, would have to comply with any new requirements in the Guidelines.

The same principle would apply to a project being processed with a Negative Declaration or with an EIR substitute under a certified program.

Subsection (c) provides an interpretation clarifying the content requirement for documents. It provides expressly that if a document met all content requirements in effect at the time when it was sent out for public review, the contents of the document would not need to be changed even if new amendments altering the content requirements took effect before the document was finally approved. Because the section uses the term "documents," the wording shows that the principle applies to Negative Declarations as well as EIRs.

Section 15007(d) was added to avoid any inconsistency with Section 15022. Section 15007(d) provides that agencies must comply with new amendments to the Guidelines either on the effective date of their own implementing procedures or the 120th day after the effective date of the Guidelines, whichever is earlier. This approach is necessary to provide agencies with enough time to revise their procedures and bring their process into conformity with the revised Guidelines.

Subsection (e) provides that agencies have the option of complying with new amendments to the Guidelines at an earlier time if they so choose. This approach allows agencies to take immediate advantage of any new efficiencies or shortcuts allowed in amendments but does not require compliance with the new amendments until later.

Article 2. General Responsibilities
Sections 15020 to 15025

15020   General

Each public agency is responsible for complying with CEQA and these Guidelines. A public agency must meet its own responsibilities under CEQA and shall not rely on comments from other public agencies or private citizens as a substitute for work CEQA requires the lead agency to accomplish. For example, a lead agency is responsible for the adequacy of its environmental documents. The Lead Agency shall not knowingly release a deficient document hoping that public comments will correct defects in the document.

Note: Authority cited: Sections 21083 and 21087, Public Resources Code. Reference:

Sections 21082 and 21082.1, Public Resources Code; *Russian Hill Improvement Association v. Board of Permit Appeals*, 44 Cal.App.3d 158 (1975).

Discussion: This section makes the point that an agency is responsible for its own compliance with CEQA.

15021 Duty to Minimize Environmental Damage and Balance Competing Public Objectives

(a) CEQA establishes a duty for public agencies to avoid or minimize environmental damage where feasible.

   (1) In regulating public or private activities, agencies are required to give major consideration to preventing environmental damage.

   (2) A public agency should not approve a project as proposed if there are feasible alternatives or mitigation measures available that would substantially lessen any significant effects that the project would have on the environment.

(b) In deciding whether changes in a project are feasible, an agency may consider specific economic, environmental, legal, social, and technological factors.

(c) The duty to prevent or minimize environmental damage is implemented through the findings required by Section 15091.

(d) CEQA recognizes that in determining whether and how a project should be approved, a public agency has an obligation to balance a variety of public objectives, including economic, environmental, and social factors and in particular the goal of providing a decent home and satisfying living environment for every Californian. An agency shall prepare a statement of overriding considerations as described in Section 15093 to reflect the ultimate balancing of competing public objectives when the agency decides to approve a project that will cause one or more significant effects on the environment.

Note: Authority cited: Sections 21083 and 21087, Public Resources Code. Reference: Public Resources Code Sections 21000, 21001, 21002, 21002.1, and 21081; *San Francisco Ecology Center v. City and County of San Francisco*, (1975) 48 Cal.App.3d 584; *Laurel Hills Homeowners Association v. City Council*, (1978) 83 Cal.App.3d 515.

Discussion: Section 15021 brings together the many separate elements that apply to the duty to minimize environmental damage. These duties appear in the policy sections

of CEQA, in the findings requirement in Section 21081, and in a number of court decisions that have built up a body of case law that is not immediately reflected in the statutory language. This section is also necessary to provide one place to explain how the ultimate balancing of the merits of the project relates to the search for feasible alternatives or mitigation measures to avoid or reduce the environmental damage.

The placement of this section early in the article on general responsibilities helps highlight this duty to prevent environmental damage. This section is an effort to provide a careful statement of the duty with its limitations and its relationship to other essential public goals.

15022 Public Agency Implementing Procedures

(a) Each public agency shall adopt objectives, criteria, and specific procedures consistent with CEQA and these Guidelines for administering its responsibilities under CEQA, including the orderly evaluation of projects and preparation of environmental documents. The implementing procedures should contain at least provisions for:

   (1) Identifying the activities that are exempt from CEQA. These procedures should contain:

      (A) Provisions for evaluating a proposed activity to determine if there is no possibility that the activity may have a significant effect on the environment.

      (B) A list of projects or permits over which the public agency has only ministerial authority.

      (C) A list of specific activities which the public agency has found to be within the categorical exemptions established by these guidelines.

   (2) Conducting initial studies.

   (3) Preparing negative declarations.

   (4) Preparing draft and final EIRs.

   (5) Consulting with and obtaining comments from other public agencies and members of the public with regard to the environmental effects of projects.

   (6) Assuring adequate opportunity and time for public review and comment on the Draft EIR or Negative Declaration.

   (7) Evaluating and responding to comments received on environmental documents.

   (8) Assigning responsibility for determining the adequacy of an EIR or negative declaration.

   (9) Reviewing and considering environmental documents by the person or decisionmaking body who will approve or disapprove a project.

   (10) Filing documents required or authorized by CEQA and these Guidelines.

   (11) Providing adequate comments on environmental documents which are submitted to the public agency for review.

   (12) Assigning responsibility for specific functions to particular units of the public agency.

   (13) Providing time periods for performing functions under CEQA.

(b) Any district, including a school district, need not adopt objectives, criteria, and procedures of its own if it uses the objectives, criteria, and procedures of another public agency whose boundaries are coterminous with or entirely encompass the district.

(c) Public agencies should revise their implementing procedures to conform to amendments to these Guidelines within 120 days after the effective date of the amendments. During the period while the public agency is revising its procedures, the agency must conform to any statutory changes in the California Environmental Quality Act that have become effective regardless of whether the public agency has revised its formally adopted procedures to conform to the statutory changes.

(d) In adopting procedures to implement CEQA, a public agency may adopt the State CEQA Guidelines through incorporation by reference. The agency may then adopt only those specific procedures or provisions described in subsection (a) which are necessary to tailor the general provisions of the Guidelines to the specific operations of the agency. A public agency may also choose to adopt a complete set of procedures identifying in one document all the necessary requirements.

Note: Authority cited: Sections 21083 and 21087, Public Resources Code. Reference: Sections 21082, 21100.2, and 21151.5, Public Resources Code.

Discussion: This section supplements the statutory requirement for every agency to have implementing procedures for CEQA. After identifying the statutory requirement, the section spells out the essential contents for the implementing procedures. Without this list of essential contents, many agencies that only occasionally work with CEQA would find that they had failed to comply with the Act when challenged over their implementing procedures.

Subsection (b) identifies the statutory allowance for a school district to use the implementing procedures of any public agency whose boundaries are coterminous with the district. The regulation then expands this authorization to allow any agency to adopt the procedures of a second agency whose boundaries are coterminous with or entirely encompass those of the first agency. This regulation is necessary to validate the common practice of many counties of having the county planning department often provide the staff work for CEQA compliance of most of the districts within the county, following county procedures.

Subsection (c) answers the often asked question of how soon agencies must bring their implementing procedures into conformance with newly adopted amendments to the Guidelines.

Subsection (d) allows a public agency to use an efficient, short method of bringing its procedures into compliance by adopting the State Guidelines through incorporation by reference. Agencies which have followed this approach have been able to reduce the size of their regulations and reduce the expense of keeping their regulations up-to-date. This section still allows public agencies the option of adopting their own complete set of procedures if they so choose.

15023   Office of Planning and Research (OPR)

(a) From time to time OPR shall review the State CEQA Guidelines and shall make recommendations for amendments to the Secretary for Resources.

(b) OPR shall receive and evaluate proposals for adoption, amendment, or repeal of categorical exemptions and shall make recommendations on the proposals to the Secretary for Resources. People making suggestions concerning categorical exemptions shall submit their recommendations to OPR with supporting information to show that the class of projects in the proposal either will or will not have a significant effect on the environment.

(c) The State Clearinghouse in the Office of Planning and Research shall be responsible for distributing environmental documents to State agencies, departments, boards, and commissions for review and comment.

(d) Upon request of a Lead Agency or a project applicant, OPR shall provide assistance in identifying the various responsible agencies and any federal agencies which have responsibility for carrying out or approving a proposed project.

(e) OPR shall ensure that state responsible agencies provide the necessary information to lead agencies in response to notices of preparation within at most 30 days after receiving a notice of preparation.

(f) OPR shall resolve disputes as to which agency is the lead agency for a project.

(g) OPR shall receive and file all notices of completion, determination, and exemption.

Note: Authority cited: Sections 21083 and 21087, Public Resources Code. Reference: Sections 21080.4, 21083, 21086, 21087, 21108, and 21161, Public Resources Code.

Discussion: This section brings together many different requirements which apply to the Office of Planning and Research. Although some of the requirements identified in this section are statutory, others are administrative in origin. The statutory and administrative requirements are combined here to provide a comprehensive view of the OPR responsibility.

15024   Secretary for Resources

(a) The Guidelines shall be adopted by the Secretary for Resources. The Secretary shall make a finding that each class of projects given a categorical exemption will not have a significant effect on the environment.

(b) The Secretary may issue amendments to these Guidelines.

(c) The Secretary shall certify state environmental regulatory programs which meet the standards for certification in Section 21080.5, Public Resources Code.

(d) The Secretary shall receive and file notices required by certified state environmental regulatory programs.

Note: Authority cited: Sections 21083 and 21087, Public Resources Code. Reference: Sections 21080.5, 21083, 21084, 21086, 21087, 21088, and 21152, Public Resources Code.

Discussion: This section brings together many different requirements under CEQA which apply to the Secretary for Resources and OPR. The section is included here to provide information to agencies and members of the public who are concerned with the CEQA process.

Subsection (d) has been changed to conform with amendments made to the statute

by Chapter 571, statutes of 1984. These amendments consolidated the filing of Notices of Completion, Determination and Exemption in OPR rather than with the Secretary of Resources, except for notices required for CEQA compliance under certified regulatory programs.

15025   Delegation of Responsibilities

(a) A public agency may assign specific functions to its staff to assist in administering CEQA. Functions which may be delegated include but are not limited to:

(1) Determining whether a project is exempt.

(2) Conducting an initial study and deciding whether to prepare a draft EIR or negative declaration.

(3) Preparing a negative declaration or EIR.

(4) Determining that a negative declaration has been completed within a period of 105 days.

(5) Preparing responses to comments on environmental documents.

(6) Filing of notices.

(b) The decisionmaking body of a public agency shall not delegate the following functions:

(1) Reviewing and considering a final EIR or approving a negative declaration prior to approving a project.

(2) The making of findings as required by Sections 15091 and 15093.

(c) Where an advisory body such as a planning commission is required to make a recommendation on a project to the decisionmaking body, the advisory body shall also review and consider the EIR or negative declaration in draft or final form.

Note: Authority cited: Sections 21083 and 21087, Public Resources Code. Reference: Section 21082, Public Resources Code; *Kleist v. City of Glendale*, (1976) 56 Cal. App.3d 770.

Discussion: This section is a recodification of former Section 15055 with one additional feature. The section is necessary in order to identify functions in the CEQA process that a decision-making body can delegate to other parts of the Lead Agency. The agency can operate more efficiently when many functions are delegated to the staff rather than requiring the decision-making body to perform all the functions.

Subsection (b) codifies the holding in *Kleist v. City of Glendale* by identifying the functions that cannot be delegated. The functions of considering the environmental document and making findings in response to significant effects identified in a final EIR are fundamental to the CEQA process. These steps bring together the environmental evaluation and the decision on the project. This section is intended to assure that the environmental analysis of a project is brought to bear on the actual decision on the project. The section also serves to guide agencies away from practices that have been ruled invalid.

Subsection (c) reflects an administrative interpretation which applies the requirements of CEQA to advisory bodies. Such bodies need not and may not certify an EIR, but they should consider the effects of a project in making their recommendations. This section also suggests that advisory bodies may consider a draft EIR.

Article 3. Authorities Granted to Public Agencies by CEQA Sections 15040 to 15045

15040   Authority Provided by CEQA

(a) CEQA is intended to be used in conjunction with discretionary powers granted to public agencies by other laws.

(b) CEQA does not grant an agency new powers independent of the powers granted to the agency by other laws.

(c) Where another law grants an agency discretionary powers, CEQA supplements those discretionary powers by authorizing the agency to use the discretionary powers to mitigate or avoid significant effects on the environment when it is feasible to do so with respect to projects subject to the powers of the agency. Prior to January 1, 1983, CEQA provided implied authority for an agency to use its discretionary powers to mitigate or avoid significant effects on the environment. Effective January 1, 1983, CEQA provides express authority to do so.

(d) The exercise of the discretionary powers may take forms that had not been expected before the enactment of CEQA, but the exercise must be within the scope of the power.

(e) The exercise of discretionary powers for environmental protection shall be consistent with express or implied limitations provided by other laws.

Note: Authority cited: Sections 21083 and 21087, Public Resources Code. Reference: Sections 21000, 21001, 21002, 21002.1, and 21004, Public Resources Code; Section 4, Chapter 1438, Statutes of 1982; *Golden Gate Bridge, etc., District v. Muzzi,* (1978)

83 Cal.App.3d 707; *E.D.F. v. Mathews,* 410 F. Supp. 366, 339 (D.D.C., 1976); *Friends of Mammoth v. Board of Supervisors,* (1972) 8 Cal.3d 247; *Pinewood Investors v. City of Oxnard* (1982) 133 Cal.App.3d 1030.

Discussion: This section conforms the Guidelines to Section 21004 as added by SB 2011 of 1982, Chapter 1438 of the Statutes of 1982, and adds clarifying interpretations of that bill. The sentences about express and implied authority show that SB 2011 is consistent with prior case law and does not require a change in an agency's manner of implementing CEQA if the agency had been careful before to base its actions on a discretionary power.

Subsection (d) shows that discretionary powers may be used to avoid or mitigate significant environmental effects even if that involves using the powers in new ways. As shown in the *Golden Gate Bridge District* case, the use of specific powers when supplemented by the implied authority in CEQA may result in the use of powers going beyond traditional ideas of the limits on those powers. The Golden Gate Bridge District was allowed to use its power of eminent domain to condemn property for mitigation outside the "take line" that was the normal limit to the use of condemnation. Subsection (e) makes the point that the exercise of discretionary powers as authorized by CEQA to avoid or mitigate environmental effects is subject to limitations provided in other laws. There have been many questions about the extent to which CEQA is or is not limited by other laws. This section shows that CEQA is just like any other law in that its general provisions may be subject to specific limitations provided in other laws. This provision is consistent with Section 21004 and with the court decision of *Pinewood Investors v. City of Oxnard,* (1982) 133 Cal.App.3d 1030.

15041   Authority to Mitigate

Within the limitations described in Section 15040 :

(a) A lead agency for a project has authority to require feasible changes in any or all activities involved in the project in order to substantially lessen or avoid significant effects on the environment, consistent with applicable constitutional requirements such as the "nexus" and "rough proportionality" standards established by case law (*Nollan v. California Coastal Commission* (1987) 483 U.S. 825, *Dolan v. City of Tigard,* (1994) 512 U.S. 374, *Ehrlich v. City of Culver City,* (1996) 12 Cal.4th 854.).

(b) When a public agency acts as a responsible agency for a project, the agency

shall have more limited authority than a lead agency. The responsible agency may require changes in a project to lessen or avoid only the effects, either direct or indirect, of that part of the project which the agency will be called on to carry out or approve.

(c) With respect to a project which includes housing development, a lead or responsible agency shall not reduce the proposed number of housing units as a mitigation measure or alternative to lessen a particular significant effect on the environment if that agency determines that there is another feasible, specific mitigation measure or alternative that would provide a comparable lessening of the significant effect.

Note: Authority cited: Sections 21083 and 21087, Public Resources Code. Reference: Sections 21002, 21002.1, and 21085, Public Resources Code; *Golden Gate Bridge, etc., District v. Muzzi* (1978) 83 Cal.App.3d 707; and *Laurel Hills Homeowners Assn. v. City Council of City of Los Angeles* (1978) 83 Cal.App.3d 515.

Discussion: This section explains the differences in authority an agency can exercise depending on whether it is acting as a Lead Agency or a Responsible Agency. Subsection (b) limits the powers of a Responsible Agency to considering the environmental effects that would be caused by the activity which the agency is called upon to approve. These environmental effects may be either direct or indirect, but they must be traced to the activity which the agency approves. This section is intended to resolve the confusion among Responsible Agencies concerning this issue. Some Responsible Agencies have believed that they could consider only the direct effects of the activity they approve.

This section reminds agencies of their responsibility to substantially lessen project impacts where feasible and of basic Constitutional principles which may act to limit the feasibility of mitigation measures. As noted in Section 15040 and Public Resources Code Section 21004, CEQA does not give an agency any new powers beyond those express or implied powers which it already holds. Recognizing the practical limitations on regulatory powers is key to preparing feasible mitigation measures.

15042   Authority to Disapprove Projects

A public agency may disapprove a project if necessary in order to avoid one or more significant effects on the environment that would occur if the project were approved as proposed. A lead agency has broader authority to disapprove a project than does a responsible agency. A responsible agency may refuse to approve a project in order to avoid direct or indirect environmental effects of that part of the project which the responsible agency would be called on to carry out or approve. For example, an air quality management district acting as a responsible agency would not have authority to disapprove a project for water pollution effects that were unrelated to the air quality aspects of the project regulated by the district.

Note: Authority cited: Sections 21083 and 21087, Public Resources Code. Reference: Sections 21002 and 21002.1, Public Resources Code; *Friends of Mammoth v. Mono County*, 8 Cal.App.3d 247; *San Diego Trust and Savings Bank v. Friends of Gill*, 121 Cal.App.3d 203.

Discussion: This section is necessary to codify the holdings of the cases cited in the note. These cases hold that a public agency has authority to disapprove a project due to environmental problems even though that authority might not be expressly stated in the enabling legislation for the agency.

15043   Authority to Approve Projects Despite Significant Effects

A public agency may approve a project even though the project would cause a significant effect on the environment if the agency makes a fully informed and publicly disclosed decision that:

(a) There is no feasible way to lessen or avoid the significant effect (see Section 15091); and

(b) Specifically identified expected benefits from the project outweigh the policy of reducing or avoiding significant environmental impacts of the project. (See: Section 15093.)

Note: Authority cited: Sections 21083 and 21087, Public Resources Code. Reference: Sections 21002 and 21002.1, Public Resources Code; *San Francisco Ecology Center v. City and County of San Francisco*, (1975) 48 Cal.App.3d 584; *San Diego Trust & Savings Bank v. Friends of Gill*, (1981) 121 Cal.App.3d 203.

Discussion: The other side of the authority to disapprove, or require changes in, a project is the authority to approve a project despite significant environmental effects. As shown by the case cited in the note, CEQA provides authority to approve projects which have significant adverse environmental effects. CEQA requires, however, that the agency make such a decision only after going through the full CEQA process and making explicit findings to support its actions. This section is a codification of case law.

15044   Authority to Comment

Any person or entity other than a responsible agency may submit comments to a lead agency concerning any environmental effects of a project being considered by the lead agency.

Note: Authority cited: Sections 21083 and 21087, Public Resources Code. Reference: Sections 21000, 21001, 21002.1, 21104, and 21153, Public Resources Code.

Discussion: This section reflects 1984 amendments enacted to Sections 21104 and 21153 of the Public Resources Code (Stats 1984, Ch 1514), which revised the duties of Responsible Agencies with regard to submitting comments to Lead Agencies on draft EIRs. The statute now limits the comments of Responsible Agencies to those areas in which the agency has expertise or jurisdiction.

15045   Fees

(a) ~~All lead agencies preparing EIRs and negative declarations for projects~~ For a project to be carried out by any person or entity other than the lead agency, ~~it-self~~ the lead agency may charge and collect a reasonable fee from ~~the person or entity proposing the project~~ ~~such per-son on entity,~~ in order to recover the estimated costs incurred in preparing ~~the EIR or negative declaration~~ environmental documents and for procedures necessary to comply with CEQA on the project. Litigation expenses, costs and fees incurred in actions alleging noncompliance with CEQA are not recoverable under this section.

(b) Public agencies may charge and collect a reasonable fee from members of the public for a copy of an environmental document not to exceed the actual cost of reproducing a copy.

Note: Authority: Sections 21083 and 21087, Public Resources Code. Reference: Section 21089 and 21105, Public Resources Code. ~~and Sections 6250 et seq., Government Code.~~

Discussion: The authority to charge fees is an essential part of any discussion of authorities granted by CEQA. This section brings together two separate statutory authorities. These are the authority to charge a fee for the preparation of an EIR or Negative Declaration and the authority to charge a fee to a person requesting a copy of an EIR or Negative Declaration. The Guideline section adds the interpretation that the authority to collect a fee for a copy shall be limited to the actual cost of reproducing a copy. This interpretation responds to an effort by some

agencies to say that the cost of the copy which they were entitled to recover included a prorata share of the cost of all studies and writing efforts in addition to the cost of printing the EIR. The Resources Agency believed that such an interpretation would be contrary to the policy of CEQA encouraging public participation. Further, the interpretation would enable agencies to charge fees twice for their cost of preparing the EIR, once to the applicant and second to people wanting a copy of the EIR. Subsection (b) of this section is necessary to protect public participation and to prevent agencies from charging exorbitant fees for copies of EIRs and Negative Declarations.

Section 21089 of the Public Resources Code gives the lead agency express authority to charge fees to cover the cost of preparing an EIR or negative declaration, as well as for reporting program.

Article 4. Lead Agency Sections 15050 to 15053

15050   Lead Agency Concept

(a) Where a project is to be carried out or approved by more than one public agency, one public agency shall be responsible for preparing an EIR or negative declaration for the project. This agency shall be called the lead agency.

(b) Except as provided in subsection (c), the decisionmaking body of each responsible agency shall consider the lead agency's EIR or negative declaration prior to acting upon or approving the project. Each responsible agency shall certify that its decisionmaking body reviewed and considered the information contained in the EIR or negative declaration on the project.

(c) The determination of the lead agency of whether to prepare an EIR or a negative declaration shall be final and conclusive for all persons, including responsible agencies, unless:

(1) The decision is successfully challenged as provided in Section 21167 of the Public Resources Code,

(2) Circumstances or conditions change as provided in Section 15162, or

(3) A responsible agency becomes a lead agency under Section 15052.

Note: Authority cited: Sections 21083 and 21087, Public Resources Code. Reference: Sections 21080.1, 21165, and 21167.2, Public Resources Code.

Discussion: This section provides a short and concise statement of the Lead Agency concept for clarity of this article. While the bulk of this article deals with identifying the appropriate Lead Agency, a summary of the Lead Agency concept is appropriate because the concept is fundamental to the CEQA process as a whole.

15051 Criteria for Identifying the Lead Agency

Where two or more public agencies will be involved with a project, the determination of which agency will be the lead agency shall be governed by the following criteria:

(a) If the project will be carried out by a public agency, that agency shall be the lead agency even if the project would be located within the jurisdiction of another public agency.

(b) If the project is to be carried out by a nongovernmental person or entity, the lead agency shall be the public agency with the greatest responsibility for supervising or approving the project as a whole.

   (1) The lead agency will normally be the agency with general governmental powers, such as a city or county, rather than an agency with a single or limited purpose such as an air pollution control district or a district which will provide a public service or public utility to the project.

   (2) Where a city prezones an area, the city will be the appropriate lead agency for any subsequent annexation of the area and should prepare the appropriate environmental document at the time of the prezoning. The local agency formation commission shall act as a responsible agency.

(c) Where more than one public agency equally meet the criteria in subsection (b), the agency which will act first on the project in question shall be the lead agency.

(d) Where the provisions of subsections (a), (b), and (c) leave two or more public agencies with a substantial claim to be the lead agency, the public agencies may by agreement designate an agency as the lead agency. An agreement may also provide for cooperative efforts by two or more agencies by contract, joint exercise of powers, or similar devices.

Note: Authority cited: Sections 21083 and 21087, Public Resources Code. Reference: Section 21165, Public Resources Code.

Discussion: The purpose of this section is to provide the criteria for identifying which of several competing agencies shall be the Lead Agency for a project. By providing these criteria, the Guidelines will enable most agencies to determine for themselves which agency is the appropriate Lead Agency in any given circumstance. Thus, most projects will be spared the additional time and cost involved in submitting a Lead Agency dispute for resolution by the Office of Planning and Research.

15052 Shift in Lead Agency Designation

(a) Where a responsible agency is called on to grant an approval for a project subject to CEQA for which another public agency was the appropriate lead agency, the responsible agency shall assume the role of the lead agency when any of the following conditions occur:

   (1) The lead agency did not prepare any environmental documents for the project, and the statute of limitations has expired for a challenge to the action of the appropriate lead agency.

   (2) The lead agency prepared environmental documents for the project, but the following conditions occur:

      (A) A subsequent EIR is required pursuant to Section 15162,

      (B) The lead agency has granted a final approval for the project, and

      (C) The statute of limitations for challenging the lead agency's action under CEQA has expired.

   (3) The lead agency prepared inadequate environmental documents without consulting with the responsible agency as required by Sections 15072 or 15082, and the statute of limitations has expired for a challenge to the action of the appropriate lead agency.

(b) When a responsible agency assumes the duties of a lead agency under this section, the time limits applicable to a lead agency shall apply to the actions of the agency assuming the lead agency duties.

Note: Authority cited: Sections 21083 and 21087, Public Resources Code. Reference: Section 21165, Public Resources Code.

Discussion: The purpose of this section is to explain how Responsible Agencies shall deal with the problem they encounter when the appropriate Lead Agency failed to comply with CEQA. As a general rule, Responsible Agencies must use the EIR or Negative Declaration prepared by the Lead Agency even if the Responsible Agency believes that the document is inadequate. The purpose for this general rule is to require Responsible Agencies to work through the normal CEQA consultation and review process to obtain adequate documents from the Lead Agency. If the Responsible Agency is dissatisfied with the end product, the Responsible Agency's only relief is to litigate the adequacy of the document within 30 days.

Section 15052 deals with the situation where the normal CEQA process broke down. The section provides three exceptions to the general rule. These are (1) where the Lead Agency prepared no document for the project, (2) where a subsequent EIR would be required, and (3) where the Lead Agency failed to consult with the Responsible Agencies as required by CEQA. If any of these situations occurs and the statute of limitations has expired for a challenge to the action of the appropriate Lead Agency, then the Responsible Agency would be required to assume the role of the Lead Agency. These exceptions are narrowly drawn in order to require Responsible Agencies to work within the normal CEQA process to the maximum extent possible. Where the normal process breaks down in any of these three ways, the Responsible Agency could not get an adequate document from the Lead Agency due to no fault of its own. This section provides an interpretation necessary to allow the Responsible Agency to obtain an adequate analysis of the environmental problems.

Subsection (b) is added to provide an interpretation as to which set of time limits would apply to the agency when it shifts roles. There has been confusion on this point because the agency could be viewed as either a Lead or a Responsible Agency. The section provides that when the agency acts in the Lead Agency role, the time limits involved will be those that apply to a Lead Agency.

15053 Designation of Lead Agency by Office of Planning and Research

(a) If there is a dispute over which of several agencies should be the lead agency for a project, the disputing agencies should consult with each other in an effort to resolve the dispute prior to submitting it to OPR. If an agreement cannot be reached, any public agency, or the applicant if a private project is involved, may submit the dispute to OPR for resolution.

(b) OPR shall designate a lead agency within 21 days after receiving a completed request to resolve a dispute.

(c) Regulations adopted by OPR for resolving lead agency disputes may be found in Title 14, California Administrative Code, Sections 16000 et seq.

(d) Designation of a lead agency by OPR shall be based on consideration of the criteria in Section 15052 as well as the capacity of the agency to adequately fulfill the requirements of CEQA.

Note: Authority cited: Sections 21083 and 21087, Public Resources Code. Reference: Section 21165, Public Resources Code; California Administrative Code, Title 14, Sections 16000–16041.

Discussion: The purpose of this section is to outline the process to be used by the Office of Planning and Research in resolving Lead Agency disputes. Because resolving a dispute involves additional costs and delays for a project, the Guidelines require the disputing agencies to try to resolve the issue among themselves. Only where an agreement cannot be reached, would the issue be submitted to OPR. Once the dispute is submitted to OPR, certain formal steps would be required in order to allow all interested parties to make their views known. These steps are contained in the regulations identified in subsection (c). This section outlines the process so that public agencies can understand the process before deciding to submit a dispute to OPR.

Article 5. Preliminary Review of Projects and Conduct of Initial Study Sections 15060 to 15065

15060   Preliminary Review

(a) A ~~public~~ lead agency is allowed 30 days to review for completeness applications for permits or other entitlements for use. While conducting this review for completeness, the agency should be alert for environmental issues that might require preparation of an EIR or that may require additional explanation by the applicant. Accepting an application as complete does not limit the authority of the lead agency to require the applicant to submit additional information needed for environmental evaluation of the project. Requiring such additional information after the application is complete does not change the status of the application.

(b) Except as provided in Section 15111, the lead agency shall begin the formal environmental evaluation of the project after accepting an application as complete and determining that the project is subject to CEQA. ~~Accepting an application as complete does not limit the authority of the lead agency to require the applicant to submit additional information needed for environmental evaluation of the project.~~

(c) Once an application is deemed complete, a lead agency must first determine whether an activity is subject to CEQA before conducting an initial study. An activity is not subject to CEQA if:

(1) The activity does not involve the exercise of discretionary powers by a public agency~~.~~;

(2) The activity will not result in a direct or reasonably foreseeable indirect physical change in the environment~~.~~; or

(3) The activity is not a project as defined in Section 15378.

(d) If the lead agency can determine that an EIR will be clearly required for a project, the agency may skip further initial review of the project and begin work directly on the EIR process described in Article 9, commencing with Section 15080. In the absence of an initial study, the lead agency shall still focus the EIR on the significant effects of the project and indicate briefly its reasons for determining that other effects would not be significant or potentially significant.

Note: Authority: Sections 21083 and 21087, Public Resources Code. Reference: ~~Section 65944, Government Code;~~ Sections 21080(b), 21080.2 and 21160, Public Resources Code.

Discussion: This section describes the actions required of the Lead Agency when it receives an application for a project. This section is necessary in order to save time that could otherwise be spent if the agency ignored environmental issues for the first 30 days of reviewing the application. The section is also necessary for allowing the efficiencies that result from moving directly to the preparation of an EIR where the agency can see that one will clearly be required. This avoids the time involved in the separate step of preparing an Initial Study where the Lead Agency believes it will perform the work of identifying effects as significant or non-significant while it does simultaneous work preparing the EIR.

This section also introduces the term "preliminary review" to apply to this early review of an application for completeness and for a possible exemption from CEQA. This term is needed to provide a shorthand way to referring to these early steps and to distinguish them from the more formal Initial Study process that follows preliminary review.

See Public Resources Code Section 21151.7 which provides that EIRs are required for certain projects.

Public Resources Code Section 21080.1, subdivision (b), requires the lead agency,

upon the request of the project applicant, to provide for consultation with responsible and trustee agencies before the filing of an application. The consultation is to cover the range of actions, potential alternatives, mitigation measures, and any potential and significant effects on the environment of the project.

The 1998 amendment emphasizes that preliminary review is the appropriate time to determine whether the project is indeed subject to CEQA. Subsection (c) offers basic guidance in that area. Further, accepting an application as complete does not restrict the lead agency from requiring additional information as may be necessary for the environmental evaluation of the project.

15060.5   Preapplication Consultation

(a) For a potential project involving the issuance of a lease, permit, license, certificate, or other entitlement for use by one or more public agencies, the lead agency shall, upon the request of a potential applicant and prior to the filing of a formal application, provide for consultation with the potential applicant to consider the range of actions, potential alternatives, mitigation measures, and any potential significant effects on the environment of the potential project.

(b) The lead agency may include in the consultation one or more responsible agencies, trustee agencies, and other public agencies who in the opinion of the lead agency may have an interest in the proposed project. The lead agency may consult the Office of Permit Assistance in the Trade and Commerce Agency for help in identifying interested agencies.

Note: Authority cited: Sections 21083 and 21087, Public Resources Code. Reference: Section 21080.1, Public Resources Code.

Discussion: This section incorporates the provisions of Public Resources Code Section 21080.1 enabling a project proponent to request a preapplication meeting with the lead agency to discuss their project. The lead agency is responsible for holding the meeting and may ask the California Office of Permit Assistance for help in identifying state and regional agencies that may be interested in the proposed project.

15061   Review for Exemption

(a) Once a lead agency has determined that an activity is a project subject to CEQA ~~As part of the preliminary review~~, a ~~public~~ lead agency shall determine whether ~~a particular activity~~ the project is exempt from CEQA.

(b) A project is exempt from CEQA if ~~Possible exemptions from CEQA include~~:

  (1) ~~The activity is not a project as defined in Section 15378.~~ The project is exempt by statute (see, e.g. Article 18, commencing with Section 15260).

  (2) The project is exempt pursuant to a ~~has been granted an exemption by statute (see Article 18, commencing with Section 15260) or by~~ categorical exemption (see Article 19, commencing with Section 15300) and the application of that categorical exemption is not barred by one of the exceptions set forth in Section 15300.2.

  (3) The activity is covered by the general rule that <u>CEQA applies only to projects which have the potential for causing a significant effect on the environment.</u> Where it can be seen with certainty that there is no possibility that the activity in question may have a significant effect on the environment, the activity is not subject to CEQA.

  (4) The project will be rejected or disapproved by a public agency. (See Section 15270(b)).

(c) Each public agency should include in its implementing procedures a listing of the projects often handled by the agency that the agency has determined to be exempt. This listing should be used in preliminary review.

(d) After determining that a project is exempt, the agency may prepare a notice of exemption as provided in Section 15062. Although the notice may be kept with the project application at this time, the notice shall not be filed with OPR or the county clerk until the project has been approved.

Note: Authority cited: Sections 21083 and 21087, Public Resources Code. Reference: Sections 21080(b), 21080.9, 21080.10, 21084, 21108(b), and 21152(b), Public Resources Code; *No Oil, Inc. v. City of Los Angeles*, (1974) 13 Cal.3d 68.

Discussion: This section outlines the review of a project to see if the project is exempt from CEQA. This review corresponds to the first steps of the process as shown on the flow chart in Appendix A. Reviewing a project for exempt status at this early time can avoid the expense of the CEQA process.

Subsection (b)(3) provides a short way for agencies to deal with discretionary activities which could arguably be subject to the CEQA process but which common sense provides should not be subject to the Act.

This section is based on the idea that CEQA applies jurisdictionally to activities which have the potential for causing environmental effects. Where an activity has no possibility of causing a significant effect, the activity will not be subject to CEQA. This approach has been noted with approval in a number of appellate court decisions including the State Supreme Court opinion in *No Oil, Inc. v. City of Los Angeles*.

Subsection (d) notes that timing and processing of the Notice of Exemption is to be compatible with the requirement in Section 15062 that the notice not be filed until after the agency has made a decision on the project. Section 15061(d) allows the Notice of Exemption to be completed during the preliminary review and to be kept with the project file during the processing of the project application. By including the notice in the file, the agency would show any people reviewing the file that CEQA had been considered, that the agency regarded the project as exempt, and that the agency would be ready to file the notice as soon as the decision was made on the project.

15062 Notice of Exemption

(a) When a public agency decides that a project is exempt <u>from CEQA</u> and the public agency approves or determines to carry out the project, the agency may file a notice of exemption. The notice shall be filed, if at all, after approval of the project. Such a notice shall include:

  (1) A brief description of the project,

  (2) A finding that the project is exempt <u>from CEQA</u>, including a citation to the State Guidelines section <u>or statute</u> under which it is found to be exempt, and

  (3) A brief statement of reasons to support the finding.

(b) A notice of exemption may be filled out and may accompany the project application through the approval process. The notice shall not be filed with the county clerk or the OPR until the project has been approved.

(c) When a public agency approves an applicant's project, either the agency or the applicant may file a notice of exemption.

  (1) When a state agency files this notice, the notice of exemption ~~shall be~~ is filed with OPR. A form for this notice is provided in Appendix E. A list of all such notices shall be posted on a weekly basis at the Office of Planning and Research, 1400 Tenth Street, Sacramento, California.

The list shall remain posted for at least 30 days.

  (2) When a local agency files this notice, the notice of exemption ~~will be~~ is filed with the county clerk of ~~the~~ each county ~~or counties~~ in which the project will be located. Copies of all such notices shall be available for public inspection and ~~a list of~~ such notices shall be posted ~~on a weekly basis~~ within 24 hours of receipt in the office of the county clerk. Each ~~such list~~ notice shall remain posted for a period of 30 days. Thereafter, the clerk shall return the notice to the local agency with a notation of the period it was posted. The local agency shall retain the notice for not less than 9 months.

  (3) All public agencies are encouraged to make postings pursuant to this section available in electronic format on the Internet. Such electronic postings are in addition to the procedures required by these guidelines and the Public Resources Code.

  (4) When an applicant files this notice, special rules apply.

    (A) The notice filed by an applicant ~~shall be~~ is filed in the same place as if it were filed by the agency granting the permit. If the permit was granted by a state agency, the notice ~~shall be~~ is filed with OPR. If the permit was granted by a local agency, the notice ~~shall be~~ is filed with the county clerk of the county or counties in which the project will be located.

    (B) The notice of exemption filed by an applicant shall contain the information required in subdivision (a) together with a certified document issued by the public agency stating that the agency has found the project to be exempt. The certified document may be a certified copy of an existing document or record of the public agency.

    (C) A notice filed by an applicant ~~shall be~~ is subject to the same posting and time requirements as a notice filed by a public agency.

(d) The filing of a Notice of Exemption and the posting on the list of notices start a 35 day statute of limitations period on legal challenges to the agency's decision that the project is exempt from CEQA. If a Notice of Exemption is not filed, a 180 day statute of limitations will apply.

Note: Authority cited: Sections 21083 and 21087, Public Resources Code. Reference: Sections 21108 and 21152, Public Resources Code.

Discussion: This section prescribes the use and content of the Notice of Exemption. Agencies are authorized but not required to file this notice. The regulation spells out minimum contents so that people can recognize whether a particular notice applies to the project with which they are concerned. The section notes that the effect of filing the notice is to start a short statute of limitations period. If the notice is not filed, a longer period would apply. Failure to comply with all of the requirements for filing notices of exemption results in the longer, 180-day, statute of limitations applying.

Subsection (c)(3) encourages agencies to post notices on the internet. This provides the public with an additional opportunity for notice of project decisions.

This section has been amended to conform with the statutory amendments made by Chapter 571 Statutes of 1984. The Notice of Exemption formerly filed with the Secretary of Resources is now filed with OPR. The filing and posting of notices at OPR now commences the 35 day statute of limitations period.

15063   Initial Study

(a) Following preliminary review, the lead agency shall conduct an initial study to determine if the project may have a significant effect on the environment. If the lead agency can determine that an EIR will clearly be required for the project, an initial study is not required but may still be desirable.

   (1) All phases of project planning, implementation, and operation must be considered in the initial study of the project.

   (2) To meet the requirements of this section, the lead agency may use an ~~initial study~~ environmental assessment or a similar analysis prepared pursuant to the National Environmental Policy Act.

   (3) An initial study may rely upon expert opinion supported by facts, technical studies or other substantial evidence to document its findings. However, an initial study is neither intended nor required to include the level of detail included in an EIR.

(b) Results.

   (1) If the agency determines that there is substantial evidence that any

aspect of the project, either individually or cumulatively, may cause a significant effect on the environment, regardless of whether the overall effect of the project is adverse or beneficial, the lead agency shall do one of the following:

   (A) Prepare an EIR, or

   (B) Use a previously prepared EIR which the lead agency determines would adequately analyze the project at hand, or

   (C) Determine, pursuant to a program EIR, tiering, or another appropriate process, which of a project's effects were adequately examined by an earlier EIR or negative declaration. Another appropriate process may include, for example, a master EIR, a master environmental assessment, approval of housing and neighborhood commercial facilities in urban areas as described in section 15181, approval of residential projects pursuant to a specific plan described in section 15182, approval of residential projects consistent with a community plan, general plan or zoning as described in section 15183, or an environmental document prepared under a State certified regulatory program. The lead agency shall then ascertain which effects, if any, should be analyzed in a later EIR or negative declaration.

   (2) The lead agency shall prepare a negative declaration if there is no substantial evidence that the project or any of its aspects may cause a significant effect on the environment.

(c) Purposes. The purposes of an initial study are to:

   (1) Provide the lead agency with information to use as the basis for deciding whether to prepare an EIR or a negative declaration;

   (2) Enable an applicant or lead agency to modify a project, mitigating adverse impacts before an EIR is prepared, thereby enabling the project to qualify for a Negative Declaration;

   (3) Assist in the preparation of an EIR, if one is required, by:

   (A) Focusing the EIR on the effects determined to be significant,

   (B) Identifying the effects determined not to be significant,

   (C) Explaining the reasons for determining that potentially significant effects would not be significant, and

   (D) Identifying whether a program EIR, tiering, or another appropriate process can be used for analysis of the project's environmental effects.

   (4) Facilitate environmental assessment early in the design of a project;

   (5) Provide documentation of the factual basis for the finding in a negative declaration that a project will not have a significant effect on the environment;

   (6) Eliminate unnecessary EIRs;

   (7) Determine whether a previously prepared EIR could be used with the project.

(d) Contents. An Initial Study shall contain in brief form:

   (1) A description of the project including the location of the project;

   (2) An identification of the environmental setting;

   (3) An identification of environmental effects by use of a checklist, matrix, or other method, provided that entries on a checklist or other form are briefly explained to indicate that there is some evidence to support the entries. The brief explanation may be either through a narrative or a reference to another information source such as an attached map, photographs, or an earlier EIR or negative declaration. A reference to another document should include, where appropriate, a citation to the page or pages where the information is found.

   (4) A discussion of the ways to mitigate the significant effects identified, if any;

   (5) An examination of whether the project would be consistent with existing zoning, plans, and other applicable land use controls;

   (6) The name of the person or persons who prepared or participated in the initial study.

(e) Submission of Data. If the project is to be carried out by a private person or private organization, the lead agency may require such person or organization to submit data and information which will enable the lead agency to prepare the initial study. Any person may submit any information in any form to assist a lead agency in preparing an initial study.

(f) Format. Sample forms for an applicant's project description and a review form for use by the lead agency are contained in Appendices G and H ~~and I~~. When used together, these forms would meet the requirements for an initial study, provided that the entries on the checklist are briefly explained pursuant to subsection (d)(3). These forms are only suggested, and public agencies are free to devise their own format for an initial study. A previously prepared EIR may also be used as the initial study for a later project.

(g) Consultation. As soon as a Lead Agency has determined that an initial study will be required for the project, the lead agency shall consult informally with all responsible agencies and all trustee agencies responsible for resources affected by the project to obtain the recommendations of those agencies as to whether an EIR or a negative declaration should be prepared. During or immediately after preparation of an initial study for a private project, the lead agency may consult with the applicant to determine if the applicant is willing to modify the project to reduce or avoid the significant effects identified in the initial study.

Note: Authority cited: Sections 21083 and 21087, Public Resources Code. Reference: Sections 21080(c), 21080.1, 21080.3, 21082.1, 21100 and 21151, Public Resources Code; *Gentry v. City of Murrieta* (1995) 36 Cal.App.4th 1359, *San Joaquin Raptor/ Wildlife Rescue Center v. County of Stanislaus* (1994) 27 Cal.App.4th 713, *Leonoff v. Monterey County Board of Supervisors* (1990) 222 Cal.App.3d 1337.

Discussion: The purpose of this section is to describe the process, contents, and use of the Initial Study. This is a device not mentioned in the statute itself. The Initial Study is necessary in order to provide the factual and analytical basis for a Negative Declaration or to focus an EIR on the significant effects of a project. This section is also necessary to authorize and encourage the use of a number of efficiencies including using a Negative Declaration when the project proponent has changed his proposal in order to mitigate or avoid the significant effects identified in an Initial Study. The section also makes the point that the Initial Study can be used to determine whether a previously prepared EIR would adequately apply to the project at hand, or whether pursuant to a program EIR, tiering, or other appropriate process one or more of the project's effects

were adequately examined by an earlier EIR or negative declaration. These two provisions would result, respectively, in the use of an EIR from an earlier project pursuant to section 15153 or in building upon a previous EIR or negative declaration as generally provided in section 15152, Article 11 (commencing with section 15160), or other provisions.

This section also clarifies that the individual conclusions reached by an initial study must be based on some evidence. Entries on a checklist or other form should be briefly explained to indicate the basis for determinations. These explanations are not intended to be as detailed as an EIR (*Leonoff v. Monterey County Board of Supervisors* (1990) 222 Cal.App.3d 1337).

Since a lead agency must consider all impacts of a project, consultation provides access to the expertise of other agencies in evaluating a project. In *Sundstrom v. Mendocino* (1988) 202 Cal.App.3d 296, the court held that "some degree of interdisciplinary consultation may be necessary on an initial study as well as in preparation of an EIR." It also stated that an agency must provide the information it used to reach its conclusions and that a checklist unsupported by data and facts is not sufficient for an adequate Initial Study. In *Antioch v. Pittsburg* (1986) 187 Cal.App.3d 1325, the court cited *City of Carmel-by-the-Sea v. Board of Supervisors of Monterey County* 183 Cal. App.3d 229, to emphasize the importance of considering in the initial study all the activities and impacts involved in planning, implementation, and operation of a project.

15064 Determining ~~Significant Effect~~ the Significance of the Environmental Effects Caused by a Project

(a) Determining whether a project may have a significant effect plays a critical role in the CEQA process.

(1) ~~When a lead agency determines that~~ If there is substantial evidence, in light of the whole record before a lead agency, that a project may have a significant effect on the environment, the agency shall prepare a draft EIR.

(2) When a final EIR identifies one or more significant effects, the lead agency and each responsible agency shall make a finding under Section 15091 for each significant effect and may need to make a statement of overriding considerations under Section 15093 for the project.

(b) The determination of whether a project may have a significant effect on the

environment calls for careful judgment on the part of the public agency involved, based to the extent possible on scientific and factual data. An ironclad definition of significant effect is not always possible because the significance of an activity may vary with the setting. For example, an activity which may not be significant in an urban area may be significant in a rural area.

(c) In determining whether an effect will be adverse or beneficial, the lead agency shall consider the views held by members of the public in all areas affected as expressed in the whole record before the lead agency. ~~If the Lead Agency expects that there will be a substantial body of opinion that considers or will consider the effect to be adverse, the Lead Agency shall regard the effect as adverse.~~ Before requiring the preparation of an EIR, the lead agency must still determine whether environmental change itself might be substantial.

(d) In evaluating the significance of the environmental effect of a project, the lead agency shall consider ~~both primary or direct and secondary or indirect consequences~~ direct physical changes in the environment which may be caused by the project and reasonably foreseeable indirect physical changes in the environment which may be caused by the project.

(1) ~~Primary consequences are~~ A direct physical change in the environment is a physical change in the environment which is caused by and immediately related to the project. Examples of direct physical changes in the environment are ~~such as~~ the dust, noise, and traffic of heavy equipment that would result from construction of a sewage treatment plant and possible odors from operation of the plant.

(2) ~~Secondary consequences are related more to effects of the primary consequences than to the project itself and may be several steps removed from the project in a chain of cause and effect.~~ An indirect physical change in the environment is a physical change in the environment which is not immediately related to the project, but which is caused indirectly by the project. If a direct physical change in the environment in turn causes another change in the environment, then the other change is an indirect physical change in the environment. For example, the construction of a new sewage treatment

plant may facilitate population growth in the service area due to the increase in sewage treatment capacity and may lead to an increase in air pollution.

(3) An indirect physical change is to be considered only if that change is a reasonably foreseeable impact which may be caused by the project. A change which is speculative or unlikely to occur is not reasonably foreseeable.

(e) ~~Some examples of physical changes which may be deemed to be a significant effect on the environment are contained in Appendix G.~~

(f)(e) Economic and social changes resulting from a project shall not be treated as significant effects on the environment. Economic or social changes may be used, however, to determine that a physical change shall be regarded as a significant effect on the environment. Where a physical change is caused by economic or social effects of a project, the physical change may be regarded as a significant effect in the same manner as any other physical change resulting from the project. Alternatively, economic and social effects of a physical change may be used to determine that the physical change is a significant effect on the environment. If the physical change causes adverse economic or social effects on people, those adverse effects may be used as ~~the basis for~~ a factor in determining ~~that~~ whether the physical change is significant. For example, if a project would cause overcrowding of a public facility and the overcrowding causes an adverse effect on people, the overcrowding would be regarded as a significant effect.

(f)(g) The decision as to whether a project may have one or more significant effects shall be based on ~~information~~ substantial evidence in the record of the lead agency.

(1) If the lead agency ~~finds~~ determines there is substantial evidence in the record that the project may have a significant effect on the environment, the lead agency shall prepare an EIR (*Friends of B Street v. City of Hayward* (1980) 106 Cal.App.3d 988). Said another way, if a lead agency is presented with a fair argument that a project may have a significant effect on the environment, the lead agency shall prepare an EIR even though it may also be presented with other substantial evidence

that the project will not have a significant effect (*No Oil, Inc. v. City of Los Angeles* (1974) 13 Cal.3d 68).

(2) If the lead agency determines there is substantial evidence in the record that the project may have a significant effect on the environment but the lead agency determines that revisions in the project plans or proposals made by, or agreed to by, the applicant would avoid the effects or mitigate the effects to a point where clearly no significant effect on the environment would occur and there is no substantial evidence in light of the whole record before the public agency that the project, as revised, may have a significant effect on the environment then a mitigated negative declaration shall be prepared.

(3) If the lead agency ~~finds~~ determines there is no substantial evidence that the project may have a significant effect on the environment, the lead agency shall prepare a negative declaration (*Friends of B Street v. City of Hayward* (1980) 106 Cal.App. 3d 988).

(h) ~~In marginal cases where it is not clear whether there is substantial evidence that a project may have a significant effect, the lead agency shall be guided by the following factors:~~

(1)(4) ~~If there is serious public controversy over the environmental effects of a project, the lead agency shall consider the effect or effects subject to the controversy to be significant and shall prepare an EIR. Controversy unrelated to an environmental issue does not require preparation of an EIR.~~

The existence of public controversy over the environmental effects of a project will not require preparation of an EIR if there is no substantial evidence before the agency that the project may have a significant effect on the environment.

(2) ~~If there is disagreement among experts over the significance of an effect on the environment, the lead agency shall treat the effect as significant and shall prepare an EIR.~~

(5) Argument, speculation, unsubstantiated opinion or narrative, or evidence that is clearly inaccurate or erroneous, or evidence that is not credible, shall not constitute substantial evidence. Substantial evidence shall include facts, reasonable

assumptions predicated upon facts, and expert opinion support by facts.

(6) Evidence of economic and social impacts that do not contribute to or are not caused by physical changes in the environment is not substantial evidence that the project may have a significant effect on the environment.

(7) The provisions of sections 15162, 15163, and 15164 apply when the project being analyzed is a change to, or further approval for, a project for which an EIR or negative declaration was previously certified or adopted (e.g. a tentative subdivision, conditional use permit). Under case law, the fair argument standard does not apply to determinations of significance pursuant to sections 15162, 15163, and 15164.

(g)(h) After application of the principles set forth above in Section 15064(g),[1] and in marginal cases where it is not clear whether there is substantial evidence that a project may have a significant effect on the environment, the lead agency shall be guided by the following principle: If there is disagreement among expert opinion supported by facts over the significance of an effect on the environment, the Lead Agency shall treat the effect as significant and shall prepare an EIR.

(h)(i)(1)(A) Except as otherwise required by Section 15065, a change in the environment is not a significant effect if the change complies with a standard that meets the definition in subsection (i) (3).[2]

(B) If there is a conflict between standards, the lead agency shall determine which standard is appropriate for purposes of this subsection based upon substantial evidence in light of the whole record.

(C) Notwithstanding subsection (i)(1)(A), if the lead agency determines on the basis of substantial evidence in light of the whole record that a standard is inappropriate to determine the significance of an effect for a particular project, the lead agency shall determine whether the effect may be significant as otherwise required by this section, Section 15065, and the Guidelines.

(2) In the absence of a standard that satisfies subsection (i)(1)(a), the lead

agency shall determine whether the effect may be significant as otherwise required by this section, Section 15065, and the Guidelines.

   (3) For the purposes of this subsection a "standard" means a standard of general application that is all of the following:

     (A) a quantitative, qualitative or performance requirement found in a statute, ordinance, resolution, rule, regulation, order, or other standard of general application;

     (B) adopted for the purpose of environmental protection;

     (C) adopted by a public agency through a public review process to implement, interpret, or make specific the law enforced or administered by the public agency;

     (D) one that governs the same environmental effect which the change in the environment is impacting; and,

     (E) one that governs within the jurisdiction where the project is located.

   (4) This definition includes thresholds of significance adopted by lead agencies which meet the requirements of this subsection.

(i)(1) _When assessing whether a cumulative effect requires an EIR, the lead agency shall consider whether the cumulative impact is significant and whether the effects of the project are cumulatively considerable. An EIR must be prepared if the cumulative impact may be significant and the project's incremental effect, though individually limited, is cumulatively considerable. "Cumulatively considerable" means that the incremental effects of an individual project are considerable when viewed in connection with the effects of past projects, the effects of other current projects, and the effects of probable future projects. "Probable future projects" are defined in Section 15130._

   (2) _A lead agency may determine in an initial study that a project's contribution to a significant cumulative impact will be rendered less than cumulatively considerable and thus is not significant. When a project might contribute to a significant cumulative impact, but the contribution will be rendered less than cumulatively considerable through_

mitigation measures set forth in a mitigated negative declaration, the initial study shall briefly indicate and explain how the contribution has been rendered less than cumulatively considerable.

   (3) _A lead agency may determine that a project's incremental contribution to a cumulative effect is not cumulatively considerable if the project will comply with the requirements in a previously approved plan or mitigation program which provides specific requirements that will avoid or substantially lessen the cumulative problem (e.g. water quality control plan, air quality plan, integrated waste management plan) within the geographic area in which the project is located. Such plans or programs must be specified in law or adopted by the public agency with jurisdiction over the affected resources through a public review process to implement, interpret, or make specific the law enforced or administered by the public agency._

   (4) _A lead agency may determine that the incremental impacts of a project are not cumulatively considerable when they are so small that they make only a de minimis contribution to a significant cumulative impact caused by other projects that would exist in the absence of the proposed project. Such de minimis incremental impacts, by themselves, do not trigger the obligation to prepare an EIR. A de minimis contribution means that the environmental conditions would essentially be the same whether or not the proposed project is implemented._

   (5) _The mere existence of significant cumulative impacts caused by other projects alone shall not constitute substantial evidence that the proposed project's incremental effects are cumulatively considerable._

Note: Authority cited: Sections 21083 and 21087, Public Resources Code. Reference: Sections 21003, 21065, 21068, 21080, 21082, 21082.1, 21082.2, 21083 and 21100; _No Oil, Inc. v. City of Los Angeles_ (1974) 13 Cal.3d 68; _San Joaquin Raptor/Wildlife Center v. County of Stanislaus_ (1996) 42 Cal.App.4th 608; _Gentry v. City of Murrieta_ (1995) 36 Cal.App.4th 1359; and _Laurel Heights Improvement Assn. v. Regents of the University of California_ (1993) 6 Cal.4th 1112.

Discussion: This section provides general criteria to guide agencies in determining the

significance of environmental effects of their project as required by Section 21083. This section is necessary because the determination of significance is one of the key decisions in the CEQA process. This decision leads to the preparation of either a Negative Declaration or an EIR which involves the additional requirements to investigate the significant effects, to propose mitigation measures and alternatives, to respond to public comments, and to make findings on the feasibility of changing the project to reduce or avoid the significant effects. This section incorporates statutory provisions which: define "substantial evidence;" specify that controversy alone, without substantial evidence of a significant effect, does not trigger the need for an EIR; limit CEQA's analysis to physical effects, except under some circumstances; and specify that determinations of significance are to be based on the whole record before the lead agency. This section also provides for the use of a mitigated negative declaration when warranted.

Regarding subsection (c), as to public controversy, the court in _Antioch v. Pittsburg_ (1986) 187 Cal.App.3d 1325, stated that the absence of controversy does not justify a negative declaration when there are otherwise significant impacts.

Subsection (f) is necessary for providing an interpretation of how economic and social effects can be used in determining the significance of physical changes. This interpretation is needed to resolve a number of potentially conflicting provisions in CEQA as explained in the discussion of Section 15130.

Regarding subsection (g), Public Resources Code section 21082.2 provides that the determination of significance shall be based upon substantial evidence in light of the whole record before the agency. This may include materials that are not part of the environmental document, but that are known to and have been considered by the agency. Public Resources Code section 21082.2 states that: "argument, speculation, unsubstantiated opinion or narrative, evidence which is clearly inaccurate or erroneous, or evidence of social or economic impacts which do not contribute to, or are not caused by, physical impacts on the environment, is not substantial evidence." Substantial evidence is defined to include: "facts, reasonable assumptions predicated upon facts, and expert opinion supported by facts." Public controversy alone, without substantial evidence of a significant effect, does not require preparation of an EIR.

Pursuant to Public Resources Code section 21084.1, a project which may result in a substantial adverse change in the significance of a historical resource may have a significant effect on the environment.

Subsection (i) promotes the use of standards and thresholds that have been adopted to protect the environment as the means for determining the significance of project impacts. Where an applicable standard or threshold exists, an environmental change which complies with that standard or threshold would not be considered significant.

"Standard" has been carefully defined to ensure that any such benchmark for determining significance has been adopted for the purpose of environmental protection, governs the same environmental effect that the project is causing, and governs within the area of the project. Further, only those standards which have been adopted by a public agency after a public review process are applicable.

Subsection (i) provides guidance for determining at an early stage whether a project will make a considerable contribution to a significant cumulative effect. When the project does not make a considerable contribution to a potentially significant cumulative effect, or if any contribution is rendered less than cumulatively considerable through mitigation, no analysis is required beyond that necessary to determine that the contribution is not considerable and a negative declaration or mitigated negative declaration is required. When the contribution is determined to be considerable, an EIR must be prepared in order to further analyze the cumulative effect.

Subsection (i) also provides that where the incremental impacts of a project are so small as to be de minimus, no EIR is required. De minimus means that the environmental conditions would essentially be the same with or without the project.

Pursuant to section 15063, this initial determination of whether the project adds a considerable contribution does not require the extent of analysis that would be required of a discussion of cumulative impacts in an EIR.

15064.5 Determining the Significance of Impacts to Archeological and Historical Resources

(a) For purposes of this section, the term "historical resources" shall include the following:

(1) A resource listed in, or determined to be eligible by the State Historical Resources Commission, for listing in the California Register of Historical Resources (Pub. Res. Code §5024.1, Title 14 CCR, Section 4850 et seq.).

(2) A resource included in a local register of historical resources, as defined in section 5020.1(k) of the Public Resources Code or identified as significant in an historical resource survey meeting the requirements section 5024.1(g) of the Public Resources Code, shall be presumed to be historically or culturally significant. Public agencies must treat any such resource as significant unless the preponderance of evidence demonstrates that it is not historically or culturally significant.

(3) Any object, building, structure, site, area, place, record, or manuscript which a lead agency determines to be historically significant or significant in the architectural, engineering, scientific, economic, agricultural, educational, social, political, military, or cultural annals of California may be considered to be an historical resource, provided the lead agency's determination is supported by substantial evidence in light of the whole record. Generally, a resource shall be considered by the lead agency to be "historically significant" if the resource meets the criteria for listing on the California Register of Historical Resources (Pub. Res. Code §5024.1, Title 14 CCR, Section 4852) including the following:

(A) Is associated with events that have made a significant contribution to the broad patterns of California's history and cultural heritage;

(B) Is associated with the lives of persons important in our past;

(C) Embodies the distinctive characteristics of a type, period, region, or method of construction, or represents the work of an important creative individual, or possesses high artistic values; or

(D) Has yielded, or may be likely to yield, information important in prehistory or history.

(4) The fact that a resource is not listed in, or determined to be eligible for listing in the California Register of Historical Resources, not included in a local register of historical resources (pursuant to section 5020.1(k) of the Public Resources Code), or identified in an historical resources survey (meeting the criteria in section 5024.1(g) of the Public Resources Code) does not preclude a lead agency from determining that the resource may be an historical resource as defined in Public Resources Code sections 5020.1(j) or 5024.1.

(b) A project with an effect that may cause a substantial adverse change in the significance of an historical resource is a project that may have a significant effect on the environment.

(1) Substantial adverse change in the significance of an historical resource means physical demolition, destruction, relocation, or alteration of the resource or its immediate surroundings such that the significance of an historical resource would be materially impaired.

(2) The significance of an historical resource is materially impaired when a project:

(A) Demolishes or materially alters in an adverse manner those physical characteristics of an historical resource that convey its historical significance and that justify its inclusion in, or eligibility for, inclusion in the California Register of Historical Resources; or

(B) Demolishes or materially alters in an adverse manner those physical characteristics that account for its inclusion in a local register of historical resources pursuant to section 5020.1(k) of the Public Resources Code or its identification in an historical resources survey meeting the requirements of section 5024.1(g) of the Public Resources Code, unless the public agency reviewing the effects of the project establishes by a preponderance of evidence that the resource is not historically or culturally significant; or

(C) Demolishes or materially alters in an adverse manner those physical characteristics of a historical resource that convey its historical significance and that justify its eligibility for inclusion in the California Register of Historical Resources as determined by a lead agency for purposes of CEQA.

(3) Generally, a project that follows the Secretary of the Interior's Standards for the Treatment of Historic Properties with Guidelines for Preserving,

Rehabilitating, Restoring, and Reconstructing Historic Buildings or the Secretary of the Interior's Standards for Rehabilitation and Guidelines for Rehabilitating Historic Buildings (1995), Weeks and Grimmer, shall be considered as mitigated to a level of less than a significant impact on the historical resource.

(4) A lead agency shall identify potentially feasible measures to mitigate significant adverse changes in the significance of an historical resource. The lead agency shall ensure that any adopted measures to mitigate or avoid significant adverse changes are fully enforceable through permit conditions, agreements, or other measures.

(5) When a project will affect state-owned historical resources, as described in Public Resources Code Section 5024, and the lead agency is a state agency, the lead agency shall consult with the State Historic Preservation Officer as provided in Public Resources Code Section 5024.5. Consultation should be coordinated in a timely fashion with the preparation of environmental documents.

(c) CEQA applies to effects on archaeological sites.

(1) When a project will impact an archaeological site, a lead agency shall first determine whether the site is an historical resource, as defined in subsection (a).

(2) If a lead agency determines that the archaeological site is an historical resource, it shall refer to the provisions of Section 21084.1 of the Public Resources Code, and this section, Section 15126.4 of the Guidelines, and the limits contained in Section 21083.2 of the Public Resources Code do not apply.

(3) If an archaeological site does not meet the criteria defined in subsection (a), but does meet the definition of a unique archeological resource in Section 21083.2 of the Public Resources Code, the site shall be treated in accordance with the provisions of section 21083.2. The time and cost limitations described in Public Resources Code Section 21083.2 (c-f) do not apply to surveys and site evaluation activities intended to determine whether the project location contains unique archaeological resources.

(4) If an archaeological resource is neither a unique archaeological nor an historical resource, the effects of the project on those resources shall not be considered a significant effect on the environment. It shall be sufficient that both the resource and the effect on it are noted in the Initial Study or EIR, if one is prepared to address impacts on other resources, but they need not be considered further in the CEQA process.

(d) When an initial study identifies the existence of, or the probable likelihood, of Native American human remains within the project, a lead agency shall work with the appropriate native americans as identified by the Native American Heritage Commission as provided in Public Resources Code §5097.98. The applicant may develop an agreement for treating or disposing of, with appropriate dignity, the human remains and any items associated with Native American burials with the appropriate Native Americans as identified by the Native American Heritage Commission. Action implementing such an agreement is exempt from:

(1) The general prohibition on disinterring, disturbing, or removing human remains from any location other than a dedicated cemetery (Health and Safety Code Section 7050.5).

(2) The requirements of CEQA and the Coastal Act.

(e) In the event of the accidental discovery or recognition of any human remains in any location other than a dedicated cemetery, the following steps should be taken:

(1) There shall be no further excavation or disturbance of the site or any nearby area reasonably suspected to overlie adjacent human remains until:

(A) The coroner of the county in which the remains are discovered must be contacted to determine that no investigation of the cause of death is required, and

(B) If the coroner determines the remains to be Native American:

1. The coroner shall contact the Native American Heritage Commission within 24 hours.

2. The Native American Heritage Commission shall identify the person or persons it believes to be the most likely descended from the deceased native american.

3. The most likely descendent may make recommendations to the landowner or the person responsible for the excavation work, for means of treating or disposing of, with appropriate dignity, the human remains and any associated grave goods as provided in Public Resources Code Section 5097.98, or

(2) Where the following conditions occur, the landowner or his authorized representative shall rebury the Native American human remains and associated grave goods with appropriate dignity on the property in a location not subject to further subsurface disturbance.

(A) The Native American Heritage Commission is unable to identify a most likely descendent or the most likely descendent failed to make a recommendation within 24 hours after being notified by the commission.

(B) The descendant identified fails to make a recommendation; or

(C) The landowner or his authorized representative rejects the recommendation of the descendant, and the mediation by the Native American Heritage Commission fails to provide measures acceptable to the landowner.

(f) As part of the objectives, criteria, and procedures required by Section 21082 of the Public Resources Code, a lead agency should make provisions for historical or unique archaeological resources accidentally discovered during construction. These provisions should include an immediate evaluation of the find by a qualified archaeologist. If the find is determined to be an historical or unique archaeological resource, contingency funding and a time allotment sufficient to allow for implementation of avoidance measures or appropriate mitigation should be available. Work could continue on other parts of the building site while historical or unique archaeological resource mitigation takes place.

Note: Authority: Sections 21083 and 21087, Public Resources Code. Reference: Sections 21083.2, 21084, and 21084.1, Public Resources Code; *Citizens for Responsible Development in West Hollywood v. City of West Hollywood* (1995) 39 Cal.App.4th 490.

Discussion: This section establishes rules for the analysis of historical resources, including archaeological resources, in order to determine whether a project may have a substantial adverse effect on the significance of the resource. This incorporates provisions previously contained in Appendix K of the Guidelines. Subsection (a) relies upon the holding in *League for Protection of Oakland's Architectural and Historic Resources v. City of Oakland* (1997) 52 Cal.App.4th 896 to describe the relative significance of resources which are listed in the California Register of Historical Resources, listed in a local register or survey or eligible for listing, or that may be considered locally significant despite not being listed or eligible for listing. Subsection (b) describes those actions which have substantial adverse effects. Subsection (c) describes the relationship between historical resources and archaeological resources, as well as limits on the cost of mitigating impacts on unique archaeological resources. Subsections (d) and (e) discuss the protocol to be followed if Native American or other human remains are discovered.

15064.7   Thresholds of Significance

(a) Each public agency is encouraged to develop and publish thresholds of significance that the agency uses in the determination of the significance of environmental effects. A threshold of significance is an identifiable quantitative, qualitative or performance level of a particular environmental effect, noncompliance with which means the effect will normally be determined to be significant by the agency and compliance with which means the effect normally will be determined to be less than significant.

(b) Thresholds of significance to be adopted for general use as part of the lead agency's environmental review process must be adopted by ordinance, resolution, rule, or regulation, and developed through a public review process and be supported by substantial evidence.

Note: Authority: Sections 21083 and 21087, Public Resources Code. Reference: Sections 21082 and 21083, Public Resources Code.

Discussion: This section encourages agencies to develop, publish, and use thresholds of significance as a means of standardizing environmental assessments. Thresholds may constitute standards for determining significance pursuant to subsection (i) of section 15064. Note that if an agency decides to adopt thresholds it must do so by ordinance, resolution, regulation or rule at the conclusion of a public review process.

15065   Mandatory Findings of Significance

A lead agency shall find that a project may have a significant effect on the environment and thereby require an EIR to be prepared for the project where any of the following conditions occur:

(a) The project has the potential to substantially degrade the quality of the environment, substantially reduce the habitat of a fish or wildlife species, cause a fish or wildlife population to drop below self-sustaining levels, threaten to eliminate a plant or animal community, reduce the number or restrict the range of a~~a~~ ~~an~~ endangered, rare or threatened ~~endangered plant or animal~~ species, or eliminate important examples of the major periods of California history or prehistory.

(b) The project has the potential to achieve short-term environmental goals to the disadvantage of long-term environmental goals.

(c) The project has possible environmental effects which are individually limited but cumulatively considerable. ~~As used in the subsection, "cumulatively considerable"~~ "Cumulatively considerable" means that the incremental effects of an individual project are considerable when viewed in connection with the effects of past projects, the effects of other current projects, and the effects of probable future projects as defined in Section 15130.

(d) The environmental effects of a project will cause substantial adverse effects on human beings, either directly or indirectly.

Note: Authority cited: Sections 21083 and 21087, Public Resources Code. Reference: Sections 21001(c) and 21083, Public Resources Code; *San Joaquin Raptor/Wildlife Center v. County of Stanislaus* (1996) 42 Cal.App.4th 608.

Discussion: This section provides additional explanation of the mandatory findings of significance required by the Legislature in Section 21083. These mandatory findings control not only the decision of whether to prepare an EIR but also the identification of effects to be analyzed in depth in the EIR, the requirement to make detailed findings on the feasibility of alternatives or mitigation measures to reduce or avoid the significant effects, and when found to be feasible, the making of changes in the project to lessen the adverse environmental impacts. This section is necessary to insure that public agencies follow the concerns of the Legislature in determining that certain effects

shall be found significant and then take the actions at the different stages of the process that are required with significant effects.

Article 6. Negative Declaration Process Sections 15070 to 15075

15070   Decision to Prepare a Negative or Mitigated Negative Declaration

A public agency shall prepare or have prepared a proposed negative declaration or mitigated negative declaration ~~shall be prepared~~ for a project subject to CEQA when ~~either~~:

(a) The initial study shows that there is no substantial evidence, in light of the whole record before the agency, that the project may have a significant effect on the environment, or

(b) The initial study ~~identified~~ identifies potentially significant effects, but:

(1) Revisions in the project plans or proposals made by, or agreed to by the applicant before ~~the~~ a proposed ~~negative declaration~~ mitigated negative declaration and initial study ~~is~~ are released for public review would avoid the effects or mitigate the effects to a point where clearly no significant effects would occur, and

(2) There is no substantial evidence, in light of the whole record before the agency, that the project as revised may have a significant effect on the environment.

Note: Authority cited: Sections 21083 and 21087, Public Resources Code. Reference: Sections 21064, 21064.5, 21080(c), and 21082.1, Public Resources Code; *Friends of B Street v. City of Hayward* (1980) 106 Cal.App.3d 988; *Running Fence Corp. v. Superior Court*, (1975) 51 Cal.App.3d 400.

Discussion: Section 15070 substantially mirrors the language of Public Resources Code section 21080(c). Under subsection (a) a Negative Declaration shall be adopted when the Initial Study shows that the project may not have a significant effect on the environment.

Subsection (b) states that the Negative Declaration shall be adopted when two conditions are met: (1) the project or plan or proposals as agreed to by the applicant prior to public review of the proposed Negative Declaration has been revised to avoid significant effects or the effects have been mitigated down to a point where the effects are clearly insignificant and (2), there is no substantial evidence before the agency that the project as revised may have a significant effect.

Subsection (b) reflects the concept of the "Mitigated Negative Declaration" as defined in Public Resources Code section 21064.5. A Mitigated Negative Declaration is not intended to be a new kind of document. It is merely a Negative Declaration prepared in a slightly different situation. The Guidelines would continue to give Lead Agencies the option of allowing applicants to modify their projects so that the Lead Agency could make a finding that the project would not have a significant effect on the environment.

The portion of this section dealing with the Mitigated Negative Declaration provides efficiencies in the process where the applicant can modify his project to avoid all potential significant effects. The applicant can avoid the time and costs involved in preparing an EIR and qualify for a Negative Declaration instead. The public is still given an opportunity to review the proposal to determine whether the changes are sufficient to eliminate the significance of the effects.

Any needed or proposed mitigation measures must be incorporated into a proposed negative declaration and the project revised accordingly before the negative declaration is released for public review. *Sundstrom v. Mendocino* (1988) 202 Cal.App.3d 296.

Under subsection (a) or (b), if there is any substantial evidence before the Lead Agency that the project as proposed or revised may have a significant effect, an EIR must be prepared.

15071   Contents

A Negative Declaration circulated for public review shall include:

(a) A brief description of the project, including a commonly used name for the project, if any;

(b) The location of the project, preferably shown on a map, and the name of the project proponent;

(c) A proposed finding that the project will not have a significant effect on the environment;

(d) An attached copy of the initial study documenting reasons to support the finding; and

(e) Mitigation measures, if any, included in the project to avoid potentially significant effects.

Note: Authority cited: Sections 21083 and 21087, Public Resources Code. Reference: Section 21080(c), Public Resources Code.

Discussion: The purpose of this section is to prescribe the contents of a Negative Declaration. The statute itself does not say what a Negative Declaration must contain. The contents described in this section appear to be the minimum required to meet the public participation and disclosure policies of CEQA.

15072   ~~Public~~ Notice of Intent to Adopt a Negative Declaration or Mitigated Negative Declaration

(a) ~~Notice that the Lead Agency proposes to~~ A lead agency shall provide a notice of intent to adopt a negative declaration or mitigated negative declaration ~~shall be provided~~ to the public, responsible agencies, trustee agencies, and the county clerk of each county within which the proposed project is located, sufficiently ~~within a reasonable period of time but not less than 20 days (unless the negative declaration is submitted to the State Clearinghouse for review, in which case the review period shall be at least 30 days)~~ prior to adoption by the lead agency of the negative declaration or mitigated negative declaration to allow the public and agencies the review period provided under Section 15105.

(b) The lead agency ~~Notice~~ shall ~~be given~~ mail a notice of intent to adopt a negative declaration or mitigated negative declaration to the last known name and address of all organizations and individuals who have previously requested such notice in writing and shall also ~~be given~~ give notice of intent to adopt a negative declaration or mitigated negative declaration by at least one of the following procedures to allow the public the review period provided under Section 15105:

(1) Publication at least one time by the lead agency in a newspaper of general circulation in the area affected by the proposed project. If more than one area is affected, the notice shall be published in the newspaper of largest circulation from among the newspapers of general circulation in those areas.

(2) Posting of notice by the lead agency on and off site in the area where the project is to be located.

(3) Direct mailing to the owners and occupants of property contiguous to the project. Owners of such property shall be identified as shown on the latest equalized assessment roll.

~~(b)~~ (c) The alternatives for providing notice specified in subsection ~~(a)~~ (b) shall not preclude a lead agency from providing additional notice by other means if the agency so desires, nor shall the requirements of this section preclude a lead agency from providing the public notice at the same time and in the same manner as public notice required by any other laws for the project.

(d) The county clerk of each county within which the proposed project is located shall post such notices in the office of the county clerk within 24 hours of receipt for a period of at least 20 days.

(e) For a project of statewide, regional, or areawide significance, the lead agency shall also provide notice to transportation planning agencies and public agencies which have transportation facilities within their jurisdictions which could be affected by the project as specified in Section 21092.4(a) of the Public Resources Code. "Transportation facilities" includes: major local arterials and public transit within five miles of the project site and freeways, highways and rail transit service within 10 miles of the project site.

(f) A notice of intent to adopt a negative declaration or mitigated negative declaration shall specify the following:

(1) A brief description of the proposed project and its location.

(2) The starting and ending dates for the review period during which the lead agency will receive comments on the proposed negative declaration or mitigated negative declaration. This shall include starting and ending dates for the review period. If the review period has been is shortened pursuant to Section 15105, the notice shall include a statement to that effect.

(3) The date, time, and place of any scheduled public meetings or hearings to be held by the lead agency on the proposed project, when known to the lead agency at the time of notice.

(4) The address or addresses where copies of the proposed negative declaration or mitigated negative declaration including the revisions developed under Section 15070(b) and all documents referenced in the proposed negative declaration or mitigated negative declaration are available for review. This location or locations shall be readily accessible to the public during the lead agency's normal working hours.

(5) The presence of the site on any of the lists enumerated under Section 65962.5 of the Government Code including, but not limited to lists of hazardous waste facilities, land designated as hazardous waste property,

and hazardous waste disposal sites, and the information in the Hazardous Waste and Substances Statement required under subsection (f) of that section.

(6) Other information specifically required by statute or regulation for a particular project or type of project.

Note: Authority cited: Sections 21083 and 21087, Public Resources Code. Reference: Sections 21091(b) and, 21092, 21092.2, 21092.4, 21092.3, 21092.6, and 21151.8, Public Resources Code; Section 6061, Government Code.

Discussion: Section 15072 prescribes the notice requirements for a Negative Declaration. Although most of these requirements are contained in Section 21092 of the statute, the Guidelines provide additional explanation and interpretation. In the interest of clarity, the requirements are combined in one place. Subsection (a)(1) explains what is required by the cross-reference in Section 21092 to Section 6061 of the Government Code. Section 6061 requires publication of a notice at least one time in a newspaper of general circulation.

Public Resources Code section 21092 requires that the notice specify the period during which comments will be received, the date, time, and place of any public meetings or hearings on the project, a brief description of the project and its location, and the address where copies of the negative declaration and all documents referenced in the negative declaration are available for review. Section 21092.3 of the Public Resources Code establishes additional requirements for the filing of notice with the County Clerk for posting during the review period.

15073 Public Review of a Proposed Negative Declaration or Mitigated Negative Declaration

(a) The lead agency shall provide a public review period for a proposed Negative Declaration. The noticed public review period shall be long enough to provide members of the public with sufficient time to respond to the proposed finding before the negative declaration is approved pursuant to Section 15105 of not less than 20 days. When a proposed negative declaration or mitigated negative declaration and initial study are submitted to the State Clearinghouse for review by state agencies, the public review period shall not be less than 30 days, unless a shorter period is approved by the State Clearinghouse under Section 15105(d).

(b) When a proposed negative declaration or mitigated negative declaration and initial study have been submitted to the State Clearinghouse for review by state agencies, the public review period shall be at least as long as the review period established by the State Clearinghouse.

(c) A copy of the notice with the proposed negative declaration or mitigated negative declaration and the initial study shall be attached to the notice of intent to adopt the proposed declaration that is sent to every responsible agency and trustee agency concerned with the project and every other public agency with jurisdiction by law over resources affected by the project.

(c)(d) Where one or more state agencies will be a responsible agency or a trustee agency or will exercise jurisdiction by law over natural resources affected by the project, or where the project is of statewide, regional, or areawide environmental significance, the lead agency shall send copies of the proposed negative declaration or mitigated negative declaration to the State Clearinghouse for distribution to the state agencies.

(d) When a negative declaration is submitted to the State Clearinghouse for review by state agencies, the public review period shall be not less than 30 days unless a shorter period is approved by the State Clearinghouse.

(e) The lead agency shall notify in writing any public agency which comments on a proposed negative declaration or mitigated negative declaration of any public hearing to be held for the project for which the document was prepared. A notice provided to a public agency pursuant to Section 15072 satisfies this requirement.

Note: Authority cited: Sections 21083 and 21087, Public Resources Code. Reference: Sections 21000(e), 21003(b), and 21080(c), 21081.6, 21091, and 21092.5, Public Resources Code; *Plaggmier v. City of San Jose* (1980) 101 Cal.App.3d 842..

Discussion: This section makes clear that a public review period is required with a Negative Declaration. The section also brings together in one easily recognizable place the requirements concerning submitting Negative Declarations to the State Clearinghouse for review.

Section 21091 of the Public Resources Code now requires that the public review period for a Negative Declaration shall not be less than 20 days. The review period for Negative Declaration which has been submitted to the State Clearinghouse is 30 days, but

the Clearinghouse may authorize a shorter state review period upon formal request by the decision-making body, if consistent with criteria adopted by the Clearinghouse. However, the revised review period so authorized shall not be less than 20 days.

15073.5 Recirculation of a Negative Declaration Prior to Adoption

(a) A lead agency is required to recirculate a negative declaration when the document must be substantially revised after public notice of its availability has previously been given pursuant to Section 15072, but prior to its adoption. Notice of recirculation shall comply with Sections 15072 and 15073.

(b) A "substantial revision" of the negative declaration shall mean:

(1) A new, avoidable significant effect is identified and mitigation measures or project revisions must be added in order to reduce the effect to insignificance, or

(2) The lead agency determines that the proposed mitigation measures or project revisions will not reduce potential effects to less than significance and new measures or revisions must be required.

(c) Recirculation is not required under the following circumstances:

(1) Mitigation measures are replaced with equal or more effective measures pursuant to Section 15074.1.

(2) New project revisions are added in response to written or verbal comments on the project's effects identified in the proposed negative declaration which are not new avoidable significant effects.

(3) Measures or conditions of project approval are added after circulation of the negative declaration which are not required by CEQA , which do not create new significant environmental effects and are not necessary to mitigate an avoidable significant effect.

(4) New information is added to the negative declaration which merely clarifies, amplifies, or makes insignificant modifications to the negative declaration.

(d) If during the negative declaration process there is substantial evidence in light of the whole record, before the lead agency that the project, as revised, may have a significant effect on the environment which cannot be mitigated or avoided, the lead agency shall prepare a draft EIR and certify a final EIR prior to approving the project. It shall circulate the draft EIR for consultation and review pursuant to Sections 15086 and 15087, and advise reviewers in writing that a proposed negative declaration had previously been circulated for the project.

Note: Authority cited: Sections 21083 and 21087, Public Resources Code. Reference: Section 21080, Public Resources Code; *Gentry v. City of Murrieta* (1995) 36 Cal.App. 4th 1359; *Leonoff v. Monterey County Board of Supervisors* (1990) 222 Cal.App. 3d 1337; *Long Beach Savings and Loan Assn. v. Long Beach Redevelopment Agency* (1986) 188 Cal.App.3d 249.

Discussion: This section clarifies the situations under which a proposed negative declaration must be recirculated for public review. The recirculation requirements have been established by case law, including *Leonoff v. Monterey County Board of Supervisors* (1990) 222 Cal.App.3d 1337 and *Gentry v. City of Murrieta* (1995) 36 Cal.App.4th 1359. By applying this section, agencies will be able to determine whether a negative declaration has been revised to such an extent that it must be recirculated before it may be adopted. The requirements will ensure that the public and other agencies have the opportunity to comment on the revised document. At the same time, this section clarifies that an EIR must be prepared if substantial evidence exists that the project may result in a significant effect. This section only applies where the proposed negative declaration has not yet been adopted and the project has not been approved.

15074   Consideration and ~~Approval~~ Adoption of a Negative Declaration or Mitigated Negative Declaration

(a) Any advisory body of a public agency making a recommendation to the decisionmaking body shall consider the proposed negative declaration or mitigated negative declaration before making its recommendation.

(b) Prior to approving ~~the~~ a project, the decisionmaking body of the lead agency shall consider the proposed negative declaration or mitigated negative declaration together with any comments received during the public review process. The decisionmaking body shall ~~approve~~ adopt the proposed negative declaration or mitigated negative declaration only if it finds on the basis of the whole record before it (including the initial study and any comments received), that there is no substantial evidence that the project

will have a significant effect on the environment and that the negative declaration or mitigated negative declaration reflects the lead agency's independent judgment and analysis.

(c) When adopting a negative declaration or mitigated negative declaration, the lead agency shall specify the location and custodian of the documents or other material which constitute the record of proceedings upon which its decision is based.

(d) When adopting a mitigated negative declaration, the lead agency shall also adopt a program for reporting on or monitoring the changes which it has either required in the project or made a condition of approval to mitigate or avoid significant environmental effects.

(e) A lead agency shall not adopt a negative declaration or mitigated negative declaration for a project within the boundaries of a comprehensive airport land use plan or, if a comprehensive airport land use plan has not been adopted, for a project within two nautical miles of a public airport or public use airport, without first considering whether the project will result in a safety hazard or noise problem for persons using the airport or for persons residing or working in the project area.

Note: Authority cited: Sections 21083 and 21087, Public Resources Code. Reference: Sections 21080(c), 21081.6, 21082.1, and 21096, Public Resources Code; *Friends of B Street v. City of Hayward* (1980) 106 Cal. App.3d 988.

Discussion: The purpose of this section is to make it clear that the decision-making body of the Lead Agency must consider the Negative Declaration before approving the project. The decision-making body is required to decide whether to approve the Negative Declaration on the basis of the Initial Study and any public comment received. This approach serves the public participation policies in CEQA by requiring the Lead Agency to consider the public comments on a proposed Negative Declaration before approving the Negative Declaration.

Section 21081.6 of the Public Resources Code provides that when a public agency adopts a Negative Declaration which includes provisions to mitigate potentially significant effects or which was issued on the basis of project revisions aimed at mitigating potential environmental effects, the agency shall also adopt a program of monitoring or reporting to ensure that the provisions or revisions are complied with during implementation of the project.

15074.1   Substitution of Mitigation Measures in a Proposed Mitigated Negative Declaration

(a) As a result of the public review process for a proposed mitigated negative declaration, including any administrative decisions or public hearings conducted on the project prior to its approval, the lead agency may conclude that certain mitigation measures identified in the mitigated negative declaration are infeasible or otherwise undesirable. Prior to approving the project, the lead agency may, in accordance with this section, delete those mitigation measures and substitute for them other measures which the lead agency determines are equivalent or more effective.

(b) Prior to deleting and substituting for a mitigation measure, the lead agency shall do both of the following:

(1) Hold a public hearing on the matter. Where a public hearing is to be held in order to consider the project, the public hearing required by this section may be combined with that hearing. Where no public hearing would otherwise be held to consider the project, then a public hearing shall be required before a mitigation measure may be deleted and a new measure adopted in its place.

(2) Adopt a written finding that the new measure is equivalent or more effective in mitigating or avoiding potential significant effects and that it in itself will not cause any potentially significant effect on the environment.

(c) No recirculation of the proposed mitigated negative declaration pursuant to Section 15072 is required where the new mitigation measures are made conditions of, or are otherwise incorporated into, project approval in accordance with this section.

(d) "Equivalent or more effective" means that the new measure will avoid or reduce the significant effect to at least the same degree as, or to a greater degree than, the original measure and will create no more adverse effect of its own than would have the original measure.

Note: Authority cited: Sections 21083 and 21087, Public Resources Code. Reference: Section 21080(f), Public Resources Code.

Discussion: Public Resources Code Section 21080 allows a lead agency to delete mitigation measures which it concludes are infeasible or otherwise undesirable when it substitutes equivalent or more effective measures. Any proposed substitute measures must be considered at a public hearing. This section defines what can be considered an "equivalent or more effective" measure and clarifies that the lead agency may consider substitute measures at the same public hearing during which it considers that project.

15075 Notice of Determination on a Project for Which a Proposed Negative or Mitigated Negative Declaration Has Been Approved

(a) After deciding to carry out or approve a project for which a negative declaration or mitigated negative declaration has been approved, the lead agency shall file a notice of determination. For projects with phases, the lead agency shall file a notice of determination after deciding to carry out or approve each phase.

(b) The notice of determination shall must include:

(1) An identification of the project including its common name where possible, and its location.

(2) A brief description of the project.

(3) The date on which the agency approved the project.

(4) The determination of the agency that the project will not have a significant effect on the environment.

(5) A statement that a negative declaration or a mitigated negative declaration has been prepared pursuant to the provisions of CEQA.

(6) The address where a copy of the negative declaration or mitigated negative declaration may be examined.

(c) If the lead agency is a state agency, the lead agency shall file the notice of determination shall be filed with OPR.

(d) If the lead agency is a local agency, the local lead agency shall file the notice of determination with the county clerk of the county or counties in which the project will be located within five working days after approval of the project by the lead agency. If the project requires a discretionary approval from any state agency, the local lead agency shall also file the notice of determination also shall be filed with OPR.

(e) All notices filed pursuant to this section shall be available for public inspection and shall be posted by the county clerk within 24 hours of receipt. Each notice shall remain posted for a period of at least 30 days. Thereafter, the clerk shall return the notice to the local lead

agency with a notation of the period it was posted. The local lead agency shall retain the notice for not less than 9 months. The filing of the notice of determination and the posting on a list of such notices starts a 30-day statute of limitations on court challenges to the approval under CEQA.

(f) Public agencies are encouraged to make copies of all notices filed pursuant to this section available in electronic format on the Internet. Such electronic notices are in addition to the posting requirements of these guidelines and the Public Resources Code.

Note: Authority cited: Sections 21083 and 21087, Public Resources Code. Reference: Sections 21080(c), 21108(a) and (c), 21152(a) and (c), and 21167(b), Public Resources Code; *Citizens of Lake Murray Area Association v. City Council,* (1982) 129 Cal.App. 3d 436.

Discussion: The purpose of this section is to describe the use and contents of the Notice of Determination. Because the Notice of Determination starts a statute of limitation period, the notice must contain enough information so that people can see whether the notice applies to the project with which they are concerned. The Guidelines expand the statutory requirements to require filing of a notice for a local project with OPR if the project will also be subject to a discretionary approval from a state agency. The purpose of this requirement is to provide a state agency with a way of learning that a local agency has approved a project which will be subject later to the state agency's permitting process. This enables state Responsible Agencies to decide whether to take action to challenge the adequacy of the Lead Agency documents as provided in Section 21167.2 and to learn that the time period for acting on the permit application may have started.

The section declares that the notice starts a statute of limitation period as a way of explaining the reason for filing the notice.

This section also establishes requirements for county clerks to post notices.

Subsection (f) encourages agencies to post notices on the internet. This provides the public with an additional opportunity for notice of project decisions.

Article 7. EIR Process
Sections 15080 to 15096

15080 General

To the extent possible, the EIR process should be combined with the existing

planning, review, and project approval process used by each public agency.

Note: Authority cited: Sections 21083 and 21087, Public Resources Code. Reference: Sections 21003, 21061, 21100, and 21151, Public Resources Code.

Discussion: The section declares the general principle that the EIR process should be combined with any other project approval process used by the agency. Private applicants have experienced hardships with the CEQA process when Lead Agencies have separated the EIR process from the permit process. That approach required completion of the EIR process before starting review of the permit application and doubles the time necessary to obtain a permit. This section is necessary to discourage that practice.

15081 Decision to Prepare an EIR

The EIR process starts with the decision to prepare an EIR. This decision will be made either during preliminary review under Section 15060 or at the conclusion of an initial study after applying the standards described in Section 15064.

Note: Authority cited: Sections 21083 and 21087, Public Resources Code. Reference: Section 21100, Public Resources Code; *No Oil, Inc. v. City of Los Angeles* (1974) 13 Cal.3d 68; *Friends of B Street v. City of Hayward* (1980) 106 Cal.App.3d 988.

Discussion: This section ties together a number of other provisions in the Guidelines. The section is necessary to show that the EIR process can start at either of two points in the early evaluation of the project. If the Lead Agency can see during preliminary review that an EIR will be required, the EIR process can begin right then rather than requiring the project to go through an Initial Study. Alternatively, the Lead Agency can conduct the Initial Study and use the information developed in the Initial Study to determine whether to prepare an EIR or a Negative Declaration. This section merely refers to the standards described in Section 15064 for determining whether a project may have a significant effect on the environment. If the Lead Agency can determine that the project may have a significant effect on the environment, then it is required to prepare an EIR for the project.

15081.5 EIRs Required by Statute

(a) A lead agency shall prepare or have prepared an EIR for the following types of projects. An initial study may be prepared to help identify the significant effects of the project.

(1) The burning of municipal wastes, hazardous wastes, or refuse-derived

fuel, including but not limited to tires, if the project is either:

(A) The construction of a new facility; or

(B) The expansion of an existing facility that burns hazardous waste that would increase its permitted capacity by more than 10 percent. This does not apply to any project exclusively burning hazardous waste for which a determination to prepare a negative declaration, or mitigated negative declaration or environmental impact report was made prior to July 14, 1989. The amount of expansion of an existing facility is calculated pursuant to subdivision (b) of Section 21151.1 of the Public Resources Code.

(C) Subsection (1) of this subdivision does not apply to:

1. Projects for which the State Energy Resources Conservation and Development Commission has assumed jurisdiction pursuant to Chapter 6 (commencing with Section 25500) of Division 15 of the Public Resources Code.

2. Any of the types of burn or thermal processing projects listed in subdivision (d) of Section 21151.1 of the Public Resources Code.

(2) The initial issuance of a hazardous waste facilities permit to a land disposal facility, as defined in subdivision (d) of Section 25199.1 of the Health and Safety Code. Preparation of an EIR is not mandatory if the facility only manages hazardous waste which is identified or listed pursuant to Section 25140 or Section 25141 of the Health and Safety Code on or after January 1, 1992; or only conducts activities which are regulated pursuant to Chapter 6.5 (commencing with Section 25100) of Division 20 of the Health and Safety Code on or after January 1, 1992. "Initial issuance" does not include the issuance of a closure or postclosure permit pursuant to Chapter 6.5 (commencing with Section 25100) of Division 20 of the Health and Safety Code.

(3) The initial issuance of a hazardous waste facility permit pursuant to Section 25200 of the Health and Safety Code to an off-site large treatment facility, as defined pursuant to

subdivision (d) of Section 25205.1 of that code. Preparation of an EIR is not mandatory if the facility only manages hazardous waste which is identified or listed pursuant to Section 25140 or Section 25141 of the Health and Safety Code on or after January 1, 1992; or only conducts activities which are regulated pursuant to Chapter 6.5 (commencing with Section 25100) of Division 20 of the Health and Safety Code on or after January 1, 1992. "Initial issuance" does not include the issuance of a closure or postclosure permit pursuant to Chapter 6.5 (commencing with Section 25100) of Division 20 of the Health and Safety Code.

(4) Any open pit mining operation which is subject to the permit requirements of the Surface Mining and Reclamation Act (beginning at Section 2710 of the Public Resources Code) and which utilizes a cyanide heap-leaching process for the purpose of extracting gold or other precious metals.

(5) An initial base reuse plan as defined in Section 15229.

(b) A lead agency shall prepare or have prepared an EIR for the selection of a California Community College, California State University, University of California, or California Maritime Academy campus location and approval of a long range development plan for that campus.

(1) The EIR for a long range development plan for a campus shall include an analysis of, among other significant impacts, those environmental effects relating to changes in enrollment levels.

(2) Subsequent projects within the campus may be addressed in environmental analyses tiered on the EIR prepared for the long range development plan.

Note: Authority cited: Sections 21083 and 21087, Public Resources Code. Reference: Sections 21080.09, 21083.8, 21083.8.1, 21151.1, and 21151.7, Public Resources Code.

Discussion: This section describes the types of projects for which CEQA mandates preparation of an EIR. No negative declaration or mitigated negative declaration can be prepared for a project which falls under any of these categories.

15082 Determination of Scope of EIR

(a) Notice of Preparation. Immediately after deciding that an environmental impact

report is required for a project, the lead agency shall send to each responsible agency a notice of preparation stating that an environmental impact report will be prepared. This notice shall also be sent to every federal agency involved in approving or funding the project and to each trustee agency responsible for natural resources affected by the project.

(1) The Notice of Preparation shall provide the responsible agencies with sufficient information describing the project and the potential environmental effects to enable the responsible agencies to make a meaningful response. At a minimum, the information shall include:

(A) Description of the project,

(B) Location of the project indicated either on an attached map (preferably a copy of a U.S.G.S. 15' or 7-1/2' topographical map identified by quadrangle name, or by a street address in an urbanized area), and

(C) Probable environmental effects of the project.

(2) A sample for a notice of preparation is shown in Appendix J.[3] Public agencies are free to devise their own formats for this notice. A copy of the initial study may be sent with the notice to supply the necessary information.

(3) To send copies of the notice of preparation, the lead agency shall use either certified mail or any other method of transmittal which provides it with a record that the notice was received.

(4) The lead agency may begin work on the draft EIR immediately without awaiting responses to the notice of preparation. The draft EIR in preparation may need to be revised or expanded to conform to responses to the notice of preparation. A lead agency shall not circulate a draft EIR for public review before the time period for responses to the notice of preparation has expired.

(b) Response to Notice of Preparation. Within 30 days after receiving the notice of preparation under subsection (a), each responsible agency shall provide the lead agency with specific detail about the scope and content of the environmental information related to the responsible agency's area of statutory responsibility which must be included in the draft EIR.

(1) The response at a minimum shall identify:

    (A) The significant environmental issues and reasonable alternatives and mitigation measures which the Responsible Agency will need to have explored in the draft EIR; and

    (B) Whether the agency will be a responsible agency or trustee agency for the project.

(2) If a responsible agency fails by the end of the 30 day period to provide the lead agency with either a response to the notice or a well justified request for additional time, the lead agency may presume that the responsible agency has no response to make.

(3) A generalized list of concerns not related to the specific project shall not meet the requirements of this section for a response.

(c) Meetings. In order to expedite the consultation, the lead agency, a responsible agency, a trustee agency, or a project applicant may request one or more meetings between representatives of the agencies involved to assist the lead agency in determining the scope and content of the environmental information which the responsible agency may require. Such meetings shall be convened by the lead agency as soon as possible, but no later than 30 days, after the meetings were requested. On request, the Office of Planning and Research will assist in convening meetings which involve state agencies.

(d) State Clearinghouse. When one or more state agencies will be a responsible agency or a trustee agency, the lead agency shall send a notice of preparation to each state responsible agency and each trustee agency with a copy to the State Clearinghouse in the Office of Planning and Research. The State Clearinghouse will ensure that the state Responsible Agencies and trustees reply to the Lead Agency within the required time.

(e) Identification Number. When the Notice of Preparation is submitted to the State Clearinghouse, the state identification number issued by the Clearinghouse shall be the identification number for all subsequent environmental documents on the project. The identification number should be referenced on all subsequent correspondence regarding the project, specifically on the title page of the draft and final EIR and on the notice of determination.

Note: Authority cited: Sections 21083 and 21087, Public Resources Code. Reference: Section 21080.4, Public Resources Code.

Discussion: The purpose of this section is to spell out the consultation process between a Lead Agency and Responsible Agencies when the Lead Agency is preparing an EIR which all the Responsible Agencies will use in approving the project. The section combines statutory and regulatory requirements in one place in the interest of clarity. This section is necessary to spell out the detailed steps involved in using the Notice of Preparation and to authorize a number of efficiencies in the process. These efficiencies include beginning work on the draft EIR before receiving responses to the notice and sending the notices directly to the individual state agencies rather than through the State Clearinghouse. The section requires that a copy of the notice be sent to the Clearinghouse in order to allow the State Clearinghouse to monitor the compliance by state agencies and to assist Lead Agencies in obtaining timely responses.

Public Resources Code section 21080.4, subdivision (a), limits the response of a responsible or trustee agency to information which is germane to the statutory responsibilities of that agency.

15083   Early Public Consultation

Prior to completing the draft EIR, the lead agency may also consult directly with any person or organization it believes will be concerned with the environmental effects of the project. Many public agencies have found that early consultation solves many potential problems that would arise in more serious forms later in the review process. This early consultation may be called scoping. Scoping will be necessary when preparing an EIR/EIS jointly with a federal agency.

(a) Scoping has been helpful to agencies in identifying the range of actions, alternatives, mitigation measures, and significant effects to be analyzed in depth in an EIR and in eliminating from detailed study issues found not to be important.

(b) Scoping has been found to be an effective way to bring together and resolve the concerns of affected federal, state, and local agencies, the proponent of the action, and other interested persons including those who might not be in accord with the action on environmental grounds.

(c) Where scoping is used, it should be combined to the extent possible with consultation under Section 15082.

Note: Authority cited: Sections 21083 and 21087, Public Resources Code. Reference:

Section 21082.1, Public Resources Code; Section 4, Chapter 480 of the Statutes of 1981; 40 Code of Federal Regulations, Part 1501.7.

Discussion: The purpose of this section is to authorize and encourage, but not require early consultation with the public. Although public consultation prior to completing the draft EIR is permissive under CEQA, this step is recommended as a way of avoiding controversy or resolving controversy early in the process. The section is also necessary for making the point that where a state or local agency is preparing an EIR/EIS with a federal agency, scoping will be required in order to meet the requirements under NEPA for the federal agency.

15083.5   City or County Consultation with Water Agencies   SB 610

This guideline addresses consultation between a city or county and affected water agencies at the notice of preparation stage of environmental review.

(a) This guideline shall apply only to projects which meet all of the following criteria:

    (1) The project consists of any of the following activities for which an application has been submitted to a city or county:

        (A) A residential development of more than 500 dwelling units.

        (B) A shopping center or business establishment that will employ more than 1,000 persons or have more than 500,000 square feet of floor space.

        (C) A commercial office building that will employ more than 1,000 persons or have more than 250,000 square feet of floor space.

        (D) A hotel, motel or both with more than 500 rooms.

        (E) An industrial, manufacturing, or processing plant, or industrial park intended to house more than 1,000 persons, occupying more than 40 acres of land, or having more than 650,000 square feet of floor area.

        (F) Any mixed-use project that would demand an amount of water equal to, or greater than, the amount of water needed to serve a 500-dwelling unit project.

    (2) As part of approval of the project, any of the following are required:

        (A) An amendment to, or revision of, the land use element of a general plan or a specific plan, which would result in a net increase in the stated population density or building intensity to provide for additional development.

(B) The adoption of a specific plan, unless the city or county has previously complied with this section for the project.

Notwithstanding the foregoing provisions of this subsection (a)(2), when a project is identified in connection with the revision of any part of a general plan, that project is subject to the requirements of this section only if the project results in a net increase in the stated population density or building intensity, and if the city or county has not previously complied with the requirements of this section for the project in question.

(3) A city or county has determined that an environmental impact report is required in connection with the project.

(b) For projects subject to this guideline, a city or county shall identify any water system that is, or may become, a public water system, as defined in Section 10912 of the Water Code, that may supply water for the project. When a city or county releases a notice of preparation for review, it shall send a copy of the notice to each public water system which serves or would serve the proposed project and request that the system both indicate whether the projected water demand associated with the proposed project was included in its last urban water management plan and assess whether its total projected water supplies available during normal, single-dry, and multiple-dry water years as included in the 20-year projection contained in its urban water management plan will meet the projected water demand associated with the proposed project, in addition to the system's existing and planned future uses.

(c) The governing body of a public water system shall approve and submit its water supply assessment to the city or county not later than 30 days after the date on which the request and notice of preparation were received. If the public water system fails to submit its assessment within the allotted time, the lead agency may assume, unless there has been a request for a specific extension of time from the public water system, that the public water system has no information to submit. If a public water

system concludes there would be insufficient water to serve the proposed project, it shall provide the city or county with its plans for acquiring additional water supplies.

(d) The lead agency shall include within the EIR the public water system's assessment and any other information provided by the water agency, up to a maximum of ten typewritten pages. The assessment and information may only exceed that length with the approval of the lead agency. The lead agency may independently evaluate the water system's information and shall determine, based on the entire record, whether projected water supplies will be sufficient to satisfy the demands of the proposed project, in addition to existing and planned future uses. If the lead agency determines that water supplies will not be sufficient, the lead agency must include that determination in its findings for the project pursuant to Sections 15091 and 15093.

(e) For purposes of this section, "public water system" means a system as defined in Section 10912 of the Water Code with 3,000 or more service connections.

(f) This section does not apply to the County of San Diego and the cities in the county as provided in Section 10915 of the Water Code.

Note: Authority cited: Sections 21083 and 21087, Public Resources Code. References: Section 21151.9, Public Resources Code.

15084   Preparing the Draft EIR

(a) The draft EIR shall be prepared directly by or under contract to the lead agency. The required contents of a draft EIR are discussed in Article 9 beginning with Section 15120.

(b) The lead agency may require the project applicant to supply data and information both to determine whether the project may have a significant effect on the environment and to assist the Lead Agency in preparing the draft EIR. The requested information should include an identification of other public agencies which will have jurisdiction by law over the project.

(c) Any person, including the applicant, may submit information or comments to the lead agency to assist in the preparation of the draft EIR. The submittal may be presented in any format, including the form of a draft EIR. The lead agency must consider all information and comments received. The information or

comments may be included in the draft EIR in whole or in part.

(d) The lead agency may choose one of the following arrangements or a combination of them for preparing a draft EIR.

(1) Preparing the draft EIR directly with its own staff.

(2) Contracting with another entity, public or private, to prepare the draft EIR.

(3) Accepting a draft prepared by the applicant, a consultant retained by the applicant, or any other person.

(4) Executing a third party contract or memorandum of understanding with the applicant to govern the preparation of a draft EIR by an independent contractor.

(5) Using a previously prepared EIR.

(e) Before using a draft prepared by another person, the lead agency shall subject the draft to the agency's own review and analysis. The draft EIR which is sent out for public review must reflect the independent judgment of the lead agency. The lead agency is responsible for the adequacy and objectivity of the draft EIR.

Note: Authority cited: Sections 21083 and 21087, Public Resources Code. Reference: Section 21082.1, Public Resources Code.

Discussion: This section brings together in one place the requirements that apply to preparing the draft EIR. This section identifies permissible options as well as the minimum requirements.

In *Sundstrom v. Mendocino* (1988) 202 Cal.App.3d 296, the court reemphasized that an EIR or Negative Declaration must show the lead agency's independent judgment in regard to the environmental impacts of the project. Further, the court, citing *Kleist v. Glendale* (1976) 56 Cal.App. 3d, 770, held that the Board of Supervisors cannot delegate the responsibility of considering the final EIR to the staff of the Planning Commission.

15085   Notice of Completion

(a) As soon as the draft EIR is completed, a notice of completion must be filed with OPR in a printed hard copy or in electronic form on a diskette or by electronic mail transmission.

(b) The notice of completion shall include:

(1) A brief description of the project,

(2) The proposed location of the project,

(3) An address where copies of the draft EIR are available, and

(4) The period during which comments will be received on the draft EIR.

(c) A form for the notice of completion is included in the appendices.

(d) Where the EIR will be reviewed through the state review process handled by the State Clearinghouse, the cover form required by the State Clearinghouse will serve as the Notice of Completion.

(e) Public agencies are encouraged to make copies of notices of completion filed pursuant to this section available in electronic format on the Internet.

Note: Authority cited: Sections 21083 and 21087, Public Resources Code. Reference: Section 21161, Public Resources Code.

Discussion: This section describes the contents and the use of the Notice of Completion. Use of this notice is required by Section 21161 in CEQA. The Guidelines provide the interpretation that this notice shall be given at the time of completing the draft EIR so the notice can serve the public disclosure and public involvement functions of CEQA.

Prior to January 1, 1985, Notices of Completion required by this section were filed with the Secretary of Resources. Public Resources code as amended by Chapter 571 Statutes of 1984 consolidated the filing of the Notice of Completion in OPR.

Subsection (e) encourages agencies to post notices on the internet. This provides the public with an additional opportunity for notice of project decisions.

15086   Consultation Concerning Draft EIR

(a) The Lead Agency shall consult with and request comments on the draft EIR from:

(1) Responsible Agencies,

(2) Trustee agencies with resources affected by the project, and

(3) Any other ~~Other~~ state, federal, and local agencies which have jurisdiction by law with respect to the project or which exercise authority over resources which may be affected by the project~~.~~, including water agencies consulted pursuant to section 15083.5.

(4) Any city or county which borders on a city or county within which the project is located.

(5) For a project of statewide, regional, or areawide significance, the transportation planning agencies and public agencies which have transportation facilities within their jurisdictions which could be affected by

the project. "Transportation facilities" includes: major local arterials and public transit within five miles of the project site, and freeways, highways and rail transit service within 10 miles of the project site.

(6) For a state lead agency, the Department of Fish and Game as to the impact of the project on the continued existence of any endangered or threatened species pursuant to Article 4 (commencing with Section 2090) of Chapter 1.5 of Division 3 of the Fish and Game Code.

(7) For a state lead agency when the EIR is being prepared for a highway or freeway project, the State Air Resources Board as to the air pollution impact of the potential vehicular use of the highway or freeway and if a non-attainment area, the local air quality management district for a determination of conformity with the air quality management plan.

(8) For a subdivision project located within one mile of a facility of the State Water Resources Development System, the California Department of Water Resources.

(b) The lead agency may consult directly with ~~any~~ :

(1) Any person who has special expertise with respect to any environmental impact involved,

(2) Any member of the public who has filed a written request for notice with the lead agency or the clerk of the governing body.

(3) Any person identified by the applicant whom the applicant believes will be concerned with the environmental effects of the project.

(c) A responsible agency or other public agency shall only make substantive comments regarding those activities involved in the project that are within an area of expertise of the agency or which are required to be carried out or approved by the responsible agency. Those comments shall be supported by specific documentation.

(d) Prior to the close of the public review period, a responsible agency or trustee agency which has identified what that agency considers to be significant environmental effects shall advise the lead agency of those effects. As to those effects relevant to its decision, if any, on the project, the responsible or trustee agency shall either submit to the lead agency complete and detailed

performance objectives for mitigation measures addressing those effects or refer the lead agency to appropriate, readily available guidelines or reference documents concerning mitigation measures. If the responsible or trustee agency is not aware of mitigation measures that address identified effects, the responsible or trustee agency shall so state.

Note: Authority cited: Sections 21083 and 21087, Public Resources Code. Reference: Sections 21081.6, 21092.4, 21092.5, 21104 and 21153, Public Resources Code.

Discussion: This section implements the statutory requirements for consultation with other public agencies and the authority to consult with people who have special expertise concerning the environmental effects of the project. The section is necessary in order to interpret the scope of the term "jurisdiction by law" as it relates to agencies which must be consulted. The section limits the required consultation with Trustee Agencies to only those agencies holding in trust resources affected by the project. The courts have held that an agency which has a certified regulatory program exemption under Guidelines Section 15251 must also consult trustee agencies in the process of preparing an EIR substitute. (See: *Environmental Protection Information Center v. Johnson*, (1985) 170 Cal. App.3d 604.) The 1998 amendment substantially expanded this section to include agencies which, by statute, are to be consulted on a project. Subsection (d) clarifies the responsibility of responsible and trustee agencies to submit comments on any significant effects to the lead agency before the review period closes, and to submit recommendations relative to mitigation measures.

15087   Public Review of Draft EIR

(a) The lead agency shall provide public notice of the availability of a draft EIR at the same time as it sends a notice of completion to OPR. This notice shall be given as provided under Section 15105. Notice shall be ~~given~~ mailed to the last known name and address of all organizations and individuals who have previously requested such notice in writing, and shall also be given by at least one of the following procedures:

(1) Publication at least one time by the public agency in a newspaper of general circulation in the area affected by the proposed project. If more than one area is affected, the notice shall be published in the newspaper of largest circulation from among

the newspapers of general circulation in those areas.

(2) Posting of notice by the public agency on and off the site in the area where the project is to be located.

(3) Direct mailing to the owners and occupants of property contiguous to the parcel or parcels on which the project is located. Owners of such property shall be identified as shown on the latest equalized assessment roll.

(b) The alternatives for providing notice specified in subsection (a) shall not preclude a public agency from providing additional notice by other means if such agency so desires, nor shall the requirements of this section preclude a public agency from providing the public notice required by this section at the same time and in the same manner as public notice otherwise required by law for the project.

(c) The notice shall disclose the following:

(1) A brief description of the proposed project and its location.

(2) The starting and ending dates for the review period during which the lead agency will receive comments. If the review period is shortened, the notice shall disclose that fact.

(3) The date, time, and place of any scheduled public meetings or hearings to be held by the lead agency on the proposed project when known to the lead agency at the time of notice.

(4) A list of the significant environmental effects anticipated as a result of the project, to the extent which such effects are known to the lead agency at the time of the notice.

(5) The address where copies of the EIR and all documents referenced in the EIR will be available for public review. This location shall be readily accessible to the public during the lead agency's normal working hours.

(6) The presence of the site on any of the lists of sites enumerated under Section 65962.5 of the Government Code including, but not limited to, lists of hazardous waste facilities, land designated as hazardous waste property, hazardous waste disposal sites and others, and the information in the Hazardous Waste and Substances Statement required under subsection (f) of that Section.

(d) The notice required under this section shall be posted in the office of the county clerk of each county in which the project will be located for a period of at least 30 days. The county clerk shall post such notices within 24 hours of receipt.

(e) In order to provide sufficient time for public review, the review ~~periods~~ period for a draft EIR ~~EIRs should not be less than 30 days nor longer than 90 days from the date of the notice except in unusual situations. The review period for draft EIRs for which a state agency is the Lead Agency or Responsible Agency shall be at least 45 days unless a shorter period is approved by the State Clearinghouse~~ shall be as provided in Section 15105. The review period shall be combined with the consultation required under Section 15086. When a draft EIR has been submitted to the State Clearinghouse, the public review period shall be at least as long as the review period established by the Clearinghouse.

~~(d)~~(f) Public agencies shall use the State Clearinghouse to distribute draft EIRs to state agencies for review and should use areawide clearinghouses to distribute the documents to regional and local agencies.

~~(e)~~(g) To make copies of EIRs available to the public, lead agencies should furnish copies of draft EIRs to public library systems serving the area involved. Copies should also be available in offices of the lead agency.

~~(f)~~(h) Public agencies should compile listings of other agencies, particularly local agencies, which have jurisdiction by law and/or special expertise with respect to various projects and project locations. Such listings should be a guide in determining which agencies should be consulted with regard to a particular project.

~~(g)~~(i) Public hearings may be conducted on the environmental documents, either in separate proceedings or in conjunction with other proceedings of the public agency. Public hearings are encouraged, but not required as an element of the CEQA process.

Note: Authority cited: Sections 21083 and 21087, Public Resources Code. Reference: Sections 21091, 21092, 21092.2, 21092.3, 21092.6, 21104, 21153, and 21161, Public Resources Code~~; Section 6061, Government Code~~.

Discussion: The purpose of this section is to combine the statutory notice requirements with other regulatory requirements that apply to the public review of draft EIRs. Although subsection (a) repeats the statutory requirements for public notice, subsection (a)(1) provides a clearer explanation of the requirement than does the statute itself. Subsection (b) allows public agencies flexibility in providing notice. This subsection allows agencies to use additional methods of notice if they so desire or to combine the CEQA notice with notice required under other statute. This approach allows agencies the opportunity to reduce costs by avoiding duplication.

Pursuant to Public Resources Code Section 21092, certain projects, generally those involving the burning of municipal waste, hazardous waste, or refuse-derived fuel, require that notice be given by all three procedures under subdivision (a). In addition, notice shall be given by direct mail to the owners and occupants of property within one-fourth of a mile of the project parcel or parcels.

Public Resources Code section 21092 requires that the notice specify the period during which comments will be received, the date, time, and place of any public meetings or hearings on the project, a brief description of the project and its location, and the address where copies of the draft EIR and all documents referenced in the draft EIR are available for review. Section 21092.3 of the Public Resources Code establishes additional requirements for the filing of notice with the County Clerk for 30-day posting.

Section 21091 of the Public Resources Code requires that the minimum public review period for a draft EIR shall be 30 days. When a draft EIR is submitted to the State Clearinghouse for review, the period shall be 45 days. A shorter period of state review may by authorized by the State Clearinghouse upon formal request by the local decision-making body, but the revised review period shall not be less than 30 days.

Subsection (d) requires public agencies to use the State Clearinghouse for distribution of EIRs and Negative Declarations to obtain review by state agencies. The reason for this is to provide a single point of contact for dealing with the state review system. It also provides the assurance that all state permitting agencies will be contacted. Frequently when a local agency does not use the Clearinghouse, it overlooks one or more state agencies which have permitting power over the project. Using the State Clearinghouse avoids these omissions. For similar reasons, the Guidelines encourage use of areawide clearinghouses as a way of communicating with regional and local agencies. The areawide clearinghouses are normally more familiar with the different agencies in their areas than are the individual local agencies.

In order to promote the public participation goals of CEQA, the Guidelines encourage use of public library systems as a way of making EIRs available to the public for review. Experience has shown that the public library systems provide a highly effective way to make documents available to the public for review.

Subsection (f) strongly encourages public agencies to compile listings of other agencies which have jurisdiction by law or special expertise with regard to types of projects and locations affected by the agency. With this information each agency can then use the Notice of Preparation process effectively to notify other agencies concerned with the project.

Although CEQA strongly encourages public participation, it does not require oral hearings to be provided as a part of the process. The review and comment part of the CEQA process may be conducted entirely by written statements if the Lead Agency so chooses. Public hearings are encouraged because hearings provide for direct communication between reviewers and the Lead Agency. Further, the hearings provide an opportunity for members of the public to learn the concerns of other people testifying about the project.

15088   Evaluation of and Response to Comments

(a) The lead agency shall evaluate comments on environmental issues received from persons who reviewed the draft EIR and shall prepare a written response. The lead agency shall respond to comments received during the noticed comment period and any extensions and may respond to late comments.

(b) The written response shall describe the disposition of significant environmental issues raised (e.g., revisions to the proposed project to mitigate anticipated impacts or objections). In particular, the major environmental issues raised when the lead agency's position is at variance with recommendations and objections raised in the comments must be addressed in detail giving reasons why specific comments and suggestions were not accepted. There must be good faith, reasoned analysis in response. Conclusory statements unsupported by factual information will not suffice.

(c) The response to comments may take the form of a revision to the draft EIR or may be a separate section in the final EIR. Where the response to comments makes important changes in the information contained in the text of the draft EIR, the lead agency should either:

(1) Revise the text in the body of the EIR, or

(2) Include marginal notes showing that the information is revised in the response to comments.

Note: Authority cited: Sections 21083 and 21087, Public Resources Code. Reference: Sections 21104 and 21153, Public Resources Code; *People v. County of Kern*, (1974) 39 Cal.App.3d 830; *Cleary v. County of Stanislaus*, (1981) 118 Cal.App.3d 348.

Discussion: The main purpose of this section is to codify the holding in *People v. County of Kern* cited in the note. The evaluation and response to public comments is an essential part of the CEQA process. Failure to comply with the requirements can lead to disapproval of a project. To avoid this problem it is necessary to identify the requirements in the Guidelines. This section is also necessary for explaining the different ways in which the responses to comments can be prepared. The options of revising the draft or adding the comments and responses as a separate section of the final EIR match the permissible approaches under the federal NEPA system. Subsection (c) encourages revisions in the draft or the use of marginal notes to show where the text of the draft EIR was changed in response to comments. Either of these approaches will make the final EIR more useful and informative to the decision-makers when they consider the EIR with the project.

In *Browning-Ferris Industries of California, Inc. v. San Jose* (1986) 181 Cal.App.3d 852, the court citing *Gallegos v. California Board of Forestry* (1978) 76 Cal.App.3d 945, *Twain Harte Homeowners Association, Inc. v. Tuolumne* (1982) 138 Cal.App.3d 664, and *Cleary v. Stanislaus* (1981) 118 Cal.App.3d 348, stated that the lead agency must respond to all significant environmental comments in a level of detail commensurate to that of the comment.

Further, while there is no legal requirement for an agency to respond in writing to comments submitted after the expiration of the comment period, an agency's failure to evaluate the substance of the comment and to respond appropriately to substantive comments in the proceedings may place the agency at risk in the event of legal challenge.

15088.5   Recirculation of an EIR Prior to Certification

(a) A lead agency is required to recirculate an EIR when significant new information is added to the EIR after public notice is given of the availability of the draft EIR for public review under Section 15087 but before certification. As used in this section, the term "information" can include changes in the project or environmental setting as well as additional data or other information. New information added to an EIR is not "significant" unless the EIR is changed in a way that deprives the public of a meaningful opportunity to comment upon a substantial adverse environmental effect of the project or a feasible way to mitigate or avoid such an effect (including a feasible project alternative) that the project's proponents have declined to implement. "Significant new information" requiring recirculation include, for example, a disclosure showing that:

(1) A new significant environmental impact would result from the project or from a new mitigation measure proposed to be implemented.

(2) A substantial increase in the severity of an environmental impact would result unless mitigation measures are adopted that reduce the impact to a level of insignificance.

(3) A feasible project alternative or mitigation measure considerably different from others previously analyzed would clearly lessen the environmental impacts of the project, but the project's proponents decline to adopt it.

(4) The draft EIR was so fundamentally and basically inadequate and conclusory in nature that meaningful public review and comment were precluded. (*Mountain Lion Coalition v. Fish and Game Com.* (1989) 214 Cal.App.3d 1043)

(b) Recirculation is not required where the new information added to the EIR merely clarifies or amplifies or makes insignificant modifications in an adequate EIR.

(c) If the revision is limited to a few chapters or portions of the EIR, the lead agency need only recirculate the chapters or portions that have been modified.

(d) Recirculation of an EIR requires notice pursuant to Section 15087, and consultation pursuant to Section 15086.

(e) A decision not to recirculate an EIR must be supported by substantial evidence in the administrative record.

(f) The lead agency shall evaluate and respond to comments as provided in Section 15088. Recirculating an EIR can result in the lead agency receiving more than one set of comments from reviewers. Following are two ways in which the lead agency may identify the set of comments to which it will respond.

This dual approach avoids confusion over whether the lead agency must respond to comments which are duplicates or which are no longer pertinent due to revisions to the EIR. In no case shall the lead agency fail to respond to pertinent comments on significant environmental issues.

(1) When the EIR is substantially revised and the entire EIR is recirculated, the lead agency may require that reviewers submit new comments and need not respond to those comments received during the earlier circulation period. The lead agency shall advise reviewers, either within the text of the revised EIR or by an attachment to the revised EIR, that although part of the administrative record, the previous comments do not require a written response in the final EIR, and that new comments must be submitted for the revised EIR. The lead agency need only respond to those comments submitted in response to the recirculated revised EIR. The lead agency shall send directly to every agency, person, or organization that commented on the prior draft EIR a notice of the recirculation specifying that new comments must be submitted.

(2) When the EIR is revised only in part and the lead agency is recirculating only the revised chapters or portions of the EIR, the lead agency may request that reviewers limit their comments to the revised chapters or portions. The lead agency need only respond to (i) comments received during the initial circulation period that relate to chapters or portions of the document that were not revised and recirculated, and (ii) comments received during the recirculation period that relate to the chapters or portions of the earlier EIR that were revised and recirculated. The lead agency's request that reviewers limit the scope of their comments shall be included either within the text of the revised EIR or by an attachment to the revised EIR.

(g) When recirculating a revised EIR, either in whole or in part, the lead agency shall, in the revised EIR or by an attachment to the revised EIR, summarize the revisions made to the previously circulated draft EIR.

Note: Authority cited: Sections 21083 and 21087, Public Resources Code. Reference: Section 21092.1, Public Resources Code;

Laurel Heights Improvement Association v. Regents of the University of California (1993) 6 Cal.4th 1112.

Discussion: The purpose of this section is to provide guidance in applying Public Resources Code section 21092.1. It codifies the interpretation of that section made by the state Supreme Court in *Laurel Heights Improvement Association v. Regents of the University of California* (1993) 6 Cal. 4th 1112.

Recirculation applies only to EIRs which have been made available for review, but which have not been certified. Once an EIR has been certified, then the procedures established under sections 15162, 15163, and 15164 apply to the question of whether or not a subsequent EIR, supplement to an EIR, or addendum must be prepared. Circulating a subsequent EIR or supplement to an EIR is not "recirculation" as described under section 15088.5.

Subsection (f) clarifies the responsibility of the lead agency to respond to comments received on the previously circulated EIR. When the previously circulated EIR has been extensively revised prior to recirculation, the lead agency is not required to respond to comments received during the previous circulation. This provision is intended to relieve the lead agency of the responsibility to respond to comments on what is essentially a different EIR than that currently being circulated. Nonetheless, the lead agency must specifically notify reviewers that it does not intend to respond to comments on the previous version of the EIR, and the lead agency must respond to all comments received during the recirculation. Subsection (g) requires the lead agency to summarize any changes made to a previously circulated EIR. This will help reviewers to familiarize themselves with the revised EIR and give them a quick indication of whether it addresses their previous concerns.

When the previously circulated EIR has not been extensively revised, the lead agency must respond to the comments received during each circulation period.

15089   Preparation of Final EIR

(a) The lead agency shall prepare a final EIR before approving the project. The contents of a final EIR are specified in Section 15132 of these guidelines.

(b) Lead Agencies may provide an opportunity for review of the final EIR by the public or by commenting agencies before approving the project. The review of a final EIR should focus on the responses to comments on the draft EIR.

Note: Authority cited: Sections 21083 and 21087, Public Resources Code. Reference: Sections 21100, 21105, and 21151, Public Resources Code; *City of Carmel-by-the-Sea v. Board of Supervisors*, (1977) 71 Cal.App. 3d 84. State Administrative Manual, Section 1060.

Discussion: This section makes clear the requirement for the Lead Agency to prepare a final EIR before approving the project. It also provides interpretations for several questions dealing with the final EIR. This section specifies that agencies need not provide a separate review period for the final EIR. In this regard, the CEQA process is deliberately made shorter than federal process under NEPA. Federal agencies must allow a 30-day review period on the contents of the final EIS to receive comments on how the final EIS deals with the problems raised with the draft EIS. In order to save time, the CEQA process requires public review only at the draft EIR stage. The final EIR can be submitted directly to the decision-making body of an agency for consideration.

Public Resources Code Section 21092.5 requires the lead agency to provide a written proposal response to each public agency which commented on the EIR. The proposed response must be provided to the pertinent public agency 10 days prior to the lead agency's certification of the final EIR.

15090   Certification of the Final EIR

(a) Prior to approving a project ~~The~~ the lead agency shall certify that:

~~(a)~~(1) The final EIR has been completed in compliance with CEQA; ~~and~~

~~(b)~~(2) The final EIR was presented to the decision-making body of the lead agency and that the decisionmaking body reviewed and considered the information contained in the final EIR prior to approving the project~~.~~; and

(3) The final EIR reflects the lead agency's independent judgment and analysis.

(b) When an EIR is certified by a non-elected decision-making body within a local lead agency, that certification may be appealed to the local lead agency's elected decision-making body, if one exists. For example, certification of an EIR for a tentative subdivision map by a city's planning commission may be appealed to the city council. Each local lead agency shall provide for such appeals.

Note: Authority cited: Sections 21083 and 21087, Public Resources Code. Reference: Sections ~~21108 and 21152~~ 21082.1, 21100, and 21151, Public Resources Code; *City of*

Carmel-by-the-Sea v. Board of Supervisors (1977) 71 Cal.App.3d 84; *Kleist v. City of Glendale* (1976) 56 Cal.App.3d 770.

Discussion: This section describes the way for a Lead Agency to implement the requirement for the decision-making body to consider the EIR. As shown in *Kleist v. City of Glendale,* the decision-making body itself must consider the information in the EIR. The section omits any mention of delegating the certification functions. Instead, the responsibility for certification rests with the Lead Agency. This approach allows Lead Agencies to determine for themselves how they will assign responsibility for completing the certification. The section also highlights the two parts of certification. The Lead Agency must certify the adequacy of the final EIR and certify that the decision-making body reviewed and considered the final EIR in reaching its decision on the project. These two separate elements of certification have always been required in the Guidelines.

Public Resources Code section 21151, subdivision (c), provides that where an EIR has been certified by a non-elected decision making body, that certification may be appealed to the agency's elected decision making body, if any.

15091   Findings

(a) No public agency shall approve or carry out a project for which an EIR has been certified which identifies one or more significant environmental effects of the project unless the public agency makes one or more written findings for each of those significant effects, accompanied by a brief explanation of the rationale for each finding. The possible findings are:

  (1) Changes or alterations have been required in, or incorporated into, the project which avoid or substantially lessen the significant environmental effect as identified in the final EIR.

  (2) Such changes or alterations are within the responsibility and jurisdiction of another public agency and not the agency making the finding. Such changes have been adopted by such other agency or can and should be adopted by such other agency.

  (3) Specific economic, legal, social, technological, or other considerations, including provision of employment opportunities for highly trained workers, make infeasible the mitigation measures or project alternatives identified in the final EIR.

(b) The findings required by subsection (a) shall be supported by substantial evidence in the record.

(c) The finding in subsection (a)(2) shall not be made if the agency making the finding has concurrent jurisdiction with another agency to deal with identified feasible mitigation measures or alternatives. The finding in subsection (a)(3) shall describe the specific reasons for rejecting identified mitigation measures and project alternatives.

(d) When making the findings required in subsection (a)(1), the agency shall also adopt a program for reporting on or monitoring the changes which it has either required in the project or made a condition of approval to avoid or substantially lessen significant environmental effects. These measures must be fully enforceable through permit conditions, agreements, or other measures.

(e) The public agency shall specify the location and custodian of the documents or other material which constitute the record of the proceedings upon which its decision is based.

(f) A statement made pursuant to Section 15093 does not substitute for the findings required by this section.

Note: Authority cited: Sections 21083 and 21087, Public Resources Code. Reference: Sections 21002, 21002.1, ~~and~~ 21081, and 21081.6, Public Resources Code; *Laurel Hills Homeowners Association v. City Council* (1978) 83 Cal.App.3d 515; *Cleary v. County of Stanislaus* (1981) 118 Cal.App.3d 348; *Sierra Club v. Contra Costa County* (1992) 10 Cal.App.4th 1212; *Citizens for Quality Growth v. City of Mount Shasta* (1988) 198 Cal.App.3d 433.

Discussion: This section brings together statutory, regulatory, and case law requirements dealing with findings which an agency must make before approving a project for which an EIR was prepared. The statute in Section 21081 provides that a separate finding must be made for each significant effect. This section avoids the problem of agencies deferring to each other, with the result that no agency deals with the problem. This result would be contrary to the strong policy declared in Sections 21002 and 21002.1 of the statute.

Substantial evidence to support the findings appears to be required to implement the legislative intent of this section. The Legislature wanted agencies to deal directly with the facts presented in the EIR. Although the courts have often drawn the distinction between quasi-adjudicatory findings which must be supported by substantial evidence

and quasi-legislative findings which need not be supported by substantial evidence, the Legislature has blurred this distinction by requiring all agencies to make these findings in response to specific facts in an EIR without regard to whether the decision could be classified as legislative or adjudicatory. In requiring this finding, the Legislature appears to have removed the partition between the two pigeon holes and required agencies to grapple with the facts as presented in the EIR.

Where the courts have required agencies to make findings, they have required three elements. First, the agency must make the ultimate finding called for in the statute. Second, the finding must be supported by substantial evidence in the record. Third, the agency must present some explanation to supply the logical step between the ultimate finding and the facts in the record. Section 15091 requires that all three elements must be addressed. This section implements many court decisions interpreting the findings requirement. The decisions include *City of Rancho Palos Verdes v. City Council of the City of Rolling Hills Estates*, (1976) 59 Cal.App.3d 869; *Mountain Defense League v. Board of Supervisors*, (1977) 65 Cal.App.3d 723; *Village Laguna of Laguna Beach, Inc. v. Board of Supervisors*, (1982) 134 Cal.App.3d 1022.

The court in *Citizens For Quality Growth v. Mount Shasta* (1988) 198 Cal.App.3d 433, found that passing reference to mitigation measures are insufficient to constitute a finding, as nothing in the lead agency's resolutions binds it to follow [those] measures. In this case, there was nothing in the lead agency findings which obligated the project proponent to implement the necessary measures to effectuate the mitigation.

In discussing the "Standard of Review," the Court in *Santee v. San Diego* (1989) 214 Cal.App.3d 1438, held that a court's inquiry into the appropriateness of an agency's action under CEQA shall extend only to whether there was a prejudicial abuse of discretion. Abuse of discretion is established if the agency has not proceeded in a manner required by law or if the determination or decision is not supported by substantial evidence. Citing *Inyo v. Los Angeles* (1977) 71 Cal.App.3d 185, the Court restated that "courts do not pass upon the correctness of an EIR's environmental conclusions, but only upon its sufficiency as an informative document."

Section 21081.6 of the Public Resources Code now requires that, upon making a finding under subdivision (1) of subsection (a), the public agency shall adopt a reporting or monitoring program for the changes to the project which it has required or mitigation measures which were adopted. The program shall be designed to ensure compliance during project implementation.

Public Resources Code section 21081, subdivision (c), now provides that a finding under paragraph (3) of subsection (a) may cite legal, technological, and employment related reasons for determining that a mitigation measure or project alternative identified in the EIR is infeasible.

15092   Approval

(a) After considering the final EIR and in conjunction with making findings under Section 15091, the lead agency may decide whether or how to approve or carry out the project.

(b) A public agency shall not decide to approve or carry out a project for which an EIR was prepared unless either:

(1) The project as approved will not have a significant effect on the environment, or

(2) The agency has:

(A) Eliminated or substantially lessened all significant effects on the environment where feasible as shown in findings under Section 15091, and

(B) Determined that any remaining significant effects on the environment found to be unavoidable under Section 15091 are acceptable due to overriding concerns as described in Section 15093.

(c) With respect to a project which includes housing development, the public agency shall not reduce the proposed number of housing units as a mitigation measure if it determines that there is another feasible specific mitigation measure available that will provide a comparable level of mitigation.

Note: Authority cited: Sections 21083 and 21087, Public Resources Code. Reference: Sections 21002, 21002.1, 21081, and 21085, Public Resources Code; *Friends of Mammoth v. Board of Supervisors*, (1972) 8 Cal. App.3d 247; *San Francisco Ecology Center v. City and County of San Francisco*, (1975) 48 Cal.App.3d 584; *City of Carmel-by-the-Sea v. Board of Supervisors*, (1977) 71 Cal.App.3d 84; *Laurel Hills Homeowners Association v. City Council*, (1978) 83 Cal.App.3d 515.

Discussion: This section is designed to bring together in one place a short statement of the sequence of actions that occur near the time of approving the project and also to

provide a simple statement of the substantive duty to reduce or avoid environmental damage where feasible. This duty is a constraint on the authority of an agency to approve a project.

The duty to reduce or avoid environmental damage was first stated in Footnote 8 in the *Friends of Mammoth* decision, 8 Cal.3d at 263. The *San Francisco Ecology Center* case established the need for the statement of the ultimate balancing of the merits of the project if the project could result in environmental damage. After the Legislature established the findings requirement in Section 21081 of CEQA focusing on the individual environmental effects of the project, the courts still required a statement of the ultimate balancing of the benefits of the project against the unavoidable environmental damage. This section brings together the requirements from case law and the express requirements in the statute.

Subsection (c) identifies the limitation on the authority of an agency to mitigate the significant effects of a housing project by reducing the number of housing units if the agency determines that there is another mitigation measure available that would provide a comparable level of mitigation. Even though this limitation is contained in the statute, it is included here in order to make this section complete and to identify the limitation at the relevant step of the process. If agencies are not made aware of this provision through the Guidelines, many agencies will be likely to overlook the limitation. The result could be increased litigation over permits and a reduction in the number of housing units that may be constructed in the state.

15093   Statement of Overriding Considerations

(a) CEQA requires the ~~decisionmaker~~ decision-making agency to balance, as applicable, the economic, legal, social, technological, or other benefits of a proposed project against its unavoidable environmental risks ~~in~~ when determining whether to approve the project. If the specific economic, legal, social, technological, or other benefits of a proposed project outweigh the unavoidable adverse environmental effects, the adverse environmental effects may be considered "acceptable."

(b) ~~Where the decision of the public agency allows~~ When the lead agency approves a project which will result in the occurrence of significant effects which are identified in the final EIR but are not ~~at least substantially mitigated~~ avoided or

substantially lessened, the agency shall state in writing the specific reasons to support its action based on the final EIR and/or other information in the record. The statement of overriding considerations shall be supported by substantial evidence in the record.

(c) If an agency makes a statement of overriding considerations, the statement should be included in the record of the project approval and should be mentioned in the notice of determination. This statement does not substitute for, and shall be in addition to, findings required pursuant to Section 15091.

Note: Authority cited: Sections 21083 and 21087, Public Resources Code. Reference: Sections 21002 and 21081, Public Resources Code; *San Francisco Ecology Center v. City and County of San Francisco* (1975) 48 Cal.App.3d 584 ~~(1975)~~; *City of Carmel-by-the-Sea v. Board of Supervisors* (1977) 71 Cal.App.3d 84 ~~(1977)~~; *Sierra Club v. Contra Costa County* (1992) 10 Cal.App.4th 1212; *Citizens for Quality Growth v. City of Mount Shasta* (1988) 198 Cal.App.3d 433.

Discussion: This section is necessary to codify the requirement from case law that when an agency approves a project which will have an adverse environmental effect, the agency must make a statement of its views on the ultimate balancing of the merits of approving the project despite the environmental damage. This requirement was originally traced to case law interpreting NEPA. The *San Francisco Ecology Center* case clearly established this balancing statement as a requirement under CEQA. The *City of Carmel-by-the-Sea* decision showed that this balancing statement is required even though an agency makes findings as to the feasibility of mitigation measures under Section 21081 of the Statute.

Subsection (c) identifies the importance of preserving the statement in the record of project approval. Mentioning the statement in the Notice of Determination will help anyone concerned with the project to find the notice. The section also helps to show that the statement is not a part of the EIR. The statement is prepared, if at all, at the end of the process after the final EIR has been completed.

The court in *Citizens For Quality Growth v. Mount Shasta* (1988) 198 Cal.App.3d 433, held that when an agency approves a project that will significantly affect the environment, CEQA places the burden on the approving agency to affirmatively show that it has considered the identified means (mitigation and/or alternatives) of lessening or avoiding the project's significant effects and to explain its decision allowing those adverse changes to occur. In other words, an agency may only get to overriding considerations after the agency has made the appropriate findings; then, and only then, may an agency go on to explain why a project may go forward notwithstanding its effects.

The requirement for a statement of overriding considerations was codified at Public Resources Code section 21081(b) by Chapter 1294 of the Statutes of 1994.

15094   Notice of Determination

(a) The lead agency shall file a notice of determination ~~following each project approval for which an EIR was considered~~ within 5 working days after approval of the project by the lead agency. The notice shall include:

  (1) An identification of the project including its common name where possible and its location.

  (2) A brief description of the project.

  (3) The date when the agency approved the project.

  (4) The determination of the agency whether the project in its approved form will have a significant effect on the environment.

  (5) A statement that an EIR was prepared and certified pursuant to the provisions of CEQA.

  (6) Whether mitigation measures were made a condition of the approval of the project.

  (7) Whether findings were made pursuant to Section 15091.

  (8) Whether a statement of overriding considerations was adopted for the project.

  (9) The address where a copy of the final EIR and the record of project approval may be examined.

(b) If a state agency is the lead agency, the notice of determination shall be filed with OPR.

(c) If a local agency is the lead agency, the notice of determination shall be filed with the county clerk of the county or counties in which the project will be located. If the project requires discretionary approval from a state agency, the notice of determination shall also be filed with OPR.

(d) A notice of determination filed with the county clerk is available for public inspection and shall be posted within 24 hours of receipt for a period of at least 30 days. Thereafter, the clerk shall return the notice to the local lead agency with a notation of the period during which it was posted. The local lead agency shall retain the notice for not less than 9 months.

(e) A notice of determination filed with OPR is available for public inspection and shall be posted for a period of at least 30 days.

(f) The filing of the notice of determination and the posting ~~on a list~~ of such notice starts a 30-day statute of limitations on court challenges to the approval under CEQA.

Note: Authority cited: Sections 21083 and 21087, Public Resources Code. Reference: Sections 21108, 21152, and 21167, Public Resources Code; *Citizens of Lake Murray Area Association v. City Council*, (1982) 129 Cal.App.3d 436.

Discussion: The Notice of Determination is required by the statute. The contents prescribed by this section are the minimum necessary for the notice to provide its public information function and to enable a person inquiring about the project to learn enough from the notice to be able to respond to it. The section contains the requirement that a notice from a local agency must be submitted to OPR if a state agency will be a Responsible Agency for the project. This additional filing is required to enable a state agency to know when the time period for action by the Responsible Agency begins to run under Government Code Section 65952. The notices are made available to state agencies in the Office of Planning and Research and the State Clearinghouse Newsletter.

Subsections (d) and (e) identify the responsibilities of the county clerk and OPR relative to posting notices.

15095   Disposition of a Final EIR

The lead agency shall:

(a) File a copy of the final EIR with the appropriate planning agency of any city, county, or city and county where significant effects on the environment may occur.

(b) Include the final EIR as part of the regular project report which is used in the existing project review and budgetary process if such a report is used.

(c) Retain one or more copies of the final EIR as public records for a reasonable period of time.

(d) Require the applicant to provide a copy of the certified, final EIR to each responsible agency.

Note: Authority cited: Sections 21083 and 21087, Public Resources Code. Reference: Sections 21105, 21151, and 21165, Public Resources Code; *County of Inyo v. Yorty*, (1973) 32 Cal.App.3d 795.

Discussion: This section prescribes the ways for dealing with the final EIR after the project has been approved. Subsection (a) codifies the ruling in *County of Inyo v. Yorty* that a copy of the EIR must be sent to the county in which the project will be located. Subsection (b) implements the statutory requirement in Section 21105 for including the EIR in the project report but limits the requirement to situations where a project report is used. This qualification is necessary to answer questions which have arisen over the use of Section 21105. Subsection (c) states that a final EIR is a public record and must be maintained as such. Subsection (d) provides a way for the Lead Agency to have a copy of the final EIR delivered to each Responsible Agency which must use the final EIR. Currently, there is no formal communication device between the Lead Agency and Responsible Agencies after the Lead Agency has approved the project. By requiring the applicant to provide copies of the final EIR to the Responsible Agencies, the Lead Agency can avoid the cost of doing the job itself and will rely on the person with the greatest interest in having the project go through the CEQA process in a legally valid way.

15096   Process for a Responsible Agency

(a) General. A responsible agency complies with CEQA by considering the EIR or negative declaration prepared by the lead agency and by reaching its own conclusions on whether and how to approve the project involved. This section identifies the special duties a public agency will have when acting as a responsible agency.

(b) Response to Consultation. A responsible agency shall respond to consultation by the lead agency in order to assist the lead agency in preparing adequate environmental documents for the project. By this means, the responsible agency will ensure that the documents it will use will comply with CEQA.

  (1) In response to consultation, a responsible agency shall explain its reasons for recommending whether the lead agency should prepare an EIR or negative declaration for a project. Where the responsible agency disagrees with the lead agency's proposal to prepare a negative declaration for a project, the responsible agency should identify the significant environmental effects which it believes could result from the project and recommend either that an

EIR be prepared or that the project be modified to eliminate the significant effects.

(2) As soon as possible, but not longer than 30 days after receiving a notice of preparation from the lead agency, the responsible agency shall send a written reply by certified mail or any other method which provides the agency with a record showing that the notice was received. The reply shall specify the scope and content of the environmental information which would be germane to the responsible agency's statutory responsibilities in connection with the proposed project. The lead agency shall include this information in the EIR.

(c) Meetings. The responsible agency shall designate employees or representatives to attend meetings requested by the lead agency to discuss the scope and content of the EIR.

(d) Comments on Draft EIRs and negative declarations. A responsible agency should review and comment on draft EIRs and negative declarations for projects which the responsible agency would later be asked to approve. Comments should focus on any shortcomings in the EIR, the appropriateness of using a negative declaration, or on additional alternatives or mitigation measures which the EIR should include. The comments shall be limited to those project activities which are within the agency's area of expertise or which are required to be carried out or approved by the agency or which will be subject to the exercise of powers by the agency. Comments shall be as specific as possible and supported by either oral or written documentation.

(e) Decision on Adequacy of EIR or Negative Declaration. If a responsible agency believes that the final EIR or negative declaration prepared by the lead agency is not adequate for use by the responsible agency, the responsible agency must either:

(1) Take the issue to court within 30 days after the lead agency files a notice of determination;

(2) Be deemed to have waived any objection to the adequacy of the EIR or negative declaration;

(3) Prepare a subsequent EIR if permissible under Section 15162; or

(4) Assume the lead agency role as provided in Section 15052(a)(3).

(f) Consider the EIR or Negative Declaration. Prior to reaching a decision on the project, the responsible agency must consider the environmental effects of the project as shown in the EIR or negative declaration. A subsequent or supplemental EIR can be prepared only as provided in Sections 15162 or 15163.

(g) Adoption of Alternatives or Mitigation Measures.

(1) When considering alternatives and mitigation measures, a responsible agency is more limited than a lead agency. A responsible agency has responsibility for mitigating or avoiding only the direct or indirect environmental effects of those parts of the project which it decides to carry out, finance, or approve.

(2) When an EIR has been prepared for a project, the Responsible Agency shall not approve the project as proposed if the agency finds any feasible alternative or feasible mitigation measures within its powers that would substantially lessen or avoid any significant effect the project would have on the environment. With respect to a project which includes housing development, the responsible agency shall not reduce the proposed number of housing units as a mitigation measure if it determines that there is another feasible specific mitigation measure available that will provide a comparable level of mitigation.

(h) Findings. The responsible agency shall make the findings required by Section 15091 for each significant effect of the project and shall make the findings in Section 15093 if necessary.

(i) Notice of Determination. The responsible agency should file a notice of determination in the same manner as a lead agency under Section 15075 or 15094 except that the responsible agency does not need to state that the EIR or negative declaration complies with CEQA. The responsible agency should state that it considered the EIR or negative declaration as prepared by a lead agency.

Note: Authority cited: Sections 21083 and 21087, Public Resources Code. Reference: Sections 21165, 21080.1, 21080.3, 21080.4, 21082.1, and 21002.1(b) and (d), Public Resources Code.

Discussion: Most of the statutory requirements for the CEQA process are focused on the Lead Agency, but the statute clearly requires Responsible Agencies to take a number of actions also. Responsible Agencies are generally freed from the need to prepare EIRs or Negative Declarations because they must use the document prepared by the Lead Agency subject to a few exceptions. This section spells out the process to be used by a Responsible Agency. The section organizes the requirements according to the probable sequence of actions as a Responsible Agency administers the process. Public Resources Code Sections 21104 and 21153 as amended by Chapter 1514, Statutes of 1985 now limit comments by responsible and other public agencies to activities which fall in an area of expertise of the agency or which are required to be carried out or approved by the agency. Further, such comments must be supported by specific documentations. Corresponding Guideline section 15044 and this section have been amended to conform to the revised provisions of the Public Resources Code.

<u>15097</u>   **Mitigation Monitoring or Reporting**

(a) This section applies when a public agency has made the findings required under paragraph (1) of subdivision (a) of Section 15091 relative to an EIR or adopted a mitigated negative declaration in conjunction with approving a project. In order to ensure that the mitigation measures and project revisions identified in the EIR or negative declaration are implemented, the public agency shall adopt a program for monitoring or reporting on the revisions which it has required in the project and the measures it has imposed to mitigate or avoid significant environmental effects. A public agency may delegate reporting or monitoring responsibilities to another public agency or to a private entity which accepts the delegation; however, until mitigation measures have been completed the lead agency remains responsible for ensuring that implementation of the mitigation measures occurs in accordance with the program.

(b) Where the project at issue is the adoption of a general plan, specific plan, community plan or other plan-level document (zoning, ordinance, regulation, policy), the monitoring plan shall apply to policies and any other portion of the plan that is a mitigation measure or adopted alternative. The monitoring plan may consist of policies included in plan-level documents. The annual report on general plan status required pursuant to the Government Code is one example of a reporting program for adoption of a city or county general plan.

(c) The public agency may choose whether its program will monitor mitigation, report on mitigation, or both. "Reporting" generally consists of a written compliance review that is presented to the decision making body or authorized staff person. A report may be required at various stages during project implementation or upon completion of the mitigation measure. "Monitoring" is generally an ongoing or periodic process of project oversight. There is often no clear distinction between monitoring and reporting and the program best suited to ensuring compliance in any given instance will usually involve elements of both. The choice of program may be guided by the following:

(1) Reporting is suited to projects which have readily measurable or quantitative mitigation measures or which already involve regular review. For example, a report may be required upon issuance of final occupancy to a project whose mitigation measures were confirmed by building inspection.

(2) Monitoring is suited to projects with complex mitigation measures, such as wetlands restoration or archeological protection, which may exceed the expertise of the local agency to oversee, are expected to be implemented over a period of time, or require careful implementation to assure compliance.

(3) Reporting and monitoring are suited to all but the most simple projects. Monitoring ensures that project compliance is checked on a regular basis during and, if necessary, after, implementation. Reporting ensures that the approving agency is informed of compliance with mitigation requirements.

(d) Lead and responsible agencies should coordinate their mitigation monitoring or reporting programs where possible. Generally, lead and responsible agencies for a given project will adopt separate and different monitoring or reporting programs. This occurs because of any of the following reasons: the agencies have adopted and are responsible for reporting on or monitoring different mitigation measures; the agencies are deciding on the project at different times; each agency has the discretion to choose its own approach to monitoring or reporting; and each agency has its own special expertise.

(e) At its discretion, an agency may adopt standardized policies and requirements to guide individually adopted monitoring or reporting programs. Standardized policies and requirements may describe, but are not limited to:

(1) The relative responsibilities of various departments within the agency for various aspects of monitoring or reporting, including lead responsibility for administering typical programs and support responsibilities.

(2) The responsibilities of the project proponent.

(3) Agency guidelines for preparing monitoring or reporting programs.

(4) General standards for determining project compliance with the mitigation measures or revisions and related conditions of approval.

(5) Enforcement procedures for non-compliance, including provisions for administrative appeal.

(6) Process for informing staff and decision makers of the relative success of mitigation measures and using those results to improve future mitigation measures.

(f) Where a trustee agency, in timely commenting upon a draft EIR or a proposed mitigated negative declaration, proposes mitigation measures or project revisions for incorporation into a project, that agency, at the same time, shall prepare and submit to the lead or responsible agency a draft monitoring or reporting program for those measures or revisions. The lead or responsible agency may use this information in preparing its monitoring or reporting program.

(g) When a project is of statewide, regional, or areawide importance, any transportation information generated by a required monitoring or reporting program shall be submitted to the transportation planning agency in the region where the project is located. Each transportation planning agency shall adopt guidelines for the submittal of such information.

Note: Authority cited: Sections 21083 and 21087, Public Resources Code. References: Sections 21081.6 and 21081.7, Public Resources Code.

Discussion: This section reflects the mitigation monitoring and reporting program requirements of Public Resources Code section 21081.6. It offers suggestions for the content of such programs and recommends that lead and responsible agencies coordinate their programs to ensure that all mitigation measures that are to be implemented will be either monitored, reported on, or both.

15100   General

(a) Public agencies shall adopt time limits to govern their implementation of CEQA consistent with this article.

(b) Public agencies should carry out their responsibilities for preparing and reviewing EIRs within a reasonable period of time. The requirement for the preparation of an EIR should not cause undue delays in the processing of applications for permits or other entitlements to use.

Note: Authority cited: Sections 21083 and 21087, Public Resources Code. Reference: Sections 21000–21176, Public Resources Code.

Discussion: Subsection (a) identifies the requirements for state and local agencies to adopt time limits to implement CEQA. Adoption of these time limits is required by Sections 21100.2 and 21151.5. Requirements for specific time limits are scattered throughout the statute, so the citation of individual code sections in the note for this section would be so long as to be of little use. Where particular time limits are discussed in the later sections of this article, the specific statutory sections are referenced. Subsection (b) states the overriding policy consideration that applies throughout CEQA for agencies to carry out their responsibilities in an expeditious manner. This concern for expeditious processing was shown when the Legislature enacted Chapter 1200 of the statutes of 1977 (AB 884). That bill added many time limits to CEQA as well as providing time limits for the processing of development permits under the Government Code.

15101   Review of Application for Completeness

A lead agency or responsible agency shall determine whether an application for a permit or other entitlement for use is complete within 30 days from the receipt of the application except as provided in Section 15111. If no written determination of the completeness of the application is made within that period, the application will be deemed complete on the 30th day.

Note: Authority cited: Sections 21083 and 21087, Public Resources Code. Reference: Section 21083, Public Resources Code; Section 65943, Government Code.

Discussion: This section is necessary for coordinating the CEQA review of an application with the review of the application for completeness under other statutes. Government

Code Section 65943 requires an agency to rule on the completeness of an application within 30 days. Government Code Section 65950 provides that the CEQA time periods shall begin on the same date as the permit processing time limits under the Government Code.

15102 Initial Study

The lead agency shall determine within 30 days after accepting an application as complete whether it intends to prepare an EIR or a negative declaration or use a previously prepared EIR or negative declaration except as provided in Section 15111. The 30 day period may be extended 15 days upon the consent of the lead agency and the project applicant.

Note: Authority cited: Sections 21083 and 21087, Public Resources Code. Reference: Section 21080.2, Public Resources Code.

Discussion: This section identifies the statutory requirement for the Lead Agency to make a determination within 30 days as to whether it will prepare an EIR or a Negative Declaration for a project. This section also allows for a 15 day extension of the 30 day period upon consent of the lead agency and the project applicant. The requirement is inserted here in the interest of clarity and completeness of this article dealing with time limits. The section adds to the statutory provisions the possibility of using a previously prepared EIR or Negative Declaration as is allowed by the Guidelines.

Public Resources Code Section 21151.5 provides that if a draft EIR, EIR, or focused EIR is to be prepared under contract to a local agency, the contract shall be executed within 45 days from the date on which the agency releases a notice of preparation. This limit may be extended in the face of compelling circumstances, with the approval of the project applicant.

15103 Response to Notice of Preparation

Responsible agencies and trustee agencies shall provide a response to a notice of preparation to the lead agency within 30 days after receipt of the notice. If a responsible agency fails to reply within the 30 days with either a response or a well justified request for additional time, the lead agency may assume that the responsible agency has no response to make and may ignore a late response.

Note: Authority cited: Sections 21083 and 21087, Public Resources Code. Reference: Sections 21080.4, Public Resources Code.

Discussion: This section identifies the statutory requirement for Responsible Agencies and Trustee Agencies to respond to a Notice of Preparation within 30 days after receiving the notice. The time period is supplemented by an interpretation allowing the Lead Agency to disregard late responses. The sanction on disregarding late responses is necessary to provide meaning to the time limit.

15104 Convening of Meetings

The lead agency shall convene a meeting with agency representatives to discuss the scope and content of the environmental information a responsible agency will need in the EIR as soon as possible but no later than 30 days after receiving a request for the meeting. The meeting may be requested by the lead agency, a responsible agency, a trustee agency, or by the project applicant.

Note: Authority cited: Sections 21083 and 21087, Public Resources Code. Reference: Section 21080.4, Public Resources Code.

Discussion: This section identifies the requirement for convening a meeting to discuss the contents of a draft EIR being prepared by a Lead Agency where such a meeting has been requested. This requirement is also statutory. This requirement is presented in the Guidelines in the logical sequence with other time limits. In this way, people implementing the law are likely to be made aware of this requirement and comply with it.

15105 Public Review Period for a Draft EIR or a Proposed Negative Declaration or Mitigated Negative Declaration

(a) The public review period for a draft EIR ~~should~~ shall not be less than 30 days nor ~~should it be~~ longer than ~~90~~ 60 days except under unusual circumstances. When a draft EIR is submitted to the State Clearinghouse for review by state agencies, the public review period shall not be less than 45 days, unless a shorter period, not less than 30 days, is approved by the State Clearinghouse.

(b) The public review period for a proposed negative declaration or mitigated negative declaration shall be ~~a reasonable period of time sufficient to allow members of the public to respond to the proposed finding before the Negative Declaration is approved~~ not less than 20 days. When a proposed negative declaration or mitigated negative declaration is submitted to the State Clearinghouse for review by state agencies, the public review period shall not be less than 30 days, unless a shorter period, not less than 20 days, is approved by the State Clearinghouse.

(c) If a draft EIR or proposed negative declaration or mitigated negative declaration has been submitted to the State Clearinghouse for review by state agencies, the public review period shall be at least as long as the review period established by the State Clearinghouse.

(d) A shortened Clearinghouse review period may be granted in accordance with the provisions of Appendix L [4] and the following principles:

(1) A shortened review shall not be granted for any proposed project of statewide, areawide, or regional environmental significance.

(2) Requests for shortened review periods shall be submitted to the Clearinghouse in writing by the decision-making body of the lead agency, or a representative authorized by ordinance, resolution, or delegation of the decision-making body.

(3) The lead agency has contacted responsible and trustee agencies and they have agreed to the shortened review period.

Note: Authority cited: Sections 21083 and 21087, Public Resources Code. Reference: ~~Section~~ Sections 21091 and 21092, Public Resources Code; *People v. County of Kern* 39 Cal.App.3d 830.

Discussion: The discussion of public review period brings together requirements from a number of different articles in the Guidelines. Both this section and Section 15106 are purely regulatory in origin. They spell out the minimum and maximum review periods under CEQA as an effort to balance the ability of the public to respond within relatively short periods against the interests of applicants and public agencies in moving expeditiously in order to reach an ultimate decision on the project. This discussion applies equally to Section 15106.

Refer to the discussions under Sections 15073 and 15087 for the statutory requirements for minimum public review periods. With specific exceptions, the review period for an EIR shall be 45 days when submitted to the State Clearinghouse and 30 days when subject to local review only. The review period for a Negative Declaration shall be 30 days when submitted to the State Clearinghouse and 20 days otherwise, with certain exceptions. This section also specifies the circumstances under which OPR may grant a shortened review period for negative declarations and EIRs which are submitted to the State Clearinghouse.

15106 [Deleted]

15107 Completion of Negative Declaration for Certain Private Projects

With a ~~project~~ projects involving the issuance of a lease, permit, license, certificate, or other entitlement for use by one or more public agencies, the negative declaration must be completed and ~~ready for approval~~ approved within ~~105~~ 180 days from the date when the lead agency accepted the application as complete. ~~The negative declaration may be approved at a later time when the permit or other entitlement is approved.~~

Note: Authority cited: Sections 21083 and 21087, Public Resources Code. Reference: Sections 21100.2 and 21151.5, Public Resources Code.

Discussion: This section reflects the statutory requirement that a Negative Declaration be completed and adopted within 180 days of the day a private project is accepted as complete for processing. Under prior law, now repealed, the time frame for completion of a Negative Declaration was 105 days.

15108 Completion and Certification of EIR

With a private project, the lead agency shall complete and certify the final EIR as provided in Section 15090 within one year after the date when the lead agency accepted the application as complete. Lead agency procedures may provide that the one-year time limit may be extended once for a period of not more than 90 days upon consent of the lead agency and the applicant.

Note: Authority cited: Sections 21083 and 21087, Public Resources Code. Reference: Sections 21100.2 and 21151.5, Public Resources Code; Government Code Section 65950.

Discussion: This section identifies the requirement to complete and certify an EIR within one year from the date when the application is received as complete, and combines the statutory one-year time limit in CEQA with the requirement in the Government Code that the one year period be measured from the date on which the application is accepted as complete. Sections 21100.2 and 21151.5 of CEQA allow a reasonable extension to the one-year time limit with the consent of the applicant. Section 15108 adds the interpretation providing that this extension should not exceed 90 days. This interpretation is added to make the extension match the limit on the extension allowed for the one-year time limit for processing permits for development projects under Government Code Section 65957. Because most development projects will be subject to time limits under both the Government Code and CEQA, the

time limits should be as similar as possible to avoid conflicts and confusion.

15109 Suspension of Time Periods

An unreasonable delay by an applicant in meeting requests by the lead agency necessary for the preparation of a negative declaration or an EIR shall suspend the running of the time periods described in Sections 15107 and 15108 for the period of the unreasonable delay. Alternatively, an agency may disapprove a project application where there is unreasonable delay in meeting requests. The agency may allow a renewed application to start at the same point in the process where the application was when it was disapproved.

Note: Authority cited: Sections 21083 and 21087, Public Resources Code. Reference: Sections 21100.2 and 21151.5, Public Resources Code; *Carmel Valley View, Ltd. v. Maggini*, 91 Cal.App.3d 318.

Discussion: This section is an interpretation responding to the question of what happens to the Lead Agency's one-year time limit if the applicant unreasonably delays providing information that was requested by the Lead Agency. The problem of unreasonable delays has plagued many agencies and has led to disputes over whether a project has been approved by operation of law. The section is necessary to resolve the disputes and to avoid the need to litigate the same. This interpretation is consistent with the court decision in *Carmel Valley View, Ltd. v. Maggini*, cited in the note.

The section also identifies the option of disapproving the project in response to unreasonable delays. The section also validates the use of a "disapproval without prejudice" that is used by some agencies. This approach allows a new application for a disapproved project to start at the same point in the process where it was when disapproved. Following this approach, an agency can avoid the time and expense for early steps in the process that would not be necessary for a project that had been partially reviewed before.

15110 Projects with Federal Involvement

(a) At the request of an applicant, the lead agency may waive the one-year time limit for completing and certifying a final EIR or the 105-day period for completing a negative declaration if:

(1) The project will be subject to CEQA and to the National Environmental Policy Act,

(2) Additional time will be required to prepare a combined EIR-EIS or

combined negative declaration-finding of no significant impact as provided in Section 15221, and

(3) The time required to prepare the combined document will be shorter than the time required to prepare the documents separately.

(b) The time limits for taking final action on a permit for a development project may also be waived where a combined EIR-EIS will be prepared.

(c) The time limits for processing permits for development projects under Government Code Sections 65950–65960 shall not apply if federal statutes or regulations require time schedules which exceed the state time limits. In this event, any state agencies involved shall make a final decision on the project within the federal time limits.

Note: Authority cited: Sections 21083 and 21087, Public Resources Code. Reference: Sections 21083.6 and 21083.7, Public Resources Code; Sections 65951 and 65954, Government Code; Public Law 91-190 as amended, 42 U.S.C.A. 4321–4347.

Discussion: This section implements the statutory provision allowing a waiver of CEQA time limits where the project will be subject to NEPA as well as CEQA. The regulation supplements the statutory provision by applying this principle to situations where a Negative Declaration under CEQA is prepared jointly with a Finding of No Significant Impact under NEPA. This approach is consistent with the principle contained in the statutory section but applies in a situation not mentioned by the statute. The section adds a requirement that any state agency involved make a final decision on the project within the federal time limit if that period is longer than the state time limit. This provision is necessary to avoid an interpretation that would provide that no time limits would apply to a state agency at all under this section. The section follows the general policy of CEQA and the Government Code of requiring action on development projects to be completed within a definite period of time.

15111 Projects with Short Time Periods for Approval

(a) A few statutes or ordinances require agencies to make decisions on permits within time limits that are so short that review of the project under CEQA would be difficult. To enable the lead agency to comply with both the permit statute and CEQA, the Lead Agency shall deem an application for a project not received for filing under the permit statute or ordinance until such time as progress toward completing the environmental documentation required by CEQA is sufficient to enable the lead agency to finish the CEQA process within the short permit time limit. This section will apply where all of the following conditions are met:

(1) The enabling legislation for a program, other than Chapter 4.5 (commencing with Section 65920) of Division 1 of Title 7 of the Government Code, requires the lead agency to take action on an application within a specified period of time that is six months or less, and

(2) The enabling legislation provides that the project will become approved by operation of law if the lead agency fails to take any action within such specified time period, and

(3) The project involves the issuance of a lease, permit, license, certificate, or other entitlement for use.

(b) Examples of time periods subject to this section include, but are not limited to:

(1) ~~Action within 50 days on a tentative subdivision map for which an EIR is being or will be prepared pursuant to Article 2 (commencing with Section 66452) of Chapter 3, Division 2, Title 2 of the Government Code, but a negative declaration for a subdivision map must be completed within the 50-day period (see Government Code Section 66452.1(e)).~~

~~(2)~~ Action on a timber harvesting plan by the Director of Forestry within 15 days pursuant to Section 4582.7 of the Public Resources Code,

~~(3)~~(2) Action on a permit by the San Francisco Bay Conservation and Development Commission within 90 days pursuant to Section 66632(f) of the Government Code, and

~~(4)~~(3) Action on an oil and gas permit by the Division of Oil and Gas within 10 days pursuant to Sections 3203 and 3724 of the Public Resources Code.

(c) In any case described in this section, the environmental document shall be completed or certified and the decision on the <u>project</u> ~~application~~ shall be made within ~~one year from the date on which an application requesting approval of such project has been received and accepted as complete for CEQA processing by such agency~~ <u>the period established under the Permit Streamlining Act</u> <u>(Government Code Sections 65920, et seq.).</u> ~~This one year limit may be extended once for a period not to exceed 90 days upon consent of the public agency and the applicant.~~

Note: Authority cited: Sections 21083 and 21087, Public Resources Code. Reference: Sections 21100.2 and 21151.5, Public Resources Code; *N.R.D.C. v. Arcata National Corp.* <u>(1976)</u> 59 Cal.App.3d 959 ~~(1976)~~

Discussion: This section provides a way of reconciling the competing and apparently inconsistent demands of different statutes. The state court of appeal decision in *N.R.D.C. v. Arcata National Corporation*, cited in the note, approved the interpretation that allowed an agency to suspend the running of the shorter time limit until the CEQA process had been completed. This is the approach taken in this section. The section was developed in the interest of treating all laws as part of one large body of law which should be read consistently wherever possible. This approach allows the purposes to be served by all these different laws to be promoted rather than forcing an agency to choose which of several laws they will ignore in order to accomplish the requirements of others.

This section is designed to call for the maximum overlap between the CEQA process and the short permit time period rather than calling for the CEQA process to be completed before the short permit time period could begin. Under this approach, the Lead Agency would suspend the short permit time period and begin the CEQA process. When the Lead Agency was far enough along in the CEQA process that it could finish the CEQA process within the permit time period, the agency would start the clock for the permit time period and begin processing the permit. This way the last part of the CEQA process and the permit process would overlap as much as possible. This would save time for the permit applicant.

Subsection (c) is intended to place a maximum time limit on the special approach allowed in this section. It also seeks to avoid conflicts with the time limits for processing development projects under the Government Code by adopting the 90-day limit on a time extension that is contained in Government Code Section 65957. This provision is necessary to avoid a conflict with the time limit on processing development projects under the Government Code because most development projects are subject to both CEQA and the Government Code time limits. The time limits should be as similar as possible.

15112   Statutes of Limitations

(a) CEQA provides unusually short statutes of limitations on filing court challenges to the approval of projects under the act.

(b) The statute of limitations periods are not public review periods or waiting periods for the person whose project has been approved. The project sponsor may proceed to carry out the project as soon as the necessary permits have been granted. The statute of limitations cuts off the right of another person to file a court action challenging approval of the project after the specified time period has expired.

(c) The statute of limitations periods under CEQA are as follows:

(1) Where the public agency filed a notice of determination in compliance with Sections 15075 or 15094, 30 days after the filing of the notice and the posting on a list of such notices.

(2) Where the public agency filed a notice of exemption in compliance with Section 15062, 35 days after the filing of the notice and the posting on a list of such notices.

(3) Where a certified state regulatory agency files a notice of decision in compliance with Public Resources Code Section 21080.5(d)(2)(v), 30 days after the filing of the notice.

(4) Where the Secretary for Resources certifies a state environmental regulatory agency under Public Resources Code Section 21080.5, the certification may be challenged only during the 30 days following the certification decision.

(5) Where none of the other statute of limitations periods in this section apply, 180 days after either:

(A) The public agency's decision to carry out or approve the project, or

(B) Commencement of the project if the project is undertaken without a formal decision by the public agency.

Note: Authority cited: Sections 21083 and 21087, Public Resources Code. Reference: Sections 21167, 21167.3, and 21080.5, Public Resources Code; *Kriebel v. City Council*, 112 Cal.App.3d 693; *Citizens of Lake Murray Area Association v. City Council*, (1982) 129 Cal.App.3d 436.

Discussion: This section discusses the various statutes of limitations under CEQA. These periods are contained in Public Resources Code Sections 21080.5 and 21167. Subsection (b) explains that the statute of limitation period is not a public review period but is merely an unusually short period during which approved projects are subject to challenge by lawsuit. In the absence of a statute of limitations as specified in Sections 21080.5 and 21167, a longer period would apply. Amended Public Resources Code section 21167 (Chapter 1294, Statutes of 1994) provides that the time period during which to file an action or proceeding commences from the date that the public agency mails a written copy of the Notice of Determination to any person requesting a copy within the posting periods for that notice. This effectively extends the potential statute of limitations.

Subsection (c) reorganizes and simplifies the presentation of the statutes of limitations under CEQA and adds an administrative interpretation. The section responds to the problem that the statute does not address the situation where an agency prepared an EIR or Negative Declaration but neglected to file a Notice of Determination.

The court in *Concerned Citizens of Costa Mesa, Inc. v. 32nd District Agricultural Assoc.* (1986) 42 Cal.3d 929, permitted a challenge to an agency's compliance with CEQA to be filed beyond the strict statutory time limitations because the agency made substantial changes in a project after filing the final EIR and failed to file a subsequent/supplemental EIR which was needed under section 21166. In this instance, a 5000 fixed seat amphitheater on six acres of land with noise directed away from residential areas was changed to 7000 fixed seats on ten acres of land and the stage was relocated to face the single-family residences. Further, the noise mitigation measures contemplated by the EIR were not taken and the noise levels generated during performances exceeded the level allowed by county law. Plaintiffs had no notice of the changes and were not afforded a hearing to comment on them. Accordingly, the challenge was permitted to be filed within 180 days of the time the plaintiff knew or should have known that the project under way differed substantially from the one described in the EIR, i.e., the construction stage that provided sufficient insight to final configuration.

Article 9. Contents of Environmental Impact Reports Sections 15120 to 15132

15120   General

(a) Environmental Impact Reports shall contain the information outlined in this article, but the format of the document may be varied. Each element must be covered, and when these elements are not separated into distinct sections, the document shall state where in the document each element is discussed.

(b) The EIR may be prepared as a separate document, as part of a general plan, or as part of a project report. If prepared as a part of the project report, it must still contain one separate and distinguishable section providing either analysis of all the subjects required in an EIR or, as a minimum, a table showing where each of the subjects is discussed. When the lead agency is a state agency, the EIR shall be included as part of the regular project report if such a report is used in the agency's existing review and budgetary process.

(c) Draft EIRs shall contain the information required by Sections 15122 through 15131. Final EIRs shall contain the same information and the subjects described in Section 15132.

(d) No document prepared pursuant to this article that is available for public examination shall include a "trade secret" as defined in Section 6254.7 of the Government Code, information about the location of archaeological sites and sacred lands, or any other information that is subject to the disclosure restrictions of Section 6254 of the Government Code.

Note: Authority cited: Sections 21083 and 21087, Public Resources Code. Reference: Sections 21100, ~~and~~ 21105 and 21160, Public Resources Code.

Discussion: This section provides general information on the EIR document. The document may be prepared in a wide variety of formats so long as the essential elements of information are included. In order to promote public understanding of the document, the Guidelines require that when the required elements are not separated into distinct sections, the document must include a statement as to where each element is discussed.

Subsection (b) is also designed to allow Lead Agencies flexibility in preparing the document. This section provides that the EIR may be a separate document by itself, or the EIR may be included within another document. Where the EIR is included within another document, the EIR must be a distinguishable section of that larger document.

The flexibility allowed by this section enables Lead Agencies to achieve efficiencies in different situations. For example, where a Local Agency Formation Commission has prepared a large document analyzing the effects of a proposed annexation, the LAFCO may reduce its cost by including the EIR within the larger document. The decision in *Russian Hill Improvement Association v. Board of Permit Appeals,* (1974) 44 Cal. App.3d 158 ruled that the EIR must be a separate, distinguishable document rather than merely a collection of reports prepared for some other purpose. This section allows agencies to combine the EIR with other documents so long as the EIR is a separate identifiable entity that would meet the standards of the Russian Hill decision.

Subsection (c) highlights the differences in contents for draft EIRs and final EIRs. The Guidelines refer so often to draft or final EIRs that the contents should be identified in the introductory section in the article on EIR contents.

Subsection (d) clarifies that limitations on the disclosure of 'trade secret' and archaeological sites established by state law outside of CEQA also apply to environmental documents. Limiting disclosure of archaeological sites and sacred lands is particularly important in order to reduce the chances that they might be damaged or destroyed by collectors.

15121   Informational Document

(a) An EIR is an informational document which will inform public agency decisionmakers and the public generally of the significant environmental effect of a project, identify possible ways to minimize the significant effects, and describe reasonable alternatives to the project. The public agency shall consider the information in the EIR along with other information which may be presented to the agency.

(b) While the information in the EIR does not control the agency's ultimate discretion on the project, the agency must respond to each significant effect identified in the EIR by making findings under Section 15091 and if necessary by making a statement of overriding consideration under Section 15093.

(c) The information in an EIR may constitute substantial evidence in the record to support the agency's action on the project if its decision is later challenged in court.

Note: Authority cited: Sections 21083 and 21087, Public Resources Code. Reference: Section 21061, Public Resources Code; *Carmel Valley View, Ltd. v. Board of Supervisors,* (1976) 58 Cal.App.3d 817.

Discussion: This section describes the fundamental role played by the EIR in CEQA. This section makes the point that the EIR provides information to assist the agency in making decisions on the project but does not control the agency's exercise of discretion.

15122   Table of Contents or Index

An EIR shall contain at least a table of contents or an index to assist readers in finding the analysis of different subjects and issues.

Note: Authority cited: Sections 21083 and 21087, Public Resources Code. Reference: Section 21061, Public Resources Code.

Discussion: This section identifies the statutory requirement for an EIR to contain either a table of contents or an index. The requirement is included here in the article on EIR contents in the interest of clarity.

15123   Summary

(a) An EIR shall contain a brief summary of the proposed actions and its consequences. The language of the summary should be a clear and simple as reasonably practical.

(b) The summary shall identify:

(1) Each significant effect with proposed mitigation measures and alternatives that would reduce or avoid that effect;

(2) Areas of controversy known to the lead agency including issues raised by agencies and the public; and

(3) Issues to be resolved including the choice among alternatives and whether or how to mitigate the significant effects.

(c) The summary should normally not exceed 15 pages.

Note: Authority cited: Sections 21083 and 21087, Public Resources Code. Reference: Section 21061, Public Resources Code.

Discussion: This section identifies the statutory requirement for an EIR to contain a summary. The section then provides additional regulatory requirements for the summary. This section requires the summary to focus on the major areas of importance to decision-makers and to use clear, simple language to promote understanding. The section suggests a 15-page limit to the summary.

15124   Project Description

The description of the project shall contain the following information but should not supply extensive detail beyond that needed for evaluation and review of the environmental impact.

(a) The precise location and boundaries of the proposed project shall be shown on a detailed map, preferably topographic.

The location of the project shall also appear on a regional map.

(b) A statement of objectives sought by the proposed project. A clearly written statement of objectives will help the lead agency develop a reasonable range of alternatives to evaluate in the EIR and will aid the decision makers in preparing findings or a statement of overriding considerations, if necessary. The statement of objectives should include the underlying purpose of the project.

(c) A general description of the project's technical, economic, and environmental characteristics, considering the principal engineering proposals if any and supporting public service facilities.

(d) A statement briefly describing the intended uses of the EIR.

(1) This statement shall include, to the extent that the information is known to the lead agency,

(A) A list of the agencies that are expected to use the EIR in their decision-making, and

(B) A list of permits and other ~~the~~ approvals required to implement the project ~~for which the EIR will be used~~.

(C) A list of related environmental review and consultation requirements required by federal, state, or local laws, regulations, or policies. To the fullest extent possible, the lead agency should integrate CEQA review with these related environmental review and consultation requirements.

(2) If a public agency must make more than one decision on a project, all its decisions subject to CEQA should be listed, preferably in the order in which they will occur. On request, the Office of Planning and Research will provide assistance in identifying state permits for a project.

Note: Authority cited: Sections 21083 and 21087, Public Resources Code. Reference: Sections 21080.3, 21080.4, 21165, 21166, and 21167.2, Public Resources Code; *County of Inyo v. City of Los Angeles* (1977) 71 Cal.App.3d 185 ~~(1977)~~.

Discussion: This section requires the EIR to describe the proposed project in a way that will be meaningful to the public, to the other reviewing agencies, and to the decision-makers. Although the statute contains no express requirement for an EIR to contain a project description, the statutory points of analysis need to be supplemented with a project description for the analysis to

make sense. This section is a codification of the ruling in *County of Inyo v. City of Los Angeles*, cited in the note. There the court noted that an accurate description of the project has been required by case law interpreting the National Environmental Policy Act. The state court of appeal declared that an accurate, stable, finite project description is an essential element of an informative and legally sufficient EIR under CEQA.

Subsection (b) emphasizes the importance of a clearly written statement of objectives. Compatibility with project objectives is one of the criteria for selecting a reasonable range of project alternatives. Clear project objectives simplify the selection process by providing a standard against which to measure possible alternatives.

Subsection (d) calls for a brief statement of how the Lead Agency and any Responsible Agencies will use the EIR in their approval or permitting processes. This is necessary to make the EIR fit the Lead Agency concept which requires all permitting agencies to use the same EIR. In addition, it encourages the lead agency to consult with other agencies and to integrate CEQA review with other related environmental reviews. This advances Public Resources Code section 21003 which provides that, to the extent possible, CEQA is to be applied concurrently with other review processes.

15125   Environmental Setting

(a) An EIR must include a description of the physical environmental conditions in the vicinity of the project, as ~~it exists~~ they exist ~~before the commencement of the project~~ at the time the notice of preparation is published, or if no notice of preparation is published, at the time environmental analysis is commenced, from both a local and regional perspective. This environmental setting will normally constitute the baseline physical conditions by which a lead agency determines whether an impact is significant. The description of the environmental setting shall be no longer than is necessary to an understanding of the significant effects of the proposed project and its alternatives.

(b) When preparing an EIR for a plan for the reuse of a military base, lead agencies should refer to the special application of the principle of baseline conditions for determining significant impacts contained in Section 15229.

(~~a~~ c) Knowledge of the regional setting is critical to the assessment of environmental impacts. Special emphasis should be placed on environmental resources that are rare or unique to that region and would be affected by the project. The EIR must demonstrate that the significant environmental impacts of the proposed project were adequately investigated and discussed and it must permit the significant effects of the project to be considered in the full environmental context.

(b d) The EIR shall discuss any inconsistencies between the proposed project and applicable general plans and regional plans. Such regional plans include, but are not limited to, the applicable air quality attainment or maintenance plan Air Quality Management Plan (or State Implementation Plan once adopted) , area-wide waste treatment and water quality control plans, regional transportation plans, regional housing allocation plans, habitat conservation plans, natural community conservation plans and regional land use plans for the protection of the coastal zone, Lake Tahoe Basin, San Francisco Bay, and Santa Monica Mountains.

(e e) Where a proposed project is compared with an adopted plan, the analysis shall examine the existing physical conditions at the time the notice of preparation is published, or if no notice of preparation is published, at the time environmental analysis is commenced as well as the potential future conditions discussed in the plan.

Note: Authority cited: Sections 21083 and 21087, Public Resources Code. Reference: Sections 21061 and 21100, Public Resources Code; *E.P.I.C. v. County of El Dorado* (1982) 131 Cal.App.3d 350; *San Joaquin Raptor/Wildlife Rescue Center v. County of Stanislaus* (1994) 27 Cal.App.4th 713; *Bloom v. McGurk* (1994) 26 Cal.App. 4th 1307.

Discussion: Because the concept of a significant effect on the environment focuses on changes in the environment, this section requires an EIR to describe the environmental setting of the project so that the changes can be seen in context. The description of the pre-existing environment also helps reviewers to check the Lead Agency's identification of significant effects. A number of agencies have been required to spend large amounts of public funds to develop regional plans as a way of dealing with large-scale environmental problems involving air and water pollution, solid waste, and transportation. Where individual projects would run counter to the efforts identified as desirable or approved by agencies in the regional plans, the Lead Agency should address the

inconsistency between the project plans and the regional plans. As a result of this analysis, Lead Agencies may be able to find ways to modify the project to reduce the inconsistency.

Subsection (a) clarifies that the 'environmental setting' is intended to mean the environmental conditions as they exist at the time the Notice of Preparation is filed. This gives the lead agency greater certainty regarding the setting which must be described. The subsection goes on to provide that normally the environmental setting describes the baseline conditions against which the significance of any physical change in the environment that may occur as a result of the project will be measured.

Regarding subsection (c), in *Antioch v. Pittsburg* (1986) 187 Cal.App.3d 1325, the court underscored that mere conformity with a general plan (in and of itself) will not justify a finding that the project has no significant environmental effects. In the instant case, a developer sought a site development permit from the City of Pittsburg and the initiation of an assessment district for the construction of major infrastructure for three parcels of land. Although consistent with the general plan, the court found the project level environmental review to be inadequate and ordered an EIR prepared. Subsection (c) further emphasizes the importance of examining the project in its regional context. This is intended to ensure that the environmental setting is comprehensively described.

Subsection (d) reflects the decision in *Environmental Information and Planning Council v. County of El Dorado* (1982) 131 Cal.App.3d 350, which held that in comparing an old general plan with a new county general plan that would allow less growth than the old plan, the EIR had to address the existing level of actual physical development in the county as the base line for the comparison. The two plans could not be compared with each other without showing how they would relate to the existing level of development.

15126 Consideration and Discussion of Environmental Impacts

All phases of a project must be considered when evaluating its impact on the environment: planning, acquisition, development, and operation. The following subjects listed below shall be discussed as directed in Sections 15126.2, 15126.4 and 15126.6, preferably in separate sections or paragraphs of the EIR. If they are not discussed separately, the EIR shall include a table showing where each of the subjects is discussed.

(a) Significant Environmental Effects of the Proposed Project.

(b) Significant Environmental Effects Which Cannot be Avoided if the Proposed Project is Implemented.

(c) Significant Irreversible Environmental Changes Which Would be Involved in the Proposed Project Should it be Implemented.

(d) Growth-Inducing Impact of the (Proposed Project.

(e) The Mitigation Measures Proposed to Minimize the Significant Effects.

(f) Alternatives to the Proposed Project.

(A) The Significant Environmental Effects of the Proposed Project. An EIR shall identify and focus on the significant environmental effects of the proposed project. Direct and indirect significant effects of the project on the environment shall be clearly identified and described, giving due consideration to both the short-term and long-term effects. The discussion should include relevant specifics of the area, the resources involved, physical changes, alterations to ecological systems, and changes induced in population distribution, population concentration, the human use of the land (including commercial and residential development), health and safety problems caused by the physical changes, and other aspects of the resource base such as water, scenic quality, and public services. The EIR shall also analyze any significant environmental effects the project might cause by bringing development and people into the area affected. For example, an EIR on a subdivision astride an active fault line should identify as a significant effect the seismic hazard to future occupants of the subdivision. The subdivision would have the effect of attracting people to the location and exposing them to the hazards found there.

(b) Any Significant Environmental Effects Which Cannot be Avoided if the Proposal is Implemented. Describe any significant impacts, including those which can be mitigated but not reduced to a level of insignificance. Where there are impacts that cannot be alleviated without imposing an alternative design, their implications and the reasons why the project is being proposed, notwithstanding their effect, should be described.

(c) Mitigation Measures Proposed to Minimize the Significant Effects. Describe measures which could minimize significant adverse impacts, including where relevant, inefficient and unnecessary consumption of energy. The discussion of mitigation measures shall distinguish between the measures which are proposed by project proponents to be included in the project and other measures that are not included but could reasonably be expected to reduce adverse impacts if required as conditions of approving the project. This discussion shall identify mitigation measures for each significant environmental effect identified in the EIR. Where several measures are available to mitigate an impact, each should be discussed and the basis for selecting a particular measure should be identified if one has been selected. Energy conservation measures, as well as other appropriate mitigation measures, shall be discussed when relevant. Examples of energy conservation measures are provided in Appendix F. If a mitigation measure would cause one or more significant effects in addition to those that would be caused by the project as proposed, the effects of the mitigation measure shall be discussed but in less detail than the significant effects of the project as proposed. (Stevens v. City of Glendale, 125 Cal.App.3d 986.)

(d) Alternatives to the Proposed Action. Describe a range of reasonable alternatives to the project, or to the location of the project, which would feasibly attain most of the basic objectives of the project but would avoid or substantially lessen any of the significant effects of the project, and evaluate the comparative merits of the alternatives.

(1) Purpose. Because an EIR must identify ways to mitigate or avoid the significant effects that a project may have on the environment (Public Resources Code Section 21002.1), the discussion of alternatives shall focus on alternatives to the project or its location which are capable of avoiding or substantially lessening any significant effects of the project, even if these alternatives would impede to some degree the attainment of the project objectives, or would be more costly.

(2) Selection of a range of reasonable alternatives. The range of potential alternatives to the proposed project shall include those that could feasibly accomplish most of the basic purposes of the project and could avoid or substantially lessen one or more of the significant effects. The EIR should briefly describe the

rationale for selecting the alternatives to be discussed. The EIR should also identify any alternatives that were considered by the lead agency but were rejected as infeasible during the scoping process and briefly explain the reasons underlying the lead agency's determination. Additional information explaining the choice of alternatives may be included in the administrative record.

(3) Evaluation of alternatives. The EIR shall include sufficient information about each alternative to allow meaningful evaluation, analysis, and comparison with the proposed project. A matrix displaying the major characteristics and significant environmental effect of each alternative may be used to summarize the comparison. If an alternative would cause one or more significant effects in addition to those that would be caused by the project as proposed, the significant effects of the alternative shall be discussed, but in less detail than the significant effects of the project as proposed. (County of Inyo v. City of Los Angeles, 124 Cal.App.3d 1)

(4) "No project" alternative. The specific alternative of "no project" shall also be evaluated along with its impact. The "no project" analysis shall discuss the existing conditions, as well as what would be reasonably expected to occur in the foreseeable future if the project were not approved, based on current plans and consistent with available infrastructure and community services. If the environmentally superior alternative is the "no project" alternative, the EIR shall also identify an environmentally superior alternative among the other alternatives.

(5) Rule of reason. The range of alternatives required in an EIR is governed by a "rule of reason" that requires the EIR to set forth only those alternatives necessary to permit a reasoned choice. The alternatives shall be limited to ones that would avoid or substantially lessen any of the significant effects of the project. of those alternatives, the EIR need examine in detail only the ones that the lead agency determines could feasibly attain most of the basic objectives of the project. The range of feasible alternatives shall be selected and discussed in a manner to foster

meaningful public participation and informed decision-making.

(A) Feasibility. Among the factors that may be taken into account when addressing the feasibility of alternatives are site suitability, economic viability, availability of infrastructure, general plan consistency, other plans or regulatory limitations, jurisdictional boundaries (projects with a regionally significant impact should consider the regional context), and whether the proponent can reasonably acquire, control or otherwise have access to the alternative site (or the site is already owned by the proponent). No one of these factors establishes a fixed limit on the scope of reasonable alternatives. (Citizens of Goleta Valley v. Board of Supervisors, (1990) 52 Cal.3d 553; see Save Our Residential Environment v. City of West Hollywood, (1992) 9 Cal.App.4th 1745, 1753, fn. 1).

(B) Alternative locations.

1. Key question. The key question and first step in analysis is whether any of the significant effects of the project would be avoided or substantially lessened by putting the project in another location. Only locations that would avoid or substantially lessen any of the significant effects of the project need be considered for inclusion in the EIR.

2. None feasible. If the lead agency concludes that no feasible alternative locations exist, it must disclose the reasons for this conclusion, and should include the reasons in the EIR. For example, in some cases there may be no feasible alternative locations for a geothermal plant or mining project which must be close proximity to natural resources at a given location.

3. Limited new analysis required. Where a previous document has sufficiently analyzed a range of reasonable alternative locations and environmental impacts for projects with the same

basic purpose, the lead agency should review the previous document. The EIR may rely on the previous document to help it assess the feasibility of potential project alternatives to the extent the circumstances remain substantially the same as they relate to the alternative. (Citizens of Goleta Valley v. Board of Supervisors, (1990) 52 Cal.3d 553, 573).

(C) An EIR need not consider an alternative whose effect cannot be reasonably ascertained and whose implementation is remote and speculative. (Residents Ad Hoc Stadium Committee v. Board of Trustees, (1979) 89 Cal.App. 3d 274).

(e) The Relationship Between Local Short-Term Uses of Man's Environment and the Maintenance and Enhancement of Long-Term Productivity. Describe the cumulative and long-term effects of the proposed project which adversely affect the state of the environment. Special attention should be given to impacts which narrow the range of beneficial uses of the environment or pose long-term risks to health or safety. In addition, the reasons why the proposed project is believed by the sponsor to be justified now, rather than reserving an option for further alternatives, should be explained.

(f) Any Significant Irreversible Environmental Changes Which Would be Involved in the Proposed Action Should it be Implemented. Uses of nonrenewable resources during the initial and continued phases of the project may be irreversible since a large commitment of such resources makes removal or nonuse thereafter unlikely. Primary impacts and, particularly, secondary impacts (such as highway improvement which provides access to a previously inaccessible area) generally commit future generations to similar uses. Also irreversible damage can result from environmental accidents associated with the project. Irretrievable commitments of resources should be evaluated to assure that such current consumption is justified.

(g) The Growth-Inducing Impact of the Proposed Action. Discuss the ways in which the proposed project could foster economic or population growth, or the construction of additional housing, either directly or indirectly, in the

surrounding environment. Included in this are projects which would remove obstacles to population growth (a major expansion of a waste water treatment plant might, for example, allow for more construction in service areas). Increases in the population may further tax existing community service facilities so consideration must be given to this impact. Also discuss the characteristic of some projects which may encourage and facilitate other activities that could significantly affect the environment, either individually or cumulatively. It must not be assumed that growth in any area is necessarily beneficial, detrimental, or of little significance to the environment.

Note: Authority cited: Sections 21083 and 21087, Public Resources Code. Reference: ~~Section~~ Sections 21002, 21003, 21100, and 21081.6, Public Resources Code; *Citizens of Goleta Valley v. Board of Supervisors* (1990) 52 Cal.3d 553 ~~(1990)~~; *Laurel Heights Improvement Association v. Regents of the University of California* (1988) 47 Cal.3d 376 ~~(1988)~~; *Gentry v. City of Murrieta* (1995) 36 Cal.App.4th 1359; and *Laurel Heights Improvement Association v. Regents of the University of California* (1993) 6 Cal.4th 1112.

Discussion: This section specifies that an EIR must discuss, preferably separately, a project's significant environmental effects, mitigation measures, and a range of alternatives. The 1998 amendments to the Guidelines moved the comprehensive discussion of each of these EIR components, which once resided in section 15126, into sections 15126.2, 15126.4, and 15126.6, respectively.

15126.2 Consideration and Discussion of Significant Environmental Impacts

(a) The Significant Environmental Effects of the Proposed Project. An EIR shall identify and focus on the significant environmental effects of the proposed project. In assessing the impact of a proposed project on the environment, the lead agency should normally limit its examination to changes in the existing physical conditions in the affected area as they exist at the time the notice of preparation is published, or where no notice of preparation is published, at the time environmental analysis is commenced. Direct and indirect significant effects of the project on the environment shall be clearly identified and described, giving due consideration to both the short-term and long-term effects. The discussion should include relevant specifics of the area, the resources involved,

physical changes, alterations to ecological systems, and changes induced in population distribution, population concentration, the human use of the land (including commercial and residential development), health and safety problems caused by the physical changes, and other aspects of the resource base such as water, historical resources, scenic quality, and public services. The EIR shall also analyze any significant environmental effects the project might cause by bringing development and people into the area affected. For example, an EIR on a subdivision astride an active fault line should identify as a significant effect the seismic hazard to future occupants of the subdivision. The subdivision would have the effect of attracting people to the location and exposing them to the hazards found there.

(b) Significant Environmental Effects Which Cannot be Avoided if the Proposed Project is Implemented. Describe any significant impacts, including those which can be mitigated but not reduced to a level of insignificance. Where there are impacts that cannot be alleviated without imposing an alternative design, their implications and the reasons why the project is being proposed, notwithstanding their effect, should be described.

(c) Significant Irreversible Environmental Changes Which Would be Caused by the Proposed Project Should it be Implemented. Uses of nonrenewable resources during the initial and continued phases of the project may be irreversible since a large commitment of such resources makes removal or nonuse thereafter unlikely. Primary impacts and, particularly, secondary impacts (such as highway improvement which provides access to a previously inaccessible area) generally commit future generations to similar uses. Also irreversible damage can result from environmental accidents associated with the project. Irretrievable commitments of resources should be evaluated to assure that such current consumption is justified.

(d) Growth-Inducing Impact of the Proposed Project. Discuss the ways in which the proposed project could foster economic or population growth, or the construction of additional housing, either directly or indirectly, in the surrounding environment. Included in this are projects which would remove obstacles to population growth (a major expansion of a waste water treatment plant might, for example, allow for more construction in service areas). Increases in the population may tax existing community service facilities, requiring construction of new facilities that could cause significant environmental effects. Also discuss the characteristic of some projects which may encourage and facilitate other activities that could significantly affect the environment, either individually or cumulatively. It must not be assumed that growth in any area is necessarily beneficial, detrimental, or of little significance to the environment.

Note: Authority cited: Sections 21083 and 21087, Public Resources Code. Reference: Sections 21002, 21003, and 21100, Public Resources Code; *Citizens of Goleta Valley v. Board of Supervisors*, (1990) 52 Cal.3d 553; *Laurel Heights Improvement Association v. Regents of the University of California*, (1988) 47 Cal.3d 376; *Gentry v. City of Murrieta* (1995) 36 Cal.App.4th 1359; and *Laurel Heights Improvement Association v. Regents of the University of California* (1993) 6 Cal.4th 1112; *Goleta Union School Dist. v. Regents of the Univ. of Calif* (1995) 37 Cal.App.4th 1025.

Discussion: This section describes how an EIR must identify and focus on the significant environmental effects, unavoidable significant environmental effects, significant irreversible environmental changes, and growth-inducing impacts which may result from a project. Subsection (a) reiterates the baseline discussion contained in section 15125. Subsection (d), discussing growth-inducing impacts, clarifies that the construction of new facilities may be important because that construction itself may have significant effects.

15126.4 Consideration and Discussion of Mitigation Measures Proposed to Minimize Significant Effects

(a) Mitigation Measures in General.

(1) An EIR shall describe feasible measures which could minimize significant adverse impacts, including where relevant, inefficient and unnecessary consumption of energy.

(A) The discussion of mitigation measures shall distinguish between the measures which are proposed by project proponents to be included in the project and other measures proposed by the lead, responsible or trustee agency or other persons which are not included but the lead agency determines could reasonably be expected to reduce adverse impacts if required as conditions of

approving the project. This discussion shall identify mitigation measures for each significant environmental effect identified in the EIR.

(B) Where several measures are available to mitigate an impact, each should be discussed and the basis for selecting a particular measure should be identified. Formulation of mitigation measures should not be deferred until some future time. However, measures may specify performance standards which would mitigate the significant effect of the project and which may be accomplished in more than one specified way.

(C) Energy conservation measures, as well as other appropriate mitigation measures, shall be discussed when relevant. Examples of energy conservation measures are provided in Appendix F.

(D) If a mitigation measure would cause one or more significant effects in addition to those that would be caused by the project as proposed, the effects of the mitigation measure shall be discussed but in less detail than the significant effects of the project as proposed. (*Stevens v. City of Glendale*(1981) 125 Cal.App.3d 986.)

(2) Mitigation measures must be fully enforceable through permit conditions, agreements, or other legally-binding instruments. In the case of the adoption of a plan, policy, regulation, or other public project, mitigation measures can be incorporated into the plan, policy, regulation, or project design.

(3) Mitigation measures are not required for effects which are not found to be significant.

(4) Mitigation measures must be consistent with all applicable constitutional requirements, including the following:

(A) There must be an essential nexus (i.e. connection) between the mitigation measure and a legitimate governmental interest. *Nollan v. California Coastal Commission*, 483 U.S. 825 (1987); and

(B) The mitigation measure must be "roughly proportional" to the impacts of the project. *Dolan v.*

City of Tigard, 512 U.S. 374 (1994). Where the mitigation measure is an ad hoc exaction, it must be "roughly proportional" to the impacts of the project. *Ehrlich v. City of Culver City* (1996) 12 Cal.4th 854.

(5) If the lead agency determines that a mitigation measure cannot be legally imposed, the measure need not be proposed or analyzed. Instead, the EIR may simply reference that fact and briefly explain the reasons underlying the lead agency's determination.

(b) Mitigation Measures Related to Impacts on Historical Resources.

(1) Where maintenance, repair, stabilization, rehabilitation, restoration, preservation, conservation or reconstruction of the historical resource will be conducted in a manner consistent with the Secretary of the Interior's Standards for the Treatment of Historic Properties with Guidelines for Preserving, Rehabilitating, Restoring, and Reconstructing Historic Buildings (1995), Weeks and Grimmer, the project's impact on the historical resource shall generally be considered mitigated below a level of significance and thus is not significant.

(2) In some circumstances, documentation of an historical resource, by way of historic narrative, photographs or architectural drawings, as mitigation for the effects of demolition of the resource will not mitigate the effects to a point where clearly no significant effect on the environment would occur.

(3) Public agencies should, whenever feasible, seek to avoid damaging effects on any historical resource of an archaeological nature. The following factors shall be considered and discussed in an EIR for a project involving such an archaeological site:

(A) Preservation in place is the preferred manner of mitigating impacts to archaeological sites. Preservation in place maintains the relationship between artifacts and the archaeological context. Preservation may also avoid conflict with religious or cultural values of groups associated with the site.

(B) Preservation in place may be accomplished by, but is not limited to, the following:

1. Planning construction to avoid archaeological sites;

2. Incorporation of sites within parks, greenspace, or other open space;

3. Covering the archaeological sites with a layer of chemically stable soil before building tennis courts, parking lots, or similar facilities on the site.

4. Deeding the site into a permanent conservation easement.

(C) When data recovery through excavation is the only feasible mitigation, a data recovery plan, which makes provision for adequately recovering the scientifically consequential information from and about the historical resource, shall be prepared and adopted prior to any excavation being undertaken. Such studies shall be deposited with the California Historical Resources Regional Information Center. Archaeological sites known to contain human remains shall be treated in accordance with the provisions of Section 7050.5 Health and Safety Code.

(D) Data recovery shall not be required for an historical resource if the lead agency determines that testing or studies already completed have adequately recovered the scientifically consequential information from and about the archaeological or historical resource, provided that the determination is documented in the EIR and that the studies are deposited with the California Historical Resources Regional Information Center.

Note: Authority cited: Sections 21083 and 21087, Public Resources Code. Reference: Sections 21002, 21003, 21100, and 21084.1, Public Resources Code; *Citizens of Goleta Valley v. Board of Supervisors*, (1990) 52 Cal.3d 553; *Laurel Heights Improvement Association v. Regents of the University of California*, (1988) 47 Cal.3d 376; *Gentry v. City of Murrieta* (1995) 36 Cal.App.4th 1359; and *Laurel Heights Improvement Association v. Regents of the University of California* (1993) 6 Cal.4th 1112; *Sacramento Old City Assn. v. City Council of Sacramento* (1991) 229 Cal.App.3d 1011.

Discussion: This section describes the requirements for and selection of feasible mitigation measures. Subsection (a) reminds EIR

preparers that the formulation of mitigation measures should not be deferred to a later time, but that mitigation measures may specify performance standards that will result in mitigation and may be undertaken in more than one way. Subsection (a) specifies that measures must be fully enforceable through permit conditions or other requirements. It also offers a reminder that mitigation measures can be subject to Constitutional 'takings' principles. Further, it clarifies that mitigation measures are not required for impacts which are not significant.

Subsection (b) describes how impacts to historical resources may be mitigated. It provides that compliance with federal standards for the treatment of historic properties will generally avoid a significant effect on the resource. It also clarifies that where a historic resource is to be demolished, documentation of the resource usually falls short of full mitigation. In addition, subsection (b) describes the factors to be considered and discussed in an EIR for a project involving an archaeological site.

15126.6 Consideration and Discussion of Alternatives to the Proposed Project

(a) Alternatives to the Proposed Project. An EIR shall describe a range of reasonable alternatives to the project, or to the location of the project, which would feasibly attain most of the basic objectives of the project but would avoid or substantially lessen any of the significant effects of the project, and evaluate the comparative merits of the alternatives. An EIR need not consider every conceivable alternative to a project. Rather it must consider a reasonable range of potentially feasible alternatives that will foster informed decisionmaking and public participation. An EIR is not required to consider alternatives which are infeasible. The lead agency is responsible for selecting a range of project alternatives for examination and must publicly disclose its reasoning for selecting those alternatives. There is no ironclad rule governing the nature or scope of the alternatives to be discussed other than the rule of reason. (*Citizens of Goleta Valley v. Board of Supervisors* (1990) 52 Cal.3d 553 and *Laurel Heights Improvement Association v. Regents of the University of California* (1988) 47 Cal.3d 376).

(b) Purpose. Because an EIR must identify ways to mitigate or avoid the significant effects that a project may have on the environment (Public Resources Code Section 21002.1), the discussion of alternatives shall focus on alternatives to the

project or its location which are capable of avoiding or substantially lessening any significant effects of the project, even if these alternatives would impede to some degree the attainment of the project objectives, or would be more costly.

(c) Selection of a range of reasonable alternatives. The range of potential alternatives to the proposed project shall include those that could feasibly accomplish most of the basic objectives of the project and could avoid or substantially lessen one or more of the significant effects. The EIR should briefly describe the rationale for selecting the alternatives to be discussed. The EIR should also identify any alternatives that were considered by the lead agency but were rejected as infeasible during the scoping process and briefly explain the reasons underlying the lead agency's determination. Additional information explaining the choice of alternatives may be included in the administrative record. Among the factors that may be used to eliminate alternatives from detailed consideration in an EIR are:(i) failure to meet most of the basic project objectives, (ii) infeasibility, or (iii) inability to avoid significant environmental impacts.

(d) Evaluation of alternatives. The EIR shall include sufficient information about each alternative to allow meaningful evaluation, analysis, and comparison with the proposed project. A matrix displaying the major characteristics and significant environmental effects of each alternative may be used to summarize the comparison. If an alternative would cause one or more significant effects in addition to those that would be caused by the project as proposed, the significant effects of the alternative shall be discussed, but in less detail than the significant effects of the project as proposed. (*County of Inyo v. City of Los Angeles* (1981) 124 Cal.App.3d 1).

(e) "No project" alternative.

(1) The specific alternative of "no project" shall also be evaluated along with its impact. The purpose of describing and analyzing a no project alternative is to allow decisionmakers to compare the impacts of approving the proposed project with the impacts of not approving the proposed project. The no project alternative analysis is not the baseline for determining whether the proposed project's environmental impacts may be significant, unless it is

identical to the existing environmental setting analysis which does establish that baseline (see Section 15125).

(2) The "no project" analysis shall discuss the existing conditions at the time the notice of preparation is published, or if no notice of preparation is published, at the time environmental analysis is commenced, as well as what would be reasonably expected to occur in the foreseeable future if the project were not approved, based on current plans and consistent with available infrastructure and community services. If the environmentally superior alternative is the "no project" alternative, the EIR shall also identify an environmentally superior alternative among the other alternatives.

(3) A discussion of the "no project" alternative will usually proceed along one of two lines:

(A) When the project is the revision of an existing land use or regulatory plan, policy or ongoing operation, the "no project" alternative will be the continuation of the existing plan, policy or operation into the future. Typically this is a situation where other projects initiated under the existing plan will continue while the new plan is developed. Thus, the projected impacts of the proposed plan or alternative plans would be compared to the impacts that would occur under the existing plan.

(B) If the project is other than a land use or regulatory plan, for example a development project on identifiable property, the "no project" alternative is the circumstance under which the project does not proceed. Here the discussion would compare the environmental effects of the property remaining in its existing state against environmental effects which would occur if the project is approved. If disapproval of the project under consideration would result in predictable actions by others, such as the proposal of some other project, this "no project" consequence should be discussed. In certain instances, the no project alternative means "no build" wherein the existing environmental

setting is maintained. However, where failure to proceed with the project will not result in preservation of existing environmental conditions, the analysis should identify the practical result of the project's non-approval and not create and analyze a set of artificial assumptions that would be required to preserve the existing physical environment.

(C) After defining the no project alternative using one of these approaches, the lead agency should proceed to analyze the impacts of the no project alternative by projecting what would reasonably be expected to occur in the foreseeable future if the project were not approved, based on current plans and consistent with available infrastructure and community services.

(f) Rule of reason. The range of alternatives required in an EIR is governed by a "rule of reason" that requires the EIR to set forth only those alternatives necessary to permit a reasoned choice. The alternatives shall be limited to ones that would avoid or substantially lessen any of the significant effects of the project. Of those alternatives, the EIR need examine in detail only the ones that the lead agency determines could feasibly attain most of the basic objectives of the project. The range of feasible alternatives shall be selected and discussed in a manner to foster meaningful public participation and informed decision making.

(1) Feasibility. Among the factors that may be taken into account when addressing the feasibility of alternatives are site suitability, economic viability, availability of infrastructure, general plan consistency, other plans or regulatory limitations, jurisdictional boundaries (projects with a regionally significant impact should consider the regional context), and whether the proponent can reasonably acquire, control or otherwise have access to the alternative site (or the site is already owned by the proponent). No one of these factors establishes a fixed limit on the scope of reasonable alternatives. (*Citizens of Goleta Valley v. Board of Supervisors* (1990) 52 Cal.3d 553; see *Save Our Residential Environment v. City of West Hollywood* (1992) 9 Cal.App.4th 1745, 1753, fn. 1).

(2) Alternative locations.

(A) Key question. The key question and first step in analysis is whether any of the significant effects of the project would be avoided or substantially lessened by putting the project in another location. Only locations that would avoid or substantially lessen any of the significant effects of the project need be considered for inclusion in the EIR.

(B) None feasible. If the lead agency concludes that no feasible alternative locations exist, it must disclose the reasons for this conclusion, and should include the reasons in the EIR. For example, in some cases there may be no feasible alternative locations for a geothermal plant or mining project which must be in close proximity to natural resources at a given location.

(C) Limited new analysis required. Where a previous document has sufficiently analyzed a range of reasonable alternative locations and environmental impacts for projects with the same basic purpose, the lead agency should review the previous document. The EIR may rely on the previous document to help it assess the feasibility of potential project alternatives to the extent the circumstances remain substantially the same as they relate to the alternative. (*Citizens of Goleta Valley v. Board of Supervisors* (1990) 52 Cal.3d 553, 573).

(3) An EIR need not consider an alternative whose effect cannot be reasonably ascertained and whose implementation is remote and speculative. (*Residents Ad Hoc Stadium Committee v. Board of Trustees* (1979) 89 Cal.App.3d 274).

Note: Authority cited: Sections 21083 and 21087, Public Resources Code. Reference: Sections 21002, 21002.1, 21003, and 21100, Public Resources Code; *Citizens of Goleta Valley v. Board of Supervisors*, (1990) 52 Cal.3d 553; *Laurel Heights Improvement Association v. Regents of the University of California*, (1988) 47 Cal.3d 376; *Gentry v. City of Murrieta* (1995) 36 Cal.App.4th 1359; and *Laurel Heights Improvement Association v. Regents of the University of California* (1993) 6 Cal.4th 1112.

Discussion: This section examines the required discussion of project alternatives.

Subsection (b) states that the discussion shall focus on alternatives to the project or its location which can avoid or substantially lessen any of the significant impacts of the project and shall evaluate their comparative merits. Subsection (c) includes guidance on the selection of a reasonable range of feasible alternatives, including the need to document the process of selecting alternatives. Subsection (e) describes the 'no project' alternative, including its relationship to the baseline conditions under which the project is evaluated for potential significance and the analysis of the potential impacts if the project is not undertaken. Subsection (f) discusses the 'rule of reason' in detail, including such factors as feasibility, location, and speculation, which help agencies select a reasonable range of alternatives.

15127 Limitations on Discussion of Environmental Impact

The information required by Section 15126(e) [5] concerning short-term uses versus long-term productivity, and (f) concerning irreversible changes, need be included only in EIRs prepared in connection with any of the following activities:

(a) The adoption, amendment, or enactment of a plan, policy, or ordinance of a public agency;

(b) The adoption by a local agency formation commission of a resolution making determinations; or

(c) A project which will be subject to the requirement for preparing an environmental impact statement pursuant to the requirements of the National Environmental Policy Act of 1969, 42 U.S.C. 4321–4347.

Note: Authority cited: Sections 21083 and 21087, Public Resources Code. Reference: Section 21100.1, Public Resources Code.

Discussion: The reference in this section to previous subsection (e) of Section 15126 has been deleted. The statutory requirement for a discussion of the relationship between short-term uses and long-term productivity was repealed by Chapter 1230 of the Statutes of 1994.

15128 Effects Not Found to Be Significant

An EIR shall contain a statement briefly indicating the reasons that various possible significant effects of a project were determined not to be significant and were therefore not discussed in detail in the EIR. Such a statement may be contained in an attached copy of an initial study.

Note: Authority cited: Sections 21083 and 21087, Public Resources Code. Reference: Section 21100, Public Resources Code.

Discussion: This section repeats the statutory requirement from Section 21100 for an EIR to contain a brief statement explaining why various effects of the project were found not to be significant. The section then adds the administrative interpretation that this statement may be provided by an attached copy of the Initial Study. Using the Initial Study would help the Lead Agency avoid duplication in writing and would provide a relatively simple way of meeting this requirement.

15129 Organizations and Persons Consulted

The EIR shall identify all federal, state, or local agencies, other organizations, and private individuals consulted in preparing the draft EIR, and the persons, firm, or agency preparing the draft EIR, by contract or other authorization.

Note: Authority cited: Sections 21083 and 21087, Public Resources Code. Reference: Sections 21104 and 21153, Public Resources Code.

Discussion: This section requires the Lead Agency to disclose the agencies, organizations, and individuals whom it consulted pursuant to Sections 21104 or 21153.

15130 Discussion of Cumulative Impacts

(a) An EIR shall discuss cumulative Cumulative impacts of a project shall be discussed when they are significant the project's incremental effect is cumulatively considerable, as defined in section 15065(c). Where a lead agency is examining a project with an incremental effect that is not "cumulatively considerable," a lead agency need not consider that effect significant, but shall briefly describe its basis for concluding that the incremental effect is not cumulatively considerable.

(1) As defined in Section 15355, a cumulative impact consists of an impact which is created as a result of the combination of the project evaluated in the EIR together with other projects causing related impacts. An EIR should not discuss impacts which do not result in part from the project evaluated in the EIR.

(2) When the combined cumulative impact associated with the project's incremental effect and the effects of other projects is not significant, the EIR shall briefly indicate why the cumulative impact is not significant and is not discussed in further detail in the EIR. A lead agency shall identify facts and analysis supporting the lead

agency's conclusion that the cumulative impact is less than significant.

(3) An EIR may determine that a project's contribution to a significant cumulative impact will be rendered less than cumulatively considerable and thus is not significant. A project's contribution is less than cumulatively considerable if the project is required to implement or fund its fair share of a mitigation measure or measures designed to alleviate the cumulative impact. The lead agency shall identify facts and analysis supporting its conclusion that the contribution will be rendered less than cumulatively considerable.

(4) An EIR may determine that a project's contribution to a significant cumulative impact is de minimus and thus is not significant. A de minimus contribution means that the environmental conditions would essentially be the same whether or not the proposed project is implemented.

(b) The discussion of cumulative impacts shall reflect the severity of the impacts and their likelihood of occurrence, but the discussion need not provide as great detail as is provided of for the effects attributable to the project alone. The discussion should be guided by standards of practicality and reasonableness, and should focus on the cumulative impact to which the identified other projects contribute rather than the attributes of other projects which do not contribute to the cumulative impact. The following elements are necessary to an adequate discussion of significant cumulative impacts:

(1) Either:

(A) A list of past, present, and reasonably anticipated probable future projects producing related or cumulative impacts, including, if necessary, those projects outside the control of the agency, or

(B) A summary of projections contained in an adopted general plan or related planning document, or in a prior environmental document which has been adopted or certified, which described or evaluated is designed to evaluate regional or areawide conditions contributing to the cumulative impact. Any such planning document shall be referenced and made available to the public at a location specified by the lead agency;

1. When utilizing a list, as suggested in paragraph (1) of subdivision (b), factors to consider when determining whether to include a related project should include the nature of each environmental resource being examined, the location of the project and its type. Location may be important, for example, when water quality impacts are at issue since projects outside the watershed would probably not contribute to a cumulative effect. Project type may be important, for example, when the impact is specialized, such as a particular air pollutant or mode of traffic.

2. "Probable future projects" may be limited to those projects requiring an agency approval for an application which has been received at the time the notice of preparation is released, unless abandoned by the applicant; projects included in an adopted capital improvements program, general plan, regional transportation plan, or other similar plan; projects included in a summary of projections of projects (or development areas designated) in a general plan or a similar plan; projects anticipated as later phase of a previously approved project (e.g. a subdivision); or those public agency projects for which money has been budgeted.

3. Lead agencies should define the geographic scope of the area affected by the cumulative effect and provide a reasonable explanation for the geographic limitation used.

(2) A summary of the expected environmental effects to be produced by those projects with specific reference to additional information stating where that information is available; and

(3) A reasonable analysis of the cumulative impacts of the relevant projects. An EIR shall examine reasonable, feasible options for mitigating or avoiding the project's contribution to any significant cumulative effects of a proposed project.

(c) With some projects, the only feasible mitigation for cumulative impacts may involve the adoption of ordinances or regulations rather than the imposition of conditions on a project-by-project basis.

(d) Previously approved land use documents such as general plans, specific plans, and local coastal plans may be used in cumulative impact analysis. A pertinent discussion of cumulative impacts contained in one or more previously certified EIRs may be incorporated by reference pursuant to the provisions for tiering and program EIRs. No further cumulative impacts analysis is required when a project is consistent with a general, specific, master or comparable programmatic plan where the lead agency determines that the regional or areawide cumulative impacts of the proposed project have already been adequately addressed, as defined in section 15152(e), in a certified EIR for that plan.

(e) If a cumulative impact was adequately addressed in a prior EIR for a community plan, zoning action, or general plan, and the project is consistent with that plan or action, then an EIR for such a project should not further analyze that cumulative impact, as provided in Section 15183(j).

Note: Authority cited: Sections 21083 and 21087, Public Resources Code. Reference: Sections 21083(b), 21093, 21094, and 21100, Public Resources Code; *Whitman v. Board of Supervisors* (1979) 88 Cal.App.3d 397; *San Franciscans for Reasonable Growth v. City and County of San Francisco* (1984) 151 Cal.App.3d 61; *Kings County Farm Bureau v. City of Hanford* (1990) 221 Cal. App.3d 692; *Laurel Heights Homeowners Association v. Regents of the University of California* (1988) 47 Cal.3d 376; *Sierra Club v. Gilroy* (1990) 220 Cal.App.3d 30; *Citizens to Preserve the Ojai v. County of Ventura* (1985) 176 Cal.App.3d 421; *Concerned Citizens of South Cent. Los Angeles v. Los Angeles Unified Sch. Dist.* (1994) 24 Cal.App.4th 826; *Las Virgenes Homeowners Fed'n v. County of Los Angeles* (1986) 177 Cal.App.3d 300; *San Joaquin Raptor/Wildlife Rescue Ctr v. County of Stanislaus* (1994) 27 Cal.App.4th 713; and *Fort Mojave Indian Tribe v. Cal. Dept. of Health Services* (1995) 38 Cal.App.4th 1574.

Discussion: This section is necessary to explain how to discuss cumulative impacts in an EIR. The section limits the discussion to situations where the cumulative effects are found to be significant. Further, the section

codifies the requirements for analysis of cumulative effects as spelled out in *Whitman v. Board of Supervisors*, cited in the note, but the section allows the alternative approach of summarizing projections from a planning document. The options allow the Lead Agency to choose the method of analysis that may be best suited to the situation at hand. Essential guidance is also provided on approaches to mitigating cumulative effects, since cumulative effects can rarely be mitigated in the same way as the primary effects of an individual project.

When analyzing the cumulative impacts of a project under 15130 (b)(1)(A), the Lead Agency is required to discuss not only approved projects under construction and approved related projects not yet under construction, but also unapproved projects currently under environmental review with related impacts or which result in significant cumulative impacts. This analysis should include a discussion of projects under review by the Lead Agency and projects under review by other relevant public agencies, using reasonable efforts to discover, disclose, and discuss the other related projects. The cumulative impact analysis requires a discussion of projects with related cumulative impacts which required EIRs, Negative Declarations, or were exempt from CEQA. (See: *San Franciscans for Reasonable Growth v. City and County of San Francisco*, (1984) 151 Cal.App.3d 61.) The court in SFFRG took note of the problem of where to draw the line on projects undergoing environmental review since application of new projects are constantly being submitted. A reasonable point might be after the preparation of the draft EIR. Additional project information could be included in the final EIR if cumulative impacts were originally analyzed in the draft EIR and if the new project information doesn't warrant the preparation of a subsequent or supplemental EIR as required by Section 15162 of the Guidelines.

Subsection (b)(1)(B) authorizes a lead agency to limit its analysis of probable future projects to those which are planned or which have had an application made at the time the NOP is released for review. This describes a reasonable point in time at which to begin the cumulative impact analysis. Without this guideline, the cumulative impact analysis may suffer frequent revision as new, incremental projects are identified. If additional projects are identified later, they may be addressed during completion of the final EIR.

Cumulative impacts analysis must include reasonably anticipated future activities of a project or associated with the project. Whether these activities are addressed in the cumulative impact analysis section or in the impacts associated with the project, as defined, if there is substantial evidence indicating reasonable foreseeable future projects or activities, an EIR must analyze the impacts of those future activities. The Court in *Laurel Heights* set forth the following two pronged test to determine whether an EIR must include an analysis of the environmental effects of future activities: (1) it is a reasonably foreseeable consequence of the initial project; and (2) the future action will be significant in that it will likely change the scope or nature of the initial project or its environmental effects. Absent these two circumstances, potential future expansion need not be considered. *Laurel Heights Improvement Association v. Regents of the University of California* (1988) 47 Cal.3d 376.

Consistent with the holding in *Antioch v. Pittsburg* (see discussion with Section 15126), a cumulative impact analysis should address the most probable development patterns.

This section describes the analysis necessary where a project will make a considerable contribution to a cumulative effect (see also section 15064). Based on the holding in *San Joaquin Raptor/Wildlife Rescue Center v. County of Stanislaus* (1996) 42 Cal. App.4th 608, subdivision (a) provides that when the lead agency determines that a project makes only a de minimus contribution to a cumulative effect no analysis of the cumulative effect is needed. This subsection also provides that an EIR may determine that a project's contribution, originally thought to be considerable, is less than considerable with mitigation. Any such conclusion must be documented in the EIR.

Subsection (b) discusses the elements necessary for an adequate discussion of significant cumulative impacts. It recommends that the discussion focus on the particular cumulative impact to which other projects contribute rather than on the non-contributing aspects of those projects. This subsection offers further guidance on focusing the discussion on impacts rather than on other projects per se.

Subsection (d) links cumulative impact analysis to tiering and other similar approaches which seek to limit redundant analyses. Where cumulative impacts have been adequately addressed in the EIR certified for a general plan or other programmatic plan, and the project is consistent with that plan, the discussion contained in the prior EIR may be incorporated by reference.

No further cumulative impact analysis would be necessary.

15131 Economic and Social Effects

Economic or social information may be included in an EIR or may be presented in whatever form the agency desires.

(a) Economic or social effects of a project shall not be treated as significant effects on the environment. An EIR may trace a chain of cause and effect from a proposed decision on a project through anticipated economic or social changes resulting from the project to physical changes caused in turn by the economic or social changes. The intermediate economic or social changes need not be analyzed in any detail greater than necessary to trace the chain of cause and effect. The focus of the analysis shall be on the physical changes.

(b) Economic or social effects of a project may be used to determine the significance of physical changes caused by the project. For example, if the construction of a new freeway or rail line divides an existing community, the construction would be the physical change, but the social effect on the community would be the basis for determining that the effect would be significant. As an additional example, if the construction of a road and the resulting increase in noise in an area disturbed existing religious practices in the area, the disturbance of the religious practices could be used to determine that the construction and use of the road and the resulting noise would be significant effects on the environment. The religious practices would need to be analyzed only to the extent to show that the increase in traffic and noise would conflict with the religious practices. Where an EIR uses economic or social effects to determine that a physical change is significant, the EIR shall explain the reason for determining that the effect is significant.

(c) Economic, social, and particularly housing factors shall be considered by public agencies together with technological and environmental factors in deciding whether changes in a project are feasible to reduce or avoid the significant effects on the environment identified in the EIR. If information on these factors is not contained in the EIR, the information must be added to the record in some other manner to allow the agency to consider the factors in reaching a decision on the project.

Note: Authority cited: Sections 21083 and 21087, Public Resources Code. Reference: Sections 21001(e) and (g), 21002, 21002.1, 21060.5, 21080.1, 21083(c), and 21100, Public Resources Code.

Discussion: This section is necessary because there has been confusion over the authority of a Lead Agency to include economic and social information in an EIR. This section resolves the controversy by providing the authority with the rationale for including the information.

The term "significant effect on the environment" is defined in Section 21068 of CEQA as meaning "a substantial or potentially substantial adverse change in the environment." This focus on physical changes is further reinforced by Sections 21100 and 21151.

Despite the implication of these sections, CEQA does not focus exclusively on physical changes, and it is not exclusively physical in concern. For example, in Section 21083(c), CEQA requires an agency to determine that a project may have a significant effect on the environment if it will cause substantial adverse effects on human beings, either directly or indirectly. This section was added to CEQA by the same bill in 1972 (AB 889, Chapter 1154 of the Statutes of 1972) that added the definition of the term "environment" and the term "project".

The interpretation provided in Section 15131 starts with the analysis as used in the *Friends of Mammoth* decision, (1972) 8 Cal.3d 247. The analysis begins with the question of whether the governmental action involved will culminate in a physical change. There must be a physical change resulting from the project directly or indirectly before CEQA will apply. Direct physical changes are easy to identify. Indirect examples could include the increased traffic, fuel consumption, and air pollution as the potential results of a bus system fare increase in *Shaw v. Golden Gate Bridge etc. District*, (1976) 60 Cal.App.3d 699.

Once a physical change or a potential physical change has been identified, the Lead Agency must determine whether substantial evidence exists indicating that the physical change will be significant and thereby require preparation of an EIR. Public Resources Code section 21082.2, subdivision (c), states that evidence of social or economic impacts which do not contribute to or are not caused by physical impacts on the environment is not "substantial evidence" that would show those impacts to be significant.

Under the interpretation provided in this section, effects on facilities or services are not automatically regarded as significant effects of a project. The changes must be related to or caused by physical changes. If the project causes a direct physical change in a facility by pumping ground water and causing ground settling under the facility, the resulting deterioration can be easily regarded as a significant effect. If the project causes physical changes that affect the use of the facility, the effects on use may be considered a significant effect in the same way as increases in traffic are often treated as significant effects.

In *Citizens Association for Sensible Development of Bishop Area v. Inyo* (1985) 172 Cal.App.3d 151, the court held that "economic or social change may be used to determine that a physical change shall be regarded as a significant effect of the environment. Where a physical change is caused by economic or social effects of a project, the physical change may be regarded as a significant effect in the same manner as any other physical change resulting from the project. Alternatively, economic and social effects of a physical change may be used to determine that the physical change is a significant effect on the environment." In this case, the Court held that an EIR for a proposed shopping center located away from the downtown shopping area must discuss the potential economic and social consequences of the project, if the proposed center would take business away from the downtown and thereby cause business closures and eventual physical deterioration of the downtown.

15132 Contents of Final Environmental Impact Report

The final EIR shall consist of:

(a) The Draft EIR or a revision of the draft.

(b) Comments and recommendations received on the Draft EIR either verbatim or in summary.

(c) A list of persons, organizations, and public agencies commenting on the draft EIR.

(d) The responses of the Lead Agency to significant environmental points raised in the review and consultation process.

(e) Any other information added by the lead agency.

Note: Authority cited: Sections 21083 and 21087, Public Resources Code. Reference: Section 21100, Public Resources Code.

Discussion: This section is necessary in order to explain the difference between a draft EIR and the final EIR which is ultimately considered by the decision-makers in each agency prior to granting an approval for the project. The final EIR is a necessary document because it brings together a number of subjects such as comments and responses to comments which would not be available in the draft EIR that is sent out for public review. The list of contents is also necessary in order to show that the findings on the feasibility of avoiding or reducing significant effects and the statement of overriding considerations are not part of the final EIR. The findings and the statement of overriding considerations are made after the decision-makers have considered the final EIR. The findings and statement are included in the public record but not in the final EIR.

Article 10. Considerations in Preparing EIRs and Negative Declarations Sections 15140 to 15154

15140 Writing

EIRs shall be written in plain language and may use appropriate graphics so that decisionmakers and the public can rapidly understand the documents.

Note: Authority cited: Sections 21083 and 21087, Public Resources Code. Reference: Sections 21003 and 21100, Public Resources Code.

Discussion: This section is intended to improve the clarity of EIRs. The section is also necessary to provide an interpretation resolving the question of who is the appropriate audience for the EIR.

15141 Page Limits

The text of draft EIRs should normally be less than 150 pages and for proposals of unusual scope or complexity should normally be less than 300 pages.

Note: Authority cited: Sections 21083 and 21087, Public Resources Code. Reference: Section 21100, Public Resources Code.

Discussion: The recommended page limits encourage agencies to reduce unneeded bulk in EIRs and to help the documents disclose the key environmental issues to the decision-makers and the public. Further, the page limits match the page limits under the federal system. Adopting the same limits as used in the federal system improves compatibility of the two systems.

15142 Interdisciplinary Approach

An EIR shall be prepared using an interdisciplinary approach which will ensure the integrated use of the natural and social sciences and the consideration of qualitative as well as quantitative factors. The interdisciplinary analysis shall be conducted by competent individuals, but no single discipline shall be designated or required to undertake this evaluation.

Note: Authority cited: Sections 21083 and 21087, Public Resources Code. Reference Sections 21000, 21001, and 21100, Public Resources Code.

Discussion: This section is necessary to show that an EIR must use many disciplines in order to find the interrelationships among the various factors in the environmental effects. The requirement for an interdisciplinary is also part of NEPA. Accordingly, this requirement comes from the legislative history of CEQA. This section also makes the essential point that an EIR must consider qualitative factors as well as quantitative, economic, and technical factors.

15143 Emphasis

The EIR shall focus on the significant effects on the environment. The significant effects should be discussed with emphasis in proportion to their severity and probability of occurrence. Effects dismissed in an Initial Study as clearly insignificant and unlikely to occur need not be discussed further in the EIR unless the Lead Agency subsequently receives information inconsistent with the finding in the Initial Study. A copy of the Initial Study may be attached to the EIR to provide the basis for limiting the impacts discussed.

Note: Authority cited: Sections 21083 and 21087, Public Resources Code. Reference: Sections 21003, 21061, and 21100, Public Resources Code.

Discussion: This section provides an interpretation that the Initial Study can be used to show which effects were examined and found to be insignificant and, therefore, not worthy of further discussion.

15144 Forecasting

Drafting an EIR or preparing a negative declaration necessarily involves some degree of forecasting. While foreseeing the unforeseeable is not possible, an agency must use its best efforts to find out and disclose all that it reasonably can.

Note: Authority cited: Sections 21083 and 21087, Public Resources Code. Reference: Sections 21003, 21061, and 21100, Public Resources Code.

Discussion: This section limits the requirement for forecasting to that which could be reasonably expected under the circumstances and is part of the effort to provide a general "rule of reason" for EIR contents.

In regard to forecasting, the *Laurel Heights* Court commented that an agency is required to forecast only to the extent that an activity could be reasonably expected under the circumstances. An agency cannot be expected to predict the future course of governmental regulation or exactly what information scientific advances may ultimately reveal. *Laurel Heights Improvement Association v. Regents of the University of California* (1988) 47 Cal.3d 376.

15145 Speculation

If, after thorough investigation, a lead agency finds that a particular impact is too speculative for evaluation, the agency should note its conclusion and terminate discussion of the impact.

Note: Authority cited: Sections 21083 and 21087, Public Resources Code. Reference: Sections 21003, 21061, and 21100, Public Resources Code; *Topanga Beach Renters Association v. Department of General Services,* (1976) 58 Cal.App.3d 712.

Discussion: This section deals with a difficulty in forecasting where a thorough investigation is unable to resolve an issue and the answer remains purely speculative. This section is necessary to relieve the Lead Agency from a requirement to engage in idle speculation. Once an agency finds that a particular effect is too speculative for evaluation, discussion of that effect should be terminated. This section provides authority to do so.

In *Laurel Heights Improvement Association v. Regents of the University of California* (1988) 47 Cal.3d 376, the court noted that where future development is unspecified and uncertain, no purpose can be served by requiring an EIR to engage in sheer speculation as to future environmental consequences.

15146 Degree of Specificity

The degree of specificity required in an EIR will correspond to the degree of specificity involved in the underlying activity which is described in the EIR.

(a) An EIR on a construction project will necessarily be more detailed in the specific effects of the project than will be an EIR on the adoption of a local general plan or comprehensive zoning ordinance because the effects of the construction can be predicted with greater accuracy.

(b) An EIR on a project such as the adoption or amendment of a comprehensive zoning ordinance or a local general plan should focus on the secondary effects that can be expected to follow from the adoption or amendment, but the EIR need not be as detailed as an EIR on the specific construction projects that might follow.

Note: Authority cited: Sections 21083 and 21087, Public Resources Code. Reference: Sections 21003, 21061, and 21100, Public Resources Code.

Discussion: This section is necessary to deal with the wide range of activities which are subject to the CEQA process. Some activities such as the adoption of local general plans may deal with issues on a level of broad generalities. At the other end of the scale, CEQA also applies to conditional use permits for specific development projects. While CEQA requirements cannot be avoided by chopping the proposed project into pieces to render its impacts insignificant the EIR need not engage in a speculative analysis of environmental consequences for future and unspecified development. (*Atherton v. Board of Supervisors of Orange County*, (1983) 146 Cal.3d 346.)

As with the range of alternatives, the level of analysis provided in an EIR is subject to the rule of reason. The level of specificity for a given EIR depends upon the type of project. The analysis must be specific enough to permit informed decision making and public participation. The need for thorough discussion and analysis is not to be construed unreasonably, however, to serve as an easy way of defeating projects. What is required is the production of information sufficient to understand the environmental impacts of the proposed project and to permit a reasonable choice of alternatives so far as environmental aspects are concerned. See *Laurel Heights Improvement Association v. Regents of the University of California* (1988) 47 Cal.3d 376. In *Antioch v. Pittsburg* (1986) 187 Cal.App.3d 1325, the court held that EIR requirements must be sufficiently flexible to encompass vastly differing projects with varying levels of specificity. When the alternatives have been set forth in this manner, an EIR does not become vulnerable because it fails to consider in detail each and every conceivable variation of the alternatives stated.

15147 Technical Detail

The information contained in an EIR shall include summarized technical data, maps, plot plans, diagrams, and similar relevant information sufficient to permit full assessment of significant environmental impacts by reviewing agencies and members of the public. Placement of highly technical and specialized analysis and data in the body of an EIR should be avoided through inclusion of supporting information and analyses as appendices to the main body of the EIR. Appendices to the EIR may be prepared in volumes separate from the basic EIR document, but shall be readily available for public examination and shall be submitted to all clearinghouses which assist in public review.

Note: Authority cited: Sections 21083 and 21087, Public Resources Code. Reference: Sections 21003, 21061, and 21100, Public Resources Code.

Discussion: This section is designed to achieve a balance between the technical accuracy of the EIR and the public information function of the document. Accuracy can be maintained by moving the technical details into appendices and summarizing the technical information in the body of the EIR itself. This approach may help reduce the cost of the EIR. The Lead Agency may reproduce fewer copies of the appendices than of the basic EIR. This section follows the federal NEPA regulations which already encourage placement of technical details in appendices.

15148 Citation

Preparation of EIRs is dependent upon information from many sources, including engineering project reports and many scientific documents relating to environmental features. These documents should be cited but not included in the EIR. The EIR shall cite all documents used in its preparation including, where possible, the page and section number of any technical reports which were used as the basis for any statements in the EIR.

Note: Authority cited: Sections 21083 and 21087, Public Resources Code. Reference: Sections 21003, 21061, and 21100, Public Resources Code.

Discussion: This section recognizes source documents but discourages their inclusion in the EIR. Citations are required for accountability and to allow statements to be verifiable. This section is necessary to keep the size of the EIRs down to manageable levels and at the same time maintain the accuracy of the information in the document.

15149 Use of Registered Professionals in Preparing EIRs

(a) A number of statutes provide that certain professional services can be provided to the public only by individuals who have been registered by a registration board established under California law. Such statutory restrictions apply to a number of professions including but not limited to engineering, land surveying, forestry, geology, and geophysics.

(b) In its intended usage, an EIR is not a technical document that can be prepared only by a registered professional.

The EIR serves as a public disclosure document explaining the effects of the proposed project on the environment, alternatives to the project, and ways to minimize adverse effects and to increase beneficial effects. As a result of information in the EIR, the lead agency should establish requirements or conditions on project design, construction, or operation in order to protect or enhance the environment. State statutes may provide that only registered professionals can prepare technical studies which will be used in or which will control the detailed design, construction, or operation of the proposed project and which will be prepared in support of an EIR.

Note: Authority cited: Sections 21083 and 21087, Public Resources Code. Reference: Sections 21003, 21061, and 21100, Public Resources Code.

Discussion: This section is necessary for declaring that an EIR is not the kind of technical document which can be prepared only by a person registered under a professional registration law in California. The section recognizes that some technical background documents may be legally prepared only by registered professionals.

15150   Incorporation by Reference

(a) An EIR or negative declaration may incorporate by reference all or portions of another document which is a matter of public record or is generally available to the public. Where all or part of another document is incorporated by reference, the incorporated language shall be considered to be set forth in full as part of the text of the EIR or negative declaration.

(b) Where part of another document is incorporated by reference, such other document shall be made available to the public for inspection at a public place or public building. The EIR or negative declaration shall state where the incorporated documents will be available for inspection. At a minimum, the incorporated document shall be made available to the public in an office of the lead agency in the county where the project would be carried out or in one or more public buildings such as county offices or public libraries if the lead agency does not have an office in the county.

(c) Where an EIR or negative declaration uses incorporation by reference, the incorporated part of the referenced document shall be briefly summarized where possible or briefly described if the data or information cannot be summarized.

The relationship between the incorporated part of the referenced document and the EIR shall be described.

(d) Where an agency incorporates information from an EIR that has previously been reviewed through the state review system, the state identification number of the incorporated document should be included in the summary or designation described in Subsection (c).

(e) Examples of materials that may be incorporated by reference include but are not limited to:

   (1) A description of the environmental setting from another EIR.

   (2) A description of the air pollution problems prepared by an air pollution control agency concerning a process involved in the project.

   (3) A description of the city or county general plan that applies to the location of the project.

(f) Incorporation by reference is most appropriate for including long, descriptive, or technical materials that provide general background but do not contribute directly to the analysis of the problem at hand.

Note: Authority cited: Sections 21083 and 21087, Public Resources Code. Reference Sections 21003, 21061, and 21100, Public Resources Code.

Discussion: Incorporation by reference is a necessary device for reducing the size of EIRs. This section authorizes use of incorporation by reference and provides guidance for using it in a manner consistent with the public involvement and full disclosure functions of CEQA.

15151   Standards for Adequacy of an EIR

An EIR should be prepared with a sufficient degree of analysis to provide decision-makers with information which enables them to make a decision which intelligently takes account of environmental consequences. An evaluation of the environmental effects of a proposed project need not be exhaustive, but the sufficiency of an EIR is to be reviewed in the light of what is reasonably feasible. Disagreement among experts does not make an EIR inadequate, but the EIR should summarize the main points of disagreement among the experts. The courts have looked not for perfection but for adequacy, completeness, and a good faith effort at full disclosure.

Note: Authority cited: Sections 21083 and 21087, Public Resources Code. Reference: Sections 21061 and 21100, Public Resources Code; *San Francisco Ecology Center v. City*

and County of San Francisco, (1975) 48 Cal.App.3d 584.

Discussion: This section is a codification of case law dealing with the standards for adequacy of an EIR.

In *Concerned Citizens of Costa Mesa, Inc. v. 32nd District Agricultural Assoc.* (1986) 42 Cal.3d 929, the court held that "the EIR must contain facts and analysis, not just the agency's bare conclusions or opinions." In *Browning-Ferris Industries of California, Inc. v. San Jose* (1986) 181 Cal.App.3d 852, the court reasserted that an EIR is a disclosure document and as such an agency may choose among differing expert opinions when those arguments are correctly identified in a responsive manner. Further, the state Supreme Court in its 1988 *Laurel Heights* decision held that the purpose of CEQA is to compel government at all levels to make decisions with environmental consequences in mind. CEQA does not, indeed cannot, guarantee that these decisions will always be those which favor environmental considerations, nor does it require absolute perfection in an EIR.

15152   Tiering

(a) "Tiering" refers to using the analysis of general matters contained in a broader EIR (such as one prepared for a general plan or policy statement) with later EIRs and negative declarations on narrower projects; incorporating by reference the general discussions from the broader EIR; and concentrating the later EIR or negative declaration solely on the issues specific to the later project.

(a)(b) Agencies are encouraged to tier the EIRs environmental analyses which they prepare for separate but related projects including general plans, zoning changes, and development projects. This approach can eliminate repetitive discussions of the same issues and focus the later EIR or negative declaration on the actual issues ripe for decision at each level of environmental review. Tiering is appropriate when the sequence of analysis is from an EIR prepared for a general plan, policy, or program to an EIR or negative declaration for another plan, policy, or program of lesser scope, or to a site-specific EIR or negative declaration. Tiering does not excuse the lead agency from adequately analyzing reasonably foreseeable significant environmental effects of the project and does not justify deferring such analysis to a later tier EIR or negative declaration. However, the level of detail contained in a first tier EIR need not be greater than that of the program, plan, policy, or ordinance being analyzed.

(b)(c) Where a lead agency is using the tiering process in connection with an EIR for a large-scale planning approval, such as a general plan or component thereof (e.g., an area plan or community plan), the development of detailed, site-specific information may not be feasible but can be deferred, in many instances, until such time as the lead agency prepares a future environmental document in connection with a project of a more limited geographical scale, as long as deferral does not prevent adequate identification of significant effects of the planning approval at hand.

(c)(d) Where an EIR has been prepared and certified for a program, plan, policy, or ordinance consistent with the requirements of this section, any lead agency for a later project pursuant to or consistent with the program, plan, policy, or ordinance should limit the EIR or negative declaration on the later project to effects which:

(1) Were not examined as significant effects on the environment in the prior EIR; or

(2) Are susceptible to substantial reduction or avoidance by the choice of specific revisions in the project, by the imposition of conditions, or other means.

(e)(e) Tiering under this section shall be limited to situations where the project is consistent with the general plan and zoning of the city or county in which the project is located, except that a project requiring a rezone to achieve or maintain conformity with a general plan may be subject to tiering.

(d)(f) The initial study shall be used to decide whether and to what extent the prior EIR is still sufficient for the present project. A later EIR shall be required when the initial study or other analysis finds that the later project may cause significant effects on the environment that were not adequately addressed in the prior EIR. A negative declaration shall be required when the provisions of Section 15070 are met.

(1) Where a lead agency determines that a cumulative effect has been adequately addressed in the prior EIR, that effect is not treated as significant for purposes of the later EIR or negative declaration, and need not be discussed in detail.

(2) When assessing whether there is a new significant cumulative effect,

the lead agency shall consider whether the incremental effects of the project would be considerable when viewed in the context of past, present, and probable future projects. At this point, the question is not whether there is a significant cumulative impact, but whether the effects of the project are cumulatively considerable. For a discussion on how to assess whether project impacts are cumulatively considerable, see Section 15064(i).

(3) Significant environmental effects have been "adequately addressed" if the lead agency determines that:

(A) they have been mitigated or avoided as a result of the prior environmental impact report and findings adopted in connection with that prior environmental report;

(B) they have been examined at a sufficient level of detail in the prior environmental impact report to enable those effects to be mitigated or avoided by site specific revisions, the imposition of conditions, or by other means in connection with the approval of the later project; or

(C) they cannot be mitigated to avoid or substantially lessen the significant impacts despite the project proponent's willingness to accept all feasible mitigation measures, and the only purpose of including analysis of such effects in another environmental impact report would be to put the agency in a position to adopt a statement of overriding considerations with respect to the effects.

(f)(g) When tiering is used, the later EIRs or negative declarations shall refer to the prior EIR and state where a copy of the prior EIR may be examined. The later EIR or negative declaration should state that the lead agency is using the tiering concept and that the EIR it is being tiered with the earlier EIR.

(g)(h) There are various types of EIRs that may be used in a tiering situation. These include, but are not limited to, the following:

(1) General plan EIR (Section 15166).

(2) Staged EIR (Section 15167).

(3) Program EIR (Section 15168).

(4) Master EIR (Section 15175).

(5) Multiple-family residential development/residential and commercial or

retail mixed-use development (Section 15179.5).

(6) Redevelopment project (Section 15180).

(7) Housing / neighborhood commercial facilities in an urbanized area (Section 15181).

(8) Projects consistent with community plan, general plan, or zoning (Section 15183).

Note: Authority cited: Sections 21083 and 21087, Public Resources Code. Reference: Sections 21003, 21061, 21093, 21094, 21100, and 21151, Public Resources Code; *Stanislaus Natural Heritage Project, Sierra Club v. County of Stanislaus* (1996) 48 Cal.App. 4th 182; *Al Larson Boat Shop, Inc. v. Board of Harbor Commissioners* (1993) 18 Cal. App.4th 729; and *Sierra Club v. County of Sonoma* (1992) 6 Cal.App.4th 1307.

Discussion: The tiering concept authorized in this section is designed to promote efficiency in the process and to improve the compatibility of the CEQA process with the NEPA process. This section recognizes that the approval of many projects will move through a series of separate public agency decisions, going from approval of a general plan, to approval of an intermediate plan or zoning, and finally to approval of a specific development proposal. Each of these approvals is subject to the CEQA process. Often, the EIR prepared for a particular approval re-examines all the environmental issues analyzed in the EIRs prepared for the earlier approvals. This approach involves unnecessary expense when a particular issue has been fully analyzed before. Tiering is an effort to focus environmental review on the environmental issues which are relevant to the approval being considered. At the same time, tiering requires the lead agency to analyze reasonably foreseeable significant effects and does not allow deferral of such analysis to a later tier document.

This section expands the guidance on use of tiering. This section follows the general approach taken in Public Resources Code Section 21083.3. That section authorizes tiering of EIRs for projects which were consistent with an adopted community plan for which an EIR was prepared. This section extends the tiering concept to all programs, plans, or policies for which an EIR was prepared. This section improves efficiency by encouraging the Lead Agency to limit the EIR or the Negative Declaration on a later project, which is pursuant to or consistent with the program, plan, or policy, to examining the significant effects which were not examined as significant effects in the prior EIR or are susceptible to substantial reduction or avoidance by specific revisions in the project. The section allows use of tiering even where the action on the prior project and EIR did not include mitigation for every significant effect.

This approach recognizes that not all effects can be mitigated at each step of the process. There will be some effects for which mitigation will not be feasible at an early step of approving a particular development project, and the section would allow a Lead Agency to defer mitigation of that kind of effect to a later step. Such effects may include site specific effects such as aesthetics or parking, depending on the circumstances. At the same time, this section makes clear that tiering does not excuse the Lead Agency from analyzing reasonably foreseeable significant effects, or justify deferring analysis to a later tier EIR or Negative Declaration.

Where tiering is used, the Lead Agency will need to determine whether, in the light of changing circumstances, the EIR prepared earlier in the process would still provide an adequate description of the broad effects considered at that stage. Tiering enables an agency to rely upon the analysis contained in a previous document when it adequately addresses a later project. Subdivision (e) describes what is meant by 'adequately addressed' in such a way as to ensure that prior mitigation measures will be applied to the later project.

To make the process understandable, any EIR or Negative Declaration using the tiering principle must refer to the prior EIR, state where a copy of that document may be examined, and state that tiering is being used.

15153   Use of an EIR from an Earlier Project

(a) The lead agency may employ a single EIR to describe more than one project, if such projects are essentially the same in terms of environmental impact. Further, the lead agency may use an earlier EIR prepared in connection with an earlier project to apply to a later project, if the circumstances of the projects are essentially the same.

(b) When a lead agency proposes to use an EIR from an earlier project as the EIR for a separate, later project, the lead agency shall use the following procedures:

  (1) The lead agency shall review the proposed project with an initial study, using incorporation by reference if necessary, to determine whether the EIR would adequately describe:

    (A) The general environmental setting of the project,

    (B) The significant environmental impacts of the project, and

    (C) Alternatives and mitigation measures related to each significant effect.

  (2) If the lead agency believes that the EIR would meet the requirements of subsection (1), it shall provide public review as provided in Section 15087 stating that it plans to use the previously prepared EIR as the draft EIR for this project. The notice shall include as a minimum:

    (A) An identification of the project with a brief description;

    (B) A statement that the agency plans to use a certain EIR prepared for a previous project as the EIR for this project;

    (C) A listing of places where copies of the EIR may be examined; and

    (D) A statement that the key issues involving the EIR are whether the EIR should be used for this project and whether there are any additional, reasonable alternatives or mitigation measures that should be considered as ways of avoiding or reducing the significant effects of the project.

  (3) The lead agency shall prepare responses to comments received during the review period.

  (4) Before approving the project, the decisionmaker in the lead agency shall:

    (A) Consider the information in the EIR including comments received during the review period and responses to those comments,

    (B) Decide either on its own or on a staff recommendation whether the EIR is adequate for the project at hand, and

    (C) Make or require certification to be made as described in Section 15090.

    (D) Make findings as provided in Sections 15091 and 15093 as necessary.

  (5) After making a decision on the project, the lead agency shall file a notice of determination.

(c) An EIR prepared for an earlier project may also be used as part of an initial study to document a finding that a later project will not have a significant effect. In this situation a negative declaration will be prepared.

(d) An EIR prepared for an earlier project shall not be used as the EIR for a later project if any of the conditions described in Section 15162 would require preparation of a subsequent or supplemental EIR.

Note: Authority cited: Sections 21083 and 21087, Public Resources Code. Reference: Sections 21100, 21151, and 21166, Public Resources Code.

Discussion: The purpose of this section is to grant Lead Agencies clear authority to use an EIR prepared for one project over again for a second project which has essentially the same impacts as the project for which the EIR was originally prepared. The section places necessary conditions on the use of a prior EIR to avoid abuse of this approach. Where two projects are essentially the same in terms of environmental impact, there is little reason to require preparation of a separate EIR for the second project.

Subsection (b) prescribes the procedures for an agency to use in implementing this authority. Use of a Negative Declaration is not appropriate. Although a Negative Declaration does state than an EIR will not be prepared, the reason for preparing a Negative Declaration is that the project will not have a significant effect. An EIR is needed if the project may have a significant effect although under some circumstances a previously prepared EIR may be used as the basis for review. The procedures prescribed in subsection (b) should reduce the confusion that has often been experienced in this situation.

This section is different from tiering in that this process does not involve a series of approvals moving from the general to the specific with EIRs omitting issues fully addressed at the earlier stages. The use of a previously prepared EIR is most appropriate where an EIR was prepared earlier for a project very similar to the one currently being examined by the Lead Agency.

15154   Projects Near Airports

(a) When a lead agency prepares an EIR for a project within the boundaries of a comprehensive airport land use plan or, if a comprehensive airport land use plan has not been adopted for a project within two nautical miles of a public airport or public use airport, the agency shall utilize the Airport Land Use Planning Handbook published by Caltrans' Division of Aeronautics to assist in the preparation of the EIR relative to potential airport-related safety hazards and noise problems.

(b) A lead agency shall not adopt a negative declaration or mitigated negative declaration for a project described in subsection (a) unless the lead agency considers whether the project will result in a safety hazard or noise problem for persons using the airport or for persons residing or working in the project area.

Note: Authority cited: Sections 21083 and 21087, Public Resources Code. Reference: Section 21096, Public Resources Code.

Article 11. Types of EIRs
Sections 15160 to 15170

15160   General

This article describes a number of examples of variations in EIRs as the documents are tailored to different situations and intended uses. These variations are not exclusive. Lead agencies may use other variations consistent with the guidelines to meet the needs of other circumstances. All EIRs must meet the content requirements discussed in Article 9 beginning with Section 15120.

Note: Authority cited: Sections 21083 and 21087, Public Resources Code. Reference: Sections 21061, 21100, and 21151, Public Resources Code.

15161   Project EIR

The most common type of EIR examines the environmental impacts of a specific development project. This type of EIR should focus primarily on the changes in the environment that would result from the development project. The EIR shall examine all phases of the project including planning, construction, and operation.

Note: Authority cited: Sections 21083 and 21087, Public Resources Code. Reference: Sections 21061, 21100, and 21151, Public Resources Code.

**15162   Subsequent EIRs and
             Negative Declarations**

(a) When an EIR has been certified or a negative declaration adopted for a project, no subsequent EIR shall be prepared for that project unless the lead agency determines, on the basis of substantial evidence in the light of the whole record, one or more of the following:

(1) Substantial changes are proposed in the project which will require major revisions of the previous EIR or negative declaration due to the involvement of new significant environmental effects or a substantial increase in the severity of previously identified significant effects;

(2) Substantial changes occur with respect to the circumstances under which the project is undertaken which will require major revisions of the previous EIR or negative declaration due to the involvement of new significant environmental effects or a substantial increase in the severity of previously identified significant effects; or

(3) New information of substantial importance, which was not known and could not have been known with the exercise of reasonable diligence at the time the previous EIR was certified as complete or the negative declaration was adopted, shows any of the following:

(A) The project will have one or more significant effects not discussed in the previous EIR or negative declaration;

(B) Significant effects previously examined will be substantially more severe than shown in the previous EIR;

(C) Mitigation measures or alternatives previously found not to be feasible would in fact be feasible, and would substantially reduce one or more significant effects of the project, but the project proponents decline to adopt the mitigation measure or alternative; or

(D) Mitigation measures or alternatives which are considerably different from those analyzed in the previous EIR would substantially reduce one or more significant effects on the environment, but the project proponents decline to adopt the mitigation measure or alternative.

(b) If changes to a project or its circumstances occur or new information becomes available after adoption of a negative declaration, the lead agency shall prepare a subsequent EIR if required under subsection (a). Otherwise the lead agency shall determine whether to prepare a subsequent negative declaration, an addendum, or no further documentation.

(c) Once a project has been approved, the lead agency's role in project approval is completed, unless further discretionary approval on that project is required. Information appearing after an approval does not require reopening of that approval. If after the project was is approved, any of prior to the occurrence

of the conditions described in Ssubsection (a) occurs, a the subsequent EIR or negative declaration shall only be prepared by the public agency which grants the next discretionary approval for the project, if any. In this situation no other responsible agency shall grant an approval for the project until the subsequent EIR has been certified or subsequent negative declaration adopted.

(d) A subsequent EIR or subsequent negative declaration shall be given the same notice and public review as required under Section 15087 or Section 15072. A subsequent EIR or negative declaration shall state where the previous document is available and can be reviewed.

Note: Authority cited: Public Resources Code Sections 21083 and 21087. Reference: Section 21166, Public Resources Code; *Bowman v. City of Petaluma* (1986) 185 Cal. App.3d 1065 (1986); and *Benton v. Board of Supervisors* (1991) 226 Cal.App.3d 1467 (1991); and *Fort Mojave Indian Tribe v. California Department of Health Services et al.* (1995) 38 Cal.App.4th 1574

Discussion: This section implements the requirements in Section 21166 of CEQA which limit preparation of a subsequent EIR to certain situations. This section provides interpretation of the three situations in which the statute requires preparation of a subsequent EIR. These interpretations are necessary to add certainty to the process.

This section also clarifies that a subsequent EIR may be prepared where a negative declaration had previously been adopted. Further, a subsequent negative declaration may be adopted where none of the situations described in subsection (a) have occurred.

Subsections (b) and (c) explain which agency would have responsibility for preparing a subsequent EIR under different circumstances. A subsequent EIR must, of course, receive the same circulation and review as the previous EIR.

Fund for Environmental Defense v. Orange (1988) 204 Cal.App.3d 1538, contains a discussion of the application of §15162 and §15163. The Court in *Bowman v. Petaluma* (1986) 185 Cal.App.3d 1065 distinguished requirements for a subsequent EIR from the threshold required for initial EIR preparation, saying "whereas §15064 (§21151 PRC) requires an EIR if the initial project may have a significant effect on the environment, §15162 (§21166 PRC) indicates a quite different intent, namely, to restrict the powers of agencies by prohibiting them from requiring a subsequent or supplemental EIR unless "substantial changes" in the project or its circumstances will require major revisions to the EIR. §15162 (§21166 PRC) comes into play precisely because in-depth review has already occurred, the time for challenging the sufficiency of the original EIR has long since expired, and the question is whether circumstances have changed enough to justify repeating a substantial portion of the process.

15163   Supplement to an EIR

(a) The lead or responsible agency may choose to prepare a supplement to an EIR rather than a subsequent EIR if:

    (1) Any of the conditions described in Section 15162 would require the preparation of a subsequent EIR, and

    (2) Only minor additions or changes would be necessary to make the previous EIR adequately apply to the project in the changed situation.

(b) The supplement to the EIR need contain only the information necessary to make the previous EIR adequate for the project as revised.

(c) A supplement to an EIR shall be given the same kind of notice and public review as is given to a draft EIR under Section 15087.

(d) A supplement to an EIR may be circulated by itself without recirculating the previous draft or final EIR.

(e) When the agency decides whether to approve the project, the decision-making body shall consider the previous EIR as revised by the supplemental EIR. A finding under Section 15091 shall be made for each significant effect shown in the previous EIR as revised.

Note: Authority cited: Sections 21083 and 21087, Public Resources Code. Reference: Section 21166, Public Resources Code.

Discussion: This section provides a short-form method where only minor additions or changes would be necessary in the previous EIR to make that EIR apply in the changed situation. The section also provides essential interpretations of how to handle public notice, public review, and circulation of the supplement.

A supplement to an EIR may be distinguished from a subsequent EIR by the following: a supplement augments a previously certified EIR to the extent necessary to address the conditions described in section 15162 and to examine mitigation and project alternatives accordingly. It is intended to revise the previous EIR through supplementation. A subsequent EIR, in contrast, is a complete EIR which focuses on the conditions described in section 15162.

15164   Addendum to an EIR or Negative Declaration

(a) The lead agency or a responsible agency shall prepare an addendum to a previously certified EIR if some changes or additions are necessary but none of the conditions described in Section 15162 calling for preparation of a subsequent EIR have occurred.

(b) An addendum to an adopted negative declaration may be prepared if only minor technical changes or additions are necessary or none of the conditions described in Section 15162 calling for the preparation of a subsequent EIR or negative declaration have occurred.

(c) An addendum need not be circulated for public review but can be included in or attached to the final EIR or adopted negative declaration.

(d) The decision-making body shall consider the addendum with the final EIR or adopted negative declaration prior to making a decision on the project.

(e) A brief explanation of the decision not to prepare a subsequent EIR pursuant to Section 15162 should be included in an addendum to an EIR, the lead agency's findings on the project, or elsewhere in the record. The explanation must be supported by substantial evidence.

Note: Authority cited: Sections 21083 and 21087, Public Resources Code. Reference: Section 21166, Public Resources Code; *Bowman v. City of Petaluma* (1986) 185 Cal.App.3d 1065 (1986); and *Benton v. Board of Supervisors* (1991) 226 Cal.App. 3d 1467 (1991).

Discussion: This section is designed to provide clear authority for an addendum as a way of making minor corrections in EIRs and negative declarations without recirculating the EIR or negative declaration.

15165   Multiple and Phased Projects

Where individual projects are, or a phased project is, to be undertaken and where the total undertaking comprises a project with significant environmental effect, the lead agency shall prepare a single program EIR for the ultimate project as described in Section 15168. Where an individual project is a necessary precedent for action on a larger project, or commits the lead agency to a larger project, with significant environmental effect, an EIR must address itself to the scope of the larger project. Where one project is one of several similar projects of a public agency, but is not deemed a part of a larger undertaking or a larger project, the agency may prepare one EIR for all projects, or one for each project, but shall in either case comment upon the cumulative effect.

Note: Authority cited: Sections 21083 and 21087, Public Resources Code. Reference: Sections 21061, 21100, and 21151, Public Resources Code; *Whitman v. Board of Supervisors*, 88 Cal.App.3d 397 (1979).

Discussion: This section follows the principle that the EIR on a project must show the big picture of what is involved. If the approval of one particular activity could be expected to lead to many other activities being approved in the same general area, the EIR should examine the expected effects of the ultimate environmental changes. This section is consistent with the *Whitman* decision cited in the note interpreting CEQA.

15166   EIR as Part of a General Plan

(a) The requirements for preparing an EIR on a local general plan, element, or amendment thereof will be satisfied by using the general plan, or element document, as the EIR and no separate EIR will be required, if:

    (1) The general plan addresses all the points required to be in an EIR by Article 9 of these guidelines, and

    (2) The document contains a special section or a cover sheet identifying where the general plan document addresses each of the points required.

(b) Where an EIR rather than a negative declaration has been prepared for a general plan, element, or amendment thereto, the EIR shall be forwarded to the State Clearinghouse for review. The requirement shall apply regardless of whether the EIR is prepared as a separate document or as a part of the general plan or element document.

Note: Authority cited: Sections 21083 and 21087, Public Resources Code. Reference: Sections 21003, 21061, 21083, 21100, 21104, 21151, and 21152, Public Resources Code.

Discussion: A separate section is provided to authorize combining the general plan document with the EIR. This section allows the use of the general plan document as the EIR if the document contains a special section or a cover sheet identifying where each of the points required in an EIR may be found. This section also identifies the special requirement for an EIR on a general plan to be submitted to the State Clearinghouse for review as a project of areawide, regional, or statewide significance as provided in Section 15207.

15167 Staged EIR

(a) Where a large capital project will require a number of discretionary approvals from government agencies and one of the approvals will occur more than two years before construction will begin, a staged EIR may be prepared covering the entire project in a general form. The staged EIR shall evaluate the proposal in light of current and contemplated plans and produce an informed estimate of the environmental consequences of the entire project. The aspect of the project before the public agency for approval shall be discussed with a greater degree of specificity.

(b) When a staged EIR has been prepared, a supplement to the EIR shall be prepared when a later approval is required for the project, and the information available at the time of the later approval would permit consideration of additional environmental impacts, mitigation measures, or reasonable alternatives to the project.

(c) Where a statute such as the Warren-Alquist Energy Resources Conservation and Development Act provides that a specific agency shall be the lead agency for a project and requires the lead agency to prepare an EIR, a responsible agency which must grant an approval for the project before the lead agency has completed the EIR may prepare and consider a staged EIR.

(d) An agency requested to prepare a staged EIR may decline to act as the lead agency if it determines, among other factors, that:

(1) Another agency would be the appropriate lead agency; and

(2) There is no compelling need to prepare a staged EIR and grant an approval for the project before the appropriate lead agency will take its action on the project.

Note: Authority cited: Sections 21083 and 21087, Public Resources Code. Reference: Section 21003, Public Resources Code.

Discussion: The staged EIR was developed as a device to deal with the problem of a large development project which would require many years for planning, engineering, and construction but would need a number of approvals from public agencies before the final plans for the project would be available. Where those final plans would not be available, the Lead Agency preparing an EIR for one of the early approvals would have difficulty providing enough information about the project to evaluate the effects of the entire project as would otherwise be required.

The device of the staged EIR provides a special relaxation of the requirement for the EIR on a development project to examine the entire project in detail. To make up for this lack of detail with the early approval, the section requires preparation of a supplement with later approvals when additional information becomes available. The section also allows this device to be used in the troublesome situation where an agency with limited control over the project is asked to grant the first approval for the project long before the normal Lead Agency would be called upon to act. The Responsible Agency needs some document to use in order to comply with CEQA. At the same time, due to its limited control over the project, it would not be a prime candidate for being Lead Agency. This approach allows the Responsible Agency to do a limited EIR examining the effects of its approval but noting in a general way the larger scope of the project and the general environmental effects expected.

15168 Program EIR

(a) General. A program EIR is an EIR which may be prepared on a series of actions that can be characterized as one large project and are related either:

(1) Geographically,

(2) As logical parts in the chain of contemplated actions,

(3) In connection with issuance of rules, regulations, plans, or other general criteria to govern the conduct of a continuing program, or

(4) As individual activities carried out under the same authorizing statutory or regulatory authority and having generally similar environmental effects which can be mitigated in similar ways.

(b) Advantages. Use of a program EIR can provide the following advantages. The program EIR can:

(1) Provide an occasion for a more exhaustive consideration of effects and alternatives than would be practical in an EIR on an individual action,

(2) Ensure consideration of cumulative impacts that might be slighted in a case-by-case analysis,

(3) Avoid duplicative reconsideration of basic policy considerations,

(4) Allow the lead agency to consider broad policy alternatives and programwide mitigation measures at an early time when the agency has greater flexibility to deal with basic problems or cumulative impacts,

(5) Allow reduction in paperwork.

(c) Use with Later Activities. Subsequent activities in the program must be examined in the light of the program EIR to determine whether an additional environmental document must be prepared.

(1) If a later activity would have effects that were not examined in the program EIR, a new initial study would need to be prepared leading to either an EIR or a negative declaration.

(2) If the agency finds that pursuant to Section 15162, no new effects could occur or no new mitigation measures would be required, the agency can approve the activity as being within the scope of the project covered by the program EIR, and no new environmental document would be required.

(3) An agency shall incorporate feasible mitigation measures and alternatives developed in the program EIR into subsequent actions in the program.

(4) Where the subsequent activities involve site specific operations, the agency should use a written checklist or similar device to document the evaluation of the site and the activity to determine whether the environmental effects of the operation were covered in the program EIR.

(5) A program EIR will be most helpful in dealing with subsequent activities if it deals with the effects of the program as specifically and comprehensively as possible. With a good and detailed analysis of the program, many subsequent activities could be found to be within the scope of the project described in the program EIR, and no further environmental documents would be required.

(d) Use with Subsequent EIRs and Negative Declarations. A program EIR can be used to simplify the task of preparing environmental documents on later parts of the program. The program EIR can:

(1) Provide the basis in an initial study for determining whether the later activity may have any significant effects.

(2) Be incorporated by reference to deal with regional influences, secondary effects, cumulative impacts, broad alternatives, and other factors that apply to the program as a whole.

(3) Focus an EIR on a subsequent project to permit discussion solely of new effects which had not been considered before.

(e) Notice with Later Activities. When a law other than CEQA requires public notice when the agency later proposes to carry out or approve an activity within the program and to rely on the program EIR for CEQA compliance, the notice for the activity shall include a statement that:

(1) This activity is within the scope of the program approved earlier, and

(2) The program EIR adequately describes the activity for the purposes of CEQA.

Note: Authority cited: Sections 21083 and 21087, Public Resources Code. Reference: Section 21003, Public Resources Code; *County of Inyo v. Yorty*, 32 Cal.App.3d 795 (1973).

Discussion: The program EIR is a device originally developed by federal agencies under NEPA. Use of this approach was recommended for CEQA in the court decision of *County of Inyo v. Yorty* cited in the note.

The detailed description of the permissible uses of this document are provided in an effort to encourage its use. The program EIR can be used effectively with a decision to carry out a new governmental program or to adopt a new body of regulations in a regulatory program. The program EIR enables the agency to examine the overall effects of the proposed course of action and to take steps to avoid unnecessary adverse environmental effects.

Use of the program EIR also enables the Lead Agency to characterize the overall program as the project being approved at that time. Following this approach when individual activities within the program are proposed, the agency would be required to examine the individual activities to determine whether their effects were fully analyzed in the program EIR. If the activities would have no effects beyond those analyzed in the program EIR, the agency could assert that the activities are merely part of the program which had been approved earlier, and no further CEQA compliance would be required. This approach offers many possibilities for agencies to reduce their costs of CEQA compliance and still achieve high levels of environmental protection.

15169   Master Environmental Assessment

(a) General. A public agency may prepare a master environmental assessment, inventory, or data base for all, or a portion of, the territory subject to its control in order to provide information which may be used or referenced in EIRs or negative declarations. Neither the content, the format, nor the procedures to be used to develop a master environmental

assessment are prescribed by these guidelines. The descriptions contained in this section are advisory. A master environmental assessment is suggested solely as an approach to identify and organize environmental information for a region or area of the state.

(b) Contents. A master environmental assessment may contain an inventory of the physical and biological characteristics of the area for which it is prepared and may contain such additional data and information as the public agency determines is useful or necessary to describe environmental characteristics of the area. It may include identification of existing levels of quality and supply of air and water, capacities and levels of use of existing services and facilities, and generalized incremental effects of different categories of development projects by type, scale, and location.

(c) Preparation.

(1) A master environmental assessment or inventory may be prepared in many possible ways. For example, a master environmental assessment may be prepared as a special, comprehensive study of the area involved, as part of the EIR on a general plan, or as a data base accumulated by indexing EIRs prepared for individual projects or programs in the area involved.

(2) The information contained in a master environmental assessment should be reviewed periodically and revised as needed so that it is accurate and current.

(3) When advantageous to do so, master environmental assessments may be prepared through a joint exercise of powers agreement with neighboring local agencies or with the assistance of the appropriate Council of Governments.

(d) Uses.

(1) A master environmental assessment can identify the environmental characteristics and constraints of an area. This information can be used to influence the design and location of individual projects.

(2) A master environmental assessment may provide information agencies can use in initial studies to decide whether certain environmental effects are likely to occur and whether certain effects will be significant.

(3) A master environmental assessment can provide a central source

of current information for use in preparing individual EIRs and negative declarations.

(4) Relevant portions of a master environmental assessment can be referenced and summarized in EIRs and negative declarations.

(5) A master environmental assessment can assist in identifying long range, areawide, and cumulative impacts of individual projects proposed in the area covered by the assessment.

(6) A master environmental assessment can assist a city or county in formulating a general plan or any element of such a plan by identifying environmental characteristics and constraints that need to be addressed in the general plan.

(7) A master environmental assessment can serve as a reference document to assist public agencies which review other environmental documents dealing with activities in the area covered by the assessment. The public agency preparing the assessment should forward a completed copy to each agency which will review projects in the area.

Note: Authority cited: Sections 21083 and 21087, Public Resources Code. Reference: Section 21003, Public Resources Code.

Discussion: The Master Environmental Assessment was developed as a way of providing a data base for use with later EIRs. If an agency prepared a Master Environmental Assessment, the agency could reduce the amount of work necessary to prepare later EIRs. The environmental setting would have been fully analyzed, and the likely environmental effects in the area could be anticipated. Thus, the Master Environmental Assessment could help focus initial studies as well as EIRs.

15170   Joint EIR-EIS

A lead agency under CEQA may work with a federal agency to prepare a joint document which will meet the requirements of both CEQA and NEPA. Use of such a joint document is described in Article 14, beginning with Section 15220.

Note: Authority cited: Sections 21083 and 21087, Public Resources Code. Reference: Sections 21083.5 and 21083.7, Public Resources Code.

Discussion: This section identifies the joint EIR-EIS as a special type of EIR. This special treatment is appropriate because many unusual steps would be required in order to meet the requirements of NEPA as well as CEQA. These steps may include formal scoping hearings, publication of notice in the Federal Register, and public review of the final EIR-EIS. This section also clearly establishes the validity of this joint document.

Article 11.5 Master Environmental Impact Report Sections 15175 to 15179.5

15175   Master EIR

(a) The Master EIR procedure is an alternative to preparing a project EIR, staged EIR, or program EIR for certain projects which will form the basis for later decision making. It is intended to streamline the later environmental review of projects or approval included within the project, plan or program analyzed in the Master EIR. Accordingly, a Master EIR shall, to the greatest extent feasible, evaluate the cumulative impacts, growth inducing impacts, and irreversible significant effects on the environment of subsequent projects.

(b) A lead agency may prepare a Master EIR for any of the following classes of projects:

(1) A general plan, general plan update, general plan element, general plan amendment, or specific plan.

(2) Public or private projects that will be carried out or approved pursuant to, or in furtherance of, a redevelopment plan.

(3) A project that consists of smaller individual projects which will be carried out in phases.

(4) A rule or regulation which will be implemented by later projects.

(5) Projects that will be carried out or approved pursuant to a development agreement.

(6) A state highway project or mass transit project which will be subject to multiple stages of review or approval.

(7) A plan proposed by a local agency, including a joint powers authority, for the reuse of a federal military base or reservation that has been closed or is proposed for closure by the federal government.

(8) A regional transportation plan or congestion management plan.

(9) Regulations adopted by the California Department of Fish and Game for the regulation of hunting and fishing.

(c) A lead agency may develop and implement a fee program in accordance with

applicable provisions of law to generate the revenue necessary to prepare a Master EIR.

Note: Authority cited: Sections 21083 and 21087, Public Resources Code. Reference: Sections 21156, 21157, and 21089, Public Resources Code.

Discussion: This section introduces the master EIR concept and lists the types of projects for which a master EIR may be prepared.

15176   Contents of a Master EIR

A lead agency shall include in a Master EIR all of the following:

(a) A detailed discussion as required by Section 15126.

(b) A description of anticipated subsequent projects that are within the scope of the Master EIR, including information with regard to the kind, size, intensity, and location of the subsequent projects, including, but not limited to all of the following:

(1) The specific type of project anticipated to be undertaken such as a single family development, office-commercial development, sewer line installation or other activities.

(2) The maximum and minimum intensity of any anticipated subsequent project, such as the number of residences in a residential development, and with regard to a public works facility, its anticipated capacity and service area.

(3) The anticipated location for any subsequent development projects, and, consistent with the rule of reason set forth in Section 15126, subdivision (d)(5),[6] alternative locations for any such projects.

(4) A capital outlay or capital improvement program, or other scheduling or implementing device that governs the submission and approval of subsequent projects, or an explanation as to why practical planning considerations render it impractical to identify any such program or scheduling or other device at the time of preparing the Master EIR.

(c) A description of potential impacts of anticipated projects for which there is not sufficient information reasonably available to support a full assessment of potential impacts in the Master EIR. This description shall not be construed as a limitation on the impacts which may be considered in a focused EIR.

(d) Where a Master EIR is prepared in connection with a project identified in subdivision (b)(1) of section 15175, the anticipated subsequent projects included within a Master EIR may consist of later planning approvals, including parcel-specific approvals, consistent with the overall planning decision (e.g., general plan, or specific plan, or redevelopment plan) for which the Master EIR has been prepared. Such subsequent projects shall be adequately described for purposes of subdivision (b) or of this section (15176) if the Master EIR and any other documents embodying or relating to the overall planning decision identify the land use designations and the permissible densities and intensities of use for the affected parcel(s). The proponents of such subsequent projects shall not be precluded from relying on the Master EIR solely because that document did not specifically identify or list, by name, the subsequent project as ultimately proposed for approval.

Note: Authority cited: Sections 21083 and 21087, Public Resources Code. Reference: Section 21157, Public Resources Code.

Discussion: This section details the minimum requirements for the content of a master EIR. A master EIR must identify the subsequent projects which will be considered within its scope and thereby eligible for streamlined review.

Subsection (b)(4) clarifies that in some cases, it may be impractical for the lead agency to specify a capital improvement program, or other scheduling or implementing device for future projects when preparing a master EIR. Where it is not possible to specify a scheduling device, the agency must describe the practical planning considerations which render it impractical.

Subsection (d) clarifies that the lead agency is not required to identify or list subsequent projects by name in order for them to qualify for streamlined review. For example, where the master EIR was prepared for a city general plan, a subsequent project consistent with the land use designation and permitted density and intensity of development established in that plan is considered to be within the scope of the master EIR.

15177   Subsequent Projects within the Scope of the MEIR

(a) After a Master EIR has been prepared and certified, subsequent projects which the lead agency determines as being within the scope of the Master EIR will be subject to only limited environmental review.

(b) Except as provided in subsection (2) of this subdivision, neither a new environmental document nor the preparation of findings pursuant to section 15091 shall be required of a subsequent project when all the following requirements are met:

(1) The lead agency for the subsequent project is the lead agency or any responsible agency identified in the Master EIR.

(2) The lead agency for the subsequent project prepares an initial study on the proposal. The initial study shall analyze whether the subsequent project was described in the Master EIR and whether the subsequent project may cause any additional significant effect on the environment which was not previously examined in the Master EIR.

(3) The lead agency for the subsequent project determines, on the basis of written findings, that no additional significant environmental effect will result from the proposal, no new additional mitigation measures or alternatives may be required, and that the project is within the scope of the Master EIR. "Additional significant environmental effect" means any project-specific effect which was not addressed as a significant effect in the Master EIR.

(c) Whether a subsequent project is within the scope of the Master EIR is a question of fact to be determined by the lead agency based upon a review of the initial study to determine whether there are additional significant effects or new additional mitigation measures or alternatives required for the subsequent project that are not already discussed in the Master EIR.

(d) Prior to approval of the proposed subsequent project, the lead agency shall incorporate all feasible mitigation measures or feasible alternatives appropriate to the project as set forth in the Master EIR and provide notice in the manner required by Section 15087.

(e) When the lead agency approves a project pursuant to this section, the lead agency shall file a notice in the manner required by Section 15075.

Note: Authority cited: Sections 21083 and 21087, Public Resources Code. References: Sections 21157, 21157.6 and 21158, Public Resources Code.

Discussion: This section discusses the circumstances under which the master EIR can be applied to subsequent projects which are within its scope, avoiding the need to prepare a subsequent EIR or negative declaration. The master EIR can be certified as the environmental analysis for subsequent projects that are within its scope and which do not have project-specific effects that were not previously discussed. As specified in statute, an initial study must be performed on all projects to determine whether the master EIR can be applied and no additional environmental document is needed.

15178 Subsequent Projects Identified in the MEIR

(a) When a proposed subsequent project is identified in the Master EIR, but the lead agency cannot make a determination pursuant to Section 15177 that the subsequent project is within the scope of the Master EIR, and the lead agency determines that the cumulative impacts, growth inducing impacts and irreversible significant effects analysis in the Master EIR is adequate for the subsequent project, the lead agency shall prepare a mitigated negative declaration or a focused EIR if, after preparing an initial study, the lead agency determines that the project may result in new or additional significant effects. Whether the cumulative impacts, growth inducing impacts and irreversible significant effects analyses are adequate is a question of fact to be determined by the lead agency based upon a review of the proposed subsequent project in light of the Master EIR.

(b) A lead agency shall prepare a mitigated negative declaration for any proposed subsequent project if both of the following occur:

(1) The initial study prepared pursuant to Section 15177 has identified potentially new or additional significant environmental effects that were not analyzed in the Master EIR; and

(2) Feasible mitigation measures or alternatives will be incorporated to revise the subsequent project before the negative declaration is released for public review pursuant to Section 15073 in order to avoid or mitigate the identified effects to a level of insignificance.

(c) A lead agency shall prepare a focused EIR if the subsequent project may have a significant effect on the environment and a mitigated negative declaration pursuant to subdivision (b) of this section cannot be prepared.

(1) The focused EIR shall incorporate by reference the Master EIR and analyze only the subsequent project's additional significant environmental effects and any new or additional mitigation measures or alternatives that were not identified and analyzed by the Master EIR. "Additional significant environmental effects" are those project-specific effects on the environment which were not addressed as significant in the Master EIR.

(2) A focused EIR need not examine those effects which the lead agency, prior to public release of the focused EIR, finds, on the basis of the initial study, related documents, and commitments from the proponent of a subsequent project, have been mitigated in one of the following manners:

(A) Mitigated or avoided as a result of mitigation measures identified in the Master EIR which the lead agency will require as part of the approval of the subsequent project;

(B) Examined at a sufficient level of detail in the Master EIR to enable those significant effects to be mitigated or avoided by specific revisions to the project, the imposition of conditions of approval, or by other means in connection with approval of the subsequent project; or

(C) The mitigation or avoidance of which is the responsibility of and within the jurisdiction of another public agency and is, or can and should be, undertaken by that agency.

(3) The lead agency's findings pursuant to subdivision (2) shall be included in the focused EIR prior to public release pursuant to Section 15087.

(4) A focused EIR prepared pursuant to this section shall analyze any significant environmental effects when:

(A) Substantial new or additional information shows that the adverse environmental effect may be more significant than was described in the Master EIR; or

(B) Substantial new or additional information shows that mitigation measures or alternatives which were previously determined to be infeasible are feasible and will avoid or reduce the significant effects of the subsequent project to a level of insignificance.

(d) A lead agency shall file a notice of determination shall be filed pursuant to Section 15075 if a project has been approved for which a mitigated negative declaration has been prepared pursuant to this section and a notice of determination shall be filed pursuant to Section 15094 if a project has been approved for which a focused EIR has been prepared pursuant to this section.

(e) When a lead agency determines that the cumulative impacts, growth inducing impacts and irreversible significant effects analysis in the Master EIR is inadequate for the subsequent project, the subsequent project is no longer eligible for the limited environmental review available under the Master EIR process and shall be reviewed according to Article 7 (commencing with Section 15080) of these guidelines. The lead agency shall tier the project specific EIR upon the Master EIR to the extent feasible under Section 15152.

Note: Authority cited: Sections 21083 and 21087, Public Resources Code. References: Sections 21081(a)(2), 21157.5 and 21158, Public Resources Code.

Discussion: This section discusses the circumstances under which the master EIR must be supplemented with either a focused EIR or a mitigated negative declaration before it can be applied to subsequent projects. This section only applies to subsequent projects that are within the scope of the master EIR and whose cumulative impacts, growth inducing impacts and irreversible significant effects have been sufficiently analyzed in the master EIR.

This section defines the term "focused EIR." A focused EIR works in conjunction with a master EIR and contains project-specific analysis that was absent from the master EIR. The link to a master EIR distinguishes a focused EIR from subsequent or supplemental EIRs (as described in Sections 15162 and 15163) which focus the analysis of subsequent actions under a project that was previously analyzed in an EIR or negative declaration.

15179 Limitations on the Use of the Master EIR

The certified Master EIR shall not be used in accordance with this article if either (i) it was certified more than five years prior to the filing of an application for a later project, or (ii) a project not identified in the certified Master EIR as an anticipated subsequent project is approved and the approved project may affect the adequacy of the

Master EIR, unless the lead agency does one of the following:

(a) Reviews the Master EIR and finds that no substantial changes have occurred with respect to the circumstances under which the Master EIR was certified, or that there is no new available information which was not known and could not have been known at the time the Master EIR was certified; or

(b) Prepares a subsequent or supplemental EIR that updates or revises the Master EIR and which either (i) is incorporated into the previously certified Master EIR, or (ii) references any deletions, additions or other modifications to the previously certified Master EIR.

Note: Authority cited: Sections 21083 and 21087, Public Resources Code. Reference: Section 21157.6, Public Resources Code.

Discussion: A master EIR must be periodically reviewed, in light of changing circumstances, to determine that it is still an adequate analysis of the significant environmental effects of the project for which it was prepared. Updating the master EIR, including preparing subsequent or supplemental EIRs, maintains its effectiveness as the basis for streamlined review of projects that are within its scope.

15179.5 Focused EIRs and Small Projects

(a) When a project is a multiple family residential development of 100 units or less or is a residential and commercial or retail mixed-use commercial development of not more then 100,000 square feet, whether or not the project is identified in the Master EIR, a focused EIR shall be prepared pursuant to this section when the following conditions are met:

(1) The project is consistent with a general plan, specific plan, community plan, or zoning ordinance for which an EIR was prepared within five years of certification of the focused EIR; and

(2) The parcel on which the project is to be developed is either:

(A) Surrounded by immediately contiguous urban development;

(B) Previously developed with urban uses; or

(C) Within one-half mile of an existing rail transit station.

(b) A focused environmental impact report prepared pursuant to this section shall be limited to a discussion of potentially significant effects on the environment specific to the project, or which

substantial new information shows will be more significant than described in the prior environmental impact report. No discussion shall be required of alternatives to the project, cumulative impacts of the project, or the growth inducing impacts of the project.

(c) This section does not apply where the lead agency can make a finding pursuant to Section 15177 that the subsequent project is within the scope of the Master EIR, where the lead agency can prepare a mitigated negative declaration or focused EIR pursuant to Section 15178, or where, pursuant to Section 15162 or Section 15163, the environmental impact report referenced in subdivision (a)(1) of this section must be updated through the preparation of a subsequent environmental impact report or a supplemental environmental impact report.

Note: Authority cited: Sections 21083 and 21087, Public Resources Code. Reference: Section 21158.5, Public Resources Code.

Discussion: Public Resources Code Section 21158.5 provides that a focused EIR may be used for certain urban infill projects which are otherwise outside the scope of a master EIR. This section describes the circumstances under which this may occur.

Article 12. Special Situations Sections 15180 to 15190

15180 Redevelopment Projects

(a) All public and private activities or undertakings pursuant to or in furtherance of a redevelopment plan constitute a single project, which shall be deemed approved at the time of adoption of the redevelopment plan by the legislative body. The EIR in connection with the redevelopment plan shall be submitted in accordance with Section 33352 of the Health and Safety Code.

(b) An EIR on a redevelopment plan shall be treated as a program EIR with no subsequent EIRs required for individual components of the redevelopment plan unless a subsequent EIR or a supplement to an EIR would be required by Section 15162 or 15163.

Note: Authority cited: Sections 21083 and 21087, Public Resources Code. Reference: Section 21090, Public Resources Code.

Discussion: This section identifies the special requirements that apply to redevelopment projects. Subsection (a) identifies the statutory requirements that apply in this situation.

Subsection (b) is an effort to relate the provisions applying to redevelopment projects to other provisions in CEQA. The language in CEQA Section 21090 providing that a redevelopment plan and undertakings in furtherance thereof are a single project, is consistent with the theory of a program EIR. Case law interpreting program EIRs has provided that the various undertakings in furtherance of a program for which a program EIR was prepared must be analyzed in the light of that program EIR. If the later activities in the program involve no new significant effects beyond those analyzed in the program EIR and are adequately handled by mitigation measures identified in the program EIR, there is no need for further documentation in the EIR process. If, however, a particular activity would involve a new significant effect, then there must be additional CEQA compliance for that effect.

This approach is also consistent with Sections 21166 and 21090 which speaks in terms of a single project. They provide that where an EIR has been prepared for a project under CEQA, no subsequent or supplemental EIR shall be required by the Lead Agency or any other Responsible Agency unless one of the three described events occurs.

15181 Housing and Neighborhood Commercial Facilities in Urbanized Areas

(a) A Lead Agency may approve a project involving the construction of housing or neighborhood commercial facilities in an urbanized area with the use of an EIR or negative declaration previously prepared for a specific plan, local coastal program, or port master plan if the lead agency complies with the requirements of this section.

(b) The procedures for complying with this section are as follows:

(1) The lead agency shall conduct an initial study to determine whether the project may have one or more significant effects on the environment.

(2) The lead agency shall give notice of its proposed use of a previously prepared EIR to all persons who had submitted a written request for notice and shall also give notice by either:

(A) Posting notice on and off the site in the area where the project would be located, or

(B) Mailing notice directly to owners of property contiguous to the project site.

(3) The lead agency shall make the following findings with regard to planning and the previously prepared EIR.

(A) That the project is consistent with either:

1. A specific plan which was adopted for the area pursuant to Article 8 (commencing with Section 65450), Article 9 (commencing with Section 65500), and Article 10 (commencing with Section 65550) of Chapter 3 of Title 7 of the Government Code, or

2. A local coastal program or port master plan certified pursuant to Article 2 (commencing with Section 30510) of Chapter 6 of Division 20 of the Public Resources Code.

(B) That the specific plan, local coastal program, or port master plan was adopted not more than five years prior to the finding made pursuant to this subsection and that the method of adoption was the procedure specified by Article 9 (commencing with Section 65500) of Chapter 3 of Title 7 of the Government Code for adopting specific plans and regulations.

(C) That the specific plan or local coastal program or port master plan was the subject of a certified environmental impact report.

(D) That the environmental impact report is sufficiently detailed so that all the significant effects of the project on the environment and measures necessary to mitigate or avoid any such effects can be determined. This examination of the previously prepared EIR shall include a further, specific finding as to:

1. Whether there would be any significant physical effects on existing structures and neighborhoods of historical or aesthetic significance if any exist in the area covered by the plan or program, and

2. Whether measures necessary to mitigate or avoid such effects are included in the EIR.

(E) That a subsequent EIR is not required pursuant to Public Resources Code Section 21166 and Guidelines Section 15162.

(4) The lead agency shall make one or more findings as required by Section 15091 with regard to mitigating or avoiding each significant effect that the project would have on the environment.

(5) The lead agency shall file a notice of determination with the county clerk if the lead agency approves the project.

(c) As used in this section, "neighborhood commercial facilities" means those commercial facilities which are an integral part of a project involving the construction of housing and which will serve the residents of such housing.

(d) As used in this section, "urbanized area" means only those areas mapped and designated as urbanized by the U. S. Bureau of the Census.

Note: Authority cited: Sections 21083 and 21087, Public Resources Code. Reference: Section 21080.7, Public Resources Code.

Discussion: This section describes and interprets the special rules that apply to construction of housing and neighborhood commercial facilities in urbanized areas. Subsection (a) provides a brief summary and introduction to the concepts in this section. Subsection (b) spells out the procedures to be followed and the detailed findings which must be made in order to comply with the section.

15182 Residential Projects Pursuant to a Specific Plan

(a) Exemption. Where a public agency has prepared an EIR on a specific plan after January 1, 1980, no EIR or negative declaration need be prepared for a residential project undertaken pursuant to and in conformity to that specific plan if the project meets the requirements of this section.

(b) Scope. Residential projects covered by this section include but are not limited to land subdivisions, zoning changes, and residential planned unit developments.

(c) Limitation. This section is subject to the limitation that if after the adoption of the specific plan, an event described in Section 15162 should occur, this exemption shall not apply until the city or county which adopted the specific plan completes a subsequent EIR or a supplement to an EIR on the specific plan. The exemption provided by this section shall again be available to residential projects after the lead agency has filed a Notice of Determination on the specific plan as reconsidered by the subsequent EIR or supplement to the EIR.

(d) Alternative. This section provides an alternative to the procedure described in Section 15181.

(e) Fees. The Lead Agency has authority to charge fees to applicants for projects which benefit from this section. The fees shall be calculated in the aggregate to defray but not to exceed the cost of developing and adopting the specific plan including the cost of preparing the EIR.

(f) Statute of Limitations. A court action challenging the approval of a project under this section for failure to prepare a supplemental EIR shall be commenced within 30 days after the lead agency's decision to carry out or approve the project in accordance with the specific plan.

Note: Authority cited: Section 21083, Public Resources Code. Reference: Section 65453, Government Code.

Discussion: This section is added to reorganize and interpret the special provisions of AB 1151 (Roos) of 1979 dealing with specific plans. This section is necessary to draw attention to Government Code Section 65453.

15183 Residential Projects Consistent with a Community Plan, General Plan, or Zoning

(a) CEQA mandates that projects which are consistent with the development density established by existing zoning, community plan, or general plan policies for which an EIR was certified shall not require additional environmental review, except as might be necessary to examine whether there are project-specific significant effects which are peculiar to the project or its site. This streamlines the review of such projects and reduces the need to prepare repetitive environmental studies.

(b) In approving a ~~residential~~ project meeting the requirements of this section, a public agency shall limit its examination of environmental effects ~~under CEQA to effects~~ to those which the agency determines, in an initial study or other analysis:

(1) Are peculiar to the project or the parcel on which the project would be located, ~~although the effect may occur on or off the site of the project, and~~

(2) Were not analyzed as significant effects in a prior EIR on the zoning action, general plan, or community plan, with which the ~~residential~~ project is consistent,

(3) Are potentially significant off-site impacts and cumulative impacts which were not discussed in the prior EIR prepared for the general plan, community plan or zoning action, or

(4) Are previously identified significant effects which, as a result of substantial new information which was not known at the time the EIR was certified, are determined to have a more severe adverse impact than discussed in the prior EIR.

(c) If an impact is not peculiar to the parcel or to the project, has been addressed as a significant effect in the prior EIR, or can be substantially mitigated by the imposition of uniformly applied development policies or standards, as contemplated by subdivision (e) below, then an additional EIR need not be prepared for the project solely on the basis of that impact.

(b)(d) This section shall apply only to ~~residential~~ projects which meet the following conditions:

(1) The project is consistent with:

(A) A community plan adopted as part of a general plan, ~~or~~

(B) A zoning action which zoned or designated the parcel on which the project would be located to accommodate a particular density of ~~residential~~ development, or

(B)(C) A general plan of a local agency, and

(2) An EIR was certified by the lead agency for the zoning action, the community plan, or the general plan.

(c)(e) This section shall limit the analysis of only those significant environmental effects for which:

(1) Each public agency with authority to mitigate any of the significant effects on the environment identified in the planning or zoning action undertakes or requires others to undertake mitigation measures specified in the EIR which the lead agency found to be feasible, and

(2) The lead agency makes a finding at a public hearing as to whether the feasible mitigation measures will be undertaken.

(d)(f) An effect of a project on the environment shall not be considered peculiar to the project or the parcel for the purposes of this section if uniformly applied development policies or standards have been previously adopted by the city or county with a finding that the development policies or standards will

substantially mitigate that environmental effect when applied to future projects, unless substantial new information shows that the policies or standards will not substantially mitigate the environmental effect. The finding shall be based on substantial evidence which need not include an EIR. Such development policies or standards need not apply throughout the entire city or county, but can apply only within the zoning district in which the project is located, or within the area subject to the community plan on which the lead agency is relying. Moreover, such policies or standards need not be part of the general plan or any community plan, but can be found within another pertinent planning document such as a zoning ordinance. Where a city or county, in previously adopting uniformly applied development policies or standards for imposition on future projects, failed to make a finding as to whether such policies or standards would substantially mitigate the effects of future projects, the decisionmaking body of the city or county, prior to approving such a future project pursuant to this section, may hold a public hearing for the purpose of considering whether, as applied to the project, such standards or policies would substantially mitigate the effects of the project. Such a public hearing need only be held if the city or county decides to apply the standards or policies as permitted in this section.

(g) Examples of uniformly applied development policies or standards include, but are not limited to:

(1) Parking ordinances.

(2) Public access requirements.

(3) Grading ordinances.

(4) Hillside development ordinances.

(5) Flood plain ordinances.

(6) Habitat protection or conservation ordinances.

(7) View protection ordinances.

(e)(h) An environmental effect shall not be considered peculiar to the project or parcel solely because no uniformly applied development policy or standard is applicable to it.

(f)(i) Where ~~a~~ the prior EIR relied upon by the lead agency was prepared for a general plan or community plan that meets the requirements of this section, any rezoning action consistent with the general plan or community plan shall be treated as a ~~residential~~ project subject to this section.

(1) "Community plan" is defined as a part of the general plan of a city or county which applies to a defined geographic portion of the total area included in the general plan, includes or references each of the mandatory elements specified in Section 65302 of the Government Code, and contains specific development policies and implementation measures which will apply those policies to each involved parcel.

(2) For purposes of this section, "consistent" means that the density of the proposed project is the same or less than the standard expressed for the involved parcel in the general plan, community plan or zoning action for which an EIR has been certified, and that the project complies with the density-related standards contained in that plan or zoning. Where the zoning ordinance refers to the general plan or community plan for its density standard, the project shall be consistent with the applicable plan.

(j) This section does not affect any requirement to analyze potentially significant offsite or cumulative impacts if those impacts were not adequately discussed in the prior EIR. If a significant offsite or cumulative impact was adequately discussed in the prior EIR, then this section may be used as a basis for excluding further analysis of that offsite or cumulative impact.

Note: Authority cited: Sections 21083 and 21087, Public Resources Code. Reference: Section 21083.3, Public Resources Code.

Discussion: This section implements Public Resources Code Section 21083.3(a) as amended by the Legislature in 1984. Formerly Section 21083.3(a) authorized a limited EIR for residential projects which were consistent with a community plan or zoning. The section was amended to include projects consistent with a general plan for which an EIR has been certified.

Public Resources Code section 21083.3 was further amended in 1992 (Chapter 1102) to broaden its application to all qualifying development projects, not simply residential projects. In addition, the conditions which would trigger the application of CEQA to such projects have been expanded to include situations where "substantial new information" shows an effect addressed in the previous EIR will be "more significant" than previously described. Further, uniformly applied standards or policies are negated by substantial new information indicating that they will not offer substantial mitigation.

Subsection (f) clarifies that uniformly applied development standards or policies do not have to apply jurisdiction-wide in order to substantially mitigate the impacts of a project. They do have to apply within a zoning district or a community plan. Some ordinances, such as hillside development and floodplain protection zones, are applied only in areas subject to environmental constraints such as steep slopes and flooding. Yet, they establish standards that are uniformly applied within those zoning classifications to mitigate environmental effects. This subsection further provides that if at the time these standards or policies were adopted no finding had been made regarding their use for future projects, such findings may be made after a public hearing for that purpose.

15184   State Mandated Local Projects

Whenever a state agency issues an order which requires a local agency to carry out a project subject to CEQA, the following rules apply:

(a) If an EIR is prepared for the project, the local agency shall limit the EIR to considering those factors and alternatives which will not conflict with the order.

(b) If a local agency undertakes a project to implement a rule or regulation imposed by a certified state environmental regulatory program listed in Section 15251, the project shall be exempt from CEQA with regard to the significant effects analyzed in the document prepared by the state agency as a substitute for an EIR. The local agency shall comply with CEQA with regard to any site-specific effect of the project which was not analyzed by the certified state agency as a significant effect on the environment. The local agency need not re-examine the general environmental effects of the state rule or regulation.

Note: Authority cited: Sections 21083 and 21087, Public Resources Code. Reference: Sections 21080, 21080.5, and 21154, Public Resources Code.

Discussion: This section brings together two separate provisions dealing with state-mandated local projects. The first provision implements Section 21154 of the statute. This requirement in subsection (a) is straightforward and needs little interpretation.

This section exempts the local agency from complying with CEQA as to any effects as discussed as significant in an EIR substitute document prepared by a state environmental regulatory agency certified under Section 21080.5 of CEQA. The local agency would still need to comply with CEQA with regard to any site-specific effects of the project

which were not analyzed as significant effects by the certified state agency. The main benefit to local agencies from this provision is that it frees them from the need to re-examine the purpose and general environmental effects of the state rule or regulation. This purpose and general effect are matters outside the hands of the local agency. The section makes it clear that the local agency need not reconsider these matters.

15185   Administrative Appeals

(a) Where an agency allows administrative appeals upon the adequacy of an environmental document, an appeal shall be handled according to the procedures of that agency. Public notice shall be handled in accordance with individual agency requirements and Section 15202(e).

(b) The decisionmaking body to which an appeal has been made shall consider the environmental document and make findings under Sections 15091 and 15093 if appropriate.

Note: Authority cited: Sections 21083 and 21087, Public Resources Code. Reference: Sections 21082 and 21083, Public Resources Code.

Discussion: This section deals with the problem of how to handle appeals from decisions for which an EIR or Negative Declaration was prepared under CEQA. Subsection (a) relies on the procedures which individual agencies have adopted for appeals. Subsection (b) identifies the requirement for the body hearing the appeal to consider the EIR or Negative Declaration and make findings if necessary in the same way as the original decision-making body.

15186   School Facilities

(a) CEQA establishes a special requirement for certain school projects, as well as certain projects near schools, to ensure that potential health impacts resulting from exposure to hazardous materials, wastes, and substances will be carefully examined and disclosed in a negative declaration or EIR, and that the lead agency will consult with other agencies in this regard.

(b) When a project located within one-fourth mile of a school involves the construction or alteration of a facility which might reasonably be anticipated to emit hazardous or acutely hazardous air emissions, or which would handle acutely hazardous material or a mixture containing acutely hazardous material in a quantity equal to or greater than that specified in subdivision (a) of Section 25536 of the Health and Safety Code, which may impose a health or safety hazard to persons who would attend or would be employed at the school, the lead agency must:

(1) Consult with the affected school district or districts regarding the potential impact of the project on the school when circulating the proposed negative declaration or draft EIR for review.

(2) Notify the affected school district of the project, in writing, not less than 30 days prior to approval or certification of the negative declaration or EIR. This subdivision does not apply to projects for which an application was submitted prior to January 1, 1992.

(c) When the project involves the purchase of a school site or the construction of a secondary or elementary school, the negative declaration or EIR prepared for the project shall not be approved or certified by the school board unless:

(1) The negative declaration or EIR contains sufficient information to determine whether the property is:

(A) The site of a current or former hazardous waste or solid waste disposal facility and, if so, whether wastes have been removed.

(B) A hazardous substance release site identified by the Department of Toxic Substances Control in a current list adopted pursuant to Section 25356 of the Health and Safety Code for removal or remedial action pursuant to Chapter 6.8 (commencing with Section 25300) of Division 20 of the Health and Safety Code.

(C) The site of one or more buried or above ground pipelines which carry hazardous substances, acutely hazardous materials, or hazardous wastes, as defined in Division 20 of the Health and Safety Code. This does not include a natural gas pipeline used only to supply the school or neighborhood.

(2) The lead agency has notified in writing and consulted with the county or city administering agency (as designated pursuant to Section 25502 of the Health and Safety Code) and with any air pollution control district or air quality management district having jurisdiction, to identify facilities within one-fourth mile of the proposed school site which might reasonably be anticipated to emit hazardous emissions or handle hazardous or acutely hazardous material, substances, or waste. The notice shall include a list of the school sites for which information is sought. Each agency or district receiving notice shall provide the requested information and provide a written response to the lead agency within 30 days of receiving the notification. If any such agency or district fails to respond within that time, the negative declaration or EIR shall be conclusively presumed to comply with this section as to the area of responsibility of that agency.

(3) The school board makes, on the basis of substantial evidence, one of the following written findings:

(A) Consultation identified none of the facilities specified in paragraph (2).

(B) The facilities specified in paragraph (2) exist, but one of the following conditions applies:

1. The health risks from the facilities do not and will not constitute an actual or potential endangerment of public health to persons who would attend or be employed at the proposed school.

2. Corrective measures required under an existing order by another agency having jurisdiction over the facilities will, before the school is occupied, mitigate all chronic or accidental hazardous air emissions to levels that do not constitute any actual or potential public health danger to persons who would attend or be employed at the proposed school. When the school district board makes such a finding, it shall also make a subsequent finding, prior to occupancy of the school, that the emissions have been so mitigated.

This finding shall be in addition to any findings which may be required pursuant to Sections 15074, 15091 or 15093.

(d) When the lead agency has carried out the consultation required by paragraph (2) of subdivision (b), the negative declaration or EIR shall be conclusively presumed to comply with this section, notwithstanding any failure of the consultation to identify an existing facility.

(e) The following definitions shall apply for the purposes of this section:

(1) "Acutely hazardous material," is as defined in 22 C.C.R. §66260.10.

(2) "Administering agency," is as defined in Section 25501 of the Health and Safety Code.

(3) "Hazardous air emissions," is as defined in subdivisions (a) to (f), inclusive, of Section 44321 of the Health and Safety Code.

(4) "Hazardous substance," is as defined in Section 25316 of the Health and Safety Code.

(5) "Hazardous waste," is as defined in Section 25117 of the Health and Safety Code.

(6) "Hazardous waste disposal site," is as defined in Section 25114 of the Health and Safety Code.

Note: Authority cited: Sections 21083 and 21087, Public Resources Code. References: Sections 21151.4 and 21151.8, Public Resources Code.

Discussion: CEQA contains requirements applicable to school projects and projects proposed near schools which are intended to limit the exposure of school children and others to toxic or hazardous substances. This section brings the requirements of Public Resources Code sections 21151.4 and 21151.8 together in a single place for ease of reference.

15187 Environmental Review of New Rules and Regulations

(a) At the time of the adoption of a rule or regulation requiring the installation of pollution control equipment, establishing a performance standard, or establishing a treatment requirement, the California Air Resources Board, Department of Toxic Substances Control, Integrated Waste Management Board, State Water Resources Control Board, all regional water quality control boards, and all air pollution control districts and air quality management districts, as defined in Section 39025 of the Health and Safety Code, must perform an environmental analysis of the reasonably foreseeable methods by which compliance with that rule or regulation will be achieved.

(b) If an EIR is prepared by the agency at the time of adoption of a rule or regulation, it satisfies the requirements of this section provided that the document contains the information specified in subdivision (c) below. Similarly, for those State agencies whose regulatory programs have been certified by the Resources Agency pursuant to Section 21080.5 of the Public Resources Code, an environmental document prepared pursuant to such programs satisfies the requirements of this section, provided that the document contains the information specified in subdivision (c) below.

(c) The environmental analysis shall include at least the following:

(1) An analysis of reasonably foreseeable environmental impacts of the methods of compliance;

(2) An analysis of reasonably foreseeable feasible mitigation measures relating to those impacts; and

(3) An analysis of reasonably foreseeable alternative means of compliance with the rule or regulation, which would avoid or eliminate the identified impacts.

(d) The environmental analysis shall take into account a reasonable range of environmental, economic, and technical factors, population and geographic areas, and specific sites. The agency may utilize numerical ranges and averages where specific data is not available, but is not required to, nor should it, engage in speculation or conjecture.

(e) Nothing in this section shall require the agency to conduct a project level analysis.

(f) Nothing in this section is intended, or may be used, to delay the adoption of any rule or regulation for which this section requires an environmental analysis.

Note: Authority cited: Sections 21083 and 21087, Public Resources Code. References: Sections 21159 and 21159.4, Public Resources Code.

Discussion: This section provides that an environmental assessment must be prepared prior to the enactment of specified regulations and outlines the minimum contents of such an assessment. An EIR may be substituted for this assessment when otherwise available, but this section does not mandate preparation of an EIR.

15188   Focused EIR for Pollution Control Equipment

This section applies to projects consisting solely of the installation of pollution control equipment and other components necessary to the installation of that equipment which are undertaken for the purpose of complying with a rule or regulation which was the subject of an environmental analysis as described in Section 15187.

(a) The lead agency for the compliance project may prepare a focused EIR to analyze the effects of that project when the following occur:

(1) the agency which promulgated the rule or regulation certified an EIR on that rule or regulation, or reviewed it pursuant to an environmental analysis prepared under a certified regulatory program and, in either case, the review included an assessment of growth inducing impacts and cumulative impacts of, and alternatives to, the project;

(2) the focused EIR for the compliance project is certified within five years of the certified EIR or environmental analysis required by subdivision (a)(1); and

(3) the EIR prepared in connection with the adoption of the rule or regulation need not be updated through the preparation of a subsequent EIR or supplemental EIR pursuant to section 15162 or section 15163.

(b) The discussion of significant environmental effects in the focused EIR shall be limited to project-specific, potentially significant effects which were not discussed in the environmental analysis required under Section 15187. No discussion of growth-inducing or cumulative impacts is required. Discussion of alternatives shall be limited to alternative means of compliance, if any, with the rule or regulation.

Note: Authority: Sections 21083 and 21087, Public Resources Code. Reference: Section 21159.1, Public Resources Code.

Discussion: This section applies to lead agencies which are permitting projects consisting of the installation of pollution control equipment where a regulatory agency has already prepared an environmental assessment or EIR under section 15187 for the rule or regulation mandating such equipment. If an EIR is required in order to analyze the effects of complying with the rule or regulation, the lead agency may prepare a focused EIR when the environmental assessment or EIR prepared by the regulatory agency for the rule or regulation included an assessment of the growth inducing impacts and cumulative impacts of, and alternatives to, the project. If no EIR is necessary for the compliance project, this section does not apply.

15189   Compliance with Performance Standard or Treatment Requirement Rule or Regulation

This section applies to projects consisting solely of compliance with a performance standard or treatment requirement which was the subject of an environmental analysis as described in Section 15187.

(a) If preparing a negative declaration, mitigated negative declaration or EIR on the compliance project the lead agency for the compliance project shall, to the greatest extent feasible, use the environmental analysis prepared pursuant to Section 15187. The use of numerical averages or ranges in the environmental analysis prepared under Section 15187 does not relieve the lead agency on the compliance project from its obligation to identify and evaluate the environmental effects of the project.

(b) Where the lead agency determines that an EIR is required for the compliance project, the EIR need address only the project-specific issues or other issues that were not discussed in sufficient detail in the environmental analysis prepared under Section 15187. The mitigation measures imposed by the lead agency shall be limited to addressing the significant effects on the environment of the compliance project. The discussion of alternatives shall be limited to a discussion of alternative means of compliance, if any, with the rule or regulation.

Note: Authority cited: Sections 21083 and 21087, Public Resources Code. Reference: Section 21159.2, Public Resources Code.

Discussion: This section enables the lead agency for a compliance project to tier a negative declaration or EIR for that project on the environmental analysis prepared by the regulatory agency which promulgated the underlying rule or regulation which prompts the compliance project.

15190   Deadlines for Compliance with Sections 15188 and 15189

(a) The lead agency for a compliance project under either Section 15188 or Section 15189 shall determine whether an EIR or negative declaration should be prepared within 30 days of its determination that the application for the project is complete.

(b) Where the EIR will be prepared under contract to the lead agency for the compliance project, the agency shall issue a request for proposal for preparation of the EIR not later than 30 days after the deadline for response to the notice of preparation has expired. The contract shall be awarded within 30 days of the response date on the request for proposals.

Note: Authority cited: Sections 21083 and 21087, Public Resources Code. Reference: Section 21159.3, Public Resources Code.

Article 13. Review and Evaluation of EIRs and Negative Declarations Sections 15200 to 15209

15200   Purposes of Review

The purposes of review of EIRs and Negative Declarations include:

(a) Sharing expertise,

(b) Disclosing agency analyses,

(c) Checking for accuracy,

(d) Detecting omissions,

(e) Discovering public concerns, and

(f) Soliciting counter proposals.

Note: Authority cited: Sections 21083 and 21087, Public Resources Code. Reference: Sections 21000, 21108, and 21152, Public Resources Code; *Environmental Defense Fund v. Coastside County Water District,* (1972) 27 Cal.App.3d 695; *County of Inyo v. City of Los Angeles*, (1977) 71 Cal.App. 3d 185.

Discussion: This interpretation of the purposes of review is added to show the different purposes which review serves.

15201   Public Participation

Public participation is an essential part of the CEQA process. Each public agency should include provisions in its CEQA procedures for wide public involvement, formal and informal, consistent with its existing activities and procedures, in order to receive and evaluate public reactions to environmental issues related to the agency's activities. Such procedures should include, whenever possible, making environmental information available in electronic format on the Internet, on a web site maintained or utilized by the public agency.

Note: Authority cited: Sections 21083 and 21087, Public Resources Code. Reference: Sections 21000, 21082, 21108, and 21152, Public Resources Code; *Environmental Defense Fund v. Coastside County Water District*, (1972) 27 Cal.App.3d 695; *People v. County of Kern*, (1974) 39 Cal.App.3d 830; *County of Inyo v. City of Los Angeles*, (1977) 71 Cal.App.3d 185.

Discussion: This section declares the importance of public participation as an element of the CEQA process. This section encourages agencies to provide notice on the internet when possible. Internet posting offers the public yet another means of being informed about a project.

In *Concerned Citizens of Costa Mesa, Inc. v. 32nd District Agricultural, Assoc.* (1986) 42 Cal.3d 929, the court emphasized that the public holds a "privileged position" in the CEQA process "based on a belief that citizens can make important contributions to environmental protection and on notions of democratic decision making."

15202   Public Hearings

(a) CEQA does not require formal hearings at any stage of the environmental review process. Public comments may be restricted to written communication.

(b) If an agency provides a public hearing on its decision to carry out or approve a project, the agency should include environmental review as one of the subjects for the hearing.

(c) A public hearing on the environmental impact of a project should usually be held when the lead agency determines it would facilitate the purposes and goals of CEQA to do so. The hearing may be held in conjunction with and as a part of normal planning activities.

(d) A draft EIR or negative declaration should be used as a basis for discussion at a public hearing. The hearing may be held at a place where public hearings are regularly conducted by the lead agency or at another location expected to be convenient to the public.

(e) Notice of all public hearings shall be given in a timely manner. This notice may be given in the same form and time as notice for other regularly conducted public hearings of the public agency. To the extent that the public agency maintains an Internet web site, notice of all public hearings should be made available in electronic format on that site.

(f) A public agency may include, in its implementing procedures, procedures for the conducting of public hearings pursuant to this section. The procedures may adopt existing notice and hearing requirements of the public agency for regularly conducted legislative, planning, and other activities.

(g) There is no requirement for a public agency to conduct a public hearing in connection with its review of an EIR prepared by another public agency.

Note: Authority cited: Sections 21083 and 21087, Public Resources Code. Reference: Sections 21000, 21082, 21108, and 21152, Public Resources Code; *Concerned Citizens of Palm Desert, Inc. v. Board of Supervisors*, (1974) 38 Cal.App.3d 272.

Discussion: The section encourages agencies to include environmental issues in the agenda when the agency provides a public hearing on the project itself. The section also provides that the draft EIR or Negative Declaration should be used as a basis for discussion of environmental issues at a hearing if one is held. In an effort to simplify procedures, the section allows agencies to conduct hearings on environmental issues according to the same rules that the agency applies to its other hearings. This section also acknowledges that there is no requirement for a public agency to conduct a public hearing concerning its review of an EIR.

Subsection (e) encourage agencies to provide public hearing notice on the internet when possible. Internet posting offers the public another means of being informed about a project.

15203   Adequate Time for Review and Comment

The lead agency shall provide adequate time for other public agencies and members of the public to review and comment on a draft EIR or negative declaration that it has prepared.

(a) Public agencies may establish time periods for review in their implementing procedures and shall notify the public and reviewing agencies of the time for receipt of comments on EIRs. These time periods shall be consistent with applicable statutes, the State CEQA Guidelines, and applicable clearinghouse review periods.

(b) A review period for an EIR does not require a halt in other planning or evaluation activities related to a project. Planning should continue in conjunction with environmental evaluation.

Note: Authority cited: Sections 21083 and 21087, Public Resources Code. Reference: Sections 21082, 21108 and 21152, Public Resources Code. Formerly Sections 15160 (a) and (e).

Discussion: This section establishes the requirement that the Lead Agency provide adequate time for other agencies and the public to review draft EIRs and Negative Declarations. The section allows public agencies to establish time periods for review in their implementing procedures but requires that the time periods be consistent with requirements from other sources. The section requires, however, that notices to the public and reviewing agencies shall identify time limits and deadlines for receipt of comments. The section also provides that the review period for an EIR does not require a halt in other planning or evaluation activities related to the project.

15204 Focus of Review

(a) In reviewing draft EIRs, ~~people~~ persons and public agencies should focus on the sufficiency of the document in identifying and analyzing the possible impacts on the environment and ways in which the significant effects of the project might be avoided or mitigated. Comments are most helpful when they suggest additional specific alternatives or mitigation measures that would provide better ways to avoid or mitigate the significant environmental effects. At the same time, reviewers should be aware that the adequacy of an EIR is determined in terms of what is reasonably feasible, in light of factors such as the magnitude of the project at issue, the severity of its likely environmental impacts, and the geographic scope of the project. CEQA does not require a lead agency to conduct every test or perform all research, study, and experimentation recommended or demanded by commentors. When responding to comments, lead agencies need only respond to significant environmental issues and do not need to provide all information requested by reviewers, as long as a good faith effort at full disclosure is made in the EIR.

(b) In reviewing negative declarations, ~~people~~ persons and public agencies should focus on the proposed finding that the project will not have a significant effect on the environment. If ~~people~~ persons and public agencies believe that the project ~~would~~ may have a significant effect, they should:

(1) Identify the specific effect,

(2) Explain why they believe the effect would occur, and

(3) Explain why they believe the effect would be significant.

(c) Reviewers should explain the basis for their comments, and ~~whenever possible,~~ should submit data or references offering facts, reasonable assumptions based on facts, or expert opinion supported by facts in support of the comments. Pursuant to Section 15064, an effect shall not be considered significant in the absence of substantial evidence.

(d) Reviewing agencies or organizations should include with their comments the name of a contact person who would be available for later consultation if necessary. Each responsible agency and trustee agency shall focus its comments on environmental information germane to that agency's statutory responsibility.

(e) This section shall not be used to restrict the ability of reviewers to comment ~~on broader issues and~~ on the general adequacy of a document or of the lead agency to reject comments not focused as recommended by this section.

(f) Prior to the close of the public review period for an EIR or mitigated negative declaration, a responsible or trustee agency which has identified significant effects on the environment may submit to the lead agency proposed mitigation measures which would address those significant effects. Any such measures shall be limited to impacts affecting those resources which are subject to the statutory authority of that agency. If mitigation measures are submitted, the responsible or trustee agency shall either submit to the lead agency complete and detailed performance objectives for the mitigation measures, or shall refer the lead agency to appropriate, readily available guidelines or reference documents which meet the same purpose.

Note: Authority cited: Sections 21083 and 21087, Public Resources Code. Reference: Sections 21080, 21081.6, and 21080.4, 21104 and 21153, Public Resources Code~~,~~. Formerly Section 15161; *San Joaquin Raptor/Wildlife Rescue Center v. County of Stanislaus* (1996) 42 Cal.App.4th 608; and *Leonoff v. Monterey County Board of Supervisors* (1990) 222 Cal.App.3d 1337.

Discussion: This section helps the public and public agencies to focus their review of environmental documents and their comments to lead agencies. Case law has held that the lead agency is not obligated to undertake every suggestion given them, provided that the agency responds to significant environmental issues and makes a good faith effort at disclosure. Subsection (a) clarifies this for reviewers. The guideline encourages reviewers to examine the sufficiency of the environmental document, particularly in regard to significant effects, and to suggest specific mitigation measures and project alternatives. Given that an effect is not considered significant in the absence of substantial evidence, subsection (c) advises reviewers that comments should be accompanied by factual support. Subsection (d) reminds responsible and trustee agencies that, under statute, they should focus their comments on environmental information germane to their statutory responsibilities. Subsection (f) advises responsible an [sic]

15205 Review by State Agencies

(a) Draft EIRs and negative declarations to be reviewed by state agencies shall be submitted to the State Clearinghouse, 1400 Tenth Street, Sacramento, California 95814. When submitting such documents to the State Clearinghouse, the public agency shall include, in addition to the printed copy, a copy of the document in electronic form on a diskette or by electronic mail transmission, if available.

(b) The following environmental documents shall be submitted to the State Clearinghouse for review by state agencies:

(1) Draft EIRs and negative declarations prepared by a state agency where such agency is a lead agency.

(2) Draft EIRs and negative declarations prepared by a public agency where a state agency is a responsible agency, trustee agency, or otherwise has jurisdiction by law with respect to the project.

(3) Draft EIRs and negative declarations on projects identified in Section 15206 as being of statewide, regional, or areawide significance.

(4) Draft EISs, environmental assessments, and findings of no significant impact prepared pursuant to NEPA, the Federal Guidelines (Title 40 CFR, Part 1500, commencing with Section 1500.1).

(c) Public agencies may send environmental documents to the State Clearinghouse for review where a state agency has special expertise with regard to the environmental impacts involved. The areas of statutory authorities of state agencies are identified in Appendix B. Any such environmental documents submitted to the State Clearinghouse shall include, in addition to the printed copy, a copy of the document in electronic format, on a diskette or by electronic mail transmission, if available.

(d) When an EIR or negative declaration is submitted to the State Clearinghouse for review, the review period set by the lead agency shall be at least as long as the period provided in the state review system operated by the State Clearinghouse. In the state review system, the normal review period is 45 days for EIRs and 30 days for negative declarations. In exceptional circumstances, the State Clearinghouse may set shorter review periods when requested by the lead agency.

(e) The number of copies of an EIR or negative declaration submitted to the State

Clearinghouse shall not be less than ten unless the State Clearinghouse approves a lower number in advance.

(f) While the lead agency is encouraged to contact the regional and district offices of state responsible agencies, the lead agency must, in all cases, submit documents to the State Clearinghouse for distribution in order to comply with the review requirements of this section.

Note: Authority cited: Sections 21083 and 21087, Public Resources Code. Reference: Sections 21083, 21104, and 21153, Public Resources Code. Formerly Section 15161.5.

Discussion: This section spells out the requirement for sending draft EIRs and Negative Declarations to the State Clearinghouse to obtain review by state agencies.

Use of the Clearinghouse insures that all state agencies concerned with the project will be consulted.

15206 Projects of Statewide, Regional, or Areawide Significance

(a) Projects meeting the criteria in this section shall be deemed to be of statewide, regional, or areawide significance.

(1) A draft EIR or negative declaration prepared by any public agency on a project described in this section shall be submitted to the State Clearinghouse and should be submitted also to the appropriate metropolitan area council of governments for review and comment.

(2) When such documents are submitted to the State Clearinghouse, the public agency shall include, in addition to the printed copy, a copy of the document in electronic format on a diskette or by electronic mail transmission, if available.

(b) The lead agency shall determine that a proposed project is of statewide, regional, or areawide significance if the project meets any of the following criteria:

(1) A proposed local general plan, element, or amendment thereof for which an EIR was prepared. If a negative declaration was prepared for the plan, element, or amendment, the document need not be submitted for review.

(2) A project has the potential for causing significant effects on the environment extending beyond the city or county in which the project would be located. Examples of the effects include generating significant amounts of traffic or interfering with the attainment or maintenance of state or national air quality standards. Projects subject to this subsection include:

(A) A proposed residential development of more than 500 dwelling units.

(B) A proposed shopping center or business establishment employing more than 1,000 persons or encompassing more than 500,000 square feet of floor space.

(C) A proposed commercial office building employing more than 1,000 persons or encompassing more than 250,000 square feet of floor space.

(D) A proposed hotel/motel development of more than 500 rooms.

(E) A proposed industrial, manufacturing, or processing plant, or industrial park planned to house more than 1,000 persons, occupying more than 40 acres of land, or encompassing more than 650,000 square feet of floor area.

(3) A project which would result in the cancellation of an open space contract made pursuant to the California Land Conservation Act of 1965 (Williamson Act) for any parcel of 100 or more acres.

(4) A project for which an EIR and not a negative declaration was prepared which would be located in the following areas of critical environmental sensitivity:

(A) The Lake Tahoe Basin.

(B) The Santa Monica Mountains Zone as defined by Section 67463['] of the Government Code.

(C) The California Coastal Zone as defined in, and mapped pursuant to, Section 30103 of the Public Resources Code.

(D) An area within 1/4 mile of a wild and scenic river as defined by Section 5093.5 of the Public Resources Code.

(E) The Sacramento-San Joaquin Delta, as defined in Water Code Section 12220.

(F) The Suisun Marsh as defined in Public Resources Code Section 29101.

(G) The jurisdiction of the San Francisco Bay Conservation and Development Commission as defined in Government Code Section 66610.

(5) A project which would substantially affect sensitive wildlife habitats including but not limited to riparian lands, wetlands, bays, estuaries, marshes, and habitats for ~~rare and~~ endangered, rare and threatened species as defined by ~~Fish and Game Code Section 903~~ Section 15380 of this Chapter.

(6) A project which would interfere with attainment of regional water quality standards as stated in the approved areawide waste treatment management plan.

(7) A project which would provide housing, jobs, or occupancy for 500 or more people within 10 miles of a nuclear power plant.

Note: Authority cited: Sections 21083 and 21087, Public Resources Code. Reference: Section 21083, Public Resources Code.

Discussion: This section implements the requirement in Section 21083 for the Guidelines to contain criteria for determining whether a project is of sufficient statewide, regional, or areawide environmental significance that it should be submitted to state agencies for review, even when no state agency has any direct jurisdiction by law over the project. When a project is of statewide, regional or areawide significance, as defined in this section, its environmental document must be submitted to the State Clearinghouse for distribution to state agencies for their review and comment.

Section 15206 lists many kinds of projects which have been determined to be of statewide, regional, or areawide significance. In some cases, the basis for determining whether the project has such significance is based on whether an EIR or Negative Declaration was prepared for the project. With these activities such as adoption or amendment of local general plans, the activity is declared to be of more than local significance only if an EIR was prepared. Negative Declarations on these activities are not required to be sent to the Clearinghouse. This distinction was drawn in an effort to focus state review on only the larger or more important general plan changes.

Another criterion for determining areawide, regional, or statewide significance is the location of the activity in an area of critical environmental sensitivity. These areas are listed in subsection (b)(4). In the listed geographical areas of environmental sensitivity, only projects for which an EIR was prepared must be submitted to the State Clearinghouse.

Subsection (b)(5) focuses on environmental effects. Under this subsection, any project which would substantially affect sensitive wildlife habitats must be submitted to the Clearinghouse, even if a Negative Declaration was prepared. The sensitive wildlife habitats are regarded as even more critical and subject to damage than the larger geographical areas identified by name in subsection (b)(4).

A proposed project falling under Section 15206 (b)(2)(E) on a site of 40 acres or more includes not only the land actually to be occupied by the structures but also includes access roads and railroad tracks serving the site. This is particularly important if the project is also part of an annexation proposal. (See: *Guardians for Turlock's Integrity v. City Council of Turlock*, (1983) 149 Cal.App.3d 584.)

15207   Failure to Comment

If any public agency or person who is consulted with regard to an EIR or Negative Declaration fails to comment within a reasonable time as specified by the lead agency, it shall be assumed, absent a request for a specific extension of time, that such agency or person has no comment to make. Although the lead agency need not respond to late comments, the lead agency may choose to respond to them.

Note: Authority cited: Sections 21083 and 21087, Public Resources Code. Reference: Sections 21104 and 21153, Public Resources Code; *Cleary v. County of Stanislaus*, (1981) 118 Cal.App.3d 348. Formerly Section 15162.

Discussion: This section is added to provide certainty in the review process. At the expiration of the review period, the Lead Agency will know what comments it must respond to. It need not hold its process open to prepare formal responses to comments which come in later. The section provides flexibility by allowing agencies to request additional time to comment if they find that they will be unable to submit their comments by the deadline. This approach has been approved in the Cleary decision cited in the note.

15208   Retention and Availability of Comments

Comments received through the consultation process shall be retained for a reasonable period and available for public inspection at an address given in the final EIR. Comments which may be received on a draft EIR or negative declaration under preparation shall also be considered and kept on file.

Note: Authority cited: Sections 21083 and 21087, Public Resources Code. Reference:

Sections 21104, 21082.1 and 21153, Public Resources Code; Section 4, Chapter 480, Statutes of 1981; *People v. County of Kern*, (1974) 39 Cal.App.3d 830.

Discussion: This section is added so that Lead Agencies will retain comments as public records pertaining to the EIR process.

15209   Comments on Initiative of Public Agencies

Every public agency may comment on environmental documents dealing with projects which affect resources with which the agency has special expertise regardless of whether its comments were solicited or whether the effects fall within the legal jurisdiction of the agency.

Note: Authority cited: Sections 21083 and 21087, Public Resources Code. Reference: Sections 21002, 21104, and 21153, Public Resources Code.

Discussion: This section was added to make it clear that public agencies may comment on any project with which they are concerned, regardless of whether the Lead Agency requests their comments or whether the project effects may fall within the legal jurisdiction of the agency. Many agencies have expertise which reaches beyond the jurisdiction of the agency. This section provides that an agency may submit comments from its staff experts even if the agency is not directly involved with the environmental problems of a proposed project.

Public Resources Code Sections 21104 and 21153 have since been revised to provide that a responsible agency "shall only make substantive comments regarding those activities. . . which are within an area of expertise of the agency or which are required to be carried out or approved by the agency."

Article 14. Projects Also Subject to the National Environmental Policy Act (NEPA) Sections 15220 to 15229

15220   General

This article applies to projects that are subject to both CEQA and NEPA. NEPA applies to projects which are carried out, financed, or approved in whole or in part by federal agencies. Accordingly, this article applies to projects which involve one or more state or local agencies and one or more federal agencies.

Note: Authority cited: Sections 21083 and 21087, Public Resources Code. Reference: Sections 21083.5, 21083.6, and 21083.7, Public Resources Code; National Environmental Policy Act of 1969, Public Law 91-

190 as amended, 42 U.S.C.A. 4321-4347; NEPA Regulations, 40 Code of Federal Regulations (C.F.R.) Parts 1500-1508.

Discussion: This section identifies the contents of this article in the interest of clarity. The section adds a brief identification of NEPA and the NEPA regulations in order to put this section into context.

15221   NEPA Document Ready Before CEQA Document

(a) When a project will require compliance with both CEQA and NEPA, state or local agencies should use the EIS or finding of no significant impact rather than preparing an EIR or negative declaration if the following two conditions occur:

(1) An EIS or finding of no significant impact will be prepared before an EIR or negative declaration would otherwise be completed for the project; and

(2) The EIS or finding of no significant impact complies with the provisions of these guidelines.

(b) Because NEPA does not require separate discussion of mitigation measures or growth inducing impacts, these points of analysis will need to be added, supplemented, or identified before the EIS can be used as an EIR.

Note: Authority cited: Sections 21083 and 21087, Public Resources Code. Reference: Sections 21083.5 and 21083.7, Public Resources Code; Section 102(2)(C) of NEPA, 43 U.S.C.A. 4322(2)(C).

Discussion: This section complies with the mandate in CEQA Section 21083.5 for the Guidelines to provide that an Environmental Impact Statement prepared under NEPA may be used in the place of an EIR under CEQA. The section also provides guidance on how to make the EIS cover all the points required in CEQA. Normally, EISs do not contain separate discussions of mitigation measures or growth-inducing impacts because those points are not required as separate subjects for analysis under NEPA. The subjects are mentioned in the NEPA regulations and will normally be found somewhere in an EIS. Where the EIS is used in the place of an EIR, the discussion of mitigation measures or growth-inducing impacts should be located and identified. If an EIS did not include these two points of analysis, the EIS would need to be supplemented before it could be used in the place of an EIR.

15222   Preparation of Joint Documents

If a lead agency finds that an EIS or finding of no significant impact for a project would not be prepared by the federal agency by the time when the lead agency will need to consider an EIR or negative declaration, the lead agency should try to prepare a combined EIR-EIS or negative declaration-finding of no significant impact. To avoid the need for the federal agency to prepare a separate document for the same project, the lead agency must involve the federal agency in the preparation of the joint document.

This involvement is necessary because federal law generally prohibits a federal agency from using an EIR prepared by a state agency unless the federal agency was involved in the preparation of the document.

Note: Authority cited: Sections 21083 and 21087, Public Resources Code. Reference: Sections 21083.5 and 21083.7, Public Resources Code; Section 102(2)(D) of NEPA, 43 U.S.C.A. 4322(2)(D); 40 C.F.R. Part 1506.2.

Discussion: This section is added in the interest of efficiency. It strongly encourages state and local agencies to try to work with the federal agency involved with the same project. Where the agencies can work together to provide a combined EIR-EIS, or a combined Negative Declaration-Finding of No Significant Impact, duplication between different levels of government will be avoided. The section is also necessary for providing guidance about the need for involvement of the federal agency in preparing the joint document. The federal NEPA Guidelines strongly encourage federal agencies to cooperate in such situations.

15223   Consultation with Federal Agencies

When it plans to use an EIS or finding of no significant impact or to prepare such a document jointly with a federal agency, the lead agency shall consult as soon as possible with the federal agency.

Note: Authority cited: Sections 21083 and 21087, Public Resources Code. Reference: Sections 21083.5 and 21083.7, Public Resources Code.

Discussion: This section highlights the need for consulting with federal agencies prior to using a NEPA document or preparing a document jointly with a federal agency. This consultation is required by CEQA Section 21083.7.

15224   Time Limits

Where a project will be subject to both CEQA and the National Environmental Policy Act, the one year time limit and the 105-day time limit may be waived pursuant to Section 15110.

Note: Authority cited: Sections 21083 and 21087, Public Resources Code. Reference: Section 21083.6, Public Resources Code.

Discussion: This section provides a cross-reference to the waiver of time limits discussed in Section 15110. This cross-reference will bring the possible waiver to the attention of Lead Agencies and applicants who use the Guidelines.

15225   Circulation of Documents

(a) Where the federal agency circulated the EIS or finding of no significant impact for public review as broadly as state or local law may require and gave notice meeting the standards in Section 15072(a) or 15087(a), the lead agency under CEQA may use the federal document in the place of an EIR or negative declaration without recirculating the federal document for public review. One review and comment period is enough. Prior to using the federal document in this situation, the lead agency shall give notice that it will use the federal document in the place of an EIR or negative declaration and that it believes that the federal document meets the requirements of CEQA. The notice shall be given in the same manner as a notice of the public availability of a draft EIR under Section 15087.

(b) If an EIS has been prepared and filed pursuant to NEPA on the closure and reuse of a military base and the Lead Agency decides that the EIS does not fully meet the requirements of CEQA or has not been circulated for public review as state and local law may require, the Lead Agency responsible for preparation of an EIR for a reuse plan for the same base may proceed in the following manner:

(1) Prepare and circulate a notice of preparation pursuant to Section 15082. The notice shall include a description of the reuse plan, a copy of the EIS, an address to which to send comments, and the deadline for submitting comments. The notice shall state that the lead agency intends to utilize the EIS as a draft EIR and requests comments on whether the EIS provides adequate information to serve as a draft EIR and what specific additional information, if any, is necessary.

(2) Upon the close of the comment period, the lead agency may proceed with preparation and circulation for comment of the draft EIR for the reuse plan. To the greatest extent feasible, the lead agency shall avoid

duplication and utilize the EIS or information in the EIS as all or part of the draft EIR. The EIR shall be completed in compliance with the provisions of CEQA.

Note: Authority cited: Sections 21083 and 21087, Public Resources Code. References: Sections 21083.5, 21083.8, and 21092, Public Resources Code..

Discussion: This section is added to avoid the need for a second public review period under CEQA where a Lead Agency uses a document prepared under NEPA. This section should save time and expense. The section is limited, however, to situations where the federal review met the requirements in CEQA for public review. Generally, the public review requirements in CEQA are broader than those applying to federal agencies under NEPA.

A lead agency utilizing an EIS prepared for a military base reuse plan may recirculate it for full CEQA review and comment when it decides that the EIS does not fully meet the requirements of CEQA or has not been previously circulated for public review as CEQA may require.

15226   Joint Activities

State and local agencies should cooperate with federal agencies to the fullest extent possible to reduce duplication between the California Environmental Quality Act and the National Environmental Policy Act. Such cooperation should, to the fullest extent possible, include:

(a) Joint planning processes,

(b) Joint environmental research and studies,

(c) Joint public hearings,

(d) Joint environmental documents.

Note: Authority cited: Sections 21083 and 21087, Public Resources Code. Reference: Sections 21083.5 and 21083.7, Public Resources Code; 40 C.F.R. Part 1506.2.

Discussion: This section mirrors a section contained in the federal NEPA regulations encouraging joint activities. The President's Council on Environmental Quality urged states with environmental review statutes to include such a section in their Guidelines in order to promote cooperation between state and federal agencies. The Council of State Governments also recommended that such a section be adopted.

15227   State Comments on a Federal Project

When a state agency officially comments on a proposed federal project which may have a significant effect on the environment, the comments shall include or reference a discussion of the material specified in Section 15126. An EIS on the federal project may be referenced to meet the requirements of this section.

Note: Authority cited: Sections 21083 and 21087, Public Resources Code. Reference: Section 21101, Public Resources Code.

Discussion: This section is intended to implement the requirements of CEQA Section 21101 which requires the state comments on a federal project which would have a significant effect to contain the points of analysis required in an EIR. Most federal projects on which the state prepares official comments will have been the subject of an EIS.

Accordingly, this section allows the state agency preparing the state comments to reference the discussion in the EIS to meet the requirements of Section 21101. This approach is necessary in order to avoid duplication.

15228   Where Federal Agency Will Not Cooperate

Where a federal agency will not cooperate in the preparation of joint document and will require separate NEPA compliance for the project at a later time, the state or local agency should persist in efforts to cooperate with the federal agency. Because NEPA expressly allows federal agencies to use environmental documents prepared by an agency of statewide jurisdiction, a local agency should try to involve a state agency in helping prepare an EIR or Negative Declaration for the project. In this way there will be a greater chance that the federal agency may later use the CEQA document and not require the applicant to pay for preparation of a second document to meet NEPA requirements at a later time.

Note: Authority cited: Sections 21083 and 21087, Public Resources Code. Reference: Section 21083.5, Public Resources Code; Section 102(2)(D) of NEPA, 42 U.S.C.A. 4322(2)(D).

Discussion: Despite inclusion of the section on joint activities in the federal NEPA regulations, there are occasional problems with federal agencies which will not cooperate with state or local agencies under environmental review statutes. This section provides guidance on how to handle that situation.

15229   Baseline Analysis for Military Base Reuse Plan EIRs

When preparing and certifying an EIR for a plan for the reuse of a military base, including when utilizing an Environmental Impact Statement pursuant to Section 21083.5 of the Public Resources Code, in addition to the procedure authorized pursuant to subdivision (b) of Section 21083.8 of the Public Resources Code, the determination of whether the reuse plan may have a significant effect on the environment may, at the discretion of the lead agency, be based upon the physical conditions which were present at the time that the federal decision for the closure or realignment of the base or reservation became final. These conditions shall be referred to as the "baseline physical conditions." Impacts which do not exceed the baseline physical conditions shall not be considered significant.

(a) Prior to circulating a draft EIR pursuant to the provisions of this Section, the lead agency shall do all of the following, in order:

(1) Prepare proposed baseline physical conditions, identify pertinent responsible and trustee agencies and consult with those agencies prior to the public hearing required by subdivision (a)(2) as to the application of their regulatory authority and permitting standards to the proposed baseline physical conditions, the proposed reuse plan, and specific, planned future nonmilitary land uses of the base or reservation. The affected agencies shall have not less than 30 days prior to the public hearing to review the proposed baseline physical conditions and the proposed reuse plan and to submit their comments to the lead agency.

(2) Hold a public hearing at which is discussed the federal EIS prepared for, or being prepared for, the closure or realignment of the military base or reservation. The discussion shall include the significant effects on the environment, if any, examined in the EIS, potential methods of mitigating those effects, including feasible alternatives, and the mitigative effects of federal, state, and local laws applicable to future nonmilitary activities. Prior to the close of the hearing, the lead agency shall specify whether it will adopt any of the baseline physical conditions for the reuse plan EIR and identify those conditions. The lead agency shall specify particular baseline physical conditions, if any, which it will examine in greater detail than they were examined in the EIS. Notice of the hearing shall be given pursuant to Section 15087. The hearing may be continued from time to time.

(3) Prior to the close of the hearing, the lead agency shall do all of the following:

(A) Specify the baseline physical conditions which it intends to adopt for the reuse plan EIR, and specify particular physical conditions, if any, which it will examine in greater detail than were examined in the EIS.

(B) State specifically how it intends to integrate its discussion of the baseline physical conditions in the EIR with the reuse planning process, taking into account the adopted environmental standards of the community, including but not limited to, the adopted general plan, specific plan or redevelopment plan, and including other applicable provisions of adopted congestion management plans, habitat conservation or natural communities conservation plans, air quality management plans, integrated waste management plans, and county hazardous waste management plans.

(C) State the specific economic or social reasons, including but not limited to, new job creation, opportunities for employment of skilled workers, availability of low and moderate-income housing, and economic continuity which support selection of the baseline physical conditions.

(b) An EIR prepared under this section should identify any adopted baseline physical conditions in the environmental setting section. The baseline physical conditions should be cited in discussions of effects. The no-project alternative analyzed in an EIR prepared under this section shall discuss the conditions on the base as they exist at the time of preparation, as well as what could be reasonably expected to occur in the foreseeable future if the reuse plan were not approved, based on current plans and consistent with available infrastructure and services.

(c) All public and private activities taken pursuant to or in furtherance of a reuse plan for which an EIR was prepared and certified pursuant to this section shall be deemed to be a single project. A subsequent or supplemental EIR shall be required only if the lead agency determines that any of the circumstances described in Section 15162 or 15163 exist.

(d) Limitations:

(1) Nothing in this section shall in any way limit the scope of review or determination of significance of the presence of hazardous or toxic wastes, substances, and materials, including but not limited to, contaminated soils and groundwater. The regulation of hazardous or toxic wastes, substances, and materials shall not be constrained by this section.

(2) This section does not apply to hazardous waste regulation and remediation projects undertaken pursuant to Chapter 6.5 (commencing with Section 25100) or Chapter 6.8 (commencing with Section 25300) of Division 20 of the Health and Safety Code or pursuant to the Porter-Cologne Water Quality Control Act (Water Code Section 13000, et seq.)

(3) All subsequent development at the military base or reservation shall be subject to all applicable federal, state, or local laws, including but not limited to, those relating to air quality, water quality, traffic, threatened and endangered species, noise, and hazardous or toxic wastes, substances, or materials.

(e) "Reuse plan" means the initial plan for the reuse of military base adopted by a local government, including a redevelopment agency or joint powers authority, in the form of a general plan, general plan amendment, specific plan, redevelopment plan, or other planning document. For purposes of this section, a reuse plan also shall include a statement of development policies, a diagram or diagrams illustrating its provisions, including a designation of the proposed general distribution, location, and development intensity for housing, business, industry, open space, recreation, natural resources, public buildings and grounds, roads, and other transportation facilities, infrastructure, and other categories of proposed uses, whether public or private.

(f) This section may be applied to any reuse plan EIR for which a notice of preparation is issued within one year from the date that the federal record of decision was rendered for the military base or reservation closure or realignment and reuse, or prior to January 1, 1997, whichever is later, but only if the EIR is completed and certified within five years from the date that the federal record of decision was rendered.

Note: Authority cited: Sections 21083 and 21087, Public Resources Code. Reference: Section 21083.1, Public Resources Code.

Discussion: This section offers agencies that are preparing a military base reuse plan EIR the option of identifying a baseline for their environmental analysis. The baseline establishes the level of previously existing impacts beyond which the agency will consider impacts significant. The section details the procedures for establishing the baseline.

Article 15. Litigation
Sections 15230 to 15233

15230 Time Limits and Criteria

Litigation under CEQA must be handled under the time limits and criteria described in Sections 21167 et seq. of the Public Resources Code and Section 15112 of these guidelines in addition to provisions in this article.

Note: Authority cited: Sections 21083 and 21087, Public Resources Code. Reference: Sections 21167 et seq., Public Resources Code.

Discussion: This section provides a cross-reference to the statutory sections which govern litigation under CEQA.

15231 Adequacy of EIR or Negative Declaration for Use By Lead and Responsible Agencies

A final EIR prepared by a lead agency or a negative declaration adopted by a lead agency shall be conclusively presumed to comply with CEQA for purposes of use by responsible agencies which were consulted pursuant to Sections 15072 or 15082 unless one of the following conditions occurs:

(a) The EIR or negative declaration is finally adjudged in a legal proceeding not to comply with the requirements of CEQA, or

(b) A subsequent EIR is made necessary by Section 15162 of these guidelines.

Note: Authority cited: Sections 21083 and 21087, Public Resources Code. Reference: Sections 21080.1, 21166, 21167.2, and 21167.3, Public Resources Code.

Discussion: This section is added to clarify the ways in which a Responsible Agency is affected by litigation involving the adequacy of environmental documents prepared by the Lead Agency. This section implements CEQA Section 21167.2 but provides additional interpretation. This Guideline section limits the conclusive presumption that an EIR complies with CEQA to situations where the Lead Agency consulted with the Responsible Agency. The statutory presumption was based on the idea that the Responsible Agency had been consulted and had an opportunity to make its views known to the Lead Agency.

15232 Request for Hearing

In a writ of mandate proceeding challenging approval of a project under CEQA, the petitioner shall, within 90 days of filing the petition, request a hearing or otherwise be subject to dismissal on the court's own motion or on the motion of any party to the suit.

Note: Authority cited: Sections 21083 and 21087, Public Resources Code. Reference: Section 21167.4, Public Resources Code.

Discussion: Experience with Section 21167.4 of CEQA has revealed an ambiguity that needs interpretation in the Guidelines. Section 21167.4 provides in part: ". . . the petitioner shall request a hearing within 90 days of filing the petition or otherwise be subject to dismissal. . . ." The section does not make it clear whether only the request must be made within 90 days after filing the petition, or whether the hearing must be had within 90 days.

15233 Conditional Permits

If a lawsuit is filed challenging an EIR or negative declaration for noncompliance with CEQA, responsible agencies shall act as if the EIR or negative declaration complies with CEQA and continue to process the application for the project according to the time limits for responsible agency action contained in Government Code Section 65952.

(a) If an injunction or a stay has been granted in the lawsuit prohibiting the project from being carried out, the responsible agency shall have authority only to disapprove the project or to grant a conditional approval of the project. A conditional approval shall constitute permission to proceed with a project only when the court action results in a final determination that the EIR or negative declaration does comply with the provisions of CEQA (Public Resources Code Section 21167.3a).

(b) If no injunction or stay is granted in the lawsuit, the responsible agency shall assume that the EIR or negative declaration fully meets the requirements of CEQA. The responsible agency shall approve or disapprove the project within the time limits described in Article 8, commencing with Section 15100, of these guidelines and described in Government Code Section 65952. An approval granted by a responsible agency in this situation provides only permission to proceed with the project at the applicant's risk prior to a final decision in the lawsuit (Public Resources Code Section 21167.3b).

Note: Authority cited: Sections 21083 and 21087, Public Resources Code. Reference: Section 21167.3, Public Resources Code; *Kriebel v. City Council* (1980) 112 Cal.App. 3d 693.

Discussion: This section combines the statutory provision dealing with conditional permits with administrative interpretations. While the statute limits the authority of the Responsible Agency to granting a conditional approval for a project, this Guideline section follows case law by providing authority to disapprove the application as well.

Article 16. EIR Monitor
Section 15240

15240   EIR Monitor

The Secretary for Resources may provide for publication of a bulletin entitled "California EIR Monitor" on a subscription basis to provide public notice of amendments to the guidelines, the completion of draft EIRs, and other matters as deemed appropriate. Inquiries and subscription requests should be sent to the following address:

Secretary for Resources
Attention: California EIR Monitor
1416 Ninth Street, Room 1311
Sacramento, California 95814

Note: Authority cited: Sections 21083 and 21087, Public Resources Code. Reference: Section 21088, Public Resources Code.

Discussion: This section is included to identify the California EIR Monitor and to provide an address where further information may be obtained.

Article 17. Exemption for Certified State Regulatory Programs
Sections 15250 to 15253

15250   General

Section 21080.5 of the Public Resources Code provides that a regulatory program of a state agency shall be certified by the Secretary for Resources as being exempt from the requirements for preparing EIRs, negative declarations, and initial studies if the Secretary finds that the program meets the criteria contained in that code section. A certified program remains subject to other provisions in CEQA such as the policy of avoiding significant adverse effects on the environment where feasible. This article provides information concerning certified programs.

Note: Authority cited: Sections 21083 and 21087, Public Resources Code. Reference: Section 21080.5, Public Resources Code.

Discussion: This section clarifies the scope of the exemption provided by certification under Section 21080.5. The exemption applies only to Chapter 3 of CEQA, the chapter which requires state agencies to prepare EIRs and Negative Declarations. Other provisions of CEQA continue to apply to a certified program where relevant. In *EPIC v. Johnson*, (1985) 170 Cal.App.3d 604, the court held that PRC Section 21080.5 provided a limited exemption from CEQA and that the Forest Practices Act (FPA) and administrative rules though exempt from Chapter 3 of CEQA, remained subject to the other policies of CEQA such as avoiding significant environmental effects. The court added that exemptions specified in the statute precluded additional exemptions from being implied or presumed absent specific legislative intent.

The court in *EPIC v. Johnson* further held that under certified regulatory exempt programs state agencies must consult with trustee agencies even though they are exempt from the need to prepare an EIR.

The exemption for the certified state regulatory programs is not a blanket exemption from CEQA as the agency must still comply with CEQA's policies, evaluation criteria and standards. The required environmental review must address all activities and impacts associated with a project. *Laupheimer v. California* (1988) 200 Cal.App.3d 440, *Environmental Protection Information Center, Inc. v. Johnson* (1985) 170 Cal. App.3d 604. Only activities of the agency specified in the certified regulatory program are subject to partial exemptions. Thus while some of the agency's activities may be within the certified program, others may not be exempt and would still be subject to review under CEQA. *Citizens for Non-Toxic Pest Control v. Department of Food and Agriculture* (1986) 187 Cal.App.3d 1575.

15251   List of Certified Programs

The following programs of state regulatory agencies have been certified by the Secretary for Resources as meeting the requirements of Section 21080.5:

(a) The regulation of timber harvesting operations by the California Department of Forestry and the State Board of Forestry pursuant to Chapter 8, commencing with Section 4511 of Part 2 of Division 4 of the Public Resources Code.

(b) The regulatory program of the Fish and Game Commission pursuant to the Fish and Game Code.

(c) The regulatory program of the California Coastal Commission and the regional coastal commissions dealing with the consideration and granting of coastal development permits under the California Coastal Act of 1976, Division 20 (commencing with Section 30000) of the Public Resources Code.

(d) That portion of the regulatory program of the Air Resources Board which involves the adoption, approval, amendment, or repeal of standards, rules, regulations, or plans to be used in the regulatory program for the protection and enhancement of ambient air quality in California.

(e) The regulatory program of the State Board of Forestry in adopting, amending, or repealing standards, rules, regulations, or plans under the Z'berg-Nejedly Forest Practice Act, Chapter 8 (commencing with Section 4511) of Part 2 of Division 4 of the Public Resources Code.

(f) The program of the California Coastal Commission involving the preparation, approval, and certification of local coastal programs as provided in Sections 30500 through 30522 of the Public Resources Code.

(g) The Water Quality Control (Basin)/208 Planning Program of the State Water Resources Control Board and the Regional Water Quality Control Boards.

(h) The permit and planning programs of the San Francisco Bay Conservation and Development Commission under the McAteer-Petris Act, Title 7.2 (commencing with Section 66600) of the Government Code and the Suisun Marsh Preservation Act, Division 19 (commencing with Section 29000) of the Public Resources Code.

(i) The pesticide regulatory program administered by the Department of Food and Agriculture and the county agricultural commissioners insofar as the program consists of:

(1) The registration, evaluation, and classification of pesticides.

(2) The adoption, amendment, or repeal of regulations and standards for the licensing and regulation of pesticide dealers and pest control operators and advisors.

(3) The adoption, amendment, or repeal of regulations for standards dealing with the monitoring of pesticides

and of the human health and environmental effects of pesticides.

(4) The regulation of the use of pesticides in agricultural and urban areas of the state through the permit system administered by the county agricultural commissioners.

(j) The regulations of weather resources management projects through the issuance of operating permits by the State Department of Water Resources pursuant to the California Weather Resources Management Act of 1978 (Water Code Sections 400 et seq.).

(k) The power plant site certification program of the State Energy Resources Conservation and Development Commission under Chapter 6 of the Warren-Alquist Act, commencing with Public Resources Code Section 25500.

(l) The regulatory program of the State Water Resources Control Board to establish instream beneficial use protection programs.

(m) That portion of the regulatory program of the South Coast Air Quality Management District which involves the adoption, amendment, and repeal of regulations pursuant to the provisions of the Health and Safety Code.

(n) The program of the Delta Protection Commission involving the preparation and adoption of a Resource Management Plan for the Sacramento-San Joaquin Delta (Pub. Resources Code §29760 ff.), and the Commission's review and action on general plan amendments proposed by local governments to make their plans consistent with the provisions of the Commission's Resource Management Plan (Pub. Resources Code §29763.5).

(o) The program of the Department of Fish and Game for the adoption of regulations under the Fish and Game Code.

Note: Authority cited: Sections 21083 and 21087, Public Resources Code. Reference: Section 21080.5, Public Resources Code.

Discussion: Section 15251 lists the programs which have been certified by the Secretary for Resources as meeting the requirements in Section 21080.5. The certifications of individual programs have been handled as rule-making proceedings characterized as proposed amendments to this section. Certification of a program formally recognizes that an environmental analysis undertaken in compliance with the certified program is the functional equivalent of a CEQA analysis.

15252 Substitute Document

The document used as a substitute for an EIR or negative declaration in a certified program shall include at least the following items:

(a) A description of the proposed activity, and

(b) Either:

(1) Alternatives to the activity and mitigation measures to avoid or reduce any significant or potentially significant effects that the project might have on the environment, or

(2) A statement that the agency's review of the project showed that the project would not have any significant or potentially significant effects on the environment and therefore no alternatives or mitigation measures are proposed to avoid or reduce any significant effects on the environment. This statement shall be supported by a checklist or other documentation to show the possible effects that the agency examined in reaching this conclusion.

Note: Authority cited: Sections 21083 and 21087, Public Resources Code. Reference: Section 21080.5, Public Resources Code.

Discussion: This section allows the use of a short-form document equivalent to a Negative Declaration as an alternative to a document that would be a substitute for an EIR. Section 21080.5 describes the short-form document only in terms of a document to be used in the place of an EIR. The statute requires the document to include a discussion of alternatives and mitigation measures to avoid or reduce any significant or potentially significant effects of the project. This requirement overlooks the possibility that the project at hand may have no significant effect. Where there is no significant effect, there would be no alternatives or mitigation measures that would substantially lessen any significant effect.

A cumulative impacts analysis as defined in §15130(b) is not required to be contained within the substitute document prepared under a certified program. In *Laupheimer v. California* (1988) 200 Cal.App.3d 440, the court found that the state's requirements for cumulative impacts analysis in "Certified Programs" differs from that defined in §15130, i.e., "cumulative impacts need not be considered as a 'cumulative analysis' but recognized as to the cumulative aspects of a project." What is required is for the certified program to have looked for and in some reasonable manner assessed potential cumulative environmental effects

to have given sufficient consideration to any such effect it should reasonably have considered to be significant. In this case, potential cumulative environmental impacts of a proposed timber harvesting plan were vividly and repeatedly brought to the State Department of Forestry and Fire Protection's attention, by correspondence and at a public hearing and the court determined that at an absolute minimum the Department of Forestry was required to incorporate an adequate response into its major issue statement even, if for reasons stated, the expressed concerns were deemed too remote and speculative to be significant.

15253 Use of an EIR Substitute by a Responsible Agency

(a) An environmental analysis document prepared for a project under a certified program listed in Section 15251 shall be used by another agency granting an approval for the same project where the conditions in Subsection (b) have been met. In this situation, the certified agency shall act as lead agency, and the other permitting agencies shall act as responsible agencies using the certified agency's document.

(b) The conditions under which a public agency shall act as a responsible agency when approving a project using an environmental analysis document prepared under a certified program in the place of an EIR or negative declaration are as follows:

(1) The certified agency is the first agency to grant a discretionary approval for the project.

(2) The certified agency consults with the responsible agencies, but the consultation need not include the exchange of written notices.

(3) The environmental analysis document identifies:

(A) The significant environmental effects within the jurisdiction or special expertise of the responsible agency.

(B) Alternatives or mitigation measures that could avoid or reduce the severity of the significant environmental effects.

(4) Where written notices were not exchanged in the consultation process, the responsible agency was afforded the opportunity to participate in the review of the property by the certified agency in a regular manner designed to inform the certified agency of the concerns of the responsible

agency before release of the EIR substitute for public review.

    (5) The certified agency established a consultation period between the certified agency and the responsible agency that was at least as long as the period allowed for public review of the EIR substitute document.

    (6) The certified agency exercised the powers of a lead agency by considering all the significant environmental effects of the project and making a finding under Section 15091 for each significant effect.

(c) Certified agencies are not required to adjust their activities to meet the criteria in Subsection (b). Where a certified agency does not meet the criteria in Subsection (b):

    (1) The substitute document prepared by the agency shall not be used by other permitting agencies in the place of an EIR or negative declaration, and (2) Any other agencies granting approvals for the project shall comply with CEQA in the normal manner. A permitting agency shall act as a lead agency and prepare an EIR or a negative declaration. Other permitting agencies, if any, shall act as responsible agencies and use the EIR or negative declaration prepared by the lead agency.

Note: Authority cited: Sections 21083 and 21087, Public Resources Code. Reference: Sections 21002.1(d), 21080.5, and 21165, Public Resources Code.

Discussion: The purpose of this section was to allow a certified state environmental regulatory agency to act as a Lead Agency and, thereby, enable other agencies that would have to grant a permit for the same project to use the EIR substitute prepared by the certified agency. In this way, the other permitting agencies would act in the role of Responsible Agencies.

The criteria outlined in subsection (b) are modeled after the consultation requirement that applies to Lead and Responsible Agencies under the normal EIR process. The same basic steps would be required. The certified agency would be required to consult with the other permitting agencies for the project, and the expressed concerns of other agencies.

Section 15253 is not intended to require certified agencies to act as Lead Agencies. Rather, the section serves as authority for certified agencies to act in the Lead Agency role if they choose to consult with other permitting agencies as outlined in the

section. Subsection (c) is added to show that a certified agency does not need to act as a Lead Agency if it does not choose to do so. If the certified agency does not consult with the other agencies, it will complete its process on its own. The other permitting agencies would then be required to comply with CEQA in the normal manner. One of the permitting agencies would act as Lead Agency and prepare an EIR or a Negative Declaration. The other permitting agencies would act as Responsible Agencies and use the EIR or Negative Declaration prepared by the Lead Agency.

Article 18. Statutory Exemptions Sections 15260 to 15285

15260   General

This article describes the exemptions from CEQA granted by the Legislature. The exemptions take several forms. Some exemptions are complete exemptions from CEQA. Other exemptions apply to only part of the requirements of CEQA, and still other exemptions apply only to the timing of CEQA compliance.

Note: Authority cited: Sections 21083 and 21087, Public Resources Code. Reference: Section 21080(b), Public Resources Code.

Discussion: This section serves as an introduction to this article on statutory exemptions. The section notes that the exemptions take basically three forms, being either complete exemptions, partial exemptions, or special timing requirements.

The court in *Western Municipal Water District of Riverside County v. Superior Court of San Bernardino County* (1986) 187 Cal. App.3d 1104, pointed out that "the self-evident purpose of a [statutory] exemption is to provide an escape from the EIR requirement despite a project's clear, significant impact." This is in contrast to categorical exemptions which are disallowed if the project would otherwise have an environmental impact.

By way of example, the Supreme Court held in *Napa Valley Wine Train, Inc. v. Public Utilities Commission* (1990) 50 Cal 3d 370, that CEQA is a legislative act subject to legislative limitations and legislative amendment. Through that premise, the court held that statutory exemptions were enacted to avoid the environmental review process for an entire class of projects. In the specific case, an excursion train proposed for operation within an existing railroad right-of-way fell within the exemption language in Public Resources Code Section 21080(b)(11),

even though the use might have potential environmental consequences. Subsequent legislation enacted Public Resources Code Section 21080.04 making the wine train project subject to CEQA.

15261   Ongoing Project

(a) If a project being carried out by a public agency was approved prior to November 23, 1970, the project shall be exempt from CEQA unless either of the following conditions exist:

    (1) A substantial portion of public funds allocated for the project have not been spent, and it is still feasible to modify the project to mitigate potentially adverse environmental effects, or to choose feasible alternatives to the project, including the alternative of "no project" or halting the project; provided that a project subject to the National Environmental Policy Act (NEPA) shall be exempt from CEQA as an on-going project if, under regulations promulgated under NEPA, the project would be too far advanced as of January 1, 1970, to require preparation of an EIS.

    (2) A public agency proposes to modify the project in such a way that the project might have a new significant effect on the environment.

(b) A private project shall be exempt from CEQA if the project received approval of a lease, license, certificate, permit, or other entitlement for use from a public agency prior to April 5, 1973, subject to the following provisions:

    (1) CEQA does not prohibit a public agency from considering environmental factors in connection with the approval or disapproval of a project, or from imposing reasonable fees on the appropriate private person or entity for preparing an environmental report under authority other than CEQA. Local agencies may require environmental reports for projects covered by this paragraph pursuant to local ordinances during this interim period.

    (2) Where a project was approved prior to December 5, 1972, and prior to that date the project was legally challenged for noncompliance with CEQA, the project shall be bound by special rules set forth in Section 21170 of CEQA.

    (3) Where a private project has been granted a discretionary governmental

approval for part of the project before April 5, 1973, and another or additional discretionary governmental approvals after April 5, 1973, the project shall be subject to CEQA only if the approval or approvals after April 5, 1973, involve a greater degree of responsibility or control over the project as a whole than did the approval or approvals prior to that date.

Note: Authority cited: Sections 21083 and 21087, Public Resources Code. Reference: Sections 21169, 21170, and 21171, Public Resources Code; *County of Inyo v. Yorty*, 32 Cal.App.3d 795.

Discussion: While not specifically mentioned among the statutory exemptions contained in CEQA, the ongoing project exemption is a result of the prospective application of statutes when they are enacted. Accordingly, CEQA clearly applies to governmental projects approved after November 23, 1970, the effective date of CEQA. This section seeks to codify case law interpreting the application of CEQA to projects which were in process at the time of CEQA's effective date but not yet finally approved or still capable of being changed to avoid environmental damage. This section is also complicated by the special rules that apply to private projects approved after the *Friends of Mammoth* decision in 1972 and before April 5, 1973, the end of the statutory moratorium on the application of CEQA to private projects. The special rules are included here with some administrative interpretation in the interest of completeness of the ongoing project exception.

15262   Feasibility and Planning Studies

A project involving only feasibility or planning studies for possible future actions which the agency, board, or commission has not approved, adopted, or funded does not require the preparation of an EIR or negative declaration but does require consideration of environmental factors. This section does not apply to the adoption of a plan that will have a legally binding effect on later activities.

Note: Authority cited: Sections 21083 and 21087, Public Resources Code. Reference: Sections 21102 and 21150, Public Resources Code.

Discussion: This section provides an interpretation of the exception in CEQA for feasibility and planning studies. This section provides an interpretation holding clearly that feasibility and planning studies are exempt from the requirements to prepare EIRs or Negative Declarations. These studies must still include consideration of environmental factors. This interpretation is consistent with the intent of the Legislature as reflected in Sections 21102 and 21150. The section also adds a necessary limitation on this exemption to show that if the adoption of a plan will have a legally binding effect on later activities, the adoption will be subject to CEQA. This clarification is necessary to avoid a conflict with Section 15378(a)(1) that the adoption of a local general plan is a project subject to CEQA.

15263   Discharge Requirements

The State Water Resources Control Board and the regional boards are exempt from the requirement to prepare an EIR or a negative declaration prior to the adoption of waste discharge requirements, except requirements for new sources as defined in the Federal Water Pollution Control Act or in other acts which amend or supplement the Federal Water Pollution Control Act. The term "waste discharge requirements" as used in this section is the equivalent of the term "permits" as used in the Federal Water Pollution Control Act.

Note: Authority cited: Sections 21083 and 21087, Public Resources Code. Reference: Section 13389, Water Code.

Discussion: This section identifies and interprets the exemption for waste discharge requirements from existing sources under the Federal Water Pollution Control Act. This exemption is contained in the Water Code and would not be readily discovered by anybody reviewing CEQA. This Guideline section specifies that this partial exemption applies only to the preparation of EIRs and Negative Declarations. This is not a total exemption in CEQA. This section is included in the interest of completeness of this article and as part of the effort to bring together in one place the many different exemptions which are scattered throughout the codes.

15264   Timberland Preserves

Local agencies are exempt from the requirement to prepare an EIR or negative declaration on the adoption of timberland preserve zones under Government Code Sections 51100 et seq. (Gov. Code, Sec. 51119).

Note: Authority cited: Sections 21083 and 21087, Public Resources Code. Reference: Government Code Section 51119, Government Code.

Discussion: This exemption is also a partial exemption applying only to the requirement to prepare an EIR or Negative Declaration. This section repeats the exemption found in Section 51119 of the Government Code. The exemption located there would

be difficult for people to find when they are reviewing the CEQA statute and trying to determine its application to the activity.

15265   Adoption of Coastal Plans and Programs

(a) CEQA does not apply to activities and approvals pursuant to the California Coastal Act (commencing with Section 30000 of the Public Resources Code) by:

   (1) Any local government, as defined in Section 30109 of the Public Resources Code, necessary for the preparation and adoption of a local coastal program, or

   (2) Any state university or college, as defined in Section 30119, as necessary for the preparation and adoption of a long-range land use development plan.

(b) CEQA shall apply to the certification of a local coastal program or long-range land use development plan by the California Coastal Commission.

(c) This section shifts the burden of CEQA compliance from the local agency or the state university or college to the California Coastal Commission. The Coastal Commission's program of certifying local coastal programs and long-range land use development plans has been certified under Section 21080.5, Public Resources Code. See Section 15192.

Note: Authority cited: Sections 21083 and 21087, Public Resources Code. Reference: Sections 21080.9, Public Resources Code.

Discussion: This section identifies and explains the exemption which applies to the certification of coastal plans and programs. The section shows that the exemption amounts to a shift in responsibility from local governments and the state university and college system to the California Coastal Commission. The section also notes that the process used by the Coastal Commission in approving the local coastal programs or the long-range land use development plans by the state university or colleges has been certified as a "functional equivalent" program so that the Coastal Commission can use a short form of CEQA compliance. This section is necessary to explain how CEQA applies to local coastal programs and long-range land use development plans.

15266   General Plan Time Extension

CEQA shall not apply to the granting of an extension of time by the Office of Planning and Research to a city or county for the preparation and adoption of one or more elements of a city or county general plan.

Note: Authority cited: Sections 21083 and 21087, Public Resources Code. Reference: Section 21080.10(a), Public Resources Code.

Discussion: This section is necessary to make it clear that CEQA does not apply at all to the actions of the Office of Planning and Research in granting an extension of time to a city or county for the preparation and adoption of one or more elements of a local general plan.

15267 Financial Assistance to Low or Moderate Income Housing

CEQA does not apply to actions taken by the Department of Housing and Community Development to provide financial assistance for the development and construction of residential housing for persons and families of low or moderate income, as defined in Section 50093 of the Health and Safety Code. The residential project which is the subject of the application for financial assistance will be subject to CEQA when approvals are granted by another agency.

Note: Authority cited: Sections 21083 and 21087, Public Resources Code. Reference: Section 21080.10(b), Public Resources Code.

Discussion: This section identifies and interprets the exemption granted to the financial assistance activities of the state Department of Housing and Community Development which involve the development and construction of residential housing for persons of low or moderate income. The section notes that this exemption is not an exemption for the project which receives the funds. CEQA will apply to the approvals of the housing project by other agencies.

15268 Ministerial Projects

(a) Ministerial projects are exempt from the requirements of CEQA. The determination of what is "ministerial" can most appropriately be made by the particular public agency involved based upon its analysis of its own laws, and each public agency should make such determination either as a part of its implementing regulations or on a case-by-case basis.

(b) In the absence of any discretionary provision contained in the local ordinance or other law establishing the requirements for the permit, license, or other entitlement for use, the following actions shall be presumed to be ministerial:

   (1) Issuance of building permits.

   (2) Issuance of business licenses.

   (3) Approval of final subdivision maps.

   (4) Approval of individual utility service connections and disconnections.

(c) Each public agency should, in its implementing regulations or ordinances, provide an identification or itemization of its projects and actions which are deemed ministerial under the applicable laws and ordinances.

(d) Where a project involves an approval that contains elements of both a ministerial action and a discretionary action, the project will be deemed to be discretionary and will be subject to the requirements of CEQA.

Note: Authority cited: Sections 21083 and 21087, Public Resources Code. Reference: Section 21080(b)(1), Public Resources Code; *Day v. City of Glendale*, 51 Cal.App.3d 817.

Discussion: This section provides an interpretation of the exemption for ministerial projects. The term "ministerial" is defined in Section 15369. This section provides additional explanation. The key point is that the determination of whether a particular project is ministerial must be based on an examination of the law or ordinance authorizing the particular permit. The problem is that ordinances vary. Ordinances in adjacent counties requiring permits for the same kind of activity may provide different kinds of controls over the activity. In one county, the ordinance may be ministerial, and in the other the permit may be discretionary and therefore subject to CEQA. The section identifies four types of permits or licenses which are normally ministerial in most jurisdictions. The section creates a presumption that these activities are ministerial unless evidence is presented showing that there are discretionary provisions in the relevant local ordinance.

The section encourages public agencies to identify their ministerial permits in their implementing procedures. This approach will simplify the administration of the process in the individual agency. This section also codifies the ruling in *Day v. City of Glendale* cited in the note and other court decisions which have held that where a project approval involves elements of both ministerial action and discretionary action, the project will be deemed to be discretionary and therefore subject to CEQA.

The court in *Friends of Westwood, Inc. v. Los Angeles* (1986) 191 Cal.App.3d 259, provided guidance, and held that the legislative history of CEQA indicates that the term 'Ministerial' is limited to those approvals which can be legally compelled without substantial modification or change. "It is enough that the [agency] possesses discretion to require changes which would mitigate in whole or part one or more of the [significant or potentially significant]

environmental consequences an EIR might conceivably uncover."

15269 Emergency Projects

The following emergency projects are exempt from the requirements of CEQA.

(a) Projects to maintain, repair, restore, demolish, or replace property or facilities damaged or destroyed as a result of a disaster in a disaster stricken area in which a state of emergency has been proclaimed by the Governor pursuant to the California Emergency Services Act, commencing with Section 8550 of the Government Code. This includes projects that will remove, destroy, or significantly alter an historical resource when that resource represents an imminent threat to the public of bodily harm or of damage to adjacent property or when the project has received a determination by the State Office of Historic Preservation pursuant to Section 5028(b) of Public Resources Code.

(b) Emergency repairs to ~~public~~ publicly or privately owned service facilities necessary to maintain service essential to the public health, safety or welfare.

(c) Specific actions necessary to prevent or mitigate an emergency. This does not include long-term projects undertaken for the purpose of preventing or mitigating a situation that has a low probability of occurrence in the short-term.

(d) Projects undertaken, carried out, or approved by a public agency to maintain, repair, or restore an existing highway damaged by fire, flood, storm, earthquake, land subsidence, gradual earth movement, or landslide, provided that the project is within the existing right of way of that highway and is initiated within one year of the damage occurring. This exemption does not apply to highways designated as official state scenic highways, nor any project undertaken, carried out, or approved by a public agency to expand or widen a highway damaged by fire, flood, storm, earthquake, land subsidence, gradual earth movement, or landslide.

(e) Seismic work on highways and bridges pursuant to Section 180.2 of the Streets and Highways Code, Section 180 et seq.

Authority: Sections 21083 and 21087, Public Resources Code. Reference: Sections ~~5028,~~ 21080(b)(2), (3), and (4), 21080.33 and 21172, Public Resources Code; *Castaic Lake Water Agency v. City of Santa Clarita (1995) 41 Cal.App.4th 1257; and Western Municipal Water District of Riverside*

County v. Superior Court of San Bernardino County (1987) 187 Cal.App.3d 1104.

Discussion: This section identifies the emergency exemptions from CEQA. The exemptions for emergency repairs to existing highways and for emergency projects involving historical resources that are an imminent threat to the public reflect statutory provisions. Highway repairs are limited to those which do not expand or widen the highway.

In *Western Municipal Water District of Riverside County v. Superior Court of San Bernardino County* (1987) 187 Cal.App.3d 1104, the court held that an emergency is an occurrence, not a condition, and that the occurrence must involve a clear and imminent danger, demanding immediate attention. In this case, the water district proposed to dewater areas that could potentially be subject to liquefaction in the event of an earthquake. The excess water was to be pumped out to reduce the hazard as an emergency project. The court, however, ruled that this was not the proper use of this exemption. The imminence of an earthquake is not a condition but a potential event and no real change had yet occurred or could be incontestably foreseen as being mitigated by the proposed actions. The standard of review is there must be substantial evidence in the record to support the agency findings of an emergency, [sic] in this case, the Court found inadequate evidence of imminent danger and the subsequent need for immediate action. This holding is now codified in subsection (c).

15270   Projects Which Are Disapproved

(a) CEQA does not apply to projects which a public agency rejects or disapproves.

(b) This section is intended to allow an initial screening of projects on the merits for quick disapprovals prior to the initiation f the CEQA process where the agency can determine that the project cannot be approved.

(c) This section shall not relieve an applicant from paying the costs for an EIR or negative declaration prepared for his project prior to the lead agency's disapproval of the project after normal evaluation and processing.

Note: Authority cited: Sections 21083 and 21087, Public Resources Code. Reference: Section 21080(b)(5), Public Resources Code.

Discussion: This section identifies and interprets the exemption for disapprovals. This exemption was originally added to CEQA to clarify that a public agency could turn down a permit application without first preparing an EIR or Negative Declaration. Subsection (c) makes the point that if the public agency

prepares an EIR or Negative Declaration for the project, and then the agency decides to disapprove the project, the project applicant must still pay the cost of that EIR or Negative Declaration.

This section may also be used to avoid automatic approvals. If an applicant was not cooperative in providing requested information in a timely manner, and as a result the agency could not complete the CEQA process in the required time, the agency can disapprove the project to prevent the permit from being granted by operation of law without the mitigation measures that would have been developed through the CEQA process.

15271   Early Activities Related to Thermal Power Plants

(a) CEQA does not apply to actions undertaken by a public agency relating to any thermal power plant site or facility, including the expenditure, obligation, or encumbrance of funds by a public agency for planning, engineering, or design purposes, or for the conditional sale or purchase of equipment, fuel, water (except groundwater), steam, or power for such a thermal power plant, if the thermal power plant site and related facility will be the subject of an EIR or negative declaration or other document or documents prepared pursuant to a regulatory program certified pursuant to Public Resources Code Section 21080.5, which will be prepared by:

(1) The State Energy Resources Conservation and Development Commission,

(2) The Public Utilities Commission, or

(3) The city or county in which the power plant and related facility would be located.

(b) The EIR, negative declaration, or other document prepared for the thermal power plant site or facility, shall include the environmental impact, if any, of the early activities described in this section.

(c) This section acts to delay the timing of CEQA compliance from the early activities of a utility to the time when a regulatory agency is requested to approve the thermal power plant and shifts the responsibility for preparing the document to the regulatory agency.

Note: Authority cited: Sections 21083 and 21087, Public Resources Code. Reference: Section 15080(b)(6), Public Resources Code.

Discussion: This section identifies and interprets the exemption for early activities related to thermal electric power plants. This

section delays the CEQA compliance for thermal power plants for all utilities until the power plant needed approval from a regulatory agency. The statutory exception provides that when an EIR, Negative Declaration, or a document under a certified program is prepared, that document must include the environmental impacts of any of the early activities described in the section as being exempt from CEQA compliance.

Subsection (c) explains the purpose as shifting both the timing and the responsibility for preparing the EIR. Although the utility would ultimately pay for the cost, preparing the document would be the responsibility of the regulatory agency.

15272   Olympic Games

CEQA does not apply to activities or approvals necessary to the bidding for, hosting or staging of, and funding or carrying out of, Olympic Games under the authority of the International Olympic Committee, except for the construction of facilities necessary for such Olympic Games. If the facilities are required by the International Olympic Committee as a condition of being awarded the Olympic Games, the lead agency need not discuss the "no project" alternative in an EIR with respect to those facilities.

Note: Authority cited: Sections 21083 and 21087, Public Resources Code. Reference: Section 21080(b)(7), Public Resources Code.

15273   Rates, Tolls, Fares, and Charges

(a) CEQA does not apply to the establishment, modification, structuring, restructuring, or approval of rates, tolls, fares, or other charges by public agencies which the public agency finds are for the purpose of:

(1) Meeting operating expenses, including employee wage rates and fringe benefits,

(2) Purchasing or leasing supplies, equipment, or materials,

(3) Meeting financial reserve needs and requirements,

(4) Obtaining funds for capital projects, necessary to maintain service within existing service areas, or

(5) Obtaining funds necessary to maintain such intra-city transfers as are authorized by city charter.

(b) Rate increases to fund capital projects for the expansion of a system remain subject to CEQA. The agency granting the rate increase shall act either as the lead agency if no other agency has prepared environmental documents for the capital project or as a responsible agency if another agency has already complied with CEQA as the lead agency.

(c) The public agency shall incorporate written findings in the record of any proceeding in which an exemption under this section is claimed setting forth with specificity the basis for the claim of exemption.

Note: Authority cited: Sections 21083 and 21087, Public Resources Code. Reference: Section 21080(b)(8), Public Resources Code.

Discussion: This section identifies and interprets the exemption that applies to the adoption of rates, tolls, fares, and other charges. The section spells out the provisions of the statutory exemption for these charges and in summary form provides an interpretation of the kinds of rate increases that still remain subject to CEQA. The section also identifies the requirement to make written findings to support the claim that the rate change falls within the specific exemptions provided in this section. These findings are an unusual requirement with an exemption and need to be highlighted.

15274 ~~Responses to Revenue Shortfalls~~ Family Day Care Homes

~~(a) CEQA does not apply to actions taken prior to January 1, 1982, by a public agency.~~

~~(1) To implement the transition from the property taxation systems in effect prior to June 1, 1978, to the system provided for by Article XIII A of the California Constitution (Proposition 13), or~~

~~(2) To respond to a reduction in federal funds.~~

~~(b) This exemption is limited to projects directly undertaken by an public agency and to projects which are supported in whole or in part through contracts, grants, subsides, loans, or other forms of assistance from one or more public agencies where the projects:~~

~~(1) Initiate or increase fees, rates, or charges charged for any existing public service, program, or activity, or~~

~~(2) Reduce or eliminate the availability of an existing public service program, or activity, or~~

~~(3) Close publicly owned or operated facilities, or~~

~~(4) Reduce or eliminate the availability of existing publicly owned transit service, program, or activity.~~

(a) CEQA does not apply to establishment or operation of a large family day care home, which provides in-home care for

up to twelve children, as defined in Section 1596.78 of the Health and Safety Code.

(b) Under the Health and Safety Code, local agencies cannot require use permits for the establishment or operation of a small family day care home, which provides in-home care for up to six children, and the establishment or operation of a small family day care home is a ministerial action which is not subject to CEQA.

Note: Authority cited: Sections 21083 and 21087, Public Resources Code. Reference: Section ~~21080(b)(9)~~ 21083, Public Resources Code.

15275 Specified Mass Transit Projects

CEQA does not apply to the following mass transit projects:

(a) The institution or increase of passenger or commuter service on rail lines or high-occupancy vehicle lanes already in use, including the modernization of existing stations and parking facilities;

(b) Facility extensions not to exceed four miles in length which are required for transfer of passengers from or to exclusive public mass transit guideway or busway public transit services.

Note: Authority cited: Sections 21083 and 21087, Public Resources Code. Reference: Section 21080(b)(11), (12), and (13), Public Resources Code.

Discussion: This section combined several exemptions that apply to mass transit projects. The revised description of these projects clarifies the nature of the exemption and the activities to which the exemption applies.

15276 ~~State and Regional~~ Transportation Improvement and Congestion Management Programs

(a) CEQA does not apply to the development or adoption of a regional transportation improvement program or the state transportation improvement program. Individual projects developed pursuant to these programs shall remain subject to CEQA.

(b) CEQA does not apply to preparation and adoption of a congestion management program by a county congestion management agency pursuant to Government Code Section 65089, et seq.

Note: Authority cited: Sections 21083 and 21087, Public Resources Code. Reference: Section ~~21080(b)(14)~~ 21080(b)(13), Public Resources Code.

Discussion: This section identifies and interprets the exemptions that apply to the

development or adoption of state and regional transportation improvement programs, as well as congestion management plans. The section clarifies that the exemption for transportation improvement programs does not apply to individual projects undertaken pursuant to such programs.

The California Supreme Court held, in *Napa Valley Wine Train, Inc. v. Public Utilities Commission* (1990) 50 Cal 3d 370, that rail passenger service is to be construed with reference to the existence of a rail right of way and not the physical rail line, its condition, or type of rail traffic. In this case, the fact that the existing rail right of way had not been formally abandoned, not its physical existence or frequency of recent pattern of use of the line was the pertinent criteria. See also the discussion for Section 15260.

15277 Projects Located Outside California

CEQA does not apply to any project or portion thereof located outside of California which will be subject to environmental impact review pursuant to the National Environmental Policy Act of 1969 or pursuant to a law of that state requiring preparation of a document containing essentially the same points of analysis as in an environmental impact statement prepared under the National Environmental Policy Act of 1969. Any emissions or discharges that would have a significant effect on the environment in the State of California are subject to CEQA where a California public agency has authority over the emissions or discharges.

Note: Authority cited: Sections 21083 and 21087, Public Resources Code. Reference: Section 21080(b)(15), Public Resources Code; 58 Opinions of the California Attorney General 614 (S.O. 75/50).

Discussion: The section identifies and interprets the exemption that applies to projects located in another state. The section repeats part of the statutory language and provides further explanation.

This partial exemption from CEQA was a response to an Attorney General's opinion stating that when a California public agency takes an action outside of the State of California, the California agency is still bound by the requirements in CEQA to prepare an EIR if the agency's action would cause a significant effect on the environment. The Attorney General's opinion noted that the definition of the term "environment" in CEQA did not stop at the borders of the State of California. It said that CEQA applies to any exercise of powers by a California state or local agency. Where the agency was exercising powers granted by the Legislature, they were also subject to constraints enacted by the Legislature. Accordingly, when the California Department of Water Resources proposed to build a power plant in Nevada, the Department prepared an EIR analyzing the effects of its proposed action on the environment. This section will apply mostly where California public agencies undertake their own projects outside the state.

15278 Application of Coatings

(a) CEQA does not apply to a discretionary decision by an air quality management district for a project consisting of the application of coatings within an existing facility at an automotive manufacturing plant if the district finds all of the following:

(1) The project will not cause a net increase in any emissions of any pollutant for which a national or state ambient air quality standard has been established after the internal emission accounting for previous emission reductions achieved at the facility and recognized by the district.

(2) The project will not cause a net increase in adverse impacts of toxic air contaminants as determined by a health risk assessment. The term "net increase in adverse impacts of toxic air contaminants as determined by a health risk assessment" shall be determined in accordance with the rules and regulations of the district.

(3) The project will not cause any other adverse effect on the environment.

(b) The district shall provide a 10-day notice, at the time of the issuance of the permit, of any such exemption. Notice shall be published in two newspapers of general circulation in the area of the project and shall be mailed to any person who makes a written request for such a notice. The notice shall state that the complete file on the project and the basis for the district's findings of exemption are available for inspection and copying at the office of the district.

(c) Any person may appeal the issuance of a permit based on an exemption under subdivision (a) to the hearing board as provided in Section 42302.1 of the Health and Safety Code. The permit shall be revoked by the hearing board if there is substantial evidence in light of the whole record before the board that the project may not satisfy one or more of the criteria established pursuant to subdivision (a). If there is no such substantial evidence, the exemption shall be upheld. Any appeal under this subdivision shall be scheduled for hearing on the calendar of the hearing board within 10 working days of the appeal being filed. The hearing board shall give the appeal priority on its calendar and shall render a decision on the appeal within 21 working days of the appeal being filed. The hearing board may delegate the authority to hear and decide such an appeal to a subcommittee of its body.

Note: Authority cited: Sections 21083 and 21087, Public Resources Code. Reference: Chapter 1131, Statutes of 1993, Section 1.

15279 Housing for Agricultural Employees

(a) CEQA does not apply to any development project which consists of the construction, conversion, or use of residential housing for agricultural employees, as defined below, provided the development is either:

(1) Affordable to lower income households, as defined in Section 50079.5 of the Health and Safety Code, there is no public financial assistance for the development project, and the developer provides sufficient legal commitments to the appropriate local agency to ensure that the housing units will continue to be available to lower-income households for a period of at least 15 years; or

(2) Affordable to low and moderate-income households, as defined in paragraph (2) of subdivision (h) of Section 65589.5 of the Government Code, at monthly housing costs determined pursuant to paragraph (2) of subdivision (h) of Section 65589.5 of the Government Code, there is public financial assistance for the project, and the developer provides sufficient legal commitments to the appropriate local agency to ensure that the housing units will continue to be available to low and moderate-income households for a period of at least 15 years.

(b) The development must also meet all the following criteria:

(1) It is consistent with the applicable city, county, or city and county general plan as it existed on the date the project application was deemed complete.

(2) It is consistent with the local zoning, as it existed on the date the project application was deemed complete, unless the zoning is inconsistent with the general plan because the city, county, or city and county has not rezoned the property to bring it into consistency with the general plan.

(3) If the project is proposed in an urbanized area, it does not exceed 45 dwelling units, or if it consists of dormitories, barracks or other group living facilities houses not more than 45 agricultural employees, and its site is adjacent on at least two sides to land that has been previously developed.

(4) If the project is proposed in a nonurbanized area, its site is zoned for general agricultural use and the project consists of not more than 20 dwelling units or, if it consists of dormitories, barracks or other group living facilities, it houses not more than 20 agricultural employees.

(5) Its site is not more than five acres in area, except that a project located in an area with a population density of at least 1000 persons per square mile shall not be more than two acres in area.

(6) Its site is, or can be, adequately served by utilities.

(7) Its site has no value as wildlife habitat.

(8) Its site is not included on any list of hazardous waste or other facilities and sites compiled pursuant to Section 65962 of the Government Code.

(9) It will not involve the demolition of, or any substantial adverse change in, any structure that is listed, or determined to be eligible for listing in the California Register of Historical Resources.

(c) As used in this section, "residential housing for agricultural employees" means housing accommodations for an agricultural employee, as defined in subdivision (b) of Section 1140.4 of the Labor Code.

(d) As used in this section, "urbanized area" means either of the following:

(1) an area with a population density of at least 1000 persons per square mile; or

(2) an area with a population density of less than 1000 persons per square mile that is identified as an urban area in the general plan adopted by the applicable city, county, or city and county and was not designated at the time the application was deemed complete as an area reserved for future urban growth.

(e) This section does not apply if the public agency which is carrying out or approving the development project determines that there is a reasonable possibility that the project would have a significant effect on the environment due to unusual circumstances or that the cumulative impact of successive projects of the same type in the same area over time would be significant.

Note: Authority cited: Sections 21083 and 21087, Public Resources Code. Reference: Section 21080.10, Public Resources Code.

Discussion: Public Resources Code section 21080.10 establishes a statutory exemption for agricultural employees housing. The conditions and limitations of this exemption are detailed in this section.

15280 Lower-Income Housing Projects

(a) CEQA does not apply to any development project which consists of the construction, conversion, or use of residential housing consisting of not more than 45 units in an urbanized area, provided that it is either:

(1) Affordable to lower-income households, as defined in Section 50079.5 of the Health and Safety Code, and the developer provides sufficient legal commitments to the appropriate local agency to ensure that the housing units will continue to be available to lower income households for a period of at least 15 years; or

(2) Affordable to low and moderate-income households, as defined in paragraph (2) of subdivision (h) of Section 65589.5 of the Government Code, at monthly housing costs determined pursuant to paragraph (2) of subdivision (h) of Section 65589.5 of the Government Code.

(b) The development must also meet all the following criteria:

(1) It is consistent with the local jurisdiction's general plan as it existed on the date the project application was deemed complete.

(2) It is consistent with the local zoning as it existed on the date the project application was deemed complete, unless the zoning is inconsistent with the general plan because the city, county, or city and county has not rezoned the property to bring it into consistency with the general plan.

(3) Its site has been previously developed or is currently developed with urban uses, or the immediately contiguous properties surrounding the site are or have been previously developed with urban uses.

(4) Its site is not more than two acres in area.

(5) Its site is, or can be, adequately served by utilities.

(6) Its site has no value as wildlife habitat.

(7) It will not involve the demolition of, or any substantial adverse change in, any district, landmark, object, building, structure, site, area, or place that is listed, or determined to be eligible for listing in the California Register of Historical Resources.

(8) Its site is not included on any list of hazardous waste or other facilities and sites compiled pursuant to Section 65962.5 of the Government Code, and the site has been subject to an assessment by a California registered environmental assessor to determine both the presence of hazardous contaminants, if any, and the potential for exposure of site occupants to significant health hazards from nearby properties and activities.

(c) For purposes of this section, "urbanized area" means an area that has a population density of at least 1000 persons per square mile.

(d) If hazardous contaminants are found on the site, they must be removed or any significant effects mitigated to a level of insignificance in order to apply this exemption. If a potential for exposure to significant health hazards from nearby properties and activities is found to exist, the effects of the potential exposure must be mitigated to a level of insignificance in order to apply this exemption. Any removal or mitigation to insignificance must be completed prior to any residential occupancy of the project.

(e) This section does not apply if there is a reasonable possibility that the project would have a significant effect on the environment due to unusual circumstances or due to the related or cumulative impacts of reasonably foreseeable other projects in the vicinity.

Note: Authority cited: Sections 21083 and 21087, Public Resources Code. Reference: Section 21080.14, Public Resources Code.

Discussion: Public Resources Code section 21080.14 establishes a statutory exemption for lower-income residential projects in urban areas. The conditions and limitations of this exemption are detailed in this section.

15281 Air Quality Permits

CEQA does not apply to the issuance, modification, amendment, or renewal of any permit by an air pollution control district or air quality management district pursuant to Title V, as defined in Section 39053.3 of the Health and Safety Code, or pursuant to an air district Title V program established under Sections 42301.10, 42301.11, and 42301.12 of the Health and Safety Code, unless the issuance, modification, amendment, or renewal authorizes a physical or operational change to a source or facility.

Note: Authority cited: Sections 21083 and 21087, Public Resources Code. Reference: Section 21080.24, Public Resources Code.

15282 Other Statutory Exemptions

The following is a list of existing statutory exemptions. Each subsection summarizes statutory exemptions found in the California Code. Lead agencies are not to rely on the language contained in the summaries below but must rely on the actual statutory language that creates the exemption. This list is intended to assist lead agencies in finding them, but not as a substitute for them. This section is merely a reference tool.

(a) The notification of discovery of Native American burial sites as set forth in Section 5097.98(c) of the Public Resources Code .

(b) Specified prison facilities as set forth in Sections 21080.01, 21080.02, 21080.03 and 21080.07 of the Public Resources Code.

(c) The lease or purchase of the rail right-of-way used for the San Francisco Peninsula commute service between San Francisco and San Jose as set forth in Section 21080.05 of the Public Resources Code.

(d) Any activity or approval necessary for or incidental to project funding or authorization for the expenditure of funds for the project, by the Rural Economic Development Infrastructure Panel as set forth in Section 21080.08 of the Public Resources Code.

(e) The construction of housing or neighborhood commercial facilities in an urbanized area pursuant to the provisions of Section 21080.7 of the Public Resources Code.

(f) The conversion of an existing rental mobilehome park to a resident initiated subdivision, cooperative, or condominium for mobilehomes as set forth in Section 21080.8 of the Public Resources Code.

(g) Settlements of title and boundary problems by the State Lands Commission and to exchanges or leases in connection with those settlements as set forth in Section 21080.11 of the Public Resources Code.

(h) Any railroad grade separation project which eliminates an existing grade crossing or which reconstructs an existing grade separation as set forth in Section 21080.13 of the Public Resources Code.

(i) The adoption of an ordinance regarding second units in a single-family or multifamily residential zone by a city or county to implement the provisions of Sections 65852.1 and 65852.2 of the Government Code as set forth in Section 21080.17 of the Public Resources Code.

(j) The closing of any public school or the transfer of students from that public school to another school in which kindergarten or any grades 1 through 12 is maintained as set forth in 21080.18 of the Public Resources Code.

(k) A project for restriping streets or highways to relieve traffic congestion as set forth in Section 21080.19 of the Public Resources Code.

(l) The installation of new pipeline or maintenance, repair, restoration, removal, or demolition of an existing pipeline as set forth in Section 21080.21 of the Public Resources Code, as long as the project does not exceed one mile in length.

(m) The activities and approvals by a local government necessary for the preparation of general plan amendments pursuant to Public Resources Code §29763 as set forth in Section 21080.22 of the Public Resources Code. Section 29763 of the Public Resources Code refers to local government amendments made for consistency with the Delta Protection Commission's regional plan.

(n) Minor alterations to utilities made for the purposes of complying with Sections 4026.7 and 4026.8 of the Health and Safety Code as set forth in Section 21080.26 of the Public Resources Code.

(o) The adoption of an ordinance exempting a city or county from the provisions of the Solar Shade Control Act as set forth in Section 25985 of the Public Resources Code.

(p) The acquisition of land by the Department of Transportation if received or acquired within a statewide or regional priority corridor designated pursuant to Section 65081.3 of the Government Code as set forth in Section 33911 of the Public Resources Code .

(q) The adoption or amendment of a nondisposal facility element as set forth in Section 41735 of the Public Resources Code.

(r) Cooperative agreements for the development of Solid Waste Management Facilities on Indian country as set forth in Section 44203(g) of the Public Resources Code .

(s) Determinations made regarding a city or county's regional housing needs as set forth in Section 65584 of the Government Code.

(t) Any action necessary to bring a general plan or relevant mandatory element of the general plan into compliance pursuant to a court order as set forth in Section 65759 of the Government Code.

(u) Industrial Development Authority activities as set forth in Section 91543 of the Government Code .

(v) Temporary changes in the point of diversion, place of use, of purpose of use due to a transfer or exchange of water or water rights as set forth in Section 1729 of the Water Code.

(w) The preparation and adoption of Urban Water Management Plans pursuant to the provisions of Section 10652 of the Water Code.

Note: Authority: Sections 21083 and 21087, Public Resources Code. References: Sections 5097.98(c), 21080.01, 21080.02, 21080.03, 21080.05, 21080.07, 21080.08, 21080.7, 21080.8, 21080.11, 21080.13, 21080.17, 21080.18, 21080.19, 21080.21, 21080.22, 21080.26, 25985, 33911, 41735, and 44203(g), Public Resources Code.

Discussion: There are numerous statutory exemptions from CEQA, not all of which can be found in CEQA itself. This section identifies many of these exemptions and provides the reader with cross references to the pertinent statutes.

15283   Housing Needs Allocation

CEQA does not apply to regional housing needs determinations made by the Department of Housing and Community Development, a council of governments, or a city or county pursuant to Section 65584 of the Government Code.

Note: Authority cited: Sections 21083 and 21087, Public Resources Code. Reference: Section 65584, Government Code.

Discussion: This section describes the statutory exemption for regional housing need allocations made prior to and during the

preparation of city and county general plan housing elements.

15284   Pipelines

(a) CEQA does not apply to any project consisting of the inspection, maintenance, repair, restoration, reconditioning, relocation, replacement, or removal of an existing hazardous or volatile liquid pipeline or any valve, flange, meter, or other piece of equipment that is directly attached to the pipeline.

(b) To qualify for this exemption, the diameter of the affected pipeline must not be increased and the project must be located outside the boundaries of an oil refinery. The project must also meet all of the following criteria:

(1) The affected section of pipeline is less than eight miles in length and actual construction and excavation activities are not undertaken over a length of more than one-half mile at a time.

(2) The affected section of pipeline is not less than eight miles distance from any section of pipeline that had been subject to this exemption in the previous 12 months.

(3) The project is not solely for the purpose of excavating soil that is contaminated by hazardous materials.

(4) To the extent not otherwise required by law, the person undertaking the project has, in advance of undertaking the project, prepared a plan that will result in notification of the appropriate agencies so that they may take action, if necessary, to provide for the emergency evacuation of members of the public who may be located in close proximity to the project, and those agencies, including but not limited to the local fire department, police, sheriff, and California Highway Patrol as appropriate, have reviewed and agreed to that plan.

(5) Project activities take place within an existing right-of-way and that right-of-way will be restored to its pre-project condition upon completion of the project.

(6) The project applicant will comply with all conditions otherwise authorized by law, imposed by the city or county as part of any local agency permit process, and to comply with the Keene-Nejedly California Wetlands Preservation Act (Public Resources Code Section 5810, et seq.),

the California Endangered Species Act (Fish and Game Code Section 2050, et seq.), other applicable state laws, and all applicable federal laws.

(c) When the lead agency determines that a project meets all of the criteria of subdivisions (a) and (b), the party undertaking the project shall do all of the following:

(1) Notify in writing all responsible and trustee agencies, as well as any public agency with environmental, public health protection, or emergency response authority, of the lead agency's invocation of this exemption.

(2) Mail notice of the project to the last known name and address of all organizations and individuals who have previously requested such notice and notify the public in the affected area by at least one of the following procedures:

(A) Publication at least one time in a newspaper of general circulation in the area affected by the proposed project. If more than one area is affected, the notice shall be published in the newspaper of largest circulation from among the newspapers of general circulation in those areas.

(B) Posting of notice on and off site in the area where the project is to be located.

(C) Direct mailing to the owners and occupants of contiguous property shown on the latest equalized assessment roll.

The notice shall include a brief description of the proposed project and its location, and the date, time, and place of any public meetings or hearings on the proposed project. This notice may be combined with the public notice required under other law, as applicable, but shall meet the preceding minimum requirements.

(3) In the case of private rights-of-way over private property, receive from the underlying property owner permission for access to the property.

(4) Immediately inform the lead agency if any soil contaminated with hazardous materials is discovered.

(5) Comply with all conditions otherwise authorized by law, imposed by the city or county as part of any local agency permit process, and to comply with the Keene-Nejedly Cali-

fornia Wetlands Preservation Act (Public Resources Code Section 5810, et seq.), the California Endangered Species Act (Fish and Game Code Section 2050, et seq.), other applicable state laws, and all applicable federal laws.

(d) For purposes of this section, "pipeline" is used as defined in subdivision (a) of Government Code Section 51010.5. This definition includes every intrastate pipeline used for the transportation of hazardous liquid substances or highly volatile liquid substances, including a common carrier pipeline, and all piping containing those substances located within a refined products bulk loading facility which is owned by a common carrier and is served by a pipeline of that common carrier, and the common carrier owns and serves by pipeline at least five such facilities in California.

Note: Authority cited: Sections 21083 and 21087, Public Resources Code. Reference: Section 21080.23, Public Resources Code.

Discussion: This section describes the statutory exemption for the inspection, maintenance, repair, restoration, reconditioning, relocation, replacement, or removal of existing hazardous or volatile liquid pipelines. The Legislature's purpose in creating this exemption was to encourage the upkeep of existing pipelines by limiting the review required of particular activities.

Subsection (b) establishes the criteria under which a pipeline project qualifies for this exemption. These include a prohibition on increasing the diameter of the existing pipeline, limitations on the length of pipeline which may be worked on at any one time, provision of an emergency notification plan to local safety agencies and the California Highway Patrol for their review and agreement, site restoration, and compliance with local, state, and federal environmental laws. Subsection (c) clarifies that the lead agency is responsible for determining that the criteria described in subsection (b) have been met. This exemption is to be invoked by the lead agency, not the project applicant. The project applicant is responsible for providing public notice, obtaining property owner's permission where the pipeline crosses private property, and complying with all regulatory requirements.

15285 Transit Agency Responses to Revenue Shortfalls

(a) CEQA does not apply to actions taken on or after July 1, 1995 to implement

budget reductions made by a publicly owned transit agency as a result of a fiscal emergency caused by the failure of agency revenues to adequately fund agency programs and facilities. Actions shall be limited to those directly undertaken by or financially supported in whole or in part by the transit agency pursuant to Section 15378(a)(1) or (2), including actions which reduce or eliminate the availability of an existing publicly owned transit service, facility, program, or activity.

(b) When invoking this exemption, the transit agency shall make a specific finding that there is a fiscal emergency. Before taking its proposed budgetary actions and making the finding of fiscal emergency, the transit agency shall hold a public hearing. After this public hearing, the transit agency shall respond within 30 days at a regular public meeting to suggestions made by the public at that initial hearing. The transit agency may make the finding of fiscal emergency only after it has responded to public suggestions.

(c) For purposes of this subdivision, "fiscal emergency" means that the transit agency is projected to have negative working capital within one year from the date that the agency finds that a fiscal emergency exists. "Working capital" is defined as the sum of all unrestricted cash, unrestricted short-term investments, and unrestricted short-term accounts receivable, minus unrestricted accounts payable. Employee retirements funds, including deferred compensation plans and Section 401(k) plans, health insurance reserves, bond payment reserves, workers' compensation reserves, and insurance reserves shall not be included as working capital.

(d) This exemption does not apply to the action of any publicly owned transit agency to reduce or eliminate a transit service, facility, program, or activity that was approved or adopted as a mitigation measure in any environmental document certified or adopted by any public agency under either CEQA or NEPA. Further, it does not apply to actions of the Los Angeles County Metropolitan Transportation Authority.

Note: Authority cited: Sections 21083 and 21087, Public Resources Code. References: Sections 21080 and 21080.32, Public Resources Code.

Discussion: This section describes the statutory exemption established for certain public transit agency budget reductions.

Article 19. Categorical Exemptions
Sections 15300 to 15329

15300 Categorical Exemptions

Section 21084 of the Public Resources Code requires these guidelines to include a list of classes of projects which have been determined not to have a significant effect on the environment and which shall, therefore, be exempt from the provisions of CEQA.

In response to that mandate, the Secretary for Resources has found that the following classes of projects listed in this article do not have a significant effect on the environment, and they are declared to be categorically exempt from the requirement for the preparation of environmental documents.

Note: Authority cited: Sections 21083 and 21087, Public Resources Code. Reference: Section 21084, Public Resources Code.

15300.1 Relation to Ministerial Projects

Section 21080 of the Public Resources Code exempts from the application of CEQA those projects over which public agencies exercise only ministerial authority. Since ministerial projects are already exempt, Categorical Exemptions should be applied only where a project is not ministerial under a public agency's statutes and ordinances. The inclusion of activities which may be ministerial within the classes and examples contained in this article shall not be construed as a finding by the Secretary for resources that such an activity is discretionary.

Note: Authority cited: Sections 21083 and 21087, Public Resources Code. Reference: Section 21084, Public Resources Code.

15300.2 Exceptions

(a) Location. Classes 3, 4, 5, 6, and 11 are qualified by consideration of where the project is to be located—a project that is ordinarily insignificant in its impact on the environment may in a particularly sensitive environment be significant. Therefore, these classes are considered to apply all instances, except where the project may impact on an environmental resource of hazardous or critical concern where designated, precisely mapped, and officially adopted pursuant to law by federal, state, or local agencies.

(b) Cumulative Impact. All exemptions for these classes are inapplicable when the cumulative impact of successive projects of the same type in the same place, over time is significant for example, annual additions to an existing building under Class 1.

(c) Significant Effect. A categorical exemption shall not be used for an activity where there is a reasonable possibility that the activity will have a significant effect on the environment due to unusual circumstances.

(d) Scenic Highways. A categorical exemption shall not be used for a project which may result in damage to scenic resources, including but not limited to, trees, historic buildings, rock outcroppings, or similar resources, within a highway officially designated as a state scenic highway. This does not apply to improvements which are required as mitigation by an adopted negative declaration or certified EIR.

(e) Hazardous Waste Sites. A categorical exemption shall not be used for a project located on a site which is included on any list compiled pursuant to Section 65962.5 of the Government Code.

(f) Historical Resources. A categorical exemption shall not be used for a project which may cause a substantial adverse change in the significance of a historical resource.

Note: Authority cited: Sections 21083 and 21087, Public Resources Code. Reference: Section Sections 21084 and 21084.1, Public Resources Code; *Wildlife Alive v. Chickering* (1977) 18 Cal.3d 190; *League for Protection of Oakland's Architectural and Historic Resources v. City of Oakland* (1997) 52 Cal.App.4th 896; *Citizens for Responsible Development in West Hollywood v. City of West Hollywood* (1995) 39 Cal.App.4th 925; *City of Pasadena v. State of California* (1993) 14 Cal.App.4th 810; *Association for the Protection etc. Values v. City of Ukiah* (1991) 2 Cal.App.4th 720; and *Baird v. County of Contra Costa* (1995) 32 Cal. App.4th 1464

Discussion: In *McQueen v. Mid-Peninsula Regional Open Space* (1988) 202 Cal.App. 3d 1136, the court reiterated that categorical exemptions are construed strictly, shall not be unreasonably expanded beyond their terms, and may not be used where there is substantial evidence that there are unusual circumstances (including future activities) resulting in (or which might reasonably result in) significant impacts which threaten the environment.

Public Resources Code Section 21084 provides several additional exceptions to the use of categorical exemptions. Pursuant to that statute, none of the following may qualify as a categorical exemption: (1) a project which may result in damage to scenic resources, including but not limited to, trees, historic buildings, rock outcroppings, or

similar resources within a scenic highway (this does not apply to improvements which are required as mitigation for a project for which a negative declaration or EIR has previously been adopted or certified, (2) a project located on a site included on any list compiled pursuant to Government Code section 65962.5 (hazardous and toxic waste sites, etc.); and (3) a project which may cause a substantial adverse change in the significance of a historical resource.

15300.3 Revisions to List of Categorical Exemptions

A public agency may, at any time, request that a new class of categorical exemptions be added, or an existing one amended or deleted. This request must be made in writing to the Office of Planning and Research and shall contain detailed information to support the request. The granting of such request shall be by amendment to these Guidelines.

Note: Authority cited: Sections 21083 and 21087, Public Resources Code. Reference: Section 21084, Public Resources Code.

15300.4 Application by Public Agencies

Each public agency shall, in the course of establishing its own procedures, list those specific activities which fall within each of the exempt classes, subject to the qualification that these lists must be consistent with both the letter and the intent expressed in the classes. Public agencies may omit from their implementing procedures classes and examples that do not apply to their activities, but they may not require EIRs for projects described in the classes and examples in this article except under the provisions of Section 15300.2.

Note: Authority cited: Sections 21083 and 21087, Public Resources Code. Reference: Section 21084, Public Resources Code.

15301 Existing Facilities

Class 1 consists of the operation, repair, maintenance, permitting, leasing, licensing, or minor alteration of existing public or private structures, facilities, mechanical equipment, or topographical features, involving negligible or no expansion of use beyond that previously existing at the time of the lead agency's determination. The types of "existing facilities" itemized below are not intended to be all-inclusive of the types of projects which might fall within Class 1. The key consideration is whether the project involves negligible or no expansion of an existing use.

Examples include including but are not limited to:

(a) Interior or exterior alterations involving such things as interior partitions, plumbing, and electrical conveyances;

(b) Existing facilities of both investor and publicly-owned utilities used to provide electric power, natural gas, sewerage, or other public utility services;

(c) Existing highways and streets, sidewalks, gutters, bicycle and pedestrian trails, and similar facilities (this includes road grading for the purpose of public safety). except where the activity will involve removal of a scenic resource including a stand of trees, a rock out cropping, or an historic building;

(d) Restoration or rehabilitation of deteriorated or damaged structures, facilities, or mechanical equipment to meet current standards of public health and safety, unless it is determined that the damage was substantial and resulted from an environmental hazard such as earthquake, landslide, or flood;

(e) Additions to existing structures provided that the addition will not result in an increase of more than:

   (1) 50 percent of the floor area of the structures before the addition, or 2,500 square feet, whichever is less; or

   (2) 10,000 square feet if:

     (A) The project is in an area where all public services and facilities are available to allow for maximum development permissible in the General Plan and

     (B) The area in which the project is located is not environmentally sensitive.

(f) Addition of safety or health protection devices for use during construction of or in conjunction with existing structures, facilities, or mechanical equipment, or topographical features including navigational devices;

(g) New copy on existing on and off-premise signs;

(h) Maintenance of existing landscaping, native growth, and water supply reservoirs (excluding the use of economic poisons, as defined in Division 7, Chapter 2, California Agricultural Code);

(i) Maintenance of fish screens, fish ladders, wildlife habitat areas, artificial wildlife waterway devices, streamflows, springs and waterholes, and stream channels (clearing of debris) to protect fish and wildlife resources;

(j) Fish stocking by the California Department of Fish and Game;

(k) Division of existing multiple family ~~rental units~~ or single-family residences into ~~condominiums~~ common-interest ownership and subdivision of existing commercial or industrial buildings, where no physical changes occur which are not otherwise exempt;

(l) Demolition and removal of individual small structures listed in this subsection ~~except where the structures are of historical, archaeological, or architectural significance~~;

   (1) ~~Single-family residences not in conjunction with the building demolition of two or more such units.~~ One single-family residence. In urbanized areas, up to three single-family residences may be demolished under this exemption.

   (2) ~~Apartments, duplexes and~~ A duplex or similar multifamily residential structures ~~with no more than four dwelling units if not in conjunction with the demolition of two or more such structures~~. In urbanized areas, this exemption applies to ~~single apartments,~~ duplexes, and similar structures ~~designed for~~ where not more than six dwelling units ~~if not~~ will be demolished ~~in conjunction with the demolition of two or more such structures~~.

   (3) A ~~Stores~~ store, motel, office, restaurant, or similar small commercial structure if designed for an occupant load of 30 persons or less, ~~if designed for an occupant load of 30 persons or less if not demolished in conjunction with the demolition of four or more such structures~~. In urbanized areas, the exemption also applies to the demolition of up to three such commercial buildings on sites zoned for such use.

   (4) Accessory (appurtenant) structures including garages, carports, patios, swimming pools, and fences.

(m) Minor repairs and alterations to existing dams and appurtenant structures under the supervision of the Department of Water Resources.

(n) Conversion of a single family residence to office use.

(o) ~~The conversion of existing commercial units in one structure from single to condominium type ownership.~~ Installation, in an existing facility occupied by a medical waste generator, of a steam sterilization unit for the treatment of medical waste generated by that facility provided that the unit is installed and operated in accordance with the Medical Waste Management Act (Section ~~25015~~ 117600, et seq., of the Health and Safety Code) and accepts no offsite waste.

(p) Use of a single-family residence as a small family day care home, as defined in Section 1596.78 of the Health and Safety Code.

Note: Authority cited: Sections 21083 and 21087, Public Resources Code. References: ~~Section~~ Sections 21084 and 21084.2, Public Resources Code; *Bloom v. McGurk* (1994) 26 Cal.App.4th 1307.

Discussion: This section describes the class of projects wherein the proposed activity will involve negligible or no expansion of the use existing at the time the exemption is granted. Application of this exemption, as all categorical exemptions, is limited by the factors described in section 15300.2. Accordingly, a project with significant cumulative impacts or which otherwise has a reasonable possibility of resulting in a significant effect does not qualify for a Class 1 exemption.

15302   Replacement or Reconstruction

Class 2 consists of replacement or reconstruction of existing structures and facilities where the new structure will be located on the same site as the structure replaced and will have substantially the same purpose and capacity as the structure replaced, including but not limited to:

(a) Replacement or reconstruction of existing schools and hospitals to provide earthquake resistant structures which do not increase capacity more than 50 percent.

(b) Replacement of a commercial structure with a new structure of substantially the same size, purpose, and capacity.

(c) Replacement or reconstruction of existing utility systems and/or facilities involving negligible or no expansion of capacity.

(d) Conversion of overhead electric utility distribution system facilities to underground including connection to existing overhead electric utility distribution lines where the surface is restored to the condition existing prior to the undergrounding.

Note: Authority cited: Sections 21083 and 21087, Public Resources Code. Reference: Section 21084, Public Resources Code.

15303   New Construction or Conversion of Small Structures

Class 3 consists of construction and location of limited numbers of new, small facilities or structures; installation of small new equipment and facilities in small structures; and the conversion of existing small structures from one use to another where only minor modifications are made in the exterior of the structure. The numbers of structures described in this section are the maximum allowable on any legal parcel ~~or to be associated with a project within a two year period~~. Examples of this exemption include, but are not limited to:

(a) ~~Single family residences not in conjunction with the building of two or more such units~~ One single-family residence, or a second dwelling unit in a residential zone. In urbanized areas, up to three single-family residences may be constructed or converted under this exemption.

(b) ~~Apartments, duplexes~~ A duplex ~~and~~ or similar multi-family residential ~~structures~~ structure, ~~with~~ totaling no more than four dwelling units ~~if not in conjunction with the building or conversion of two or more such structures~~. In urbanized areas, this exemption applies to ~~single~~ apartments, duplexes and similar structures designed for not more than six dwelling units ~~if not constructed in conjunction with the building or conversion of two or more such structures~~.

(c) ~~Stores, motels, offices, restaurants, and~~ A store, motel, office, restaurant or similar ~~small commercial structures~~ structure not involving the use of significant amounts of hazardous substances, ~~if designed for an occupant load of 30 persons or less if not constructed in conjunction with the building of two or more such structures~~ and not exceeding 2500 square feet in floor area. In urbanized areas, the exemption also applies to up to four such commercial buildings not exceeding 10,000 square feet in floor area on sites zoned for such use, ~~if designed for an occupant load of 30 persons or less if not constructed in conjunction with the building of four or more such structures and~~ if not involving the use of significant amounts of hazardous substances where all necessary public services and facilities are available and the surrounding area is not environmentally sensitive.

(d) Water main, sewage, electrical, gas, and other utility extensions, including street improvements, of reasonable length to serve such construction.

(e) Accessory (appurtenant) structures including garages, carports, patios, swimming pools, and fences.

(f) An accessory steam sterilization unit for the treatment of medical waste at ~~an ex-isting~~ a facility occupied by a medical waste generator, provided that the unit is installed and operated in accordance with the Medical Waste Management Act (Section ~~25015~~ 117600, et seq., of the Health and Safety Code) and accepts no offsite waste.

Note: Authority cited: Sections 21083 and 21087, Public Resources Code. Reference: ~~Section~~ Sections 21084 and 21084.2, Public Resources Code.

Discussion: This section describes the class of small projects involving new construction or conversion of existing small structures. The 1998 revisions to the section clarify the types of projects to which it applies. In order to simplify and standardize application of this section to commercial structures, the reference to 'occupant load of 30 persons or less' contained in the prior guideline was replaced by a limit on square footage. Subsection (c) further limits the use of this exemption to those commercial projects which have available all necessary public services and facilities, and which are not located in an environmentally sensitive area.

15304   Minor Alterations to Land

Class 4 consists of minor public or private alterations in the condition of land, water, and/or vegetation which do not involve removal of healthy, mature, scenic trees except for forestry or agricultural purposes. Examples include, but are not limited to:

(a) Grading on land with a slope of less than 10 percent, except that grading shall not be exempt in a waterway, in any wetland, in an officially designated (by federal, state, or local government action) scenic area, or in officially mapped areas of severe geologic hazard such as an Alquist-Priolo Earthquake Fault Zone or within an official Seismic Hazard Zone, as delineated by the State Geologist.

(b) New gardening or landscaping, including the replacement of existing conventional landscaping with water efficient or fire resistant landscaping.

(c) Filling of earth into previously excavated land with material compatible with the natural features of the site;

(d) Minor alterations in land, water, and vegetation on existing officially designated wildlife management areas or fish production facilities which result in improvement of habitat for fish and wildlife resources or greater fish production;

(e) Minor temporary use of land having negligible or no permanent effects on the environment, including carnivals, sales of Christmas trees, etc;

(f) Minor trenching and backfilling where the surface is restored;

(g) Maintenance dredging where the spoil is deposited in a spoil area authorized by all applicable state and federal regulatory agencies;

(h) The creation of bicycle lanes on existing rights-of-way.

(i) Fuel management activities within 30 feet of structures to reduce the volume of flammable vegetation, provided that the activities will not result in the taking of endangered, rare, or threatened plant or animal species or significant erosion and sedimentation of surface waters. This exemption shall apply to fuel management activities within 100 feet of a structure if the public agency having fire protection responsibility for the area has determined that 100 feet of fuel clearance is required due to extra hazardous fire conditions.

Note: Authority cited: Sections 21083 and 21087, Public Resources Code. Reference: Section 21084, Public Resources Code.

Discussion: This section describes the class of projects involving minor alterations to the land. The 1998 revision to the section specified that this exemption applies to fuel management activities which will not impact threatened or endangered species or result in significant erosion or sedimentation.

15305   Minor Alterations in Land Use Limitations

Class 5 consists of minor alterations in land use limitations in areas with an average slope of less than 20%, which do not result in any changes in land use or density, including but not limited to:

(a) Minor lot line adjustments, side yard, and set back variances not resulting in the creation of any new parcel;

(b) Issuance of minor encroachment permits;

(c) Reversion to acreage in accordance with the Subdivision Map Act.

Note: Authority cited: Sections 21083 and 21087, Public Resources Code. Reference: Section 21084, Public Resources Code.

15306   Information Collection

Class 6 consists of basic data collection, research, experimental management, and resource evaluation activities which do not result in a serious or major disturbance to an environmental resource. These may be strictly for information gathering purposes, or as part of a study leading to an action which a public agency has not yet approved, adopted, or funded.

15307 Actions by Regulatory Agencies for Protection of Natural Resources

Class 7 consists of actions taken by regulatory agencies as authorized by state law or local ordinance to assure the maintenance, restoration, or enhancement of a natural resource where the regulatory process involves procedures for protection of the environment. Examples include but are not limited to wildlife preservation activities of the State Department of Fish and Game. Construction activities are not included in this exemption.

Note: Authority cited: Sections 21083 and 21087, Public Resources Code. Reference: Section 21084, Public Resources Code.

15308 Actions by Regulatory Agencies for Protection of the Environment

Class 8 consists of actions taken by regulatory agencies, as authorized by state or local ordinance, to assure the maintenance, restoration, enhancement, or protection of the environment where the regulatory process involves procedures for protection of the environment. Construction activities and relaxation of standards allowing environmental degradation are not included in this exemption.

Note: Authority cited: Sections 21083 and 21087, Public Resources Code. Reference: Section 21084, Public Resources Code; *International Longshoremen's and Warehousemen's Union v. Board of Supervisors*, (1981) 116 Cal.App.3d 265.

Discussion: This section reflects the ruling in *International Longshoremen's and Warehousemen's Union v. Board of Supervisors*, (1981) 116 Cal.App.3d 265. That decision ruled that the use of categorical exemption Class 8 was improper for a change in a county air pollution rule that allowed a doubling of the emissions of oxides of nitrogen. The court followed the ruling in *Wildlife Alive v. Chickering*, (1976) 18 Cal.3d 190 that provided that where there is a reasonable possibility that a project or activity may have a significant effect on the environment, an exemption is improper.

15309 Inspections

Class 9 consists of activities limited entirely to inspections, to check for performance of an operation, or quality, health, or safety of a project, including related activities such as inspection for possible mislabeling, misrepresentation, or adulteration of products.

Note: Authority cited: Sections 21083 and 21087, Public Resources Code. Reference: Section 21084, Public Resources Code.

15310 Loans

Class 10 consists of loans made by the Department of Veterans Affairs under the Veterans Farm and Home Purchase Act of 1943, mortgages for the purchase of existing structures where the loan will not be used for new construction and the purchase of such mortgages by financial institutions. Class 10 includes but is not limited to the following examples:

(a) Loans made by the Department of Veterans Affairs under the Veterans Farm and Home Purchase Act of 1943.

(b) Purchases of mortgages from banks and mortgage companies by the Public Employees Retirement System and by the State Teachers Retirement System.

Note: Authority cited: Sections 21083 and 21087, Public Resources Code. Reference: Section 21084, Public Resources Code.

15311 Accessory Structures

Class 11 consists of construction, or placement of minor structures accessory to (appurtenant to) existing commercial, industrial, or institutional facilities, including but not limited to:

(a) On-premise signs;

(b) Small parking lots;

(c) Placement of seasonal or temporary use items such as lifeguard towers, mobile food units, portable restrooms, or similar items in generally the same locations from time to time in publicly owned parks, stadiums, or other facilities designed for public use.

Note: Authority cited: Sections 21083 and 21087, Public Resources Code. Reference: Section 21084, Public Resources Code.

15312 Surplus Government Property Sales

Class 12 consists of sales of surplus government property except for parcels of land located in an area of statewide, regional, or areawide concern identified in Section 15206(b)(4). However, even if the surplus property to be sold is located in any of those areas, its sale is exempt if:

(a) The property does not have significant values for wildlife habitat or other environmental purposes, and

(b) Any of the following conditions exist:

(1) The property is of such size, shape, or inaccessibility that it is incapable of independent development or use; or

(2) The property to be sold would qualify for an exemption under any other class of categorical exemption in these guidelines; or

(3) The use of the property and adjacent property has not changed since the time of purchase by the public agency.

Note: Authority cited: Sections 21083 and 21087, Public Resources Code. Reference: Section 21084, Public Resources Code.

Discussion: In *McQueen v. Midpeninsula Regional Open Space District* (1988) 202 Cal.App.3d 1136, the court stated that the terms 'sale' and 'acquisition' are not interchangeable and reaffirmed that exemptions must comply with the "specific terms" of the exemption which are to be narrowly construed.

15313 Acquisition of Lands for Wildlife Conservation Purposes

Class 13 consists of the acquisition of lands for fish and wildlife conservation purposes including preservation of fish and wildlife habitat, establishing ecological reserves under Fish and Game Code Section 1580, and preserving access to public lands and waters where the purpose of the acquisition is to preserve the land in its natural condition.

Note: Authority cited: Sections 21083 and 21087, Public Resources Code. Reference: Section 21084, Public Resources Code.

15314 Minor Additions to Schools

Class 14 consists of minor additions to existing schools within existing school grounds where the addition does not increase original student capacity by more than 25% or ten classrooms, whichever is less. The addition of portable classrooms is included in this exemption.

Note: Authority cited: Sections 21083 and 21087, Public Resources Code. Reference: Section 21084, Public Resources Code.

15315 Minor Land Divisions

Class 15 consists of the division of property in urbanized areas zoned for residential, commercial, or industrial use into four or fewer parcels when the division is in conformance with the General Plan and zoning, no variances or exceptions are required, all services and access to the proposed parcels to local standards are available, the parcel was not involved in a division of a larger parcel within the previous 2 years, and the parcel does not have an average slope greater than 20 percent.

Note: Authority cited: Sections 21083 and 21087, Public Resources Code. Reference: Section 21084, Public Resources Code.

15316 Transfer of Ownership of Land in Order to Create Parks

Class 16 consists of the acquisition, ~~or sale,~~ or other transfer of land in order to establish a park where the land is in a natural condition or contains ~~historic sites~~ historical or archaeological ~~sites~~ resources and either:

(a) The management plan for the park has not been prepared, or

(b) The management plan proposes to keep the area in a natural condition or preserve the historic or archaeological ~~site~~ resources. CEQA will apply when a management plan is proposed that will change the area from its natural condition or ~~significantly~~ cause substantial adverse change in the significance of the historic or archaeological ~~site~~ resource.

Note: Authority cited: Sections 21083 and 21087, Public Resources Code. Reference: ~~Section~~ Sections 21084, 21083.2, and 21084.1, Public Resources Code.

Discussion: In *McQueen v. Midpeninsula Regional Open Space District* (1988) 202 Cal. App.3d 1136, the court ruled that the taking or acquiring property "as-is" does not constitute a "natural condition" when there is substantial evidence in the record that hazardous waste has been upon it.

15317 Open Space Contracts or Easements

Class 17 consists of the establishment of agricultural preserves, the making and renewing of open space contracts under the Williamson Act, or the acceptance of easements or fee interests in order to maintain the open space character of the area. The cancellation of such preserves, contracts, interests, or easements is not included and will normally be an action subject to the CEQA process.

Note: Authority cited: Sections 21083 and 21087, Public Resources Code. Reference: Section 21084, Public Resources Code.

15318 Designation of Wilderness Areas

Class 18 consists of the designation of wilderness areas under the California Wilderness System.

Note: Authority cited: Sections 21083 and 21087, Public Resources Code. Reference: Section 21084, Public Resources Code.

15319 Annexations of Existing Facilities and Lots for Exempt Facilities

Class 19 consists of only the following annexations:

(a) Annexations to a city or special district of areas containing existing public or private structures developed to the density allowed by the current zoning or pre-zoning of either the gaining or losing governmental agency whichever is more restrictive, provided, however, that the extension of utility services to the existing facilities would have a capacity to serve only the existing facilities.

(b) Annexations of individual small parcels of the minimum size for facilities exempted by Section 15303, New Construction or Conversion of Small Structures.

Note: Authority cited: Sections 21083 and 21087, Public Resources Code. Reference: Section 21084, Public Resources Code.

Discussion: The exemption under subsection (a) is not allowed if it is foreseeable that utility services would extend into the annexed parcels and have the potential to serve a greater capacity than existing uses. The exemption is also unavailable if "unusual circumstances" under Section 15300.2(c) are found. For example, in *City of Santa Clara v. LAFCO of Santa Clara County*, (1983) 139 Cal.App.3d 923, the court found that unusual circumstances existed when the annexing city's general plan called for the newly annexed parcels to eventually become residential and industrial rather than the prezoned agricultural use. The unusual circumstances arose from the inconsistency between the prezoned agricultural use and the general plan's designated land use and thus precluded the use of this categorical exemption.

15320 Changes in Organization of Local Agencies

Class 20 consists of changes in the organization or reorganization of local governmental agencies where the changes do not change the geographical area in which previously existing powers are exercised. Examples include but are not limited to:

(a) Establishment of a subsidiary district.

(b) Consolidation of two or more districts having identical powers.

(c) Merger with a city of a district lying entirely within the boundaries of the city.

Note: Authority cited: Sections 21083 and 21087, Public Resources Code. Reference: Section 21084, Public Resources Code.

15321 Enforcement Actions by Regulatory Agencies

Class 21 consists of:

(a) Actions by regulatory agencies to enforce or revoke a lease, permit, license, certificate, or other entitlement for use issued, adopted, or prescribed by the regulatory agency or enforcement of a law, general rule, standard, or objective, administered or adopted by the regulatory agency. Such actions include, but are not limited to, the following:

(1) The direct referral of a violation of lease, permit, license, certificate, or entitlement for use or of a general rule, standard, or objective to the Attorney General, District Attorney, or City Attorney as appropriate, for judicial enforcement;

(2) The adoption of an administrative decision or order enforcing or revoking the lease, permit, license, certificate, or entitlement for use or enforcing the general rule, standard, or objective.

(b) Law enforcement activities by peace officers acting under any law that provides a criminal sanction;

(c) Construction activities undertaken by the public agency taking the enforcement or revocation action are not included in this exemption.

Note: Authority cited: Sections 21083 and 21087, Public Resources Code. Reference: Section 21084, Public Resources Code.

Discussion: The exemption for law enforcement activities by peace officers acting under any law that provides a criminal sanction is based largely on the rationale explained by the court in *Pacific Water Conditioning Association v. City Council*, (1977) 73 Cal.App.3d 546. There the court noted that enforcement actions are taken long after the public agency, or possibly the State Legislature, has exercised its discretion to set standards governing a certain kind of activity.

15322 Educational or Training Programs Involving No Physical Changes

Class 22 consists of the adoption, alteration, or termination of educational or training programs which involve no physical alteration in the area affected or which involve physical changes only in the interior of existing school or training structures. Examples include but are not limited to:

(a) Development of or changes in curriculum or training methods.

(b) Changes in the grade structure in a school which do not result in changes in student transportation.

Note: Authority cited: Sections 21083 and 21087, Public Resources Code. Reference: Section 21084, Public Resources Code.

15323 Normal Operations of Facilities for Public Gatherings

Class 23 consists of the normal operations of existing facilities for public gatherings for which the facilities were designed, where there is a past history of the facility being used for the same or similar kind of purpose. For the purposes of this section, "past history" shall mean that the same or similar kind of activity has been occurring for at least three years and that there is a reasonable expectation that the future occurrence of the activity would not represent a change in the operation of the facility. Facilities included within this exemption include, but are not limited to, racetracks, stadiums, convention centers, auditoriums, amphitheaters, planetariums, swimming pools, and amusement parks.

Note: Authority cited: Sections 21083 and 21087, Public Resources Code. Reference: Section 21084, Public Resources Code.

Discussion: This section clarifies what is meant by the term "a past history of the facility being used for the same kind of purpose." The section relates the concept of past history to public expectations for use of the facility in the future. Where the facility has been used for a particular purpose for several years and people expect the use to continue in the future, continuation of that use would not represent a change in the environmental conditions. For example, if a county fair had included a stock car racing meet for each of three consecutive years, people living in the area would have come to expect that the county fair would involve stock car racing in the future. Continuing racing activity would not represent a substantial change in the environment from what people had come to expect. However, in *Lewis v. 17th District Agricultural Ass'n* (1985) 165 Cal.App.3d 823, the court found that the existence of residential areas near a racetrack constituted "unusual circumstances" (Guidelines section 15300.2 (c)) which removed the racing activity from the exemption. Additionally, the court found that imposing mitigation measures to offset the possible significant adverse change in the environment caused by the activity will not cause the exemption to be applicable unless the mitigation measures result in the elimination of the possibility of a significant adverse change in the environment. The decision to allow stock car racing at a county fair in the first place could well call for some kind of CEQA analysis before starting that activity. Once the activity has been established, however, continuing the activity does not represent a change, and absent a significant change in the use and absent a significant change in the use and absent the

existence of unusual circumstances. Concerning what are considered normal operations of facilities for public gatherings see *Campbell v. Third District Agricultural Association* (1987) 195 Cal.App.3d 115.

15324 Regulations of Working Conditions

Class 24 consists of actions taken by regulatory agencies, including the Industrial Welfare Commission as authorized by statute, to regulate any of the following:

(a) Employee wages,

(b) Hours of work, or

(c) Working conditions where there will be no demonstrable physical changes outside the place of work.

Note: Authority cited: Sections 21083 and 21087, Public Resources Code. Reference: Section 21084, Public Resources Code.

15325 Transfers of Ownership of Interest in Land to Preserve ~~Open Space~~ Existing Natural Conditions and Historical Resources

Class 25 consists of transfers of ownership in interests in land in order to preserve open space, habitat, or historical resources. Examples include but are not limited to:

(a) Acquisition, sale, or other transfer of areas to preserve existing natural conditions, including plant or animal habitats.

(b) Acquisition, sale, or other transfer of areas to allow continued agricultural use of the areas.

(c) Acquisition, sale, or other transfer to allow restoration of natural conditions, including plant or animal habitats.

(d) Acquisition, sale, or other transfer to prevent encroachment of development into flood plains.

(e) Acquisition, sale, or other transfer to preserve historical resources.

Note: Authority cited: Sections 21083 and 21087, Public Resources Code. Reference: Section 21084, Public Resources Code.

Discussion: In *McQueen v. Midpeninsula Regional Open Space District* (1988) 202 Cal. App.3d 1136, stated that the terms 'sale' and 'acquisition' are not interchangeable and reaffirmed that exemptions must comply with the "specific terms" of the exemption which are to be narrowly construed.

The class of project described by this section consists of transfers of ownership that are made to preserve open space, habitat, or historical resources. The 1998 revisions to this section clarify that sale or other transfer of lands is included among the exempt activities. Use of this exemption, like all categorical exemptions, is limited by the factors described in section 15300.2.

15326 Acquisition of Housing for Housing Assistance Programs

Class 26 consists of actions by a redevelopment agency, housing authority, or other public agency to implement an adopted Housing Assistance Plan by acquiring an interest in housing units. The housing units may be either in existence or possessing all required permits for construction when the agency makes its final decision to acquire the units.

Note: Authority cited: Sections 21083 and 21087, Public Resources Code. Reference: Section 21084, Public Resources Code.

15327 Leasing New Facilities

(a) Class 27 consists of the leasing of a newly constructed or previously unoccupied privately owned facility by a local or state agency where the local governing authority determined that the building was exempt from CEQA. To be exempt under this section, the proposed use of the facility:

(1) Shall be in conformance with existing state plans and policies and with general, community, and specific plans for which an EIR or negative declaration has been prepared;

(2) Shall be substantially the same as that originally proposed at the time the building permit was issued;

(3) Shall not result in a traffic increase of greater than 10% of front access road capacity, and

(4) Shall include the provision of adequate employee and visitor parking facilities.

(b) Examples of Class 27 include, but are not limited to:

(1) Leasing of administrative offices in newly constructed office space.

(2) Leasing of client service offices in newly constructed retail space.

(3) Leasing of administrative and/or client service offices in newly constructed industrial parks.

Note: Authority cited: Sections 21083 and 21087, Public Resources Code. Reference: Section 21084, Public Resources Code.

15328 Small Hydroelectric Projects at Existing Facilities

Class 28 consists of the installation of hydroelectric generating facilities in connection with existing dams, canals, and pipelines where:

(a) The capacity of the generating facilities is 5 megawatts or less,

(b) Operation of the generating facilities will not change the flow regime in the affected stream, canal, or pipeline including but not limited to:

(1) Rate and volume of flow,

(2) Temperature,

(3) Amounts of dissolved oxygen to a degree that could adversely affect aquatic life, and

(4) Timing of release.

(c) New power lines to connect the generating facilities to existing power lines will not exceed one mile in length if located on a new right of way and will not be located adjacent to a wild or scenic river.

(d) Repair or reconstruction of the diversion structure will not raise the normal maximum surface elevation of the impoundment.

(e) There will be no significant upstream or downstream passage of fish affected by the project.

(f) The discharge from the power house will not be located more than 300 feet from the toe of the diversion structure.

(g) The project will not cause violations of applicable state or federal water quality standards.

(h) The project will not entail any construction on or alteration of a site included in or eligible for inclusion in the National Register of Historic Places, and

(i) Construction will not occur in the vicinity of any endangered, rare, or threatened or endangered species.

Note: Authority cited: ~~Section~~ Sections 21083 and 21087, Public Resources Code. Reference: Section 21084, Public Resources Code.

15329 Cogeneration Projects at Existing Facilities

Class 29 consists of the installation of cogeneration equipment with a capacity of 50 megawatts or less at existing facilities meeting the conditions described in this section.

(a) At existing industrial facilities, the installation of cogeneration facilities will be exempt where it will:

(1) Result in no net increases in air emissions from the industrial facility, or will produce emissions lower than the amount that would require review under the new source review rules applicable in the county, and

(2) Comply with all applicable state, federal, and local air quality laws.

(b) At commercial and industrial facilities, the installation of cogeneration facilities will be exempt if the installation will:

(1) Meet all the criteria described in Subsection (a),

(2) Result in no noticeable increase in noise to nearby residential structures,

(3) Be contiguous to other commercial or institutional structures.

Note: Authority cited: Sections 21083 and 21087, Public Resources Code. Reference: Section 21084, Public Resources Code.

15330 Minor Actions to Prevent, Minimize, Stabilize, Mitigate or Eliminate the Release or Threat of Release of Hazardous Waste or Hazardous Substances

Class 30 consists of any minor cleanup actions taken to prevent, minimize, stabilize, mitigate, or eliminate the release or threat of release of a hazardous waste or substance which are small or medium removal actions costing $1 million or less. No cleanup action shall be subject to this Class 31 exemption if the action requires the onsite use of a hazardous waste incinerator or thermal treatment unit, with the exception of low temperature thermal desorption, or the relocation of residences or businesses, or the action involves the potential release into the air of volatile organic compounds as defined in Health and Safety Code section 25123.6, except for small scale in situ soil vapor extraction and treatment systems which have been permitted by the local Air Pollution Control District or Air Quality Management District. All actions must be consistent with applicable state and local environmental permitting requirements including, but not limited to, air quality rules such as those governing volatile organic compounds and water quality standards, and approved by the regulatory body with jurisdiction over the site. Examples of such minor cleanup actions include but are not limited to:

(a) Removal of sealed, non-leaking drums or barrels of hazardous waste or substances that have been stabilized, containerized and are designated for a lawfully permitted destination;

(b) Maintenance or stabilization of berms, dikes, or surface impoundments;

(c) Construction or maintenance of interim or temporary surface caps;

(d) Onsite treatment of contaminated soils or sludges provided treatment system meets Title 22 requirements and local air district requirements;

(e) Excavation and/or offsite disposal of contaminated soils or sludges in regulated units;

(f) Application of dust suppressants or dust binders to surface soils;

(g) Controls for surface water run-on and run-off that meets seismic safety standards;

(h) Pumping of leaking ponds into an enclosed container;

(i) Construction of interim or emergency ground water treatment systems;

(j) Posting of warning signs and fencing for a hazardous waste or substance site that meets legal requirements for protection of wildlife.

Note: Authority cited: Sections 21083 and 21087, Public Resources Code. Reference: Section 21084, Public Resources Code.

Discussion: This defines certain minor hazardous waste or hazardous substances cleanup actions as a class of exempt projects. This exemption is intended to speed such cleanups, while at the same time providing sufficient safeguards to ensure that no significant environmental effects may occur as a result. Application of this exemption, as all categorical exemptions, is limited by the factors described in section 15300.2.

15331 Historical Resource Restoration/Rehabilitation

Class 31 consists of projects limited to maintenance, repair, stabilization, rehabilitation, restoration, preservation, conservation or reconstruction of historical resources in a manner consistent with the Secretary of the Interior's Standards for the Treatment of Historic Properties with Guidelines for Preserving, Rehabilitating, Restoring, and Reconstructing Historic Buildings (1995), Weeks and Grimmer.

Note: Authority cited: Section 21083 and 21087, Public Resources Code. Reference: Section 21084, Public Resources Code.

Discussion: This section establishes an exemption for projects involving the maintenance, rehabilitation, restoration, preservation, or reconstruction of historical resources, provided that the activity meets published federal standards for the treatment of historic properties. These federal standards describe means of preserving, rehabilitating, restoring, and reconstructing historic buildings without adversely affecting their historic significance. Use of this exemption, like all categorical exemptions, is limited by the factors described in section 15300.2 and is not to be used where the activity would cause a substantial adverse change in the significance of a historical resource.

15332 In-Fill Development Projects

Class 32 consists of projects characterized as in-fill development meeting the conditions described in this section.

(a) The project is consistent with the applicable general plan designation and all applicable general plan policies as well as with applicable zoning designation and regulations.

(b) The proposed development occurs within city limits on a project site of no more than five acres substantially surrounded by urban uses.

(c) The project site has no value, as habitat for endangered, rare or threatened species.

(d) Approval of the project would not result in any significant effects relating to traffic, noise, air quality, or water quality.

(e) The site can be adequately served by all required utilities and public services.

Note: Authority cited: Section 21083, Public Resources Code. Reference: Section 21084, Public Resources Code.

Article 20. Definitions
Sections 15350 to 15387

15350 General

The definitions contained in this article apply to terms used throughout the guidelines unless a term is otherwise defined in a particular section.

Note: Authority cited: Sections 21083 and 21087, Public Resources Code. Reference: Section 21083, Public Resources Code.

15351 Applicant

"Applicant" means a person who proposes to carry out a project which needs a lease, permit, license, certificate, or other entitlement for use or financial assistance from one or more public agencies when that person applies for the governmental approval or assistance.

Note: Authority cited: Sections 21083 and 21087, Public Resources Code. Reference: Section 21065, Public Resources Code.

Discussion: This section defines a term used frequently in the Guidelines to refer to a person who applies to a public agency for a lease, permit, license, certificate, or other entitlement in the Guidelines apply only to applicants and not to governmental agencies that carry out projects directly.

15352 Approval

(a) "Approval" means the decision by a public agency which commits the agency to a definite course of action in regard to a project intended to be carried out by any person. The exact date of approval of any project is a matter determined by each public agency according to its rules, regulations, and ordinances. Legislative action in regard to a project often constitutes approval.

(b) With private projects, approval occurs upon the earliest commitment to issue or the issuance by the public agency of a discretionary contract, grant, subsidy, loan, or other form of financial assistance, lease, permit, license, certificate, or other entitlement for use of the project.

Note: Authority cited: Sections 21083 and 21087, Public Resources Code. Reference: Sections 21061 and 21065, Public Resources Code.

Discussion: The term "approval" needs definition because the term is critical to the CEQA process. A public agency must comply with CEQA when the agency proposes to approve some kind of project. The statute does not define the term, and it is often difficult to identify the time when the project is approved. This section spells out criteria for determining when the approval occurs.

15353 CEQA

"CEQA" means the California Environmental Quality Act, California Public Resources Code Sections 21000 et seq.

Note: Authority cited: Sections 21083 and 21087, Public Resources Code. Reference: Section 21050, Public Resources Code.

15354 Categorical Exemption

"Categorical exemption" means an exemption from CEQA for a class of projects based on a finding by the Secretary for Resources that the class of projects does not have a significant effect on the environment.

Note: Authority cited: Sections 21083 and 21087, Public Resources Code. Reference: Sections 21080(b)(10) and 21084, Public Resources Code.

Discussion: This section provides a simple term and definition to apply to the administrative exemptions from CEQA established by the Secretary for Resources under Section 21084 in CEQA. These exemptions apply to classes of projects for which the Secretary for Resources has made a finding that the class of projects will not have a significant effect on the environment.

15355 Cumulative Impacts

"Cumulative impacts" refer to two or more individual effects which, when considered together, are considerable or which compound or increase other environmental impacts.

(a) The individual effects may be changes resulting from a single project or a number of separate projects.

(b) The cumulative impact from several projects is the change in the environment which results from the incremental impact of the project when added to other closely related past, present, and reasonably foreseeable probable future projects. Cumulative impacts can result from individually minor but collectively significant projects taking place over a period of time.

Note: Authority cited: Sections 21083 and 21087, Public Resources Code. Reference: Section 21083(b), Public Resources Code; *Whitman v. Board of Supervisors*, 88 Cal. App.3d 397.

Discussion: The definition of the term "cumulative impacts" is provided because the term is related to one of the mandatory findings of significant effect required by Section 21083. A common understanding of the term is needed in order to implement the section. Further, this definition is needed to codify the court rulings in *Whitman v. Board of Supervisors* and *San Franciscans for Reasonable Growth v. City and County of San Francisco*.

15356 Decision-Making Body

"Decision-making body" means any person or group of people within a public agency permitted by law to approve or disapprove the project at issue.

Note: Authority cited: Sections 21083 and 21087, Public Resources Code. Reference: Section 21003(b), Public Resources Code; *Kleist v. City of Glendale*, (1976) 56 Cal. App.3d 770.

Discussion: This definition is added because there is a need for a term to apply to the person or group which has authority to make the decision to approve or carry out a project. The individuals or groups which are granted this authority seem to have no one common name or common description among the many agencies subject to CEQA. Accordingly, the Guidelines must provide a term which could apply to these people in all situations.

15357 Discretionary Project

"Discretionary project" means a project which requires the exercise of judgment or deliberation when the public agency or body decides to approve or disapprove a particular activity, as distinguished from situations where the public agency or body merely has to determine whether there has been conformity with applicable statutes, ordinances, or regulations. A timber harvesting plan submitted to the State Forester for approval under the requirements of the Z'berg-Nejedly Forest Practice Act of 1973 (Pub. Res. Code Sections 4511 et seq.) constitutes a discretionary project within the meaning of the California Environmental Quality Act. Section 21065(c).

Note: Authority cited: Sections 21083 and 21087, Public Resources Code. Reference: Section 21080(a), Public Resources Code; *Johnson v. State of California* (1968) 69 Cal.2d 782; *People v. Department of Housing and Community Development* (1975) 45 Cal.App.3d 185; *Day v. City of Glendale* (1975) 51 Cal.App.3d 817; *N.R.D.C. v. Arcata National Corp.* (1976) 59 Cal.App.3d 959.

Discussion: A definition of the term "discretionary project" is essential for defining the scope of activities subject to CEQA. The Act provides that it applies to discretionary projects, but the Act does not define the term. The definition offered here is taken from the State Supreme Court decision in *Johnson v. State of California*, a 1968 decision. The definition in this section has been approved in a number of court decisions since that time. Several of these decisions are cited in the note. See also discussion for Section 15268.

15358 Effects

"Effects" and "impacts" as used in these Guidelines are synonymous.

(a) Effects include:

(1) Direct or primary effects which are caused by the project and occur at the same time and place.

(2) Indirect or secondary effects which are caused by the project and are later in time or farther removed in distance, but are still reasonably foreseeable. Indirect or secondary effects may include growth-inducing effects and other effects related to induced changes in the pattern of land use, population density, or growth rate, and related effects on air and water and other natural systems, including ecosystems.

(b) Effects analyzed under CEQA must be related to a physical change.

Note: Authority cited: Sections 21083 and 21087, Public Resources Code. Reference: Sections 21068 and 21100, Public Resources Code.

Discussion: Confusion has arisen in interpreting CEQA because the law uses the terms "effects" and "impacts" without making clear whether the words have different or identical meanings. This section is intended to eliminate that confusion and to use the federal definition of the term from the NEPA regulations to the extent that the statutes are similar. Subsection (a) is identical to part of Section 1508.8 in the NEPA regulations, but subsection (b) is different because CEQA is more focused on physical changes than is NEPA.

15359 Emergency

"Emergency" means a sudden, unexpected occurrence, involving a clear and imminent danger, demanding immediate action to prevent or mitigate loss of, or damage to life, health, property, or essential public services. Emergency includes such occurrences as fire, flood, earthquake, or other soil or geologic movements, as well as such occurrences as riot, accident, or sabotage.

Note: Authority cited: Sections 21083 and 21087, Public Resources Code. Reference: Section 21080(b)(2), (3), and (4), Public Resources Code.

Discussion: The definition of the term "emergency" was originally developed in these Guidelines. Later legislation added the definition to the statute.

15360 Environment

"Environment" means the physical conditions which exist within the area which will be affected by a proposed project including land, air, water, minerals, flora, fauna, ambient noise, and objects of historical or aesthetic significance. The area involved shall be the area in which significant effects would occur either directly or indirectly as a result of the project. The "environment" includes both natural and man-made conditions.

Note: Authority cited: Sections 21083 and 21087, Public Resources Code. Reference: Section 21060.5, Public Resources Code.

Discussion: This definition combines statutory language in the first sentence with administrative interpretation in the second and third sentences.

15361 Environmental Documents

"Environmental documents" means initial studies, negative declarations, draft and final EIRs, documents prepared as substitutes for EIRs and negative declarations under a program certified pursuant to Public Resources Code Section 21080.5, and documents prepared under NEPA and used by a state or local agency in the place of an initial study, negative declaration, or an EIR.

Note: Authority cited: Sections 21083 and 21087, Public Resources Code. Reference: Sections 21061, 21080(b), 21080.5, 21108, and 21152, Public Resources Code.

Discussion: The term "environmental documents" is intended to provide a shorthand way of referring to all the documents listed in the definition.

15362 EIR–Environmental Impact Report

"EIR" or "Environmental Impact Report" means a detailed statement prepared under CEQA describing and analyzing the significant environmental effects of a project and discussing ways to mitigate or avoid the effects. The contents of an EIR are discussed in Article 9, commencing with Section 15120 of these Guidelines. The term "EIR" may mean either a draft or a final EIR depending on the context.

(a) Draft EIR means an EIR containing the information specified in Sections 15122 through 15131.

(b) Final EIR means an EIR containing the information contained in the draft EIR, comments either verbatim or in summary received in the review process, a list of persons commenting, and the response of the lead agency to the comments received. The final EIR is discussed in detail in Section 15132.

Note: Authority cited: Sections 21083 and 21087, Public Resources Code. Reference: Sections 21061, 21100, and 21151, Public Resources Code.

Discussion: This section identifies the abbreviation "EIR" and provides a short definition of the term "Environmental Impact Report" although the term "Environmental Impact Report" is defined in detail with a number of other requirements in Section 21061 of the statute. This section provides a more focused definition and introduces the terms "draft EIR" and "final EIR."

15363 EIS–Environmental Impact Statement

"EIS" or "Environmental Impact Statement" means an environmental impact document prepared pursuant to the National Environmental Policy Act (NEPA). NEPA uses the term EIS in the place of the term EIR which is used in CEQA.

Note: Authority cited: Sections 21083 and 21087, Public Resources Code. Reference: Sections 21083.5, 21083.6, and 21083.7, Public Resources Code; 43 U.S.C.A. 4322(2)(c).

Discussion: This section introduces the abbreviation "EIS" and provides a short definition of the term "Environmental Impact Statement." This definition is needed because CEQA and the Guidelines refer to EISs in many places where the CEQA process may involve overlaps with NEPA.

15364 Feasible

"Feasible" means capable of being accomplished in a successful manner within a reasonable period of time, taking into account economic, environmental, legal, social, and technological factors.

Note: Authority cited: Sections 21083 and 21087, Public Resources Code. Reference: Sections 21002, 21002.1, 21004, 21061.1, 21080.5, and 21081, Public Resources Code; Section 4, Chapter 1438 of the Statutes of 1982.

Discussion: This section provides an additional interpretation of the statutory language by adding the word "legal" to the statutory language. The legal limitation is incorporated in the concept of feasibility as it applies to the findings an agency must make concerning whether to mitigate or avoid significant effects identified in an EIR. The lack of legal powers of an agency to use in imposing an alternative or mitigation measure may be as great a limitation as any economic, environmental, social, or technological factor.

15365 Initial Study

"Initial Study" means a preliminary analysis prepared by the lead agency to determine whether an EIR or a negative declaration must be prepared or to identify the significant environmental effects to be analyzed in an EIR. Use of the initial study is discussed in Article 5, commencing with Section 15060.

Note: Authority cited: Sections 21083 and 21087, Public Resources Code. Reference: Sections 21080.1, 21080.2, 21080.3, and 21100, Public Resources Code.

Discussion: This definition is added to define a term which is created in these Guidelines.

15366 Jurisdiction by Law

(a) "Jurisdiction by law" means the authority of any public agency:

(1) To grant a permit or other entitlement for use,

(2) To provide funding for the project in question, or

(3) To exercise authority over resources which may be affected by the project.

(b) A city or county will have jurisdiction by law with respect to a project when the city or county having primary jurisdiction over the area involved is:

(1) The site of the project;

(2) The area in which the major environmental effects will occur; and/or

(3) The area in which reside those citizens most directly concerned by any such environmental effects.

(c) Where an agency having jurisdiction by law must exercise discretionary authority over a project in order for the project to proceed, it is also a Responsible Agency, see Section 15381, or the lead agency, see Section 15367.

Note: Authority cited: Sections 21083 and 21087, Public Resources Code. Reference: Sections 21080.3, 21080.4, 21104, and 21153, Public Resources Code.

Discussion: This section defines the term "jurisdiction by law" in order to establish which agencies must be consulted by the Lead Agency in preparing an EIR. The statute does not define this term.

15367 Lead Agency

"Lead Agency" means the public agency which has the principal responsibility for carrying out or approving a project. The lead agency will decide whether an EIR or negative declaration will be required for the project and will cause the document to be prepared. Criteria for determining which agency will be the lead agency for a project are contained in Section 15051.

Note: Authority cited: Sections 21083 and 21087, Public Resources Code. Reference: Section 21165, Public Resources Code.

Discussion: This section combines the statutory definition of the term "Lead Agency" with a more complete explanation in terms related to the CEQA process. The fundamental point is that CEQA gives the Lead Agency the tasks of determining whether an EIR or a Negative Declaration will be required for the project and preparing the document.

15368 Local Agency

"Local agency" means any public agency other than a state agency, board, or commission. Local agency includes but is not limited to cities, counties, charter cities and counties, districts, school districts, special districts, redevelopment agencies, local agency formation commissions, and any board, commission, or organizational subdivision of a local agency when so designated by order or resolution of the governing legislative body of the local agency.

Note: Authority cited: Sections 21083 and 21087, Public Resources Code. Reference: Sections 21062 and 21151, Public Resources Code.

Discussion: This section supplements the definition of the term "local agency" contained in the Public Resources Code to recognize the possibility that a city may designate a particular sub-unit of the city government as being a separate Lead Agency for a particular project. In this situation, the subunit would qualify as a local agency under these Guidelines, and all the requirements placed on a local agency would apply to that unit.

An agency created by state statute such as an agricultural district may be considered a local agency for the purposes of CEQA even though it may be considered a state agency for other purposes; this is possible because the agency's activities are most likely to affect only the local area in which it operates. (See: *Lewis v. 17th District Agricultural Ass'n.* (1985) 165 Cal.App.3d 823. Agencies should be aware that the notice and filing requirements stated either in Sections 21150 et seq. or Sections 21100 et seq. of CEQA may apply depending upon whether the agency is defined as "state" or "local" for CEQA purposes.

15369 Ministerial

"Ministerial" describes a governmental decision involving little or no personal judgment by the public official as to the wisdom or manner of carrying out the project. The public official merely applies the law to the facts as presented but uses no special discretion or judgment in reaching a decision. A ministerial decision involves only the use of fixed standards or objective measurements, and the public official cannot use personal, subjective judgment in deciding whether or how the project should be carried out. Common examples of ministerial permits include automobile registrations, dog licenses, and marriage licenses. A building permit is ministerial if the ordinance requiring the permit limits the public official to determining whether the zoning allows the structure to be built in the requested location, the structure would meet the strength requirements in the Uniform Building Code, and the applicant has paid his fee.

Note: Authority cited: Sections 21083 and 21087, Public Resources Code. Reference: Section 21080(b)(1), Public Resources Code; *Johnson v. State of California*, 69 Cal.2d 782; *Day v. City of Glendale*, 51 Cal.App. 3d 817.

Discussion: This definition draws upon earlier judicial definitions of "ministerial" and discretionary governmental actions and provides examples. Neither term is technically precise.

As carefully pointed out in *Friends of Westwood, Inc. v. Los Angeles* (1987) 191 Cal.

App.3d 259, usually building permits are ministerial but the approval process for a project unusual in size, dimension and location involve discretionary aspects which are subject to CEQA; it is enough the [agency] possesses discretion to require changes which would mitigate in whole or in part one or more of the [significant] environmental consequences an EIR might conceivably uncover. See also discussion for Section 15268.

15369.5   Mitigated Negative Declaration

"Mitigated negative declaration" means a negative declaration prepared for a project when the initial study has identified potentially significant effects on the environment, but (1) revisions in the project plans or proposals made by, or agreed to by, the applicant before the proposed negative declaration and initial study are released for public review would avoid the effects or mitigate the effects to a point where clearly no significant effect on the environment would occur, and (2) there is no substantial evidence in light of the whole record before the public agency that the project, as revised, may have a significant effect on the environment.

Note: Authority cited: Sections 21083 and 21087, Public Resources Code. Reference: Section 21064.5, Public Resources Code.

15370   Mitigation

"Mitigation" includes:

(a) Avoiding the impact altogether by not taking a certain action or parts of an action.

(b) Minimizing impacts by limiting the degree or magnitude of the action and its implementation.

(c) Rectifying the impact by repairing, rehabilitating, or restoring the impacted environment.

(d) Reducing or eliminating the impact over time by preservation and maintenance operations during the life of the action.

(e) Compensating for the impact by replacing or providing substitute resources or environments.

Note: Authority cited: Sections 21083 and 21087, Public Resources Code. Reference: Sections 21002, 21002.1, 21081, and 21100(c), Public Resources Code.

Discussion: This definition of the term "mitigation" adopts the definition contained in the federal NEPA regulations. The federal definition is used so that this term will have identical meanings under NEPA and CEQA for projects which are subject to both acts.

15371   Negative Declaration

"Negative declaration" means a written statement by the lead agency briefly describing the reasons that a proposed project, not exempt from CEQA, will not have a significant effect on the environment and therefore does not require the preparation of an EIR. The contents of a negative declaration are described in Section 15071.

Note: Authority cited: Sections 21083 and 21087, Public Resources Code. Reference: Section 21080(c), Public Resources Code.

Discussion: This definition is added in order to provide a clear, short identification of the term "Negative Declaration." The section identifies four essential concepts dealing with the document. First, the Negative Declaration applies to projects which are not exempt. Second, the document must be written and provide a brief explanation of its conclusion. Third, the document is used where the agency concludes that the project will not have a significant effect on the environment. Fourth, the document serves as a statement that the agency will not prepare an EIR, but the statement is used only where it is based on a finding that the project will not cause a significant effect on the environment.

15372   Notice of Completion

"Notice of Completion" means a brief notice filed with the OPR by a lead agency as soon as it has completed a draft EIR and is prepared to send out copies for review. The contents of this notice are explained in Section 15085.

Note: Authority cited: Sections 21083 and 21087, Public Resources Code. Reference: Section 21161, Public Resources Code.

Discussion: This section defines the term "Notice of Completion" to provide a commonly used and recognized term for the notice which the statute requires a Lead Agency to file when an EIR has been completed.

15373   Notice of Determination

"Notice of determination" means a brief notice to be filed by a public agency after it approves or determines to carry out a project which is subject to the requirements of CEQA. The contents of this notice are explained in Sections 15075 and 15094.

Note: Authority cited: Sections 21083 and 21087, Public Resources Code. Reference: Sections 21108(a) and 21152, Public Resources Code.

Discussion: This section defines the term "Notice of Determination" to provide a commonly used and recognized term for the notice which the statute requires an

agency to file after it has approved the project at the end of the CEQA process. One cross-reference describes the contents of the notice when used with a Negative Declaration. The other describes the contents after an EIR has been prepared.

15374   Notice of Exemption

"Notice of Exemption" means a brief notice which may be filed by a public agency after it has decided to carry out or approve a project and has determined that the project is exempt from CEQA as being ministerial, categorically exempt, an emergency, or subject to another exemption from CEQA. Such a notice may also be filed by an applicant where such a determination has been made by a public agency which must approve the project. The contents of this notice are explained in Section 15062.

Note: Authority cited: Sections 21083 and 21087, Public Resources Code. Reference: Sections 21108(b) and 21152(b), Public Resources Code.

Discussion: This section provides a definition for the notice which an agency is authorized to file when it determines that a particular project is exempt from the requirements of CEQA. The statute authorizes the use of this notice but does not provide a name or detailed explanation for it.

15375   Notice of Preparation

"Notice of preparation" means a brief notice sent by a lead agency to notify the responsible agencies, trustee agencies, and involved federal agencies that the lead agency plans to prepare an EIR for the project. The purpose of the notice is to solicit guidance from those agencies as to the scope and content of the environmental information to be included in the EIR. Public agencies are free to develop their own formats for this notice. The contents of this notice are described in Section 15082.

Note: Authority cited: Sections 21083 and 21087, Public Resources Code. Reference: Section 21080.4, Public Resources Code.

Discussion: This definition provides a commonly used and easily recognizable name for the notice which a Lead Agency is required to send to Responsible Agencies to obtain the views of Responsible Agencies on the contents of an EIR which the Lead Agency will prepare. The reference to federal agencies was added because Section 15082 requires this notice to be sent to federal agencies.

15376   Person

"Person" includes any person, firm, association, organization, partnership, business, trust, corporation, <u>limited liability company</u>, company, district, city, county, city and county, town, the state, and any of the agencies or political subdivisions of such entities.

Note: Authority cited: Sections 21083 and 21087, Public Resources Code. Reference: Section ~~21065~~ <u>21066</u>, Public Resources Code.

Discussion: This definition indicates the broad scope of the term "person" as used in CEQA. This term is used in a number of different places in the Guidelines and the statute in ways that require use of such a broad definition. Legislation enacted in 1998 specifies that "person" includes federal agencies to the extent permitted by federal law (AB 2397—Chapter 272, Statutes of 1998). This addition is pertinent where federal law has delegated regulatory responsibility for actions on federal land or by federal agencies to the state.

15377   Private Project

A "private project" means a project which will be carried out by a person other than a governmental agency, but the project will need a discretionary approval from one or more governmental agencies for:

(a) A contract or financial assistance, or

(b) A lease, permit, license, certificate, or other entitlement for use.

Note: Authority cited: Sections 21083 and 21087, Public Resources Code. Reference: Section 21065, Public Resources Code.

Discussion: This section defines a term to be used in the place of a much longer phrase several places in the statute. In a number of different contexts, the statute sets up special requirements that apply by way of a cross-reference to activities which involve the issuance of a lease, license, certificate, permit, or other entitlement for use. It is clearer in these situations to refer to private projects.

15378   Project

(a) "Project" means the whole of an action, which has a potential for resulting in <u>either</u> a <u>direct</u> physical change in the environment, ~~directly or ultimately~~ <u>or a reasonably foreseeable indirect physical change in the environment</u>, and that is any of the following:

  (1) An activity directly undertaken by any public agency including but not limited to public works construction and related activities clearing or grading of land, improvements to existing public structures, enactment and amendment of zoning ordinances, and the adoption and amendment of local General Plans or elements thereof pursuant to Government Code Sections 65100– 65700.

  (2) An activity undertaken by a person which is supported in whole or in part through public agency contracts, grants, subsidies, loans, or other forms of assistance from one or more public agencies.

  (3) An activity involving the issuance to a person of a lease, permit, license, certificate, or other entitlement for use by one or more public agencies.

(b) Project does not include:

  ~~(1) Anything specifically exempted by state law;~~

  ~~(2)~~<u>(1)</u> Proposals for legislation to be enacted by the State Legislature;

  ~~(3)~~<u>(2)</u> Continuing administrative or maintenance activities, such as purchases for supplies, personnel-related actions, general policy and procedure making (except as they are applied to specific instances covered above);

  ~~(4)~~<u>(3)</u> The submittal of proposals to a vote of the people of the state or of a particular community. (*Stein v. City of Santa Monica*, <u>(1980)</u> 110 Cal.App.3d 458);

  ~~(5)~~<u>(4)</u> The creation of government funding mechanisms or other government fiscal activities<u>,</u> which do not involve any commitment to any specific project which may result in a potentially significant physical impact on the environment.

  ~~(5) Organizational or administrative activities of governments which are political or which are not physical changes in the environment (such as the reorganization of a school district or detachment of park land).~~

(c) The term "project" refers to the activity which is being approved and which may be subject to several discretionary approvals by governmental agencies. The term "project" does not mean each separate governmental approval.

(d) Where the lead agency could describe the project as either the adoption of a particular regulation under Subsection (a)(1) or as a development proposal which will be subject to several governmental approvals under Subsections (a)(2) or (a)(3), the lead agency shall describe the project as the development proposal for the purpose of environmental analysis. This approach will implement the lead agency principle as described in Article 4.

Note: Authority: Sections 21083 and 21087, Public Resources Code. Reference: Section 21065, Public Resources Code; *Kaufman and Broad-South Bay, Inc. v. Morgan Hill Unified School District* <u>(1992)</u> 9 Cal.App. 4th 464 ~~(1992)~~; and *Fullerton Joint Union High School District v. State Board of Education* <u>(1982)</u> 32 Cal.3d 779 ~~(1982)~~; <u>*Simi Valley Recreation and Park District v. Local Agency Formation Commission of Ventura County*</u> (1975) 51 Cal.App.3d 648

Discussion: This section provides a more complete explanation of the term "project." This term describes activities which are subject to CEQA. This definition brings together a number of separate provisions in the Act. These are the definition of the term contained in Section 21065 of the statute, the Lead Agency concept in Section 21165 of the statute, and the result of a number of court decisions interpreting this term. Chapter 1230 of the Statutes of 1994 codifies the emphasis on "physical change" in the environment.

Following the State Supreme Court's decision in *Friends of Mammoth*, the Legislature added a definition of the term "project" to the statute. The definition provided that "project" meant activities directly undertaken by government, activities financed by government, or activities requiring a permit or other approval from government. The Legislature then added the words "or approve" to the section requiring that agencies shall prepare an EIR "on any project they proposed to carry out or approve which may have a significant effect on the environment."

Reading the language of Sections 21065 and 21100 together, the project which is to be analyzed in the EIR is not the approval itself but is that which is being approved.

With some activities carried out by government, the plan, control, or regulation being adopted may need to be regarded as the project even though the plan, etc., is being adopted to control activities to be initiated later by other people. For example, in approving a new general plan for a city, the city council would properly regard the general plan itself as the project. The EIR would examine the environmental changes that would probably result from adopting the new plan. In this situation, the governmental plan would not be proposed in conjunction with a proposal for a specific development project, and the EIR on the plan would need to examine the range of possible effects of the plan. If, however, a small amendment to the general plan was requested as one of several approvals necessary for a specific development project, the city should characterize the proposed development as the project. In this way, the city would implement the Lead Agency concept by designating as the project the activity which would be approved by a number of agencies. This approach would result in only one EIR being prepared for the proposed development as required by Sections 21165 and 21166 of CEQA.

In *Livermore v. Local Agency Formation Commission of Alameda County* (1986) 184 Cal.App.3d 531 (1986) 183 Cal.App.3d 681, the court ruled that LAFCO's guideline revisions fit within CEQA's broad definition of a project because they are a discretionary activity of a public agency that will unquestionably have an ultimate impact on the environment, i.e., major policy decisions that determine whether growth will occur in unincorporated areas and whether agricultural land will be preserved or developed.

However, in marked contrast, *Northwood Homes, Inc. v. Moraga* (1989) 216 Cal.App.3d 1197 concluded that general guidelines enacted as administrative activities for procedural implementation as to definitions of terms and application procedures of land use decisions are not a project.

Items (4) and (5) under subsection (b) codify the decisions in *Kaufman and Broad-South Bay, Inc. v. Morgan Hill Unified School District* (1992) 9 Cal.App.4th 464 and *Simi Valley Recreation and Park District v. Local Agency Formation Commission of Ventura County* (1975) 51 Cal.App.3d 648 which clarify that CEQA does not apply to activities which do not result, either directly or in a reasonably foreseeable indirect way, in a physical change to the environment.

15379 Public Agency

"Public agency" includes any state agency, board, or commission and any local or regional agency, as defined in these guidelines. It does not include the courts of the state. This term does not include agencies of the federal government.

Note: Authority cited: Sections 21083 and 21087, Public Resources Code. Reference: Section 21063, Public Resources Code.

Discussion: This definition is necessary in order to show that the scope of the term "public agency" under CEQA does not include agencies of the federal government.

15380 ~~Rare or~~ Endangered, Rare or Threatened Species

(a) "Species" as used in this section means a species or subspecies of animal or plant or a variety of plant.

(b) A species of animal or plant is:

(1) "Endangered" when its survival and reproduction in the wild are in immediate jeopardy from one or more causes, including loss of habitat, change in habitat, overexploitation, predation, competition, disease, or other factors; or

(2) "Rare" when either:

(A) Although not presently threatened with extinction, the species is existing in such small numbers throughout all or a significant portion of its range that it may become endangered if its environment worsens; or

(B) The species is likely to become endangered within the foreseeable future throughout all or a significant portion of its range and may be considered "threatened" as that term is used in the Federal Endangered Species Act.

(c) A species of animal or plant shall be presumed to be ~~rare or~~ endangered, rare or threatened, as it is listed in:

(1) Sections 670.2 or 670.5, Title 14, California ~~Administrative~~ Code of Regulations; or

(2) Title 50, Code of Federal Regulations Section 17.11 or 17.12 pursuant to the Federal Endangered Species Act as rare, threatened, or endangered.

(d) A species not included in any listing identified in subsection (c) shall nevertheless be considered to be ~~rare or~~ endangered, rare or threatened, if the species can be shown to meet the criteria in subsection (b).

(e) This definition shall not include any species of the Class Insecta which is a pest whose protection under the provisions of CEQA would present an overwhelming and overriding risk to man as determined by:

(1) The Director of Food and Agriculture with regard to economic pests; or

(2) The Director of Health Services with regard to health risks.

Note: Authority cited: Sections 21083 and 21087, Public Resources Code. Reference: Section 21001(c), Public Resources Code; ~~and Fish and Game Code Sections 1900-1913 and 2050-2166~~.

Discussion: This definition is modeled after the definition in the Federal Rare and Endangered Species Act and the sections of the California Fish and Game Code dealing with rare or endangered plants or animals.

The definition provides that plants or animals already listed by a governmental agency as being rare or endangered shall be presumed rare or endangered for the purposes of CEQA. This presumption allows a Lead Agency to consider a listed species as rare or endangered without the need for any further proof. The section also provides that a plant or animal may be treated as rare or endangered even if it has not been placed on an official list. The section also adds the concept that rare or endangered status shall not be applied to insect pests designated by the Director of Food and Agriculture as meeting the criteria in this section.

15381 Responsible Agency

"Responsible Agency" means a public agency which proposes to carry out or approve a project, for which a lead agency is preparing or has prepared an EIR or negative declaration. For the purposes of CEQA, the term "responsible agency" includes all public agencies other than the lead agency which have discretionary approval power over the project.

Note: Authority cited: Sections 21083 and 21087, Public Resources Code. Reference: Sections 21002.1, 21069, 21080.1, 21080.3, 21080.4, 21167.2, and 21167.3, Public Resources Code.

Discussion: This section provides explanation of the term "Responsible Agency".

15382 Significant Effect on the Environment

"Significant effect on the environment" means a substantial, or potentially substantial, adverse change in any of the physical conditions within the area affected by the project, including land, air, water, minerals, flora, fauna, ambient noise, and objects of historic or aesthetic significance. An economic or social change by itself shall not be considered a significant effect on the environment. A social or economic change related to a physical change may be considered in determining whether the physical change is significant.

Note: Authority cited: Sections 21083 and 21087, Public Resources Code. Reference: Sections 21068, 21083, 21100, and 21151, Public Resources Code; *Hecton v. People of the State of California*, 58 Cal.App.3d 653.

Discussion: The first sentence combines the statutory language in the definitions of "significant effect" and "environment" in the interest of clarity because they are interrelated.

The second and third sentences pose a problem of interpretation that has caused controversy for many years. The controversy centers around the extent to which CEQA applies to economic and social effects of projects. In determining whether an effect is significant, however, Section 21083(c) of CEQA requires an effect to be found significant if the activity would cause an adverse effect on people.

This section also codifies the holding in *Hecton v. People of the State of California*, 58 Cal.App.3d 653, which ruled that a claim that a project would cause a decline in property values was not enough by itself to require an EIR to be prepared.

In *Cathay Mortuary, Inc. v. San Francisco Planning Commission* (1989) 207 Cal.App. 3d 275, the court in analyzing significant effect' offered inverse guidance regarding whether an alternative site for a proposed park would have better access to sunlight, i.e., it is irrelevant whether some body of opinion views some other alternative site as" better suited" (essentially as a planning determination), if the net impact of the project site is not an adverse change, no EIR is required. In this case, demolition of a building would provide access to sunlight in a portion of the impacted area that currently did not have access to sunlight — in other words, access to sunlight when none currently exists is not an adverse change.

15383   State Agency

"State agency" means a governmental agency in the executive branch of the State Government or an entity which operates under the direction and control of an agency in the executive branch of State Government and is funded primarily by the State Treasury.

Note: Authority cited: Sections 21083 and 21087, Public Resources Code. Reference: Section 21100, Public Resources Code.

Discussion: This section distinguishes state agencies from local agencies. Different requirements may apply depending on whether a state or local agency is involved. For example, if a project will require a permit from a state agency, the EIR or Negative Declaration on the project must be sent to the State Clearinghouse for review. This term is not defined in the Public Resources Code, and there is often confusion as to whether a particular agency with a limited geographical jurisdiction is a state agency or a local agency. For example, the San Francisco Bay Conservation and Development Commission is a state agency, but the Bay Area Air Quality Management District is a local agency for all but Section 21080.5 of CEQA. The definition is an effort to provide a clearer basis for the distinction.

15384   Substantial Evidence

(a) "Substantial evidence" as used in these guidelines means enough relevant information and reasonable inferences from this information that a fair argument can be made to support a conclusion, even though other conclusions might also be reached. Whether a fair argument can be made that the project may have a significant effect on the environment is to be determined by examining the ~~entire record~~ whole record before the lead agency. ~~Mere uncorroborated opinion or rumor~~ Argument, speculation, unsubstantiated opinion or narrative, evidence which is clearly erroneous or inaccurate, or evidence of social or economic impacts which do not contribute to or are not caused by physical impacts on the environment does not constitute substantial evidence.

(b) Substantial evidence shall include facts, reasonable assumptions predicated upon facts, and expert opinion supported by facts. ~~This definition is intended to be informative and does not constitute a change in, but is merely reflective of, existing law.~~

Note: Authority cited: Sections 21083 and 21087, Public Resources Code. References: Sections 21080, 21082.2, 21168, and 21168.5, Public Resources Code; *No Oil, Inc. v. City of Los Angeles* (1974) 13 Cal.3d 68; *Running Fence Corp. v. Superior Court* (1975) 51 Cal.App.3d 400; *Friends of B Street v. City of Hayward* (1980) 106 Cal. App.3d 988.

Discussion: "Substantial evidence" as used in the Guidelines is the same as the standard of review used by courts in reviewing agency decisions. Some cases suggest that a higher standard, the so called "fair argument standard" applies when a court is reviewing an agency's decision whether or not to prepare an EIR.

Public Resources Code section 21082.2 was amended in 1993 (Chapter 1131) to provide that substantial evidence shall include "facts, reasonable assumptions predicated upon facts, and expert opinion supported by facts." The statute further provides that "argument, speculation, unsubstantiated opinion or narrative, evidence which is clearly inaccurate or erroneous, or evidence of social or economic impacts which do not contribute to, or are not caused by, physical impacts on the environment, is not substantial evidence."

15385   Tiering

"Tiering" refers to the coverage of general matters in broader EIRs (such as on general plans or policy statements) with subsequent narrower EIRs or ultimately site-specific EIRs incorporating by reference the general discussions and concentrating solely on the issues specific to the EIR subsequently prepared. Tiering is appropriate when the sequence of EIRs is:

(a) From a general plan, policy, or program EIR to a program, plan, or policy EIR of lesser scope or to a site-specific EIR;

(b) From an EIR on a specific action at an early stage to a subsequent EIR or a supplement to an EIR at a later stage. Tiering in such cases is appropriate when it helps the lead agency to focus on the issues which are ripe for decision and exclude from consideration issues already decided or not yet ripe.

Note: Authority cited: Sections 21083 and 21087, Public Resources Code. Reference: Sections 21003, 21061, and 21100, Public Resources Code.

Discussion: This definition of "tiering" is modeled closely after the definition in the federal NEPA regulations. Tiering is needed in order to provide increased efficiency in the CEQA process. It allows agencies to deal with broad environmental issues in EIRs at planning stages and then to provide more detailed examination of specific effects in EIRs on later development projects that are consistent with or implement the plans. These later EIRs are excused by the tiering concept from repeating the analysis of the broad environmental issues examined in the general plan EIRs.

15386   Trustee Agency

"Trustee Agency" means a state agency having jurisdiction by law over natural resources affected by a project which are held in trust for the people of the State of California. Trustee Agencies include:

(a) The California Department of Fish and Game with regard to the fish and wildlife of the state, to designated rare or endangered native plants, and to game refuges, ecological reserves, and other areas administered by the department.

(b) The State Lands Commission with regard to state owned "sovereign" lands such as the beds of navigable waters and state school lands.

(c) The State Department of Parks and Recreation with regard to units of the State Park System.

(d) The University of California with regard to sites within the Natural Land and Water Reserves System.

Note: Authority cited: Sections 21083 and 21087, Public Resources Code. Reference:

Sections 21080.3 and 21080.4, Public Resources Code.

Discussion: This section is included to provide a commonly used and clearly recognizable term to use in place of the statutory phrase describing state agencies "having jurisdiction by law over natural resources affected by the project which are held in trust for the people of the State of California." The section also identifies the four agencies which have been found to meet the statutory formula.

Agencies are designated as Trustee Agencies where they administer lands to protect the natural resources on those lands or where a law gives the agency responsibility for protecting the state's interest in a natural resource as with the Department of Fish and Game's responsibility for fish and wildlife. The Department of Fish and Game is listed as a Trustee Agency for designated rare and endangered native plants because Fish and Game Code Section 1913(c) gives the department special responsibilities for protecting these plants after they have been designated rare or endangered by the Fish and Game Commission

15387   Urbanized Area

"Urbanized area" means a central city or a group of contiguous cities with a population of 50,000 or more, together with adjacent densely populated areas having a population density of at least 1,000 persons per square mile. A lead agency shall determine whether a particular area meets the criteria in this section either by examining the area or by referring to a map prepared by the U.S. Bureau of the Census which designates the area as urbanized. Maps of the designated urbanized areas can be found in the California EIR Monitor of February 7, 1979. The maps are also for sale by the Superintendent of Documents, U.S. Government Printing Office, Washington, DC 20402. The maps are sold in sets only as Stock Number 0301-3466. Use of the term "urbanized area" in Section 15182 is limited to areas mapped and designated as urbanized by the U.S. Bureau of the Census.

Note: Authority cited: Sections 21083 and 21087, Public Resources Code. Reference: Sections 21080.7 and 21083, and 21084, Public Resources Code.

Discussion: This section is included to provide certainty and precision for the portions of CEQA that allow special treatment of projects in urbanized areas. These special provisions apply to residential projects in urbanized areas as well as categorical exemptions for certain kinds of activities. The revisions in this section allows a Lead Agency to determine on its own whether a project is located in an area meeting the criteria for being "urbanized" even if the area is not included on the Census Bureau maps. This change allows the special relaxations of the CEQA process to be applied in areas.

NOTES

[1] The reference to section 15064, subdivision (g), should be a reference to subdivision (f) of that section.

[2] References in subsection (h) to subsection (i) should refer to subsection (h). Thus, "the definition in subsection (i)(3)" is found at subsection (h)(3).

[3] This reference should be to Appendix I.

[4] After the 1998 revisions to the Guidelines, the reference should be to appendix K.

[5] This reference should be to section 15126.2, subdivision (c).

[6] The reference should be to section 15126.6, subdivision (f).

[7] Section 67463 of the Government Code no longer defines the Santa Monica Mountains Zone. (Repealed by Stats. 1978, ch. 230, §5.) Instead, the zone is defined at Public Resources Code, section 33105.

Appendix A
CEQA Process Flow Chart

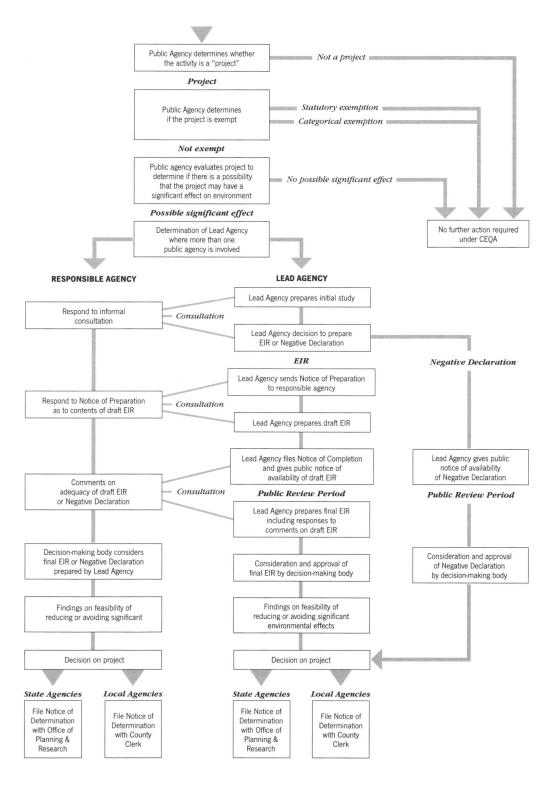

Public Agency determines whether the activity is a "project" — *Not a project*

Project

Public Agency determines if the project is exempt — *Statutory exemption* — *Categorical exemption*

Not exempt

Public agency evaluates project to determine if there is a possibility that the project may have a significant effect on environment — *No possible significant effect*

Possible significant effect

Determination of Lead Agency where more than one public agency is involved

No further action required under CEQA

RESPONSIBLE AGENCY | **LEAD AGENCY**

Respond to informal consultation — *Consultation* — Lead Agency prepares initial study

Lead Agency decision to prepare EIR or Negative Declaration

EIR | ***Negative Declaration***

Respond to Notice of Preparation as to contents of draft EIR — *Consultation* — Lead Agency sends Notice of Preparation to responsible agency

Lead Agency prepares draft EIR

Comments on adequacy of draft EIR or Negative Declaration — *Consultation* — Lead Agency files Notice of Completion and gives public notice of availability of draft EIR | Lead Agency gives public notice of availability of Negative Declaration

Public Review Period | ***Public Review Period***

Lead Agency prepares final EIR including responses to comments on draft EIR

Decision-making body considers final EIR or Negative Declaration prepared by Lead Agency | Consideration and approval of final EIR by decision-making body | Consideration and approval of Negative Declaration by decision-making body

Findings on feasibility of reducing or avoiding significant | Findings on feasibility of reducing or avoiding significant environmental effects

Decision on project | Decision on project

State Agencies | ***Local Agencies*** | ***State Agencies*** | ***Local Agencies***

File Notice of Determination with Office of Planning & Research | File Notice of Determination with County Clerk | File Notice of Determination with Office of Planning & Research | File Notice of Determination with County Clerk

Appendix B
Statutory Authority of State Departments

Bay Conservation and Development Commission	Air Resources Board	Resources Agency	Health Services	Savings and Loan	Real Estate	Caltrans	Dept. of Housing and Community Development	Dept. of Motor Vehicles	Corporations	Calif. Highway Patrol	Aeronautics	Food and Agriculture	
	✖		✖					✖		16	✖	1	1. Air quality and air pollution control
			✖									✖	2. Chemical contamination and food products
26			7										3. Coastal areas, wetlands, estuaries, waterfowl refuges, and beaches
	24		8		✖		✖						4. Congestion in urban areas, housing, and building displacement
			✖									✖	5. Disease control
	✖		✖										6. Electric energy generation and supply
			9		✖	✖	✖						7. Environmental effects with special impact in low-income neighborhoods
					✖							✖	8. Flood plains and watersheds
			✖									✖	9. Food additives and food sanitation
		✖	✖									✖	10. Herbicides
						✖							11. Historic and archaeological sites
	✖		✖									2	12. Human ecology
			✖									✖	13. Microbiological contamination
													14. Mineral land reclamation
													15. Natural gas energy development generation and supply
	16		10								✖		16. Navigable airways
25													17. Navigable waterways
			✖							✖	✖		18. Noise control and abatement
25												✖	19. Parks, forests, trees, and outdoor recreation areas
		✖	✖									✖	20. Pesticides
		✖	✖										21. Radiation and radiological health
	24		11	✖	✖	✖	✖				✖		22. Regional comprehensive planning
			✖									✖	23. Rodent control
			✖									3	24. Sanitation and waste systems
			✖										25. Shellfish sanitation
												✖	26. Soil and plant life, sedimentation, erosion, and hydrologic conditions
			✖									✖	27. Toxic Materials
			✖					✖		✖		4	28. Transportation and handling of hazardous materials
			✖									✖	29. Water quality and water pollution control
			12									5	30. Fish and wildlife
25			13										31. Activities with special impact jurisdictions
	24												32. Water project formulation
	24												33. Geothermal energy
													34. Oil and petroleum development, generation, and supply
													35. Statewide land use patterns
	24												36. Open space policy
						✖							37. Statewide overview — cumulative impact of separate projects
							✖						38. Seismic hazards

OPR	Native American Heritage	Water Resources	State Water Resources Control Board	State Reclamation Board	State Lands Commission	Solid Waste Mgmt Board	Parks and Recreation	Forestry	Fish and Game	Energy Commission	Conservation	Colorado River Board	CTRPA	Coastal Commission	Boating and Waterways	
			X								X		27			1. Air quality and air pollution control
			X						X							2. Chemical contamination and food products
		X	X		X		X		X		X	14	27	26	X	3. Coastal areas, wetlands, estuaries, waterfowl refuges, and beaches
			21										27	26		4. Congestion in urban areas, housing, and building displacement
			X					22	X			14				5. Disease control
		X					X	23	X	X		14		26	X	6. Electric energy generation and supply
								19								7. Environmental effects with special impact in low-income neighborhoods
		X		20	X		X		X		X	14	27	26		8. Flood plains and watersheds
																9. Food additives and food sanitation
			X				X	22	X			14				10. Herbicides
	X				X		X						27	26		11. Historic and archaeological sites
X							X		X				27	26		12. Human ecology
			X						X			14				13. Microbiological contamination
					X		X		X		X		27	26		14. Mineral land reclamation
					X				15	X	X			26		15. Natural gas energy development generation and supply
									16							16. Navigable airways
				20	X				X			14	27	26	X	17. Navigable waterways
									17							18. Noise control and abatement
	X				X		X		X		X	14	27	26	X	19. Parks, forests, trees, and outdoor recreation areas
		X	X				X	22	X							20. Pesticides
									X	X		14				21. Radiation and radiological health
X		X	X		X		X		X	X	X	14	27	26	X	22. Regional comprehensive planning
							X	22	X							23. Rodent control
		X	X			X			18		X	14		26		24. Sanitation and waste systems
			X						X							25. Shellfish sanitation
		X	X		X		X		X		X	14	27	26		26. Soil and plant life, sedimentation, erosion, and hydrologic conditions
			X			X	X		X			14				27. Toxic Materials
			X							X	X					28. Transportation and handling of hazardous materials
		X	X						X		X	14	27	26	X	29. Water quality and water pollution control
			21				X		X			14	27	26		30. Fish and wildlife
		X		20			X					14	27	26		31. Activities with special impact on regional jurisdictions
		X	X	20			X	23	X			14			X	32. Water project formulation
		X	21		X				X	X	X	14				33. Geothermal energy
			21		X				X	X	X			26		34. Oil and petroleum development, generation, and supply
X					X				X	X	X		27	26		35. Statewide land use patterns
X	X				X				X		X		27	26		36. Open space policy
X										X						37. Statewide overview — cumulative impact of separate projects
		X								X	X		27	26		38. Seismic hazards

Appendix B
Footnotes

1. **Food and Agriculture.** Effects on plants and animals.

2. **Food and Agriculture.** Protection of food and fiber.

3. **Food and Agriculture.** Agricultural, dairy and feed lot Systems.

4. **Food and Agriculture.** As pertains to transportation, handling, storage and decontamination of pesticides.

5. **Food and Agriculture.** Pesticide effects, predatory animal control, bird control.

6. **California Highway Patrol.** Enforcement of motor vehicle regulations.

7. **Health Services.** Beach sanitation, water pollution, solid waste and mosquito control.

8. **Health Services.** Pertains to health component.

9. **Health Services.** Most if these are strongly related to health.

10. **Health Services.** Pertains to noise.

11. **Health Services.** Pertains to personal and environmental health components.

12. **Health Services.** As it may pertain to human health hazards.

13. **Health Services.** Pertains to comprehensive health planning.

14. **Colorado River Board.** As pertains to the Colorado, New and Alamo Rivers.

15. **Fish and Game.** As field development and distribution systems may affect fish and wildlife.

16. **Fish and Game.** As may affect migrating and resident wildlife.

17. **Fish and Game.** As excessive noise may affect wildlife.

18. **Fish and Game.** As water quality may affect fish and wildlife.

19. **Parks and Recreation.** In impacted areas only.

20. **Reclamation Board.** In areas of Board's jurisdiction only — the Sacramento-San Joaquin Valley.

21. **State Water Resources Control Board.** As may pertain to water quality.

22. **Forestry.** With respect to forest land.

23. **Forestry.** (6) and (32). As related to fire protection or State (fire protection) responsibility land.

24. **Air Resources Board.** (4), (22), (32), (33), and (36). As may pertain to residential, commercial, industrial or transportation growth.

25. **San Francisco Bay Conservation and Development Commission.** (3), (17), (19), and (30). With respect to San Francisco Bay, Suisun Bay and adjacent shore areas.

26. **California Coastal Commission.** (3), (4), (6), (8), (11), (12), (14), (15), (17), (19), (22), (23), (26), (29), (30), (31), (34), (35), and (36). With respect to effects within the California Coastal Zone.

27. **California Tahoe Regional Planning Agency.** With respect to effects in the Tahoe Basin.

28. **Native American Heritage Commission.** With respect to places of special religious or social significance to Native Americans including archaeological sites, cemeteries, and places of worship.

NOTE

Authority cited: Section 21083, Public Resources Code; Reference:
Sections 21080.3, 21080.4, 21104, and 21153, Public Resources Code.

Appendix C
Notice of Completion

State of California
Office of Planning and Research
1400 Tenth Street
Sacramento, CA 95814

Project Title

Project Location – Specific

Project Location – City   **Project Location – County**

Description of Nature, Purpose, and Beneficiaries of Project

Lead Agency   **Division**

Address Where Copy of EIR Is Available

Review Period

Contact Person   **Area Code / Phone / Extension**

Revised March 1986

Notice of Completion and Environmental Document Transmittal Form

See NOTE below

SCH # _____

1. Project Title _____ 3. Contact Person _____
2. Lead Agency _____ 3. Contact Person _____
3a. Street Address _____ 3b. City _____
3c. County _____ 3d. Zip _____ 3e. Phone _____

Project Location _____

4. County _____ 4a. City/Community _____
4b. Assessor's Parcel No. _____ 4c. Section _____ Twp. _____ Range _____
5a. Cross Streets _____ 5b. For Rural, Nearest Community _____
6. Within 2 miles: a. State Hwy # _____ b. Airports _____
             c. Railways _____ d. Waterways _____

---

7. Document Type

CEQA
01. ❏ NOP
02. ❏ Early Cons
03. ❏ Neg Dec
04. ❏ Draft EIR

05. ❏ Supplement/Subsequent EIR
    (Prior SCH No.:_____)
06. ❏ NOE
07. ❏ NOC
08. ❏ NOD

NEPA
09. ❏ NOI
10. ❏ FONSI
11. ❏ Draft EIS
12. ❏ EA

OTHER
13. ❏ Joint Document
14. ❏ Final Document
15. ❏ Other _____

---

8. Local Action Type

01. ❏ General Plan Update
02. ❏ New Element
03. ❏ General Plan Amendment
04. ❏ Master Plan

05. ❏ Annexation
06. ❏ Specific Plan
07. ❏ Community Plan
08. ❏ Redevelopment

09. ❏ Rezone
10. ❏ Land Division (Subdivision, Parcel Map, Tract Map, etc.)
11. ❏ Use Permit

12. ❏ Waste Mgmt Plan
13. ❏ Cancel Ag Preserve
14. ❏ Other

---

9. Development Type

01. ❏ Residential: Units _____ Acres _____
02. ❏ Office: Sq.ft. _____ Acres _____ Employees _____
03. ❏ Shopping/Commercial: Sq.ft. _____ Acres _____ Employees _____
04. ❏ Industrial: Sq.ft. _____ Acres _____ Employees _____
05. ❏ Water Facilities: MGD _____
06. ❏ Transportation: Type _____

07. ❏ Mining: Mineral _____
08. ❏ Power: Type _____ Watts _____
09. ❏ Waste Treatment: Type _____
10. ❏ OCS Related
11. ❏ Other: _____

---

10. Total Acres _____

11. Total Jobs Created _____

---

12. Project Issues Discussed in Document

01. ❏ Aesthetic/Visual
02. ❏ Agricultural Land
03. ❏ Air Quality
04. ❏ Archaeological/Historical
05. ❏ Coastal Zone
06. ❏ Economic
07. ❏ Fire Hazard
08. ❏ Flooding/Drainage

09. ❏ Geologic/Seismic
10. ❏ Jobs/Housing Balance
11. ❏ Minerals
12. ❏ Noise
13. ❏ Public Services
14. ❏ Schools
15. ❏ Septic Systems
16. ❏ Sewer Capacity

17. ❏ Social
18. ❏ Soil Erosion
19. ❏ Solid Waste
20. ❏ Toxic/Hazardous
21. ❏ Traffic/Circulation
22. ❏ Vegetation
23. ❏ Water Quality
24. ❏ Water Supply

25. ❏ Wetland/Riparian
26. ❏ Wildlife
27. ❏ Growth Inducing
28. ❏ Incompatible Land Use
29. ❏ Cumulative Effects
30. ❏ Other _____

---

13. Funding (approx.) Federal $ _____ State $ _____ Total $ _____

---

14. Present Land Use and Zoning

---

15. Project Description

---

16. Signature of Lead Agency Representative _____ Date _____

NOTE: Clearinghouse will assign identification numbers for all new projects. If a SCH number already exists for a project (e.g. from a Notice of Preparation or previous draft document) please fill it in.

Form Revised 4/86 — Replaces CA189   *Mark Distribution on Reverse*

Reviewing Agencies

- ❏ Resources Agency
- ❏ Boating / Waterways
- ❏ Conservation
- ❏ Fish and Game
- ❏ Forestry
- ❏ Colorado River Board
- ❏ Dept. Water Resources
- ❏ Reclamation
- ❏ Parks and Recreation
- ❏ Office of Historic Preservation
- ❏ Native American Heritage Commission
- ❏ S.F. Bay Conservation and Development Commission
- ❏ Coastal Commission
- ❏ Energy Commission
- ❏ State Lands Commission
- ❏ Air Resources Board
- ❏ Solid Waste Management Board
- ❏ SWRCB: Sacramento
- ❏ RWQCB: Region #
- ❏ Water Rights
- ❏ Water Quality

- ❏ Caltrans District
- ❏ Dept. of Transportation Planning
- ❏ Aeronautics
- ❏ California Highway Patrol
- ❏ Housing and Community Development
- ❏ Statewide Health Planning
- ❏ Health
- ❏ Food and Agriculture
- ❏ Public Utilities Commission
- ❏ Public Works
- ❏ Corrections
- ❏ General Services
- ❏ OLA
- ❏ Santa Monica Mountains
- ❏ TRPA
- ❏ OPR — OLGA
- ❏ OPR — Coastal
- ❏ Bureau of Land Management
- ❏ Forest Service
- ❏ Other_____
- ❏ Other_____

For SCH Use Only:

Date Received at SCH _____   Catalog Number _____

Date Review Starts _____   Applicant _____

Date to Agencies_____   Consultant _____

Date to SCH _____   Contact_____ Phone _____

Clearance Date _____   Address_____

Notes: _____

_____

_____

Appendix D
Notice of Determination

To _____   Office of Planning and Research   **From** (*Public Agency*) _____
             1400 Tenth Street, Room 121   _____
             Sacramento, CA 95814   Address

_____   County Clerk
             County of _____

             _____

             _____

Subject   Filing of Notice of Determination in compliance with Section 21108 or 21152 of the Public Resources Code.

Project Title

State Clearinghouse Number   **Contact Person**   **Area Code / Telephone / Extension**
(*If submitted to Clearinghouse*)

Project Location (*include county*)

Project Description

This is to advise that the _____ has approved the above described project on
                    ❑ *Lead Agency*   ❑ *Responsible Agency*

_____ and has made the following determinations regarding the above described projects.
    (*Date*)

1. The project [❑ will ❑ will not] have a significant effect on the environment.
2. ❑ An Environmental Impact Report was prepared for this project pursuant to the provisions of CEQA.
   ❑ A Negative Declaration was prepared for this project pursuant to the provisions of CEQA.
3. Mitigation measures [❑ were ❑ were not] made a condition of the approval of the project.
4. A statement of Overriding Considerations [❑ was ❑ was not] adopted for this project.

This is to certify that the final EIR with comments and responses and record of project approval is available to the General Public at:

_____

_____

Signature (Public Agency)   *Date*   *Title*

Date received for filing and posting at OPR:

Revised March 1986

Appendix E
Notice of Exemption

To _____ Office of Planning and Research **From** (*Public Agency*) _____
1400 Tenth Street, Room 121
Sacramento, CA 95814   _____
                             Address
                           _____

_____ County Clerk
County of_____

_____

_____

Project Title _____

Project Location – Specific _____

_____

Project Location – City_____ **Project Location – County** _____

Description of Nature, Purpose, and Beneficiaries of Project _____

_____

_____

_____

Name of Public Agency Approving Project _____

Name of Person or Agency Carrying Out Project _____

Exempt Status (check one)

      ❏ Ministerial (Sec. 21080(b)(1); 15268);

      ❏ Declared Emergency (Sec. 21080(b)(3); 15269(a));

      ❏ Emergency Project (Sec. 21080(b)(4); 15269(b)(c)).

Reasons why project is exempt _____

_____

_____

Lead Agency Contact Person_____ **Area Code / Telephone / Extension** _____

If filed by applicant

    1. Attach certified document of exemption finding.

    2. Has a Notice of Exemption been filed by the public agency approving the project? ❏ Yes ❏ No

_____
Signature   *Date*   *Title*

Date received for filing at OPR:

Revised March 1986

Appendix F
Energy Conservation

I. Introduction

The goal of conserving energy implies the wise and efficient use of energy. The means of achieving this goal include:

(1) decreasing overall per capita energy consumption,

(2) decreasing reliance on natural gas and oil, and

(3) increasing reliance on renewable energy sources.

In order to assure that energy implications are considered in project decisions, the California Environmental Quality Act requires that EIRs include a discussion of the potential energy impacts of proposed projects, with particular emphasis on avoiding or reducing inefficient, wasteful and unnecessary consumption of energy.

Energy conservation implies that a project's cost effectiveness be reviewed not only in dollars, but also in terms of energy requirements. For many projects, lifetime costs may be determined more by energy efficiency than by initial dollar costs.

II. EIR Contents

Potentially significant energy implications of a project should be considered in an EIR. The following list of energy impact possibilities and potential conservation measures is designed to assist in the preparation of an EIR. In many instances, specific items may not apply or additional items may be needed.

A. Project Description may include the following items:

1. Energy consuming equipment and processes which will be used during construction, operation, and/or removal of the project. If appropriate, this discussion should consider the energy intensiveness of materials and equipment required for the project.

2. Total energy requirements of the project by fuel type and end use.

3. Energy conservation equipment and design features.

4. Initial and life-cycle energy costs or supplies.

5. Total estimated daily trips to be generated by the project and the additional energy consumed per trip by mode.

B. Environmental Setting may include existing energy supplies and energy use patterns in the region and locality.

C. Environmental Impacts may include:

1. The project's energy requirements and its energy use efficiencies by amount and fuel type for each stage of the project's life cycle including construction, operation, maintenance and/or removal. If appropriate, the energy intensiveness of materials may be discussed.

2. The effects of the project on local and regional energy supplies and on requirements for additional capacity.

3. The effects of the project on peak and base period demands for electricity and other forms of energy.

4. The degree to which the project complies with existing energy standards.

5. The effects of the project on energy resources.

6. The project's projected transportation energy use requirements and its overall use of efficient transportation alternatives.

D. Mitigation Measures may include:

1. Potential measures to reduce wasteful, inefficient and unnecessary consumption of energy during construction, operation, maintenance and/or removal. The discussion should explain why certain measures were incorporated in the project and why other measures were dismissed.

2. The potential of siting, orientation, and design to minimize energy consumption, including transportation energy.

3. The potential for reducing peak energy demand.

4. Alternate fuels (particularly renewable ones) or energy systems.

5. Energy conservation which could result from recycling efforts.

E. Alternatives should be compared in terms of overall energy consumption and in terms of reducing wasteful, inefficient and unnecessary consumption of energy.

F. Unavoidable Adverse Effects may include wasteful, inefficient and unnecessary consumption of energy during the project construction, operation, maintenance and/or removal that cannot be feasibly mitigated.

G. Irreversible Commitment of Resources may include a discussion of how the project preempts future energy development or future energy conservation.

H. Short-Term Gains versus Long-Term Impacts can be compared by calculating the energy costs over the lifetime of the project.

I. Growth Inducing Effects may include the estimated energy consumption of growth induced by the project.

Appendix G
Environmental Checklist Form

1. Project title

2. Lead agency name and address

3. Contact person and phone number

4. Project location

5. Project sponsor's name and address

6. General plan designation   7. Zoning

8. Description of Project. (Describe the whole action involved, including but not limited to later phases of the project, and any secondary, support, or off-site features necessary for its implementation. Attach additional sheets if necessary.)

9. Surrounding land uses and setting. (Briefly describe the project's surroundings.)

10. Other agencies whose approval is required (e.g., permits, financing approval, or participation agreement).

ENVIRONMENTAL FACTORS POTENTIALLY AFFECTED

The environmental factors checked below would be potentially affected by this project, involving at least one impact that is a "Potentially Significant Impact" as indicated by the checklist on the following pages.

❏ Aesthetics   ❏ Agriculture Resources   ❏ Air Quality

❏ Biological Resources   ❏ Cultural Resources   ❏ Geology / Soils

❏ Hazards & Hazardous Materials ❏ Hydrology / Water Quality   ❏ Land Use / Planning

❏ Mineral Resources   ❏ Noise   ❏ Population / Housing

❏ Public Services   ❏ Recreation   ❏ Transportation / Traffic

❏ Utilities / Service Systems   ❏ Mandatory Findings of Significance

DETERMINATION. (To be completed by the Lead Agency)

On the basis of this initial evaluation:

❑ I find that the proposed project COULD NOT have a significant effect on the environment, and a NEGATIVE DECLARATION will be prepared.

❑ I find that although the proposed project could have a significant effect on the environment, there will not be a significant effect in this case because revisions in the project have been made by or agreed to by the project proponent. A MITIGATED NEGATIVE DECLARATION will be prepared.

❑ I find that the proposed project MAY have a significant effect on the environment, and an ENVIRONMENTAL IMPACT REPORT is required.

❑ I find that the proposed project MAY have a "potentially significant impact" or "potentially significant unless mitigated" impact on the environment, but at least one effect 1) has been adequately analyzed in an earlier document pursuant to applicable legal standards, and 2) has been addressed by mitigation measures based on the earlier analysis as described on attached sheets. An ENVIRONMENTAL IMPACT REPORT is required, but it must analyze only the effects that remain to be addressed.

❑ I find that although the proposed project could have a significant effect on the environment, because all potentially significant effects (a) have been analyzed adequately in an earlier EIR or NEGATIVE DECLARATION pursuant to applicable standards, and (b) have been avoided or mitigated pursuant to that earlier EIR or NEGATIVE DECLARATION, including revisions or mitigation measures that are imposed upon the proposed project, nothing further is required.

_____   _____
Signature   Date

_____   _____
Printed Name   For

EVALUATION OF ENVIRONMENTAL IMPACTS

1) A brief explanation is required for all answers except "No Impact" answers that are adequately supported by the information sources a lead agency cites in the parentheses following each question. A "No Impact" answer is adequately supported if the referenced information sources show that the impact simply does not apply to projects like the one involved (e.g., the project falls outside a fault rupture zone). A "No Impact" answer should be explained where it is based on project-specific factors as well as general standards (e.g., the project will not expose sensitive receptors to pollutants, based on a project-specific screening analysis).

2) All answers must take account of the whole action involved, including off-site as well as on-site, cumulative as well as project-level, indirect as well as direct, and construction as well as operational impacts.

3) Once the lead agency has determined that a particular physical impact may occur, then the checklist answers must indicate whether the impact is potentially significant, less than significant with mitigation, or less than significant. "Potentially Significant Impact" is appropriate if there is substantial evidence that an effect may be significant. If there are one or more "Potentially Significant Impact" entries when the determination is made, an EIR is required.

4) "Negative Declaration: Less Than Significant With Mitigation Incorporated" applies where the incorporation of mitigation measures has reduced an effect from "Potentially Significant Impact" to a "Less Than Significant Impact." The lead agency must describe the mitigation measures, and briefly explain how they reduce the effect to a less than significant level (mitigation measures from Section XVII, "Earlier Analyses," may be cross-referenced).

5) Earlier analyses may be used where, pursuant to the tiering, program EIR, or other CEQA process, an effect has been adequately analyzed in an earlier EIR or negative declaration. Section 15063(c)(3)(D). In this case, a brief discussion should identify the following:

    a) Earlier Analysis Used. Identify and state where they are available for review.

    b) Impacts Adequately Addressed. Identify which effects from the above checklist were within the scope of and adequately analyzed in an earlier document pursuant to applicable legal standards, and state whether such effects were addressed by mitigation measures based on the earlier analysis.

    c) Mitigation Measures. For effects that are "Less than Significant with Mitigation Measures Incorporated," describe the mitigation measures which were incorporated or refined from the earlier document and the extent to which they address site-specific conditions for the project.

6) Lead agencies are encouraged to incorporate into the checklist references to information sources for potential impacts (e.g., general plans, zoning ordinances). Reference to a previously prepared or outside document should, where appropriate, include a reference to the page or pages where the statement is substantiated.

7) Supporting Information Sources: A source list should be attached, and other sources used or individuals contacted should be cited in the discussion.

8) This is only a suggested form, and lead agencies are free to use different formats; however, lead agencies should normally address the questions from this checklist that are relevant to a project's environmental effects in whatever format is selected.

9) The explanation of each issue should identify:

    a) the significance criteria or threshold, if any, used to evaluate each question; and

    b) the mitigation measure identified, if any, to reduce the impact to less than significance.

SAMPLE QUESTION

ISSUES	Potentially Significant Impact	Less Than Significant With Mitigation Incorporatation	Less Than Significant Impact	No Impact
I. AESTHETICS. Would the project:				
a) Have a substantial adverse effect on a scenic vista?	❑	❑	❑	❑
b) Substantially damage scenic resources, including, but not limited to, trees, rock outcroppings, and historic buildings within a state scenic highway?	❑	❑	❑	❑
c) Substantially degrade the existing visual character or quality of the site and its surroundings?	❑	❑	❑	❑
d) Create a new source of substantial light or glare which would adversely affect day or nighttime views in the area?	❑	❑	❑	❑
II. AGRICULTURE RESOURCES. In determining whether impacts to agricultural resources are significant environmental effects, lead agencies may refer to the California Agricultural Land Evaluation and Site Assessment Model (1997) prepared by the California Dept. of Conservation as an optional model to use in assessing impacts on agriculture and farmland. Would the project:				
a) Convert Prime Farmland, Unique Farmland, or Farmland of Statewide Importance (Farmland), as shown on the maps prepared pursuant to the Farmland Mapping and Monitoring Program of the California Resources Agency, to non-agricultural use?	❑	❑	❑	❑

ISSUES	Potentially Significant Impact	Less Than Significant With Mitigation Incorporation	Less Than Significant Impact	No Impact
b) Conflict with existing zoning for agricultural use, or a Williamson Act contract?	❏	❏	❏	❏
c) Involve other changes in the existing environment which, due to their location or nature, could result in conversion of Farmland, to non-agricultural use?	❏	❏	❏	❏

III. AIR QUALITY. Where available, the significance criteria established by the applicable air quality management or air pollution control district may be relied upon to make the following determinations. Would the project:

	Potentially Significant Impact	Less Than Significant With Mitigation Incorporation	Less Than Significant Impact	No Impact
a) Conflict with or obstruct implementation of the applicable air quality plan?	❏	❏	❏	❏
b) Violate any air quality standard or contribute substantially to an existing or projected air quality violation?	❏	❏	❏	❏
c) Result in a cumulatively considerable net increase of any criteria pollutant for which the project region is non-attainment under an applicable federal or state ambient air quality standard (including releasing emissions which exceed quantitative thresholds for ozone precursors)?	❏	❏	❏	❏
d) Expose sensitive receptors to substantial pollutant concentrations?	❏	❏	❏	❏
e) Create objectionable odors affecting a substantial number of people?	❏	❏	❏	❏

IV. BIOLOGICAL RESOURCES. Would the project:

	Potentially Significant Impact	Less Than Significant With Mitigation Incorporation	Less Than Significant Impact	No Impact
a) Have a substantial adverse effect, either directly or through habitat modifications, on any species identified as a candidate, sensitive, or special status species in local or regional plans, policies, or regulations, or by the California Department of Fish and Game or U.S. Fish and Wildlife Service?	❏	❏	❏	❏
b) Have a substantial adverse effect on any riparian habitat or other sensitive natural community identified in local or regional plans, policies, regulations or by the California Department of Fish and Game or US Fish and Wildlife Service?	❏	❏	❏	❏
c) Have a substantial adverse effect on federally protected wetlands as defined by Section 404 of the Clean Water Act (including, but not limited to, marsh, vernal pool, coastal, etc.) through direct removal, filling, hydrological interruption, or other means?	❏	❏	❏	❏
d) Interfere substantially with the movement of any native resident or migratory fish or wildlife species or with established native resident or migratory wildlife corridors, or impede the use of native wildlife nursery sites?	❏	❏	❏	❏

ISSUES	Potentially Significant Impact	Less Than Significant With Mitigation Incorporation	Less Than Significant Impact	No Impact
e) Conflict with any local policies or ordinances protecting biological resources, such as a tree preservation policy or ordinance?	❑	❑	❑	❑
f) Conflict with the provisions of an adopted Habitat Conservation Plan, Natural Community Conservation Plan, or other approved local, regional, or state habitat conservation plan?	❑	❑	❑	❑

V. CULTURAL RESOURCES. Would the project:

	Potentially Significant Impact	Less Than Significant With Mitigation Incorporation	Less Than Significant Impact	No Impact
a) Cause a substantial adverse change in the significance of a historical resource as defined in §15064.5?	❑	❑	❑	❑
b) Cause a substantial adverse change in the significance of an archaeological resource pursuant to §15064.5?	❑	❑	❑	❑
c) Directly or indirectly destroy a unique paleontological resource or site or unique geologic feature?	❑	❑	❑	❑
d) Disturb any human remains, including those interred outside of formal cemeteries?	❑	❑	❑	❑

VI. GEOLOGY AND SOILS. Would the project:

	Potentially Significant Impact	Less Than Significant With Mitigation Incorporation	Less Than Significant Impact	No Impact
a) Expose people or structures to potential substantial adverse effects, including the risk of loss, injury, or death involving:				
i) Rupture of a known earthquake fault, as delineated on the most recent Alquist-Priolo Earthquake Fault Zoning Map issued by the State Geologist for the area or based on other substantial evidence of a known fault? Refer to Division of Mines and Geology Special Publication 42.	❑	❑	❑	❑
ii) Strong seismic ground shaking?	❑	❑	❑	❑
iii) Seismic-related ground failure, including liquefaction?	❑	❑	❑	❑
iv) Landslides?	❑	❑	❑	❑
b) Result in substantial soil erosion or the loss of topsoil?	❑	❑	❑	❑
c) Be located on a geologic unit or soil that is unstable, or that would become unstable as a result of the project, and potentially result in on- or off-site landslide, lateral spreading, subsidence, liquefaction or collapse?	❑	❑	❑	❑
d) Be located on expansive soil, as defined in Table 18-1-B of the Uniform Building Code (1994), creating substantial risks to life or property?	❑	❑	❑	❑

VII. HAZARDS AND HAZARDOUS MATERIALS. Would the project:

	Potentially Significant Impact	Less Than Significant With Mitigation Incorporation	Less Than Significant Impact	No Impact
a) Create a significant hazard to the public or the environment through the routine transport, use, or disposal of hazardous materials?	❑	❑	❑	❑

	Potentially Significant Impact	Less Than Significant With Mitigation Incorporation	Less Than Significant Impact	No Impact
b) Create a significant hazard to the public or the environment through reasonably foreseeable upset and accident conditions involving the release of hazardous materials into the environment?	❑	❑	❑	❑
c) Emit hazardous emissions or handle hazardous or acutely hazardous materials, substances, or waste within one-quarter mile of an existing or proposed school?	❑	❑	❑	❑
d) Be located on a site which is included on a list of hazardous materials sites compiled pursuant to Government Code Section 65962.5 and, as a result, would it create a significant hazard to the public or the environment?	❑	❑	❑	❑
e) For a project located within an airport land use plan or, where such a plan has not been adopted, within two miles of a public airport or public use airport, would the project result in a safety hazard for people residing or working in the project area?	❑	❑	❑	❑
f) For a project within the vicinity of a private airstrip, would the project result in a safety hazard for people residing or working in the project area?	❑	❑	❑	❑
g) Impair implementation of or physically interfere with an adopted emergency response plan or emergency evacuation plan?	❑	❑	❑	❑
h) Expose people or structures to a significant risk of loss, injury or death involving wildland fires, including where wildlands are adjacent to urbanized areas or where residences are intermixed with wildlands?	❑	❑	❑	❑

VIII. HYDROLOGY AND WATER QUALITY. Would the project:

a) Violate any water quality standards or waste discharge requirements?	❑	❑	❑	❑
b) Substantially deplete groundwater supplies or interfere substantially with groundwater recharge such that there would be a net deficit in aquifer volume or a lowering of the local groundwater table level (e.g., the production rate of pre-existing nearby wells would drop to a level which would not support existing land uses or planned uses for which permits have been granted)?	❑	❑	❑	❑
c) Substantially alter the existing drainage pattern of the site or area, including through the alteration of the course of a stream or river, in a manner which would result in substantial erosion or siltation on- or off-site?	❑	❑	❑	❑
d) Substantially alter the existing drainage pattern of the site or area, including through the alteration of the course of a stream or river, or substantially increase the rate or amount of surface runoff in a manner which would result in flooding on- or off-site?	❑	❑	❑	❑

ISSUES	Potentially Significant Impact	Less Than Significant With Mitigation Incorporatation	Less Than Significant Impact	No Impact
e) Create or contribute runoff water which would exceed the capacity of existing or planned stormwater drainage systems or provide substantial additional sources of polluted runoff?	❑	❑	❑	❑
f) Otherwise substantially degrade water quality?	❑	❑	❑	❑
g) Place housing within a 100-year flood hazard area as mapped on a federal Flood Hazard Boundary or Flood Insurance Rate Map or other flood hazard delineation map?	❑	❑	❑	❑
h) Place within a 100-year flood hazard area structures which would impede or redirect flood flows?	❑	❑	❑	❑
i) Expose people or structures to a significant risk of loss, injury or death involving flooding, including flooding as a result of the failure of a levee or dam?	❑	❑	❑	❑
j) Inundation by seiche, tsunami, or mudflow?	❑	❑	❑	❑

IX. LAND USE AND PLANNING. Would the project:

ISSUES				
a) Physically divide an established community?	❑	❑	❑	❑
b) Conflict with any applicable land use plan, policy, or regulation of an agency with jurisdiction over the project (including, but not limited to the general plan, specific plan, local coastal program, or zoning ordinance) adopted for the purpose of avoiding or mitigating an environmental effect?	❑	❑	❑	❑
c) Conflict with any applicable habitat conservation plan or natural community conservation plan?	❑	❑	❑	❑

X. MINERAL RESOURCES. Would the project:

ISSUES				
a) Result in the loss of availability of a known mineral resource that would be of value to the region and the residents of the state?	❑	❑	❑	❑
b) Result in the loss of availability of a locally-important mineral resource recovery site delineated on a local general plan, specific plan or other land use plan?	❑	❑	❑	❑

XI. NOISE. Would the project result in:

ISSUES				
a) Exposure of persons to or generation of noise levels in excess of standards established in the local general plan or noise ordinance, or applicable standards of other agencies?	❑	❑	❑	❑
b) Exposure of persons to or generation of excessive groundborne vibration or groundborne noise levels?	❑	❑	❑	❑
c) A substantial permanent increase in ambient noise levels in the project vicinity above levels existing without the project?	❑	❑	❑	❑

ISSUES	Potentially Significant Impact	Less Than Significant With Mitigation Incorporatation	Less Than Significant Impact	No Impact
d) A substantial temporary or periodic increase in ambient noise levels in the project vicinity above levels existing without the project?	❏	❏	❏	❏
e) For a project located within an airport land use plan or, where such a plan has not been adopted, within two miles of a public airport or public use airport, would the project expose people residing or working in the project area to excessive noise levels?	❏	❏	❏	❏
f) For a project within the vicinity of a private airstrip, would the project expose people residing or working in the project area to excessive noise levels?	❏	❏	❏	❏

XII. POPULATION AND HOUSING. Would the project:

	Potentially Significant Impact	Less Than Significant With Mitigation Incorporatation	Less Than Significant Impact	No Impact
a) Induce substantial population growth in an area, either directly (for example, by proposing new homes and businesses) or indirectly (for example, through extension of roads or other infrastructure)?	❏	❏	❏	❏
b) Displace substantial numbers of existing housing, necessitating the construction of replacement housing elsewhere?	❏	❏	❏	❏
c) Displace substantial numbers of people, necessitating the construction of replacement housing elsewhere?	❏	❏	❏	❏

XIII. PUBLIC SERVICES

	Potentially Significant Impact	Less Than Significant With Mitigation Incorporatation	Less Than Significant Impact	No Impact
a) Would the project result in substantial adverse physical impacts associated with the provision of new or physically altered governmental facilities, need for new or physically altered governmental facilities, the construction of which could cause significant environmental impacts, in order to maintain acceptable service ratios, response times or other performance objectives for any of the public services:	❏	❏	❏	❏
Fire protection?	❏	❏	❏	❏
Police protection?	❏	❏	❏	❏
Schools?	❏	❏	❏	❏
Parks?	❏	❏	❏	❏
Other public facilities?	❏	❏	❏	❏

XIV. RECREATION

	Potentially Significant Impact	Less Than Significant With Mitigation Incorporatation	Less Than Significant Impact	No Impact
a) Would the project increase the use of existing neighborhood and regional parks or other recreational facilities such that substantial physical deterioration of the facility would occur or be accelerated?	❏	❏	❏	❏
b) Does the project include recreational facilities or require the construction or expansion of recreational facilities which might have an adverse physical effect on the environment?	❏	❏	❏	❏

ISSUES	Potentially Significant Impact	Less Than Significant With Mitigation Incorporation	Less Than Significant Impact	No Impact

XV. TRANSPORTATION / TRAFFIC. Would the project:

ISSUES	Potentially Significant Impact	Less Than Significant With Mitigation Incorporation	Less Than Significant Impact	No Impact
a) Cause an increase in traffic which is substantial in relation to the existing traffic load and capacity of the street system (i.e., result in a substantial increase in either the number of vehicle trips, the volume to capacity ratio on roads, or congestion at intersections)?	❑	❑	❑	❑
b) Exceed, either individually or cumulatively, a level of service standard established by the county congestion management agency for designated roads or highways?	❑	❑	❑	❑
c) Result in a change in air traffic patterns, including either an increase in traffic levels or a change in location that results in substantial safety risks?	❑	❑	❑	❑
d) Substantially increase hazards due to a design feature (e.g., sharp curves or dangerous intersections) or incompatible uses (e.g., farm equipment)?	❑	❑	❑	❑
e) Result in inadequate emergency access?	❑	❑	❑	❑
f) Result in inadequate parking capacity?	❑	❑	❑	❑

XVI. UTILITIES AND SERVICE SYSTEMS. Would the project:

ISSUES	Potentially Significant Impact	Less Than Significant With Mitigation Incorporation	Less Than Significant Impact	No Impact
a) Exceed wastewater treatment requirements of the applicable Regional Water Quality Control Board?	❑	❑	❑	❑
b) Require or result in the construction of new water or wastewater treatment facilities or expansion of existing facilities, the construction of which could cause significant environmental effects?	❑	❑	❑	❑
c) Require or result in the construction of new storm water drainage facilities or expansion of existing facilities, the construction of which could cause significant environmental effects?	❑	❑	❑	❑
d) Have sufficient water supplies available to serve the project from existing entitlements and resources, or are new or expanded entitlements needed?	❑	❑	❑	❑
e) Result in a determination by the wastewater treatment provider which serves or may serve the project that it has adequate capacity to serve the project's projected demand in addition to the provider's existing commitments?	❑	❑	❑	❑
f) Be served by a landfill with sufficient permitted capacity to accommodate the project's solid waste disposal needs?	❑	❑	❑	❑
g) Comply with federal, state, and local statutes and regulations related to solid waste?	❑	❑	❑	❑

ISSUES	Potentially Significant Impact	Less Than Significant With Mitigation Incorporatation	Less Than Significant Impact	No Impact

XVII. MANDATORY FINDINGS OF SIGNIFICANCE

a) Does the project have the potential to degrade the quality of the environment, substantially reduce the habitat of a fish or wildlife species, cause a fish or wildlife population to drop below self-sustaining levels, threaten to eliminate a plant or animal community, reduce the number or restrict the range of a rare or endangered plant or animal or eliminate important examples of the major periods of California history or prehistory?	❏	❏	❏	❏
b) Does the project have impacts that are individually limited, but cumulatively considerable? ("Cumulatively considerable" means that the incremental effects of a project are considerable when viewed in connection with the effects of past projects, the effects of other current projects, and the effects of probable future projects)?	❏	❏	❏	❏
c) Does the project have environmental effects which will cause substantial adverse effects on human beings, either directly or indirectly?	❏	❏	❏	❏

Appendix H
Environmental Information Form

(To Be Completed by Applicant)

Date Filed _____

General Information

1. Name and address of developer or project sponsor: _____
   _____

2. Address of project: _____

   Assessor's Block and Lot Number: _____

3. Name, address, and telephone number of person to be contacted concerning this project:
   _____

4. Indicate number of the permit application for the project to which this form pertains: _____

5. List and describe any other related permits and other public approvals required for this project, including those required by city, regional, state, and federal agencies:
   _____
   _____

6. Existing zoning district: _____

7. Proposed use of site (project for which this form is filed): _____
   _____

Project Description

8. Site size.

9. Square footage.

10. Number of floors of construction.

11. Amount of off-street parking provided.

12. Attach plans.

13. Proposed scheduling.

14. Associated project.

15. Anticipated incremental development.

16. If residential, include the number of units, schedule of unit sizes, range of sale prices or rents, and type of household size expected.

17. If commercial, indicate the type, whether neighborhood, city, or regionally oriented, square footage of sales area, and loading facilities.

18. If industrial, indicate type, estimated employment per shift, and loading facilities.

19. If institutional, indicate the major function, estimated employment per shift, estimated occupancy, loading facilities, and community benefits to be derived from the project.

20. If the project involves a variance, conditional use, or rezoning application, state this and indicate clearly why the application is required.

Are the following items applicable to the project or its effects? Discuss below all items checked yes (attach additional sheets as necessary).

		Yes	No
21.	Change in existing features of any bays, tidelands, beaches, or hills, or substantialalteration of ground contours.	❏	❏
22.	Change in scenic views or vistas from existing residential areas or public lands or roads.	❏	❏
23.	Change in pattern, scale, or character of general area of project.	❏	❏
24.	Significant amounts of solid waste or litter.	❏	❏
25.	Change in dust, ash, smoke, fumes, or odors in vicinity.	❏	❏
26.	Change in ocean, bay, lake, stream, or ground water quality or quantity, or alteration of existing drainage patterns.	❏	❏
27.	Substantial change in existing noise or vibration levels in the vicinity.	❏	❏
28.	Site on filled land or on slope of 10 percent or more.	❏	❏
29.	Use or disposal of potentially hazardous materials, such as toxic substances, flammables, or explosives.	❏	❏
30.	Substantial change in demand for municipal services (police, fire, water, sewage, etc.).	❏	❏
31.	Substantially increase fossil fuel consumption (electricity, oil, natural gas, etc.).	❏	❏
32.	Relationship to a larger project or series of projects.	❏	❏

Environmental Setting

33. Describe the project site as it exists before the project, including information on topography, soil stability, plants and animals, and any cultural, historical, or scenic aspects. Describe any existing structures on the site, and the use of the structures. Attach photographs of the site. Snapshots or polaroid photos will be accepted.

34. Describe the surrounding properties, including information on plants and animals and any cultural, historical, or scenic aspects. Indicate the type of land use (residential, commercial, etc.), intensity of land use (one-family, apartment houses, shops, department stores, etc.), and scale of development (height, frontage, set-back, rear yard, etc.). Attach photographs of the vicinity. Snapshots or polaroid photos will be accepted.

Certification

I hereby certify that the statements furnished above and in the attached exhibits present the data and information required for this initial evaluation to the best of my ability, and that the facts, statements, and information presented are true and correct to the best of my knowledge and belief.

Date _____   Signature _____

For _____

(Note: This is only a suggested form. Public agencies are free to devise their own format for initial studies.)

Appendix I
Notice of Preparation

TO _____   FROM _____

_____   _____
(Address)   *(Address)*

_____   _____

Subject: **Notice of Preparation of a Draft Environmental Impact Report**

_____ will be the Lead Agency and will prepare an environmental impact report for the project identified below. We need to know the views of your agency as to the scope and content of the environmental information which is germane to your agency's statutory responsibilities in connection with the proposed project. Your agency will need to use the EIR prepared by our agency when considering your permit or other approval for the project.

The project description, location, and the probable environmental effects are contained in the attached materials. A copy of the Initial Study (❏ is ❏ is not) attached.

Due to the time limits mandated by State law, your response must be sent at the earliest possible date but **not later than 30 days** after receipt of this notice.

Please send your response to _____ at the address shown above. We will need the name for a contact person in your **agency.**

Project Title _____

Project Applicant, if any _____

Date _____   Signature _____

                                          Title _____

                                          Telephone _____

Reference: California Administrative Code, Title 14, Sections 15082(a), 15103, 15375.

Appendix J
Examples of Tiering EIRs

FIRST TIER EIR (15152)	• project encompasses separate but related projects such as general plan, zoning, development • later tiers move from general to specific analysis of projects

Later Project EIR	• later project is consistent with general plan or zoning • initial study must examine significant effects not covered in prior EIR • later EIR must state lead agency is using tiering concept and must comply with section 15152

STAGED EIR (15167)	• one large project will require a number of discretionary approvals from government agencies and one of those approvals will occur more than two years before construction commences

Supplement to the Staged EIR	• supplements to the staged EIR are prepared for later government agency approvals on the same overall project if information available at the time of that later approval would permit consideration of additional environmental impacts, mitigation measures, or reasonable alternatives

PROGRAM EIR (15168)	• series of actions or activities that can be characterized as one large project and are related either:
	  – geographically
	  – as logical parts of a chain of activities
	  – in connection with rules, regulations, plans, or other general criteria governing a continuing program
	  – as individual activities carried out under common authority (statutory or regulatory) and having similar environmental effects which can be mitigated in similar ways

Subsequent Project EIR	• only if subsequent activity has effects not examined in the previously certified program EIR will additional environmental documentation be required (if subsequent activity has no new effects, that activity is covered by the program EIR)

Appendix J

continued

MASTER EIR
(15175)
	• alternative to project, staged, or program EIR
	• can be used for:
	  – general plan (or general plan element, amendment, or update)
	  – redevelopment plan projects (public or private)
	  – project consisting of phases of smaller individual projects
	  – other activities described in 15175
	• after five years from initial certification, adopting authority must review the Master EIR and prepare subsequent or supplemental EIR if substantial changes have occurred with respect to circumstances under which the original Master EIR was adopted
	• no new EIR is required for subsequent projects within the scope of the Master EIR which cause no additional significant effect

Focused EIR
(15177)
	• a subsequent, Focused EIR is required only where:
	  – substantial new/additional information shows adverse environmental effects not examined in the Master EIR or more significant than described in the EIR, or
	  – substantial new/additional information shows mitigation measures previously determined to be infeasible are now feasible and will avoid/reduce the significant effects to a level of insignificance

SPECIAL SITUATIONS/EIRs

Multiple-Family Residential Development/Residential and Commercial or Retail Mixed-Use Development (PRC 21158.5 and Guideline §15179.5)

- project is multiple-family residential development up to 100 units or is a residential and commercial or retail mixed-use development of not more than 100,000 square feet
- if project complies with procedures in section 21158.5, only a focused EIR need be prepared, notwithstanding the fact that the project wasn't identified in the Master EIR

Redevelopment Project (15180)

- all public and private activities or undertakings in furtherance of a redevelopment plan (public or private) constitute a single project
- the redevelopment plan EIR is treated as a program EIR
- no subsequent EIR is required for individual components of the redevelopment plan unless substantial changes or substantial new information triggers a subsequent EIR or supplement to an EIR pursuant to sections 15162 or 15163

Housing/Neighborhood Commercial Facilities (15181)

- a project involving construction of housing or neighborhood commercial facilities in an urbanized area
- a prior EIR for a specific plan, local coastal program, or port master plan may be used as the EIR for such a project (no new EIR need be prepared) provided section 15181 procedures are complied with

Projects Consistent with Community Plan, General Plan, or Zoning (15183)

- a project which is consistent with a community plan adopted as part of a general plan or zoning ordinance or a general plan of a local agency and where there was an EIR certified for the zoning action or master plan
- the EIR for the residential project need only examine certain significant environmental effects, as outlined in section 15183

Regulations on Pollution Control Equipment (PRC section 21159)

- section 21159 requires environmental analysis of reasonably foreseeable methods of compliance at the time of adoption of a rule or regulation requiring the installation of pollution control equipment
- an EIR prepared at the time of adoption of the rule or regulation is deemed to satisfy the requirement of section 21159

Installation of Pollution Control Equipment (PRC section 21159.1)

- a focused EIR is permitted where project 1) consists solely of installation of pollution control equipment; 2) is required by rule or regulation adopted by the State Air Resources Board, an air pollution control district or air quality management district, the State Water Resources Control Board, a California regional water quality control board, the Department of Toxic Substances Control, or the California Integrated Waste Management Board; and 3) meets the procedural requirements outlined in section 21159.1

Appendix K
Criteria for Shortened Clearinghouse Review

Under exceptional circumstances, and when requested in writing by the lead agency, the State Clearinghouse in the Office of Planning and Research (OPR) may shorten the usual review periods for proposed negative declarations, mitigated negative declarations, and draft EIRs submitted to the Clearinghouse. A request must be made by the decision-making body of the lead agency, or by a properly authorized representative of the decision-making body.

A shortened review period may be granted when any of the following circumstances exist:

(1) The lead agency is operating under an extension of the one-year period for completion of an EIR and would not otherwise be able to complete the EIR within the extended period.

(2) The public project applicant is under severe time constraints with regard to obtaining financing or exercising options which cannot be met without shortening the review period.

(3) The document is a supplement to a draft EIR or proposed negative declaration or mitigated negative declaration previously submitted to the State Clearinghouse.

(4) The health and safety of the community would be at risk unless the project is approved expeditiously.

(5) The document is a revised draft EIR, or proposed negative declaration or mitigated negative declaration, where changes in the document are primarily the result of comments from agencies and the public.

Shortened review cannot be provided to a draft EIR or proposed negative declaration or mitigated negative declaration which has already begun the usual review process. Prior to requesting shortened review, the lead agency should have already issued a notice of preparation and received comments from applicable State agencies, in the case of an EIR, or consulted with applicable State agencies, in the case of a proposed negative declaration or mitigated negative declaration. No shortened review period shall be granted unless the lead agency has contacted and obtained prior approval for a shortened review from the applicable state responsible and trustee agencies. No shortened review shall be granted for any project which is of statewide, regional, or areawide significance, as defined in Section 15206 of the guidelines.

Appendix 3

OPR Regulations for Designation of Lead Agency

Source

Governor's Office of Planning and Research (OPR). This document is reprinted with permission from the Governor's Office of Planning and Research, 1400 10th Street, Sacramento, California 95814. For additional information please call (916) 322-4245.

Solano Press Books has made every effort to see that no changes have been made to the contents of this state document as a result of reformatting and reprinting. Any omissions or changes to the contrary are entirely the responsibility of Solano Press Books and not the State of California.

Division 6.3
Office of Planning and Research

Chapter 1. Regulations for Designation of Lead Agency for the Preparation of Environmental Documents

Article 1. General

Article 2. Purpose

Article 3. Policy

Article 4. Submission of Dispute to OPR

Article 5. Designation on the Statements

Article 6. Hearing

Article 7. Administrative Record

Detailed Analysis

Article 1. General

16000   Authority
The regulations contained herein are prescribed by the Director of the Office of Planning and Research pursuant to authority granted in Div. 13, Pub. Resources Code and Title 7, Division 1, Chapter 1.5, Gov. Code, and to implement, interpret or make specific Section 21165 of the Pub. Resources Code consistent with the Guidelines for Implementation of the California Environmental Quality Act of 1970 (Div. 6, Title 14, Cal. Adm. Code) and to establish criteria and procedures for designation of the lead agency for the preparation of environmental documents in the event of a dispute between two or more public agencies.

Note: Authority cited: Section 21082, Public Resources Code and Title 7, Division 1, Chapter 1.5, Gov. Code. Reference: Section 21165, Public Resources Code.

History
1. New Division 6.3 (§§ 16000 through 16041) filed 4-12-74; effective thirtieth day thereafter (Register 74, No. 15).
2. Amendment filed 11-22-78; effective thirtieth day thereafter (Register 78, No. 47).

Article 2. Purpose

16001   Purpose
The purpose of these regulations is to specify the criteria and procedures to be followed by the Office of Planning and Research in resolving lead agency disputes.

Article 3. Policy

16002   Policy
It is the policy of the Office of Planning and Research that these regulations implement the principles, objectives and criteria for the designation of a lead agency specified in the State Guidelines.

Article 4. Submission of Dispute to OPR

16010   Definitions
Words used in these regulations, unless otherwise defined, shall have the meaning ascribed to them in the State Guidelines. In addition, the following definitions not contained in the State Guidelines are used:

(a) State Guidelines means the Guidelines for Implementation of the California Environmental Quality Act of 1970 adopted by the Secretary for Resources (Div. 6, Title 14, Cal. Adm. Code Sections 15000–15180).

(b) OPR means the Office of Planning and Research.

(c) Director means the Director of the Office of Planning and Research or the Director's designee.

(d) Interested Person means public agencies having jurisdiction over the project, public agencies which approve or comment on the project, consultants hired with respect to the project, and individuals or groups known to be interested in the project.

Note: Authority cited: Division 13, Public Resources Code; Title 7, Division 1, Chapter 1.5, Government Code. Reference: Section 21165, Public Resources Code.

History

1. Repealer of Article 4 (Sections 16010–16017) and new Article 4 (Sections 16010–16016, not consecutive) filed 11-22-78; effective thirtieth day thereafter (Register 78, No. 47).

16011   General

In the event a dispute arises between two or more public agencies as to which agency shall be a "lead agency" pursuant to the State Guidelines, the following procedures and criteria shall apply.

Note: Authority cited: Division 13, Public Resources Code; Title 7, Division 1, Chapter 1.5, Government Code. Reference: Section 21165, Public Resources Code.

16012   Dispute, What Constitutes

As used in these regulations, "dispute" means a contested, active difference of opinion between two or more public agencies as to which shall prepare environmental documents. A dispute exists where each such public agency claims that it either has or does not have the obligation to prepare such environmental documents. OPR will not designate the lead agency in the absence of such a dispute.

Note: Authority cited: Division 13, Public Resources Code; Title 7, Division 1, Chapter 1.5, Government Code. Reference: Section 21165, Public Resources Code.

16013   Public Agency Consultation

Prior to submission of a request for designation to OPR, the disputing agencies, or the disputing agencies and the project applicant for a project described in subdivision (c) of Section 21065 if such applicant requests the designation, shall consult with each other in an effort to resolve the dispute pursuant to the State Guidelines. Such consultation should include efforts to designate a lead agency by agreement. Such agencies or applicant may request OPR to assist in arranging for this consultation.

Note: Authority cited: Division 13, Public Resources Code; Title 7, Division 1, Chapter 1.5, Government Code. Reference: Section 21165, Public Resources Code.

16014   Request for Designation

A request for designation of the lead agency pursuant to this Article shall be made in writing to the Director. It shall be signed by an executive of the public agency making the request, or by the project applicant for a project described in subdivision (c) of Section 21065 if such applicant requests the designation. A complete request shall set forth:

(a) The general nature of the dispute,

(b) The other disputing agencies,

(c) Written information showing that the requesting agency of project applicant and the other disputing agencies have consulted pursuant to Section 16013 in an effort to resolve the dispute,

(d) A statement of contentions pursuant to Section 16015 from the agency or project applicant requesting the designation, and

(e) Written information showing that the agency or applicant requesting the designation has given notice in writing to, and such notice has been received by, all disputing agencies and the project applicant, stating that; i) the dispute is being submitted to OPR for resolution; and that, ii) each disputing agency is required to prepare and send a statement of contentions to OPR within 10 days after receipt of such notice.

OPR may require as a part of the application that notice of the request be published in newspapers of general circulation where the lead agency dispute exists. Such notice may allow for submission of written comments on or before a specified date, and it may also state whether or not a hearing will be held, and may specify the time and place of the hearing.

Note: Authority cited: Division 13, Public Resources Code; Title 7, Division 1, Chapter 1.5, Government Code. Reference: Section 21165, Public Resources Code.

16015   Statement of Contentions: List of Interested Persons

(a) In the event that the lead agency dispute is not resolved by consultation pursuant to Section 16013, and upon a request for designation made pursuant to Section 16014, the Director shall require a statement of contentions from each disputing agency and from the project applicant if requesting the designation, and may require a statement

of contentions from the project applicant if not requesting the designation.

(b) Each disputing agency shall prepare a written statement of contentions in support of its claim as to which agency should or should not be the lead agency. The statement shall contain the following information:

(1) A description of the project.

(2) A description of the agency's responsibility for constructing, approving, supervising, and financing the project as a whole.

(3) Citation of the agency's general governmental powers relating to the project.

(4) Data outlining all aspects of the agency's relationship to the project.

(5) The date the agency first undertook formal action, if any, on the project and a chronology of actions taken and to be taken concerning the project.

(6) A list of all interested persons who might comment on the project.

(7) Such other information as the Director may require.

(c) The project applicant requesting the designation, or a project applicant required by the Director pursuant to subdivision (a), shall prepare a written statement of contentions which shall contain the following information:

(1) A description of the project.

(2) A list of all interested persons who might comment on the project.

(3) A brief statement as to which disputing agency, if any, the applicant believes is appropriate to adequately fulfill the requirements of CEQA and complies with the lead agency criteria set forth in State Guidelines Section 15065, and the applicant's reasons in support thereof.

(4) Such other information as the Director determines would assist in designating the appropriate lead agency.

Note: Authority cited: Division 13, Public Resources Code; Title 7, Division 1, Chapter 1.5, Government Code. Reference: Section 21165, Public Resources Code.

16016   Distribution of Statement

Each disputing agency shall mail a copy of the statement of contentions to all other disputing agencies, to the applicant, and to OPR within 10 calendar days after the agency receives the notice specified in Section 16014. If an agency requested the designation, the agency shall mail such statement to all other disputing agencies and to the applicant when the agency submits a completed request to OPR. Each disputing agency shall make such statement or an informative summary thereof available to all interested persons upon request. If an informative summary is used, interested persons shall be given the full statement of contentions upon request.

Note: Authority cited: Division 13, Public Resources Code; Title 7, Division 1, Chapter 1.5, Government Code. Reference: Section 21165, Public Resources Code.

Article 5. Designation on the Statements

16020 Designation on the Statements
The Director may designate a lead agency on the basis of the completed requests and written statements, or may require a hearing. The Director may request additional written information from any disputing agency, applicant, or interested person without extending the time period for designation provided in Section 16021. Written notice of such request shall be given to all disputing agencies and the project applicant if the applicant has been required to submit a statement of contentions.

Note: Authority cited: Division 13, Public Resources Code; Title 7, Division 1, Chapter 1.5, Government Code. Reference: Section 21165, Public Resources Code.

History
1. Amendment filed 11-22-78; effective thirtieth day thereafter (Register 78, No. 47).

16021 Designation: Findings
In making a designation of lead agency, the Director shall find which of the disputing agencies is most appropriate to carry out the obligations of a lead agency. In making this finding, the Director shall consider the capacity of each such agency adequately to fulfill the requirements of CEQA. In addition, the Director shall consider the lead agency criteria set forth in the State Guidelines Section 15065. Generally, such criteria will control unless the Director finds that another agency has greater capacity to carry out the requirements of CEQA. The designation shall be made within 21 calendar days of receipt by OPR of the completed request for designation.

Note: Authority cited: Division 13, Public Resources Code; Title 7, Division 1, Chapter 1.5, Government Code. Reference: Section 21165, Public Resources Code.

History
1. Amendment filed 11-22-78; effective thirtieth day thereafter (Register 78, No. 47).

16022 Designation: Form
The designation shall be in writing and it shall be published in the *California EIR Monitor* and made available to all public agencies involved in the dispute and to all interested persons. The designation shall name the lead agency and it shall include findings upon which the designation is made. It shall be signed by the director.

Article 6. Hearing

16030 Hearing: When Called
If the Director finds on the basis of consultation pursuant to Section 16013 or the completed request for designation that the dispute involves issues of general application to other projects, or is of regional or statewide impact, or that the project involves substantial public interest or concern, the Director may require a hearing prior to making a designation. Notice of the time and place of the hearing shall be published in newspapers of general circulation where the dispute exists and be sent to all interested parties, disputing agencies, and the applicant not later than 7 calendar days after receiving the completed request for designation.

Note: Authority cited: Division 13, Public Resources Code; Title 7, Division 1, Chapter 1.5, Government Code. Reference: Section 21165, Public Resources Code.

History
1. Amendment filed 11-22-78; effective thirtieth day thereafter (Register 78, No. 47).

16031 Presiding Officer
The presiding officer at the hearing shall be the Director or any other person designated by the Director.

Note: Authority cited: Division 13, Public Resources Code; Title 7, Division 1, Chapter 1.5, Government Code. Reference: Section 21165, Public Resources Code.

History
1. Amendment filed 11-22-78; effective thirtieth day thereafter (Register 78, No. 47).

16032 Order of Proceedings
(a) The hearing will ordinarily proceed in the following order:
  (1) Identification of the dispute and a brief, fair summary of correspondence received by the presiding officer.
  (2) Presentation by or on behalf of the disputing agency which initially submitted a request for certification pursuant to Section 16014, if

such agency wishes to expand upon the material contained in its statement of contentions.
  (3) Other disputing agencies wishing to expand upon the material contained in their statement of contentions.
  (4) Other speakers concerning the dispute. Any person wishing to speak shall be heard.
(b) Questions by the presiding officer may be asked at any time during any presentations.
(c) A record of the testimony may be made.

16033 Presentations
Presentations shall be to the point, shall be as brief as possible and shall assume that OPR is familiar with the dispute from reading the statement of contentions.

16034 Summary of Hearing
The presiding officer may prepare a summary of the testimony at the hearing and shall prepare a recommended decision. The director shall consider the summary and recommended decision together with the statement of contentions and any other material presented at the hearing in making his decision.

16035 Designation: Findings
The provisions of Section 16021 shall apply to a designation made pursuant to this Article.

Article 7. Administrative Record

16040 Administrative Record
For the purposes of any court proceeding, the administrative record of OPR shall be deemed to be the request or requests for designation, the statement of contentions, the correspondence received with regard to the dispute, evidence introduced at the hearing, if any, the record of the hearing, if one is made, the hearing summary and recommended decision, and any other evidence considered by the Director.

Note: Authority cited: Division 13, Public Resources Code; Title 7, Division 1, Chapter 1.5, Government Code. Reference: Section 21165, Public Resources Code.

History
1. Amendment filed 11-22-78; effective thirtieth day thereafter (Register 78, No. 47).

16041 Final Decision
The decision of the director, whether made under Article 5. or 6. of this Division, shall be final and binding on the parties to the dispute.

Appendix 4

Tracking CEQA Mitigation Measures Under AB 3180

CEQA Technical Advice Series

Source

"Tracking CEQA Mitigation Measures Under AB 3180" (Third Edition, March 1996) CEQA Technical Advice Series. This document is reprinted with permission from the Governor's Office of Planning and Research, 1400 10th Street, Sacramento, California 95814. For additional information please call (916) 322-4245.

Solano Press Books has made every effort to see that no changes have been made to the contents of this state document as a result of reformatting and reprinting. Any omissions or changes to the contrary are entirely the responsibility of Solano Press Books and not the State of California.

Introduction

Newton's Law provides that for every action there is an equal and opposite reaction. CEQA on the other hand provides that whenever a proposed project will result in potential significant adverse environmental impacts, measures must be taken which will limit or avoid that impact. These may include conditions of approval, revisions to the project, and, less frequently, approving an alternative project with fewer impacts. Where such measures are imposed, there must be a program for monitoring or reporting on the project's compliance with those measures.

Section 21081.6 of the Public Resources Code requires all state and local agencies to establish monitoring or reporting programs whenever approval of a project relies upon a mitigated negative declaration or an environmental impact report (EIR). The monitoring or reporting program must ensure implementation of the measures being imposed to mitigate or avoid the significant adverse environmental impacts identified in the mitigated negative declaration or EIR.

The Office of Planning and Research (OPR) has written this advisory publication to offer local governments basic information and practical advice about how they may comply with the mitigation monitoring and reporting program requirements. It is supplementary to, and not an amendment or revision of, the *California Environmental Quality Act Guidelines.* Accordingly, this publication represents the informal guidance of OPR regarding compliance with Section 21081.6, but is not a regulation. This is part of OPR's public education and training program for planners, developers, and others.

The following suggestions are not the only methods of implementing Section 21081.6. The examples that follow are illustrative and not limiting. Agencies can develop their own programs to the meet the variety of projects and unique circumstances which they encounter.

The third edition of *Tracking CEQA Mitigation Measures Under AB 3180* is based upon the law as it existed on January 1, 1996. Readers should refer to the most recent CEQA statute to ensure that they are meeting all current requirements. Code citations in this document are to the Public Resources Code, unless otherwise noted.

A Brief History of AB 3180

Despite CEQA's emphasis on mitigation, until 1988 the Act did not require that agencies take actions to ensure that required mitigation measures and project revisions were indeed being implemented. When reports of gross disregard for mitigation requirements reached the State Legislature in that year, it responded by enacting AB 3180 (Cortese). Section 21081.6 of the Public Resources Code, added by this bill, provides that whenever a mitigated negative declaration is adopted or a public agency is responsible for mitigation pursuant to an EIR, the agency must adopt a program for monitoring or reporting on project compliance with the adopted mitigation. The legislation was signed into law by Governor Deukmejian in September of 1988 (Chapter 1232, Statutes 1988) and took effect on January 1, 1989.

OPR published the first edition of Tracking Mitigation Measures in early 1989 to provide guidance to local agencies in complying with the requirements of Section 21081.6. Expert publications and the efforts of U.C. Extension instructors have continued this education. As a result, by 1993, approximately 75% of cities and counties had enacted measures to comply with AB 3180. This edition of Tracking Mitigation Measures updates the advice offered by its predecessor.

Programs Required by Section 21081.6

Section 21081.6 establishes two distinct requirements for agencies involved in the CEQA process. Subdivisions (a) and (b) of the section relate to mitigation monitoring and reporting, and the obligation to mitigate significant effects where possible. Subdivision (c), which was amended into the code by AB 375 of 1992, is almost a non-sequitur. Its subject is the responsibility of responsible and trustee agencies during consultation on a negative declaration or EIR.

Pursuant to subdivision (a), whenever a public agency either: (1) adopts a mitigated negative declaration, or (2) completes an EIR and makes a finding pursuant to Section 21081(a) of the Public Resources Code taking responsibility for mitigation identified in the EIR, the agency must adopt a program of monitoring or reporting which will ensure that mitigation measures are complied with during implementation of the project. When changes have been incorporated into the project at the request of an agency having jurisdiction by law over natural resources affected by the project, that agency, if so requested by the lead or responsible agency, must prepare and submit a proposed reporting or monitoring program for the changes.

A project which is exempt from CEQA, or for which a simple (i.e., not mitigated) negative declaration has been prepared requires no AB 3180 program. In addition, no program is required for projects which are disapproved by the agency. Nor is a program required to address those mitigation measures which the agency has found to be either the responsibility of another agency or infeasible, pursuant to subdivisions (b) and (c) of Section 21081.

Besides ensuring implementation of mitigation measures, as required by statute, a monitoring or reporting program may provide feedback to staff and decisionmakers regarding the effectiveness of mitigating actions. Such experiential information can be used by staff and decisionmakers to shape future mitigation measures.

Subdivision (b) of Section 21081.6 requires that mitigation measures be "fully enforceable through permit conditions, agreements, or other measures." Incorporating the mitigation measures into the conditions of approval applied to the project meets this requirement. Where the project consists of a general plan (or other type of policy plan), a regulation, or a public project, the mitigation measures can be incorporated into the policies of the plan, the regulations themselves, or the design of the project to meet the enforceability requirement.

Subdivision (c) of Section 21081.6 creates a requirement for responsible or trustee agencies which have identified a significant impact during consultation on a negative declaration or EIR. This requirement is not directly related to mitigation monitoring or reporting programs, nor is it limited to those situations which require mitigation monitoring or reporting. We will discuss it only briefly before moving on.

Pursuant to subdivision (c), when a responsible or trustee agency suggests mitigation measures to address a significant impact which that agency has identified during consultation, it must either provide the lead agency with "complete and detailed performance objectives" (i.e., standards by which to meet specific objectives of the responsible or trustee agency) for those measures or refer the lead agency to readily available guidelines which would be the functional equivalent of such objectives. The mitigation measures suggested by a responsible or trustee agency are limited to those within the statutory authority of that agency (Section 21080.4). In effect, a responsible or trustee agency is required to limit its requests for mitigation measures to those subjects over which it has regulatory powers and to provide the lead agency with sufficient information to allow the lead agency to effectively fashion such measures.

The requirements of subdivision (c) impact the lead agency's mitigation monitoring or reporting program to the extent that the lead agency imposes such measures on the project. It does not alter the lead agency's responsibility for determining, on the basis of the evidence before it, whether a significant effect exists and how it may be mitigated. When the lead agency does not adopt those measures, it need not address them in a monitoring or reporting program.

Mitigation Monitoring or Reporting Programs

CEQA requires that each public agency adopt objectives, criteria, and specific procedures to administer its responsibilities under the Act and the *CEQA Guidelines* (Section 21082). Accordingly,

local agencies should revise their adopted CEQA guidelines and procedures as necessary to include the requirements of Section 21081.6.

The task of designing monitoring and reporting programs is the responsibility of the public agency which is approving the project. Although a public agency may delegate this work, the agency cannot escape its responsibility for ensuring the adequacy of the program.

Each city and county may adopt programs which match their unique circumstances. The contents and complexity of the programs may be expected to vary based on the characteristics of the project being approved, the environmental effects being mitigated, and the nature of the mitigation measures themselves. Further, the public agency may choose whether its program will monitor mitigation, report on mitigation, or both.

The statute does not define the terms "reporting" or "monitoring," leaving this to the interpretation of the affected agency. Later in this section, we will offer simple definitions for discussion purposes. In practice, however, there is no clear distinction between monitoring and reporting, and the program best suited to ensuring compliance with mitigation measures will generally involve elements of both. For example, reporting requires the agency to monitor mitigation at some point in time. Likewise, a monitoring program can include regular reports to the decision-making body.

Mitigation Measures

Since the purpose of a monitoring or reporting program is to ensure the implementation of mitigation measures, a quick look at mitigation measures will be the first item in our discussion. Mitigation measures are the specific requirements which will minimize, avoid, rectify, reduce, eliminate, or compensate for significant environmental effects. See Section 15370 of the *CEQA Guidelines* for a full definition.

A monitoring and reporting program's effectiveness depends in large part upon the quality of the mitigation measures themselves. Poorly drafted measures are not only difficult to implement, they are difficult to report on and monitor.

Here are some suggestions for preparing mitigation measures:

1 **Certainty:** Avoid using the words "may" or "should" when the intent is to direct some required action. "Will" or "shall" are much better. Avoid measures that are conditioned on feasibility (i.e., required "where feasible") rather than applied directly or at a specified stage in the project.

Measures should be written in clear declaratory language. Specify what is required to be done, how is to be done, when it must be done, and who is responsible for ensuring its completion.

2 **Performance:** Include specific minimum, measurable performance standards in all quantitative measures, and if possible, contingency plans if the performance standards are not met.

3 **Authority:** CEQA does not provide independent authority to carry out mitigation (Section 21004). Measures which are not based on some other authority (i.e., zoning code, tree preservation ordinance, development agreement, impact fee ordinance, subdivision ordinance, etc.) are unenforceable. Monitoring or reporting on their implementation would clearly be problematic.

4 **Continuity and Consistency:** To the extent possible, integrate measures with existing policy and regulatory systems, and inspection or review schedules. Where the mitigation measures are regulatory in nature, for example, design them as conditions of approval within the context of the zoning, subdivision, or other ordinances. Further, mitigation measures must take applicable general plan and specific plan policies into account and not conflict with those policies.

5 **Feasibility:** Above all, measures must be feasible to undertake and complete. Avoid the trap of imposing mitigation measures that are based upon future activities of uncertain outcome. For example, the court in *Sundstrom v. County of Mendocino* (1988) 202 Cal.App.3d 296 overturned the county's negative declaration for a motel project because the county required a study of potential sewage disposal methods rather than actions which would mitigate sewage impacts. A measure that did not mitigate the impact could not be the basis for a finding that impacts were mitigated.

Although infeasibility becomes obvious as the agency attempts to monitor or report on implementation, by that time it is too late. Early in the process of developing mitigation measures, the EIR or negative declaration preparer should consider how implementation of each measure is to be reported on or monitored. This offers a convenient feasibility test.

Reporting

For purposes of simplification, "reporting" may be defined as a written review of mitigation activities that is presented to the approving body by either staff or the project developer. A report may be required at various stages during project implementation and upon completion of the project.

Reporting without detailed monitoring is suited to projects which have readily measurable or quantitative mitigation measures or which already involve regular review. For example, the annual report on general plan status required under Government Code Section 65400 may serve as the reporting program for a city or county general plan as long as it meets the requirements of Section 21081.6. Reporting is also suited to simple projects where a means of reviewing project compliance already exists, such as issuance of building permits and related inspections.

A program for reporting on the implementation of mitigation measures should contain at least the following components:

1 A list of the mitigation measures being reported on.

2 Standards for determining compliance with each mitigation measure and the related condition of approval.

3 A schedule for making one or more reports to the approving agency regarding the level of compliance of the project with the required mitigation measures and related conditions of approval. The program may set out the stages of the project at which each mitigation measure must be implemented (*Christward Ministry v. County of San Diego* (1993) 13 Cal.App.4th 31, 49).

4 A statement which identifies the person or agency, public or private, responsible for reviewing the project and for preparing and making the report to the agency.

These components may be combined in a checklist, matrix, or other representation of the required mitigation measures or revisions, any related conditions of approval, the persons or agencies responsible for ensuring their completion, and the responsible person's or agency representative's affirmation of completion. In some cases, where mitigation will occur in stages during the project, or a mitigation measure contains more than one part, preparing a checklist for each mitigation measure may be an effective approach.

Monitoring

"Monitoring" can be described as a continuous, ongoing process of project oversight. Monitoring, rather than simply reporting, is suited to projects with complex mitigation measures, such as wetlands restoration or archaeological protection, which may exceed the expertise of the local agency to oversee, which are expected to be implemented over a period of time, or which require careful implementation to assure compliance.

A program for monitoring the implementation of mitigation measures should contain at least the following components:

1 A list of the mitigation measures or revisions and related conditions of approval which have been adopted for the project by the agency.

2 A schedule for regularly checking on the project's compliance with the mitigation measures or project revisions and related conditions of approval, including progress toward meeting specified standards, if any. The program may set out the stages of the project at which each mitigation measure must be implemented (*Christward Ministry v. County of San Diego* (1993) 13 Cal.App.4th 31, 49).

3 A means of recording compliance at the time of each check.

4 A statement assigning responsibility for monitoring implementation of the mitigation measures and related conditions of approval to specific persons or agencies, public or private.

5 If monitoring duties are contracted to private individuals or firms, provisions for ensuring that monitoring reflects the independent judgment of the public agency. Such provisions might include requiring the submittal of regular progress reports to the agency, establishing a mechanism for appealing actions of the contractor to the agency for decision, or selection of the contractor by the agency (as opposed to solely by the applicant). Regardless of whether monitoring is performed by the agency or a contractor, the agency retains the ultimate legal responsibility for satisfying the requirements of section 21081.6.

6 Provisions for funding monitoring activities, including the imposition of fees.

7 Provisions for responding to a failure to comply with any required mitigation measure (including conditions of approval). This might include "stop work" authority, permit revocation proceedings, or civil enforcement procedures. This can also include administrative appeal procedures.

Some agencies prepare a separate worksheet describing each mitigation measure and its monitoring requirements. These worksheets are provided to the monitors.

General Approaches to Reporting and Monitoring

Following are two basic approaches which an agency might use:

1 **Jurisdictional Framework:** A standard mitigation monitoring and reporting ordinance or guidelines adopted by the jurisdiction may establish the basis for individually tailored programs. This framework would express the relative roles of involved agencies, staff, and project proponents; establish administrative procedures; lay out a standardized format for reporting or monitoring

programs; establish general timetables; and provide or identify enforcement mechanisms. It may also include standard methods of reporting or monitoring for common mitigation measures.

Standardizing the framework for monitoring or reporting programs promotes consistency and thoroughness in reporting or monitoring activities.

2 **Project Specific:** Develop a new, specially tailored program for each project which triggers Section 21081.6. Such a program may be imposed under the regulatory authority of the agency. Compliance could be required as a condition of project approval or, if a framework ordinance is in place, by reference to that ordinance.

This may be the best way to approach large and complicated development projects which will have special monitoring requirements. It is useful where a standardized program alone may be inadequate to such a situation. This approach may also make sense for small cities and counties which adopt EIRs or mitigated negative declarations infrequently.

Regardless of the method chosen, a draft AB 3180 program should be made available to decisionmakers prior to the formal adoption of either a mitigated negative declaration or the EIR-related findings in Section 21081 (a).

Although not required to do so, some agencies choose to circulate the draft program during consultation on the draft environmental document. This allows public and agency comments on the effectiveness of both mitigation measures and the associated monitoring or reporting program. When circulating a draft, the agency should specify that the program is not final and is subject to change prior to adoption.

Ultimately, the agency must enact a program which reflects the mitigation or project revisions adopted as part of the mitigated negative declaration or subject to findings under Section 21081 (a), regardless of what might have been in the draft documents. If mitigation measures are revised, added or dropped prior to approval of the project, the adopted AB 3180 program must reflect those changes.

Program Administration

Project monitors, whether agency staff or contract personnel, should be given clear written guidance regarding the mitigation measures to be monitored and reported on. This is particularly important in those cases, such as where a large private project is involved, the applicant will perform the actual monitoring. Further, when compliance is achieved, there should be a clear "sign off" by the appropriate agency to ensure that this compliance is documented.

Worksheets offer a convenient means of tracking compliance. Worksheets can be used to express: (1) impact being mitigated; (2) mitigation measure for that impact; (3) implementor; (4) monitor; (5) monitoring requirements; (6) frequency of monitoring or reporting; (7) standards for completion or compliance; and (8) verification of compliance. Some agencies also include a checklist to summarize the monitoring or reporting record.

When the program is a relatively simple one, a checklist rather than a worksheet may suffice to guide inspections, record findings, and certify compliance.

Implementation

In order to maximize efficiency in implementing a monitoring or reporting program, the agency should make every effort to integrate the requirements of the program with its current land use regulations and inspection procedures. This applies whether the program is comprehensive or project specific. As a general rule, the more that mitigation monitoring or reporting programs can utilize existing procedures and requirements, the easier those programs may be to implement. The more that such programs work outside usual procedures, the more expensive and time consuming they may be to implement.

This is not intended to say that a program should monitor or report on zoning or other regulations that are not mitigation measures. While working within the existing regulatory system, the program's scope is limited to mitigation measures resulting from the project's mitigated negative declaration or EIR.

Enforcement

CEQA does not create new authority for agencies to carry out or enforce mitigation measures. Agencies must rely upon the authority conferred by other laws. In the case of a city or county, this would include local zoning, subdivision, and related land use regulations. Typically, enforcement procedures are enacted by ordinance and provide for administrative dispute resolution.

OPR recommends that if a jurisdiction-wide AB 3180 program is adopted, that it contain, or reference other existing regulations which would enforce compliance with the mitigation measures. A jurisdiction-wide program that includes enforcement regulations must be adopted by ordinance in order to be effective. In the absence of a jurisdiction-wide AB 3180 ordinance, individual mitigation monitoring or reporting programs should reference those existing regulations, such as the zoning ordinance, that will provide enforcement.

Cost Recovery

Section 21089 authorizes the lead agency to "charge and collect a reasonable fee from any person proposing a project subject to [CEQA] in order to recover the estimated costs incurred . . . for procedures necessary to comply with [CEQA] on the project." This express authority allows the lead agency to levy fees to cover the costs of mitigation monitoring or reporting programs. The fee is limited to the estimated cost of the program, including the agency's administrative costs. Fees may be used to cover the cost of agency staff, as well as the cost of hiring special monitors or consultants, if needed.

Fees for complex AB 3180 programs, such as those involving long-term monitoring or continuous observation over time, are often charged on the basis of time and work. Flat fees are usually charged when the AB 3180 program involves routine inspections and reporting. In practice, hourly fees and flat fees charged on a sliding scale based on project type or size are equally popular among cities and counties.

Responsible and Trustee Agencies

Lead and responsible agencies may adopt different AB 3180 programs for the same project. This is because the agencies often do not adopt the same set of mitigation measures. In general. when a lead agency approves a project for which an EIR was prepared, it adopts feasible mitigation measures for those portions of the project which it controls or regulates. In turn, the responsible agency adopts only the mitigation measures pertinent to its statutory authority. Under ideal circumstances the programs of the lead and responsible agencies, when taken together, should monitor or report upon all of the adopted mitigation measures and project revisions.

Section 21081.6 does not require agencies to duplicate monitoring programs. Agencies can avoid potential duplication by coordinating their relative roles during the consultation process.

Common Questions Regarding Section 21081.6

A number of issues commonly arise in complying with Section 21081.6. In many instances, there may be a variety of ways to resolve a particular concern; the following discussion is intended to stimulate thinking rather than to represent the only solutions. Here are some responses to commonly asked questions.

Question

What does Section 21081.6 require when an EIR for an earlier project is recertified (or certified with an addendum) and applied to a subsequent project, avoiding the need to prepare a new EIR? What is the requirement when a program EIR is used as the basis for a subsequent EIR, or a later project EIR is tiered on the earlier EIR for a plan, program, or ordinance?

Answer

The monitoring or reporting requirements of Section 21081.6 apply whenever the lead agency makes findings under Section 21081 (a) relative to the mitigation measures or alternatives being required of the project. An AB 3180 program must be adopted which addresses each mitigation measure or project change for which a finding is made. Similarly, if a project is analyzed pursuant to a program EIR or involves tiering, an AB 3180 program would be required for each mitigation measure or project change subject to findings under Section 21081 (a) or required under a mitigated Negative Declaration.

Question

What happens when an agency has a lack of trained personnel to monitor required mitigation measures?

Answer

This does not reduce the agency's responsibility to adopt and carry out an AB 3180 program. Outside consultants may be retained to provide assistance. The cost of the consultant may be borne by the agency or charged to the project proponent.

Question

What is the project planner's role in monitoring/reporting?

Answer

This is left to the discretion of the involved agency. However, the relative roles of personnel should be spelled out in either an individual or jurisdiction-wide program.

Question

What happens when the developer and the agency personnel assigned to monitor a project have differences of opinion over mitigation or monitoring requirements?

Answer

Monitoring personnel must be given sufficient authority to ensure that the mandated mitigation is being implemented. A jurisdictional framework can establish methods of resolving disputes such as administrative appeal.

Question

Have courts added any specific requirements for reporting or monitoring programs beyond those established by statute?

Answer

No. In the two cases to date *(Christward Ministry v. County of San Diego* (1993)

13 Cal.App.4th 31 and *Rio Vista Farm Bureau v. County of Solano* (1992) 5 Cal. App.4th 351), the courts have not expanded the requirements beyond those explicit in statute.

Question

Must a mitigation monitoring or reporting program address conditions of approval that are neither mitigation measures for significant effects nor revisions to the project required pursuant to the environmental document?

Answer

No. An AB 3180 program must address mitigation measures and project revisions required pursuant to the CEQA document. A program is not required to address those conditions of approval that are not related to mitigation. The agency may monitor these other conditions at its own discretion.

Question

Must a draft AB 3180 program be circulated with the draft mitigated negative declaration or draft EIR?

Answer

Nothing in CEQA requires the mitigation monitoring program to be circulated with or included in the EIR (*Christward Ministry v. County of San Diego* (1993) 13 Cal.App.4th 31, 49). Some agencies do circulate drafts in conjunction with a draft EIR. The comments received on the program can be used to fine tune the program prior to adoption. Whether an agency must respond to such comments in the final EIR is unknown. Certainly a case might be made that no response is necessary where the draft program is not an integral part of, but is merely circulated with, the draft EIR. Where the program has been incorporated into the draft EIR, there may be a need to respond to comments on the draft program.

Question

How does AB 3180 apply to actions such as adoption of a general plan or rezoning where there are no conditions of approval, and mitigation is provided by policies or regulations that are incorporated into the general plan or zoning?

Answer

In the case of a general plan, mitigation measures should be integrated directly into the plan's policies (Section 21081.6(b). The AB 3180 program can build upon the annual general plan status report required of each planning agency under Government Code Section 65400. It may not be necessary to monitor or report on site-specific mitigation measures, except to the extent of being included in the policies and standards of the plan and considered in future land use decisions (*Rio Vista Farm Bureau v. County of Solano* (1992) 5 Cal.App. 4th 351, 380).

If some of the mitigation measures for the plan are based on the subsequent adoption of new ordinances or regulations rather than being implemented by general plan policies, progress in enacting those regulations can be monitored or reported on by establishing a timetable for regular status reports to the city council or board of supervisors.

A program of regularly scheduled status reports might also be suitable for monitoring or reporting on the mitigation measures applied to a specific plan or rezoning. Recognize that where the specific plan or rezoning is associated with other actions such as a planned unit development or subdivision, i.e., actions with a finer level of detail than a plan or rezone, status reports may be only one portion of the overall AB 3180 program.

The lead agency is not allowed to *delay* adoption of a program until a subsequent discretionary permit is required. Section 21081.6 clearly mandates adoption of the monitoring or reporting program when the lead agency approves a project. Adoption of a program cannot be put off, nor may the program ignore qualifying mitigation measures or required project revisions.

Question

Should the monitoring or reporting program be adopted as a condition of project approval?

Answer

This depends upon the type of project and the existing regulatory scheme. In some cases, such as where the program is based on a framework ordinance, adopting

the program as a condition of approval may be redundant. In other instances, such as where a project specific program is being imposed, it may make sense to require compliance with the program as a condition of project approval.

Examples of AB 3180 Comprehensive Programs

The City of Encinitas

Encinitas adopted a comprehensive monitoring program in 1989, soon after AB 3180 was enacted. In addition to project-specific monitoring and reporting, the program commits the city to regular review of and reporting on city-wide impacts on development fees, the mitigation measures adopted as part of the general plan, and the progress general plan implementation.

Encinitas' program establishes the following basic provisions:

1 All mitigation measures are to be adopted as conditions of project approval. The conditions will specify a time at which implementation is expected to be complete.

2 Project approvals will be by resolution or formal notice of decision and will identify those mitigation measures being adopted as conditions. Copies of all decisions will be routed to the affected city agencies.

3 The resolution or notice of decision will be attached directly to all permits issued to the project. Mitigation which requires monitoring will be marked on the construction plans for the inspector and contractor. No permits will be issued until the Community Development Department has confirmed that any preconstruction mitigation requirements have been completed.

4 Staff is required to confirm completion of mitigation measures prior to signing off on city forms. Each department is required to confirm the measures which relate to its responsibilities, coordinated by the Community Development Department.

5 The Community Development Department is responsible for any monitoring which occurs after project completion. This includes administering the

review of long-term monitoring plans required of applicants. The program authorizes the Department to collect fees to recover its costs.

6   Each department will maintain the original program files for projects which it approves. Copies of the documentation will be given to each agency imposing mitigation.

A copy of Encinitas' community-wide program is included in the appendix.

Sacramento Metropolitan Air Quality Management District

The district's 1993 "Environmental Review Guidelines" contain standardized requirements for establishing district monitoring and reporting programs. Under these requirements, approval of the project does not become final until the adoption of a mitigation monitoring or reporting program. Compliance with the adopted program is imposed as a condition of project approval. Upon adoption, the program is forwarded to the County Recorder for recordation in order to put the requirements of the program into the chain of title and provide successors to the permittee with substantive notice of the requirements. A "program completion certificate" must be issued by the district before the project will be considered to meet all requirements of a program. This certificate is also recorded, indicating that the requirements of the program have been met.

The district's guidelines require that district programs contain the following standard elements:

1   A statement that the requirements of the program run with the property involved, as opposed to the permittee, and all successive owners.

2   A statement that the permittee must provide a copy of the adopted program to any potential lessee, buyer, or transferee of the involved property.

3   A statement of the responsibilities of the applicant and the district's environmental coordinator, as well as whether other professional expertise is necessary to complete or evaluate of any part of the program.

4   A schedule of tasks or phases which, upon completion, will allow issuance of a program completion certificate.

With regard to compliance, the *Guidelines* requires the applicant to submit regular written progress reports to the district, verified by the district environmental coordinator, and to correct any noncompliance in a timely manner.

The County of Santa Barbara

Santa Barbara County established some of the earliest mitigation monitoring programs in the State, monitoring large projects even before the passage of AB 3180. The County's Environmental Quality Assurance Programs (EQAPs), which establish comprehensive monitoring programs for large-scale environmentally sensitive projects were first developed before AB 3180. An EQAP describes the relative roles of staff, consultants, and project proponents in the monitoring process. It also provides specific performance standards for compliance and the sanctions for failure to meet those standards .

After enactment of AB 3180, the County adopted a "Permit Compliance Procedure Manual" to ensure compliance with mitigation measures and conditions of approval; to initiate county enforcement procedures; establish a systematic and consistent approach to monitoring mitigation measures and conditions of approval; maintain standard mitigation monitoring and reporting requirements, mitigation measures, and conditions of approval across departmental lines; develop a reporting program that provides feedback on the effectiveness of mitigation measures and conditions of approval; and use the feedback from monitoring programs to develop more effective comprehensive planning policies. These procedures also include reporting on the effectiveness of mitigation measures, even though AB 3180 does not require this.

The manual establishes the role and authority of the County's Permit Compliance group to monitor mitigation and conditions of approval. It also establishes detailed administrative procedures for monitoring and compliance activities, including the roles and specific responsibilities of applicable staff, and the use of outside consultants. The County's "DataEase" computerized tracking system continuously tracks

cases from initial application, to approval, to reporting, and to final compliance.

Among other things, Santa Barbara County's procedures provide for the formal exemption of qualifying minor projects from monitoring requirements. The manual includes standard administrative forms as well.

The City of Santa Maria

Santa Maria amended its adopted CEQA procedures to establish a general mitigation monitoring system. Environmental mitigation measures imposed by the city are monitored through the permit and plan check process. Santa Maria's system provides a written record of mitigation without necessitating major changes to city practices.

The key to this system is a checklist that individually identifies the mitigation measures to be monitored for a given project as well as the city department responsible for monitoring each measure. Measures are checked off when they are incorporated into project design and when they have been implemented. Monitoring generally takes place during plan check and project inspection.

On-going measures which will require monitoring over a longer period are also handled through a checklist. Projects are inspected or the developer is required to submit progress reports periodically until implementation is complete. The city makes the final verification of the adequacy of the measure before signing off on its completeness.

Fees are collected from project proponents to pay for monitoring programs. Fees are limited to actual cost, and any excess is refunded to the proponent. If consultants are needed, they are hired by the city and their cost paid by the project proponent. A copy of the city's program is included in the appendix.

South Coast Air Quality Management District

The South Coast AQMD has adopted extensive guidelines covering all aspects of CEQA compliance. The 1993 edition of the District's "CEQA Air Quality Management Handbook" contains detailed advice for establishing monitoring programs.

The District recommends that programs do the following:

1 Communicate mitigation measures and reporting responsibilities to the applicant clearly.

2 Identify the agency which will be responsible for monitoring each mitigation measure.

3 Identify the time frame within which each measure is to be completed and during which monitoring will occur.

4 Establish specific standards or criteria for completion of each mitigation measure.

5 Identify remedial measures which will be imposed in case of non-compliance.

6 Include a mechanism for periodic reporting.

The District's handbook also recommends that monitoring should be linked to a specific point in the development process, such as issuance of a grading permit, occupancy permit, building permit, or construction inspection, and that mitigation measures should be limited to those which are legally enforceable. Suggested enforcement tools include conditions of approval, impact fees, improvement security, development agreements, Memoranda of Understanding, and recorded "Conditions, Covenants, and Restrictions" (CCRs).

Bibliography

Bass, Ronald and Albert Herson, *Successful CEQA Compliance: A Step-by-Step Approach* [predecessor to *CEQA Deskbook*], 1993 edition, Solano Press, Point Arena, California, 1993

Farris, Terry, "The Story of Assembly Bill 3180: Mitigation Monitoring in California," Masters thesis, California State Polytechnic University, Pomona, 1989

Farris, Terry, unpublished mitigation monitoring survey, 1993

"Mitigation Monitoring Programs," Dominic Roques, *Environmental Monitor,* Fall 1993

Remy, Michael H., Tina A. Thomas, et al., *Guide to the Environmental Quality Act,* 1993 edition, Solano Press, Point Arena, California, 1993

Appendix 5

Focusing on Master EIRs
CEQA Technical Advice Series

Source

"Focusing on Master EIRs" (November 1997), CEQA Technical Advice Series. This document is reprinted with permission from the Governor's Office of Planning and Research, 1400 10th Street, Sacramento, California 95814. For additional information please call (916) 322-4245.

Solano Press Books has made every effort to see that no changes have been made to the contents of this state document as a result of reformatting and reprinting. Any omissions or changes to the contrary are entirely the responsibility of Solano Press Books and not the State of California.

Introduction

Assembly Bill 1888 of the 1993 legislative session (Chapter 1130, Stats. 1993) added a new word to the CEQA lexicon: "Master EIR." A Master EIR is intended to provide a detailed environmental review of plans and programs upon which the approval of subsequent related development proposals can be based. A Master EIR must, to the greatest extent feasible, evaluate the cumulative impacts, growth inducing impacts, and irreversible significant effects on the environment of specific, subsequent projects. Pursuant to AB 1888, the review of subsequent projects which have been described in the Master EIR can be limited to the extent that the Master EIR has already reviewed project impacts and set forth mitigation measures (Public Resources Code Section 21156).

The following advisory paper examines the basic requirements for preparing and using a Master EIR at the local government level, including the provisions for "Focused EIRs." This advisory reflects the *CEQA Guidelines;* it is not intended to amend or replace the regulations represented by the *Guidelines.* All code citations refer to the Public Resources Code unless otherwise noted.

This edition of Focusing on Master EIRs reflects statutes enacted by the end of the 1997 Legislative year.

The *Guidelines* now have an extensive discussion of Master EIRs, beginning at Section 15175. As always, users should refer to the most recent Public Resources Code to ensure that they are aware of any subsequent amendments. This advisory is not intended to take the place of advice by legal counsel.

The Master EIR: Another Option

The Master EIR procedure is an alternative to preparing a project EIR, staged EIR or program EIR, or tiering environmental documents for subsequent projects upon earlier EIRs. Although there are similarities between the Master EIR and these other procedures, the Master EIR requirements stand alone.

At its discretion, a Lead Agency may prepare a Master EIR for any one of the following projects:

"(1) A general plan, element, general plan amendment, or specific plan.

"(2) A project that consists of smaller individual projects which will be carried out in phases.

"(3) A rule or regulation which will be implemented by subsequent projects.

"(4) Projects which will be carried out or approved pursuant to a development agreement.

"(5) Public or private projects which will be carried out or approved pursuant to, or in furtherance of, a redevelopment plan.

"(6) A state highway project or mass transit project which will be subject to multiple stages of review or approval."

"(7) A regional transportation plan or congestion management plan.

"(8) A plan proposed by a local agency for the reuse of a federal military base or reservation that has been closed or that is proposed for closure. (Section 21157)

The above list should be viewed as classes of project for which a Master EIR may be prepared. For example, a "general plan" may include a community plan, a "project that consists of smaller individual projects" may include a capital improvement plan or drainage control project, and a "rule or regulation" may include a zoning ordinance or hillside development standards. For the sake of simplicity, throughout this advisory the categories of projects described above will be referred to simply as "plans" or "plans and programs."

Contents of a Master EIR

Section 21157 specifies the minimum contents of a Master EIR (See Appendix II for an outline). In addition to the items otherwise required of all EIRs pursuant to Section 21100, a Master EIR must include the following additional information:

1 **A description of each anticipated subsequent project that is to be considered within the scope of the Master EIR, including information with regard to the kind, size, intensity, and location of the subsequent projects.** The accuracy and completeness of these descriptions is crucial to the use of the Master EIR for

streamlining subsequent project approvals. The descriptions must include, but are not limited to, all of the following:

A **The specific type of project anticipated to be undertaken.** Describe its basic character — i.e., single-family residential subdivision, mixed residential and retail development, commercial power center, warehouse and distribution center, rail transit facility, sewage collections system, road extension, etc. — as well as its necessary entitlements such as a rezoning, subdivision, or precise development plan.

B **The maximum and minimum intensity of any anticipated subsequent project.** For a residential project, this should include the type (i.e., single family, multifamily, mixed use, etc.) and number of dwellings per acre. A commercial project's intensity might be characterized as square feet of area or floor area ratio. With regard to a public works facility, its anticipated capacity and service area can describe its intensity.

Local agencies may be able to increase their ability to rely upon a Master EIR for streamlining subsequent approvals by specifying intensity levels with respect to particular environmental impacts. The Master EIR would effectively establish an envelope of analysis for each such impact. Projects exceeding the envelope would require additional analysis — those within the envelope might not.

C **The anticipated location and alternative locations for any subsequent development projects.** Describe the location and land area (i.e., acreage, square feet) of the subsequent project. Discuss feasible alternative locations that would meet the same public objectives as the subsequent project. For linear facilities such as roads or rail transit, discuss alternative alignments and terminals. This may be done by making reference to

general or community plans where applicable.

D **A capital outlay or capital improvement program, or other scheduling or implementing device that governs the submission and approval of subsequent projects.** Describe how the jurisdiction will ensure that sufficient infrastructure will be available to serve the project, including financing mechanisms if appropriate. For public works projects, describe the mechanism or process of allocating capital funds as well as the availability of funding. Alternatively, the MEIR may explain why particular planning considerations make it impractical to identify any such program or scheduling at the time the MEIR is prepared (CEQA *Guidelines* Section 15176(b)(4)).

CEQA Guidelines Section 15176(d) provides that when an MEIR is certified for a general plan, general plan element, general plan amendment, or specific plan, subsequent projects will be considered to be adequately described for later use of the MEIR when the land use designations and permissible densities and intensities of the project site are identified in the MEIR and the general plan or specific plan. Obviously, this would apply only to projects that are consistent with the plan, element, or amendment for which the MEIR was certified.

2 **A description of the potential impacts of anticipated projects for which there is not sufficient information reasonably available to support a full assessment of potential impacts in the Master EIR.** The Lead Agency is not required to speculate about potential impacts of anticipated projects. It should specify those descriptions which are intended to generally identify and discuss potential impacts for which full information is not available in the Master EIR being prepared. Because full information is not available, inclusion of such descriptions within the Master EIR does not preclude the Focused EIR from being required to discuss the potential

impacts in greater detail and adding discussion of other impacts which had not been identified in the Master EIR. In other words, the scope of a Focused EIR is not limited to the potential impacts described in the Master EIR.

Procedural Requirements

Notice requirements, comment periods, and other procedural requirements for EIRs also apply to a Master EIR. Beyond that, the Lead Agency should specify in the document and in related notices that the document being prepared, circulated, and considered is a Master EIR.

While the procedures are identical, the greater level of detail which distinguishes a Master EIR from other subsequent review provisions such as a program EIR requires the Lead Agency to pay particular attention to maintaining strict consistency between the contents of the Master EIR and the plan or person which is the subject of the Master EIR. There is less assurance that the Master EIR can be used for later projects where such consistency is lacking.

Here are two strategies for achieving consistency. They are by no means the only ones.

Concurrent Action: Run the period for review and comment on the draft Master EIR concurrently with hearings on the draft plan. Close both the taking of public comment and testimony on the plan and the review period for the draft at the same time. Incorporate any changes made to the draft plan into the Master EIR and vice versa. Reconvene to act on both the final plan and the Master EIR. Certify the final Master EIR and adopt the plan at the same meeting.

Sequential Action: Wait to begin circulating the draft Master EIR until public testimony has been completed on the draft plan or program. Close the taking of public testimony on the plan. Circulate the draft Master EIR for comment. At the end of the comment period and prior to certification of the final Master EIR, reconvene to revise the draft plan or program to conform to changes made in the draft Master

EIR. Limit revisions to those necessary to achieve conformity. Certify the final Master EIR and adopt the plan or program at the same meeting.

Fee

Given the required level of detail, in most cases a Master EIR can be expected to be more expensive to prepare than a program or staged EIR. To help counter the cost of a Master EIR, AB 1888 augments CEQA's fee authority by specifically enabling a Lead Agency to develop and implement a Master EIR fee program (Section 21157, subdivision (c)). A city or county could, for example, establish a fee program whereunder participating developers would have their projects specifically identified in a Master EIR. The city or county would receive contributions toward completing a Master EIR; developers would benefit from streamlined environmental review for their projects.

Reevaluation

For the first five years after certification, a Master EIR may be utilized for subsequent projects without having to reevaluate its adequacy (Section 21157.6). During this period, the agency's review of subsequent projects is limited to whether any new impacts will occur and whether the proposal was identified in the Master EIR.

If an application for a subsequent project is filed more than five years from certification of the Master EIR, **or** if a project has been approved which was not described in and potentially affects the adequacy of the Master EIR, then the agency must, prior to applying the Master EIR to the subsequent project, review the adequacy of the Master EIR and **either**:

1   Make written findings that "no substantial changes have occurred with respect to the circumstances under which the [Master EIR] was certified or that no new information, which was not known and could not have been known at the time that the [Master EIR] was certified has become available." In the recent *Laurel Heights* decision, the California Supreme Court noted that the *CEQA Guidelines* "generally define 'new information' as information which shows that the

project will have new or more severe 'significant effects' on the environment not disclosed in the prior EIR." (*Laurel Heights Improvement Association v. Regents of the University of California* (1993) 6 Cal.4th 1112, citing *Guidelines* Section 15162(a)(3)) The findings should be supported by substantial evidence in the record.

2   Certify "a subsequent or supplemental EIR which has been either incorporated into the previously certified [Master EIR], or references any deletions, additions, or other modifications to the previously certified [Master EIR]." A subsequent or supplemental EIR would be required when the provisions of Section 21166 apply.

To maximize the benefits of a Master EIR, the lead agency could establish a program for keeping track of projects which are approved within the area for which the MEIR was certified (i.e., the potential impacts of those projects, whether they are within the scope of the MEIR, and whether a focused EIR, negative declaration, or other environmental document is prepared) and monitoring changes in the plan or program or other factors that would trigger the need for a subsequent or supplemental EIR. One way to do this is to prepare an annual report on the status of the plan or program.

Use With Subsequent Projects

Once a Master EIR has been certified, a subsequent project may avoid the need for a further EIR or Negative Declaration when the Lead Agency finds that the project was described in the Master EIR as being within its scope (Section 21157.1, *Guidelines* Section 15177). The Lead Agency for the subsequent project must have been either the Lead Agency for the Master EIR or a Responsible Agency identified in the Master EIR.

Initial Study

When a later development proposal is received, the Lead Agency must prepare an initial study to analyze both of the following:

1   Whether that proposal may cause any additional significant effect on the

environment not examined in the Master EIR; and

2   Whether the proposal is within the scope of the Master EIR.

A project will be considered "within the scope" of the Master EIR if it is described within that document and will:

1   Have no additional significant effect on the environment that was not identified in the Master EIR; and

2   Require no new or additional mitigation measures or alternatives. (Section 21157.1(c))

When the Lead Agency for the proposal is able to make a written finding, based on the initial study, that the subsequent project is within the scope of the project covered by the Master EIR (i.e., the plan or program), no further EIR or Negative Declaration is required. Pursuant to Section 15177 of the *CEQA Guidelines,* "[w]hether a subsequent project is within the scope of the Master EIR is a question of fact to be determined by the lead agency." This finding must be supported by substantial evidence in the record.

Prior to carrying out the subsequent project on the basis of the Master EIR, the Lead Agency must:

1   Adopt the above finding;

2   Incorporate all feasible mitigation measures or feasible alternatives appropriate to the project, as set forth in the Master EIR; and

3   Provide public notice pursuant to Section 21092 (*Guidelines* Section 15087) that it intends to use the Master EIR for the project.

When the project is approved, the Lead Agency must file a Notice of Determination. The agency is not required to make findings under Section 15091.

Subsequent Projects Outside the Scope of the MEIR

When a Lead Agency cannot find that the project is within the scope of the MEIR, it must prepare either a mitigated Negative Declaration or an EIR for the subsequent project. Whether the "fair argument" standard or the "substantial evidence" standard applies in this situation is uncertain. The provisions for preparation of a later

EIR indicate that an EIR or Focused EIR is required if the subsequent project "may have a significant effect on the environment" (Section 21157.5(b)). This language is identical to the statutory language which is the basis for court decisions establishing the "fair argument" standard (see Sections 21080 and 21151). That standard provides that an EIR must be prepared whenever it can be fairly argued on the basis of substantial evidence that a significant adverse effect may result, even when other evidence exists to the contrary. A Negative Declaration is prepared when no substantial evidence exists, including situations when potentially significant effects identified in the initial study can be avoided or mitigated by revisions in the project.

However, in the 1993 *Laurel Heights* decision, the California Supreme Court indicated that the fair argument standard derived from both the statutory language and policies underlying Section 21151, and for this reason, applies "only to the decision whether to prepare an original EIR or a negative declaration." (*Laurel Heights Improvement Association v. Regents of the University of California, supra*) Applied here, this may mean that fair argument does not apply once a Master EIR has been prepared if the Master EIR can be construed as the "original EIR" for a subsequent project. In other words, if the project is within the scope of the Master EIR.

At the same time, Section 21157.5 neither references nor closely resembles Section 21166 which establishes the criteria for determining whether to prepare a subsequent or supplemental EIR. Determinations pursuant to Section 21166 are subject to the "substantial evidence" standard; meaning that the decision of the lead agency not to prepare an EIR will be upheld when it is supported by substantial evidence, regardless of the existence of a fair argument to the contrary. The language of the statute does not clearly establish that the substantial evidence test applies to Section 21157.5.

Given this statutory uncertainty, OPR recommends that agencies adopt the cautious practice of applying the fair argument standard to the determination of whether a Negative Declaration or EIR, including a mitigated Negative Declaration or a Focused EIR, is required for a subsequent project, which is not within the scope of the Master EIR.

Projects Identified in the Master EIR

The *CEQA Guidelines* and the statute itself create two broad categories for the subsequent projects which are not within the scope of the Master EIR. The first category consists of projects which are outside the scope, but which nonetheless were identified in the MEIR and whose cumulative impacts, growth-inducing impacts and irreversible significant effects were adequately analyzed in the MEIR. These projects may be addressed by preparing either a mitigated Negative Declaration or a Focused EIR, depending upon whether their possible impacts can be fully mitigated or not.

Guidelines Section 15178(b) requires that a mitigated Negative Declaration be prepared for any proposed subsequent project if both the following occur:

1 The initial study identifies potentially new or additional significant environmental effects that were not analyzed in the Master EIR, and

2 Feasible mitigation measures or alternatives will be incorporated into the subsequent project before the mitigated Negative Declaration is released for public review, in order to avoid or mitigate potential effects to a level of insignificance.

Notice requirements, comment periods, and other procedures for preparation and review of a mitigated Negative Declaration prepared under Section 15178 are the same as for any other Negative Declaration. However, the findings made by the Lead Agency upon adoption of the mitigated Negative Declaration should specifically integrate items (1) and (2) above.

Guidelines Section 15178(c) also requires that if there is substantial evidence in light of the whole record that the subsequent project may have a significant effect on the environment, and a mitigated Negative Declaration cannot be prepared, the Lead Agency must prepare a Focused EIR. The requirements for Focused EIRs are discussed in detail in the next chapter.

Projects Not Identified in the Master EIR

Projects that were not identified in the Master EIR are subject to the usual CEQA process (as described under *CEQA Guidelines* Sections 15080–15096) and are ineligible for the limited environmental review available under the MEIR (see *CEQA Guidelines* Section 15178(e)). Such projects may require the preparation of a Negative Declaration, a mitigated Negative Declaration, or an EIR, depending upon the circumstances. To the extent feasible, the lead agency should tier the analysis of such projects upon the Master EIR.

The lead agency should keep track of all such projects and whether their approval may affect the adequacy of the Master EIR. As discussed earlier, the use of a Master EIR for projects that are identified therein may be called into question if the approval of a project that was not identified in the MEIR might affect its adequacy (*CEQA Guidelines* Section 15179).

In order to keep its Master EIR viable, when an EIR is prepared for a project that was not identified in the Master EIR, the lead agency should undertake to incorporate that EIR into the Master EIR whenever feasible. Neither CEQA nor the *CEQA Guidelines* delineate the procedure for doing this. One approach might be to use the project EIR as the basis for a subsequent EIR to be prepared for the next project that will be considered under the Master EIR.

About Focused EIRs

Prior to the enactment of AB 1888, the term "Focused EIR" was neither defined in CEQA nor in the *CEQA Guidelines*. Nonetheless, it has been commonly used to describe subsequent EIRs, or EIRs prepared subsequent to a program EIR where analysis was narrowed to those effects resulting from the subsequent project. Now, Section 21158 explicitly defines a Focused EIR as "an environmental impact report on a subsequent project identified in a master environmental impact report." Although program EIRs and other procedures for *focusing* EIRs (and environmental analysis) continue in full force, their product may no longer properly be termed a "Focused EIR."

Finding

A Focused EIR is used when, after preparation of an initial study for a subsequent project under the Master EIR, the Lead Agency specifically finds that the Master EIR's analyses of cumulative impacts, growth inducing impacts, and irreversible significant effects are adequate for the subsequent project. The finding and supporting evidence should be included in the Focused EIR (see Appendix 1). Absent this finding, a standard EIR would be required.

Limit on Analysis

A Focused EIR must incorporate by reference the Master EIR. Pursuant to *CEQA Guidelines* Section 15178(c), the analysis contained in a Focused EIR is limited to the following:

1 The subsequent project's "additional significant environmental effects" (i.e., those project-specific effects on the environment which were not addressed as significant in the Master EIR).

2 Any new or additional mitigation measures or alternatives that were not identified and analyzed by the Master EIR.

3 Any significant effects on the environment where substantial new or additional information shows that the adverse environmental effect may be more significant than was described in the Master EIR. The substantial new or additional information shows that mitigation measures or alternatives identified in the Master EIR, which were previously determined to be infeasible, are feasible and will avoid or reduce the significant effects on the environment of the subsequent project to a level of insignificance.

A Focused EIR need not examine those significant environmental effects which the lead agency, prior to releasing the draft Focused EIR for review, finds, on the basis of the initial study, related documents, and commitments from the project proponent, were either:

1 Examined at a sufficient level of detail in the Master EIR to enable those significant effects to be mitigated or avoided by specific revisions to the project, the imposition of conditions of approval, or by other means in connection with the approval of the subsequent project.

2 Mitigated or avoided as a result of mitigation measures identified in the Master EIR which the lead agency will require as part of the approval of the subsequent project. Mitigation or avoidance is the responsibility of and within the jurisdiction of another public agency and is, or can and should be, undertaken by that agency.

The draft Focused EIR must include these relevant findings of exception when it is released for review.

Note that effects for which MEIR findings were previously made pursuant to *CEQA Guidelines* Section 15091(a)(3) are not included in the above exception. Findings under paragraph (3) relate to those significant effects identified in the Master EIR for which mitigation measures or alternatives were found to be infeasible due to specific economic, social, or other considerations. The conspicuous absence of any reference to paragraph (3) seems to indicate that these significant unavoidable effects must be addressed in the Focused EIR. OPR recommends that unmitigated effects be examined in the context of the limitations on analysis described above.

Focused EIRs for Specified Projects

Section 21158.5 and *CEQA Guidelines* Section 15179.5 authorizes a streamlined review process for selected projects through use of Focused EIRs. Where a project consists of a multi-family residential development of not more than 100 dwelling units, or a residential and commercial or retail mixed-use development of not more than 100,000 square feet in area which complies with all the following, a Focused EIR shall be prepared, notwithstanding that the project was not identified in a Master EIR. In order to qualify to use this provision, a Lead Agency must make the following findings regarding the project:

1 The project is consistent with a general plan, specific plan, community plan, or zoning ordinance for which an EIR was prepared within five years of the certification of the Focused EIR.

2 The project is not within the scope of the Master EIR, a Negative Declaration or mitigated Negative Declaration cannot be prepared, and neither *Guidelines* Sections 15162 nor 15163 require a subsequent EIR.

3 The parcel on which the project is to be developed meets one or more of the following conditions:

   A It is surrounded by immediately contiguous urban development.

   B It has been previously developed with urban uses.

   C It is within one-half mile of an existing rail transit station.

The scope of a Focused EIR prepared under Section 21158.5 is limited to the following:

1 A discussion of potentially significant environmental effects specific to the project.

2 A discussion of significant effects which substantial new information shows will be more significant than described in the previous EIR.

Although the above bears passing resemblance to the seldom-used process for streamlining review of later projects under a general plan, specific plan, or zoning EIR pursuant to Section 21083.3, the two operate independently. Section 21083.3 provides that the application of CEQA to any project that is consistent with zoning, a community plan, or general plan for which an EIR was certified is limited to "those effects on the environment which are peculiar to the parcel or to the project and which were not addressed as significant effects in the prior environmental impact report, or which substantial new information shows will be more significant than described in the prior environmental impact report." Application of Section 21158.5 and *Guidelines* Section 15179.5 are qualified as noted above.

Master EIR Updates

The five year presumption of adequacy afforded a Master EIR can be periodically renewed as provided in *Guidelines*

Section 15179. This renewal may take either of two forms: (1) a finding that no substantial changes have occurred with respect to the circumstances under which the Master EIR was certified or that no new information has become available since certification of the Master EIR; or (2) preparation and certification of a subsequent or supplemental EIR that is incorporated into the previously certified MEIR or references any deletions, additions or other modifications to the MEIR. The findings under the first option should hew closely to *CEQA Guidelines* Section 15162 which describes the situations under which a subsequent or supplemental EIR need not be prepared.

If, during the five year period (and, presumably, during renewed periods), projects are approved which were not identified in the certified Master EIR and which may affect the adequacy of the Master EIR relative to subsequent projects, then the Lead Agency must review the adequacy of the Master EIR and make the findings described above before it can apply the Master EIR to subsequent projects.

The resulting updated Master EIR can then be applied to the review of subsequent projects that are described as being within its scope.

Practical Considerations

When deciding whether to prepare a Master EIR, the Lead Agency should compare the advantages and disadvantages of a Master EIR to those of other CEQA options such as tiering or a program EIR. A project suitable for a Master EIR project would have the following characteristics:

1   The plan or program for which the Master EIR is prepared will be stable for the next few years, i.e., no substantial changes are expected to occur in the plan or program which will not have been identified or discussed in the Master EIR.

2   Subsequent actions under the plan or program are well-known at the time the Master EIR is prepared and can be comprehensively described pursuant to *Guidelines* Section 15176(b).

3   The significant environmental effects of subsequent actions are sufficiently known at the time of preparing the Master EIR that they may be fully described and analyzed in that document, and measures recommended to minimize or avoid them.

4   The timetable for undertaking the project and subsequent related actions is 5 years or less, and provision is made for regular review of the Master EIR's adequacy in light of subsequent projects not described in the Master EIR.

Infrastructure or capital facilities plans, small-scale specific plans, planned unit development rezoning projects, and transit line extensions are among the projects which may be prime for Master EIRs. Section 21157(a)(1) also specifically authorizes the use of a Master EIR for a general plan. A general plan Master EIR makes practical sense where the city is largely built out, has mechanisms in place which enable it to demonstrate that later projects are "within the scope" of the Master EIR, and otherwise anticipates very little activity that would result in plan amendments.

On the other hand, Master EIRs may offer no advantages when the project is adoption of a county general plan or a large-scale specific plan. In those situations, a program EIR may be preferable. The fact that specific subsequent projects will generally arise from private applications yet to be submitted means that the county preparing the Master EIR may not know the details of subsequent projects, particularly plan amendments, at the time the document is prepared.

Once the Lead Agency has made the decision to prepare a Master EIR, it may also take the following extra steps over what would normally be involved with an EIR:

1   Take care that the Master EIR precisely matches the plan or program being approved. This means analyzing in the Master EIR all last minute changes made to the plan or program before its final approval.

2   List the known subsequent development projects which the Master EIR

has analyzed and which are to be within its scope. This list may be included in the Master EIR's project description or in an appendix. (As discussed earlier, a list is not required where a general plan or specific plan identifies land uses and the intensity and density of allowable development.)

3   Establish administrative criteria which describe when a subsequent project will be outside the scope of the Master EIR. The criteria may include thresholds which define the scope of the Master EIR's analyses of cumulative impacts, growth inducing impacts, and irreversible significant effects. For example, what future traffic levels of service were analyzed, what level of sewer service, what level of development intensity?

If the community has adopted thresholds of significance as part of their local *CEQA Guidelines* or process, they should take care to integrate the criteria related to the Master EIR into these thresholds. If the community has not adopted thresholds, they may want to consider adopting the Master EIR criteria as such.

4   Regularly review or monitor the specific assumptions made during preparation of the Master EIR (i.e., traffic levels of service, air quality standards, etc.) for changes. This is intended to inform the Lead Agency of changes which may require preparation of a subsequent or supplemental EIR to update the Master EIR pursuant to Section 21157.6 and *Guidelines* Section 15179. For example, a change in the regional air quality standards may necessitate a reassessment of the air quality discussion in the Master EIR. Keeping track of changing circumstances and making corrections will help ensure that the Master EIR will remain viable during its five year term and beyond.

Bibliography

Alling, Curtis, "Master EIR Practice Pointers," January 1994, Dames and Moore, Sacramento, California

Bass, Ronald E. and Herson, Albert I., *Successful CEQA Compliance: A Step-by-Step Approach* [predecessor to *CEQA Deskbook*], 3rd ed., 1994, Solano Press, Point Arena, California

Curtin, Daniel J. Jr. and Danforth, Ann R., "CEQA Legislation: Streamlining—Or Just More Confusion," *Los Angeles Daily Journal*

"Environmental Update," October 1993, Jones and Stokes Associates, Sacramento, California

Herson, Albert I., "1993 CEQA Amendments: Good Start, But More Streamlining Needed," *California Environmental Law Reporter,* Volume 1993, No. 12, pg. 425, Matthew Bender and Co., Inc., Conklin, New York

"Master Environmental Impact Report," Analysis by Remy and Thomas, Sacramento, California

Thomas, Tina, "Legislature Authorizes Master Environmental Impact Reports to Reduce Redundant Environmental Review," *Land Use and Environment Forum,* Winter 1994, pg. 41, California Education of the Bar, Berkeley, California

Zischke, Michael H., "CEQA 1993: The 1993 California Environmental Quality Act and Reform Legislation," presentation for the 1993 American Planning Association Legislation Workshops, December 1993, Landels, Ripley, and Diamond, San Francisco, California

Appendix 1

Findings Requirements

The following table identifies the CEQA findings requirements for actions relating to Master EIRs. Suggested language is included for findings which are peculiar to actions under the Master EIR statute. Readers should feel free to adapt these brief suggestions to their own situations. No language is suggested for common findings requirements such as *CEQA Guidelines* Section 15091.

As always, findings must be based upon substantial evidence in the record and be sufficient to bridge the gap between the evidence available and the conclusions reached. All statutory references are to the *CEQA Guidelines*, unless otherwise noted.

Certifying a Master EIR

- Section 15091 findings. (In writing these, pay particular attention to paragraphs (1) and (2) of subdivision (a) and how they would apply to subsequent proj-

ects. If possible, findings under paragraph (1) of subdivision (a) should identify the mitigation measures to be applied to future projects.)

- Section 15093 findings.

Findings When a Subsequent Project Is Adequately Addressed in the MEIR

- Section 15177 finding: Based upon the initial study, the subsequent project is within the scope of the project covered by the MEIR. Specifically, the proposed project will have no additional significant effect, as defined by subdivision (b) of Section 21158 of the Public Resources Code, on the environment that was not identified in the Master EIR and requires no new or additional mitigation measures or alternatives in order to avoid or mitigate a significant environmental effect.

- Section 15093 findings.

- No Section 15091 findings are required.

Adopting a Mitigated Negative Declaration for a Subsequent Project

- Sections 21080(c)(2) and 21157.5 combined findings:

  1 The initial study has identified potentially new or additional significant environmental effects that were not analyzed in the Master EIR, but feasible mitigation measures or alternatives will be incorporated to revise the proposed subsequent project before the Negative Declaration is released for public review in order to avoid or mitigate the identified effects to a point where clearly no significant effects would occur.

  2 There is no substantial evidence before the agency that the subsequent project, as revised, may have a significant effect on the environment.

  3 The analyses of cumulative impacts, growth inducing impacts, and irreversible significant effects on the environment contained in the Master EIR are adequate for this subsequent project.

Certifying a Focused EIR for a Subsequent Project

- Section 15178 findings:

  1 The subsequent project is identified in the Master EIR, but is not "within the scope" of the MEIR.

  2 The analyses of cumulative impacts, growth inducing impacts, and irreversible significant effects on the environment contained in the Master EIR are adequate for this subsequent project.

- Section 15178(c) findings to avoid examining specific significant effects previously examined in the Master EIR:

  1 The effect is mitigated or avoided pursuant to paragraph (1) of subdivision (a) of Section 15091 (a finding made for the Master EIR) as a result of mitigation measures identified in the Master EIR which will be required as part of approval of the subsequent project.

  2 The effect is examined in sufficient detail in the Master EIR to enable those significant effects to be mitigated or avoided by specific revisions to the project, the imposition of conditions, or by other means in connection with approval of the subsequent project.

  3 The effect is not the responsibility of the Lead Agency, pursuant to paragraph (2) of subdivision (a) of Section 15091 (a finding made for the Master EIR).

- Section 15091 findings.

- Section 15093 findings.

Certifying an EIR for a Subsequent Project

- Section 15091 findings.

- Section 15093 findings.

Extending the Time of Adequacy of a Master EIR

- Section 15079 findings (one or more must be made):

  1 No substantial changes have occurred with respect to the circumstances under which the Master EIR was certified.

  2 No new information that was not known and could not have been known at the time the Master EIR was certified has become available.

  3 A certified subsequent or supplemental EIR has either been incorporated into the previously certified Master EIR, or references any deletions, additions, or other modifications to the previously certified Master EIR.

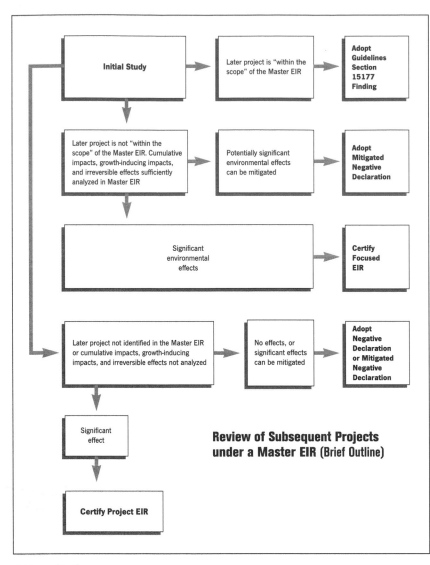

Review of Subsequent Projects under a Master EIR (Brief Outline)

Initial Study

Later project is "within the scope" of the Master EIR → Adopt Guidelines Section 15177 Finding

Later project is not "within the scope" of the Master EIR. Cumulative impacts, growth-inducing impacts, and irreversible effects sufficiently analyzed in Master EIR → Potentially significant environmental effects can be mitigated → Adopt Mitigated Negative Declaration

Significant environmental effects → Certify Focused EIR

Later project not identified in the Master EIR or cumulative impacts, growth-inducing impacts, and irreversible effects not analyzed → No effects, or significant effects can be mitigated → Adopt Negative Declaration or Mitigated Negative Declaration

Significant effect → Certify Project EIR

Appendix 2

Appendix 3

Master EIR Contents

This brief outline illustrates the basic contents of a Master EIR. Those requirements common to all EIRs are listed in plain type. The requirements peculiar to Master EIRs are in italic type.

TABLE OF CONTENTS

SUMMARY

PROJECT DESCRIPTION

Description of Each Subsequent Project to be Discussed within the Scope of the Master EIR

ENVIRONMENTAL SETTING

ENVIRONMENTAL IMPACTS

Significant Adverse Environmental Effects

Significant Effects of Subsequent Projects

Potential Effects of Subsequent Projects for Which Sufficient Information is Lacking for Full Assessment

Cumulative Impacts

Cumulative Impacts Relating to Subsequent Projects

Significant Effects Which Cannot Be Avoided

Mitigation Measures

Measures for Subsequent Projects

Project Alternatives

Alternatives to Subsequent Projects

Relationship Between Short-term Uses and Long-term Productivity

Significant Irreversible Environmental Changes

Irreversible Changes Relating to Subsequent Projects

Growth Inducing Impact

Growth Inducing Impacts Relating to Subsequent Projects

EFFECTS NOT FOUND TO BE SIGNIFICANT

ORGANIZATIONS AND PERSONS CONSULTED

Appendix 6

CEQA and Archaeological Resources
CEQA Technical Advice Series

Source

"CEQA and Archaeological Resources" (April 1994), CEQA Technical Advice Series. This document is reprinted with permission from the Governor's Office of Planning and Research, 1400 10th Street, Sacramento, California 95814. For additional information please call (916) 322-4245.

CEQA and Archaeological Resources

The California Environmental Quality Act (Public Resources Code Sections 21000, et seq.) requires that before approving most discretionary projects the Lead Agency must identify and examine the significant adverse environmental effects which may result from that project. Where a project may adversely affect a unique archaeological resource, Section 21083.2 of the Act requires that the Lead Agency treat that effect as a significant environmental effect and prepare an environmental impact report (EIR). When an archaeological resource is listed in or eligible to be listed in the California Register of Historical Resources, Section 21084.1 requires that any substantial adverse effect to that resource be considered a significant environmental effect.

The following advisory memo reviews the requirements of Public Resources Code Sections 21083.2 and 21084.1, and offers cities and counties suggestions for means of complying with those requirements. This memo is supplemental to, but does not supercede or amend the *CEQA Guidelines*. Unlike the *Guidelines* it is not a regulation. All code citations reference the Public Resources Code unless otherwise noted.

Sections 21083.2 and 21084.1

CEQA and the CEQA Guidelines

The California Environmental Quality Act (CEQA) establishes statutory requirements for the formal review and analysis of projects. The *CEQA Guidelines* have been adopted by the State to guide public agencies in implementing CEQA. CEQA's requirements for addressing impacts on archaeological resources are discussed in detail under Sections 21083.2 and 21084.1 (see Appendix 1 of this paper). Appendix K of the *Guidelines* (or Supplementary Document J of the 1992 printing of the *Guidelines*) offers a suggested method for implementing the requirements of Section 21083.2.

Sections 21083.2 and 21084.1 operate independently to ensure that potential effects on archaeological resources are considered as part of a project's environmental analysis. The latter applies to archaeological sites which are listed on or eligible for listing on the California Register, the former applies to other "unique" archaeological resources. Either of these benchmarks may indicate that a proposal may have a potential adverse effect on archaeological resources.

Initial Study

An initial study must be prepared for projects which are not exempt from CEQA in order to guide the decision whether to prepare either a Negative Declaration or EIR (*Guidelines* Section 15063). The original determination whether to prepare a Negative Declaration or an EIR is subject to the "fair argument" test (*Laurel Heights Improvement Assoc. v. U.C. Regents* (1993) 47 Cal.3d 376). In other words, if a fair argument can be raised on the basis of "substantial evidence" in the record that the project may have a significant adverse environmental impact, in this case that unique archaeological resources or archaeological sites that are historical resources would be affected, then an EIR is required even if evidence also exists to the contrary.

Section 21083.2 explicitly requires that the initial study examine whether the project may have a significant adverse effect on "unique archaeological resources." Pursuant to Part (g) of that section, a unique archaeological resource is:

"an archaeological artifact, object, or site, about which it can be *clearly demonstrated* that, without merely adding to the current body of knowledge, there is a high probability that it meets any of the following criteria:

"(1) Contains information needed to answer important scientific research questions and there is a demonstrable public interest in that information.

"(2) Has a special and particular quality such as being the oldest of its type or the best available example of its type.

"(3) Is directly associated with a scientifically recognized important prehistoric or historic event or person." [emphasis added]

In the one court case to address this definition, the Court of Appeal applied it strictly in finding that "[a]n archaeological artifact, object, or site which does not meet these criteria is a nonunique archaeological resource and 'need be given no further consideration, other than the simple recording of its existence by the lead agency if it so elects.'" (*Topanga Association for a Scenic Community v. County of Los Angeles* (1989) 214 Cal.App.3d 1348)

Appendix K of the *Guidelines* takes a broader approach, using the term "important" in place of "unique." Appendix K goes beyond Section 21083.2, suggesting additional criteria to guide the Lead Agency in making a determination of uniqueness. These include that the resource be at least 100 years old and possess "substantial stratigraphic integrity" (i.e., is substantially undisturbed); and the resource involves "important" research questions that historical research has shown can be answered only with archaeological methods.

Section 21084.1 requires an initial study to treat any substantial adverse change in the significance of a historical resource listed in or eligible to be listed in the California Register as a significant effect on the environment. The definition of "historical resource" includes archaeological resources listed in or formally determined eligible for listing in the California Register and, by reference, the National Register of Historic Places, California Historical Landmarks, Points of Historical Interest, and local registers (Sections 5020.1(j) and 5024.1).

If such an effect may occur, the Lead Agency must prepare an EIR. If there is no substantial evidence in the record for the occurrence of such effect, or if the potential effect can be reduced to a level of insignificance through project revisions, a Negative Declaration or mitigated Negative Declaration can be adopted. The Lead Agency must note the source or content of the data relied upon in preparing the initial study (*Sundstrom v. County of Mendocino* (1988) 202 Cal. App.3d 296). Supporting information may include specific studies, or references to previous environmental documents or other information sources. A thorough, referenced initial study is a crucial part of the record

supporting the Lead Agency's determination to prepare a Negative Declaration or mitigated Negative Declaration. Bear in mind, of course, that an initial study is not required to provide the full-blown analysis of a complete EIR (*Leonoff v. Monterey County Board of Supervisors* (1990) 222 Cal.App.3d 1337).

Pursuant to Sections 21083.2 and 21084.1, neither an EIR nor a Negative Declaration is required for a project which would impact only non-unique archaeological resources or archaeological sites that are not considered "historical resources" pursuant to Section 5020.1(j). Furthermore, an EIR that is required as a consequence of other significant environmental effects is not required to address non-unique archaeological resources.

Site Evaluation

The effectiveness of the initial study depends largely upon an accurate evaluation of the site's potential archaeological significance. This means determining whether there is present a unique archaeological resource (Section 21083.2) or a historical resource that is an archaeological resource (Section 21084.1).

The "unique" criterion established by Section 21083.1 is narrower and more restrictive than general, professionally accepted criteria by which the significance of an archaeological site would be evaluated. Establishing that a site is or is not "unique" may involve extensive research, analysis, field testing, and excavation. In practice, ascertaining that a significant archaeological site is not unique and therefore not subject to CEQA may involve more research, analysis, and testing than would be necessary if the resource were a significant historical resource and mitigated. This is particularly true when avoidance is a feasible alternative.

A record search to determine whether any previously identified resources exist on site is the first step in determining whether there may be archaeological resources present. Often, when the applicant submits environmental information with their project the Lead Agency requires that this include the results of a record search at the applicable California Historical Resources File System Information Center (formerly

the Archaeological Information Centers). These 11 regional centers maintain the State Archaeological Inventory as part of the Historical Resources File System. This system maintains current information on recorded archaeological sites, as well as resources listed on the California Register of Historic Resources. Alternatively, the Lead Agency itself may undertake this record search during the initial study phase of project review.

Additional sources of information on the possible presence and value of archaeological resources are colleges and universities with archaeology departments, the local historical or archaeological society, local Native American groups, or appropriate archives and repositories. Also, the Native American Heritage Commission maintains a file of Sacred Lands which contain information unavailable elsewhere. The Commission can be contacted at:

915 Capitol Mall, Room 364
Sacramento, CA 95814
(916) 653-4082

Some cities and counties have mapped areas of known archaeological sensitivity. These maps may be used as general indicators of the presence of archaeological resources, but are usually not detailed enough or current enough to be definitive. Sensitivity maps do not substitute for a record search, or archaeological field survey where necessary.

If the project area is expected to contain unique archaeological sites or historical resources that are archaeological resources, the Lead Agency should require a field survey by a qualified professional archaeologist in order to assess the significance of the resource. Certification by the Society of Professional Archaeologists (SOPA) is one indicator that an archaeologist is qualified. The State of California does not license or certify archaeologists.

Where field survey results are inconclusive, a test excavation of some type may be necessary to determine whether unique, subsurface components exist. When a unique resource is found, the archaeologist should recommend means of avoiding or mitigating impacts, including excavation plans if necessary. In such cases, the archaeologist's report should also estimate the cost of mitigation.

In order to protect the sites from unauthorized excavation, looting, or vandalism, the Lead Agency should not publicize the location of known archaeological resources beyond what is necessary. Records in the Information Centers are exempt from the California Public Records Act (Government Code Section 6250 et seq.). Government Code Section 6254.19 states that "nothing in this chapter requires disclosure of records that relate to archaeological sites information maintained by the Department of Parks and Recreation, the State Historical Resources Commission, or the State Lands Commission." Along this line, Government Code Section 6254 explicitly authorizes public agencies to withhold information from the public relating to "Native American graves, cemeteries, and sacred places maintained by the Native American Heritage Commission."

The State Office of Historic Preservation can provide additional assistance regarding archaeological resources. The Office can be contacted at:

1416 Ninth Street
Sacramento, CA 95814
(916) 653-6624

For examples of local guidelines for researching archaeological data, see Appendix 4. Appendix 3 lists the Historical Resources File System Information Centers across the State.

Mitigation

CEQA requires the Lead Agency to examine and impose mitigation measures or feasible project alternatives that would avoid or minimize any impacts or potential impacts identified in an EIR or a mitigated Negative Declaration.

When archaeological resources are involved, avoidance, or preservation in an undisturbed state is the preferable course of action. Section 21083.2 provides that preservation methods may include:

1 Planning construction to avoid archaeological sites.

2 Deeding sites into permanent conservation easements.

3 Capping or covering sites with a layer of soil before building on the sites.

4 Planning parks, greenspace, or other open space to incorporate archaeological sites.

Actual preservation measures may vary, depending upon the specific situation. For instance, capping or covering sites with soil may not be a practical solution where it might interfere with later carbon-14 or pollen dating procedures.

When avoidance is not possible, excavation may be the only feasible alternative or mitigation measure. Section 21083.2 limits excavation to those parts of the site which would otherwise be damaged or destroyed by the project. Excavation is not required if the Lead Agency determines that testing or studies already completed have adequately recovered the scientifically consequential information from and about the resource. This information must be documented in the EIR.

Part V of Appendix K suggests that any necessary excavation should be based upon an excavation plan or "research design." The contents of such a plan might include, but are not limited to:

1 A brief summary of the excavation proposed as part of the mitigation plan.

2 A list and discussion of important information the excavated resources contain or are likely to contain.

3 An explanation of how the information should be recovered to be useful in addressing scientifically valid research questions.

4 An explanation of the methods of analysis.

5 A final report for distribution.

6 An estimate of the cost of and time required to complete the excavation proposed under the plan.

7 Plans for the curation of collected materials.

An excavation plan should be prepared by a qualified archaeologist. Unless special or unusual circumstances warrant a longer period, Section 21083.2 requires that the field excavation phase of an approved mitigation plan must be completed within 90 days of final approval. Where a phased project is involved, the excavation must be completed within 90 days of the final approval of the phase to which the mitigation measures apply. The project applicant may allow additional time at their discretion.

Mitigation Monitoring and Reporting

Section 21081.6 requires a public agency to adopt a mitigation monitoring and reporting program whenever it makes a finding of significance under subdivision (a) of Section 21081 (also *CEQA Guidelines* Section 15091 (a)(1)) or adopts a mitigated Negative Declaration. This clearly applies to any EIR or mitigated Negative Declaration which identifies adverse effects or potentially adverse effects on unique archaeological resources or historical resources.

The purpose of the mitigation monitoring and reporting program is to ensure that mitigation measures such as avoiding sites during construction, following an excavation plan, or halting construction when resources are discovered, are complied with during project implementation. Where unique archaeological resources or historical resources are involved, continuous monitoring may be necessary during development. OPR's advisory memo entitled *Tracking CEQA Mitigation Measures Under AB 3180* discusses monitoring and reporting programs in detail.

Applicant Contributions

Section 21083.2 requires the applicant for a qualifying project to guarantee to the Lead Agency that the applicant will pay one-half the estimated cost of mitigating the project's effects on the resource. When determining the applicant's share, consideration must be given to the in-kind value of "project design or expenditures" that permit any or all the unique archaeological resource to be preserved in place or left undisturbed. The estimated cost of mitigation, other than avoidance or leaving the resource in an undisturbed state, should be included in the EIR.

The project applicant's share of mitigation funding is limited by statute to the following amounts:

1 For commercial or industrial projects, an amount equal to one-half of one percent of the projected cost of the project for mitigation measures undertaken within the site boundaries.

2 For a single residential unit, an amount equal to three-fourths of one percent of the projected cost of the project for mitigation measures undertaken within the site boundaries.

3 For a residential project of more than one unit, an amount equal to three-fourths of one percent of the projected cost of the project for mitigation measures undertaken within the site boundaries for the first unit plus the sum of the following:

   a $200 per unit for any of the next 99 units.

   b $150 per unit for any of the next 400 units.

   c $100 per unit in excess of 500 units.

When a final decision is made on the project, the Lead Agency shall, if necessary, reduce the specified mitigation measures to those which can be funded with the money guaranteed by the applicant and any other sources. Where such reduction results in a significant effect not being reduced to a level of insignificance, the Lead Agency must adopt findings of overriding consideration pursuant to *Guidelines* Section 15093.

Human Remains

The disposition of Native American burials (human remains) are governed by the provisions of Sections 5097.94 and 5097.98, and fall within the jurisdiction of the Native American Heritage Commission. Where human remains are known, or thought likely to exist, consultation with the Native American Heritage Commission should be initiated by the Lead Agency as early in the project planning process as possible. The Commission has statutory authority to mediate agreements relative to the disposition of Native American remains. These agreements are not subject to CEQA.

The location of old grave sites and Native American remains are often not known in advance. Appendix K suggests a specific procedure for dealing with the unexpected discovery of human remains. (Part VIII of Appendix K) If human remains are discovered, the County Coroner must be notified within 48 hours. There should be no further disturbance to the site where the remains were found. If the remains are Native American, the coroner is responsible for contacting the Native American Heritage Commission within 24 hours. The Commission, pursuant to Section 5097.98,

will immediately notify those persons it believes to be most likely to be descended from the deceased Native American.

Accidental Discoveries

CEQA authorizes, but does not require, a Lead Agency to adopt provisions in the agency's own CEQA guidelines for responding to the accidental discovery of archaeological resources during construction. A number of jurisdictions have done this, including Santa Barbara County. These measures may include, but are not limited to, the following:

1 Requirements for the immediate evaluation of the find.

2 Provisions for contingency funding and a time allotment sufficient to either allow excavation and recovery of an archaeological sample, or to employ measures which would avoid the site of the resource without disturbing it.

3 The stopping of construction work on that portion of the site where an archaeological or historical resource was discovered.

Section 21083.2 Exception

Pursuant to its subdivision (j), the requirements of Section 21083.2, including limits on the applicant's share of the cost of mitigation, may be waived for the following:

1 A public agency project, if the Lead Agency elects to comply with all other applicable provisions of CEQA.

2 A project undertaken by a person that is supported in whole or in part through contracts, grants, subsidies, loans or other forms of assistance from one or more public agencies, if the Lead Agency elects to comply with all other applicable provisions of CEQA.

3 A public agency's consideration of a private project, if the applicant and the Lead Agency jointly elect to comply with all other applicable provisions of CEQA. A private project cannot be excepted from Section 21083.2 without the applicant's consent.

When Section 21083.2 does not apply, a substantial adverse change in *any* archaeological resource should be considered a significant effect on the environment. Therefore, the project's initial study must

address the potential for significant impacts relative to any significant archaeological resource (not simply the "unique resources" defined under Section 21083.2), as well as any archaeological resource that is also a historical resource pursuant to Section 21084.1.

The majority of sub-surface archaeological sites derive their significance from their information potential, that is, the ability to yield important information which contributes to our understanding of history and pre-history. Any action, such as clearing, scraping, soil removal, mechanical excavation or digging that would alter or destroy a site's integrity (i.e., intactness), stratigraphy, or association has the potential to be a significant adverse impact.

For purposes of CEQA, "environment" is defined to include: "the physical conditions which exist within the area which will be affected by the proposed project, including... objects of historic or aesthetic significance" (Section 21060.5). This includes archaeological sites (*Society of California Archaeology v. Butte County* (1977) 65 Cal.App.3d 832).

Mitigation Measures

Although the specific mitigation provisions of Section 21083.2 do not apply, the applicant and Lead Agency may use them as a general guide to mitigation. If an archaeological survey and report is required for the project, it should recommend specific measures to mitigate the significant effect identified in the report. These recommendations should form the basis for mitigation measures or alternatives in the EIR for the project. If the project is approved on the basis of an EIR or mitigated Negative Declaration, the Lead Agency must adopt a mitigation monitoring and reporting program as required under Section 21081.6.

Appendix 7

CEQA and Historical Resources

CEQA Technical Advice Series

Source

"CEQA and Historical Resources" (May 1996), CEQA Technical Advice Series. This document is reprinted with permission from the Governor's Office of Planning and Research, 1400 10th Street, Sacramento, California 95814. For additional information please call (916) 322-4245.

Solano Press Books has made every effort to see that no changes have been made to the contents of this state document as a result of reformatting and reprinting. Any omissions or changes to the contrary are entirely the responsibility of Solano Press Books and not the State of California.

Introduction

When a proposed project may adversely affect a historical resource, the California Environmental Quality Act (CEQA) requires the Lead Agency to carefully consider the possible impacts before proceeding (Public Resources Code Sections 21084 and 21084.1). Revisions to the Act made in 1992, particularly Chapter 1075 of the Statutes of 1992, have highlighted the importance of evaluating possible impacts upon historic resources. This advisory paper discusses how CEQA applies to city and county decisions on proposed projects which may potentially impact or otherwise involve historic resources.

CEQA exists to ensure that governmental decisionmakers consider the potential significant environmental effects of proposed projects before taking action. The Lead Agency is responsible for determining whether a significant adverse environmental impact may occur and whether it can be mitigated to a level of insignificance. Where substantial evidence indicates that a significant adverse effect may occur, the lead decision-making agency is required to prepare an Environmental Impact Report (EIR) which discusses in detail the potential impact and feasible means of avoiding or reducing it. Where such an effect may be mitigated to a level of insignificance through changes in the project or other requirements, a mitigated Negative Declaration should be prepared rather than an EIR.

CEQA and Historical Resources is advisory only. Although it supplements the *CEQA Guidelines* (*Guidelines*) on this topic, it does not amend or replace the regulations represented by the *Guidelines*. All code references herein are to the Public Resources Code unless otherwise noted.

Background on Historical Resources Preservation

There are a number of ways in which local communities and the State encourage or require the preservation of California's historical resources. Before delving into how the CEQA requirements augment this preservation activity, a short overview of State and local preservation mechanisms is in order. Keep in mind that while the immediately following discussion reviews historic preservation programs, the focus of this advisory paper is on the CEQA-mandated process of evaluating development projects for potential significant effects on historical resources.

The State

The State Historic Resources Commission and the Office of Historic Preservation (SHPO) within the Department of Parks and Recreation administer California's historic preservation programs. The appointed Commission's pertinent duties include: evaluating applications and recommending properties for listing on the National Register of Historic Places; maintaining a statewide inventory of historical resources, including historical landmarks and points of interest; establishing criteria for recording and preserving historical resources; developing and adopting criteria for rehabilitating historic structures; developing and annually updating a statewide historic resources plan; overseeing administration of the California Register of Historic Places, including recommending standards for the evaluation of historic resources for inclusion in the register; and developing criteria and procedures for selecting enhancement and preservation projects for funding under the National Historic Preservation Fund, the California Heritage Fund, and other funding programs (Section 5020.4).

SHPO's duties include: serving as staff to the Commission; overseeing State agency compliance with State preservation statutes and programs; administering Federal preservation programs in California; administering State programs such as the California Register; providing information and technical assistance to agencies and the public; and reviewing and commenting on the impact on historic resources of publicly funded projects and programs (Section 5020.6).

The California Register of Historical Resources is an authoritative guide to identifying the State's historical resources. It establishes a list of those properties which are to be protected from substantial adverse change (Section 5024.1).

A historical resource may be listed in the California Register if it meets any of the following criteria: (1) it is associated with events that have made a significant contribution to the broad patterns of California's history and cultural heritage; (2) it is associated with the lives of persons important in California's past; (3) it embodies the distinctive characteristics of a type, period, region, or method of construction, or represents the work of an important creative individual, or possesses high artistic value; or (4) it has yielded or is likely to yield information important in prehistory or history. The Register includes properties which are listed or have been formally determined to be eligible for listing in the National Register, State Historical Landmarks, and eligible Points of Historical Interest.

Other resources require nomination for inclusion in the Register. These may include resources contributing to the significance of a local historic district, individual historical resources, historical resources identified in historic resources surveys conducted in accordance with SHPO procedures, historic resources or districts designated under a local ordinance consistent with Commission procedures, and local landmarks or historic properties designated under local ordinance.

An individual resource, district, or local landmark may be nominated for inclusion in the Register by a resident, a landowner, or a local government. The Commission will review each request, after providing the opportunity for affected property owners, local agencies, and interested persons to comment on the proposed listing, before determining whether to include the resource on the Register (Section 5024.1). If the local government objects to the nomination, the Commission must make supportive findings for any listing. Nominations for which there is owner objection will not be placed in the Register, but may nonetheless be listed as eligible.

There are several State and federal programs which directly promote historic preservation. In order to encourage rehabilitation, rather than demolition or removal of historic values, the State Historical Building Code (Health and Safety Section 18950, et seq.) can be applied to qualifying structures. This allows repairs, renovations, and other construction in variance to the Uniform Building Code

(UBC). The Mills Act (Revenue and Taxation Code Sections 439 et seq.) offers property tax relief in exchange for an agreement from the property owner to maintain the historic resource for a period of 10 years. The Marks Historical Rehabilitation Act authorizes cities, counties and redevelopment agencies to issue tax-exempt revenue bonds to finance the rehabilitation of significant historic buildings. In addition, Federal investment tax credits are also available for qualified rehabilitation of historic structures.

The State Office of Historic Preservation publishes a guide, The Survey of Surveys which lists all local resource surveys known to the SHPO. The State Office also provides a fact sheet about the California Register. Guidelines for the nomination of properties to the California Register are being developed by SHPO and may be available by the beginning of 1997. The SHPO can be contacted at:

1416 Ninth Street
Sacramento, CA 95814
(916) 653-6624

Other good sources of information on local surveys and designations are the city or county planning department and the local historical society. Specific information about a property identified in a formal survey can be obtained through the 11 regional Information Centers for California Historical Resources (formerly the Regional Archaeological Information Centers). A list of these centers is found in Appendix 2.

Local Government

Cities and counties use a number of tools to identify and protect historical resources. For instance, at least 60 cities and counties have adopted general plan elements containing detailed policies on historic preservation or historic structures. About 20 percent of California's cities and counties (1986) have completed historic resource surveys.

A variety of local actions directly protect historical resources by limiting the kinds of changes that can be made to them. Historic preservation ordinances for identified landmarks, historic districts, and other qualifying resources which require consideration of a use permit or other discretionary permit prior to changes in the

resource are the most effective means of protection. Architectural design controls, for example, generally require that proposed alterations receive the review and approval of an architectural review commission or board. In order to encourage owners to preserve significant properties, some localities assist owners in obtaining low-interest rehabilitation loans, help finance improvements through redevelopment or other activities (particularly in historic business districts), and may engage in outright purchase to protect the integrity of historic resources.

CEQA Provisions

CEQA does not apply to ministerial actions which may impact a historical resource. For example, a project which complies with the Uniform Building Code and for which no discretionary permit is required does not fall under CEQA, even if the project may alter a building which is considered a "qualified historic structure" under the State Historical Building Code (*Prentiss v. City of South Pasadena* (1993) 15 Cal.App.4th 85). Common ministerial actions include roof replacement, interior remodeling, or other activities which require only a non-discretionary building permit. A ministerial action applies fixed standards or objective measurements and involves "little or no personal judgment by a public official as to the wisdom or manner of carrying out the project" (*Guidelines* Section 15369).

CEQA does apply to discretionary projects and equates a substantial adverse change in the significance of a historical resource with a significant effect on the environment (Section 21084.1). Further, the Act explicitly prohibits the use of a categorical exemption within the *CEQA Guidelines* for projects which may cause such a change (Section 21084). "Substantial adverse change" is defined as demolition, destruction, relocation, or alteration activities which would impair historical significance (Section 5020.1).

This effectively requires preparation of a mitigated Negative Declaration or an EIR whenever a project may adversely impact historic resources. However, where the project meets the Secretary of Interior's

Standards for Rehabilitation (available from SHPO), and so will not result in an adverse effect, it is possible that a Negative Declaration could be adopted. Current CEQA law provides that an EIR must be prepared whenever it can be fairly argued, on the basis of substantial evidence in the administrative record, that a project may have a significant effect on a historical resource (*Guidelines* Section 15064). A mitigated Negative Declaration may be used where all potentially significant effects can be mitigated to a level of insignificance (Section 21080). For example, a mitigated Negative Declaration may be adopted for a project which meets the Secretary of Interior's Standards for Rehabilitation and local historic preservation regulations, and so will not adversely affect the resource.

Key Questions

This presents the Lead Agency with two key questions which it must address in sequence. First, does a significant historical resource exist? Absent a historical resource, the agency may proceed as usual and, depending upon the circumstances, may be able to apply a CEQA exemption to the project. Second, where a significant historical resource does exist, will the proposed project result in a substantial adverse change such that the qualities that make the resource significant are impaired or lost? This question should be answered through preparation of an initial study for the project.

Is a Historical Resource Present?

Section 21084.1 is by turns both specific and vague in distinguishing the range of resources which may be considered historic. First, any resource listed in, or eligible for listing in, the California Register of Historical Resources is presumed to be historically or culturally significant. This includes listed archaeological resources (for example, California Landmark Number 838, The Indian Village of Tsurai). The Lead Agency's first step should be to consult the applicable Historical Resources File System Information Center to ascertain whether the resource is listed in the California Register.

A side note: CEQA establishes two separate mechanisms for evaluating potential adverse effects on archaeological resources. Section 21084.1 applies to those resources that are listed in or eligible to be listed in the California Register. Section 21083.2 applies to other "unique" archaeological resources as well. For more information on the application of CEQA to archaeological resources see *CEQA and Archaeological Resources,* published by OPR.

Second, resources which are listed in a local historic register or deemed significant in a historical resource survey as provided under Section 5024.1(g) are to be presumed historically or culturally significant unless "the preponderance of evidence" demonstrates they are not. The next step is to consult the pertinent existing local register and survey. Because a local register or survey may not employ the same criteria as the California Register, listing or identification in a local survey does not necessarily establish if the property is eligible for listing on the Register. The Lead Agency will need to evaluate the resource in light of the Register's listing criteria (these will be included in guidelines expected to be released by SHPO in June 1994). The Lead Agency may determine that the preponderance of evidence demonstrates that the property in question is not historically or culturally significant despite being listed on a local register or identified in a local historic survey. When making this determination, OPR strongly recommends that the agency cite for the record the specific, concrete evidence which supports that determination.

Third, a resource that is not listed in, or determined to be eligible for listing in, the California Register of Historic Resources, not included in a local register of historic resources, or not deemed significant in a historical resource survey may nonetheless be historically significant, pursuant to Section 21084.1. This provision is intended to give the Lead Agency discretion to determine that a resource of historic significance exists where none had been identified before and to apply the requirements of Section 21084.1 to properties that have not previously been formally recognized as historic. As the last step, the local agency should employ recognized criteria to determine whether a previously unrecognized significant historical resource exists.

As always under CEQA, the lead agency must determine whether there is "substantial evidence" in the administrative record to support a finding of significant effect. Substantial evidence is defined in Public Resources Code Section 21080(e) as including "...facts, reasonable assumptions predicated upon facts, and expert opinion supported by facts." Unsubstantiated claims of historical significance do not require preparation of an EIR (*Citizen's Committee to Save Our Village v. City of Claremont* (1995) 37 Cal.App.4th 1157—no substantial evidence existed that a landscape garden planned in 1905 was ever installed or maintained).

Will There Be a Substantial Adverse Change?

When a project would potentially affect a historical resource, the Lead Agency should prepare an initial study. The initial study, and the information upon which it is based, will provide a basis for determining whether the project may result in substantial adverse changes to the resource and, at the same time, a significant adverse environmental effect.

Section 5020.1 establishes the threshold of "substantial adverse change" as demolition, destruction, relocation, or alteration activities that would impair the significance of the historic resource. One example might be the removal of a historic structure from a historic district, thereby affecting the cohesiveness of the district. Remodeling a historic structure in such a way that its distinctive nature is altered would be another. The Secretary of Interior's *Standards for Rehabilitation* provide a standard guide to recommended (and not recommended) treatments to historic properties. The *Standards* may be obtained from SHPO.

Section 21084.1 is intended to provide, in the form of CEQA mitigation measures or project alternatives, new protections for historical resources which may be adversely changed by a project. Presumably, the Lead Agency may conclude that a project will have no significant environmental effect when there is no substantial evidence of an adverse change. Buildings and other historic resources protected from adverse changes by local regulations such as a historic district designation or historic preservation ordinance, may logically be expected not to suffer such changes as long as the project complies with those regulations. Where such protective regulations exist, or where mitigating conditions of approval are imposed, the initial study for the development project may cite them as evidence that no impact will occur, or that any impacts will be mitigated to a level of insignificance. Either a Negative Declaration or mitigated Negative Declaration could be adopted under those circumstances.

In *Citizen's for Responsible Development in West Hollywood v. City of West Hollywood* (1995) 39 Cal.App.4th 925, a California appellate court upheld a city's mitigated negative declaration on essentially the same grounds as discussed above. The project consisted of a 40-unit low-income housing project which would rehabilitate and restore two craftsman-style buildings on the front of the property and demolish another four buildings in the rear. West Hollywood had established a "Craftsman District" which encompassed the front buildings for purposes of historic preservation and established a Cultural Heritage Advisory Board (CHAB) to evaluate proposed activities within the district. When creating the District, the city had considered including the rear buildings within its boundaries, but concluded that they were not historically significant. The housing project was reviewed and approved by the CHAB as being benign relative to the architectural features and historic value of the front buildings and in conformance with the Secretary of Interior's rehabilitation standards.

The court found that there was no substantial evidence to support Citizen's claim that a historical resource was being adversely impacted by the project. Those structures deemed to be of historical importance were being rehabilitated and restored in accordance with adopted city, state, and federal regulations. The structures proposed for demolition were neither on a historic register, nor eligible for listing in the California Register, and their potential historical significance had been dismissed after study by the city during creation of the Craftsman District. Under the circumstances, the city was justified in adopting a mitigated Negative Declaration.

Where there is no protective ordinance or other regulation in place or where protective actions such as mitigation measures are insufficient to avoid a "substantial adverse change" in the resource, the Lead Agency should conclude that an adverse change will occur. In that case, an EIR must be prepared. As mentioned before, for purposes of CEQA a substantial adverse change in the historical resource is the equivalent of a significant adverse environmental effect.

Historical Resources and Natural Disasters

Most projects undertaken to demolish or replace property or facilities damaged as a result of a disaster for which a state of emergency has been declared are statutorily exempt from CEQA (subdivision (b), Section 21080). Notwithstanding that exemption, actions in the aftermath of a disaster which might adversely affect historical resources are subject to State laws governing consideration of historical resources.

Section 5028 provides that no structure listed in the National Register of Historic Places, the California Register, or a local register that has been damaged as a result of a natural disaster is to be demolished, destroyed, or significantly altered (except for alterations to preserve or enhance historic value) unless: (1) the structure represents "an imminent threat to the public of bodily harm or of damage to adjacent property," or (2) the action is approved by the SHPO. That section further establishes the procedure for review of proposed actions by the SHPO.

In the wake of an earthquake, flood, fire, or other natural disaster the local agency may only demolish or destroy those structures which are an "imminent threat." In all other cases, the local agency must notify and consult with SHPO immediately if there are damaged historical resources which may require demolition, destruction, or significant alterations.

Appendix 8

Mitigated Negative Declarations

CEQA Technical Advice Series

Source

"Mitigated Negative Declarations" (December 1997), CEQA Technical Advice Series. This document is reprinted with permission from the Governor's Office of Planning and Research, 1400 10th Street, Sacramento, California 95814. For additional information please call (916) 322-4245.

Solano Press Books has made every effort to see that no changes have been made to the contents of this state document as a result of reformatting and reprinting. Any omissions or changes to the contrary are entirely the responsibility of Solano Press Books and not the State of California.

Introduction

For many years, public agencies have adopted so called "mitigated Negative Declarations" in conjunction with project revisions which prospectively avoid or mitigate all of a project's potential significant effects. In 1993, Senate Bill 919 (Chapter 1131, Stats. of 1993) and Assembly Bill 1888 (Chapter 1130, Stats. of 1993) enacted several amendments to CEQA which further encourage and support the use of mitigated Negative Declarations.

Mitigated Negative Declarations discusses Negative Declarations and mitigated Negative Declarations in light of these statutes. This brief advisory paper is aimed primarily at local public agencies and CEQA practitioners. It is intended to offer basic guidance in the preparation of mitigated Negative Declarations and to encourage their use under the proper circumstances. *Mitigated Negative Declarations* is neither a replacement of, nor an amendment to the *CEQA Guidelines*. All code citations refer to the Public Resources Code unless otherwise noted.

Negative Declarations

What Is a Negative Declaration?

When faced with a discretionary project which is not exempt from the California Environmental Quality Act (CEQA), a Lead Agency must prepare an "initial study" to determine whether the project may have a significant adverse effect on the environ-ment. If such an effect may occur, the Lead Agency must prepare an environmental impact report (EIR). If there is no substantial evidence for such an effect, or if the potential effect can be reduced to a level of insignificance through project revisions, a Negative Declaration can be adopted (Section 21080).

A mitigated Negative Declaration is used in the second situation. The statute provides that mitigated Negative Declarations are used "when the initial study has identified potentially significant effects on the environment, but (1) revisions in the project plans or proposals made by, or agreed to by, the applicant before the proposed negative declaration and initial study are released for public review would avoid the effects or mitigate the effects to a point where clearly no significant effect on the environment would occur, and (2) there is no substantial evidence in light of the whole record before the public agency that the project, as revised, may have a significant effect on the environment" (Section 21064.5).

Initial Study

An initial study formalizes the Lead Agency's preliminary analysis to determine whether an EIR or Negative Declaration must be prepared. Most commonly, the initial study is based upon a checklist which illuminates the various environmental impacts which may result from development. The checklist, however, is only part of the initial study. The initial study also must explain the reasons for supporting the checklist findings and note or reference the source or content of the data relied upon in its preparation. Simply filling out an initial study checklist without citing supporting information is insufficient to show the absence of significant effects (*Sundstrom v. County of Mendocino* (1988) 202 Cal.App.3d 296). At the same time, keep in mind that the initial study is not intended to provide the full-blown analysis expected of a complete EIR (*Leonoff v. Monterey County Board of Supervisors* (1990) 222 Cal.App.3d 1337) and *San Joaquin Raptor/Wildlife Rescue Center v. County of Stanislaus* (1996) 42 Cal.App.4th 608).

Supporting information may include specific studies which examine the potential significance of an anticipated environmental effect. It may include references to previous environmental documents or other information sources. In any case, a thorough, referenced initial study is a crucial part of the record supporting the Lead Agency's determination to prepare a mitigated Negative Declaration.

CEQA requires that the Lead Agency, through its initial study, review the whole of a project. A project must not be broken into smaller parts, each of which alone might qualify for a Negative Declaration, in an attempt to avoid preparing an EIR (*Association for Sensible Development of Bishop Area v. County of Inyo* (1985) 172 Cal. App.3d 151). The decision to prepare a mitigated Negative Declaration (and a Negative Declaration for that matter) must be grounded in an objective, good faith effort on the part of the Lead Agency to review the project's potential for significant impacts (*Sundstrom v. County of Mendocino, supra*).

Section 15071 of the *CEQA Guidelines* requires that the initial study be attached to any Negative Declaration circulated for public review. The purpose for this is to document the reasons supporting the finding that the project will not result in a significant effect. OPR recommends that prior to circulating a draft mitigated Negative Declaration the Lead Agency revise or annotate the initial study, if necessary, to reflect revisions to the project. The initial study circulated with a mitigated Negative Declaration should not indicate that there will be any significant effects of the project and should identify or reference the data which supports its determination that any potentially significant effects have been mitigated or avoided.

Fair Argument

The original determination made on the basis of the initial study whether to prepare either a Negative Declaration or an EIR is subject to the "fair argument" test (*Laurel Heights Improvement Assoc. v. U.C. Regents* (1993) 47 Cal.4th 376). In other words, if a fair argument can be raised on the basis of "substantial evidence" in the record that the project may have a significant adverse environmental impact—even if evidence also exists to the contrary—then an EIR is required. A Negative Declaration is authorized when the Lead Agency determines that no substantial evidence exists supporting a fair argument of significant effect. A mitigated Negative Declaration applies when changes to the project or other mitigation measures are imposed which such that all potentially significant effects are avoided or reduced to a level of insignificance.

SB 919 adds to CEQA a definition of the term "substantial evidence" (subdivision (e), Section 21080). Although this does not affect application of the fair argument standard, it provides the Lead Agency a means by which to gauge the quality of evidence discovered during its review of a project. Similarly, a court examining the

actions of the Lead Agency now has a consistent standard by which to judge the quality of the evidence which was before the Agency.

Pursuant to Section 21080, substantial evidence includes "facts, reasonable assumptions predicated upon facts, and expert opinion supported by facts." It does not include "argument, speculation, unsubstantiated opinion or narrative, evidence which is clearly inaccurate or erroneous, or evidence of social or economic impacts which do not contribute to, or are not caused by, physical impacts on the environment." Further, public controversy over the possible environmental effects of a project is not sufficient reason to require an EIR "if there is no substantial evidence in light of the whole record before the lead agency that the project may have a significant effect on the environment" (Section 21082.2).

Project Mitigation and Revision

There are two prerequisites to using a mitigated Negative Declaration:

1   All potentially significant effects of the project can and will be avoided or mitigated to a level of insignificance by project revisions or other requirements imposed on the project. A mitigated Negative Declaration is based on the premise that the project will not result in a *significant* effect. For example, suppose a project would increase traffic from Level of Service (LOS) B to LOS D where local guidelines have identified LOS D as the threshold for significance. If mitigation can reduce the impact to LOS C, then the project's impact would not be considered significant.

2   The project changes and mitigation measures must be agreed to or made by the proponent *before* the draft Negative Declaration is circulated for public review and comment. In other words, the draft document must reflect the revised project, with changes and mitigation measures. A few agencies apparently require proponents to submit a new project description before the draft mitigated Negative Declaration is released. This procedure is not

required by CEQA if the proponent has otherwise agreed to or made the revisions and mitigations. However, requiring or allowing an applicant to adopt prospective mitigation measures which are to be recommended in a future study, but which are not incorporated into the project before the proposed Negative Declaration is released for public review, is not allowed (*Sundstrom v. County of Mendocino, supra*).

A key question for the Lead Agency is: What level of mitigation or project revision is sufficient to avoid or eliminate a potential significant effect? There is no ironclad answer which would apply in every instance. The answer depends upon the specific situation; the Lead Agency must use its own independent and objective judgment, based on the information before it, to determine that "clearly no significant effect on the environment would occur" (Section 21064.5). Further, there must be evidence in the record as a whole to support that conclusion.

Pursuant to Section 15370 of the *CEQA Guidelines,* mitigation includes:

"(a) Avoiding the impact altogether by not taking a certain action or parts of an action.

"(b) Minimizing impacts by limiting the degree or magnitude of the action and its implementation.

"(c) Rectifying the impact by repairing, rehabilitating, or restoring the impacted environment.

"(d) Reducing or eliminating the impact over time by preservation and maintenance operations during the life of the action.

"(e) Compensating for the impact by replacing or providing substitute resources or environments."

Project revisions may include such things as changes in design, location, operations, or scope. Effective project revisions will perform any or all of the above functions (a) through (e).

Effective mitigation measures are those written in clear, declaratory language specifying what is required to be done, how it is to be done, when it is to be done, and who will be responsible for doing it. The words "will" and "shall" are preferred to "may" and "should" when directing an action. Furthermore, measures must be feasible to undertake and complete. Avoid measures that are conditional upon feasibility (i.e., required only "when feasible"), rather than applied directly or at a specified project stage. Also avoid deferred mitigation and mitigation measures consisting of monitoring and future studies not tied to performance standards and contingency plans (*Sundstrom v. County of Mendocino, supra*).

Negotiations

Some jurisdictions require the applicant to sign the draft mitigated Negative Declaration, indicating agreement with the mitigation measures or project revisions included therein, prior to circulating the document. In others, the applicant and the agency may negotiate over the revisions or mitigation measures until they are mutually acceptable and enter into a more formal agreement. Whatever the procedure, agreement must be reached before the draft mitigated Negative Declaration is circulated for review and comment.

Appendix 2 contains examples of agreements between Lead Agencies and applicants over project mitigation and revision.

Other Considerations

A mitigated Negative Declaration is subject to the same consultation and notice requirements as any Negative Declaration (see Sections 21080.3, 21091, and 21092 for details on current requirements). Practitioners should note that AB 1888 shortened the minimum local review period for Negative Declarations from 21 to 20 days (a minimum of 30 days is still required for drafts submitted to the State Clearinghouse) and revised Section 21092 to require that the notice of a draft Negative Declaration include an address where copies of the draft and all documents referenced in the draft will be available for review during the comment period.

The Lead Agency must consider the comments it receives during the review period prior to adopting a mitigated Negative Declaration. If these comments include substantial evidence that a potential environmental effect may occur despite the project revisions or mitigation measures included in the mitigated Negative Declaration, the Lead Agency must either require further revisions to the project which would effectively avoid or mitigate that effect, or if that is not possible, prepare an EIR. Although not explicitly required by CEQA, OPR recommends that under the first circumstance the Lead Agency recirculate the revised mitigated Negative Declaration for review prior to acting on the project and adopting the document. This ensures that the public will have been afforded the chance to review the new mitigation measures as well as the revised project (*Leonoff v. Monterey County Board of Supervisors* (1990) 222 Cal.App.3d 1337 and *Perley v. County of Calaveras* (1982) 137 Cal.App. 3d 424). As before, the proponent must have agreed to or made the additional project changes before the mitigated Negative Declaration is recirculated.

Upon adopting a mitigated Negative Declaration, the Lead Agency must make both of the following findings:

1 Revisions in the project plans or proposals made by, or agreed to by, the applicant before the proposed negative declaration and initial study are released for public review would avoid the effects or mitigate the effects to a point where clearly no significant effect on the environment would occur.

2 There is no substantial evidence in light of the whole record before the public agency that the project, as revised, may have a significant effect on the environment.

(Sections 21064.5 and 21080(c)).

Revising Mitigation Measures

If the lead agency concludes prior to approval of a project that one or more of the mitigation measures identified in the Negative Declaration are infeasible or otherwise undesirable, Section 21080(f) provides that the lead agency may delete those measures and substitute other equivalent or better measures without having to recirculate the mitigated Negative Declaration for review. The lead agency must: (1) hold a public hearing on the matter before substituting new mitigation measures; (2) impose the new measures as conditions of project approval or otherwise make them a part of the project approval; and (3) find that the new measures will effectively reduce potentially significant effects to a level of insignificance and will not cause any potentially significant effects of their own.

When a mitigation measure imposed as a condition of project approval is set aside by either an administrative body or a court, the lead agency's approval of the mitigated Negative Declaration for the project is invalidated and a new environmental review is required. However, pursuant to Section 21080(g), the lead agency may avoid invalidation and the need for a new environmental review if it substitutes equivalent or better measures. The procedure and findings for substituting new measures is the same as described above.

One court has held that *after* project approval an agency has some flexibility in interpreting the manner in which mitigation measures are complied with, within reasonable bounds. "[T]he agency's interpretation is reasonable in the CEQA context only if it imposes no significant new or adverse environmental impacts. Such a standard would promote the Legislature's expressed concern for balancing environmental considerations against the social and economic burdens of compliance with CEQA mandates" (*Stone v. Board of Supervisors* (1988) 205 Cal.App.3d 927, 934). Although the court allowed the defendant county to substitute one means of complying with a mitigation measure for its functional equivalent, it also implied that actually amending a mitigation measure would require further CEQA review.

Mitigation Monitoring or Reporting Program

Upon approving a project for which a mitigated Negative Declaration is adopted, the Lead Agency must also adopt a mitigation monitoring or reporting program pursuant to Section 21081.6. The purpose of the program is to ensure compliance with the required mitigation measures or project revisions during project implementation. Section 21081.6 also requires that mitigation measures be adopted as conditions of approval. A detailed discussion of program requirements is contained in OPR's publication *Tracking CEQA Mitigation Measures Under AB 3180*.

Use With Other Documents

In a number of situations where an environmental document has already been prepared, a mitigated Negative Declaration may be sufficient to address subsequent projects which have been largely examined in the previous document and which will have no unavoidable significant impacts. The most common of these and suggested findings for adopting a mitigated Negative Declaration are summarized below. In no case where a mitigated Negative Declaration is being adopted is it necessary to also adopt EIR findings pursuant to Section 21081.

Master EIR

The "Master EIR" is a 1994 statutory innovation intended to provide a detailed environmental review of plans and programs upon which the analysis of subsequent related development proposals can be based. Pursuant to AB 1888 of 1993, its enabling legislation, a Master EIR must, to the greatest extent feasible, evaluate the cumulative impacts, growth inducing impacts, and irreversible significant effects on the environment of specific, subsequent projects. The review of later projects which were described in the Master EIR can be limited to the extent that the Master EIR has already reviewed project impacts and set forth mitigation measures (Section 21156).

AB 1888 provides that a mitigated Negative Declaration shall be prepared for a later project identified in a Master EIR when there is no substantial evidence before the Lead Agency that the project may have a significant effect on the environment and both the following occur:

1 An initial study has identified potentially new or additional significant effects on the environment that were not analyzed in the Master EIR.

2 Feasible mitigation measures or alternatives will be incorporated to revise the proposed later project, before the mitigated Negative Declaration is released

for public review, such that the new potential significant effects are eliminated or reduced to a level of insignificance. (Section 21157.5)

The subsequent project must incorporate all applicable mitigation measures or project alternatives from the Master EIR, as well as the measures adopted pursuant to the mitigated Negative Declaration.

Findings — Upon adopting a mitigated Negative Declaration under these circumstances, OPR recommends that the Lead Agency make the following findings pursuant to Sections 21064.5, 21080(c), and 21157.5.

1 The subsequent project is identified in the Master EIR.

2 The project incorporates all applicable mitigation measures or project alternatives from the Master EIR.

3 There is no substantial evidence in light of the whole record before the public agency that the project, as revised, may have a significant effect on the environment.

4 Feasible mitigation measures or alternatives will be incorporated to revise the proposed later project, before the mitigated Negative Declaration is released for public review, such that the potential significant effects are eliminated or reduced to a level of insignificance.

Tiering

CEQA Guidelines Section 15152 (Section 21083.3) allows a Negative Declaration to be adopted when an EIR has previously been prepared for a program, policy, plan or ordinance, and a later project consistent with that program or other action will not result in any significant effects which were not examined in that previous EIR. In order to tier upon an EIR, the later project must be consistent with the general plan and zoning of the applicable city or county. The Negative Declaration must clearly state that it is being tiered upon a previous EIR, reference that EIR, and state where a copy of the EIR can be examined.

This section of the *Guidelines* applies equally to a mitigated Negative Declaration. Of course, any potential significant effects that were not examined in the previous

EIR must be avoided or completely mitigated if a mitigated Negative Declaration is to be adopted. This includes unavoidable significant cumulative effects. A mitigated Negative Declaration is not recommended when the document on which it is being tiered has identified unavoidable significant cumulative effects.

Findings — In addition to the findings required of a mitigated Negative Declaration pursuant to Sections 21080 and 21064.5, OPR recommends that the Lead Agency find that:

1 The project is consistent with the program, policy, plan or ordinance for which the previous EIR was prepared;

2 The project is consistent with the general plan and zoning of the applicable city or county; and

3 The project, as revised or mitigated, will not result in any significant effects which were not examined in the previous EIR.

Program EIR

Section 15168 of the *CEQA Guidelines* defines a "program EIR" as an EIR which may be prepared on a series of related actions which can be characterized as one large project. A program EIR can be used to support the determination made in an initial study to prepare either a Negative Declaration or an EIR for a later project under the program.

Pursuant to subdivision (c) of Section 15168, a mitigated Negative Declaration prepared for a later project under the program would focus on new effects which had not previously been considered in the program EIR, and which can be reduced to insignificance by mitigation measures or revisions incorporated into the project. In addition to these measures or revisions, the project must incorporate all applicable mitigation measures and alternatives identified in the program EIR (Section 15168(c)). As mentioned under tiering, a mitigated Negative Declaration is not recommended when the program EIR identified unavoidable significant cumulative effects.

Findings — OPR recommends that, in addition to the findings required under Sections 21080(c) and 21064.5, the Lead Agency find:

1. The project is consistent with the program for which the program EIR was prepared;

2. New effects which had not previously been considered in the program EIR will be be reduced to insignificance by mitigation measures or revisions incorporated into the project; and

3. The project incorporates all applicable mitigation measures and alternatives identified in the program EIR.

Subsequent Negative Declaration

Section 15162 of the *CEQA Guidelines* provides that where an EIR or Negative Declaration has been certified or adopted for a project, no additional EIR need be prepared for the same project unless there is substantial evidence before the agency that any of the following have occurred:

1. Subsequent changes are proposed in the project which will require important revisions of the previous EIR or Negative Declaration due to new significant effects not considered in the previous EIR or Negative Declaration.

2. Substantial changes occur with respect to the circumstances under which the project is undertaken which will require important revisions in the previous EIR or Negative Declaration due to the involvement of new significant effects not considered in the previous EIR or Negative Declaration.

3. New information relating to the significant effects of the project and means of reducing or avoiding those effects, which was not known and could not have been known at the time the previous EIR or Negative Declaration was certified or adopted, becomes available. "New information" is further defined in *Guidelines* Section 15162(a)(3).

Because the project has already been the subject of either an EIR or Negative Declaration and the time for challenging the adequacy of the previous document is passed, the "fair argument" test does not apply (*Bowman v. City of Petaluma* (1986) 185 Cal.App.3d 1065). Unlike under the fair argument test, the Lead Agency is judged by the "traditional substantial evidence" test. In other words, it need not

prepare an EIR when substantial evidence exists for the occurrence of a significant effect, as long as the Lead Agency has substantial evidence showing none of the three situations described above exist.

In the initial review of a project, the Lead Agency's decision to prepare an EIR is governed by the "fair argument" text: the Lead Agency must prepare an EIR if there is substantial evidence that a significant impact will result. However, after the project has already been the subject of either an EIR or Negative Declaration and the time for challenging the previous environmental document is passed, the fair argument test does not apply. Instead, the Lead Agency's decision regarding the preparation of a subsequent or supplemental EIR is governed by the "substantial evidence" test. That is, the courts will respect the Lead Agency's decision not to prepare a subsequent or supplemental EIR if there is substantial evidence in the record supporting the Lead Agency's finding that none of the three conditions exist that would warrant preparation of subsequent or supplemental EIR under Section 15162 of the *Guidelines*.

Findings—The findings required under Sections 21064.5 and 21080 should be sufficient.

Court Scoreboard

In recent years, the courts have supported the use of mitigated Negative Declarations where the lead agency has been careful neither to ignore substantial evidence of one or more significant effects, nor attempted to defer mitigation. Following are very brief summaries of additional cases involving mitigated Negative Declarations. Refer to the cases themselves for more specific information.

Mitigated Negative Declaration Upheld

San Joaquin Raptor/Wildlife Rescue Center v. County of Stanislaus (1996) 42 Cal. App.4th 608

Here the court upheld a mitigated Negative Declaration for a surface mining operation where there was no substantial evidence to support a fair argument of significant effect. The plaintiff's claim that the project would result in cumulative effects on birds, including the Swainson's Hawk, was

vague and unsubstantiated by facts or expert opinion. The County, on the other hand, had three biologists confirm that the project would have no impact on endangered species. Further, the court affirmed, based on the *Leonoff* decision, that absent substantial evidence that the project would have a considerable incremental effect, and in the presence of expert testimony that it would not, an in-depth study of potential cumulative impacts was not a prerequisite to preparing a mitigated Negative Declaration.

Citizens for Responsible Development in West Hollywood v. City of West Hollywood (1995) 39 Cal.App.4th 925

The court affirmed the city's mitigated Negative Declaration for a 40-unit low-income housing project which would rehabilitate and restore two craftsman-style homes on the front of the property and demolish another four buildings in the rear. West Hollywood had established a "Craftsman District" which encompassed the front buildings for purposes of historic preservation and established a Cultural Heritage Advisory Board (CHAB) to evaluate proposed activities within the district. The housing project was reviewed and approved by the CHAB as being benign relative to the architectural features and historic value of the front buildings and in conformance with the Secretary of Interior's rehabilitation standards.

The court found that there was no substantial evidence to support Citizen's claim that a historical resource was being adversely affected. Those structures deemed to be of historical importance were being rehabilitated and restored in accordance with adopted city, state, and federal regulations. The structures proposed for demolition were neither on a historic register nor eligible for listing in the California Register, and their potential historical significance had been duly investigated by the city during creation of the Craftsman District and dismissed.

Citizens' Committee to Save Our Village v. City of Claremont (1995) 37 Cal.App. 4th 1157

The city did not abuse its discretion by rejecting as irrelevant and untimely "new evidence" submitted by project opponents regarding a mitigated Negative Declaration for a new, two-story college building. In prior litigation on the project, the trial court had ordered the city to make findings to support the mitigated Negative Declaration. The project's opponents attempted to introduce new evidence at the hearing that the project would adversely affect a historically significant landscape garden. The court concluded that the material presented at the hearing was not new and that no substantial evidence existed that a landscape garden planned for the project site in 1905 had ever been installed or maintained. Without evidence of an impact, no EIR was required.

Mitigated Negative Declaration Overturned

League for Protection of Oakland's Architectural and Historic Resources v. City of Oakland, Feb. 10, 1997, 52 Cal.App.4th 896

The city approved a shopping center which proposed to demolish the old Montgomery Ward store. The city had adopted a mitigated Neg. Dec for the project, requiring that the store be documented before demolition, that the new center utilize design elements from the store, that a qualified archaeologist oversee the demolition, and other measures as mitigation for the impact on historical resources. Section 21084.1 provides that "[a] project that may cause a substantial adverse change in the significance of an historical resource is a project that may have a significant effect on the environment." The court held that because the Ward building is eligible for historic status and is described as historic in the city's general plan, Section 21084.1 requires the city to consider this action a significant effect requiring preparation of an EIR.

Stanislaus Audubon Society v. County of Stanislaus (1995) 33 Cal.App.4th 144

The court concluded that a country club and golf course proposed on agricultural land required preparation of an EIR. The court found that during the process of considering the project the county had been presented with an abundant amount of substantial evidence, including testimony from its own planning staff in the initial study, to support a fair argument that the project would have a significant growth-inducing effect on the surrounding agricultural area.

Gentry v. City of Murrieta (1995) 36 Cal.App.4th 1359

The court set aside and ordered the city to reconsider the mitigated Negative Declaration for a proposed 500-lot subdivision. Substantial evidence existed that the project would adversely impact the endangered Stephens kangaroo rat. In addition, Murrieta attempted to defer mitigation of this impact pending further study, as held improper in *Sundstrom v. County of Mendocino*. The city had also made a variety of procedural errors in circulating the Negative Declaration for review.

Quail Botanical Gardens Foundation v. City of Encinitas (1994) 29 Cal.App.4th 1597

The court overturned a mitigated Negative Declaration for a 40-lot subdivision adjacent to the botanical garden on "fair argument" grounds. Expert testimony presented during the city's consideration of the subdivision indicated that the project would obscure views of the ocean from the Gardens, resulting in a significant aesthetic impact that could not be completely mitigated. Since the impact could not be mitigated completely, a Negative Declaration could not be used.

Final Words

The use of mitigated Negative Declarations is nothing novel, having been affirmed by the courts as long ago as 1982 (*Perley v. County of Calaveras* (1982) 137 Cal.App.3d 424). AB 1888, by explicitly defining this term in CEQA, and SB 919, by establishing standards by which to judge the existence of substantial evidence and narrowing the importance of public controversy in the decision to require an EIR, have strengthened the grounds for using a mitigated Negative Declaration. As a result, Lead agencies should feel more confident with this CEQA tool.

The prerequisites for adopting a mitigated Negative Declaration include:

1 Making a good faith effort to determine whether there is substantial evidence that the project would result in any significant environmental effect.

2 Incorporating effective revisions or mitigation measures into the project to alleviate potential significant effects prior to circulating the draft Negative Declaration for public review.

3 Evidence in the record to support the agency's determination that there will be no significant effect as a result of the final project.

Appendix 9

CEQA, NEPA. and Base Closure:
Recipes for Streamlining Environmental Review

CEQA Technical Advice Series

Source

"CEQA, NEPA. and Base Closure: Recipes for Streamlining Environmental Review" (March 1996), CEQA Technical Advice Series. This document is reprinted with permission from the Governor's Office of Planning and Research, 1400 10th Street, Sacramento, California 95814. For additional information please call (916) 322-4245.

Introduction

The purpose of this advisory is to illustrate how local agencies may proceed through the process of evaluating a base reuse plan pursuant to the California Environmental Quality Act (CEQA) while utilizing the environmental analysis prepared by a Federal agency under the National Environmental Policy Act (NEPA). Both CEQA and the *CEQA Guidelines* contain several specific provisions which can streamline CEQA compliance where an environmental review document is also being prepared or has already been prepared under NEPA. *CEQA, NEPA, and Base Closure* offers substantive suggestions for employing those provisions to avoid repetitive work.

This paper briefly reviews the base closure and reuse process, compares CEQA and NEPA procedures, discusses the provisions in CEQA, NEPA, and the *CEQA Guidelines* for preparing joint EIS/EIR documents, and concludes with some suggestions for complying with CEQA where a joint document has not been prepared. All code citations refer to the California Public Resources Code unless otherwise noted.

Pertinent excerpts from the *CEQA Statutes and Guidelines* and the NEPA Guidelines may be found in Appendix 1. A sample Memorandum of Understanding for preparing a joint EIS/EIR is in Appendix 2.

The Base Closure and Reuse Planning Process

A brief overview of the planning process which underlies military base closure and reuse activities will put the process of assessing the potential environmental impacts of reuse into context. This section outlines the respective roles of federal and local agencies in the process. Figure 1 outlines this process.

Federal Role

Disposal of a military base is guided by the Federal Property and Administrative Services Act of 1949, the 1990 Base Closure and Realignment Act, and other laws. The product of the federal process will be a disposal plan which, having taken into account the local base reuse plan when available, will guide the disposal of base property.

When the federal government has made a final decision to close a military base, the involved services within the Department of Defense (DoD) will "screen" the base property to determine whether any DoD agency has a housing or facility need that can be met by a portion or all of that base. The secretary of the service may authorize the transfer of such property to the agency, but is not required to do so. Base property not transferred to a DoD agency is determined to be "excess" to the needs of DoD.

For this excess property, DoD undertakes a similar screening for other federal agencies' property needs. New policies enacted by the 1994 Defense Authorization Act limit this process of screening other federal agencies to six months after the date the base closure was approved. Excess property not allocated during this screening is considered "surplus" with respect to federal government needs.

In turn, surplus properties are screened for State and local agency uses, including use by the homeless under the McKinney Homeless Assistance Act. State and local entities may pursue two paths towards obtaining these surplus lands or facilities: public benefit conveyance and negotiated sale. In addition, under the new procedures enacted in 1994, the local base redevelopment agency may seek an "economic benefit conveyance."

A public benefit conveyance allows public and private nonprofit agencies to acquire property at below market value for specified uses. Typical public benefit conveyances are for such uses as public airports, prisons, recreation facilities, and public education. A public benefit conveyance must be sponsored by a federal agency (for example, a community wanting conveyance of a site for a jail facility would need the sponsorship of the U.S. Department of Justice) and will carry certain restrictions on the use of the property.

Negotiated sale, on the other hand, allows the federal government to receive fair market value for its surplus property. Eligible public agencies may request

Figure 1
Typical Military Base Disposal and Reuse Process

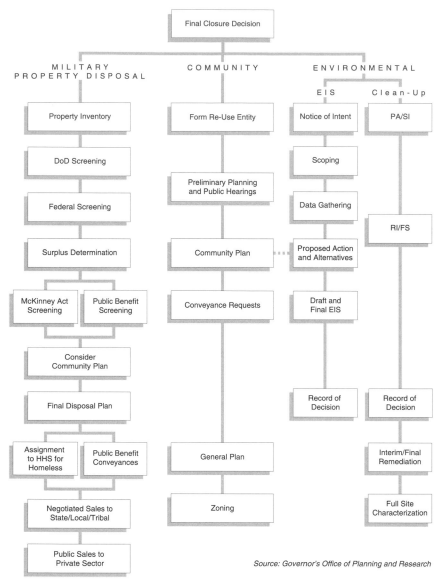

Source: Governor's Office of Planning and Research

negotiated sale without the imposition of use restrictions.

Surplus properties not claimed by State or local governments are offered for competitive sale to the public at fair market prices. Property disposed of in this manner carries no federal use restrictions and is bound by local zoning and land use regulations.

When the general disposition of the base becomes known, DoD will prepare a plan for the disposal of surplus portions of the base. An EIS, as well as hazardous waste remediation studies, will

be completed before the disposal plan is final. The planners will also consider the reuse plan prepared by the local community (where no local reuse plan exists, the DoD will prepare its own representative plan). Actual conveyances and sales of surplus properties will occur after adoption of a federal "Record of Decision" (ROD) for the final disposal plan.

The ROD must describe the decision, identify the factors involved in reaching that decision, identify the alternatives considered, and specify which alternative was considered to be environmentally

preferable (40 CFR 1505.2). The agency must also state whether all practical mitigation measures have been adopted to avoid or minimize the environmental effects of the chosen alternative, and if not, why not. A monitoring and enforcement program must be adopted where applicable.

Local Role

Affected local jurisdictions are expected to begin work on a base reuse plan concurrent with the federal activity. The California Military Base Reuse Task Force has recommended that "impacted communities establish a reuse planning entity immediately after a base closure decision becomes final, and that such entity be broadly representative of all key interests in the community, either through direct representation or inclusion in subcommittees." Where more than one community is impacted by the base closure, which is usually the case, inclusion of all impacted communities in this entity is imperative. A cooperative approach, within a formal framework, is key to smooth preparation of a reuse plan. Local reuse entities may also include ex officio State representation when advantageous.

The initial reuse planning organization is often started by local political leadership such as one or more mayors, a State legislator, or a Congressman. If a planning group does not immediately coalesce, the DoD's Office of Economic Adjustment (OEA) will attempt to bring together a representative reuse entity. The OEA can provide grant funds for reuse planning when it is satisfied that a representative group has been formed.

A local reuse organization may be established in any of several ways. The specific powers of the organization, its membership, and its governance procedures will vary depending on the circumstances of the particular base closure and the agencies involved. When a single jurisdiction is involved, the organization may consist of a steering committee appointed by the legislative body to act as a focal point for ideas and to make recommendations. Where several jurisdictions are involved, a Memorandum of Agreement (MOA) between them may be sufficient to establish their relative expectations and responsibilities. A joint powers authority (JPA) comprised of the affected jurisdictions is another alternative. The Joint Exercise of Powers Act (Government Code Section 6500, et seq.) allows member agencies to establish a JPA which meets their particular needs and wields specified powers. Additional local options are discussed in detail in the January 1994 final report of the California Military Base Reuse Task Force, available from OPR.

There are numerous good reasons for affected jurisdictions to join together to cooperatively prepare a base reuse plan. For example, the chances of receiving a reuse planning grant from the DoD's Office of Economic Adjustment are improved. Also, communication between the federal government and affected local jurisdictions is easier when there is a single point of local contact. In addition, the reuse entity can become a forum for discussing pertinent issues and resolving differences. This reduces the chance that disgruntled local jurisdictions will litigate to protect their interests. Furthermore, of interest to this discussion, a single base reuse planning entity simplifies the process of preparing the Environmental Impact Statement and Environmental Impact Report for the reuse plan.

Regardless of the form it takes, the goal of the reuse planning process should be an overall vision of and development policies for future uses of the closed facility, based on a realistic assessment of available resources and land use regulations.

NEPA and CEQA: Comparisons and Contrasts

NEPA and CEQA are similar laws with a common purpose: examining and weighing the potential environmental consequences of proposed government actions before such actions are undertaken.

National Environmental Policy Act

The National Environmental Policy Act of 1969 (NEPA) requires federal agencies to assess the possible environmental consequences of projects which they propose to undertake, fund, or approve. Under NEPA, closure of a military base usually requires preparation of an Environmental Impact Statement (EIS).

The process of preparing an EIS is as follows:

- A "Notice of Intent" (NOI) to prepare an EIS is published in the Federal Register. The NOI includes a description of the project and alternatives, the lead agency's proposed "scoping" process and any related meetings, and a contact person within the agency.

- "Scoping" of the project occurs, whereby other agencies are given the opportunity to bring to the attention of the lead agency significant issues which should be included in the EIS. This enables the lead agency to focus the EIS on a particular range of actions, alternatives, and impacts.

- A Draft EIS is prepared by the agency.

- Upon completion of the draft, a public "Notice of Availability" (NOA) of the Draft EIS is filed with the Environmental Protection Agency's (EPA's) Washington D.C. and regional offices for publication in the Federal Register.

- The Draft EIS is made available for public review.

- A Final EIS is prepared, including responses to the comments received during the review period.

- The Final EIS is circulated for public review; a second NOA, this time for the Final EIS, is sent to the EPA.

- The Final EIS is adopted and the agency renders its decision on the project.

- The "Record of Decision" (ROD) is prepared. The ROD includes a comparative discussion of the project alternatives, a discussion of the factors considered in making the decision, a description of those mitigation measures which were adopted and an explanation of why mitigation measures were not adopted, as well as a monitoring and enforcement program for adopted mitigation measures.

A Draft EIS contains the following basic components:

- A cover sheet enumerating the preparing agency, the project and its location, the agency contact person, a very brief abstract of the EIS, and final comment date.

- A summary of the EIS, including conclusions, areas of controversy, issues raised, and issues to be resolved.

- Table of Contents

- Statement of the purpose and the need fulfilled by the project and its alternatives.

- A range of alternatives, including the proposed action, comparatively analyzed and including mitigation measures for adverse environmental impacts (the agency need not adopt these measures unless so required by its own NEPA procedures).

- A list of the Federal permits required by the action

- A description of the affected environment.

- A description of the environmental consequences of the various alternatives, including direct, indirect, and cumulative effects.

- A list of preparers.

- A list of agencies and organizations consulted.

- Appendices.

- Index.

A Final EIS will include all of the above as well as incorporate or otherwise respond to the substantive comments received on the draft EIS from the public and other agencies.

The 1994 Defense Authorization Act requires DoD to complete its EIS within 12 months after receiving a community's reuse plan. The reuse plan will comprise the preferred alternative and a single NEPA document will be prepared for both disposal and reuse. However, if no community reuse plan is available before the draft EIS is prepared, the advance scoping and related information will become the basis for completion of the EIS. In this situation, the involved DoD service will devise the preferred reuse plan alternative as well as the other alternatives to be evaluated.

California Environmental Quality Act

The California Environmental Quality Act (CEQA) requires State and local public agencies to consider the environmental consequences of projects which they undertake, fund, or permit. Under CEQA, an Environmental Impact Report (EIR) must be prepared for the adoption of an initial base reuse plan by the local agency (Section 21151.1(a)(4)). An EIR may be required for later revisions to the plan and associated general plan amendments, specific plans, or redevelopment plans, depending upon whether those actions would result in environmental impacts not previously analyzed in the initial EIR. Even if the base reuse plan is not prepared to serve as a state-required plan, it may nevertheless benefit the reuse entity to subject it to an EIR to establish it as the basis for environmental review of future projects.

After an initial study and preliminary consultation or scoping have been completed and the decision is made to prepare an EIR, the process is as follows:

- A "Notice of Preparation" (NOP) is sent to interested agencies to solicit their comments on the project. The NOP includes a project description, location of the project, possible environmental impacts, and the date and time of known future meetings on the project. Where a State agency will be a responsible agency, a copy of the NOP is also sent to the State Clearinghouse. Agencies have 30 days to tender their comments.

- A Draft EIR is prepared.

- A "Notice of Completion" (NOC) and copies of the Draft EIR are submitted to the State Clearinghouse for distribution to interested State agencies. Public notice is provided by the lead agency and a copy of the NOC is posted in the office of the County Clerk of the county where the project is located. The Draft EIR is available for review and comment by the public and local agencies during this time.

- A Final EIR is completed, including responses to the comments received during the review period.

- The Final EIR is certified and the project approved.

- The Lead Agency makes findings regarding mitigation of the significant environmental impacts of the project (*Guidelines* Section 15091). It describes in writing the overriding considerations which justify project approval in the face of unavoidable impacts (*Guidelines* Section 15093). It also adopts a mitigation monitoring or reporting program upon approval of the project.

- A "Notice of Determination" (NOD) describing the project, its impacts and adopted mitigation, the environmental findings of the agency, and the location of copies for examination is filed with the county clerk. This starts a 30-day statute of limitations for court challenges to the EIR.

The *CEQA Guidelines* provide that the lead agency may determine the particular format of the EIR it prepares (*Guidelines* Section 15120). Within this flexible approach, the required contents of a Draft EIR are as follows:

- Table of contents or index

- Summary of proposed actions and expected consequences of those actions.

- Project description.

- Environmental setting of the project.

- Environmental impacts, including significant effects of the proposed action (direct and indirect); significant effects which cannot be avoided; mitigation measures proposed to minimize significant effects; feasible alternatives which would avoid or lessen the project's impacts; relationship between local short-term uses of man's environment and the maintenance and enhancement of long-term productivity; significant irreversible environmental changes; and growth-inducing impacts.

- Effects not found to be significant.

- Cumulative impacts of the project in the context of past, present, and reasonably anticipated projects.

- A list of organizations and persons consulted.

The Final EIR will include comments received on the draft and the lead agency's responses to those comments. It must also include a list of the organizations and individuals which commented on the draft.

Upon approving a project for which an EIR has been prepared, the lead agency must make findings relative to each of the mitigation measures pursuant to *Guidelines* Section 15091. These findings state whether the agency is imposing the mitigation measure, the measure is the responsibility of another agency which can and will impose it, or there are economic, social or other reasons why the mitigation measures and project alternatives are infeasible. Further, if the EIR has identified any significant environmental impacts which cannot be mitigated or avoided, the agency must make a "statement of overriding considerations" which describes the specific benefits of the project which outweigh its unavoidable environmental effects (*Guidelines* Section 15093).

Figure 2 compares the major features of EIS and EIRs, respectively.

Commonalities and Contrasts

As can be seen from the above discussion, there are many similarities between NEPA and CEQA processes, and between an EIS and an EIR. For instance, the federal NOI is analogous to the State NOP; the federal Notice of Availability performs the same function as the State Notice of Completion; both processes offer the opportunity for other agencies and the public to comment on the environmental document; and the required contents of an EIS are largely the same as those required of an EIR.

Nonetheless, there are also differences. For instance, EIS scoping and notice requirements are, understandably, oriented toward federal agencies and include State and local agencies and groups as necessary. CEQA requires public notice to be published in a local newspaper or otherwise provided locally. Under NEPA, the project and a range of alternatives to the project are examined at the same level of detail (i.e., the proposal is seen as one of several alternatives). CEQA does not require alternatives to be examined in

Figure 2
NEPA and CEQA: Parallel Processes

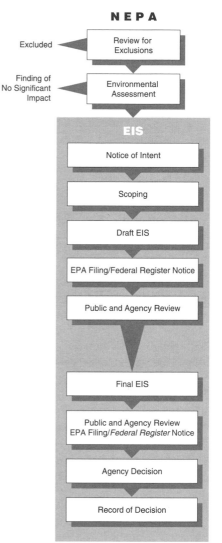

NEPA

Excluded ← Review for Exclusions

Finding of No Significant Impact ← Environmental Assessment

EIS
- Notice of Intent
- Scoping
- Draft EIS
- EPA Filing/Federal Register Notice
- Public and Agency Review
- Final EIS
- Public and Agency Review EPA Filing/*Federal Register* Notice
- Agency Decision
- Record of Decision

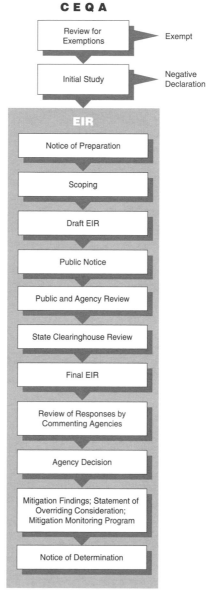

CEQA

Review for Exemptions → Exempt

Initial Study → Negative Declaration

EIR
- Notice of Preparation
- Scoping
- Draft EIR
- Public Notice
- Public and Agency Review
- State Clearinghouse Review
- Final EIR
- Review of Responses by Commenting Agencies
- Agency Decision
- Mitigation Findings; Statement of Overriding Consideration; Mitigation Monitoring Program
- Notice of Determination

as great a detail as the project (i.e., alternatives are means of avoiding the impacts associated with the project). NEPA requires, as part of the discussion of each alternative, discussion of mitigation measures and growth inducing impacts. CEQA requires a separate discussion of these issues, focusing on the project. NEPA does not require the agency to adopt the mitigation measures identified in an EIS. CEQA mandates adoption unless a measure is found to be infeasible for specific reasons.

Figure 3 summarizes these differences. Despite their minor differences, both NEPA and CEQA are flexible enough that a single environmental document can be prepared which will comply with both. For local agencies, the primary consideration is ensuring that the EIS meets the basic requirements of CEQA. Later, when the local agency uses the EIS as an EIR, it will be responsible for making the findings and statement of overriding considerations required under *Guidelines* Sections 15091 and 15093, respectively.

Preparing a Combined EIS/EIR

CEQA and the *CEQA Guidelines* strongly encourage State and local agencies to prepare a combined EIS/EIR (i.e., one document which satisfies both NEPA and CEQA) for projects where time is of the essence (Section 21083.6, *Guidelines* Section 15222). The NEPA regulations similarly encourage federal agencies to cooperate with local agencies "to the fullest extent possible to reduce duplication between NEPA and comparable State and local requirements," including the preparation of a joint document (40 CFR 1506.2). A joint document cannot be prepared solely by a State or local agency, it must include direct federal agency involvement (40 CFR 1506.2).

Preparing a combined EIS/EIR requires the close coordination and cooperation of the involved federal, State, and local agencies. This should include early agreement on the thresholds or other means of determining the significance of potential environmental effects and, where possible, upon the significant effects themselves. In many cases, the agencies preparing the joint EIS/EIR will enter into a Memorandum of Understanding (MOU) which formally establishes their roles and responsibilities in the process. Appendix II contains a model MOU for federal, State, and local agencies preparing a joint EIS/EIR. CEQA *Guidelines* section 15110 enables the State or local agency to waive the one-year time limit otherwise applicable to completion of an EIR. This lengthened period may be reflected in the MOU.

Those places where a single local entity is responsible for base reuse planning have a distinct advantage in the process. Coordination is simpler: the DoD service has fewer local agencies to deal with; a single base reuse plan, rather than competing individual plans, is agreed upon by the involved local agencies; and the plan being examined in the EIS/EIR is relatively stable.

The process of preparing an EIS/EIR proceeds most efficiently when the plan for reuse is well-defined from the beginning and not subject to change during environmental review. Obviously, this reuse plan cannot describe in detail all anticipated projects, particularly if it is prepared

Figure 3
Comparison of EIS and EIR

Draft EIS contains:

- A cover sheet enumerating the preparing agency, the project and its location, the agency contact person, a very brief abstract of the EIS, and final comment date. (40 CFR 1502.11)

- Table of contents and index. (40 CFR 1502.10)

- A summary of the EIS, including conclusions, areas of controversy, issues raised (i.e., significant effects), and issues to be resolved (i.e., mitigation and alternatives). (40 CFR 1502.12)

- Description of the purpose and need fulfilled by the project and its alternatives. (40 CFR 1502.13)

- A description of the affected environment. (40 CFR 1502.15)

- Discussion of a range of alternatives, including the proposed action and the no project alternative, comparatively analyzed and including mitigation measures. (40 CFR 1502.14)

- A list of the Federal permits required by the action. (40 CFR 1502.25)

- A description of the environmental consequences of the various alternatives, including: Direct, indirect, and cumulative environmental effects (40 CFR 1508.25); Growth-inducing effects (40 CFR 1508.8); Unavoidable significant effects; Proposed mitigation measures; Relationship between local short-term uses of man's environment and the maintenance and enhancement of long-term productivity; and Significant irreversible environmental changes. (40 CFR 1502.16)

- A list of preparers. (40 CFR 1502.17)

- A list of agencies and organizations consulted. (40 CFR 1502.10)

- Appendices. (40 CFR 1502.18)

Final EIS contains in addition:

- Comments received on the draft (40 CFR 1503.4); and

- Responses to comments, including revisions to the draft. (40 CFR 1503.4)

Draft EIR contains:

- Table of contents or index. (Guidelines Section 15122)

- Summary of the EIR, including summaries of proposed actions, significant effects, mitigation, and alternatives. (Guidelines Section 15123)

- Project description, including location, physical characteristics, objectives, and permits required from other agencies. (Guidelines Section 15124)

- Environmental setting of the project. (*Guidelines* Section 15125)

- An analysis of the environmental consequences of the project, including: Direct and indirect significant environmental effects of the proposal; Cumulative effects (*Guidelines* Section 15130); Unavoidable significant effects; Proposed mitigation measures ; Feasible alternatives; Relationship between local short-term uses of man's environment and the maintenance and enhancement of long-term productivity; Significant irreversible environmental changes; and Growth-inducing impacts. (*Guidelines* Section 15126)

- Effects not found to be significant. (*Guidelines* Section 15128)

- A list of organizations and persons consulted. (*Guidelines* Section 15129)

- Appendices. (*Guidelines* Section 15147)

Final EIR contains in addition:

- Comments received on the draft;

- A list of commenters; and

- Responses to comments, including revisions to the draft.

(*Guidelines* Section 15132)

early in the closure and reuse process. What it should do is establish the general land use objectives and policies which will be the foundation for later, more detailed, project-specific activities.

The more specific the reuse plan, the easier it may be to use its EIS/EIR as the basis for environmental review of later projects which occur pursuant to that plan. The ability of an EIS/EIR to address later projects with a minimum of additional environmental review hinges on meeting the procedural, as well as substantive requirements of CEQA. The local agency should take it upon itself to ensure that the EIS, in process and content, will meet CEQA requirements. For example, CEQA's stricter notice requirements must be complied with in addition to the requirements under NEPA.

The following chronology generally identifies those parts of the EIS and NEPA process which may need attention in order to meet CEQA standards, or which should be highlighted to illustrate their CEQA compliance, and suggests specific actions.

Notice of Intent (NOI)

The NOI performs the same function as CEQA's "Notice of Preparation" (NOP). The NOI should be supplemented with a summary of the probable environmental impacts of the project in order to meet the standards for NOP content under *CEQA Guidelines* Section 15082.

NEPA regulations require the federal agency to diligently pursue public involvement in the NOI. This includes direct notice to State and local responsible and trustee agencies as otherwise required under CEQA. The local agency may provide the federal agency a list of responsible and trustee agencies and their addresses to facilitate this notice.

Scoping

Scoping allows interested agencies the opportunity to comment on the project's potential effects and help focus the contents of the EIS/EIR. NEPA doesn't establish a specific length of time for the scoping process. This period must be at least 30 days, as provided for the review of an NOP under *CEQA Guidelines* Section 15082.

Notice of Availability (NOA)

This corresponds to the "Notice of Completion" required under the *CEQA Guidelines*. The NOA must be filed with the State Clearinghouse and an appropriate number of copies of the draft EIS/EIR must accompany it for circulation to State agencies. A copy must also be posted in the office of the County Clerk. The draft EIS/EIR must be available for public review for at least 45 days, as provided under Section 21091, and public notice of that fact must be given pursuant to Section 21092. NEPA regulations also require a 45-day review period (40 CFR 1506.10).

Draft EIS/EIR

This serves as the draft EIR. The local agency should review the draft EIS/ EIR to ensure that it meets CEQA standards before it is released for review. This can include examining the specific mitigation measures identified for the project and the EIS/EIR's discussion of the project's growth-inducing impacts, if any. The local agency may attach a cross-reference to the draft EIS/EIR to enable reviewers to locate the pertinent discussions required under CEQA.

Final EIS/EIR

In order to comply with CEQA, the local agency should highlight the responses to comments, attaching additional pages if necessary to describe them. Further, the local agency should check the FEIS/EIR to ensure that mitigation measures and any growth-inducing impacts relative to the project are specifically identified.

Distribution of the Final EIS

NEPA requires the federal lead agency to file a second NOA with the EPA and to distribute the final EIS/EIR to interested agencies, groups, and individuals at least 30 days prior to acting on the disposal and reuse plan (40 CFR 1506.10). CEQA does not have a corresponding requirement for circulating a final EIR. However, the CEQA lead agency must send to each commenting agency a proposed response to that agency's comment.

Action

After approval of the disposal and reuse plan by the DoD agency, the local agen-cy should file a Notice of Determination (NOD) for the EIS/EIR with the county clerk and the State Clearinghouse. This initiates CEQA's 30-day statute of limitations for legal challenges to an EIR.

Certification and Findings

Later, at such time as it uses the EIS/EIR, the local agency must certify the document pursuant to *Guidelines* Section 15090 and make the findings and statement of overriding considerations required under *Guidelines* Sections 15091 and 15093, respectively. Certification is the agency's voucher as to the CEQA adequacy of the EIS and its formal expression that the decision-making body has reviewed and considered the information contained in the EIS/EIR prior to approving the project. Pertinent mitigation measures must be adopted by the local agency at that time. A mitigation monitoring or reporting program must also be adopted (Section 21081.6).

An NOD must be filed within 5 days of the agency's action (Section 21152).

Boarding a Moving Train: Joining the EIS Process

As discussed above, Federal and California agencies may cooperate to prepare one document for base disposal and reuse plans which will satisfy both NEPA and CEQA requirements. The following section suggests an alternative intervention strategy for local agencies when a joint document is not being prepared and the federal agency is proceeding on its own.

CEQA specifically allows the use of an EIS in place of an EIR when the EIS meets all substantive requirements of CEQA (Section 21083.5 and *Guidelines* Section 15221). A local agency may take a number of independent actions which will help ensure that the EIS sufficiently complies with the provisions of CEQA and the *CEQA Guidelines* to qualify as an EIR. As in the case of joint preparation, the local agency must involve itself as early in the process as possible.

Typically, in this situation no locally agreed upon reuse plan is yet available. As a result, the local agency cannot expect the EIS to accurately reflect the eventual direction on reuse. In the end, the result should be an EIS which, although limited in its applicability to specific later projects, at least can be considered the equivalent of an EIR.

The primary goal of the local agency should be that the EIS will meet the basic notice and content requirements of CEQA. Tiering and application of the subsequent/ supplemental EIRs to later projects will be easier when there is no question that the prior EIS meets all substantive CEQA requirements.

Here are specific suggestions for each stage of the federal EIS process.

Notice of Intent

Request that the DoD agency submit a copy of the NOI to responsible State and local agencies and to the State Clearinghouse, pursuant to 40 CFR 1506.6 (public involvement). The local agency should provide a list of agencies and their addresses to the federal agency as part of this request. The local agency should also request that the NOI list the possible environmental impacts of the project.

Scoping

The local agency should offer comments to the DoD agency relative to the potential environmental effects, cumulative effects, growth-inducing impacts, project alternatives, and mitigation measures which would be required to comply with CEQA. The local agency's intention should be to direct the discussions in the EIS in a manner which will fulfill CEQA requirements for content.

Notice of Availability (NOA)

The local agency should request that the DoD agency send the NOA to the State Clearinghouse, as well as any other agencies that were sent the NOI, and provide a comment period that is no shorter than that established by the State Clearinghouse (at least 45 days). The NOI should contain all those elements required by Section 21092. The local agency should also request that the DoD agency send 10 copies of the Draft EIS to the Clearinghouse, or do so itself. In addition, the local agency should request that the DoD agency provide public notice of the NOA pursuant to Section 21092 (as encouraged by 40 CFR

1506.2 and 1506.6), or provide such notice itself. Notice should also be posted in the County Clerk's office for a period of not less than 30 days.

Draft EIS

Taking a tip from Section 21101, which directs State agencies to include in their comments on a draft EIS "a detailed statement" putting the comments into the context of the mandated contents of an EIR, the local agency's comments should identify that material which is otherwise required of an EIR. Particular attention should be paid to the project description, potential environmental effects, cumulative effects, growth-inducing impacts, project alternatives, and mitigation measures. Further, the local agency's comments may include additional discussion and analyses of these topics. They may also restate the contents of the EIS' discussion of the project in a format more consistent with CEQA.

For example, an EIS typically places equal emphasis on the project and alternatives. CEQA, however, emphasizes the project and relates the discussions of significant effects, cumulative effects, and growth inducing impacts directly to that project. A local agency may identify and reference, or even restate, the relevant EIS discussions as they relate to the reuse plan.

If no local base reuse plan was available during the drafting of the EIS, this is the last practical opportunity for the local agency to attempt to have such a plan incorporated into the EIS. If a local reuse plan has been completed by this stage, the local agency should submit a copy of that plan with its comments on the Draft EIS. The local agency may also include an examination of the reuse plan's significant effects, cumulative effects, and growth-inducing impacts.

Distribution of the Final EIS and Federal Action

If a base reuse plan is completed after the end of the review period for the Draft EIS, but during final distribution of the Final EIS, the local agency should immediately so inform the DoD agency and provide it with a copy of that plan. The local agency may suggest that for purposes of 40 CFR

Section 1502.9 the base reuse plan constitutes "significant new circumstances or information relevant to environmental concerns" requiring preparation of a supplement to the Final EIS. The supplement would effectively incorporate the local reuse plan into the EIS.

Applying an Existing EIS to Later Local Projects

An EIS can be used as an EIR to the extent that the EIS complies with the provisions of the *CEQA Guidelines* (Section 21083.5, *Guidelines* Section 15221). All too often, however, development opportunities arise which were not contemplated in the local reuse plan or EIS. When evaluating later proposals necessary to base reuse such as local base reuse plans, general plan amendments, specific plans, rezoning, or redevelopment plans, the local agency faces two key questions: Can the EIS suffice to address these later projects? If not, how may the information contained in the EIS be productively reused?

The local agency's first step should be to critically evaluate the adequacy of the EIS relative to the later proposal. This evaluation should pursue two broad lines of inquiry:

(1) *Content:* To what extent does the EIS comply with CEQA and, further, is the later project fully examined in the EIS? As discussed previously, the requirements of NEPA and CEQA largely overlap. Recognizing that an EIS will not necessarily look like an EIR and that *CEQA Guidelines* Section 15120 provides that there is no mandatory format for EIRs, disregard superficial differences and focus on the overall contents of the EIS.

Guidelines Section 15221 states that a separate discussion of mitigation measures and growth-inducing impacts will need to be "added, supplemented, or identified before the EIS can be used as an EIR." However, since the NEPA Guidelines require that an EIS contain these points of analysis, addition may not actually be necessary (40 CFR 1508.20). If the analysis must be supplemented, OPR recommends that the local agency prepare a supplemental EIR as provided under Section 15163 of the *CEQA Guidelines*. If the analysis is

present, but needs to be identified in order to show that it is present, the lead agency may follow the procedure for addenda provided under Section 15163 of the *Guidelines*.

(2) *Notice:* Was public notice and the opportunity for review and comment provided in accordance with CEQA procedures? If yes, then Section 15225 of the *CEQA Guidelines* enables the local agency to use the EIS as the equivalent of an EIR without additional circulation. If no, then the local agency should follow the procedure described under *Guidelines* Section 15153 for use of an EIR from an earlier project. This will include preparing an initial study and circulating the EIS for public review as a draft EIR.

Applying an Adequate EIS to Later Projects

Where the EIS complies with CEQA and adequately discusses the later project, such as a local reuse plan purposely written to match the preferred alternative set out in the EIS, Section 15221(b) of the *CEQA Guidelines* provides that the local agency need not prepare an EIR. The local agency must provide advance public notice pursuant to *Guidelines* Section 15087 that it intends to use the EIS as an EIR and that the EIS meets the requirements of CEQA. OPR recommends providing notice pursuant to Public Resource Code Section 21092. This notice does not open a new comment period.

From that point, the local agency proceeds as though using an EIR. The EIS must be certified (*Guidelines* Section 15090). Unlike NEPA, which requires federal agencies to consider, but not necessarily impose, mitigation measures and alternatives, the local agency must impose the applicable mitigation measures or alternatives identified in the EIS(EIR) if it approves the later project. It must adopt findings under *Guidelines* Section 15091 for each of the significant environmental effects identified in the EIS(EIR) and, if there are any unavoidable significant effects, a statement of overriding consideration pursuant to *Guidelines* Section 15093. A Notice of Determination must be filed with the County Clerk and, if the project will involve State agency approvals, with

OPR. The EIS (EIR) must be filed with other agencies as required under *Guidelines* Section 15095.

Using an EIS as the Basis for Additional Environmental Analysis

What if the later project was not fully addressed in the EIS? This may be the case when there was no local reuse plan available to the DoD agency during preparation of the EIS or, more commonly, when specific projects such as a specific plan or rezoning are proposed after completion of the NEPA process.

Later projects must undergo a new environmental review, beginning with an initial study to determine whether the project may have a significant adverse effect on the environment. If there is substantial evidence that such an effect may occur, the Lead Agency must prepare an EIR. If there is no substantial evidence for such an effect a negative declaration (including a mitigated negative declaration) is adopted instead (Section 21080). A mitigated negative declaration is used "when the initial study has identified potentially significant effects on the environment, but (1) revisions in the project plans or proposals made by, or agreed to by, the applicant before the proposed negative declaration is released for public review would avoid the effects or mitigate the effects to a point where clearly no significant effect on the environment would occur, and (2) there is no substantial evidence in light of the whole record before the public agency that the project, as revised, may have a significant effect on the environment" (Section 21064.5).

Where possible, the initial study should use and cite information in the EIS which is indicative of the presence or absence of a significant effect. Further, the later EIR or negative declaration may reference pertinent sections of the EIS rather than generating the same information a second time (*Guidelines* Section 15150).

Where the later activity was generally described in the EIS, but was not a focus of that document, the later review may be "tiered" upon the EIS. Pursuant to Sections 21093 and 21094, the review of the later project may avoid repetitive discussion of issues and focus on those issues which are "ripe for decision" and specific to the later project. One example of a project suitable for tiering might be adoption of specific zoning for a use described in the closure and reuse plan.

As a rule, tiering is used for "separate but related projects" (*Guidelines* Section 15152). A tiered EIR is limited to discussion of those significant effects which were not examined in the prior EIS or are susceptible to substantial reduction or avoidance by specific revisions or conditions imposed on the project. If a project's environmental review is to be tiered upon the previous EIS, the lead agency must find that the project is consistent with both of the following:

- The program, plan, policy, or ordinance for which the previous EIR (or in this case the EIS) was certified.

- The general plan and zoning of the city or county in which the project would be located (Section 21094(b)).

Recirculating an EIS

Section 21083.8 provides an optional procedure for those initial base reuse plans where an EIS has already been prepared and filed in accordance with NEPA. It involves circulating the EIS for review and comment as a precursor to using the federal document as a draft EIR.

The lead agency preparing an EIR for the initial reuse plan would proceed in the following manner:

- Issue an NOP pursuant to Section 21080.4 (or an expanded NOP pursuant to Section 21080.6) describing the proposed reuse plan and containing a copy of the EIS. The NOP would be required to state that the lead agency intends to use the accompanying EIS as a draft EIR and to request comments on whether and to what extent the EIS is adequate for that purpose and what specific additional information, if any, is needed.

- Upon the close of the NOP's comment period, continue with the EIR process, utilizing all or part of the EIS, combined with any necessary additional information, as the draft EIR.

Section 21083.8 is repealed by its own provisions on January 1, 2001.

SB 1180 and Baseline Conditions

A fundamental question in environmental analysis is what baseline conditions should be used for determining whether a proposed military base reuse plan will result in significant environmental effects. Should the potential impacts of the reuse plan be analyzed relative to the closed base, or in the context of the higher level of activity which existed before its closure or realignment?

SB 1180 of 1995 (Stats. of 1995, Chapter 861) was enacted as an optional means of establishing a baseline context for analysis. It offers a statutory "safe harbor" for agencies which follow its procedures. Although primarily designed for situations where an EIR is being prepared apart from an EIS, it is flexible enough to be used during preparation of a combined EIS/EIR.

Baseline Context

Most, but not all, armed services have opted in preparing their base closure and reuse EIS to relate their closure and reuse plan to the activity level which existed on their base when it was in full operation. Some reuse authorities and local agencies have followed the federal lead and assumed pre-closure activity as a baseline. Others have not felt comfortable with that approach and have analyzed the reuse plan as if no activity had previously existed.

SB 1180, codified in Section 21083.8.1, enables the lead agency to identify the specific physical conditions which existed when the federal decision to close or realign the base became final that will form the context for environmental review. For example, the lead agency may decide to ground its environmental analysis on pre-existing noise and traffic levels. The EIR would analyze that increment of impact, if any, which exceeds the baseline and, where that increment may result in a significant effect, address mitigation measures and alternatives accordingly. Where the reuse plan would not exceed the baseline level of activity, the lead agency could presume that no significant impact would occur. Once an EIR had been certified for a base reuse plan under this provision, all later activities consistent with or to implement that plan would avoid the need for further EIRs or negative declarations unless subject to *Guidelines* Sections 15162-15164.

There are limits to the conditions which may be included in the baseline determination. No hazardous material or waste can be included in a baseline, nor can water quality issues. In addition, although adoption of a baseline limits the review necessary for CEQA purposes, it does not forgive the plan's future compliance with federal, State, and local regulations and ordinances which might otherwise apply. For example, adopting a CEQA baseline for preexisting traffic levels at the military base would avoid the need to include mitigation measures or alternatives to address reuse plan traffic levels projected at that level or below, but would not change the requirements of the county's congestion management program or local traffic impact fees.

Reuse Plan

SB 1180 applies only to reuse plans which match the definition set out in Section 21083.8.1(a). For purposes of the statute, "reuse plan" means the initial plan for reuse of a military base adopted by a local government or redevelopment agency. The reuse plan may take the form of a general plan, general plan amendment, specific plan, redevelopment plan, or other planning document such as a community plan. The military base or reservation in question must be either closed or realigned, or slated for closure or realignment by the federal government.

A reuse plan under Section 21083.8.1 must include a statement of development policies and a diagram or diagrams illustrating that policy. The plan must designate the proposed general distribution and location, as well as the development intensity, of housing, business, industry, open space, recreation, natural resources, public buildings and grounds, roads and other transportation facilities, infrastructure, and those other public and private uses of land which may be of importance to the local government.

Section 21151.1, enacted in 1995, requires that an EIR be prepared for every

initial base reuse plan. The local lead agency has the usual options in preparing that document. For instance, a joint EIS/EIR would fulfill the requirement. Where an EIR alone is being prepared, it may incorporate pertinent portions of a previously prepared EIS. Section 21083.8.1 may be used to narrow the range of potential impacts of the proposed initial plan which must be analyzed in the required EIR.

Procedure

SB 1180 has unique requirements intended to ensure that the public, as well as responsible and trustee agencies are given ample opportunity to consider and discuss any proposed baselines. These create new responsibilities for the lead agency.

Prior to preparing its EIR, the lead agency must hold a noticed public hearing on the proposed baseline(s) at which to discuss the federal EIS prepared or being prepared for the base closure or realignment. This must include a discussion of the significant effects identified in the EIS, mitigation measures, feasible alternatives, and the mitigative effects of federal, State, and local laws applicable to planned future nonmilitary activities. Hearing notice must be provided per Section 21092. If the hearing cannot be completed at once, it may be continued to a time certain. Prior to the close of the hearing, the lead agency may specify, at its discretion:

- The baseline conditions to be used in preparation of the EIR. This should identify those particular levels of activity which existed prior to the federal base closure or realignment ROD that are to form the context within which the reuse plan's activities are analyzed. Activities might include traffic levels, housing, water use, or others.

- Any particular physical conditions to be addressed in greater detail in the EIR than in the EIS. This could include conditions which would be significant under CEQA that were not considered significant in the EIS, or adding detail to the mitigation measures discussed in the EIS.

Prior to holding the above hearing, the lead agency must consult with pertinent

responsible and trustee agencies regarding the proposed baseline(s) and provide those agencies 30 days in which to respond with their concerns. This consultation requirement neatly coincides with the NOP consultation period otherwise provided for under CEQA and can be combined with the NOP to avoid duplication of effort. Where the lead agency intends to use a previously prepared EIS as its EIR through the alternative procedure established under Section 21083.8 (see Section 5 of this advisory), it must also include a copy of the EIS with the NOP.

Section 21083.8.1 does not specify the contents of the notice sent to responsible and trustee agencies for review and comment. OPR suggests that it identify the particular activity, its specific pre-existing level, and outline any related significant effects, mitigation measures, and alternatives discussed in the EIS, and the expected mitigative effects of other regulations. Unless sent with an NOP, the notice should specify the location of the military base and the location of the activity (where applicable), the name and address of the lead agency, a contact person, and the date by which comments must be received. The notice should also provide the date, time, and place of the public hearing on the baseline, if known.

At the close of the public hearing, the lead agency must specify the following in writing:

- How it will integrate the selected baseline(s) into the CEQA analysis and the reuse planning process. Areas of discussion include community environmental standards, the applicable general plan, specific plan, and redevelopment plan, and any applicable provisions of adopted congestion management plans, habitat conservation or natural communities conservation plans, integrated waste management plans, and county hazardous waste management plans. One purpose of this requirement is to relate the baseline(s) to community environmental standards. The other is to describe the planning and regulatory context within which the baseline(s) exist.

- The economic and social reasons which support adoption of the baseline(s). These may include such things as new job creation, opportunities for the employment of skilled workers, availability of low- and moderate-income housing, and economic continuity. Although this determination resembles the finding of overriding consideration required under *Guidelines* Section 15093, it is a separate requirement which must be met before the draft EIR is circulated for review.

SB 1180 requires that the "no project" alternative analyzed in the EIR discuss the existing conditions on the base at time the EIR is being prepared, as well as what could be reasonably expected to occur in the foreseeable future if the reuse plan were not approved. The reasonable expectations must be based on current plans and be consistent with available infrastructure and services. This is identical to the requirement established in *Guidelines* Section 15126 for any discussion of a no project alternative.

After reaching this point, a lead agency which has chosen to employ Section 21083.8.1 would proceed as usual with the standard EIR process. It would release a draft EIR for review, respond to comments in the final EIR, certify the final EIR, adopt a mitigation monitoring or reporting program, and make the required findings under *Guidelines* Sections 15091 and 15093. Filing a notice of determination would fulfill the agency's responsibilities.

The provisions of SB 1180 will only be available for a limited time. If a lead agency chooses to employ Section 21083.8.1, it must release an NOP for consultation within one year from either the date of approval of the federal ROD completing the base closure or realignment, or January 1, 1997, whichever is later.

Advantages

The primary attraction of using Section 21083.8.1 is that it offers the lead agency a safe harbor within which to use pre-existing physical conditions as the context for determining whether the reuse plan may have a significant effect under CEQA.

Secondarily, the procedure ensures that interested public agencies and the public are given an opportunity to comment on the proposed baseline for analysis. And, that the lead agency makes a full disclosure of its approach to using the baseline.

Where a joint EIS/EIR is being prepared, SB 1180 offers an opportunity to publicly disclose and discuss the baseline assumptions applied in that joint document.

Bibliography

Bass, Ronald E. and Albert I. Herson, *Mastering NEPA: A Step-by-Step Approach,* 1993, Solano Press, Point Arena, California

Bass, Ronald E. and Albert I. Herson, *Successful CEQA Compliance: A Step-by-Step Approach* [predecessor to *CEQA Deskbook*], 1993, Solano Press, Point Arena, California

California Environmental Quality Act Statute and Guidelines, 1992, Governor's Office of Planning and Research, Sacramento, California

Kosta, Stephen L. and Michael H. Zischke, *Practice Under the California Environmental Quality Act,* 1993, Continuing Education of the Bar, Berkeley, California

Remy, Michael H., Tina Thomas, et al., *Guide to the California Environmental Quality Act,* 1993, Solano Press, Point Arena, California

Appendix 10

Thresholds of Significance:
Criteria for Defining Environmental Significance
CEQA Technical Advice Series

Source

"Thresholds of Significance: Criteria for Defining Environmental Significance" (September 1994), CEQA Technical Advice Series. This document is reprinted with permission from the Governor's Office of Planning and Research, 1400 10th Street, Sacramento, California 95814. For additional information please call (916) 322-4245.

Introduction

Determining whether or not a project may result in a significant adverse environmental effect is one of the key aspects of the California Environmental Quality Act (CEQA). *Thresholds of Significance* discusses how public agencies, including cities, counties, and special districts, may adopt quantitative or qualitative thresholds which represent the point at which a given environmental effect will be considered significant. Enacting thresholds helps ensure that during the initial study phase of environmental review significance determinations will be made on a consistent and objective basis.

Neither CEQA nor the *CEQA Guidelines* describes specific thresholds of significance or how they may be used. Appendix G of the *Guidelines* lists a variety of potentially significant effects, but does not provide a means of judging whether they are indeed significant in a given set of circumstances. Appendix I, the environmental checklist, prompts project reviewers to examine a spectrum of potential environmental effects, but leaves the determination of significance to the lead agency. Instead of dictating a one-size-fits-all approach, CEQA authorizes local governments to adopt by "ordinance, resolution, rule or regulation" their own "objectives, criteria, and procedures for the evaluation of projects" (Section 21082). Clearly, this enables local governments to adopt thresholds which will

assist in determining the environmental significance of a project.

By explaining thresholds of significance and the practical advantages to public agencies, the Office of Planning and Research hopes to encourage more local agencies to use them. This advisory paper is not a mandate of any kind. It does not replace, nor does it amend, the *CEQA Guidelines*. All citations refer to the Public Resources Code unless otherwise noted.

Threshold of Significance

Thresholds of significance are principally used to determine whether a project may have a significant environmental effect. They are not intended to be stand alone environmental policies, although they should certainly reflect the agency's policies. Thresholds are an analytical tool for judging significance.

When examining a project that is not exempt from CEQA, the Lead Agency usually prepares an initial study to determine whether the project may have a significant adverse effect on the environment. If no potential significant effects are identified, a negative declaration is prepared (Section 21080(c)). A mitigated negative declaration is called for if there are potential effects, but these can be mitigated to a level of insignificance (Section 21064.5). An EIR is required if there are significant environmental effects which cannot be avoided or mitigated (Sections 21100 and 21151). The *CEQA Guidelines* defines

"significant effect on the environment" as: "a substantial, or potentially substantial, adverse change in any of the physical conditions within the area affected by the project including land, air, water, minerals, flora, fauna, ambient noise, and objects of historic or aesthetic significance" (*Guidelines* Section 15382).

The "threshold of significance" for a given environmental effect is simply that level at which the Lead Agency finds the effects of the project to be significant. "Threshold of significance" can be defined as:

A quantitative or qualitative standard, or set of criteria, pursuant to which the significance of a given environmental effect may be determined.

Ideally, a threshold of significance provides a clear differentiation of whether or not the project may result in a significant environmental effect. More practically, a threshold will assist the Lead Agency in making this determination. In either case, thresholds do not substitute for the agency's use of careful judgment in determining significance (*CEQA Guidelines* Section 15064).

A threshold may be based on standards such as the following:

- A health-based standard such as air pollutant emission standards, water pollutant discharge standards, or noise levels.

- Service capacity standards such as traffic level of service, water supply capacity, or waste treatment plant capacity.

- Ecological tolerance standards such as physical carrying capacity, impacts on declared threatened or endangered species, loss of prime farmland, or wetland encroachment.
- Cultural resource standards such as impacts on historic structures or archaeological resources.
- Other standards relating to environmental quality issues, such as those listed in the *Guidelines'* Initial Study Checklist or Appendix G of the *Guidelines*.

Advantages

Adopting thresholds of significance promotes consistency, efficiency, and predictability in the initial study process.

Thresholds enable the Lead Agency to make consistent determinations of significance. Once thresholds have been adopted, every project in a given locale will be subject to a known set of impact assessment criteria. Project reviews undertaken by different staff members or at different times will employ a standard methodology. This increases certainty for both the agency and the applicant, as well as the fairness of the process.

The Lead Agency's efficiency in preparing an initial study may be improved when the anticipated effects of a project can be examined pursuant to standard thresholds. Standardizing review criteria reduces duplication of effort. It may also offer some assurance that a comprehensive review has been made.

Standard threshold criteria are also valuable as a method of "scoping" a proposed project. They may assist the Lead Agency in identifying Responsible Agencies, as well as focusing its environmental analysis on effects expected to be significant.

A threshold provides a rational basis for significance determinations. This complies with the *CEQA Guidelines'* requirement that a Lead Agency's determination of significance be "based to the extent possible on scientific and factual data" (*Guidelines* Section 15064). In this same vein, thresholds based on substantial evidence of significance bolster the defensibility of the determination.

The existence of a threshold may encourage project proponents to incorporate mitigation into the design of the project prior to submitting an application or a project's public review. The advantages of this are clear: the Lead Agency receives a project which has minimized its environmental impact; the project sponsor may avoid the need to prepare an EIR; when an EIR is required, it is properly focused on pertinent issues. Similarly, a threshold offers a target for revisions or mitigation actions which, if integrated into the project, would allow the preparation of a mitigated negative declaration rather than an EIR.

At least one court has shown a willingness to defer to local thresholds in order to decide a marginal situation where disagreement among experts or serious public controversy based on substantial evidence of a significant effect might require preparation of an EIR. In *Citizens Action to Serve All Students v. Thornley* (1990) 222 Cal.App. 3rd 748, the City of Hayward's traffic impact thresholds played some part in convincing the court that evidence did not exist to support the existence of a significant impact on traffic.

Establishing Thresholds

Only a few agencies have formally adopted a comprehensive set of significance thresholds as part of their local CEQA guidelines. Many others utilize in-house criteria which have not been adopted by the governing body (i.e., city council, board of supervisors, district board, etc.). These written, administrative rules can be as comprehensive as a formally adopted ordinance or resolution, and offer some advantages. Proponents of this approach point out that administrative thresholds are easier to adopt and amend and are less subject to conflicting political pressures than thresholds which are adopted by the governing body. In addition, they contend that administrative adoption avoids potential difficulties and misunderstandings arising from attempting to explain the technically and legally complex CEQA process. It may be cheaper as well.

Nonetheless, OPR recommends that whenever possible the governing body adopt thresholds by either resolution or ordinance after a public hearing. We believe

formal adoption is preferable because: (1) the thresholds will carry the full authority of the city or county, (2) the adoption process is a fully public undertaking, and (3) decision makers will have made a commitment to the thresholds by participating in their preparation and adoption.

Thresholds may be either qualitative or quantitative. Some effects, such as traffic or noise, lend themselves to numerical standards. Others, such as aesthetics or wildlife habitat are difficult to quantify and must rely upon qualitative descriptions. In either case, thresholds should be based on legal standards, studies, surveys, reports, or other data which can identify that point at which a given environmental effect becomes significant. Thresholds are intended to be analytic tools to assist in significance determinations, not rigid standards. They should not result in de facto policy making. Along this same vein, thresholds must reflect CEQA's fair argument standard, as discussed under the Limitations section of this paper.

The significance of an activity may vary with its setting. For instance, a subdivision which would create 10 new lots may not be significant in an urban area, but may be significant in an undeveloped rural area. In such instances, the Lead Agency could adopt more than one threshold of significance for a given effect or include flexible standards which recognize differences in setting.

Drafting Thresholds

Developing thresholds is not simple. The first step should be to identify those effects for which thresholds are to be drafted. These might be chosen from the agency's initial study work sheet or, they may be based upon the significant effects identified in Appendix G of the *Guidelines*.

The next step should be to gather and evaluate existing information relative to the chosen effects. Review past Master Environmental Assessments (MEAs), EIRs, Negative Declarations, and related environmental studies—at what point or under what circumstances was a given effect deemed significant? Are there effective criteria by which to measure significance?

The agency should also rely upon its general plan as a source of environmental standards. For instance, policies for the conservation of agricultural land may yield a threshold based on soil type, project size, and water availability. The noise element may provide noise exposure standards. The circulation element may establish level of service (LOS) standards for roads, sewers, and other services. Whenever possible, thresholds should be based on or otherwise reflect the community's adopted planning policies and regulations. The general plan and associated community plans, and specific plans can provide a long-term context for issues relating to land use, resources, and open space. By establishing thresholds, a jurisdiction is effectively recognizing the environmental ethics that are consistent with accepted local values.

A note of caution regarding the use of general plan policies: remember that a threshold represents that point at which a project's potential environmental effects are considered significant. The focus of the threshold is on actual limits to significant environmental impacts. When general plan policies or standards do not actually limit the potential impacts of a project to a particular level they are not effective measures of significance. Accordingly, at least two courts have held that "conformity with a general plan does not insulate a project from EIR review where it can be fairly argued that the project will generate significant environmental effects" (*Oro Fino Gold Mining Corp. v. County of El Dorado* (1990) 225 Cal.App.3d 872), citing *City of Antioch v. City Council* (1986) 187 Cal.App.3d 1325). In *Oro Fino Gold Mining,* the project proponent unsuccessfully argued that no significant impact existed because the proposed exploratory mine would not exceed the noise standards of the county general plan. The court dismissed this argument, marking that the county did not enforce those standards. Similarly, when examining a major road and sewer project, the *City of Antioch* court held that "general plan conformity alone does not effectively 'mitigate' significant effects of a project."

The Lead Agency should also survey other agencies for adopted standards which might lend themselves to thresholds. For example, the South Coast Air Quality Management District's *CEQA Air Quality Hand-book* promulgates quantitative pollutant emissions thresholds. A county Congestion Management Agency will have LOS standards for regionally significant roads. Neighboring cities and counties may have enacted pertinent thresholds of significance. Air, water, and toxic standards established by the Environmental Protection Agency and state and local agencies should also be reviewed. The Lead Agency should contact these other agencies to discuss incorporation of their thresholds into its own. Thresholds can and should be based on existing environmental laws and regulations whenever possible to reduce duplicative environmental reviews and take advantage of regulatory agency expertise.

Previously prepared studies and research are additional sources of thresholds, provided that they offer clear standards for assessing significance. These might include, but are not limited to, wetlands delineations, archaeological surveys, historic resources surveys or registers, capital improvement plans, and water district capacity studies.

Most agencies allow for some flexibility in the application of thresholds to individual projects. This is generally a good idea. It allows, for example, agencies to presume a certain project will have a significant effect if a threshold is exceeded, but allows case-by-case deviation from the threshold when unusual circumstances warrant.

Adoption Process

When enacting a resolution or ordinance establishing thresholds, the agency's legislative body should hold at least one public hearing before taking action. Because the thresholds relate to development projects, OPR recommends including the planning commission in the process of drafting thresholds. Through its public hearings, the commission can fine tune the work of staff as well as offer a forum for the concerns of its members and the public.

A jurisdiction may choose to offer more opportunities for public involvement. The City of Mountain View, for example, relied an informal committee of citizens, planners, environmentalists, and representatives of regional agencies to cooperatively draft its thresholds. This effort provided these interests a stake in the city's thresholds, ensured that the thresholds did not conflict with the requirements of regional agencies, and, importantly, reflected community values. The process had the further advantage of educating decision makers about the environmental review process.

If the jurisdiction decides to adopt its thresholds administratively, e.g., by an agency rather than the governing body, OPR suggests: (1) adopting a single set of thresholds for use by all agencies and departments within the jurisdiction; (2) undertaking the same broad review of sources recommended above; and (3) providing the public with opportunities to assist in drafting or at least review and comment on the proposed thresholds prior to adopting them.

Thresholds can offer the same basic advantages whether they are adopted legislatively or administratively. Jurisdictions will weigh their own political and administrative situation before deciding which style of adoption would work best for them.

Contents

A fully-fledged threshold should contain, in some form, the following elements:

- A brief definition of the potential effect.
- Reasons for its significance.
- Threshold criteria for significance.
- Geographic scope of the criteria, if applicable.
- References to the facts or data upon which the criteria are based.

The threshold may also contain a menu of standardized mitigation measures. These should be flexible enough to be tailored to individual projects. Standardized measures offer project proponents the opportunity to design their projects so that environmental effects are minimized from an early stage. Standardized measures can also assure the agency and the public that potential effects will be mitigated on a consistent basis and that the threshold represents the boundary between significance and insignificance.

The description of a threshold may be long or short depending upon its subject. In a jurisdiction with diverse locales, there may be more than one or even a sliding scale of thresholds for a single effect. For example, Ventura County has adopted two thresholds for surface water quality impacts based on project location within specified groundwater basins. Santa Barbara County uses a weighted point system to determine whether a given project will have a significant impact on agricultural lands.

OPR does not suggest that an agency establish a threshold for every conceivable environmental effect. This may be neither practical nor desirable. There may be certain effects, such as aesthetic impacts, which for one reason or another are not easily described. There is no advantage to adopting a threshold which does not clarify or otherwise improve the process of determining significance.

Once adopted, thresholds should be reviewed periodically and revised as necessary to incorporate changes as conditions and regulations change.

Appendix 2 contains excerpts from adopted thresholds. OPR does not necessarily endorse these specific thresholds; they are simply offered as representative examples of how jurisdictions have chosen to define particular levels of significance.

Ten Tips for Thresholds

1 Write the threshold criteria clearly and succinctly. Thresholds, whether quantitative or qualitative, should be as objective as possible so that they can be applied in a consistent manner.

2 Enact only those thresholds with a basis in fact (technical thresholds such as traffic levels and air quality standards) or in adopted policy (community thresholds such as aesthetics), and reference that basis. A factual basis may be developed as part of the process of preparing thresholds. Further, the standards or regulations upon which the thresholds are based must be enforceable.

3 Do not force an issue. If a clear threshold does not exist, or existing policies are vague and unenforceable, simply do not adopt a threshold for that effect.

4 Harmonize the thresholds with those of other agencies to the extent possible, particularly the technical thresholds of regulatory agencies such as an air quality management district or water quality control board.

5 Review thresholds periodically to ensure their continued relevance and accuracy.

6 Revise thresholds promptly upon the receipt of pertinent new information.

7 Adopt quantitative rather than qualitative thresholds whenever reasonably possible.

8 Base thresholds on existing standards and regulations whenever possible.

9 Adopt thresholds as part of the local CEQA guidelines, with public review, either by ordinance or resolution.

10 Place all thresholds in a single document and in a format that encourages their use during the initial study process.

Limitations

Thresholds can help determine the significance of environmental effects, but are not necessarily conclusive. A lead agency's significance determination can be challenged if opponents of the determination produce substantial evidence supporting a fair argument that a significant effect does exist. Even more troublesome, what happens when the thresholds adopted by the Lead Agency are less stringent than those adopted by another agency for the same effect? Can project opponents (other than a Responsible Agency, which is limited by Section 21167.3) reference the stricter thresholds as evidence of a significant environmental effect?

The original determination whether to prepare either a Negative Declaration or an EIR is subject to the "fair argument" test (*Laurel Heights Improvement Assoc. v. U.C. Regents* (1993) 47 Cal.3d 376). In other words, when a fair argument can be raised on the basis of substantial evidence in the record that the project may have a significant adverse environmental impact—even if evidence also exists to the contrary—then an EIR is required. If another agency's more stringent thresholds are based upon substantial evidence of environmental effects, then the fair argument test would seem to require preparation of an EIR even though the project does not exceed the Lead Agency's threshold (this would not apply to subsequent activities

under a program EIR or the decision to prepare a subsequent/supplemental EIR). Although there is no absolute means of avoiding this problem, the agency preparing the thresholds may minimize it by consulting with other agencies during the drafting process and working out inconsistencies before adoption.

Furthermore, significance thresholds may not obviate the need to provide information to support the determinations made in the initial study. Simply filling out an initial study checklist without citing supporting information is insufficient to show the absence of significant effects (*Sundstrom v. County of Mendocino* (1988) 202 Cal.App.3d 296). Proper thresholds give the checklist reviewer sufficient background to make reasonable determinations on the basis of facts and should be referenced in the initial study. An initial study is not intended to provide the full-blown analysis that would be contained in a complete EIR (*Leonoff v. Monterey County Board of Supervisors* (1990) 222 Cal.App.3d 1337) and, by inference, neither is the discussion of thresholds.

Final Word

Thresholds are an underused means of making CEQA practice more rational, predictable, and scientific. Enacting thresholds of significance offers many advantages for local agencies. A project's potential significant environmental effects may be readily identified. Carefully drawn thresholds can ensure that environmental reviews are consistent and predictable from project to project. Thresholds based on existing local policies and environmental regulations offer the opportunity to integrate those policies and regulations through the CEQA process. The background data upon which thresholds are based may offer evidence of the existence or absence of a significant effect, supporting the Lead Agency's decision to prepare an EIR or negative declaration, respectively. Thresholds may be adopted for a comprehensive list of potential effects, or for only a few effects; either approach can be useful.

Thresholds are a valuable CEQA tool that OPR recommends for more widespread use among Lead Agencies.

Appendix 11

Circulation and Notice Under the California Environmental Quality Act

CEQA Technical Advice Series

Source

"Circulation and Notice Under the California Environmental Quality Act" (January 1998), CEQA Technical Advice Series. This document is reprinted with permission from the Governor's Office of Planning and Research, 1400 10th Street, Sacramento, California 95814. For additional information please call (916) 322-4245.

Solano Press Books has made every effort to see that no changes have been made to the contents of this state document as a result of reformatting and reprinting. Any omissions or changes to the contrary are entirely the responsibility of Solano Press Books and not the State of California.

Introduction

The California Environmental Quality Act (CEQA) is, in many ways, a procedural statute. One of the challenges facing the CEQA practitioner is to keep track of all the required and suggested notice, consultation, and review periods promulgated by CEQA and the *CEQA Guidelines*. In addition, revisions are made to the statute and the *Guidelines* through legislation and changes promulgated by the Secretary of the Resources Agency. The purpose of this brief paper is to provide an overview of those requirements.

The reader is assumed to have a working knowledge of CEQA. This advisory focuses on notice, consultation, and review without delving into the other substantive requirements of the Act. For a more complete discussion of this complex law, please refer to the books listed in the bibliography.

The terms "must," "requires," and "may" are used carefully in the following advisory. "Must," or "requires" denotes a mandatory action required by CEQA or the *CEQA Guidelines*. "May" denotes a suggested, but not mandatory action.

Please note that inconsistencies may exist between the CEQA statute and the *CEQA Guidelines*. In such instances, it is important to remember that the Act prevails over the *Guidelines* where clear conflict exists.

Circulation and Notice under CEQA

"Public participation is an essential part of the CEQA process."
Guidelines Section 15201

CEQA's Guiding Policy

Two of the basic purposes of CEQA are to inform governmental decisionmakers and the public about the potential significant effects, if any, of proposed activities and to provide opportunities for other agencies and the public to review and comment on draft environmental documents. The latter is crucial to the effectiveness of the former. Along these lines, CEQA and the *CEQA Guidelines* establish a number of specific points during the review and consideration of a project when the lead agency must inform other agencies and the public of the project and its potential environmental ramifications.

Julius Caesar wrote that "All of Gaul is divided in three parts." Coincidentally, the same can be said of the CEQA process. Depending upon the characteristics of a project and its potential for significant environmental effects, CEQA review may pursue either of three basic directions: (1) an exemption (statutory or categorical); (2) a negative declaration (including a mitigated negative declaration); or (3) an environmental impact report (EIR). Requirements for review, comment, and notice vary according to the complexity of the environmental review. A project that is exempt from CEQA has fewer requirements than a project subject to an EIR. In the following sections, we will examine in detail the relative requirements for each level of environmental review.

Exempt Projects

CEQA exempts a number of specific kinds of projects from its provisions. For example, emergency repairs to public service facilities and specific actions necessary to prevent or mitigate an emergency are statutorily exempt from CEQA pursuant to Public Resources Code (PRC) Section 21080(b). In addition, the Secretary of the Resources Agency has identified 29 classes of project which are normally exempt from the Act. Exemptions cannot be used for projects which have cumulative impacts, when there is a reasonable possibility that there may be a significant impact due to unusual circumstances, or when there would be an adverse impact on historical resources, for example. Possible exemptions include, but are not limited to, the operation, repair, or minor alteration of existing facilities, replacement or reconstruction of existing structures, and construction or replacement of accessory structures (*Guidelines* Section 15301, 15302, and 15311, respectively).

In coordination with the Permit Streamlining Act (Government Code Section 65950), the lead agency **must** approve or deny a development project within 60 days from the date it determines that the project is exempt from CEQA.

- **Notice of Exemption**—PRC Sections 21108 and 21152, and *Guidelines* Section 15062 provide that after approving a project for which an exemption was employed, the lead agency (or the applicant) *may* file a Notice of Exemption with the county clerk. If a state agency files this notice, it must be filed with the Office of Planning and Research (OPR). Appendix E of the *CEQA Guidelines* contains a suggested format for the Notice of Exemption. Filing a Notice of Exemption triggers a 35-day statute of limitations for litigation. If a Notice of Exemption is not filed, the statute of limitations becomes 180 days from either the date the decision is made to carry out or approve a project, or where no formal decision is required, 180 days from the date the project is commenced. (PRC Section 21167).

There are no other notice requirements for CEQA exemptions.

Initial Study

The decision whether to prepare a negative declaration or an EIR is based on findings supported by the lead agency's initial study. CEQA and the *Guidelines* contain a number of consultation suggestions and requirements which are applicable at this stage of the environmental process. Comments received during the initial study consultation allow the lead agency to identify responsible, trustee, and other agencies and their specific concerns. Further, the initial study provides the analyses necessary to determine whether an EIR will be required or a negative declaration may be adopted. This determination is based upon whether it can be fairly argued, based on substantial evidence in light of the whole record, that a project may or may not have a significant effect on the environment. Even if a fair argument can be raised that a project will not have a significant effect on the environment, it will be outweighed where, at the same time, a fair argument can be raised that it will have a significant effect on the environment (*Guidelines* Section 15064 and *No Oil v. City of Los Angeles* (1975) 13 Cal.3d 68).

- **Preapplication Consultation**—PRC Section 21080.1 *requires* that the lead agency, upon the request of a potential applicant, provide for consultation prior to the filing of the application regarding the range of actions, potential alternatives, mitigation measures, and any potential and significant effects on the environment that the proposed project may have.
- **Preconsultation**—PRC Section 21080.3 provides that the lead agency *may* consult informally with responsible and trustee agencies before preparing the initial study.
- **Agency Consultation**—PRC Section 21080.3 *requires* the lead agency to consult with responsible and trustee agencies regarding the project during preparation of the initial study. Note that this supersedes the requirement of *Guidelines* Section 15063 for "informal" consultation.
- **Applicant Consultation**—*Guidelines* Section 15063 provides that the lead agency *may* consult with the applicant to determine whether the applicant would be willing to revise the project to mitigate or avoid potential significant effects and thereby qualify for a mitigated negative declaration.

Negative Declaration

A negative declaration may be prepared when, based upon substantial evidence in light of the whole record, the project will not have a significant effect on the environment. In situations where a potential significant effect is identified, but revisions or mitigation measures imposed on the project will avoid or reduce the effect to a level of insignificance, a negative declaration may also be prepared. The following sections summarize the consultation and notice requirements which are applicable at the time the initial study is completed and the decision is made to prepare a negative declaration (including subsequent negative declarations as provided under *CEQA Guidelines* Section 15162). Please refer to the cited sections

of CEQA and the *CEQA Guidelines* for additional information.

A Negative Declaration circulated for public review **must** include (*CEQA Guidelines* Section 15071) a brief description of the project, including a commonly used name for the project, if any; the location of the project, preferably shown on a map, and the name of the project proponent; a proposed finding that the project will not have a significant effect on the environment; an attached copy of the Initial Study documenting reasons to support the finding; and mitigation measures, if any, included in the project to avoid potentially significant effect.

- **Notice of Intent to Adopt a Negative Declaration**—PRC Section 21092 and *Guidelines* Section 15072 *require* the lead agency to provide public notice of its intent to adopt a negative declaration. Section 21092 establishes the means by which notice is to be given, as well as the contents of that notice.
- **Posting of Notice**—In addition, PRC Section 21092.3 *requires* notice to be posted for 20 days in the office of the county clerk of each county in which the project will be located (30 days if the negative declaration has been sent to the State Clearinghouse).
- **Notice to Individuals**—PRC Section 21092.2 also *requires* notice of the availability of a draft negative declaration to be mailed to any person who has filed a written request for notification with the lead agency.
- **Agency Consultation on Draft Negative Declaration**—PRC Section 21091 and *Guidelines* Section 15073 *require* that the proposed negative declaration and its initial study be attached to the Notice of Intent and sent to every responsible and trustee agency concerned with the project and every other public agency with jurisdiction by law over resources affected by the project for review and comment.
- **Additional Agency Consultation**—PRC Section 21092.4 further

requires the lead agency for a project which would have state-wide, regional, or areawide significance to consult with the regional transportation planning agency and public agencies that have transportation facilities which would be affected.

- **Review and Consultation Period**—The preceding notice and consultation opportunities are intended to occur simultaneously. Pursuant to PRC Section 21091 and *Guidelines* Section 15073, agencies and the public *must* be afforded at least 20 days to review and comment on the negative declaration. When one or more of the responsible or trustee agencies is a state agency, or when a project is of statewide, regional, or areawide significance, as defined in *Guidelines* Section 15206, a copy of the negative declaration *must* be sent to the State Clearinghouse, and *should* be sent to the appropriate metropolitan area council of governments. In these situations, the public review period shall be at least as long as the review period established by the State Clearinghouse (normally 30 days)

- **Comments**—When considering whether to approve a project, the lead agency *must* consider the comments received during its consultation and review periods together with the negative declaration (*Guidelines* Section 15074). However, unlike with an EIR, these comments are *not required* to be attached to the negative declaration, nor must the lead agency make specific written responses to public agencies. However, the lead agency must notify in writing any public agency which comments on a proposed negative declaration of any public hearing for the project for which the document was prepared.

- **Substitution of Mitigation Measures**—PRC Section 21080(f) and *CEQA Guidelines* Section 15074.1 provide that the lead agency may,

prior to project approval, delete mitigation measures from a mitigated negative declaration and substitute for them other measures which the lead agency determines are equivalent or more effective. The lead agency is *required* to hold a public hearing on the matter and adopt a written finding that the new measure is equivalent or more effective in mitigating or avoiding potential significant effects and that it in itself will not cause any potentially significant effect on the environment. If a public hearing is already being held to consider the project approval, no separate hearing is required.

- **Notice of Determination**—A local agency which approves or determines to carry out a project for which a negative declaration was adopted *must* file a Notice of Determination with the county clerk within 5 days of its action (PRC Section 21152 and *Guidelines* Section 15075). The notice *must* be posted by the clerk within 24 hours of receipt, remain posted for 30 days, and, when the posting period is over, returned to the local agency with certification of its posting. If the project also requires discretionary approval from a state agency, the notice must also be filed with the Office of Planning and Research (*Guidelines* Section 15075).

- **State Agency Notice of Determination**—A state agency which approves or determines to carry out a project for which a negative declaration was adopted *must* file a Notice of Determination with the Office of Planning and Research (PRC Section 21108 and *Guidelines* Section 15075). A list of these notices shall be posted weekly by OPR and each list shall remain posted for at least 30 days.

- **Completion/Adoption of the Negative Declaration**—When a project proponent is other than a public agency, the Negative Declaration must be completed and

adopted within 180 days from the date the lead agency accepted the application as complete. The project must be approved or denied within 60 days of adopting the Negative Declaration (PRC Section 21151.5).

Filing a Notice of Determination triggers a 30-day statute of limitations for litigation. If the notice is not filed with the County Clerk or OPR within 5 days, the statute of limitations becomes 180 days from the date the decision is made to carry out or approve a project, or where no formal decision is required, 180 days from the date the project is commenced (PRC Section 21167).

Environmental Impact Report (EIR)

An EIR is prepared when substantial evidence exists, based upon the whole record, that a project may have a significant adverse effect on the environment.

The following summarizes the consultation and notice requirements for EIRs in chronological order. Please refer to the cited sections of CEQA and the *CEQA Guidelines* for details about the requirements. This list begins after completion of the initial study and the decision to prepare an EIR.

- **Notice of Preparation**—PRC Section 21080.4 and *Guidelines* Section 15082 *require* that the lead agency immediately send notice of its determination to prepare an EIR to all affected responsible agencies, trustee agencies, and federal agencies. These agencies have 30 days to inform the lead agency with specific detail about the scope and content of the environmental information germane to the responsible, trustee, or federal agency's area of statutory responsibility which must be included in the EIR. PRC Section 21080.4 further provides that the lead agency *must* convene a scoping meeting to discuss these issues upon the request of any affected responsible or trustee agency. Upon request of a lead agency or project applicant, OPR *must* assist the scoping effort by identifying the various responsible, trustee, and federal agencies.

- **Early Public Consultation**—Prior to completing the draft EIR, *Guidelines* Section 15083 provides that the lead agency *may* also consult with other persons or organizations which may be concerned with the environmental effects of the project. PRC Section 21153 provides that, upon request of the applicant, the lead agency *must* consult with affected agencies and *may* consult with persons who the applicant believes will be concerned with environmental effects, as well as members of the public making a written request. Early consultation provides the opportunity to identify the range of actions, alternatives, mitigation measures, and significant effects to be analyzed in depth in the environmental impact report.

- **Consultation with Water Agencies**—Projects affecting water agencies and meeting the criteria established under *CEQA Guidelines* Section 15083.5 are *required* to send a notice of preparation to each public water system which serves or would serve the proposed project. These agencies have 30 days to submit a water supply assessment addressing the adequacy of the supply to support the demand created by the project. The lead agency *shall* include in the EIR the information provided by the water agency (up to ten pages) and must determine whether projected water supplies will be sufficient to meet the demand of the project, in addition to existing and planned future uses.

- **Notice of Completion**—PRC Section 21161 and *Guidelines* Section 15085 *require* the lead agency to file a Notice of Completion with OPR as soon as a draft EIR is completed. Pursuant to the *Guidelines*, this notice can be combined with the cover form required by the State Clearinghouse of EIRs submitted for state review.

- **Public Review of Draft** *EIR*—*Guidelines* Section 15087 *requires* that the lead agency give public notice of the availability of a draft EIR by one of several methods at the same time that it submits the Notice of Completion to OPR. Notice *must* also be sent to affected responsible, trustee, and federal agencies. The method and contents of this notice are prescribed by Section 15087 and PRC Section 21092. PRC Section 21092 *requires* additional notice for waste burning projects.

- **Posting of Notice**—PRC Section 21092.3 *requires* the above notice to be posted for 30 days in the office of the county clerk of each county in which the project will be located.

- **Notice to Individuals**—PRC Section 21092.2 *requires* notice of the availability of a draft EIR to be mailed to any person who has filed a written request for notification with the lead agency.

- **Agency Consultation**—When a draft EIR is completed, *Guidelines* Section 15086 *requires* the lead agency to consult with the affected responsible, trustee, and federal agencies, as well as any person which the lead agency believes has expertise in the area, and request comments on the draft EIR. PRC Sections 21104 and 21153 *require* the lead agency to also consult with any city or county which borders the city or county within which the project is proposed.

- **Additional Agency Consultation**—PRC Section 21092.4 further *requires* the lead agency for a project which would have statewide, regional, or areawide significance to consult with the regional transportation planning agency and public agencies that have transportation facilities which would be affected.

- **Caltrans Scoping Meeting**—PRC Section 21083.9 specifies that when so requested by Caltrans, a lead

agency *must* call at least one scoping meeting prior to completing an EIR to discuss any proposed project which may affect highways or other Caltrans facilities.

- **Department of Fish and Game**—PRC Section 21104.2 *requires* state lead agencies to consult, and obtain written findings from, the Department regarding the potential impacts of a project on endangered or threatened species.

- **Review and Consultation Period**—The preceding notice and consultation opportunities, beginning with "Public Review of Draft EIR," are intended to occur simultaneously. Pursuant to *Guidelines* Section 15105, the period for public and agency review of and consultation on a draft EIR shall not be less than 30 days, nor should it be longer than 60 days except under unusual circumstances. When a draft EIR is submitted to the State Clearinghouse, the review period shall not be less than 45 days, unless a shorter period of not less than 30 days is approved by the State Clearinghouse.

  Draft EIRs which *must* be submitted to the State clearinghouse for review include: EIRs prepared by a state agency; those prepared by a public agency where a state agency is a responsible or trustee agency; those prepared for a project of statewide, regional, or areawide significance; and draft EIRs prepared pursuant to NEPA. Projects of statewide, regional, or areawide significance are defined in *Guidelines* Section 15206.

- **Comments on Draft EIR**—PRC Section 21091 *requires* the lead agency to include in the final EIR responses to comments which describe the disposition of any significant effects brought up by commenters. PRC Section 21092.5 further requires that written responses to the comments submitted by public agencies must be provided to those agencies at least

10 days prior to certification of the final EIR.

- **Recirculation**—PRC Section 21092.1 and *Guidelines* Section 15088.5 *require* an EIR to be recirculated to responsible and trustee agencies for consultation and new public notice given whenever significant new information has been added to the EIR after the draft has been available for review, but prior to certification of the final EIR. The review and consultation period is the same as for a draft EIR. "Significant new information" is defined in *Guidelines* Section 15088.5.

- **Notice of Determination**—A local agency which approves or determines to carry out a project for which an EIR was certified *must* file a Notice of Determination with the county clerk within 5 days of its action (PRC Section 21152 and *Guidelines* Section 15094). The notice *must* be posted by the clerk within 24 hours of receipt, remain posted for 30 days, and, when the posting period is over, returned to the local agency with certification of its posting. If the project also requires discretionary approval from a state agency, the notice *must* also be filed with the Office of Planning and Research (*Guidelines* Section 15094).

- **State Agency Notice of Determination**—A state agency which approves or determines to carry out a project for which an EIR was certified *must* file a Notice of Determination with the Office of Planning and Research (PRC Section 21108 and *Guidelines* Section 15094). A list of these notices *must* be posted weekly by OPR and each list shall remain posted for at least 30 days.

- **Statute of Limitations**—Filing a Notice of Determination triggers a 30-day statute of limitations for litigation. If the notice is not filed with the County Clerk or OPR within 5 days, the statute of limitations becomes 180 days from the date the decision is made to carry out or approve a project, or where no formal decision is required, 180 days from the date the project is commenced (PRC Section 21167).

- **Copy of Final EIR**—*Guidelines* Section 15095 *requires* the lead agency to file a copy of the final EIR with the planning agency of any city or county where significant environmental effects may occur. In addition, the applicant *must* be required to provide a copy of the certified final EIR to each responsible agency.

- **Completion/Certification of the EIR**—When a project proponent is other than a public agency, the EIR *must* be completed and certified within one year from the date when the lead agency accepted the application as complete. The one year limit may be extended once for a period of not more than 90 days upon consent of the applicant and the lead agency.

Summary List

Exempt Projects

- No consultation or public notice required by CEQA.
- Filing of a Notice of Exemption is optional.

Initial Study

- Preconsultation with responsible and trustee agencies is optional.
- Consultation with responsible and trustee agencies is required.
- Consult with the applicant over mitigation or avoidance of potentially significant effects where pertinent.

Negative Declaration

Consultation requirements of the Initial Study apply, plus the following:

- Public notice of the availability of the draft negative declaration is required.
  - Publish and mail notices.
  - Post notice with the County Clerk.

  - Provide notice to responsible, trustee, and other agencies.
  - Provide notice to individuals upon request.
- Consultation is begun with the notice of availability.
  - Consult with responsible and trustee agencies.
  - Consult with transportation agencies (for projects of statewide, regional, or areawide significance).
- A public hearing must be held on any proposed changes to mitigation measures.
- A Notice of Determination must be filed after approving a project for which a negative declaration was adopted.

Environmental Impact Report

Consultation requirements of the Initial Study apply, plus the following:

- A Notice of Preparation must be sent to all affected responsible, trustee, and federal agencies and a scoping meeting held upon request.
  - Early public consultation must be held with affected water system agencies.
  - Early public consultation may be held with interested persons or organizations and must be held, at the request of the applicant, with affected agencies.
- A Notice of Completion must be filed with OPR when the draft EIR is completed.
- Public notice must be given of the availability of the draft EIR for review.
  - Publish and mail notices.
  - Post notice with the County Clerk.
  - Provide notice to all affected responsible, trustee, and federal agencies
  - Send notice of the draft EIR's availability to individuals upon request.
- Consultation begins at this time.
  - Consult with affected responsible, trustee, and federal agencies, cities and counties bordering the

jurisdiction within which the project is located, as well as individuals with pertinent expertise.

- Submit the draft EIR for a project involving a state agency or which is of statewide, regional, or areawide significance to the State Clearinghouse for distribution.

- Consult with transportation agencies (for projects of state-wide, regional, or areawide significance).

- Hold a scoping meeting when requested by Caltrans.

- State lead agencies must consult with the Department of Fish and Game.

• The EIR must be recirculated if significant new information has been added after the draft EIR was circulated for review and consultation, but before the final EIR is certified.

• Written draft responses to public agency comments must be provided to those agencies prior to certification of the EIR.

• A Notice of Determination must be filed after approving a project for which an EIR was certified.

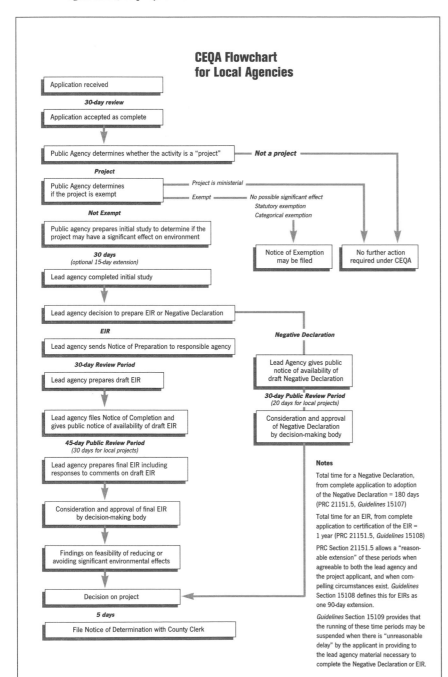

CEQA Flowchart for Local Agencies

Application received

30-day review

Application accepted as complete

Public Agency determines whether the activity is a "project" → **Not a project**

Project

Public Agency determines if the project is exempt → *Project is ministerial* / *Exempt* → No possible significant effect / Statutory exemption / Categorical exemption

Not Exempt

Public agency prepares initial study to determine if the project may have a significant effect on environment

30 days (optional 15-day extension)

Lead agency completed initial study

Notice of Exemption may be filed

No further action required under CEQA

Lead agency decision to prepare EIR or Negative Declaration

EIR

Lead agency sends Notice of Preparation to responsible agency

30-day Review Period

Lead agency prepares draft EIR

Lead agency files Notice of Completion and gives public notice of availability of draft EIR

45-day Public Review Period (30 days for local projects)

Lead agency prepares final EIR including responses to comments on draft EIR

Consideration and approval of final EIR by decision-making body

Findings on feasibility of reducing or avoiding significant environmental effects

Decision on project

5 days

File Notice of Determination with County Clerk

Negative Declaration

Lead Agency gives public notice of availability of draft Negative Declaration

30-day Public Review Period (20 days for local projects)

Consideration and approval of Negative Declaration by decision-making body

Notes

Total time for a Negative Declaration, from complete application to adoption of the Negative Declaration = 180 days (PRC 21151.5, *Guidelines* 15107)

Total time for an EIR, from complete application to certification of the EIR = 1 year (PRC 21151.5, *Guidelines* 15108)

PRC Section 21151.5 allows a "reasonable extension" of these periods when agreeable to both the lead agency and the project applicant, and when compelling circumstances exist. *Guidelines* Section 15108 defines this for EIRs as one 90-day extension.

Guidelines Section 15109 provides that the running of these time periods may be suspended when there is "unreasonable delay" by the applicant in providing to the lead agency material necessary to complete the Negative Declaration or EIR.

Bibliography

Guide to the California Environmental Quality Act, by Michael Remy, Tina Thomas, et al., Solano Press Books, P.O. Box 773, Point Arena, CA 95468, phone: (707) 884-4508. The CEQA practitioner's "Bible" is a highly respected and comprehensive discussion of the Act, including recent case law. It includes a copy of the current statutes and the State CEQA Guidelines.

Practice under the California Environmental Quality Act, by Stephen L. Kostka and Michael H. Zischke, Continuing Education of the Bar, 2300 Shattuck Avenue, Berkeley, CA 94704, phone: (800) 924-3924. Concise, authoritative, and comprehensive, this two volume set is intended for use by both environmental planners and attorneys.

State Clearinghouse Handbook, Governor's Office of Planning and Research, 1400 Tenth Street, Sacramento, CA 95814, phone: (916) 322-3170. The requirements and procedures of the State Clearinghouse regarding the review of environmental documents and federal grants are described in detail in this handbook.

CEQA Deskbook, by Ronald Bass and Albert Herson, Solano Press Books, P.O. Box 773, Point Arena, CA 95468, phone: (707) 884-4508. This is a "how-to" manual offering practical advice on complying with CEQA's procedures and legal requirements. It includes the current statutes and State CEQA Guidelines.

Glossary

Categorical Exemption

An exemption from CEQA for certain projects that the Secretary for Resources has determined generally do not have a significant effect on the environment.

Cumulative Impacts

Two or more environmental effects which, when considered together, are considerable or which compound or increase other environmental impacts.

Direct Impacts

Primary environmental effects which are caused by a project and occur at the same time and place.

Environment

The physical conditions which exist within an area which will be affected by a proposed project. The conditions include land, air, water, minerals, flora, fauna, noise, and objects of historical or aesthetic significance.

Environmental Impact Report

A detailed statement describing and analyzing the significant environmental effects of a project, and discussing ways to mitigate or avoid those effects.

Findings

Written legal conclusions prepared by a public agency that explain the disposition of each significant environmental effect and alternative identified in an EIR.

Indirect Impacts

Also referred to as secondary effects, indirect impacts are caused by a project and occur later in time or at some distance from the project; however, they are still reasonably foreseeable.

Initial Study

A preliminary analysis prepared by a Lead Agency determining whether an EIR or Negative Declaration must be prepared, and identifying the significant environmental effects to be analyzed in an EIR.

Lead Agency

The public agency that has the principal responsibility for carrying out or approving a project.

Mitigation Measure

A change in a project designed to avoid, minimize, rectify, reduce, or compensate for a significant environmental impact.

National Environmental Policy Act

The federal law that provided the model for CEQA and requires federal agencies to prepare Environmental Impact Statements (EIS) for federal actions significantly affecting the human environment.

Negative Declaration

A written statement prepared by a Lead Agency that briefly describes the reasons why a proposed project will not have a significant effect on the environment and, therefore, does not require an EIR.

Notice of Completion

A brief notice filed with the Office of Planning and Research by the Lead Agency, as soon as it has completed a draft EIR.

Notice of Determination

A brief notice filed by a pubic agency after it approves or determines to carry out a project.

Notice of Exemption

A brief notice which may be filed by a public agency after it has decided to carry out or approve a project for which an exemption to CEQA applies.

Notice of Preparation

A brief notice sent by a Lead Agency notifying Responsible, Trustee and involved federal agencies that it plans to prepare an EIR for a project.

Project

The entirety of an action which has a potential for resulting in a physical change in the environment.

Responsible Agency

A public agency which proposes to carry out or approve a project for which a Lead Agency is preparing or has prepared an EIR.

Significant Effect

A substantial, or potentially substantial, adverse change in any of the physical conditions within the area affected by a project.

Statement of Overriding Consideration

A written explanation prepared by a public agency that explains why it approved a project, despite the presence of significant, unavoidable environmental impacts.

Tiering

Refers to the concept of a "multi-tiered" approach to preparing EIRs. The first-tier EIR covers general issues in a broader program-oriented analysis. Subsequent tiers incorporate by reference the general discussions from the broader EIR, while primarily concentrating on the issues specific to the action being evaluated.

Trustee Agency

A state agency with legal jurisdiction over natural resources held in trust for the people of the state, and which are affect by a project.

Acronyms

ABAG

Association of Bay Area Governments

AEP

Association of Environmental Professionals

APA

American Planning Association

BCDC

San Francisco Bay Conservation and Development Commission

CAL EPA

California Environmental Protection Agency

Caltrans

California Department of Transportation

CEQA

California Environmental Quality Act

CFR

Code of Federal Regulations

DFG

Department of Fish and Game

DHS

Department of Health Services

EIA

Environmental Impact Assessment

EIR

Environmental Impact Report

EIS

Environmental Impact Statement

FONSI

Finding of No Significant Effect

Gov. Code

California Government Code

Guidelines

State CEQA Guidelines

LAFCO

Local Agency Formation Commission

LESA

Land Evaluation and Site Assessment

MEA

Master Environmental Assessment

MOU

Memo of Understanding

NEPA

National Environmental Policy Act

NOD

Notice of Determination

NOP

Notice of Preparation

OPR

Office of Planning and Research

PSA

Permit Streamlining Act

Pub. Res. Code

California Public Resources Code

SCH

State Clearinghouse

SMUD

Sacramento Municipal Utility District

Suggested Reading

California Environmental Law and Land Use Practice

Edited by Kenneth A. Manaster and Daniel P. Selmi
1989, with annual updates

This is a comprehensive six-volume treatise on all aspects of California environmental law and land use control. It is updated annually. Volume I contains four detailed chapters on CEQA written by Ronald E. Bass and Albert I. Herson. Available from:

Matthew Bender & Co., Inc.
201 Mission Street, 26th floor
San Francisco, CA 94105
tel (415) 908-3200 or (800) 833-9844

Curtin's California Land Use and Planning Law

By Daniel J. Curtin, Jr.
1999 (nineteenth) edition

A definitive summary of the major provisions of land use and planning law that apply to California's cities and counties. Thorough coverage is given to California land use statutes, recent federal and state court decisions, and California Attorney General Opinions—all brought up to date as of December 1998. Several chapters are devoted to CEQA and the environmental impact report (EIR) process, the Endangered Species Act, and federal and state wetland regulations. Available from:

Solano Press Books
PO Box 773
Point Arena, CA 95468
tel (800) 931-9373
fax (707) 884-4109

California Permit Handbook

1996 edition

A guidebook to the state permit process, including advice on integrating CEQA with the permit process. Copies and information can be obtained from:

Office of Permit Assistance
Trade and Commerce Agency
801 K Street, Suite 1700
Sacramento, CA 95814
tel (916) 322-4245

CEQA Guidelines

Adopted by City of Mountain View, May 26, 1992

An example of CEQA Guidelines tailored to fit the special requirements of a local jurisdiction. It contains both the required CEQA elements as well as a variety of optional procedures. Also included are locally adopted thresholds of significance and an initial study checklist. Copies and information can be obtained from:

City of Mountain View
Office of Planning and
Community Development
500 Castro Street
Mountain View, CA 94039

CEQA Statutes and Guidelines

A publication of the Governor's Office of Planning and Research, containing the CEQA statutes and the state CEQA Guidelines. Up-to-date copies of the statutes (including all amendments as of December 1995) and the Guidelines (incorporating a recently expanded "Discussions" section) are included

as part of the appendices of this book (*see* Appendices). You may also order copies from the following address:

Governor's Office of Planning
and Research (OPR)
1400 10th Street
Sacramento, CA 95814
tel (916) 322-4245

Guide to the California Environmental Quality Act (CEQA)

By Michael H. Remy, Tina A. Thomas, James G. Moose, and Whitman F. Manley
1999 (tenth) edition

A thorough examination of the substance and procedures of CEQA, including the statutes, the implementing Guidelines, and current case law as of December 1998. Also included is an appendix with summaries of important cases as of May 1998. Updated frequently, this book is available from:

Solano Press Books
PO Box 773
Point Arena, CA 95468
tel (800) 931-9373 or fax (707) 884-4109

Longtin's California Land Use

Edited by James Longtin
1986 (second edition), with updates

This document reviews laws related to land use control and planning in California. It includes a chapter on CEQA. Available from:

Local Government Publications
PO Box 10087
Berkeley, CA 94709
tel (800) 345-0899

Mastering NEPA: A Step-by-Step Approach

By Ronald E. Bass and Albert I. Herson
1999 (second) edition

A presentation of the critical steps, basic requirements and most important decision points of the National Environmental Policy Act. This book takes the reader step-by-step through the provisions of NEPA and the environmental review process. As a user's handbook, the authors include recommendations for successful NEPA compliance. Available from:

Solano Press Books
PO Box 773
Point Arena, CA 95468
tel (800) 931-9373
fax (707) 884-4109

NEPA Deskbook

Environmental Law Institute
1995 (second) edition

Contains NEPA and CEQ regulations and related material and sample documents dealing with NEPA. It is available from:

Environmental Law Institute
1616 P Street, NW, Suite 200
Washington, DC 20036
tel (800) 433-5120
fax (202) 939-3817

NEPA Law and Litigation

By Daniel R. Mandelker
1992 edition, with updates

A treatise on the National Environmental Policy Act. Updated periodically, it is available from:

Clark Boardman Callaghan
(West Group)
155 Pfingsten Road
Deerfield, IL 60015
tel (847) 948-7000

Practice under the California Environmental Quality Act

By Stephen L. Kostka
and Michael H. Zischke
1993 edition, with updates

A detailed guide to CEQA for legal professionals. Copies and information can be obtained from:

California Continuing
Education of the Bar
2300 Shattuck Avenue
Berkeley, CA 94704
tel (800) 232-3444

State Clearinghouse Handbook

1997 edition

Published by the Governor's Office of Planning and Research (OPR), this handbook explains in detail the operations of the State Clearinghouse. It provides information on the requirements of CEQA and the State Clearinghouse for state agency review of environmental documents. Copies and answers to questions may be obtained from:

The State Clearinghouse
Governor's Office of Planning
and Research (OPR)
1400 10th Street
Sacramento, CA 95814
tel (916) 445-0613

Relevant Websites

The CERES (California Environmental Resources Evaluation System) site:
http://ceres.ca.gov/ceqa

The Find California Legislation (Senate) site:
www.sen.ca.gov/~newsen/legislation/legislation.htp

The California Home Page (Your Government) site:
www.ca.gov/s/govt

Index

A page number in boldface
refers to material in a table.

Photography Credits

Pages 2, 45, 94 — Tim Messick

Page 15 — Virginia Getz

Pages 24, 71, 89, 99, 119, 148, 157 — Jones & Stokes Associates

Page 31 — Ted Beedy

Page 41 — California Department of Parks and Recreation

Pages 65, 86, 135 — Sudhir Vaikkattil

Pages 77, 114, 150 — Al Herson

Pages 109, 136 — California Department of Water Resources

Page 126 — David De Vries

Pages 145, 152 — Amy Rucker

CEQA
Deskbook

2001 Supplement

CEQA
Deskbook

2001 Supplement

Ronald E. Bass

Albert I. Herson

Kenneth M. Bogdan

Solano Press Books
Point Arena, California

CEQA Deskbook

2001 Supplement to the
1999–2000 [Second] Edition

The authors of the *CEQA Deskbook*
are employed by Jones and Stokes, a
consulting firm providing services in
environmental planning and natural
resources management with offices
throughout California and the western
United States.

November 2000

Solano Press Books
Post Office Box 773
Point Arena, California 95468
telephone (800) 931-9373
facsimile (707) 884-4109

email spbooks@solano.com
internet www.solano.com

ISBN 0-923956-69-7

IMPORTANT NOTICE

Before you rely on the information in this
book, please be sure you have the latest
edition and are aware that some changes
in statutes, guidelines, or case law may
have gone into effect since the date of
publication. The book, moreover, provides
general information about the law. Readers
should consult their own attorneys before
relying on the representations found herein.

Contents

Introduction

This 2001 Supplement to the 1999–2000 (second) edition of the *CEQA Deskbook* presents the latest developments in California Environmental Quality Act practice, including legal decisions and administrative policies, that have occurred through November 2000. Since publication of the 1999–2000 edition of the *Deskbook* in 1999 (after the Resources Agency made significant changes to the CEQA Guidelines), no major changes have been made either to the CEQA statute itself or to the Guidelines; therefore, a rewrite of the *Deskbook* was not warranted. These new developments, however, along with significant year 2000 CEQA legislation, are sufficiently important to share with our readers in this special publication.

The new developments are presented here by chapter, topic, and page number, following the format of the second edition. Please note that the information in the 1999–2000 edition of the *CEQA Deskbook* should still be considered a current representation of the California Environmental Quality Act, the CEQA Guidelines, and CEQA practice.

Chapter 1

Background and Implementation of CEQA

Administration and Oversight *page 8*

OPR Responsibilities *page 9*

OPR Must Make Notices Available on the Internet. SB 761 (Sher) (Chapter 766, Statutes of 2000) requires the Governor's Office of Planning and Research to make all Notices of Exemption, Notices of Determination, Notices of Completion, and Notices of Preparation filed with the State Clearinghouse available on the Internet.

CEQA = California Environmental Quality Act
OPR = Governor's Office of Planning and Research

Resources Agency Responsibilities *page 9*

CEQA Guidelines–1998 CEQA Guidelines Amendments Challenged. When the California State Resources Agency last amended the CEQA Guidelines in 1998, agency staff made an ambitious attempt to involve numerous stakeholders in the revision process. Generally, the CEQA Guidelines amendments have been well received and have improved the ability of state and local agencies to comply with CEQA efficiently.

However, in April 2000, a coalition of environmental organizations filed a lawsuit challenging many of the 1998 CEQA Guidelines Amendments (*Communities for a Better Environment et al. v. California Resources Agency*, Sacramento County Superior Court, No. 00CS00300). According to court documents, the plaintiffs are particularly concerned with various sections of the revised CEQA Guidelines that they claim make it easier to rely on Categorical Exemptions and Negative Declarations. At the time of this publication, the next steps in the litigation process were not known. It should be noted that filing of the lawsuit has no immediate effect on the status of the 1998 CEQA Guidelines Amendments, and CEQA practitioners should still consider the current version of the CEQA Guidelines as "good law."

It should be noted that the lawsuit filing has no immediate effect on the status of the 1998 CEQA Guidelines Amendments, and CEQA practitioners should still consider the current version of the CEQA Guidelines as "good law."

CEQA Guidelines–Resources Agency Commences Biennial Guidelines Revision. In an effort unrelated to the recent lawsuit, the Resources Agency has started on another round of CEQA Guidelines revisions, pursuant to its statutory

1

mandate to revise the CEQA Guidelines every two years (California Public Resources Code Section 21087). To kick off the effort, the Resources Agency's new General Counsel invited various interest groups to informal meetings in June and July 2000 to discuss suggested clarifications and changes to the CEQA Guidelines. It is anticipated that there will be two separate revision processes, a shorter one for minor technical changes and corrections and a longer one for substantive changes. Firm schedules for the future revisions to the CEQA Guidelines have not yet been established.

CEQA Implementation by Public Agencies *page 12*

Key Participants in the CEQA Process *page 13*

Lead Agency *page 13*

DWR = California Department of Water Resources

In Planning and Conservation League, *the court then noted that DWR had a statewide perspective and expertise in water issues and that the water district lacked such qualities.*

Wrong Lead Agency Results in EIR Being Set Aside. In *Planning and Conservation League v. Department of Water Resources* (2000) ___ Cal. App. 4th ___, the court found that State Department of Water Resources, not an individual participating water district, should have been the lead agency for a multi-agency water supply agreement. The court reaffirmed the CEQA Guidelines provision that the Lead Agency must be the agency with the principal responsibility for carrying out a project. In arriving at its conclusion the court then noted that DWR had a statewide perspective and expertise in water issues and that the water district lacked such qualities.

Chapter 2

Preliminary Review, Exemptions, and Negative Declarations

Phase One: Preliminary Review *page 19*

**Determining Whether an Action Is a
"Project" as Defined by CEQA** *page 19*

Definition of a Project *page 21*

State Supreme Court Agrees to Review CEQA/Initiative Decision. On March 1, 2000, the California State Supreme Court granted review of *Friends of Sierra Madre v. City of Sierra Madre* (1999) 76 Cal. App. 4th 1061. In the underlying case, the City of Sierra Madre's city council deferred a decision on whether to remove certain properties from the city's register of historic landmarks, and instead submitted it to a city-wide election. The petitioners challenged the decision to submit the matter to election as an action subject to CEQA. The appellate court agreed with petitioners and held that the council's submission of the matter to the voters was a project subject to CEQA because it might lead to a substantial adverse change in the significance of an historical resource. The issue before the State Supreme Court is whether an initiative put on the ballot by a city council is subject to CEQA or whether it falls within CEQA's statutory exemption for votes of the people.

Department of Fish and Game Lake/Streambed Alteration Agreements Must Comply with CEQA. In response to a court order in *Mendocino Environmental Center v. California Department of Fish and Game* (County of Mendocino, 1999; CV76761), the California Department of Fish and Game (DFG) revised its Lake/Streambed Alteration Agreement Program to comply with CEQA. Prior to the court order, DFG's regulatory process for reviewing agreement requests under the Lake/Streambed Alteration Agreement Program (California Fish and Game Code Sections 1600–1607) had varied, and, in recent years, DFG had inconsistently applied the definition of a project in determining whether CEQA compliance was necessary when issuing these agreements. The petitioners in the Mendocino case asserted that DFG was required to comply with CEQA for issuance of a Section 1603 agreement to a nonpublic entity

The California State Supreme Court has granted review of Friends of Sierra Madre v. City of Sierra Madre *to decide the issue of whether an initiative put on the ballot by a city council is subject to CEQA or whether it falls within CEQA's statutory exemption for votes of the people.*

DFG = California Department of Fish and Game

On May 1, 1999, DFG released a revised "notification package" so that the Lake/Streambed Alteration process incorporates CEQA compliance for all Section 1601 and 1603 Agreements.

http://www.dfg.ca/wahcb/1600.html

involved in sinker log operations (recovery of submerged trees from stream or river bottoms). The court stated that DFG's review of Section 1603 applications must be subject to CEQA, and DFG responded by revising their program for both the Section 1601 (for public entities) and Section 1603 processes.

On May 1, 1999, DFG released a revised "notification package" so that the Lake/Streambed Alteration Form Notification Instructions, Project Questionnaire, Fee Schedule, and Question and Answer Fact Sheet reflect the stipulations of the court order and incorporate CEQA compliance for all Section 1601 and 1603 Agreements. This information is available from DFG's website at: http://www.dfg.ca/wahcb/1600.html.

Exemptions from CEQA *page 22*

Categorical Exemptions *page 25*

Categorical Exemption for Small Commercial Building Upheld. In *Fairbank v. City of Mill Valley* (1999) 75 Cal. App. 4th 1243, the court found that a retail/office building project qualified for a categorical exemption for small commercial projects. The most surprising aspect of that case was the court's willingness to retroactively apply the 1998 CEQA Guidelines Amendments' revised exemption language to the project.

Partial Exemptions for Certified Regulatory Programs *page 31*

The Secretary of Resources has granted certified regulatory program status to the "incidental take permit" regulatory program of the Department of Fish and Game.

The Department of Fish and Game Receives Certification for Section 2081 Incidental Take Permits Under the California Endangered Species Act. The Secretary of Resources has granted certified regulatory program status to the "incidental take permit" regulatory program of DFG (Fish and Game Code 2081; California Code of Regulations, Subdivision 3, Chapter 6, Sections 783.0–783.8). DFG's incidental take permit regulatory process differentiates between when DFG would be considered "lead agency" for purposes of issuing the incidental take permit and when DFG would only be considered a responsible agency and another state or local agency has taken lead agency status (California Code of Regulations, Subdivision 3, Chapter 6, Sections 783.3, 783.5).

Phase Three: Preparation of Negative Declarations, Including Mitigated Negative Declarations *page 45*

Preparation and Review of a Negative Declaration *page 46*

Failure to Notify Trustee Agency of Negative Declaration Results Violates CEQA. In *Fall River Wild Trout Foundation v. County of Shasta* (1999) 70 Cal. App. 4th 482, the court found that the County of Shasta's failure to send a copy of a proposed Negative Declaration to DFG and the State Clearinghouse was a prejudicial abuse of discretion. In arriving at this decision, the court reiterated the importance of Responsible and Trustee Agencies' review and consultation in achieving CEQA's objectives.

Negative Declarations Upheld *page 46*

Ten-year-old Negative Declaration for Parking Garage Upheld. In *Snarled Traffic Obstructs Progress v. City and County of San Francisco* (1999) 74 Cal. App. 4th 793, the court upheld the City of San Francisco's reliance on a Negative

Declaration prepared in 1988 for a project to demolish and then build an expanded downtown parking garage when the city sought to build a smaller version of the project nine years later.

Mitigated Negative Declaration on Construction of Townhouse Upheld. In *Baldwin v. City of Los Angeles* (1999) 70 Cal. App. 4th 819, the court upheld the City of Los Angeles' Mitigated Negative Declaration prepared for a 26-unit townhouse project because the plaintiffs failed to produce any substantial evidence of a potentially significant loss of recreational opportunities in the immediate neighborhood.

Negative Declaration for Solid Waste Plan Upheld. In *Pala Band of Mission Indians v. County of San Diego* (1999) 68 Cal. App. 4th 556, the court upheld the County of San Diego's Negative Declaration for a solid waste management plan despite the county's failure to evaluate the impacts of "tentatively reserved" future landfill sites.

Negative Declarations Set Aside *page 46*

Mitigated Negative Declaration for Habitat Conservation Plan (HCP) Set Aside. In *San Bernardino Valley Audubon Society v. Metropolitan Water District of Southern California* (1999) 71 Cal. App. 4th 382, the court set aside the Metropolitan Water District of Southern California's Mitigated Negative Declaration for a proposed multi-species HCP. The court held that the Mitigated Negative Declaration was inadequate because the plaintiffs were able to make a fair argument, based on substantial evidence, that the HCP's mitigation bank would not actually mitigate all of the environmental impacts of future land development. This case demonstrates that even a project designed to protect the environment and approved by resource agencies may require an EIR; although an HCP prepared in compliance with the federal and state Endangered Species Acts is designed to mitigate the impacts of land development, the adoption of such a plan may require an EIR.

EIR = Environmental Impact Report
HCP = Habitat Conservation Plan

Although an HCP prepared in compliance with the federal and state Endangered Species Acts is designed to mitigate the impacts of land development, the adoption of such a plan may require an EIR.

Negative Declaration for "Already Built" Car Wash Set Aside. In *Woodward Park Homeowners Association v. Garreks, Inc.* (2000) 77 Cal App. 4th 880, the court set aside the City of Fresno's approval of a car wash project based on a Negative Declaration. Opponents filed a lawsuit, and the trial court found that the city had violated CEQA by not preparing an EIR. The city appealed, and, while the case was on appeal, the applicant built the project and then argued to the appellate court that the lawsuit was moot because the project was already built. The appellate court held that the case was not moot and that the city must prepare an EIR even though the project was built. The court noted that remedies such as requiring mitigation and even denying the project were possible; thus, CEQA would still be important to the decision-making process.

Subsequent Negative Declarations *page 50*

No Subsequent Negative Declaration or EIR Is Necessary If No Agency Discretion Remains. In *Cucamongans United for Reasonable Expansion v. City of Rancho Cucamonga* (2000) ___ Cal. App. 4th ___, the court held that, after the City of Rancho Cucamonga issued a Negative Declaration and approved a 40-unit subdivision, a subsequent Negative Declaration or EIR is only required if there are remaining agency discretionary decisions to be made regarding the project. If no such decisions remain, as was the situation for the city with this project, then the challenge to the Negative Declaration is moot.

Payment of Environmental Review Fees to the Department of Fish and Game *page 51*

Department of Fish and Game Environmental Review Fees Upheld Against Constitutional Challenge. In *California Association of Professional Scientists et al. v. Department of Fish and Game* (2000) 79 Cal. App. 4th 935, the court upheld DFG environmental review fees (California Fish and Game Code Section 711.4). The court held that the fees, which were adopted by a simple legislative majority, were valid regulatory fees and not an unconstitutional tax. This decision should end the debate over the validity of DFG's environmental review fees and provides a green light for DFG, through local governments and the Office of Planning and Research, to collect the fees. For any project subject to the fees, approval of the project is not considered final until the fees are paid.

In California Association of Professional Scientists et al. v. Department of Fish and Game, *the court upheld DFG environmental review fees.*

Chapter 3

Types of Environmental Impact Reports

Redevelopment Plan Program EIR May Not Rely on Tiering. In what may be the most important CEQA case of the last year, the court in *Friends of Mammoth v. Town of Mammoth Lakes* (2000) ___ Cal. App. 4th ___, set aside the Town of Mammoth's Program EIR on its redevelopment plan. The court found the Program EIR inadequate because it failed to sufficiently evaluate the impacts of seventy-two foreseeable future redevelopment projects. The court distinguished a redevelopment plan Program EIR from a tiered EIR, holding that a tiered EIR assumes that subsequent projects will be evaluated at a later stage of planning, while a redevelopment plan Program EIR precludes such second-tier review. According to the court, because a redevelopment plan and any subsequent redevelopment projects are considered to be a "single project" under CEQA, the town could not rely on tiering to evaluate the impacts of the subsequent projects.

The decision contains extensive discussions of the differences between Program EIRs, tiered EIRs, and supplements to EIRs. The court's decision called into question the use of Program EIRs as first-tier documents for any program types with known specific projects, not just redevelopment plans. As a result of this case, it would be prudent for all first-tier Program EIRs to describe reasonably foreseeable specific projects included in the program and discuss their reasonably foreseeable impacts and mitigation measures, even if more detailed, project-specific, second-tier EIRs will be prepared in the future.

In what may be the most important CEQA case of the last year, the court in Friends of Mammoth v. Town of Mammoth Lakes *set aside the Town of Mammoth's Program EIR on its redevelopment plan.*

7

Chapter 4

Preparation and Review of an EIR and Agency Decision Making

Determining the Scope, Focus, and Content of the EIR *page 70*

Notice of Preparation *page 71*

Notices of Preparation Must Be Sent to the Office of Planning and Research. AB 970 (Longville) (Chapter 387, Statutes of 2000) requires all Lead Agencies to send copies of their Notices of Preparation to the Office of Planning and Research and authorizes OPR to comment on those NOPs. Prior to this change, Notices of Preparation only had to be sent to Responsible and Trustee Agencies.

Consideration and Certification of Final EIR *page 81*

Certification *page 81*

Under CEQA's time limits, a lead agency has a statutory duty to complete and certify an EIR within one year of accepting an application as complete for a private development project.

Agency Delay Violates CEQA. In *Sunset Drive Corporation v. City of Redlands* (1999) 73 Cal App. 4th 215, the court held that the City of Redlands' four-year delay in completing and certifying an EIR was a violation of the time limits under CEQA. The court ordered the city to prepare the EIR, stating that under CEQA's time limits, a lead agency has a statutory duty to complete and certify an EIR within one year of accepting an application as complete for a private development project. In a novel remedy rectifying the effect of the city's CEQA violation, the court also held that the city could be sued for monetary damages for violating the applicant's civil rights.

Tie Vote by Board of Supervisors Does Not Certify EIR. In *Vedanta Society of Southern California v. California Quartet, Ltd.* (2000) ___ Cal. App. 4th ___, the court held that the Orange County Board of Supervisors' deadlocked vote on appeal of the Planning Commissioner's EIR certification for a 705-unit housing development did not constitute valid certification under CEQA. The court found that, while CEQA allows certification to be delegated to a planning commission, to constitute a valid certification on appeal, a majority affirmative vote of the Board of Supervisors was necessary. The court also held that an affirmative vote of the Board was also required to adopt the Findings approved by the Planning Commission.

Taking Action on Projects for Which an EIR Was Prepared *page 82*

Lead and Responsible Agency Authority *page 82*

Limitations on Authority *page 82*

CEQA Does Not Give Agency Authority to Regulate Building Occupants. In *Friends of Davis v. City of Davis* (2000) ___ Cal. App. 4th ___, the court held that CEQA did not give the City of Davis authority to regulate the specific occupants of commercial buildings when the city's design review ordinance was limited to regulating only the exterior appearance of such buildings. Plaintiffs were opposed to the city's decision to approve a commercial complex that included a nationally-known mega-bookstore, and argued that the city should rely on CEQA to deny the use to that specific occupant. In reaching its conclusion, the court relied on the well-established rule that an agency may only exercise those powers provided by law.

CEQA Compliance after an EIR Is Prepared *page 87*

Subsequent EIR and Supplemental EIR *page 87*

Standard of Judicial Review *page 88*

Initial Study Not Required to Support Decision Regarding Supplemental EIR. In *Friends of Davis v. City of Davis* (2000) ___ Cal. App. 4th ___, the court held that the city did not have to prepare an Initial Study to support its decision that no supplemental EIR was necessary, so long as the administrative record contained no substantial evidence to suggest the need for a supplement. (Despite this holding, it is good practice to prepare an Initial Study to aid in the decision whether or not to supplement a CEQA document, and to augment the administrative record supporting such a decision.)

In Friends of Davis v. City of Davis, *the court held that the city did not have to prepare an Initial Study to support its decision that no supplemental EIR was necessary, so long as the administrative record contained no substantial evidence to suggest the need for a supplement.*

Chapter 5
Contents of an EIR

Environmental Setting *page 95*
EIR Environmental Baseline Challenged

The amendments to the CEQA Guidelines in 1998 added the language in Section 15126.2(a) that "normally" the environmental baseline for determining the significant effects of a proposed project is the existing physical condition at the time the Notice of Preparation is published. Three recent cases dealt with project baseline and reveal that the baseline determination is often more complicated than it first appears.

In *Fairview Neighbors v. County of Ventura* (1999) 70 Cal. App. 4th 238, the court upheld the County of Ventura's baseline, in an EIR for a mining project, as the level of allowable truck traffic under an existing permit, rather than the actual, fluctuating daily traffic, which was lower. In *County of Amador v. El Dorado County Water Agency* (1999) 76 Cal. App. 4th 931, the court struck down the El Dorado County Water Agency's baseline in an EIR for a water supply plan because it was lacking a detailed description of baseline conditions (rather than a summary). In *Riverwatch v. County of San Diego* (1999) 76 Cal. App. 4th 1428, the court upheld the County of San Diego's baseline in an EIR for a rock quarry (but disapproved of the EIR on other grounds), stating that the environmental baseline did not have to go back in time and describe historic environmental damage that was caused by the applicant before the current project was proposed.

Failure to Adequately Describe Existing Groundwater Aquifer Results in Inadequate EIR

In *Cadiz Land Company, Inc. v. Rail Cycle, L.P. et al.* (2000) ___ Cal. App. 4th ___, the court held inadequate the County of San Bernardino's EIR on a proposed landfill in the Mojave Desert. The court held that the EIR failed to include a detailed description of a large groundwater aquifer underlying the project site and neighboring agricultural land. The court found that without a detailed description of the extent of the aquifer, the EIR could not properly assess the significance of the ground water impacts from the landfill (primarily on neighboring agricultural operations) or the extent of mitigation necessary to avoid or substantially reduce such impacts.

Environmental Impacts *page 96*

Types of Impacts *page 98*

Growth-Inducing Impacts *page 99*

An EIR for a Water Project Must Be "Predicated" on the Local General Plan. In *County of Amador v. El Dorado County Water Agency* (1999) 76 Cal. App. 4th 931, the court struck down the El Dorado County Water Agency's EIR for a water supply plan, holding that the water agency's EIR did not satisfy CEQA because it was not "predicated" on population projections in an adopted county general plan. It appears that the court was more concerned with the use of officially approved population projections to prepare the water plan, rather than the adequacy of that information as substantial evidence to support the conclusions in the EIR. Water agencies preparing water plans and EIRs should take note and consider only using population projections in adopted general plans or other adopted population projections, such as those prepared by regional councils of government.

Water agencies preparing water plans and EIRs should take note of County of Amador v. El Dorado County Water Agency, *and consider only using population projections in adopted general plans or other adopted population projections.*

Economic and Social Effects *page 102*

Psychological Effects Not an Environmental Impact. In *National Parks and Conservation Association v. County of Riverside* (1999) 71 Cal. App. 4th 1341, the court held that the County of Riverside's EIR for a landfill project 1.5 miles from the Joshua Tree National Park adequately considered the proposed project's impact on park visitors' "wilderness experience" and various other desert resources. The court, relying on well-established National Environmental Policy Act (NEPA) precedent, held that CEQA only applied to physical effects and not psychological effects and that the EIR in this case appropriately evaluated the physical environmental effects of the proposed project.

NEPA = National Environmental Policy Act

Economic and Social Effects Not Required in EIR. In *Friends of Davis v. City of Davis* (2000) ___ Cal. App. 4th ___, the court held that economic and social changes resulting from the approval of a commercial project (containing a nationally-known mega-book store) did not constitute environmental effects under CEQA and did not have to be included in the EIR.

While the court acknowledged that such changes could indirectly lead to business closures and physical deterioration in the community, in this case the record contained no substantial evidence that such physical effects would result from the project. The court found that the plaintiffs' concerns about the possibility of such effects occurring were based solely on speculation and unsubstantiated opinion.

Projects Involving Schools *page 106*

Special Requirements for Toxic Materials on Proposed School Sites. AB 2644 (Calderon) (Chapter 443, Statutes of 2000) introduces special rules (Education Code Section 17213.1) for integrating the CEQA document with the

"Preliminary Endangerment Assessment" (PEA) required by the California Department of Toxic Substances Control when a school district proposes a new school site containing hazardous materials. Under this bill a school district must test for toxics, with DTSC oversight, prior to site acquisition or building, and must present the results and proposed remediation in a PEA. Once prepared, the PEA must accompany the district's CEQA document through the environmental review process and must be adopted prior to approving the project.

Alternatives *page 107*

No-Project Alternative *page 109*

"No-Project" Alternative Must Be Given Serious Evaluation. In *Planning and Conservation League v. Department of Water Resources* (2000) ___ Cal. App. 4th ___, the court held that an EIR for a multi-agency water delivery agreement was inadequate where it contained only a cursory evaluation of the "no-project" alternative. The court also found that the Lead Agency improperly dismissed the "no-project" alternative as infeasible, when the facts of the case demonstrated that it would, in fact, be likely to occur. In arriving at this conclusion, the court pointed out the importance of the "no-project" alternative as a point of comparison for the impacts of the proposed project and other alternatives.

Mitigation Measures *page 112*

Details of Mitigation Plans May Be Deferred *page 114*

Three cases in the past year have dealt with the question of how much detail is necessary in an EIR's discussion of mitigation measures. It should be noted that CEQA requires that for each significant impact on the environment identified in the EIR, the EIR must disclose feasible measures to avoid or substantially reduce the project's significant environmental effect. CEQA Guidelines Section 15126.4(a). In all three court decisions taking place in the last year, the courts allowed agencies to include only a generalized discussion of mitigation in an EIR, with the details deferred to future environmental analysis. These cases illustrate that the courts are willing to allow agencies considerable latitude in defining mitigation when an EIR is prepared and when subsequent CEQA review will be required in the future. Agencies should be aware, however, that the courts are not so lenient when a Mitigated Negative Declaration is prepared. In those situations, a more detailed description of mitigation measures is generally necessary to satisfy CEQA.

The courts are willing to allow agencies considerable latitude in defining mitigation when an EIR is prepared and when subsequent CEQA review will later be required.

In *Dry Creek Citizen's Coalition v. County of Tulare* (1999) 70 Cal. App. 4th 20, the court upheld the County of Tulare's mitigation detail in an EIR for a sand and gravel mine, stating that a general description of the technical aspects of the project's design features to mitigate impacts was sufficient to understand the environmental impacts. In *Fairview Neighbors v. County of Ventura* (1999) 70 Cal. App. 4th 238, the court upheld the County of Ventura's treatment of mitigation in an EIR for a mining project, stating that the county appropriately concluded that the impacts were still significant and unmitigable and, as such, adopted a statement of overriding considerations. In *Riverwatch v. County of San Diego* (1999) 76 Cal. App. 4th 1428, the court upheld the County of San Diego's mitigation description in an EIR for a rock quarry (but disapproved of the EIR on other grounds), stating that obtaining details on the mitigation for a road was "not meaningfully possible" at the time.

Chapter 6

Projects Subject to
CEQA and NEPA

EIS = Environmental Impact Statement

In General—Consultation Required with Federal Agency When NEPA Document Used. AB 2848 (Chapter 387, Statutes of 2000) requires that when a state or local Lead Agency intends to use an Environmental Impact Statement (EIS) as an EIR it must consult with the federal Lead Agency and notify such agency of any scoping meetings for the proposed project.

New NEPA Book Published

As this Supplement to the *CEQA Deskbook* is being written (November 2000), Solano Press is in the final stages of publishing *The NEPA Book: A Step-by-Step Guide to the National Environmental Policy Act*. This new edition contains detailed information about how to comply with NEPA, including an entire chapter on how to integrate NEPA with other laws, and particularly state "mini-NEPA's" (e.g., CEQA).

Chapter 7

CEQA Litigation

The Role of Litigation

Legal Enforcement

Attorney General Makes CEQA Litigation a Priority. Since his election to office, California's Attorney General Bill Lockyer has made the enforcement of CEQA a key priority. Not since the early years of CEQA has the Attorney General taken such an interest in the adequacy of state and local agencies' compliance with CEQA. Through the Public Right's Division, the Attorney General's office has initiated several CEQA lawsuits, intervened in a variety of others, and served as a public watchdog over CEQA compliance, particularly for large, controversial projects. The Attorney General's role in CEQA was summarized in an article by Attorney General Lockyer in the April 2000 edition of *Western City Magazine*, published by the League of California Cities.

Since his election to office, California's Attorney General Bill Lockyer has made the enforcement of CEQA a key priority.

Typical Defenses

Procedural Defenses

Standing

Economic Competitor Does Not Have Standing to Bring CEQA Challenge. In *Waste Management of Alameda County, Inc. v. County of Alameda* (2000) 79 Cal. App. 4th 223, a landfill company opposed a competitor's proposed landfill, alleging that the company's commercial and competitive interests would be harmed by the project; therefore, the landfill company argued it had standing to challenge the adequacy of the County of Alameda's EIR on the landfill project. The court held that commercial and competitive interests were not within the environmental "zone of interests" that CEQA was designed to protect, and thus the opponent lacked standing to maintain the CEQA challenge.

The court held that commercial and competitive interests are not within the environmental "zone of interests" that CEQA was designed to protect.

Exhaustion of Administrative Remedies

Failure to File Administrative Appeal on CEQA Issues Precludes Legal Challenge. In *Tahoe Vista Concerned Citizens v. County of Placer* (2000) 81 Cal. App. 4th

577, the court did not allow a CEQA lawsuit to move forward against Placer County's Mitigated Negative Declaration for a motel expansion on Lake Tahoe. The opponents of the proposed project had appealed the County of Placer's Planning Commission approval of a conditional use permit to the Board of Supervisors, but failed to appeal the Planning Commission's adoption of the Mitigated Negative Declaration. The court held that by not raising the CEQA issues in their appeal to the Board of Supervisors, the opponents did not exhaust administrative remedies and thus could not challenge the Mitigated Negative Declaration in court.

In Cucamongans United for Reasonable Expansion v. City of Rancho Cucamonga, *the court held that a supplemental environmental document is only required if there are remaining discretionary decisions to be made regarding the project.*

Lack of Discretionary Decision Renders Challenge "Moot." As stated previously, in *Cucamongans United for Reasonable Expansion v. City of Rancho Cucamonga* (2000) ___ Cal. App. 4th ___, the court held that a supplemental environmental document is only required if there are remaining discretionary decisions to be made regarding the project; if no such decisions remain, then the challenge to the environmental document is moot.

Chapter 8

Is CEQA Effective?

Have CEQA's Objectives Been Achieved? *page 151*

AEP's Environmental Mitigation Monitoring and Reporting Under CEQA

In May 2000, The Association of Environmental Professionals (AEP) released a report entitled "Environmental Mitigation Monitoring and Reporting under the California Environmental Quality Act," which revealed that public agencies are improving their compliance with CEQA's monitoring requirements. The report, based in part on a survey of cities and counties conducted by private environmental consultants, showed that agencies are routinely requiring monitoring programs, despite being understaffed and underfunded. The report noted considerable improvement in monitoring since an earlier study in 1992. According to the report, while monitoring has generally been successfully integrated into day-to-day CEQA practice by most agencies, there is still inconsistent implementation from jurisdiction to jurisdiction and from project to project. The full report is available from the Association of Environmental Professionals (1333 36th Street, Sacramento, California 95816; telephone (916) 737-2371).

AEP = Association of Environmental Professionals

While monitoring has generally been successfully integrated into day-to-day CEQA practice by most agencies, there is still inconsistent implementation from jurisdiction to jurisdiction and from project to project.

Notes

Notes

Notes

Notes

Notes

Other Guides and References

PLANNING . LAND USE . URBAN AFFAIRS . ENVIRONMENTAL ANALYSIS . REAL ESTATE DEVELOPMENT

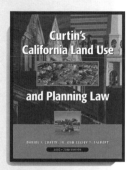

Curtin • Updated annually

Curtin's California Land Use and Planning Law

Well known, heavily quoted, definitive summary of California's planning laws that includes expert commentary on the latest statutes and case law. Cited by the California Courts, including the California Supreme Court, as an Authoritative Source.

Michael H. Remy et al. • 1999–2000 (tenth) edition

Guide to CEQA

Professional and legal guide offering an understandable, in-depth description of CEQA's requirements for adequate review and preparation of EIRs and other documents. With case law through December 1998 and the complete text of the Statutes and Guidelines. Cited as an Authoritative Source by the California Courts.

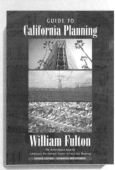

Fulton • 1999 (second) edition

Guide to California Planning

Describes how planning really works in California, how cities, counties, developers, and citizen groups all interact with each other on a daily basis to shape California communities and the California landscape, for better and for worse. Recipient of the California Chapter APA Award for Planning Education.

Ballot Box Navigator
A Practical and Tactical Guide to Land Use Initiatives and Referenda in California

This book is the authoritative resource on securing a ballot title, qualifying an initiative or referendum for the ballot, and submitting a measure for an election. With short articles, practice tips, drawings, an index, glossary, and a table of authorities.

Durkee et al. • 2002 edition

California Transportation Law

The first complete collection of the most important laws and regulations affecting transportation planning in California. Includes ISTEA provisions, Title VI guidelines for urban mass transit, STIP Guidelines, provisions relating to air quality conformity and equal employment opportunity, a subject index, and more.

March • 2000 edition

Code Enforcement

A detailed guide to creating, implementing, and enforcing a land use, zoning, and building code enforcement program. Includes short articles, practice tips, case references, legal notes, and citations as well as photographs, figures, flow charts, and graphs.

Schilling & Hare • 1994 edition

Eminent Domain A Step-by-Step
Guide to the Acquisition of Real Property

A step-by-step guide through the process California public agencies must follow to acquire private property for public purposes through eminent domain. Includes case law, legal references, tips, a table of authorities, sample letters and forms, a glossary, and an index.

Rypinski • 2002 (second) edition

TO ORDER, CALL TOLL-FREE
(800) 931-9373 OR FAX (707) 884-4109

PLEASE INQUIRE ABOUT PRICE AND AVAILABILITY.

Solano Press Books

Exactions and Impact Fees in California

This book is designed to help public officials, citizens, attorneys, planners, and developers understand exactions. Includes case studies, practice tips, photographs, and drawings to illustrate key considerations and legal principles along with a glossary, a table of authorities, and an index. Formerly called Public Needs and Private Dollars.

Abbott et al. • 2001 edition

Guide to Hazardous Materials and Waste Management

Adapted from a very popular course that has trained hundreds of environmental managers, this Guide is a valuable reference for students and professionals in the field. Provides the information necessary to understand and manage hazardous materials and wastes.

Kindschy • 1997 edition

Mastering NEPA A Step-by-Step Approach

A practitioner's handbook that takes you through the critical steps, basic requirements, and most important decision points of the National Environmental Policy Act. With short articles, practice tips, charts, tables, illustrations, and sources of additional information.

Bass & Herson • 1999 (second) edition

Putting TDRs to Work in California

Using twenty-seven case studies, the author explains how development rights can be formally and legally traded or transferred to protect open space and agricultural land, as well as natural resources, historic properties, and areas of historic value. Includes short articles, a model program, photographs, and tables.

Pruetz • 1993 edition

Redevelopment in California

A definitive guide to both the law and practice of redevelopment in California cities and counties, together with codes, case law, and commentary. Contains short articles, notes, photos, charts, graphs, and illustrative time schedules.

Beatty et al. • 1995 edition, plus annual supplement

Subdivision Map Act Manual

All-new desk reference containing the latest information to understand the legal provisions of the Act, recent court-made law, and the review and approval processes. Includes the full text of the Map Act, practice tips, sample forms, a table of authorities, and an index.

Curtin & Merritt • 2001 (tenth) edition

Telecommunications The Local Government Role in Managing the Connected Community

Detailed summary and analysis of federal and state laws governing the location and regulation of physical facilities including cable, traditional telephone systems, wireless (cellular, paging, and Internet), satellite dishes, and antennas. With practice tips, photographs, a glossary, table of authorities, and an index.

Valle-Riestra • 2002 edition

Wetlands, Streams, and Other Waters Regulation, Conservation, and Mitigation Planning

A practical guide to federal and state wetland identification and regulation and permitting processes. With detailed information, commentary, and practice tips for those who work with federal and state laws and are engaged in wetland conservation planning.

Cylinder et al. • 2002 edition